SEEDS OF FAMINE

SEEDS OF FAMINE

Ecological Destruction and the Development Dilemma in the West African Sahel

by
RICHARD W. FRANKE
and BARBARA H. CHASIN

LandMark Studies
ROWMAN & ALLANHELD

ROWMAN & ALLANHELD PUBLISHERS

Published in the United States of America in 1980
by Allanheld, Osmun & Co. Publishers, Inc.
(A Division of Littlefield, Adams & Company)
81 Adams Drive, Totowa, New Jersey 07512

LIBRARY OF CONGRESS CATALOGING IN PUBLICATION DATA

Franke, Richard W.
Seeds of famine.

Bibliography: p.
Includes index.
1. Sahel—Famines. 2. Sahel—Rural conditions.
3. Rural development—Sahel. I. Chasin, Barbara H., joint author. II. Title.
HC591.S253F3433 338.1'9'66 79-52471
ISBN 0-916672-26-3
ISBN 0-86598-053-5 (PBK)

85 / 10 9 8 7 6 5

Printed in the United States of America

Contents

Tables and Figures

TABLES

FIGURES

Preface and Acknowledgments

We began this study in 1974, not as experts on the Sahel, but as two social scientists concerned with the problems of inequality, poverty, and the growing world food crisis, which was highlighted in that year by major food shortages and famines in many parts of the world. To us, the Sahel drought and famine of 1968-74 seemed to be a particularly horrible case study in the dual problems of environmental destruction—a major news story at the time—and the loss of human life through the collapse of a food-producing system.

Richard W. Franke spent two years in Indonesia studying food production projects of the Green Revolution, whereas Barbara H. Chasin was developing a course on the sociology of violence. In 1973, campus actions and urban rebellions were still fresh in peoples' minds, and "crime in the streets" was a popular theme in political campaigns. The direct violence of protests and crime seemed always to dominate the awareness of the subtler, more pervasive destruction of lives and resources caused by the daily workings of a particular kind of society.

From these related but different backgrounds, we began preliminary research on the famine. At first we collected newspaper and magazine articles and discussed our interest with our students. In 1975, we began historical research into the background of the region while continuing to teach at Montclair State College.

In 1976, we were able to join the World Agricultural Research Project, financed by the Ford Foundation, at Harvard University's School of Public Health. The project is concerned with food production problems in many parts of the world and brings together people from several different scientific disciplines.

We were granted leaves of absence from teaching while we worked with the Harvard project in 1976-78. In 1977, we spent three months in France, consulting with experts familiar with the Sahel region. In 1978, with the support of the Harvard project, we traveled for five months in Senegal, Mali, and Niger, three of the Sahel countries. We spoke with academics and officials of development agencies and visited projects that were designed to overcome, it was hoped, the effects of the 1968-74 drought and famine and to render the region less vulnerable to future vagaries of climate.

The design of the book follows our own development of the project, but we believe it is also the most logical presentation. In Part I we argue that, despite the terrible famine described in the Introduction, the Sahel region is not a wasteland. This is demonstrated by an analysis of its ecology (Chapter 1), and of the societies that developed there in the past (Chapter 2). We then show how colonial (Chapter 3) and pre-famine international economic and political relationships (Chapter 4) were the main factors leading to the vastly increased vulnerability of the region to the droughts which are a recurring phenomenon.

In Part 2, we examine the response of the scientific and development communities of the West to the famine and the extent to which scientists (Chapter 5) and development planners and agencies (Chapters 6 and 7) have assimilated the historical lessons from the Sahel.

In Part 3 we analyze several of the major contradictions which we believe are plaguing the implementation of the Sahel Development Program both at the international level (Chapter 8) and within several Sahelian societies themselves (Chapter 9). In the final chapter we discuss what we consider to be the highly significant lessons to be drawn from the experiences of the smaller, more marginal projects, and pose what appear to be the major options for an ecologically sound rehabilitation of the region.

We have prepared this book with two audiences in mind. The text has been kept as free as possible of academic side remarks in the hope that the study will be readable and useful for students and the general public who are concerned with ecological and food problems in general. We also hope the book will be of value to scholars whose particular interest is West Africa, those who are studying the food and environmental crisis from a technical perspective, and Sahelian experts who are already familiar with the region. The Notes at the end of each chapter can be ignored by the general reader without losing the essentials of our argument, while the specialist or advanced student will find suggestions for further research there. We have divided the Bibliography into Part I which gives references cited that are the most accessible and would be of greatest value to the nonspecialist reader; and Part II, which includes the many specialized reports and documents used in the preparation of this study. All translations from French and Dutch sources have been made by the authors.

In this work, we were helped by many people who patiently answered our questions, made suggestions, helped us with contacts or references, and shared their own research findings. We especially want to thank our friends and colleagues at Montclair State College, the members of the World Agricultural Research Project at the Harvard School of Public Health, the directors and staff of the many projects we visited, the farmers and elected officers of the Federation of Soninke Peasants in Senegal and the many other Sahelians who aided us in our travel and research.

SEEDS OF FAMINE

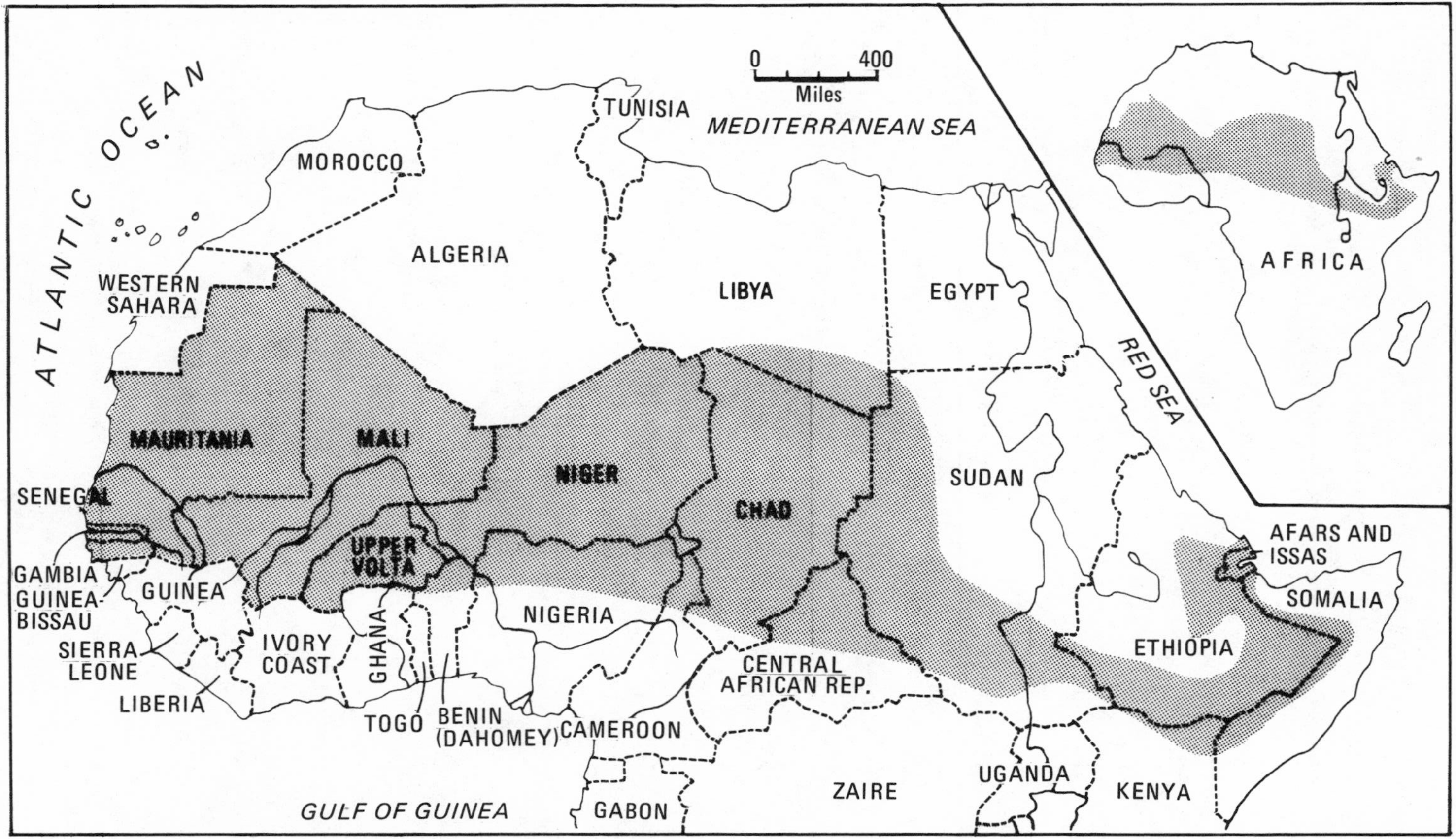

Figure A Sahel Drought and Famine: 1968–1974

Introduction

FOOD CRISIS—ECOLOGY CRISIS

Except perhaps for nuclear war, nothing in our time so threatens a majority of the world's people as does the spector of hunger and starvation. Despite all the development programs, the technology transfer, and the "miracle seeds" of the so-called Green Revolution, the prospects for eating a reasonably nutritional diet seem increasingly dim for hundreds of millions in the 1980s and beyond. Bad weather, bad harvests, rising food prices, food riots, malnutrition, poor health, misery—all seem to be part of our times. Even in such food-rich nations as the United States, evidence is accumulating that seems to indicate hard times ahead. It is surely not accidental, for example, that the Los Angeles Police Department began training 7,200 officers for a special riot force in anticipation of possible food disturbances in that city.[1]

In the poorest, "underdeveloped" nations of the world, however, the food problem is, and appears to be, increasingly severe and even insurmountable. In 1974, *The Wall Street Journal* estimated that up to 30 million people would die of starvation in a 12-month period.[2] Norman Borlaug, one of the developers of the "miracle seeds" of the Green Revolution, asserted that between 10 and 50 million people would die in India alone in a single year.[3] More recently, the FAO estimates that a conservative figure for the undernourished of the world in 1978 would be

420 million people.[4] Other experts have predicted worldwide famines leading to major political upheavals, and some have proclaimed that it is more "humane" to withold food from poor nations, arguing that food gives an incentive to reproduce, thus contributing to growing population, which in turn exacerbates the food problem in the long run.[5]

The issue of food, and its production and distribution, has been the subject of much discussion in recent years. Several major studies have appeared, and a wide-ranging debate is underway. On one side are those who, like the journalists of the New York *Times*, high-ranking foundation and governmental officials, and many academics, view the essential problems as overpopulation, inefficiency, and lack of adequate technology; on the other are those who, like Susan George, Francis Lappé, and Joe Collins, see the problem as arising primarily from the general nature of international economic relations and the production priorities deriving from those relations.[6]

Simultaneously, the ecology movement has grown, with its principal concern being what is happening to the environment. At its most trivial, the ecology movement worries about beer cans marring the scenic beauty of our national parks; in its more serious form, it has raised questions about alternate energy sources, industrial pollution, chemicals in food and in the workplace, and the many ways that the by-products of modern life seem contradictory to the promise of health and happiness implicit in the great technological achievements of the 20th century.[7]

But while the ecology movement has principally been directed at problems having to do with the quality of the environment, it has also concerned itself with the subject of food. On campuses, in churches, and in community groups across the United States, activities have developed around the specific relationships between food and environment. Is growing grain to feed cattle the most efficient way to use land resources? Can enough food be produced without the use of potentially dangerous pesticides? Is it ethical to eat meat? Should we fast one day each month in order to save food for those who are starving today and may starve tomorrow?

Critics of this movement, however, and undoubtedly many of its adherents as well, realize that the problem of hunger abroad is not merely the wastefulness of 78 percent of American grain production going to feed cattle (which is a much less efficient source of calories and proteins, at least in the amounts eaten in this country) (Heiser, 1973, p. 36). We would go even further and argue that this fasting will do almost no good, no matter how admirably motivated. For there is another way in which the ecology and food crises are related, and one that requires the most thorough understanding for all of us who are working for the end of hunger and malnutrition.

In the poorer countries of the world, hunger is often *directly* connected to the deterioration or the destruction of ecological systems that could provide a harvest of plenty instead of continuing food shortages. And this ecological deterioration has been and continues to be brought about by forces that cannot be altered by individual acts such as fasting, but only by political organization and action to change the structure of society. A few examples from the past may help us set the stage for this argument.

On the Indonesian island of Java, less than 23 percent of the land had been forested by 1962, despite the insistence by forestry experts that a 30 percent covering is required to hold the soil in place. By 1972, the amount of forest had declined to only 15 percent.[8] As a result of the cutting of the forests, land washes down from the mountains and silts up the irrigation canals, thus causing saltwater to back up onto rice fields in the lowlands, which kills the crops. The ecological crisis on Java is thus part and parcel of the crisis of hunger and malnutrition, and it is among the worst cases in the world today (Franke, 1974 and 1975).

But why have the forests been cut? They were cut when Dutch colonialists wanted sugar, coffee, and tea plantations, and when the Japanese imperial occupiers needed lumber for their World War II production. And they were cut when peasants, desperate for farmland, moved their farms ever higher into the mountains during the 1950s and 1960s. Today, a large part of central Java, a region formerly covered with lush forest, is a barren wasteland. Similarly, some of the eastern parts of the island are now savanna grasslands, where formerly rice fields alternated with stands of trees (Buchanan, 1968, pp. 52-55).

Northeast Brazil was once a region verdant and blooming, with great potential for food production. Today, however, it is a semiwasteland, frequently ravaged by drought and constantly poor. The terrible process of ecological destruction in this area has been analyzed by many Latin American scholars. One of them, Eduardo Galeano (1973, pp. 72, 74), writes:

> The Northeast was Brazil's richest area and is now its poorest. . . . The humid coastal fringe, well watered by rains, had a soil of great fertility, rich in humus and mineral salts and covered by forests from Bahia to Ceara. This region of tropical forests was turned into a region of savannas. Naturally fitted to produce food, it became a place of hunger.

Brazilian nutritionist Josué de Castro (1966, p. 31) explains further:

> . . . once the river banks were stripped of trees and the valleys through which the rivers flowed were left naked to the sun, the same waterways became a menace. In flood they tore up the moist soil of the flatlands, dissolved minerals and humus, and washed everything away.

Whether from the grinding poverty of this denuded coast or from the periodic droughts of the inland *sertão*, this once rich and fertile land could thus be described in geographical terms by De Castro as "600,000 square miles of suffering" (ibid., pp. 22-64).[9] Why did this happen? Ask the sugar barons who grew wealthy there but did not have the interest to plan for the permanent use of the area for food production. Their profits on sugar could be turned into capital, and when the land became useless to them, they could shift their capital elsewhere—into mines or industry, or perhaps into sugar plantations in other parts of the world where the soil had not been depleted.

In the most recent past, we have seen yet another pattern of ecological devastation: In Vietnam, this process was used as a weapon of war against a people trying to restructure their society. The fertile rice-producing lands of the Tonkin Delta and the Mekong River—along with the upland forests that secure the waters and help hold and gradually distribute the soils for lowland food-producing areas—made Vietnam a potentially food-rich nation. These valuable resources were, from 1962 to 1974, so massively bombed and defoliated that the National Academy of Sciences, many of whose members had willingly participated in research for that very same war of destruction, eventually estimated that as much as 36 percent of the mangrove forests of the Mekong Delta had been chemically poisoned and destroyed, along with 10 percent of the inland forests. These estimates were considered extremely low by other forestry experts. The mangrove forests could take up to 100 years to recover, while the loss of soil from erosion may never be accurately known (Lewallen, 1971, p. 66).[10]

The relationship between ecological destruction and food production is thus direct and close. Whenever an environment is degraded, deprived of its basic resources—or often of even *one* of the key resources—that environment becomes a part of the world food crisis, and the people who live there become its victims.

The crisis of food and the crisis of ecology are not always easy to see in their proper relationships. We are often led to think that if we eat, other people will go hungry. Many people in the United States—which imports much of its food from poor countries—are honestly concerned about other people's hunger, and they are willing to undergo limited personal sacrifice in an effort to improve the situation.[11] Underlying these well-intentioned motivations, however, is a paternalistic attitude: The world's starving need our food because they seem unable to produce enough for themselves.[12]

We will argue that these attitudes reflect a critical misunderstanding of the major causes of the world food crisis and its ecological counterpart. The catastrophic famine in West Africa, between 1968 and 1974, is a dramatic and compelling example of a food and ecology disaster. Americans read that the famine was the result of a drought, or, simply, another blow at an already impoverished and backward part of the world—the border of the Sahara Desert.

In many ways, the events surrounding the Sahel famine exemplify what may be in store for other regions. For the delicate ecological relationships in the Sahel make it at once more vulnerable to changes in climate *or* to misuse by irrational and uncautious production systems; and because its people are already impoverished, food deficits can turn quickly into famine. The Sahel is also worthy of attention because in the aftermath of the famine this region has become the scene of one of the most intensive international development efforts yet to appear in the Third World.

Thus the Sahel famine, its historical background, and the current development programs offer a particularly significant case study of the processes of ecological deterioration and its relation to food production. And in the current wide-ranging debate over the origins of and solutions for the world food crisis, detailed examinations of particular cases are, in our view, the next step needed.

We believe that a careful study of this famine can demonstrate in both scientific and human terms how the concerns about food and ecology are bound together, connected with the structure of our own economy and society in ways that require far-reaching changes in the structure of our society and those abroad. A study of the famine can tell us of the many intricate relationships among the primary sources of food: soil, water, wind, plants, fungi, fertilizers, human labor, social organization. It can also tell us about that specific phenomenon of so much of the world's production systems, *profits*, and the institutions that serve it, and the small minority of people who benefit from it.

We will argue that the evidence from the Sahel famine shows that ecological deterioration and food shortages are not only linked with each other but also are structurally related to a specific form of production—international capitalism—and the many secondary effects it produces in even the most marginal and faraway environments.

This study attempts to place the great West African famine of 1968-74 within the context of the food and ecological crises of our times. It attempts to explain how and why this major famine took place, why major ecological destruction occurred, and why the development programs emanating from the Western capitalist nations are *not* likely to bring about a solution to the crisis. It is the thesis of this study that by understanding this famine we can begin to think more clearly about the causes and implications of other forms of ecological destruction, other famines, and the food crisis in general.

THE GREAT WEST AFRICAN FAMINE OF 1968-74

By all counts, the famine in West Africa ranks among the greatest tragedies of the 20th century. Food stands at the center of life for all individuals and for all human social organizations. When the production of food becomes difficult, the effects are devastating.

Many thousands of people die the slow and painful death that comes from eating too little and then nothing at all. In a famine, food is not available in sufficient amounts to sustain human life. A chain reaction is set in motion, a reaction affected by the intricate relationships among people, animals, plants, soil, weather, and many other factors in that complex set of elements called human ecology.

In Senegal, a cattle herder said: "I never saw a drought so bad. And my father and grandfather never told me of so terrible a drought where so many people have lost everything."[13] Michael Latham, professor of international nutrition at Cornell University, after a tour of the area, described the situation as "the most serious and perhaps the most spectacular drought and famine in African history." Elaborating on this, he noted: "This famine was important and different because (a) its duration was much longer than usual (perhaps six years), (b) it involved a very large area including at least six countries . . . and (c) it has some elements which contribute to make it a recurring or chronic problem (whereas most famines are acute, not chronic)" (US Senate, June 1975, p. 26).[14]

In 1973, Jerry Rosenthal of USAID reported: "The opinion of everyone with experience in the area is that the Sahel is on the edge of catastrophe."[15] U.N. Secretary-General Kurt Waldheim, after visiting the region in the fall of 1974, declared that there "has not been such a disaster in two centuries. I have never been so shaken by what I have seen here in all my life." And one eyewitness told of seeing "young children, men and women, pulling at the intestines of dead cows for something to eat" (US Senate, March 1974, p. 16).

The whole landscape of West Africa was changed. "Giant Lake Chad withdrew from its shore; by mid-1974 it was no longer a single lake, but four ponds. The harbor at Timbuktu dried up. Boats that usually delivered food to the surrounding areas were unable to go up the river to the city."[16] The Senegal and Niger rivers, usually imposing waterways, became shrunken streams in many places (Sheets and Morris, 1974, p. 11).[17] In 1972, the Niger River was at its lowest point in 30 years (FAO, 1973, p. 3).[18] The canals usually used as shipping channels up the Niger were sandy and unnavigable.[19] With the loss of the river came a decrease in nutrition. Dried river fish is an important source of protein for people in the area, but with the lack of rain and the change in water levels the fish supply declined. In Mali, in 1972-73, fish production dropped to one-fifth of the normal levels, and Chad also experienced a dramatic drop in its fish tonnage (Messiant, in Copans ed. 1975, p. 63). The change in river depth had another effect as well. The Senegal River normally acts as a barrier to the desert. Now, in the words of a Senegalese official, "the desert has crossed the river."[20] Wells, springs, and pools of water that could not be replenished shrank or altogether disappeared. Grasses wilted either before they flowered, or, if they reached that stage, their seeds were unable to germinate (FAO, 1973, pp. 2-3).

Food sources and export crops naturally were affected. Irrigated crops such as sorghum and beans in some parts of Senegal could be grown on only a fraction of their normal area. Rice growing along the riverbanks was curtailed (Messiant, 1975, in Copans ed. p. 63). In Mali, 40 percent of the harvests of millet and sorghum, staple foods, were lost in 1973. Mauritania harvested only 28,000 tons of grain in 1972-73; the usual yield is 95,000 tons (Messiant, in Copans ed. 1975, pp. 68-69). In Senegal, where peanuts provide 80 percent of the country's total export earnings, the crop in 1975 was expected to be half that of 1974.[21] In a good year, Mali produces about 850,000 tons of grain, but in 1973 it harvested only 450,000.[22]

With normal food supplies so sharply curtailed, people were forced to take extremely drastic measures to obtain any nourishment at all. These measures, necessary to the temporary preservation of life, broke the delicate ecological chain of inputs that might have sustained life in the future. An official in Mali described families who were eating only once every three days, and most ominously they were eating the seeds needed for planting next year's crop.[23] An African diplomat commented on this: "In my country, a farmer keeps his seed religiously. Year after year he selects the very best grain from his crop and keeps that for seed. But this year, they are eating the seed. I never saw that in my life."[24]

Nor did the famine stop at death. Entire ways of life were overturned. The nomads seem to have suffered even more than the settled agriculturalists; their herds, on which their whole social structure was based, were decimated. As of 1974, 25 percent of the total herds in the areas, or 3.5 million head, were wiped out. USAID estimated losses that ranged from a low of 33 percent in Niger to virtual extinction in Mali (Sheets and Morris, 1974, p. 11). Mauritania had 600,000 head left from a total of 2.5 million before the drought. But none of the experts can say exactly what the figures are (Sterling, 1974, p. 100).[25]

Cattle were slaughtered for food by their owners, or they were driven to areas where there was still water, which resulted in overgrazing. "In effect, cattle have died where there is grass but no water and where there is water but no grass."[26] Weakened animals were driven from the most parched areas of the north southward in search of water, where they were attacked by foxes, hyenas, and lions.[27]

Animals were the economic basis for nomadic society. Without them, it was difficult to provide dowries for prospective brides or for the necessary tent, furnishings, and utensils for a newly married couple. Traditional gatherings such as the Cure Salée (salt cure)—an annual gathering of nomadic groups in a northern pasture where the animals lick salt and drink from salty ponds—could not take place. The herdspeople believed, based on generations of experience, that the salt was necessary for the continued good health of the animals. The waters were described as "cleaning the animals' interiors." Necessary minerals were added to the diet of the livestock, and they browsed in pastures that were free of insects, animals, and human waste (Rupp, 1976, pp. 9-10). For the people, the Cure Salée was a time of feasting and ceremonies, where they played music, danced, and created and recited poetry (Clarke, 1978, pp. 51-75). With their herds weakened, and with insufficient pack animals, it was impossible to make the trek to the northern oases where these ceremonies were held.

Another consequence of the drought was that milk became scarce. The cattle that survived produced less, so little was available for the calves. This reduced the size of future herds even further (FAO, 1973, p. 5), and it meant that less milk was available for trading to the agricultural peoples, which was a loss to both groups.

Ironically, while the cattle were starving to death, potential feed in the form of cottongrain and peanut cake was being exported to Japan and Europe. In any case, these necessities for survival were priced beyond the means of the herdspeople (FAO, 1973, p. 6). The death of the cattle resulted in a loss in foreign exchange to Mali, Niger, and Upper Volta that was estimated by the United Nations at a quarter of a billion U.S. dollars (ibid., p. 4). The whole way of life of the herdspeople was threatened as their cattle perished in the sands or were sold for a pittance to buy some food. Even pregnant animals turned up at the slaughterhouses (ibid., p. 5).

Conditions were also difficult for the agriculturalists. Their crops failed, and they were left with no income. But dismal as the situation was for the farmers, it was worse for the herdspeople. If the farmers could hold onto their lands—and it is not certain how many actually lost them—they could pursue their livelihood when weather conditions improved. A U.N. official in Niger pointed out that the herdsman "is not like a farmer, who, if the rains come, can plant a crop and recover his losses at least in part. A herd takes four or five years to build. Where and how can the nomads do it?"[28]

The nomads are well aware of their dependence on their animals. A Tuareg woman, quoted in the *Christian Science Monitor,* starkly recounted her perceptions:

> Last year it was the animals, we could do nothing as we watched them die, watched them withering away until they would just stop and sit down with no strength to fight any longer. But for some reason there was hope while they lived. We knew that after they were gone we were next. Last year it was the animals. This year it is us. [Quoted in US Senate, August 1974, p. 142]

Similarly, a Tuareg man described his view of the situation to an American sociologist: "We have seen changes in nature. We are in a very serious situation where we no longer have enough to eat." He was asked by the sociologist: "And your future, how do you see your future?" The bleak response: "My future is patience and suffering" (Rupp, 1976, p. 6).

The nomads took desperate measures, including cutting down trees to feed the animals. The trees had served as barriers to the desert, and so the ecological problem of desert encroachment was compounded. They tried other things too. Cattle were moved in some places into areas where they were exposed to *trypanosomiasis* (FAO, 1973, p. 11). In normal times, these areas would have been avoided. In addition, with their usual herding patterns disrupted, the nomads found themselves quarreling with the farmers.[29] The traditional trading patterns between farmers and herdspeople were disrupted, as the New York *Times* put it, "to a serious, although unknown extent."[30] The nomads were driven by their very realistic fear of starvation. To stave it off, they ate cottonseed, intended for animal feed.[31]

Other forms of death were considered preferable to starvation. A 1974 New York *Times* account told of a tribe in northern Chad whose cattle had died, whose children had contracted diphtheria. But they told Moise Mensah, FAO administrator for West Africa, not to send aid. Diphtheria would be a quick death, better than the slow agonies of starvation (US Senate, March 1974, p. 174).

With their children and old people starving to death and their cattle dying, and with no way to stop the catastrophe, some people went mad.[32] An official in Mauritania described the mental condition of the nomads to

Claire Sterling, an American journalist. "They are dazed, stupefied, some go crazy. They simply can't take in the fact that their herds have been wiped out overnight" (Sterling, 1974, p. 99). An American Friends Service Committee worker told a U.S. Senate hearing: "Many of the social structures seem to have broken down under the stress of the drought. There were innumerable accounts of suicides, of men abandoning women and children in the desert, of mothers abandoning children, and that sort of thing, which does not normally happen in these societies. (US Senate, July 1973, p. 6). This was corroborated by Thomas Johnson of the New York *Times*:

> The region abounds in tales of suicide by men unable to support their families. Herdsmen near Asjoujt, Mauritania, tell of nomads who got tired of waiting for relief supplies and just walked out into the desert to die. In Niger and Mali there are numerous accounts of *Fulani* cattle raisers who, sitting in the sands near where their cattle had perished, said they were waiting for death themselves. [US Senate, July 1973, p. 6; cf. Sterling, 1974, p. 100]

It would be wrong, however, to view the nomads as simply passive victims of a tragedy. Many made strenuous efforts to provide for themselves and those dependent upon them. Although it was not an accustomed activity for the higher-caste Tuaregs, some of them tried gardening, expressing a desire to learn new types of economic activity so that they would not be solely dependent on their animals (Rupp, 1976, p. 32). They wanted jobs created in their areas, and they made it clear that they preferred work to charity (Rupp, 1976, p. 27; Sawadogo, 1975, p. 10).

For most herdspeople, gardening was not a viable alternative given the ecological situation and the lack of seeds, tools, and draft animals. There were other methods for dealing with the drought. In some instances, traditional forms of social assistance could be relied upon. Relatives who had not been badly stricken might help, and people assisted not only kinspeople but strangers, if they came from their village or tribe (Clarke, 1978, pp. 154, 196).

Emigration was another form of action. Some of the Tuaregs in Niger went to the uranium-mining town of Arlit; others went to Sahelian capitals and even the coastal cities in Nigeria and Ghana. The men found jobs as herders, woodcutters, brickmakers, food and water sellers, and laborers of various sorts. The Tuareg men habitually wear swords and knives and have an exotic countenance with their veil-covered faces. Their general appearance and warrior tradition created a demand for Tuareg nightwatchmen and guards for homes and businesses (Clarke, 1978, p. 244). For those who could not find work, there was a chance in the cities to sell their handicrafted possessions, swords and knives, amulets worn as a protection against calamity, and finely crafted camelskin boxes. Some women became prostitutes to earn money.

On a large scale, however, these solutions could not be effective, nor could they re-create the basis of nomadic society—the herds. Individual attempts to solve a major social problem could add to the dimensions of that problem. Thousands of people became refugees, wandering through the arid landscape with their families and belongings until they came to a refugee station or town. One description of such a trek gives some glimmering of what life had become for those forced to leave their homes and traditional occupations. In Niger, a family of ten, Sidi Mohammed, his brother, mother, and wife, who had recently given birth, and six children, including the infant, began to head south. They took with them two camels and three donkeys. They left their home after their herds had died, their destination a town where food was supposedly available. The wife died on the way, and the infant son, without his mother's milk, "wasted away to skin and bones." He too would die. Sidi desperately tried to give away his two youngest daughters, since he could not feed them, but no one was able to take them on. When they arrived in Maradi, they discovered there was no food, so they sold their animals and the sons went begging. The family took up residence in a refugee camp, hoping that the rains would come next year and somehow they could go back north and begin again (US Senate, March 1974, p. 136).

This scene, multiplied by thousands of families, led to the sudden swelling of cities and towns. In Mauritania, the capital city, Nouakchott, rose from 50-60,000 before the famine to twice that by June 1975 (US Senate, June 1975, p. 27). The situation was similar throughout the Sahel. Cornell University nutritionist Michael Latham made an analogy: "It is as if 5 million unemployed people were camped outside of New York City, and another 1 to 3 million each outside Chicago, Los Angeles, Philadelphia and some other U.S. cities" (US Senate, June 1975, p. 29). This may have been exceedingly unpleasant for both the refugees and the townspeople, but at least one U.S. relief official found a ray of sunshine in a seemingly gloomy situation. Referring to the camps and squatter villages, he remarked: "This in a way is good, because if we get food to the cities where most of the people are it's easier to distribute."[33]

Food may have been more accessible, but life was grim. In the camps, people were "subsisting idly on meager handouts of unaccustomed foods, living in a confined and ugly place, a world away from the freedom to which they are accustomed."[34] There were two million people in these camps (Sheets and Morris, 1974, p. 29). Many needed medical attention, but there was little medical personnel could do for people who primarily needed food. A doctor in Mauritania took reporter Martin Walker on a tour of his makeshift hospital, where scores of families were living in tents. He pointed out the "wards":

> Here is where we keep those with T.B. There are the typhoid patients. They all have anemia and soon they will have jaundice. There is not very much I can do. I write to doctors who were at medical school with me in France, asking for their free samples. But what they really need is protein—meat and milk from the animals that died last year. [Walker, 1974, p. 11]

As the doctor and the reporter walked through the tents, they saw "feet that had swollen, like footballs, from protein deficiency, at eyelids chalk-white from anemia, at limbs so like sticks that the knee joints looked gross and deformed" (ibid.). Walker observed a silent and grim scene:

> Something seemed to be missing, and it suddenly occurred to me that there were no children following us. In most villages in Africa, a white man strolling around bears a long train of giggling, thumb-sucking children. But here, not one child had the strength to play or to follow or even to wave away the flies that crawled on his sores. [ibid.]

Malnutrition was pervasive. A 1973 survey conducted by medical experts from the Center for Disease Control in Atlanta, Georgia, "found nomadic camps in Mali where 70% of the children were below the 'acute malnutrition threshold' as compared to 11.6% in the 1972 famine in Bangladesh." It was not much better away from the camps. The same study found that in settled villages in Mali, 47 percent of the children were "suffering severely from malnutrition." Throughout the Gao area in Mali, the survey found the people to be on a starvation diet of less than 400 calories daily. In Mauritania, the same report documented acute malnutrition rates of 18, 25, and 22 percent in various villages and camps (Sheets and Morris, 1974, p. 43).

Children were in such an advanced state of malnutrition that they could not even digest solid foods, and they needed a special milk ration, a ration that did not arrive in time for many of them. Technically, they died of edema; others died from measles. In Niger, the incidence of measles went from 2,886 recorded cases in 1971 to more than ten times that in 1972, 29,000, and by 1973 the incidence was more than 35,000. Similarly in Mali, the number of cases doubled between 1971 and 1973, while the death rate increased tenfold (Sheets and Morris, 1974, p. 50).

As is the case with so many of the statistics for the Sahel, no one is sure exactly how many people died. The usual estimate is about 100,000, most of them children. "On a proportional basis, it is as if a million Americans had been struck down" (Sheets and Morris, 1974, p. 1).[35]

The Famine Relief

Needless to say, the West African famine did not go unnoticed by the outside world. From many countries, relief programs were organized and certain efforts made to alleviate the immediate suffering and death. But the relief effort never came close to the real needs of the population.

The relief efforts got underway in 1973, a full six years after the famine began. The aid was slow in coming and fraught with delays and difficulties. Months passed between the time a country's needs were assessed and the arrival of food, medicine, and other relief supplies.[36] Several observers have commented on the inadequacy of the relief. Jeffrey Hodes, director of the student and young adult division of the United Nations Association of the United States of America commented in the *New York Times:*

> The international response to the region's needs offers a distressing example of the low premium placed on life in black Africa by western governments, the slowness of

the United Nations in mobilizing itself to respond to a natural disaster, and Washington's stinginess when there is no immediate political gain in giving sustenance to the "humanitarian" aspects of United States foreign policy.[37]

William Raspberry, writing in the *Washington Post,* noted: "It is a desperate situation. Yet there is in this country no air of crisis, no sense of the magnitude of the problem and hardly any knowledge of the catastrophe."[38] Hal Sheets and Roger Morris, in their report for the Carnegie Endowment for International Peace, stated:

The catastrophe of the drought did not happen suddenly. For at least four years, scores of officials from the U.S. and the U.N. were in the region, observing that the States of the Sahel were essentially helpless to deal with the drought, reporting the gathering disaster and dispensing some relief. Yet neither the U.S. nor the U.N. had contingency plans to deal with the tragedy as it reached overwhelming proportions by the fall of 1972. Aid that American and European medical experts believed might have saved many of the lives lost, such as measles immunizations among hunger weakened children, had not been planned. For tens of thousands it apparently came too late. [Sheets and Morris, 1974, p. 2]

Neither the United States nor the U.N. responded, but it was not because of a lack of information on the region. In Maryland, the World Climatic Record kept data on the water tables in the Sahel. Norman MacLeod, an agronomist at American University, remarked: "I don't think that people thought that an examination of climatic data was really worthwhile." USAID agents in the Sahel did report on growing shortages of water and the poor crops that were being harvested (Sheets and Morris, 1974, p. 19).

Scientific information could have been obtained, but it was not until the last moment. The Center for Disease Control in Atlanta had been conducting ongoing research into the epidemiology of famines. Some of the personnel there even had experience in the Sahel with smallpox and measles programs. But the doctors were not called in as advisers. They finally volunteered to assist in 1973 and went to Africa in June and July, providing information to both the United States and African governments (Sheets and Morris, 1974, p. 92). However, many USAID officials connected with the relief effort seemed unaware of the Center's report, and the same was true of FAO, which was handling relief work for the U.N. (ibid., p. 45). Some of the Center's findings might have been embarrassing for USAID in view of their measles innoculation program. Its data showed a high death rate from measles among nomads, and its statement on this was: "A well-planned immunization campaign . . . could have reduced measles morbidity and mortality" (ibid., p. 49).

Transportation of food when it was finally allocated was a major problem. American ports were clogged with ships carrying the grain that had been sold to the Soviet Union—grain that meant sales and profits for U.S. grain dealers. Even when food arrived in Africa, transportation facilities were inadequate and roads were poor or lacking altogether. An airlift was one solution, and the U.N. regarded the United States as the only nation with the resources to provide the needed air transport.

FAO requested 20 C-130s from the United States to transport 35,000 tons of seeds from the Sudan. The cost was $1,000 per flying hour, which was considered prohibitive by the director of USAID's Central and West African regional office. The FAO finally lowered its allotment to 1,000 tons and hired a private company, Alaska Airlines, to do the carrying. USAID "donated" $300,000 for this effort.[39] Three C-130 cargo planes were finally provided by Washington. Altogether, 63 planes from 14 countries were made available for the relief effort. They were mainly in operation from May to November 1973. Because the airlift was so slow in getting started, large quantities of food that had been stored outdoors were ruined in the rain (Mohamed El-Khawas, in Glantz, ed., 1976). One journalist noted: "The obstacles to an airlift cited by the donors . . . could have been overcome easily by the sophisticated logistical skills of the donors' armies" (Clarke, 1978, p. 194).

Nevertheless, in May 1978, the United States was quickly able to put a fleet of planes at the disposal of France and Belgium for a massive incursion into Zaire for the ostensible purpose of bringing out European "hostages." There is a vivid difference between this type of relief operation quickly mounted to save the lives of a few hundred, and the slow, cumbersome efforts put forth for the tens of thousands of African drought victims.

The same point with a very different sort of example is made by Thurston Clarke, a journalist who traveled in Niger and wrote of the effects of the drought on the Tuaregs.

> On October 29, 1973, a party of young Frenchmen left Abidjan in 50 Citroën cars for a 4,490 mile road rally, the first "Raid Afrique." Their route lay through Upper Volta and then to Niamey, Tahoua [towns in Niger], the Tenere desert, and north across the Sahara to Tunis. The rally was organized by Citroën (a French automobile company that also made trucks) and the Total gasoline company (with stations in Niger) that was under the patronage of the French Secretary of State for Youth and Sport. The rally arrived on November 2, and the following day the cars raced on through Tahoua, In Waggeur, and Agadez. A chartered plane patrolled the route, reporting to mechanics and support vehicles whenever a car broke down or needed replacement parts. [Clarke, 1978, p. 194]

Hundreds of thousands of tons of grain were ultimately sent to the Sahel. At least some of it ended up in the black markets at very high prices (Meunier, 1975, in Copans, ed. p. 123).[40] But even when it was distributed to the people, there were problems. "Many who ate food sent from the U.S. were weakened further by violent diarrhea because their systems could not digest the coarse sorghum" (Sheets and Morris, 1974, p. 36). At least some of the sorghum distributed was originally processed for animal feed and was contaminated with "foreign material" (ibid., p. 38). Even the American ambassador to Mali, Ralph McGuire, agreed with the Malian officials that "a large shipment of grain from the United States was not fit for human consumption." Michael Latham gave testimony to the Senate corroborating this point: "There is sufficient corruption in grain shipments to make it very plausible that such cargo is often underweight and the grain spoiled. As a consequence, people dependent on this food will die" (US Senate, June 1975, p. 31).

All this stands in contrast to a statement to the President from Maurice J. Williams, special coordinator for Emergency Relief to Sub-Sahara Africa, in August 1973. He smugly remarked:

We can take pride in the generous American response to the dire need of the peoples of Sahel Africa. Our response has been timely and has been in the great humanitarian tradition of America to help people sustain their lives in the face of catastrophic disasters beyond their control. [Sheets and Morris, 1974, p. 128]

One unexpected result of the drought should be noted. The U.S. government was able to distribute millions of pounds of civil-defense biscuits, made originally in 1962 and stored in New York for use in case of nuclear attack. Since that apparently was not too imminent, the biscuits were offered to CARE, which shipped them to Africa.[41]

Aid came from other sources too. The European Economic Community contributed several million dollars to the relief effort. France, long the dominant colonial and neocolonial power in this region, provided only about one-fifth of the total emergency assistance (Meunier, 1975, in Copans, ed. p. 117).

As far as the United States is concerned, Africa, and particularly West Africa, was not at the time a region of much political priority, and this partially accounts for the slowness of response. When Thomas Johnson, West African correspondent for the *New York Times*, testified before House hearings on the famine, he was asked by Representative Diggs (D-Michigan) why the U.S. government was so slow in responding to the disaster. Johnson replied: "Africa does not enjoy the priority of other areas with the U.S. government" (US Senate, July 1973, p. 8). The *New York Times*, on September 25, 1976, reporting on then Secretary of State Henry Kissinger's presumed settlement of Rhodesia's racial problems, noted that "the Secretary had been stunned by Soviet and Cuban success in Angola and conceded that he had ignored this continent in earlier policy considerations." Kissinger had been secretary of state throughout the famine period. One critic of the aid effort commented:

The United States was the largest donor to the Sahel with a total $130 million contributed during the 1973-74 crop year. Yet this amount is relatively small in comparison with the $2.2 billion of emergency military aid airlifted to Israel during the Yom Kippur War of October 1973. The amount of Sahel assistance also is much smaller in size and scope than the considerable amount of American aid given to the Thieu regime in South Vietnam for a similar period. [El-Khawas, 1976, in Glantz, ed., p. 95]

Again in 1973, the U.S. government expended about $50 million on the resettling of Soviet Jews. This works out to about $1,500 per capita. The per capita donation to 22 million starving West Africans comes to less than $5.00 (Laurie Wiseberg, 1976, in Glantz, ed., p. 113).

The Sahel region, even less than the rest of Africa, has never been one of major diplomatic or political interest.[42] There has been some interest in its potential economic resources, as will be discussed later. The famine, however, did not impede the development schemes envisioned by USAID.

It may even have helped them. A USAID official in Senegal, commenting on the shortage of meat as a consequence of the drought, remarked: "It's a sign that the overgrazing problem has been ended for a time at least."[43]

The nomads, thinking about their dead herds and dead children, and with no idea about their future, could not take such a sanguine view of the events. Had cognizance been taken of what was happening in the Sahel, their situation might have been less desperate.

1977 and Beyond: New Droughts?

After 1974, the rains were once again sufficient. The area's reprieve from drought, however, was a short one. The rains failed again in 1977 and in some countries even in 1976. The director of the FAO, Edward Saouma, warned of a new drought situation.[44]

Several months previous to this warning, the Foreign Minister of Niger had appealed for 200,000 tons of food and $12.7 million to fight rodents, birds, and insects that were attacking the crops.[45] The donor countries disagreed with this estimate and thought it should be lower, but some aid experts believed an oversupply was necessary in order to be sure that the poor distribution system would be able to provision the remote areas of Niger.[46]

In Mali by December 1977, new patients suffering from malnutrition had begun to arrive at the hospital that served the region of Timbuktu. It was this northern livestock-raising part of Mali that had been most affected by the 1968-74 drought. The regional commander described the situation as "very grave, people don't have enough to eat. It's impossible to save cereal. There are those who are eating nothing, who just live from one day to the next."[47]

In Mauritania, in 1977, production was only 30 percent of its normal levels.[48] The northwest section of the country had only 5 to 10 percent of its normal rainfall in 1977, and the north was receiving only 60 percent of its normal rainfall.[49]

Farmers in these countries were sowing their seeds several times. In Senegal, for example, when an early rain occurred in June 1977, farmers planted only to see their plants wither when the rains were insufficient. The process was repeated several more times.[50] Peanut production fell by 60 percent.[51] In addition, cereals were attacked by insects.[52] The cattle herds that were slowly being reconstituted were again threatened. The problem was compounded by the fact that large herds of animals, particularly goats, were crossing the Senegal River from Mauritania, searching for food on the Senegalese side.[53] With a lack of rain, the flooding of the Senegal and Niger rivers did not occur, so pastures and farmlands usually watered by this event were left dry.

The events we have described in this chapter make it dramatically clear that the Sahel environment has been greatly damaged, and the deterioration continues. In following chapters, we will describe the region in more detail, showing how this ecological degradation results from a series of social developments that have been occurring for several hundred years.

NOTES

1. *New York Times*, January 26, 1975.
2. *Wall Street Journal*, September 12, 1974.
3. *New York Times*, July 26, 1974.
4. This statistic is to appear in the 1979 FAO *State of Food and Agriculture* (forthcoming). The prepublication information was kindly provided to us by Francis Moore Lappe and Joseph Collins of the Institute for Food and Development Policy in San Francisco from their interview of July 17, 1979, with Keith C. Abercrombie, deputy director, Policy Analysis Division of the FAO, Rome. While malnutrition and undernutrition statistics are controversial, the experts mostly agree that the problem is extremely serious. The U.S. Department of Agriculture accepted a 1974 UN figure of 460 million as "malnourished" (Perelman, 1977, p. xii) while Charles Heiser cites an estimate of 400 million as "well-fed or over-fed, 650 million . . . more-or-less adequately fed, and 2,400 million . . . underfed" (1973, p. 203). Alan Berg estimated (1973, p. 5) from World Health Organization sources that 230-260 million of the world's children had mild to acute malnutrition by the early 1970s.
5. The Paddocks (1967), for example, propose dividing the world's poor nations into three categories: "Can't-be-Saved," "Walking Wounded," and "Should Receive Food." Any food we give to the first two categories is wasted, or harmful, in their view.
6. For studies appearing in recent years, see George, 1977; Lappé and Collins, 1977; *New York Times*, 1975; Hightower, 1975 and Hightower and DeMarco, 1973; and DeMarco and Sechler, 1975. An earlier study by De Castro (orig. 1952) has also been updated and re-edited (1977). In addition, Congress has conducted several lengthy hearings on the world food crisis; see President's Science Advisory Committee, 1967; and Senate and House Hearings on the World Food Problem, 1973, 1974, and 1975. See also Lester Brown's many contributions, e.g., 1974 and 1976, and Lerza and Jacobson, 1975.
7. Among the more important studies are Commoner, 1974 and 1976, and the many publications of the Sierra Club. Another major contribution is Erik Eckholm, 1976.
8. *New York Times*, March 26, 1972.
9. The expression is also the title of Chapter 2 of his work. cf. Freyre, pp. 53-57 and Hall, 1978.
10. See also Langer and Stanford Biology Group. Lewallen gives a figure of 18 percent for forests sprayed at least once with defoliants. The National Academy of Sciences report was summarized in the *New York Times*, April 29, 1974. The U.S. bombing of North Vietnam's dikes and its effects on rice production are documented by French geographer Yves Lacoste in *The Nation*, October 9, 1972, pp. 298-301.
11. In 1965, for example, 334 million pounds of vegetables were produced in Mexico but consumed in the United States. By 1974, this figure had risen to 1.1 *billion*, about half of it tomatoes. See McCaughan and Baird, 1976, p. 11.
12. Two members of the Hudson Institute, Max Singer and Paul Bracken, have responded to what they feel is the American "sense of guilt" about world poverty. Their argument boils down to saying that development was painful for us and will be painful for them—the poor countries. *New York Times Magazine*, November 7, 1976.
13. *New York Times*, September 25, 1975.
14. Not all experts are agreed, however, that the drought itself was the worst in recorded history. One French writer has concluded, using the statistical technique of "moving averages," that the rainfall shortages in 1912-16 were worse than for 1968-74, at least for the eight principal metereological stations in Niger (Derriennic, 1976, pp. 176-80).
15. *Washington Post*, July 1, 1973.
16. Ibid.; c.f. Albouy and Boulenger, in Copans, ed., 1975, vol. I, p. 53.
17. The Carnegie Endowment has also published Jack Shepard's *The Politics of Starvation* (1975), another work relevant to famine in Africa. Shepard discusses the political concerns that contributed to the disinterest of international donors in the situation, and he also analyzes the ways in which the Ethiopian class structure affected the aid when it was given.
18. For a survey of quantitative measurements on annual rainfall, monthly variations, timing of rainfall with plant growing seasons, and waterflow of major rivers, all with comparisons between normal or average amounts versus 1972-73, see Albouy and Boulenger in Copans, ed., 1975, vol. I, pp. 41-59.

19. *Washington Post,* June 16, 1973.
20. Ibid., July 1, 1973.
21. Ibid., January 20, 1975.
22. Ibid., June 17, 1973.
23. Ibid.
24. Ibid., June 29, 1973.
25. One detailed local study from Upper Volta reveals the extent of cattle losses as recorded by the veterinary attendant in the "Cercle," or district, of Oudalan. According to his records, in the villages served by the Markoye veterinary station the following data can be obtained:

Village	*Name of Pastoralist*	*Head of Cattle Before the Drought*	*Lost*	*Remaining in 1974*
Koinse	Souaibo dit Kouira	40	40	0
	Guibrila Gourankie	40	40	0
	Ousmane Kaissara	13	13	0
Ziguiberi	Azida ag Gouhoun	65	60	5
	Abdoulaye ag Takamades	70	63	7
	Maguiel	81	70	11
	Rali ag Higoum	50	48	2
	El Moustapha ag Ibrahim	13	5	8
	Mohammed ag Gourigoum	40	40	0
	Ibrahim ag Akilou	50	45	5
Goumgam	Sita Baye	80	40	40
	Tazoudi	160	130	30
Tangmole	Moussa Hamidou	65	36	29
	Sekou Dibi	10	4	6

Records of cattle holdings are always somewhat suspect, since nomads may try to underestimate them in order to reduce their taxes. But records from the same veterinary station were also obtained for vaccinations rendered. It is not likely that herdspeople would keep their cattle away from the vaccination team. In the town of Markoye, 1,913 cattle were vaccinated in 1972-73. In the vaccination campaign of 1973-74, only 809 could be found for vaccination. This sharp drop in numbers, while not quite so drastic as that given in areas further from town, is nonetheless dramatic evidence for large-scale destruction of the essential resource of the nomads (Garcia, p. 9).
26. *Washington Post,* July 1, 1973.
27. *New York Times,* August 23, 1973.
28. *Washington Post,* July 1, 1973.
29. *New York Times,* May 26, 1973.
30. Ibid., November 25, 1973.
31. Ibid., August 12, 1973.
32. Ibid., August 12, 1973.
33. *Washington Post,* June 17, 1974.
34. *New York Times,* September 27, 1974.
35. For a series of case studies of the effects of the drought and famine on farming and herding peoples of the Sahel, see Gallais, 1977. After the initial scare stories of perhaps 6 million people facing death, it has become fashionable in some quarters to *downplay* the number of fatalities by estimating them as a percentage of the general death rate for the entire region. By this approach, one author is able to claim that the demographic effects of the famine were very slight on a large-scale statistical basis (Caldwell, 1975). On a more folksy level, one American adviser to USAID explained that "the newspapers just kept showing a photograph of the same starving baby." In one of the few technically controlled studies, Mark Greene and a team of medical personnel from the Center for Disease Control in Atlanta, were able to calculate that for the nomadic population of Mauritania, a total of 960,000 people suffered 44,160 deaths from the famine alone (Greene, 1975, p. 19). If this death rate is representative of the entire region, given the estimate that one-half of all Sahelian nomads are found in Mauritania, and that the nomads represent about 15 percent of the population of the

Sahel, and that mortality among sedentary Mauritanians was not notably affected, one comes up with the figure of 100,000.

36. *New York Times,* May 21, 1973; October 3, 1974.

37. Ibid., January 9, 1974.

38. *Washington Post,* June 29, 1973.

39. Ibid.

40. One particularly sharp attack was leveled against the government of Senegal by the president of the General Union of Senegalese Workers in France, Sally N'Dongo, who charged the Senghor administration with lack of planning, corruption, and cover-up. See N'Dongo, 1975, pp. 106-30.

41. *New York Times,* June 2, 1974.

42. See, for example, Edward M. Korry's State Department Report, reprinted in Sheets and Morris, 1974, pp. 69-75.

43. *New York Times,* January 25, 1976.

44. *Le Monde Diplomatique,* October 1977.

45. *New York Times,* February 11, 1976.

46. Ibid., February 10, 1976.

47. Ibid., January 3, 1978.

48. *Le Monde,* April 18, 1978.

49. *International Herald Tribune,* November 21, 1977.

50. *Le Monde,* August 14-15, 1977.

51. Ibid., April 18, 1978.

52. *Le Soleil,* April 14, 1978.

53. Ibid., May 5, 1978.

part one

THE MAKING OF THE SAHEL FAMINE

1

Wasteland of Potential Plenty: Ecology of the Sahel

For most people who have read or written about it, the West African famine is primarily a "drought" in a region called "the Sahel." Press and journalistic accounts dwell upon the local definitions of "sahel" or "Sahel-Sudan," labeling the Sahel from its Arabic origins, as "border," meaning border of the Sahara Desert, or "shore" (Copans, 1975, vol. I, p. 5), implying the desert's oceanlike appearance to the caravan traders who crossed it for so many centuries. In a completely different vein, "sudan" derives from the Arabic word for *black,* a reference to the physical characteristics of the African populations farther from the southern "shore" of the desert. Sahara comes from the Arabic *sahra,* meaning wilderness (Fitzgerald, 1966, p. 56). These terms, while picturesque and perhaps of social importance to the caravan traders, are clearly not sufficient for a concept of the Sahel and Sudan as areas of human habitation and human production systems. How can we understand the nature of these areas?

In the simplest terms, both the Sahel and Sudan can be thought of as "transitional zones" connecting the desert on the north to the more lush and tropical regions of Africa. Thus the Sahel can be defined as "a belt, varying in width from 200 to 300 miles and extending from north of the Senegal River almost to the Red Sea coast" (Fitzgerald, 1966, p. 54), cutting across Africa from West to East along the southern edge of the Sahara Desert. As a region near the desert, it is dry and hot and lacks the resources to support large and wealthy populations. Indeed, the presumed dessication and poverty of the region constitutes a major element in the acceptance of the famine as just one more terrible blow to an area always on the brink of disaster. The Sahel is often pictured as "sparse," "impoverished," "undernourished," a place where people "eke out a living." Especially in the journalistic accounts of the famine, writers have warmed to the fascination of the cruelty of the Sahel toward the people who try to exist there. During the height of the famine, *Time* summed up everything for its millions of readers: "Even in the best of years, much of sub-Saharan Africa is stalked by the grim spector of famine."[1] Other writers were more specific. Syndicated columnist Carl Rowan told millions of newspaper readers of "that miserably poor, slightly inhabitable border of land just south of the great Sahara Desert," and he went on to point out that "this is forbidding land under the best of circumstances."[2] Claire Sterling joined the attack on the Sahel's potential in a popular account appearing in *The Atlantic Monthly*: "Intensely hot and eternally parched for rain, it [the Sahel] was never much good at sustaining life; its people are among the poorest in the world."[3]

These accounts evoke a paternalistic sympathy for the poor, helpless people of the region trying to make a substandard living in a hostile environment. But such accounts neglect two important aspects of the Sahel. First, this region has historically supported large empires, many of them among the greatest in Africa before the period of European colonialism. Second, the Sahel cannot be viewed as a region separate from the rest of West Africa. Both as a major link in the caravan routes and as part of a much larger set of ecological zones, the Sahel has a potential for supporting human life that is too often vastly underestimated. To understand fully the causes of the great famine, it is important to understand this potential. To understand why this is so, we must first see the Sahel-Sudan in the context of the larger geographical region of which it is a part: the entire geographical area known by the term West Africa.

West Africa constitutes an enormous region, with 2.38 million square miles. The usable area, according to well-known geographer William Hance, equals 40 percent of the size of the United States (Hance, 1964, p. 165).

From the Senegalese capital of Dakar on the farthest western tip, to Lake Chad, which marks the rough eastern boundary of West Africa, runs a distance of 2,100 miles, crossing 15 different nations, eight formerly French colonies, five formerly British, one formerly Portuguese, and Liberia. The political boundaries of West African nations run generally north-south, exactly cross-cutting the climatic zones that run east-west. Hance (p. 170) has noted: "West Africa has the greatest political fragmentation of any African area, explained in part by its length of contact with Europe."

West Africa is a region well defined geographically. Bordered on the south and west by the Atlantic Ocean and on the north by the harsh barrier of the Sahara Desert, the general area consists of a series of gradual transitions, moving from south to north. Tropical rain forests and swamps give way to thickly wooded "bush," to sparse woodlands, to grasslands, to steppes, or "sub-desert," and finally to the almost vegetation-free desert. In addition, several special features of West Africa have added to its great fascination for travelers and explorers: the Niger River, the *harmattan,* or desert wind, and the *tsetse* fly. These will be discussed below.

ECOLOGICAL COMPONENTS

Rainfall

One of the most important determinants of the human potential for any area of the earth is the amount and yearly distribution of rainfall. Climate specialists usually describe various rainfall zones by drawing boundaries, or "isohets," at specified intervals, usually in hundreds of millimeters or numbers of inches per year. These isohets serve as reference lines to allow the creation of technical definitions for the various climate/vegetation zones of an area as well. For West Africa, the zones and their isohet limits are shown in Figure 1.1.

What factors bring about these rainfall patterns? In the broadest sense, world weather is determined primarily by temperature differences in the atmosphere, which reflect varying amounts of solar heat reaching different parts of the earth. Areas near the North and South poles receive less heat than those at the equator, and these heat differences set in motion movements of air masses, which are also influenced by the presence of land or water on the earth's surface. In simple terms, the region of West Africa is influenced by a series of interacting factors. On the edge of the North Polar air cap is a region of sharp temperature rise that produces a jet stream, a band of westerly winds that blow across Europe from Spain, Portugal, and the Mediterranean. Around the edge of this jet stream are several swirling wind patterns known as "anticyclones," in which air masses sink, producing dry zones, such as the extremely dry air over North Africa and the Sahara Desert.

Moving in the opposite direction, off the Atlantic Ocean are warm, moist air currents known as the monsoons (from the Arabic word for "season"). As the earth's tilt changes its angle to the sun during a revolution around it, the temperature changes in the polar region set in motion a back-and-forth pattern: The monsoon winds blow northward toward the southern edge of the Sahara and are then pushed backward by the dry harmattan wind that blows off the desert, thus creating the dry season. The zone in which the two wind systems meet moves north or south, producing varying amounts of rain. This zone is known as the Intertropical Convergence (see Figure 1.2).

The Harmattan

For the people of the Sahel and its surrounding areas, weather patterns are summed up and perceived primarily in terms of the movements of the

Zone	Rainfall/Year	
	(in mm.)	(in inches)
Desert	Less than 100	4 or less
Steppe	100-300	4 to 12
Sahel	300-600	12 to 23
Sudan	650-900	26 to 34
Woodland	More than 900	Over 35
Rain Forest	2000-2600	80 to 100

Copans, 1975, vol. I p. 6; Rosevear, 1965, p. 385; Seifert and Kamrany, 1974, p. A7; see Pitot, pp. 218-19 for slightly different isohets and definitions. British geographer R. J. Harrison Church places the Sahel between the 100 and 500 mm. isohets and divides this into two parts, the Arid Zone and the Semi-Arid Zone (Dalby, 1973, p. 62).

northeasterly wind, the *harmattan*, which blows across cloudless skies and often carries large amounts of dust. It dries the mucous membranes of the eyes, nose, and throat. Skin becomes parched and cracks. Epidemics of cerebrospinal meningitis occur most often during these dry periods.

Days are hot and nights are cold. During parts of the harmattan, thick layers of dust in the air severely limit visibility (Church, 1968, pp. 24-25). The harmattan is so powerful that it often coats the shoreward sides of ships with red dust at distances of 100 miles off the coast of west Africa (Lateef, 1975, p. 390). In 1977, the U.S. National Weather Service claimed that a sandstorm in the Sahara was responsible for producing a haze over the skies of Miami, Florida.[4]

The harmattan is more than a carrier of dry air, difficult vision, and irritating dust, however. One effect of the dry air is that moisture evaporates from the atmosphere and soil, a process known as evapotranspiration (de Wilde, 1967, vol. 2, p. 15). It thus becomes a potential source of erosion, picking up and blowing away topsoils that have been deprived of the plant cover or water content that would hold them down. The harmattan, however, is also a carrier of deposits of fine materials, including clay, and thus brings about the possible *improvement* of soils in some areas. One British study in northern Nigeria, conducted in the 1930s found that the harmattan brought with it valuable elements for local soils: silica, alumina, titanium oxide, ferric oxide, lime, magnesia, potash, and soda. Perhaps it is with good reason that local farmers in the area of northern Nigeria believe that "a good harmattan means a good harvest" (Jones, 1938, p. 410).

A refinement of the total annual rainfall can be made by charting the annual distribution of rain. In the case of West Africa, this results in a generally consistent pattern, with a rainy season and a dry season. In the tropical rain forest regions, the rainy season accounts for most of the year,

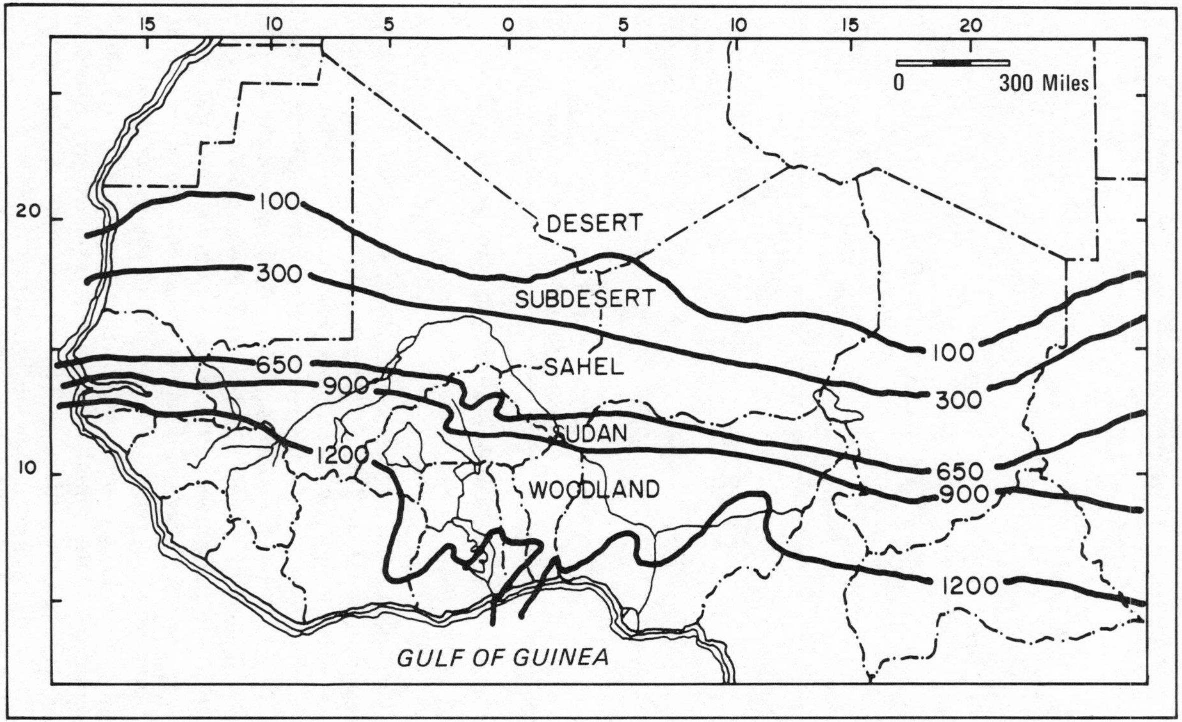

Source: Glantz (ed.), 1976, p. 234.

Figure 1.1. Climatic Zones of the Sahel Region

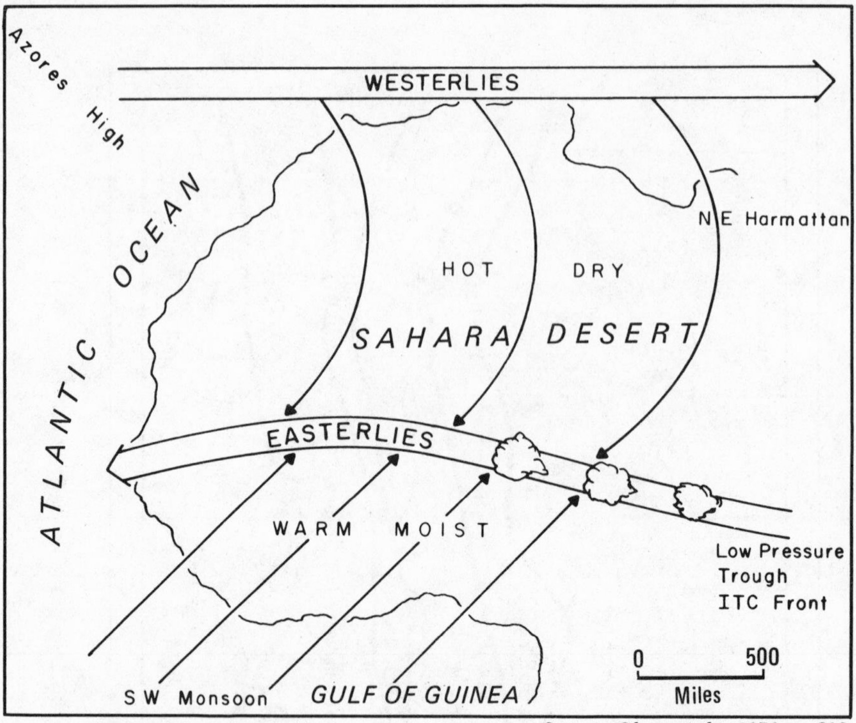

Source: Glantz (ed.), 1976, p. 218.

Figure 1.2. Regional Atmospheric Circulation in West Africa

with dry months in July and August. These dry months correspond to the only wet periods in the regions near the desert, so the Sahel-Sudan zone receives nearly all its rain in July and August, while the remaining months are dry. As with the amount of rain per year, its distribution over a 12-month period varies gradually between the formerly designated zones. In northern Nigeria, it has been calculated that the length of the wet season decreases by one day for every 3.4 miles one moves northward (Kowal and Adeoye, 1973, cited in Caldwell, 1975, p. 19). An important characteristic of rainfall in the regions near the desert is its extreme variation over long periods (Seifert and Kamrany, 1974, p. C 17), or the tendency toward wet years and dry years. Even more specifically, in a region with low rainfall, the correspondence of the rainfalls and the timing of seed germination and plant growth is of great significance. Thus, for example, at Niamey, Niger, rainfall in July 1972 was normal, while for August it was 60 percent below normal. The effect on plant life was to diminish the active growing season by 80 percent, since the August rainfall deficit corresponded with a period of the time when plants would normally have been in their active growing period (Albouy and Boulenger, in Copans, 1975, vol. 1, p. 46).

Another way to divide rainfall data over time is through the concept of a "useful rain." This means more than 3 mm. in a single downpour followed by another rain within one week at most. The importance of the timing can be seen from the rainfall data at Agades, Niger. In 1968, more rain fell than in 1967, but in 1968 there were 50.2 mm. within six days at the end of April, followed by only 0.5 mm. for all of May. The April rains caused rapid seed germination, but most of the seedlings withered and died during May (Bernus, 1973, p. 129). Some Sahelian farmers have developed careful techniques for determining whether rainfall is sufficient to plant cereal seeds. One Niger farmer interviewed in 1974 was asked how farmers knew when it was time to sow. His answer was: "We dig the ground. If the humidity extends to just over the distance between the extremity of the fingers and the first quarter of the forearm (about 22 cm.), the quantity is excellent for sowing" (Laya, 1975, p. 51). Useful as it is, this technique cannot predict whether the rains will continue, and one historical account tells of farmers in 1931 who tried sowing their seeds seven times before the failure of the rains to recur forced them to give up (Salifou, 1975, p. 24).

One important effect of the uneveness and irregularity of rainfall is the manner in which it complicates the uses of modern technology and, indeed, perhaps even exacerbates some of its potential negative effects. For example, many West African crops respond well to heavy doses of fertilizer containing nitrogen. If the rainfall patterns are irregular, however, a heavy dose may cause the plant to grow too fast for the water supply, so if late-season rains are not on time, the plant will create its own drought conditions, having used up too much of the water through rapid growth induced by the application of the fertilizer (Russell, in Moss, ed., 1968, p. 131; cf. Péhaut, 1970, p. 83).[5]

A final aspect of Sahelian rainfall is its harshness. Although the total amount of rain in a season or year may not be great, the rain that does fall falls torrentially, often washing away sandy soils left from the previous months of dry, hot weather, or carrying off small amounts of hardened, caked soils, which, over long distances, become large masses of moved earth.[6]

The erratic spacing and timing of rainfall, increasing as one approaches the desert fringe, produces the conditions for pastoral nomadism. Only with the nomadic form of society can a viable economy be constructed in some regions, with people looking for pockets of good pasture that have been created from "chance" showers (Caldwell, 1975, p. 19; cf. Swift, 1973, p. 74). In between these pockets, the herds of cattle, sheep, goats, and sometimes camels serve to store the energy from water and grasses, making it available for human uses.

The Niger River

Although rainfall is undoubtedly the major source of freshwater in most parts of the world, rivers are also important for transporting water to large regions that receive inconsistent rainfall. Rivers also often bring rich soils from steep highland regions and fan these soils out over large flatlands or deltas, creating areas with a good combination of earth and water for agriculture. So important are rivers that it is commonplace in historical and anthropological studies to attribute a large role in the rise of ancient civilizations to rivers such as the Nile, the Indus, the Yangzi (Yangtze) and the Tigris-Euphrates.

As everywhere, West Africa's rivers are greatly affected by the topography. West Africa is generally a rather flat region, with most of the area lying from 600 to 1,600 feet above sea level. Except for the Fouta Jallon highland plateau of Guinea in the southwest corner, the Guinea highlands, and a few mountains in Sierra Leone and Liberia, for the most part West Africa is like a platter gradually tilted from the desert down to the sea. Only the Volta River is rough and rugged through much of its course. The Senegal and Gambia rivers provide some useful transportation services as well as irrigation functions. Furthermore, the Senegal River, curving north and west from the Fouta Jallon highlands of Guinea, has carved a basin of 333,800 square kms., an area of 12 percent of the total surface of Guinea, Mali, Mauritania, and Senegal. This river basin holds great potential for the development of irrigated rice and other grain production (Maiga, 1974, 1976) and has been the subject of an enormous amount of research and development proposals in the past 12 years.

But it is the Niger River that dominates much of the geography and history of West Africa. The Niger begins in the Fouta Jallon highlands and runs a large S-curve for 2,600 miles through almost every climatic zone (Church, 1968, p. 18). Its strange course, up to the edge of the desert and then back to the sea, has led some people to postulate that it was once two separate rivers running in opposite directions. One, now called the Upper Niger, flowed north from the Fouta Jallon into a salt lake, which is now a dried up part of the Sahara. Recent satellite photographs of the Upper Niger seem to indicate a dry river bed that might have once carried the stream north and east toward the current Senegal River, however, so the Niger may never have flowed straight into the desert (MacLeod, et al., 1977, pp. 282-83). Nonetheless, the satellite images strengthen the case for two or more different river paths in ancient times.

Sanche de Gramont has summed up the beauty and fascination of the Upper Niger (1976, p. 34):

> To see the Niger flowing through the desert is one of nature's wonders, as incongruous as the umbrellas on the operating table made famous by the Surrealists. A great river is passing through an area which is by definition without water. Tuareg tents are pitched in the sand, camels drink from the river, and on a gently sloping rose dune indigo tunics have been stretched out to dry, like flags. In the afternoon, the dunes throw shadows, a wind flurry scoops up sand, and wild ducks fly in formation across the lilac sky.

The Lower Niger had its source in the now desolate Ahaggar mountains the Sahara and flowed south into the Gulf of Guinea. As the Sahara dried up at the end of the last ice age, the two rivers changed courses until one captured the other. The dry river beds are said to be still observable in the desert.

But the curious shape and odd history of the Niger are only the beginning of the fascination of this river. For, owing to the slightness of the slope through which it runs and to the great seasonal variations in its supply of rainfall, the Niger encompasses two major features of great importance to the potential for human production of wealth along its banks. First, the Niger is highly erratic in its current. Differences up to 35 feet have been recorded between its high and low levels (Sanche de Gramont, 1976, pp. 27-28). This renders the Niger difficult for boat transportation.

Even more significant, however, is the great inland delta of the Niger, which is found in present-day Mali. One geographer has described its great size: "In and after the rainy season the river floods areas between Segou and Timbuktu as extensive as England and Wales" (Church, 1968, pp. 18-19).

Much of this inland delta is swampy and its potential for agricultural production has yet to be developed. The great inland delta of the Niger may be one of the earth's most important potential sources of agricultural production.

The Tsetse Fly

Interacting with the rainfall, the rivers, and the harmattan is one of Africa's most important insects. The *tsetse* fly has long been thought of with a kind of romanticized dread outside of Africa as the carrier of "sleeping sickness," a disease that debilitates thousands if not millions of Africans as well as foreigners. Probably more important, however, to human habitation in West Africa, is the indirect effect of the tsetse as a regulator of the giant cattle herds of the Sudan and Sahel. These herds are the mainstay of life for a large part of the population of the entire region. Although there are more than 30 known species of tsetse, all can be broken down into two main types: those living in the rivers and those living in the bush of the southern Sudan (Stenning, 1960, p. 143; Church, 1968, p. 187). The tsetse carries an infection known as *trypanosomiasis*, a highly debilitating disease of the larger types of West African cattle. As a result, those nomadic groups that herd cattle must stay clear of the tsetse zone.

The tsetse itself, however, is far from immobile. During the rainy season, the fly moves north with the damp air and water pools and full river beds; during the dry season it moves south toward the rain forest. The cattle herders, in turn, follow the patterns of absence of the fly, making the best use of the richer southern pastures during the dry season and moving north toward the Sahel, chased by the fly, into regions where the pastures are more dispersed (Stenning, 1960, pp. 143-47). Needless to say, the nomadic herdspeople are acutely aware of the relationship between the tsetse and diseases in their cattle.[7] Ironically, however, it is during the driest periods, when rainfall patterns become abnormal, that infections rise. This comes about because the cattle in long dry periods seek water in ever more dangerous places, moving south along the rivers and toward the bush until they drink in tsetse-infected puddles or river gullies (Stenning, 1960, p. 147). It is thus drought and not a long wet season that brings on the tsetse and its infection.

In addition to the tsetse, other pests influence the movements of the animals kept by humans. In particular, many cattle and sheep have parasites in their intestines, which, when excreted, can rapidly infect an entire pasture area. The West African Fulani herdspeople have dealt with this problem for centuries before the introduction of veterinary medicine by moving their herds after a maximum of seven days at a single pasturing site (Veyret, 1954, p. 76). They have also pastured cattle late in the day (after the dew has burned off the grass) during the rainy season to reduce the possibility of spreading bacteria and parasites (van Raay and de Leeuw, 1974, p. 9). Other practices noted by outside observers include the use of branding of infections, which may help to convert them from chronic to acute status, speeding the recovery (Consortium, 1977), and herbal medicines. Cattle herders in one region of eastern Senegal appear to distinguish six different kinds of animal diseases and have four specific types of treatments using local products (République du Sénégal, 1977a, p. 21).

Soils

As with rainfall patterns, soils in West Africa vary rather consistently from the southern coast to the northern edge of the desert. The soils of the tropical rain forest are, surprisingly to many people, poor in important minerals such as silica and phosphorous, both of which are necessary for the growth of plants, especially plants with nutritional value to humans. Indeed, the technique of "slash-and-burn" agriculture practiced in the rain forest appears to be a rational adaptation to this problem. After a site has been selected, the trees and brush are chopped down at the beginning of the dry season and left to dry. Near the end of the dry season, the recently cleared field will be fired, and soon after the planting can begin. Although early observers sometimes proclaimed the burning as a testimony to the laziness of non-European farmers, modern scientists have discovered that the burning of the dry bush has many positive effects. These include the releasing of phosphorous, silicone, and other minerals that tend to accumulate in the leaves of tropical plants, thus turning the ash into an organic fertilizer, as well as possibly killing harmful bacteria while stimulating beneficial ones in a way that improves the nitrogen cycle (Geertz, 1963, p. 15; Russell, 1973, p. 95). The slash-and-burn system has thus recently come to be appreciated as a sophisticated system of transforming, as one Indonesian agricultural scientist has explained, "a natural forest . . . into a harvestable forest" (quoted in Geertz, 1963, p. 25).

In the woodland and savanna regions, the tropical soils are weathered sandstones, ferruginous, pure silicates of aluminum, and red argils. The soils of these regions are eroded by torrential rains—even though these rains occur only at certain times of the year—and by the harmattan

(Skinner, 1965, p. 3; FAO, 1962, p. 9). These soils, and the desert sands of the Sahara itself, have been formed from erosion of underlying crystalline rock, which tends to resist water seepage (Jones, 1938, p. 407). As a result, wind and water movements often push the sands, which results in the shifting of dunes. Similarly, and of far greater consequence for human habitation and the development of the famine, *the potential for soil erosion in the areas closer to the desert is very great* (Comité, 1974, p. 50). An erosion survey conducted by ORSTOM (French Overseas Scientific Research Institute), found the highest rates of soil-loss potential are in ferruginous soils of the Sahel, where more than 200 tons per square km. may be lost each year (cited in Berry, n.d., p. 14). African farmers have responded to the differences in soil and climate by adopting different patterns of slash-and-burn techniques. In Nigeria, for instance, farmers in the rain-forest crop a particular field for one to two years and then put it under fallow for eight to fourteen years to allow the forest secondary growth to recover. Farmers on the Nigerian savanna-woodland region crop their fields for four years and follow it with a fallow of up to 30 years (Russell, 1973, p. 92).

Some experts consider the poverty of African soils in general to be a major factor in the poverty of the continent's people in this time period. Several FAO and IBRD (World Bank) experts have pointed out, for example, that the soils of Africa are poor in calcium. They have also noted a total organic content of only 0.2 percent to 0.5 percent as compared with 2 percent (i.e., 4 to 10 times as rich) in the cultivated soils of Europe. High temperatures and high acid content inhibit the growth and activity of bacteria, which could improve the soil for food-producing processes (de Wilde, 1967, p. 16). But, as one soil specialist has noted, in calling for increased attention to the nitrogen cycle in savanna areas of Africa, "The soils may be inherently far less infertile than is commonly thought" (Vine, in Moss, ed., 1968, p. 107).

Vegetation

Most descriptions of West Africa's ecology choose the vegetation as the major feature distinguishing one zone from another. Plants and plant associations are relatively easy to chart, and they provide a backdrop for any consideration of human subsistence.

Along the southern coast, and reaching for several miles inland, the region is covered with a tropical rain forest. Rain forests are usually pictured as disease ridden and mosquito infested, with dangers lurking behind every tree. In actuality, the tropical rain forest is one of the earth's most important life-givers and sustainers. As one ecologist puts it: "The tropical rain forest is the most complex ecosystem on the earth" (Richards, 1973, p. 59). Rain forests are the "climax" or evolutionary outcome of a long process of development through selection in which eventually several types of zones or niches come to coexist. At the very top is a canopy of trees, sometimes reaching 150 or even 200 feet in height. This canopy receives most of the sunlight, helps to hold in the moisture underneath, and keeps the temperature of the forest cool and relatively even.

Below this canopy are several ecological niches, including an undergrowth or "brush" that receives only flecks of sunlight. Surprisingly, the rain forest is not so thickly grown that it must be hacked through with a machete. Instead, the forest, at ground level, is characterized by a wide variety of different plants, interspersed but not very close together. The variety and intermixing of single examples of different species makes the rain forest the polar opposite of its ecological counterpart, the single-species plantation in which one type of crop is grown tightly spaced over a wide area. It is probably of ecological significance that the slash-and-burn agricultural system replicates the mixed character of the forest with harvestable plants, and thus it has a less distorting effect on the myriad species of plants and animals than does modern "scientific" agriculture.

Contrary also to widely held views, the rain forest rarely is devastated by pests or blight (Richards, 1973, p. 62). These become widespread usually as a result of imbalances brought about by certain features of human intervention. The most spectacular case appears to be that of the sickle cell, still known to many in the United States as a genetic disease. Scientists have been able to show that the sickle cell occurs in various parts of the world *and in all races* as a survival adaptation wherever there is a high incidence of malaria. Malaria in turn becomes a major problem with the increase in the population of the *anopheles* mosquito. The mosquito, however, cannot breed in shady or fast-flowing water, the main characteristics of water in tropical rain forests. With the increase in agriculture in West Africa, unshaded puddles result from forest clearing for the fields, and malaria spreads (Livingstone, 1958).

Conditions in the zones near the forest have also worsened in some cases. In the 19th and 20th centuries, the incidence of malaria increased dramatically following the construction by French colonial engineers of large irrigation works. Particularly during the dry season, the canals would turn into puddles of stagnant water and the number of mosquitoes—and mosquito bites—would increase (Magasa, 1978, p. 95).

Today, most of the rain forest of the world has been destroyed. Particularly in West Africa, little remains of this once environmentally rich formation. Plantation fields and groves have replaced the forest, and the "climax" environment has been "degraded."

In addition to the various forest environments, there are at least two types of swamps in West Africa: the brackish-water (mosquitoes do not breed in brackish water) or mangrove swamps found in estuaries and tidal areas of rivers, and the freshwater swamps, where the soil is continually waterlogged (Rosevear, 1965, p. 386).

Savanna and Woodlands

Savanna (grassland) and *woodland* (forest) have come to refer to the same general regions of West Africa. Savanna denotes the presence of grasses.

Grasses are nearly absent from the rain forest and are a sign of degradation of the climax forest. At the same time, the West African savannas in fact are interspersed with trees, and thus the term woodland also has its application (Rosevear, 1965, p. 386).

The savanna-woodland areas of West Africa begin in the mid to northern areas of the coastal nations of Ivory Coast, Ghana, Togo, Dahomey, and Nigeria and extend into the southern portions of the former French West Africa, including Senegal, Mali, Upper Volta, and Niger, the principal nations affected by the Great Famine. The savanna-woodland vegetation area corresponds to the terms *sudan* and *sahel* on rainfall charts and in newspaper accounts.

The regions closest to the rain forest contain stands of five- to eight-feet-high grasses interspersed with small trees spaced so that their crowns usually do not touch. Each year the grasses are burnt off in the dry season, but these sprout quickly back. The trees, which range from about 12 to 20 feet in height, also seem to recover from the fires. In a few areas, tropical rain forests remain as islands within the southern woodland areas, particularly along river banks (Rosevear, 1965, p. 387).

As the savanna-woodland region approaches the desert to the north, several changes gradually occur. The grasses become shorter and thinner, reaching a height of only four to five feet. One short tree, the acacia, begins to appear. One species of this tree has a bright yellow-and-orange bark, while others appear more as shrubs, and some have a grayish color. The acacia is an important source of food for herds, for its leaves have a 20 percent protein content (Gillet, n.d., p. 24) and it offers other benefits as well. Research in Senegal indicates that its leaves are rich in nitrogen and calcium. Plants growing near the leaf droppings from the *acacia albida* give greater yield and better quality harvest (Pélissier, 1966, p. 273). Some species of palm trees are also found, such as the fan palm, whose point is a favorite of elephants in more easterly parts of Africa. The strange baobab tree, with its trunk shaped like an upside-down carrot (Lateef, 1975, p. 389), also appears in this region where the harmattan blows and rainfall becomes increasingly scarce. Like the acacia, the baobab tree provides many useful resources. Its fruit pulp is a souring agent for drinks, while the seeds, fermented or dried, offer nutritious elements. The leaves, dried and powdered for use in soups (Owens, 1973, p. 10), contain vitamin A and minerals such as calcium and iron (important because millet is deficient in these), and are used in many medicinal preparations. One study indicated that baobab leaves had 15 times the calcium content of cow's milk by weight (Pelissier, 1966, p. 265).

Sahel

The northernmost reaches of the savanna-woodland are the regions known to readers of the press accounts of the famine. This is the Sahel proper, a region cutting across the nations of Senegal, Mali, Upper Volta, Niger, northeast Nigeria, and Chad, and reaching even across the Sudan and down to Uganda and Tanzania in East Africa. The most prominent characteristic of this region is the appearance of a single species of acacia (*raddiana*, a favorite food of the camel), which rises to a height of only two to three feet. Despite the wide spacing of these trees, they nonetheless form a sort of woodland area along with another shrublike tree, *commiphora* (Rosevear, 1965, pp. 389-390). Even when spaced far apart, the tree "cover" in the Sahel remains of great ecological importance. The trees hold water in the soil and therefore prevent erosion. They provide forage for animals, particularly toward the end of the dry season. In addition, these sparse trees provide firewood and building materials, and food (fruits and leaves), as well as pharmaceutical products for human use (Centre Technique, n.d., p. 43). Just as the animals are dependent on trees, so the acacia is dependent on cattle, which ingest the seeds, carry them to new areas, and excrete them. The seeds, having passed through the animal's digestive tract, are able to germinate and grow (Centre Technique, n.d., p. 43; c.f. Pélissier, 1966, p. 268).

The ground between trees is generally covered with low grasses, which make excellent pasturage. Two types of plants in this region have very different responses to weather patterns. Those living in hydromorphic soils are extremely sensitive to seasonal changes in weather; during the rainy season these grasses multiply rapidly, so much that they can generally withstand heavy grazing. Other grasses, called psammophilic, or sand-loving, are less season-sensitive because the sand dunes on which they live retain moisture at a more or less even depth. These plants in turn can produce seeds at very young ages, allowing for plants to reproduce even if eaten early in life by foraging animals (Gillet, n.d., p. 23).

An important part of the plant life of the Sahel consists of floodwater pastures (pâturages de décrue). These pastures are made up of several species of grasses growing close to the beds of West African rivers, including particularly the great Niger inland delta. The floodwater grasses supplement the seasonal pastures in good years and become the major pasturage, along with the sand-loving grasses, in years of low rainfall.

The Sahel grades gradually into a region identified as steppe or subdesert in which all the trees disappear and the grass grows only in scattered tufts, which appear shortly after the rainfall periods. Here the plant cover may represent less than 30 percent of the total land surface (Gillet, n.d., p. 21), but much of this is *panicum turgidum*, a grass much sought after by pastoralists. Also growing here in a region sometimes referred to as the Northern Sahel are *aristida longifora* and *aristida acutiflora*, the latter providing good food for camels, gazelles, and addax antelopes right up to the edge of the desert (Gillet, n.d., p. 22). Beyond this final border stretches the great Sahara Desert itself, where all plant life is concentrated in a few areas near oases or other sources of localized water.

Yet the desert is a more intricate system of different environments than might appear at first glance. Even in summary form, the Sahara can be broken down into at least six major types of landscape. There are the palm groves, which thrive at oases, where underground water comes close to the land surfaces, and the date palm groves, which "seem to flourish only in almost rainless districts where there is subterranean water which its roots may reach" (Fitzgerald, 1966, p. 60). These date palms grow by the millions in various parts of the desert and remain both a major means of nourishment and an uncharted potential resource for future development of this wasteland. There are also regions of small shrubs, rocky wastelands, and gravel and pebble deserts. Finally, there are the great stretches of sand alone, the *ergs*, which the caravans avoid, such as the great Libyan Desert, a stretch of sand running for 800 miles (Fitzgerald, 1966, pp. 59-60).

WEST AFRICA AS AN ENVIRONMENT FOR HUMAN PRODUCTION

Farming

In all the regions of West Africa, whether defined principally in terms of rainfall, soil, or plant types, human groups have developed the means of subsistence and much surplus wealth. In the forest regions with high rainfall, an incomplete list of the resources (adapted from Church, pp. 97-137) available and used in the support of human life includes:

rice	Melegueta pepper	bananas
red rice	okra	pineapples
oranges	tomatoes	sugar cane
limes	chilis	tobacco
lemons	cocoa	oil palm
avocado pear	ginger	coconut palm
Turkish tobacco	fluted pumpkins	kola nut
pawpaw	coffee	cassava
yams	maize	cocoyams
beans (many types)	peas	breadfruit
rubber	piassava	raphia
African spinach	cucumbers	gourds
onions	shallots	melons
chickens	rabbits	bees
giant snails	ducks	turkeys

Moving into the savanna zones, we find most of the vegetables from this forest list, with millet or sorghum taking over from yams and rice as the main staples, along with additional foods such as the shea-butter tree, peppers, and eggplant. Fruits are reduced mostly to mango and curcurbits. Millet may reach a height of 12 feet in the southern savannas. Millet seeds grow abundantly in loose-flowering heads on the ends of the stems.

The savanna zone also provides conditions for growing cotton, sesame, and sweet potatoes. Small-sized cattle that are immune to the tsetse also are found, along with chickens and rabbits. In Chad, manioc (cassava) has recently been moving south into climatically richer zones as a "hunger crop" and "is becoming increasingly popular" (Reyna and Bouquet, in Caldwell, ed., 1975, p. 569).

As one approaches the Sahel region, agriculture continues to depend upon millet, but here the plants grow to heights of only six feet. Sorghum, a grain similar to millet, is also widely grown in the Sahel and nearby regions, but millet is the more drought resistant of the two plants and can survive with as little as 300 mm. of rain per year, the driest isohet of the Sahel (Copans, ed., 1975, vol. 1, p. 6).

Along the Atlantic coastal fringe of the Sahel and Savanna zones lies a remarkable agricultural zone stretching from Cape Verde and Dakar, Senegal, northward all the way to the Mauritanian border at St. Louis. In this region are many thousands of hectares of *niayes,* or depressions, surrounded by sand dunes held in place by coconut or palm rows. The depressions contain rich soil and hold water during the rainy season while maintaining a water level just three to twelve feet below the surface even in the dry months. These niayes are becoming major sources of tomatoes, onions, green beans, green peppers, and other products (Centre for Horticultural Development, 1975).[8]

Pasturage

North of 12 to 14 degrees latitude, the tsetse disappears, and small cattle are replaced by the larger, humped or Zebu cattle, which give more milk than the smaller cattle to the south. Zebu cattle, genetically adapted to the low-water and low-protein diets, are able to feed on sorghum stalks and the residues of various other crops. Their dung provides fertilizer for the next season's planting (Dalby, 1973, p. 17). Zebu cattle represented 80 percent of the 4.5 million head of cattle in Chad in 1967. The Arab-Zebu strain weighs about 550 to 1,000 pounds and gives about one-half gallon of milk per day. The Bororo-Zebu (belonging mostly to Fulani tribespeople) weigh 900 pounds, while the Kouri strain, found around Lake Chad, weigh up to 1,100 pounds and give more than one and a half gallons of milk per day (Reyna and Bouquet, in Caldwell, ed., 1975, p. 570; cf. Deshler, 1963).

The almost flat terrain of West Africa creates special conditions and difficulties for Sahelian animal herders. Unlike the western United States for example, where there are many mountain ranges and thus many alternating ecological zones within short distances of each other, Sahelian herders must travel many hundreds and even thousands of kilometers to achieve the changed pasture conditions necessary for different seasons.[9] As a result, herders pass through many different human culture areas, resulting in a wide variety of herder-farmer contacts and economic transactions. For example, in much of the Sahel, an important set of economic and social relationships is based on the exchange of milk and millet. This exchange network links together herdspeople of the more northerly regions on the edge of the desert with agriculturalists farther to the south, who in turn are in contact with the rich climatic zones of the savanna and, eventually, the rain forest. (More will be said of these relationships in Chapter 2.) Zebu cattle are thus a resource of great significance for all of West Africa.

However, they are susceptible to trypanosomiasis, carried by the tsetse, and move south only during parts of the dry season. Sheep and goats appear in increasing numbers in the Sahel and provide meat, milk, and skins, which are used for various types of containers, clothing, tent material, rope, and many other valuable items (Nicolaisen, 1963, pp. 404-5). Goats have been described as having a "pernicious" effect on the environment since they prefer to eat buds and will devour those of virtually any plant in the region. At the same time, milk goats, when properly managed, can forage on rocky slopes where other animals cannot.

Camels are also found throughout the northern Sahel. They are used primarily for milk and for transport. Camel milk, however, is less dependable than goat's milk, for it cannot, for biochemical reasons, be easily made into cheese. These facts further increase the importance of goats, particularly on the desert fringe (Nicolaisen, 1963, pp. 404-5). Camels, however, have the great value of being able to retrieve water from vegetable foods directly and to store it for several months (Monod, 1975, p. 106).

In addition to domesticated animals, many wild species live in the pasturage zones of the Sahel. Antelopes, gazelles, and oryx provide game for hunters. These animals are well adapted ecologically to their environment. They forage by plucking out the plant stems without harming the more vital parts of the plants (Gillet, n.d., p. 27). Wildlife is a great potential resource in the Sahel for many reasons. Wildlife, which only minimally disturbs the environment, is a low-cost source of protein and uses several layers of the ecosystem, in effect speeding up the circulation of nutrients among these layers, which is beneficial to the environment.

In the northern savanna (Sudan) and southern, or wettest, part of the Sahel the peanut, or groundnut, is grown over extremely large areas. Peanuts supply oil for cooking and for many industrial products as well as protein. The residue from nuts that have been crushed for their oil can be made into cattle cake and can also be fed to pigs.

Farther north at the edge of the desert, agriculture disappears, and we find nomadic herdspeople with cattle and especially sheep and goats, which are able to eat the leaves of the thorny acacia shrub of the region (Mountjoy, 1966, pp. 614, 621; Nicolaisen, 1963, p. 45).

Through all the regions, wherever the rivers flow—in particular, the Niger—ducks can be found, and there are turkeys in many areas, as well as bees (and thus honey). Horses and donkeys live in areas with Zebu cattle. From the ocean waters of the south and west to the lagoons of the Guinea coast, and in the Senegal River and the great bend of the Niger River and Lake Chad, fish are abundant.

THE SAHEL: WASTELAND OR LAND OF PLENTY?

From these summaries of the major ecological features of West Africa, the question of the poverty of the Sahel and its susceptibility to drought and famine can be seen in a new light. The Sahel is without sufficient rain to support a thriving and fully autonomous agriculture—and yet there is much water under the surface that can be tapped with wells. A study conducted in Upper Volta, for example, estimates that yearly water replenishment in underground containment exceeds by 10 to 100 times the present needs of the population (Levinson, 1976, p. 30, citing Seifert and Kamrany, 1974). The absence of the tsetse and the tenderness of grasses growing in low-rain, sandy soils means that the Sahel has a rich potential for herding and for the production of milk, meat, hides, and other products of goats, sheep, and cattle. The Sahel taken by itself is a region of vastly greater resources than the poverty of most of its inhabitants justify. Two studies by U.S. researchers have noted the potential of the region. One, by an M.I.T. group, has determined that the Sahel has the capacity to support two million more people than are currently there under present conditions. With a minimum of modernization of technology, the region could, according to this study, support 30 percent more people. (Seifert and Kamrany, 1974). Similarly, a Kansas State University study claims that Mali could increase grain production by 28 times present amounts without taking land from present crops (Ackels et al., 1970, p. ii). Estimates for Upper Volta stand at 13 times present production and Senegal 3.7 times, even without reducing the land in other crops, which include mainly peanuts grown for export (*ibid.*, pp. iii-iv). At a more specific level, studies conducted by the Department of Theoretical Biology at Wageningen, The Netherlands, have indicated that Sahelian pastures can produce 50 kg./ha. of dry matter (e.g., grasses) for each mm. of rainfall. Thus a pasture in a region with 300 mm. could provide 15 tons (metric) of grasses on a one-hectare plot. Test plots taken in the region of Niono, Mali, indicate that only two to four tons of dry matter is currently produced, showing the potential for a possible three to four fold increase in cattle-feed availability under improved conditions of soil and water control (interviews conducted at Projet Production Primaire Sahel, PPS, Niono, Mali, March 17, 1978).[10]

Finally, it is necessary to consider the Sahel again within the context of West Africa as a whole. In this context, the Sahel appears not as an isolated fringe of an impassable desert barrier; rather it is a major element in what could be a wealthy community of various ecological zones, each with much to offer the others (cf. Copans, ed., 1975, vol. I, p. 6). From the tropical rain forest through the Sahel and right up to the edge of the Sahara, West Africa is a region with great potential for providing sustenance for the people who live there. Sahelian animal products could be exchanged for grains, cotton, coffee, and other products of the tropical forests and woodlands to the south. Enough could be produced and exchanged from one zone to the other so that a drought would not have to result in famine.

Indeed, for many centuries Sahelian people *did* produce and exchange from the resources of the land, and a generally prosperous life was not only possible but a reality. To see how this prosperity was achieved, we will discuss the early history and anthropology of the Sahel.

NOTES

1. *Time*, April 30, 1973, p. 25.
2. *Newark Star Ledger*, September 7, 1973.
3. Claire Sterling, "The Making of the Sub-Saharan Wasteland," *The Atlantic Monthly*, May 1974, p. 98.
4. *New York Times*, June 26, 1977.
5. It also appears that increased applications of nitrogen fertilizer heightens the susceptibility of millet to rust (CILSS, 1977, Plant Protection, pp. 110-11). Robert Charlick (n.d.) reports that the Hausa farmers of the Zinder region of southeastern Niger are very concerned with the problems of rainfall undependability and its effects on fertilizer.
6. The erosive effects of this torrential rainfall are diminished somewhat by the flatness of much of the Sahelian landscape, but in mountainous areas, such as the Cape Verde Islands, this rainfall causes great soil loss wherever the tree cover has been lost. Rainfall data from the Cape Verde station of Sierra de Malagueta indicates that during the period 1961-70, there were twelve occasions where daily rainfall exceeded 100 mm., and one station, São Jorge dos Orgaos, once received 534.5 mm. in a single day (République du Cap Vert, 1976, and Petit Monographie).
7. Indeed, the awareness of African farmers and herders of the effects and the ecological position of the *tsetse* in East Africa has aided one researcher in discovering an entire hidden history of precolonial ecological control. Previous to the German-British occupation of modern-day Tanzania, Kenya, and Uganda, huge cattle herds were protected against *tsetse*-borne infection by methods including bush-clearing, night travel, and burning dung and other chemicals to create a natural fly repellant. The intrusions of the colonial government, warfare, and forcible movements of the populations resulted in a breakdown of this traditional system and the very rapid *spread* of *tsetse* infestation to areas where it had not previously been known (Kjekshus, pp. 52-56 and passim). The testing of this thesis for West Africa should be of high priority for historians and ecologists of the area. A beginning has been made in Dorward and Payne, 1975.
8. The property relations of the region of the *niayes* have been studied at length and in great detail, more than any of the Sahelian regions. See Dia, 1972.
9. This comparison was made by a range expert in the USAID Niger Range and Livestock Project Outline, p. 122 (1977, No. 683-0202).
10. In a separate study undertaken in the Zaria-Katsina region of northern Nigeria, where rainfall averages over 800 mm. per year, van Raay and de Leeuw (1974, p. 19) found that upland savanna pastures actually yielded 1,500 kg./ha. in the month of November; but this dropped to only 50 kg./ha. in May.

2

Farmers, Herders, and Empires: West Africa Before Colonialism

In the past, the peoples of West Africa evolved very effective means for using the area's resources, organizing types of productive systems that were well suited to specific ecological conditions. Herding and agricultural societies each developed and established exchange relationships with one another. Land that was unsuitable for crops was often very well adapted for cattle grazing. Not only did people exchange animal products for agrarian ones, but the animals became one of the principal means of preserving the land's fertility. For hundreds of years, both pastoral and farming peoples benefited from this division of labor.[1]

The savanna region of West Africa was the scene of several successive major empires, whose prosperity rested on their intermediate position between the forest zone and North Africa. These large kingdoms, incorporating ethnically diverse peoples, maintained for the most part a general level of prosperity very different from the contemporary situation in West Africa. Organizing trade between different regions, having a thriving agricultural base, effectively using the livestock of the pastoral peoples, these states maintained relationships of equality with the countries of North Africa. Their international relationships contrast sharply with the dependency situation existing in modern West Africa. In these empires, towns thrived, centers for international and regional trade. These settlements have either completely disappeared or have been much reduced in size and wealth.

PASTORALISM

Herding has been important since early agricultural times. Although some sedentary groups maintained animals, for the most part the raising of livestock was an activity of the several pastoral peoples of West Africa, in particular the Maures (whose name has been given to Mauritania), the Tuaregs, and the Fulani.* Pastoral nomadism is an effective way to use land that is marginal for agriculture: too steep, too dry, or at too high an altitude for crops to be raised successfully.[2] Animals could be moved with the weather cycle to take advantage of available water and pasture. The herders moved according to the locations of food and water for their animals at a given time of year. Groups established traditional rights to particular pastures and wells. This mitigated both the possibilities of disputes and their overuse. Decisions as to when and exactly where to move were not simple or automatic for a given time of year. The state of the pastures in a given locale, the exact timing of the rains, and the compositions of the herds had to be taken into account. Since animals differed in their needs for food and water, the herders' camps were located at an optimal distance from each of these necessities and within the physical limits of movement of the younger animals (Smith, 1978, p. 85).

The material culture of the pastoral societies reflected the necessity of frequent travel. Goods were light, with utensils made of wood rather than of heavier pottery. Shelters were easily dismantled and assembled, such as the tents of the Tuaregs or the simple huts of the Fulani.

The animals were the nomads' most important possessions, the basis on which their societies were built. Pastoral groups maintained several types of animals; the exact number and composition was a combination of ecological considerations, i.e., what food and water was available, the owner's social status, and the necessity to take precautions against possible disasters. In good times the herds would be allowed to grow, taking full advantage of plentiful resources. In a drought or epidemic, a proportion of the animals would die (Monod, 1975, p. 117). If the herds were always small, then in bad times pastoralists might find themselves without any animals at all. If half of the livestock was lost, it was better to have begun with a herd of fifty than of twelve (van Raay, 1974, p. 9).

A diverse herd was another way to hedge against disaster, and several types of animals were maintained. In the more northerly desert fringe, groups such as the Tuaregs raised camels in addition to cattle, donkeys, goats, and in some instances sheep. Groups such as the Fulani, more to the south in the savanna itself, principally kept cattle and small ruminants. Camels, cattle, sheep, and goats all have different biological needs. Conditions fatal to one species may be quite appropriate for the well-being of another. Camels, of course, are the best adapted to arid zones, able to go

*In this chapter, the past tense is used throughout, even though, in varying degrees, some of the conditions described still exist.

for a week without food or water during the hottest times of year and able to travel relatively long distances in a day. Cows or sheep, however, can go for only two days without sustenance, while a goat in the cool season can do without water for up to two weeks (Smith, 1978, p. 85).

Different species are able to make use of different kinds of vegetation. Cattle and sheep require grass; camels graze and browse, eating the branches and leaves of trees and shrubs. The hardy goat can live entirely on browsing, requiring no grasses at all (Swift, 1973, p. 73). Should food resources for one species become drastically reduced, it is possible that the other species in the nomad's herd would still be able to survive and produce food.

The various animals raised in West Africa also differ in their breeding cycles. Cows and camels deliver their young once a year, in the rainy season, a time when food and water are readily available. Sheep and goats can breed more often, and the owners decide how frequently mating takes place, depending on local conditions. Goats are the hardiest and quickest breeding of all the domesticated species in West Africa, and they provide milk for most of the year unless conditions are exceptionally bad (Swift, 1973, p. 73).

Animals served many functions. Live herds were the principal way in which the nomadic populations stored their food. Animals were usually not slaughtered for meat unless they were old or sterile. Goats were the one exception, although they were not eaten regularly. The main food staple was milk, fresh or soured, and milk products. Animal skins provided leather, which was used for a wide range of goods. One anthropologist found that contemporary Tuaregs made fifty different items from goatskins alone (Nicolaisen, 1963, p. 41). There is no reason to believe that leather would have been any less important than it is today. Animal skins were also the basis for tents, saddles, shoes, and sandals. The urine of the animals was used in making medicines. The animals themselves were a means of transport, and in difficult times they could become trade items (Smith, 1978, p. 94).

The social relationships of the pastoralists reflected the importance of protecting themselves against adverse conditions. The internal social relationships among the people certainly served this end. In addition, an important aspect of life in West Africa was the way in which pastoralists were integrated with the agricultural peoples to allow each to benefit from the other's resources. The Tuaregs and the Fulani will be examined in some detail to illustrate these points.

Pastoralists

The Tuaregs, now numbering about 500,000 people, are believed to be descendents of North African Berbers who fled into the Hogghar Mountains of what is now southern Algeria, from there moving further south into the Air Mountains of Niger and the northern plateaus of Niger and Mali (Clarke, 1978, p. 32).[3] Living in the most arid zones of West Africa, the

Tuaregs developed a variety of mechanisms for coping with a harsh climate and a lack of abundant vegetation.[4]

The Tuareg social system was one of marked inequality, although, the status of women was relatively high. There were several social strata, principally those of nobles, their vassals, marabouts (Islamic religious functionaries), artisans, and slaves. The slaves were captured by raiding parties, mounted on camels, that swooped down into the savanna, pillaging and retreating. The nobles were the warriors and slaveholders and owned the largest numbers of animals. Among the nobles were differences in wealth, as reflected in herd sizes.

Despite the inequalities, there were mechanisms for redistributing the livestock so that more people had access to the animals' milk and other products. There were systems of loans to friends and relatives. The loans could be recalled any time the lenders felt they needed the animal for their own use, and the nobles were also expected to lend each other animals upon request. The poorer members of a Tuareg group would be loaned lactating females, and they were not expected in turn to lend animals to anyone else. The loans might be for a very long time but the owners had the right to demand a return at any time. The poor could also be given animals as outright gifts and there was some religious and moral pressure to do so.[5]

Slavery, although hardly a desirable condition, was not comparable to slavery in the plantation economies in the New World.[6] Slaves were not engaged in producing for a large market, although some labored under very bad conditions in the salt mines (Derriennic, 1976, p. 76). Only newly captured slaves could be sold, and after about a generation in captivity, the slave or his/her descendents were integrated into a family unit. Slaves could be given to another master in exchange for an injury the slave had allegedly inflicted on a free person. Some researchers think this was a way in which slaves could manipulate the system to acquire a new owner. They might deliberately injure, in some small way, an animal belonging to a person whose ownership they preferred. That person might then demand the slave as compensation for the damage (Bernus and Bernus, 1975, p. 33).

Slaves might live in their owners' camps or they might be installed on farms in the savanna zones, where they would grow crops. A portion of the crops would be owed to the owner, who usually passed by once a year for his share. The slaves in the camps would care for animals, garden in areas where there was sufficient water, and collect wild grains. These, an important dietary supplement in bad times, were sometimes secreted in leather pouches near group wells to be used as a reserve source of food (Smith, 1978, p. 79). Some varieties, in addition, were used as medicines.

The savanna grain was another source of protection for the Tuaregs should the herds be diminished (Baier, 1976, p. 50). The Tuaregs were warriors and conducted raids on the villages to the south, which were widely scattered and unable to offer effective resistance (Lovejoy and Baier, 1976, p. 134). The millet, sorghum, or rice that the villagers had stored would be appropriated in part by the raiders. They might even capture the villages, and the inhabitants would then be forced to pay their Tuareg overlords a grain tribute each year. In addition, the agriculturalists provided the nomads with food and accommodation when they would pass through. The villagers also paid some Tuaregs grain for their "protection" against other Tuareg raiders. This pressure from the pastoralists meant that the farmers had a strong motivation to produce more grain than would be needed for just their own use (Baier, 1976, pp. 4-5).

In bad times, the Tuaregs might send some of their animals to pasture in the savanna or even move south themselves. The villages provided one of the most important safety mechanisms for the Tuaregs in times of drought. The inhabitants were obligated to care for their visitors from the north, and while this was certainly an unwelcome burden, the villagers did not seem to starve as a result—and the Tuaregs had an alternative to remaining in an area that could not support them or their animals. When times improved, the nomads collected their herds and dependents from the savanna lands and returned north again to make use of the pastures and waters of the Sahel and desert zones.

In addition to demanding grain as tribute from savanna agriculturalists, the Tuaregs were very much involved with the caravan trade that passed through the Sahara from North Africa and into the cities of the Sudan to the south. Grain was one of the commodities carried by the caravans. The trade will be discussed in more detail below, but at this point the Tuaregs' relationship to it should be pointed out. The Tuaregs had control of certain salt supplies, an important trade item, and they also had animals and their products, as well as dates from oases to exchange for grain, cloth, swords, and so forth.

The Tuaregs were able to capitalize on their knowledge of desert routes and water sources by becoming caravan guides. Some Tuaregs took up residence within the trading towns themselves, following the occupations of merchants and brokers, lending their services to their fellow tribesmen when these came on trading missions (Lovejoy and Baier, 1976, p. 159).

In sum, the Tuaregs, inhabiting what might seem to be barren wastes, developed ways in which they could use existing resources. Having a somewhat exploitative relationship with the peoples to their south, they nevertheless performed certain important functions in the life of pre-colonial West Africa and were significant factors in the caravan trade, the lifeblood of the empires that eventually developed. The Tuaregs maintained the wells, which provided water for the thirsty desert travelers, and their keen knowledge of the desert and Sahel were vital to a caravan's safe journey. They raised food in the form of herds in areas where not much else could be grown. These animals provided sustenance for the Tuaregs and their dependents, and when traded, they could be used by those living in the agricultural zones.

In the next chapter, we will discuss the ways in which the roles of the Tuaregs have been drastically reduced. The traveler in the northern reaches of modern West Africa, however, can still get a sense of the life of these people. Riding in a Landrover across a seemingly endless tract of sand, rock, and scrub, one will sometimes encounter a band of Tuareg men gracefully astride their camels, wearing long robes and veiled to the eyes by traditional face coverings. They are a vivid reminder of the vitality that once existed here and could perhaps exist again under the right conditions.

Fulani Herders and Farmers

More numerous than the Tuaregs, and living in a more southerly zone, are another primarily pastoral people, the Fulani.[7] They are one of the most numerous and widespread of the West African ethnic groups with a modern population of around 6 million (Mabogunje, 1972, p. 26). They appear to have originated as a distinct group in the 11th century in Senegal, most likely as a result of mixing between the Tukulor of this area and invading Berbers from North Africa (Murdock, 1959, p. 405). The Berbers and their herds, it is thought, penetrated into areas that were not well suited to agriculture, and they eventually intermarried with the sedentary peoples living nearby. Some of the descendents remained agriculturalists, while others continued in the pastoral traditions of the Berbers (Mabogunje, 1972, p. 26).

During the 12th and 13th centuries, the pastoral Fulani migrated eastward. Traveling either as individual family units or in very small groups, they posed no threat to existing social groups. They were not competing with them for land, since, like their ancestors, they were able to make use of areas that were of no value to the farmers. Coexisting in a symbiotic relationship with the farmers, they remained a distinct ethnic minority with their own language and culture (Forde, 1960, p. 132).[8]

The Fulani had several forms of social organization: completely pastoral, semisedentary, and completely sedentary, practicing agriculture and raising a few animals. The semisedentary social grouping seems to have been a temporary form, occurring when herds became greatly reduced (Dupire, 1962, p. 39). Under the latter circumstances, the Fulani established farms, usually of a smaller size than those of the more exclusively agricultural peoples. The household might split, with the sons herding the animals away from the farm and coming back to help at the busiest seasons. Alternatively, the entire family might reside on the farm until harvest time, then store its grain and move off to the dry-season pastures. When they were able to reconstitute their herds, they would usually return to a completely pastoral life (Stenning, 1959, p. 8).

As pastoralists, the Fulani and their Zebu cattle (described in Chapter 1) moved with the seasons, taking account of the availability of food and water, the presence of cattle diseases, the presence or absence of the tsetse fly and the possibilities of exchange with farmers. As was mentioned previously, the tsetse fly is a problem south of 12-14 degrees latitude, and so the Fulani would begin moving north, keeping ahead of the fly, going as far as the northern limits of the Sahel and the semidesert scrub zone. With the coming of the dry season, they would move in the reverse direction.[9]

It was especially during the dry season that the exchanges of food and services would take place between herders and farmers. The farmer's harvested fields would become the Zebu's temporary pasturing grounds. Edward Stenning, who has studied the Fulani, describes their approach to the farmers. The pastoral Fulani

> appointed Functionaries whose duty it was . . . to herald the approach of the herds and to give gifts of milk and butter or of bulls for slaughter to the [people] in whose territory pasture was sought. Cattle might be coralled on fallow land shortly to come into cultivation. These relationships . . . set in train a further relationship of mutual advantage—the women's trade in dairy produce against grain and root foods. That relationship . . . was a symbiotic one of simple economic reciprocity between face-to-face units of comparable scale and organization. [Stenning, 1960, p. 154]

During the rainy season, the Fulani might also care for the farmer's cattle. In the states which developed later, the pastoralists would also have to pay a tribute to the ruler or his representative, and they might be asked to furnish warriors in exchange for slaves and horses (Stenning, 1960, p. 154).

Important as the farmer's grain might be to the Fulani and the Fulani's milk a supplement to the farmer's diet, the cattle themselves provided a most valuable service to the land. The animals, grazing on the harvested stalks, would manure the land, an essential part of the process of keeping the agricultural lands fertile. Modern studies have found that the organic carbon content, a rule-of-thumb indicator of fertility, was two- to three-times higher in fields where cattle had been present than where they were not. There is no reason to believe this would have been different in the past, since the cattle breed and their fodder is the same (van Raay, 1974, pp. 17-18).[10]

In addition to providing fertilizer, the cattle broke up the ridges on which crops had been planted and stripped the stalks that were left from the harvest. These were used for house and fence construction. Both of these actions were great conveniences for the farmers. In return, the farmers would, beside giving grain to the nomads, allow them access to trek routes and water supplies. This mutually advantageous relationship existed for centuries in West Africa.

AGRICULTURE

Agricultural activities filled the lives of the savanna peoples. The invention of agriculture, in the words of Africanist A. G. Hopkins, was "one of the outstanding achievements of the indigenous inhabitants of Africa" (Hopkins, 1973, p. 29). By the end of the second millenium B.C., the cultivation of crops had replaced the gathering of wild foods (Levtzion, 1973, p. 11).[11]

West African agricultural development was greatly enhanced by the use of iron implements. The exact origin of ironworking is still disputed by Africanists (Mabogunje, 1972, p. 13), but there is general agreement that techniques for using iron have existed in West Africa since around 500 B.C. (Hopkins, 1973, p. 44). Iron provided implements for spears, enabling military conquest and the formation of the African states, but it also had advantages for more peaceful enterprises. The iron hoe, or *daba*, was the principal West African farming tool.[12] Draft animals and plowing were not used. (The plow is unsuitable to the relatively thin soils.) Through their contacts with North Africa, people had probably become aware of the plow but had made a conscious and rational decision not to use it (Hopkins, 1973, p. 37). With a relatively simple technology and the use of irrigation on certain crops (Forde, 1960, p. 126), people were able to meet not only their subsistence needs but could produce a surplus that was able to support a state apparatus (Stride and Ifeka, 1971, p. 14; Levtzion, 1973, p. 117).

Slash-and-burn agriculture was characteristic of West African farming. Trees were cut down, their stumps left in the ground. The branches and other debris were burned and the ashes spread over the ground, where they acted as a fertilizer. A plot could be cultivated for several years, then the depleted soil was allowed to recover. A new field was cleared, while on the previous one the stumps of the trees regenerated and new trees grew from seeds carried in by the wind, birds, or animals. After a period of fallow, the field was again ready for planting. Slash-and-burn, a method widely used throughout the world, is very effective as long as there is sufficient land to allow for the fallowing of depleted fields (Mauny, 1961, p. 251; Russell, 1973, pp. 86-101; Suret-Canale, 1973, pp. 77-78). Archaeological evidence indicates that throughout West Africa, areas that are now populated with farming peoples have been so since the time of the European Middle Ages (Mauny, 1961, p. 252). This is indirect evidence, at least, that the agricultural practices did not so deplete the soils that the populations were forced to migrate elsewhere, and it is testimony to the ability of the people to make use of local resources without endangering their own subsistence base.

The valleys of the Senegal and Niger rivers provided excellent crop land. Millet and sorghum were among the most important staple crops. These grains are well suited to the conditions of brief, intense rains and intense heat that characterize the area, and they can do well even in impoverished soils. Millet has many uses: (1) it is an excellent food; (2) it can be brewed into a nourishing alcoholic drink; (3) the bran and leaves from mature plants can be fed to animals; (4) the stems can be used to make fences, mats, thatchpoles, brooms, and also fuel; and (5) the stems of a red-seeded variety provide medicine and dye. Fonio, a low-yielding variety of millet, was grown as a "hunger crop." Requiring very little moisture, fonio has a short growing season and thrives in soils that are too depleted for other crops. If planted earlier, it can be harvested while waiting for the more desirable grains to ripen (July, 1975, p. 75). Rice seems to have been developed in West Africa by the Mande people, independently of rice production in Asia (Portères, 1970, in Fage and Oliver, eds., p. 47). The Bambara groundnut, a plant somewhat resembling the peanut, was cultivated and used to make flour. It was also the basis of a porridge that was eaten with milk (Lewicki, 1974, p. 3). Several types of beans were grown, as well as cucumbers and corn.[13]

Several different kinds of crops may have been grown as a form of protection and as a way to use available resources, analogous to that of the pastoralist's mixed herds. The Wolof of Senegal, for example, grew one variety of millet near a village and another farther out, while sorghum was cultivated on patches of clay soil. Near their dwellings, manioc and cotton were grown (Curtin, 1975, p. 125). Some of the more isolated Wolof villages, which were relatively unaffected by later changes in agriculture, seem to have been in the same locale for as long as four hundred years. The cultivated fields were surrounded by forest, and much use was made of the various trees that grew there (Pélissier, 1966, pp. 471-72), as described in Chapter 1.

The exchange of products between agriculturalists and herders has been discussed above. Some peoples, such as the Serer of Senegambia, kept their own animals in addition to farming. The Serer grew millet as a principal crop and kept animals in the fields that were lying fallow. The manure made it possible to continue using some fields for many years. The cattle were fed with the leaves of the *acacia albida* during the dry season, when there was a scarcity of other food (Curtin, 1975, p. 27).

The Balantas in the Casamance region of Senegal also kept their own herds, whose manure made it possible to raise millet on long-lasting fields. In the dry season, the animals would be tethered outside the house at night. Each May, before the rains started, the dwelling would be moved to a place where the yields had not been good, and the animals would be allowed to manure this land (Pélissier, 1966, pp. 600-602, passim). In the rainy season, the herds would be taken to the forest, returning at night to the farm. Women carefully collected the droppings of the young cattle and spread these on the fields. The Balantas were also rice growers, and the collected manure would be used on the rice fields as well.

Relatively little is known about the details of the history of the stateless societies of West Africa such as the Balantas. However, some general statements can be made that give a sense of the achievements of the peoples of this area. Basil Davidson, the well-known African historian, writes:

> Though without any knowledge of modern science, West Africans had already solved many of the essential problems of living in their vast and difficult region. The had developed a degree of immunity against dangerous fevers. They had learnt the secret of many medicinal herbs and how to use them to cure sickness. They had discovered how to look after cattle in conditions of great heat. They had become expert at growing food in the forest. They had found how to recognize minerals in rocks, how to sink mines, how to get the ore and smelt and work it. [Davidson, 1966, p. 151]

THE WEST AFRICAN EMPIRES

Although information is available about the organization of the African empires that cover the period from about the 6th to the 16th centuries, the record is not as full as would be wished. Arab travelers, geographers, historians, and Islamic scholars have left a record of life in these kingdoms, and their writings provide the main source of information about the West African states.

There seems to be general agreement on the relative abundance and prosperity in West Africa. Before the Europeans came to dominate the continent and its trade, Africans themselves were able to take advantage of the regional differences between the southern forest zones and the northernmost parts of the continent and establish trading networks between them. One of the most important preconditions for this was the introduction of the camel into Africa by the Romans sometime during the first century A.D. The metaphor of the camel as a "ship of the desert" may have a trite ring, but this gangly animal, which really does rock back and forth like a boat, made it possible to traverse the Sahara, which previously had been a forbidding ocean. Towns on each side of the desert have been compared to port cities, and the analogy seems appropriate (e.g., Levtzion, 1973, p. 10).

The beginnings of each of the empires and the details of their internal histories are not yet thoroughly known, but all arose in the savanna region, where contact among many different groups was occurring and movement was easier than in the more impenetrable forest zones to the south. Each of the empires included similar occupations: cultivation, pastoralism, and trade with the different regions of West Africa. Militarily, each had large numbers of calvary armed with iron spears and iron-tipped weapons. Most important for their development, however, were the links they sustained between the forest zones and North Africa. The approximate boundaries of the major empires, along with the locations of important towns, and the principal trade routes of West and Northern Africa are shown in Figure 2.1.

Each state had a class of nobles and warriors as the highest social stratum and a king at the apex. The majority of the population cultivated the land. The court's wealth came from control over trade rather than from heavy tributes from the peasantry, although there was certainly taxation, and presumably much of this was unwelcome. The class system seems to have been based more on the advantages the upper strata gained from controlling trade revenues than from oppressive exploitation of the producers. Taxes formed one of the bases for the kingdom's wealth. These were mostly paid in kind, in some cases in gold. Customs duties were another source of revenue, as was booty and pillaging; control of the gold supply sometimes enriched the treasury (Diop, 1960, pp. 80-82). Trade was usually conducted by Moslem merchants, originating from North Africa in about the seventh century (Trimingham, 1962, p. 28). These were the agents of conversion of some of the West Africans to Islam. The great majority of the population, however, maintained their traditional animist faiths, and Islam remained mostly confined to the urban centers.

The most famous empires were Ghana, A.D. 500-A.D. 1200 (dates in each case are approximate); Mali, A.D. 1224-A.D. 1464; and Songhay, A.D. 1473-A.D. 1600. In addition to these, there were large kingdoms in Mossi country (present-day Upper Volta), in Kanem-Bornu (present-day Chad), and in the valleys of the Senegal River.

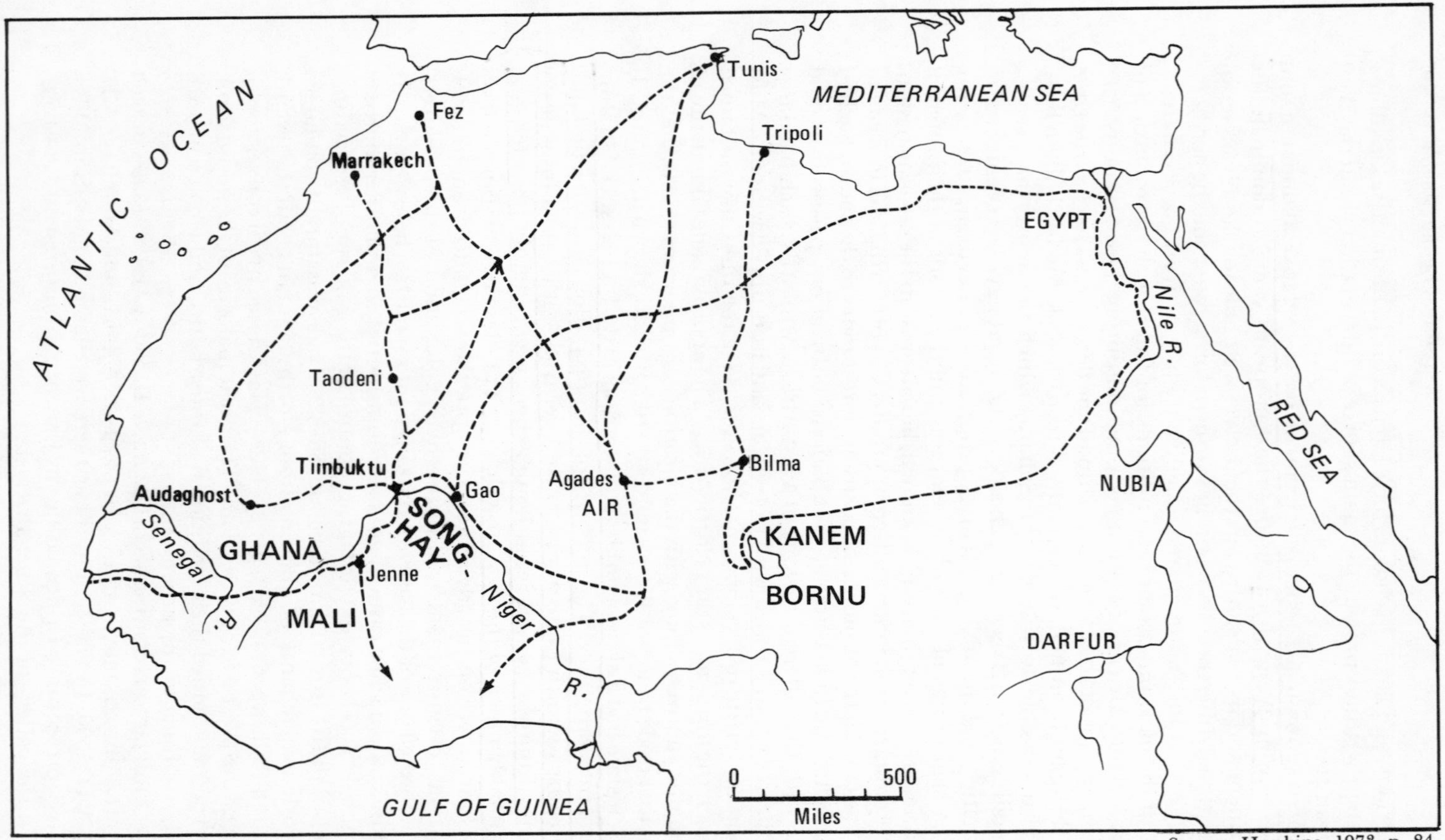

Source: Hopkins, 1973, p. 84.

Figure 2.1. Precolonial West Africa: Trans-Saharan Trade Routes, Early Empires, and Major Urban Centers.

The Empire of Ghana

At its height in about 1068, the empire of Ghana occupied the area that is now present-day Mauritania, Senegal, and Mali. Its capital is believed to have been a city called Kumbi-Saleh, located about 200 miles north of present-day Bamako. The Soninke were the dominant ethnic group. The term *Ghana* was actually the title of the ruler, and it came to be extended to the lands he ruled. Ghana is first mentioned by Arab writers in the 9th century, and not much is known of its history prior to that time.[14]

The empire was strategically located just to the north of the gold-producing areas of the forest zones and at the southern end of an important trans-Saharan caravan route. Ghana could take advantage of its geographical position only by having peace and order in the region, a goal it achieved with the use of a large calvary and iron weapons.

In A.D. 992, Ghana captured a major trading city, Audoghast, from the Berbers, and this added to its hegemony over the region. Audoghast, which no longer exists, was in southeastern Mauritania near the border of present-day Mali. The city was reputed to be a fine one, surrounded by date palms. In addition to dates, other crops included wheat, millet, figs, and gourds. Audoghast acquired a reputation as a place of luxurious living, and both its chefs and its women were spoken of highly elsewhere (Bovill, 1968, p. 11).

The most important source of revenue in Ghana was gold, although slaves and salt also figured prominently in trade. The amount of gold in this region made a very strong impression on one Arab commentator, who described Ghana as "a country where gold grows like plants in the sand in the same way as carrots do" (quoted in Boahen, 1966, p. 5). The gold itself was mined in a place called Wangara and brought into the empire. The trade was reputed to have occurred by means of silent barter, with the miners bringing the gold to a customary place but leaving it only after merchants had deposited their goods and had moved out of sight. If the goods were satisfactory, the gold would be left in exchange. There were occasional attempts to force the forest people to reveal the origin of the gold, but these were not successful (Bovill, 1968, p. 82). The court essentially held a monopoly on all the gold brought into the country. The ruler decided how much would be allowed to enter into trading and thus could control the price. Each load of gold entering or leaving Ghana was taxed, as were other import and export items. Moslem merchants did the actual trading. They had their own town about six miles from the court, and their mosques were there as well. The ruler practiced the traditional animist faith.

The court at Kumbi-Saleh was quite lavish. An eyewitness description conveys some sense of how wealthy the upper strata were:

When the king gives audience to his people to listen to their complaints and to set them to rights, he sits in a pavillion around which stand the pages holding shields and gold mounted swords. On his right hand are the sons of the princes of his empire, splendidly clad with gold plaited in their hair. The governor of the city is seated on the ground in front of the king and all around him are his counselors in the same position. The gate of the chamber is guarded by dogs of an excellent breed. These dogs never leave their place of duty. They wear collars of gold and silver ornamented with metals. The beginning of a royal audience is announced by the beating a kind of drum they call *deba*. This drum is made of a long piece of hollowed wood. The people gather when they hear its sound. . . . [quoted in Davidson, 1966, pp. 42–43]

Unfortunately, the Arab commentators were not as interested in describing the life of the ordinary cultivators and exactly how they fared under this system.

In the 11th century, Berber tribespeople inhabiting what is now Mauritania were themselves attacked by North Africans. The Berber cities were looted and their farms ruined. Facing disaster, they rallied around an Islamic leader and developed a sect known as the Almoravids. The Almoravids embarked on a holy war, one branch going north and conquering Morocco and Spain, while another went south toward Ghana. The city of Audoghast was retaken in 1055. In 1076, the capital of Ghana, Kumbi-Saleh, was captured.

The invasion had a disastrous effect on the ecology. Around Kumbi, the inhabitants had been able to grow vegetables, using the wells that also provided their drinking water. When the Almoravids attacked, the population retreated, and the wells were neglected and became filled with sand. Berber herds destroyed the vegetation and erosion occurred. Only a very careful tilling of the soil had made this land productive. Once the activities of the agricultural peoples were disrupted by the invaders, the environment was unable to support the population that had lived there (Levtzion, 1973, p. 8).

As the empire came under attack, rebellions occurred among the subject peoples, and this strengthened the position of the Almoravids. Attempts to oust the Berbers failed, and Ghana's importance as a trading center declined. The Moslem merchants sought more peaceful spots to pursue their trade, moving from the Ghanian towns. Many of the Soninke traders also dispersed to other parts of the Sudan. This movement helped in the spreading of Islam (Awe, 1965, p. 61).

The Empire of Mali

A weakened Ghana was also attacked by the founders of the Malian empire. In approximately A.D. 1200, a leader named Sumanguru, with a reputation for great ferocity, led his army against the peoples of Ghana. Three years later he conquered Kumbi-Saleh, only to be attacked in turn by a more powerful force led by a man named Sundiata, who became the first ruler, or *Mansa*, of Mali. In 1240, Kumbi-Saleh was totally destroyed, and its remains were not rediscovered until this century. Sundiata established his own capital at a town called Niani and entered on a series of conquests. By the time of Sundiata's death in 1255, Mali, according to a leading African historian, "controlled the sources of most of the important articles of trade such as the salt mines of Taghaza, the copper mines of Takedda and the gold mines of the south" (Awe, 1965, p. 63). Agriculture was encouraged, as was trade, and the growing of cotton was promoted (Stride and Ifeka, 1971, p. 50).

Sundiata's successors continued his expansionist ways. Mali achieved its greatest size between 1307 and 1359. At its zenith, it "extended from the lower Senegal and Gambia rivers in the west, to the Songhay country on the Niger below Gao in the east; from the upper Niger in the south to the fringes of the Sahara in the north" (Levtzion, 1973, p. 72). The heart of the Malian empire was the savanna, where rice, millet, and fonio were produced. The vast majority of the population were engaged in food production. The Bambara, Malinke, and Soninke grew sorghum, millet, and fonio. The Fulani herded cattle within the empire's borders, and the Bozo, Somono, and Sorko peoples fished in the waters of the Niger River. These products and rice from Gambia were traded among the various regions of the Malian empire. Internal traffic in foodstuffs, iron, and salt flourished (Levtzion, 1973, p. 117).

To expand production in the absence of new techniques, the royal authorities brought new land under cultivation. Villages were established and populated with slaves, who were obligated to send a portion of their produce to the royal granaries.[15] Even with the relatively primitive tools at their disposal, the farmers, slave and free, were able to produce enough surplus to support the administration, the army, and the merchant class (Levtzion, 1973, p. 117).

The savanna was the terminus of several major caravan routes. Nearly all of these intersected the Niger River, where pirogues, large canoelike boats, carried goods along the waterway. The major cities of the empire—Jenne, Gao, Diaka, Timbuktu—were located along the Niger River (see Figure 2.1). Varied products were traded, including the agricultural items already mentioned that provisioned the commercial towns and the salt mines. Kola nuts were an important item of commerce. The nuts, acting as a stimulant and also staving off the effect of thirst, were in great demand. Shea butter, dried fish, textiles, and dates were items in the caravan traffic, as were tobacco and gold. European cloths such as silk were brought into the Sudan for sale to the aristocracy. While Mali imported silk and wool, cotton goods were exported. Timbuktu, in particular, came to be a center for embroidered robes. This craft was the monopoly of certain families, and special Koranic training was one of the qualifications for entering into this occupation (Sundstrom, 1965, p. 147).

Gold continued to be an item of commerce, with the demand for Sudanese gold growing from the 10th century until the opening up of gold mines in the New World. European gold mines were exhausted by the 14th century at a time when commercial expansion was increasing the demand for this metal. Sudanese gold reached Europe through North Africa, particularly Morocco.[16] Rivalry for the control of this trade existed between

Portugal and Italy. The Italians even sent an agent into the interior of Mali to try to locate the sources, but he was not successful (Levtzion, 1973, p. 133).[17]

If any single item dominated the trade, however, it was salt. This spice, which seems so ordinary to us, has been compared in importance with petroleum today (Cissoko, 1975, p. 143) or the modern gold traffic (Gautier, 1935, p. 114) to indicate the place it held in exchange relationships. Salt was used not only to season food but also in the preparation of tobaccos and medicines. In many areas, it was a luxury item, with a status comparable to that of pepper in medieval Europe (Sundstrom, 1965, p. 124). It was used in some places for payment of fines, as bridal money, and for other formal payments, and could be used to purchase other items (Sundstrom, 1965, p. 129).

The trade was conducted by merchants, some of Mande descent, others from North Africa, who settled in the towns and established trading communities. Islam gave the scattered merchants a common religious bond, while Arabic provided a common language. Islam offered the traders a means of seeing themselves as part of a larger community distinct from the particular locale in which they were residing, and it also provided a set of regulations for the governing of the trade (Meillassoux, 1971, p. 72). Since much of the commerce was done on the basis of credit, it was necessary for the merchants to have a certain amount of trust in each other. The common bond of Islam may have served this function as well. The merchants were immigrants to the area, outside the traditional peasant groupings and kinship lineages. They were thus freed of the traditional gift exchanges and obligations, which would have hampered their ability to trade, since much of their merchandise would have stayed within their home villages (Meillassoux, 1971, p. 72).

The state did not control trade directly, as was the case with the kingdoms of Ashanti and Dahomey, which developed later in the forest regions. Private traders, local and foreign, organized commerce, while the central administration protected the routes used and improved roads. Government revenues were obtained from taxes and customs duties (Levtzion, 1973, p. 123).

As was the case in the previous kingdom of Ghana, the court of the Malian emperor was magnificent. In 1352, the Arab traveler Ibn Batuta described the pomp, ceremony, and splendor:

> The lord of this kingdom has a great balcony in his palace. There he has a great seat of ebony. . . . It is flanked by elephant's tusks. The king's arms stand near him. They are all of gold; sword and lance, quiver of bows and arrows. . . .
>
> Before him stand about twenty Turkish or other pages, who are brought from Cairo. One of these, standing on his left, holds a silk umbrella that is topped by a dome and bird of gold. The bird is like a hawk. The king's officers are seated in a circle near him, in two rows, one to the right, and the other to the left. Beyond him sit the commanders of the cavalry.
>
> In front of him there is a person who never leaves him and who is his executioner; and another who is his official spokesman. . . . In front of him there are also

drummers. Others dance before their king and make him merry. . . . [quoted in Davidson, 1966, p. 177]

Others before Batuta had been impressed by the splendor of the Malian ruler. In 1324-26, Mansa Musa, one of the most famous of the kings, went on a pilgramage to Mecca. Although his was not the first royal visit to the holy city, it seems to have been the most spectacular, and it had the consequence of simultaneously boosting the importance of Islam in the Sudan and the status of the Sudan in the Arab countries that were its trading partners. Mansa Musa's trip took him through Cairo, where it was reputed the price of gold declined as a result of the huge amounts that he liberally spent. He was preceded into Mecca itself by a procession of 500 slaves, each bearing a gold staff (Bovill, 1968, p. 87). Each Friday, when the Mansa stopped for prayers, he would order a mosque built on the location (Stride and Ifeka, 1971, p. 51).

On his return from Mecca, Mansa Musa brought with him a Spanish Islamic scholar and architect, As-Sahali. Under As-Sahali's direction, a number of mosques were built in a distinctive style that came to characterize Sudanic mosques. Mansa Musa also ordered that Islamic practices be followed more strictly, and he had students sent to Morocco for special religious training. It was also under his direction that the foundations for Timbuktu's commercial and educational importance were laid. Scholars settled there and attracted numerous students. The reigns of Mansa Musa and his successor seem to have been of both Islamic devotion and ethnic tolerance in the empire of Mali. There seems to have existed great security as well, so commerce could occur unimpeded over very great distances (Boahen, 1966, p. 21).

The question of succession to the throne was never satisfactorily resolved, and the second half of the 14th century saw intrigues for power. Extravagant spending led to a loss of revenues, which in turn meant a lessened ability to dispense patronage, a crucial means of ensuring loyal supporters. There was a period of coups and civil wars as well as external invasions. The Mossi and Tuaregs attacked the empire from the southern and northern regions, respectively.

The Songhay Empire

Songhay dealt the final blow to the Malian empire. This state had also begun as a small principality, located on the banks of the Niger River with its capital at Gao. Agriculture, herding, and fishing were the dominant economic activities. By the end of the 9th century, Gao itself was the terminus of three important caravan routes. Ibn Batuta described the city in 1353, when it was still a vassal of Mali. Gao, he wrote, was "one of the finest towns in the Negroland. It is also one of their biggest and best-provisioned towns with rice in plenty, milk and fish and there is a species of cucumber there which has no equal" (quoted in Boahen, 1966, p. 23).

In 1375, Gao broke loose from Mali, and in 1464, Sunni Ali became the ruler, reigning for 28 years. Under his leadership, the Songhay empire was formed. Sunni Ali was looked upon as a liberator from Tuareg oppression, the Tuaregs having successfully established their rule in a portion of the old Malian state. He recaptured Timbuktu, then laid siege to Jenne, capturing that city in 1473. Sunni Ali seems to have been disinterested in Islam, although he was a nominal believer. Nevertheless, he sought to win support from the populace by respecting its traditional animist beliefs (Awe, 1965, p. 67). He died in 1492, and from 1493-1528, its zenith, Songhay was governed by Mohammed Askia.

Each year, after the rainy season, the Songhay went to war, the objectives being pacification and/or booty, including slaves. The Songhay empire became the most vast in the history of the Western Sudan, covering the area from the north of Dahomey, up to Mauritania, and from Mossi country in the south into the heart of the Sahara. Gao remained the seat of government, and Mohammed Askia built his palace there with 700 eunuchs in attendance upon him. The political and administrative dignitaries were to be found in this city, along with important marabouts, and members of the royal family and its entourages, including the griots, or praise singers, and official genealogists. The Askia personally nominated the administrative agents of the state and could revoke their position at any time. The post of agricultural minister was held by one of the king's sons or another blood relative. This position involved the distribution of grain to the poor and probably the settling of disputes among peasants (Cissoko, 1975, p. 105).

Gao was the political center, but Timbuktu continued to be the religious and intellectual capital. Timbuktu had a more exposed position and was difficult to defend from Tuareg raids. For this reason, the administrative apparatus was not located there. Under the rule of Askia I, there were 150 Koranic schools in the city, and a university functioned as the mosque of Sankoré. At Sankoré, noted jurists, theologians, and historians attracted students from all over Islamic Africa. One of the historians residing in the city, Mahmoud Kati, described this period:

> In those days, Timbuktu did not have its equal . . . from the province of Mali to the extreme limits of the region of the Maghrib for the solidity of its institutions, its political liberties, the purity of its morals, the security of persons, its consideration and compassion toward foreigners, its courtesy toward students and men of learning and the financial assistance which it provided for the latter; the scholars of this period were the most respected among the believers for their generosity, force of character and their discretion. [Boahen, 1966, p. 31]

An eyewitness account by Leo Africanus about 1520, conveys a similar impression of bustling intellectual activity.

> In Timbuktu, there are numerous judges, professors and holy men, all being handsomely maintained by the king who holds scholars in much honor. Here too, they sell many handwritten books from North Africa. More profit is made from selling books in Timbuktu than from any other branch of Trade. [quoted in Davidson, 1966, p. 166]

Other kinds of commerce were vital to the empire's prosperity. Together, Timbuktu and Gao, in the words of one historian, "controlled trans-Saharan trade, desert-side exchange and river traffic on the Niger" (Lovejoy, 1978, p. 179). Some of the pirogues plying the Niger were quite large, able to carry as much as six tons of merchandise. Trade goods were transported also on the heads of slaves, on donkeys, and on camels. According to Ibn Khaldoun, an Arab historian, caravans of nearly 12,000 camels visited Timbuktu annually from Egypt (Cissoko, 1975, p. 37). Muhammad Askia and his administration unified weights and measures and supplied market inspectors. For a while, they were even able to pacify the Tuaregs.

Tuaregs, along with other merchants, handled the trade between the desert salt pans and the river ports. As was mentioned earlier, they also provided transport for the trans-Saharan commerce and produced livestock, one of the elements in the traffic. The overland routes to the south and the river traffic were in the hands of Songhay merchants, who have been described as "the financiers and brokers of Songhay's imperial economy. Their prosperity was linked to Songhay success, while their economic activities were a necessity for the consolidation of the empire" (Lovejoy, 1978, p. 176). They lived in endogamous communities, including in their ranks not only merchants but craftsmen and legal specialists. Their kinship networks connected them with distant towns, facilitating their trading networks. In some cases, they even intermarried with the nobility (Lovejoy, 1978, p. 177).

Commerce and education were important, but the food produced by the largest sector of the population, the peasantry, was crucial to the maintenance of a large empire. Agriculture was concentrated in the southern regions and the river valleys. The empire was able to feed its own people and also produce a surplus for trading. In December, the river would begin its annual flooding, and its recession left fertile soils where cereals could be cultivated. The dominant crops were millet and sorghum, but rice was cultivated for consumption by the elite. Wheat was grown and used to make couscous and a cake that Timbuktu became famous for. Melons, beans, onions, cotton, indigo, and other crops were raised as well.

The crown established "imperial villages," which were worked by slaves and had special obligations to the ruler. A typical royal estate might send 50 tons of grain annually to the court (Cissoko, 1975, p. 113). Royal estates specialized, some producing rice, others dried fish. The slaves were also used in some cases to produce boats, spears, and arrows, which were used directly but also put into trade (Boahen, 1966, p. 29). Some of the grains produced in the imperial villages were distributed to the urban poor in Timbuktu, at least, there was a special garden to benefit the poor of the Islamic community (Cissoko, 1975, p. 114).

Some modern historians surveying these empires have come to the conclusion that conditions in the past were better than they are today. Agriculture, herding, and fishing supplied the population with necessary foods. Commerce thrived in the relatively peaceful conditions. The population in the countryside was dense, and the cities were rich and well-populated centers of Sudanese and Islamic culture (Cissoko, 1975, p. 163). Localized famines occurred, but they seem never to have reached the catastrophic proportions of modern ones (Derriennic, 1976, p. 72) and were alleviated with stores from the royal granaries (Cissoko, 1975, p. 162).[18]

Moroccan Invasion

The relatively tranquil conditions in Songhay were disrupted in 1591, when Morroccans attacked, armed with European muskets, the most modern weapons of the day. The Moroccans themselves had been invaded by the Portuguese in 1578 and had defeated them. The North Africans then felt encouraged to turn southward to Songhay and its reputed riches. The sovereign of Morocco, Al-Mansur, said of his goals: "I have resolved to attack the Sudan. It is an exceedingly rich country and will furnish us with large taxes and we shall thus be enabled to give greater importance to the Mohammaden armies" (quoted in Boahen, 1966, p. 34).

The Moroccan army was made up of 4,000 men, half of whom were Portuguese and Spanish prisoners who had agreed to convert to Islam as an alternative to being executed or languishing in Moroccan jails. In addition to the muskets, the 1,500-strong light cavalry unit carried a cannon. The Songhay on their side had a large army with thousands of cavalry and infantry, but they could not match the North Africans' weapons. Their cities were seized. The people fought a guerrilla war in the countryside, using raiding parties and harassing the invaders, but they were not very successful.

After 1621, the Moroccans stopped reinforcing their garrisons in the cities of Gao, Jenne, and Timbuktu. The situation was very unstable. The Moroccans never established a centralized government to replace the one they had conquered; and various ethnic groups, Tuaregs, Fulani, Bambara, and the descendents of the invaders, fought for control of the region.

The consequences of the Moroccan conquest were described by an Arab observer: "This expeditionary force found the Sudan one of God's most favored countries in prosperity, comfort, security and vitality. . . . Then all that changed; security gave way to danger, prosperity made way for misery and calamity; whilst affliction and stress succeeded well-being" (quoted in Levtzion, 1973, p. 91). Morocco did not even benefit from her victory. The caravan trade was disrupted, and this had an adverse effect on the Moroccan economy (Barry, 1972, p. 135).

Local Sahelian rulers, 230 years after the Moroccan invasion, attempted to recover some of the ground lost by the disruptions in the social and ecological relationships. The regime of Cheikou Amadou reinstated peaceful relations between herders and agriculturalists, with a strict code of practices in the Niger inland delta area south of Timbuktu. Maximum herd sizes were established and trek routes strictly defined. Farmers were made to keep their fields at a safe distance from the trek routes, and the flood-recession pastures were legally divided among different groups of Fulani herders so that each group had collective ownership of a specified pasture. Regulations were also codified to ensure the exchange of grain stalks to be eaten by cattle and the dropping of cattle dung on the fields. Thus the same lands were used, as the river flood retreated, both for agriculture and herding in a mutually beneficial relationship.[19]

Other states, about which much less is known, existed in West Africa. Moslem kingdoms in the area that is now Chad were known as the states of Chad-Kanem and Bornu. Ruled at certain periods by women, these kingdoms were linked in trading relationships to Egypt, Libya, and the Mediterannean (Martin, 1969).

Mossi states arose in the region of the Volta River basin. This area also was intersected with trade routes passing from the Sahel through the forest zones. Trade was carried on by Moslem traders who had relationships with their counterparts in the Sudan. The Mossi nobles formed cavalry units and used their horses to attack caravans, capturing slaves and other booty. As was the case elsewhere, the majority of people practiced agriculture, growing yams, cereals, and legumes. These were taxed and the surplus passed upward from local chiefdoms, who maintained their own small courts, to the king himself (Echenberg, 1971; Wilks, 1972).

The Wolof States

Kingdoms developed in the Senegal River valleys as well. The earliest mention of these is by an Arab historian writing in the 10th century, so they were certainly older than this. Tekrur, founded by the Tukulor, was the first of the states in this locale. North Africans came to the capital city, also named Tekrur, to trade. Gold and silver were exchanged for wool, copper, and beads. The people were reputedly prosperous, producing large quantities of grain, vegetables, herbs, fish, cattle, and milk products. Tekrur also acquired a reputation for its weaving, using locally produced wool and cotton (Stride and Ifeka, 1971, pp. 18-19).

State societies developed among the Wolof peoples and the Serer of Sine and Saloum. The Wolof empire came to include the Serer states as well as those of Kayor, Baol, and Waalo. Each of these had its own ruler but was expected to cooperate with the highest leader, the Jolof (Stride and Ifeka, 1971, pp. 24 ff.). While one or another ethnic group predominated in a given state, they were ethnically diverse.

The outlines of social organization were similar for all the states. There were several social classes, each with its own internal strata. All levels of society had representatives at the court. The free people had at their apex a group of nobles, and from its ranks a sovereign would be chosen. Another strata of nobles provided the chiefs of territories or villages. Below them were the descendents of nobles and captives who had a hereditary right to the headship of certain cantons, or villages. The artisan caste was another social layer, subdivided into ironworkers, jewelry-makers, shoemakers, woodworkers, weavers, musicians, and griots. At the bottom were the peasants. There seem to have been no great distinctions in life style among these different strata, and there was a relative absence of social confict (Barry, 1972, p. 85).

There were also several strata of slaves. The position of the slaves reflected that of their owners. The crown's slaves furnished the royal guard and the warrior caste, called the *tyeddo.* These could become powerful in their own right and could depose kings and pillage peasants. Domestic slaves were part of the extended family of their owner and to sell them was unusual. Five mornings a week they worked for their master; the rest of the time they produced for their own consumption. The owner was obligated to find a spouse for each slave. When they married, the slaves could set up their own households with the obligation of giving homage to the master, along with a certain portion of grain each year (Barry, 1972, pp. 89-91; Klein, 1968, pp. 9-13).

The nobility's revenues came from taxes on animals and on millet and was paid in kind. Each village had a field that was worked for the royal household. In addition, there were royal monopolies such as the salt trade. Criminal acts were punished by fines, which were divided between the king and the judge. The wealth collected from these various sources was used by the Jolof to maintain his entourage and keep its loyalty.

Like the Niger, the Senegal River watered the fields with its annual floods. The valley constituted a millet granary and was an excellent zone for pasturage. When the flood waters receded between November and June, the pastoralists brought their cattle to the river. Agricultural products were exchanged for those derived from the animals. The abundance of uncleared land could be worked or left for the herds. French explorers in the 17th century remarked on the excellence of the farming (Barry, 1972, p. 77), but fishing, hunting, and gathering also added to the food supply.

Commerce was brisk, particularly in salt. Gum arabic was traded by the Maures, while horses and other goods were also exchanged. The slave trade increased in importance as the Europeans established trading centers on the coast. Waalo, located at the mouth of the Senegal River, early became a point of contact between Africans and Europeans. The rulers of Waalo and eventually of the other coastal states in the Wolof empire saw an opportunity to profit from commerce with the Europeans, even if done at the expense of their relationship with the Jolof. Serious internal dissensions resulted from this contact in the late 15th century.

The Europeans' main interest at this date was the slave trade. The French attempted to build a fort on the strategically located island they named St. Louis, at the mouth of the Senegal River. The Waalo fought them, but the fort was erected in 1659. The island was useful for the slave traders because it was easily defended and escape was difficult.

Senegal's hinterland was not densely populated, so raids provided fewer slaves for the new world than other regions of Africa. Nevertheless, the trade had important repercussions on life in the Wolof and Serer kingdoms. Instead of slaves being integrated into the domestic unit, as was the case traditionally, there was now the alternative of receiving desirable gifts from the Europeans, whose appetite for slaves seemed limitless. The kings and nobles could obtain brandy, sugar, and tobacco in exchange for captives. Slavery came to replace fines as a penalty for crimes, and prisoners of war were sold rather than incorporated into the domestic slave system (Klein, 1968, p. 29). The Europeans supplied the tyeddo, the warrior slaves, with arms and ammunition. The tyeddo in turn used these to raid their neighbors for slaves. Throughout the region, the trade produced general insecurity, internal dissensions, and civil wars, which disrupted agricultural production and led to famines, such as the one in 1676. In desperation, during these catastrophes, people sold themselves into captivity rather than face starvation (Barry, 1972, p. 155).

The insecurity produced by the slave trade seems to have been a major factor in the peasant's willingness to accept Islam in the second half of the 17th century. Islam became a source of resistance to the social changes that were harming the peasantry. The impetus for conversion came from the Maures. This group had been very much involved in commerce with Waalo and the other Senegalese kingdoms. When the Europeans installed themselves on the coast, trade was reoriented and the Maures found themselves largely eliminated from the commerce between the French and the people in the river valley.

In the 17th century, a mystical movement led by Nasir Al-Din sought to convert the inhabitants of the Wolof kingdoms. The aims of the movement included having the kings purify their life style and stop pillaging their subjects. The king, it was preached, should serve the people, not the people the king. Nasir Al-Din raised an army, won the support of many peasants, and succeeded in replacing the kings in the Wolof states. After his death, however, there was a counter-offensive from the king of Waalo allied with the French. In 1678, the Islamic forces were defeated (Barry, 1972, pp. 137 ff.).

THE SAHEL ON THE EVE OF COLONIAL CONQUEST

In Chapter 1, we described the Sahel as one of a complex series of environmental zones, each with its own properties and each having much to contribute to the others in a region of potential plenty. In this chapter, we have seen how the long history of West African societies shows a series of adaptations to these environmental zones, accompanied in the more recent past by the rise of empires and warring states. These states occasionally upset local adaptations while, often at the same time, helping to spread and secure the trade routes.

The overall picture that emerges from the available historical documents is one of relatively prosperous and stable communities. However, a contradiction developed between the farmers and herders, who created ecologically sound production systems, and the ruling elite of the empires, who pushed the system toward excessive output to support the lavish life styles of the courts. The elite also sometimes caused the ruin of a particular region in the course of a war. The balance, nonetheless, was clearly on the side of environmental preservation.

With the dawning of the 17th century, forces came into play to upset the balance of the Sahel, greatly overwhelming the positive adaptations with ecologically devastating policies. These forces were first and most conspicuously represented by the arrival of the European colonial system.

NOTES

1. West Africa has been the home of more than twenty ethnic groups, each characterized by its own language and culture. In addition, the major groupings have several subdivisions. There are more than 126 principal languages, not including dialect variations. See Suret-Canale, 1973, p. 64.

2. Useful discussions of nomadism can be found in D. Johnson, 1969; Forde, 1963, pp. 394-410; Irons and Dyson-Hudson, 1972; and Monod, 1975. A suggested classification of types of African pastoralists appears in Jacobs, 1965.

3. The Tuaregs have fascinated anthropologists and historians because it is the *men* who cover their faces with veils. A summary of current evidence and interpretations appears in Keenan, 1977, pp. 127-35.

4. This is not to say that everything about their society was admirable, nor to suggest that there might not have been alternate ways of adapting to their environment, but that the Tuaregs had learned how to make a living under difficult circumstances. The disruption of their traditional ways of life as a result of French colonialism helped create dreadful suffering when the recent drought occurred.

5. For descriptions of these mechanisms, see Swift, 1973; and Smith, 1978.

6. For a discussion of various aspects of African slavery, see Meillassoux, ed., 1975.

7. *Fulani* is the British term for these people. The French referred to them as *Peuls*. Their own name for themselves is *Fulbe;* the singular is *Pullo* (Stenning, 1959, p. 2).

8. In the 18th and 19th centuries, several Islamic Fulani states were established (Davidson, 1966, pp. 269-72; Last, 1973, pp. 1-29). These will not be discussed here, however, since the main interest is the use the pastoral people made of the environment.

9. See Stenning, 1960, for a description of the several patterns of movement that were followed.

10. The variations in the findings depend on whether the cattle are grazed or corralled and on the time of year.

11. A summary of currently available archaeological studies on the origins of agriculture in West Africa is given in Cohen, 1977, pp. 109-11.

12. On the advantages of the *daba*, see Suret-Canale, 1973, p. 77; see also July, 1975, p. 79.

13. In addition to the references cited, Mauny, 1961, has a useful discussion of West African agriculture during the European Middle Ages. Gray, 1962, presents a summary of some of the debates about the origins of West African agriculture that have been occurring among historians.

14. The name *Ghana* was taken by the region known as the Gold Coast when independence was achieved from the British in 1957. It does not fall within the boundaries of the old empire.

15. African historian A. G. Hopkins (1978, p. 25) argues that slavery was a response to a labor shortage, because it was less expensive to acquire and use slaves than to compensate free labor.

16. For discussions of Sudanese gold in Europe, see Braudel, 1946; and Gautier, 1935.

17. It is interesting to note that Mali and Portugal exchanged ambassadors in 1534.

18. Evidence on this point comes also from a 16th-century observer who commented on the famine and pestilence that accompanied the Moroccan invasion. All the aged people were unanimous in their claims that they had never seen such calamaties (Diop, 1960, p. 108).

19. Gallais, 1967, vol. 1, pp. 93-96, and vol. II, pp. 362-65; and Bremen, 1976, p. 128. This organization of herder-farmer relationship was based, however, on a forced sedentarization of the herders.

3

Planting the Seeds of Famine: European Colonialism in the Sahel

African historical development was harshly interrupted by the expansion of European colonialism. This new system, growing out of the capitalist economies that were replacing feudalism in Europe, had different periods and different effects on the Sahel and its surrounding environments. The essence of colonialism was the economic and political control of an overseas region that would make it susceptible to the same profit-making economy that was developing in the home country. In the process of extending this system, Europeans intervened in West Africa in several ways with many destructive effects—effects that in turn would greatly influence the development of the ecology of the region, making it increasingly vulnerable to droughts. To see how this happened, we must look at the history of this colonialism in French West Africa.

EARLY COLONIAL HISTORY

As was shown in Chapter 2, West Africa had been a trading center for centuries before the Europeans became interested in the commercial possibilities of the area. In the second half of the 15th century, the Portuguese became the first to engage in trade. In 1659, the French established a colonial outpost at St. Louis on the coast of what is now Senegal but was then called Senegambia. Richelieu, in the 17th century, organized the Normand Co., which sought commercial opportunities in that region. Profits were to be found in the exchange of slaves, ivory, skins, gold, and gum arabic for French cloth, guns, gunpowder, and paper. Gum arabic was used for paper, candy, and the textile industry, and by the 18th century, Senegambia was "the only significant supplier to Europe" (Curtin, 1975, p. 216). When the slave trade was abolished, the French looked for other possibilities too. In 1820, a government botanist introduced plants from the Antilles and the West Indies—coffee, sugarcane, cinammon, and pepper. None of these proved to be successful, however (Fouquet, 1951, p. 18).

Under the aggressive leadership of Governor Faidherbe, the French expanded from the coasts into the interior. By 1861, their main indigenous rival, Ali Halig Uma, organizer of an empire stretching from Medina to Timbuktu, had been defeated. By 1865, the area of modern Senegal was under French control.

In the region of the Upper Niger River, the French ran into powerful and skillful adversaries. El Hadj Omar, who had founded an empire extending from Timbuktu to the source of the Niger River, occupied it militarily for 40 years, from 1850-90 (De Gramont, 1976, p. 244). Another formidable opponent was Samory, also the founder of a large West African empire, who had sought to destroy tribalism and create a political structure uniting many different groups with Islam as the cementing force. He introduced compulsory education through Moslem schools set up not only to teach the Islamic religion but also to inculcate hatred for the alien invaders. He also made it mandatory for all the villages to set aside certain fields to be sowed in common and used to feed the army (Sik, 1970, vol. I, p. 315). Using an army of 20,000 men, and a people's militia five times that size, he was able to hold off the French for 16 years, from 1882-98 (De Gramont, 1976, pp. 252-53).

There were also other talented African political and military leaders, such as Rabah, who organized an empire in Chad. He was defeated in 1900, with the French taking the women of the area and parcelling them out among themselves and their African accomplices. Women were also taken and given to individuals in other battles as well (N'Dongo, 1976, p. 27).

With French officers as teachers, schools were established even as military operations occurred. The schools were simply another, more subtle form of weaponry. Guns would subdue their bodies, but education would, it was hoped, control their minds. Textbooks, produced in France, were meant to turn rebellious blacks into loyal, patriotic French subjects. The students would learn that "my new fatherland, today, is France. I am French. . . . When I am big, I will place the tricolor flag on top of my house every Sunday and I will tell everyone: Look at the fine flag" (De Gramont, 1976, p. 266).

THE NINETEENTH CENTURY

When France was defeated in the Franco-Prussian War (1870-71), her African colonies assumed a new importance: Colonial enterprises would be the compensation for France's European losses (Chamberlain, 1974, p. 50). Geographical societies were organized to give an intellectual veneer to the commercial and military interests agitating for new conquests. In 1873, the general secretary of the Paris Society wrote: "There is great danger for a people in indifference to the conditions of other peoples and in ignorance of the resources available in far-away countries for commercial and colonial purposes" (quoted in Brunschwig, 1966, p. 24). Expansion was, of course, not only in the interests of the French but of the conquered peoples as well. The president of the Marseilles Geographical Society in 1877 neatly summarized this aspect of the "white man's burden" when he said: "Trade is always, though often unconsciously, the great driving force, bringing the benefits of civilization and the fortunate discoveries of science to the furthest outposts of the inhabitable world" (ibid., p. 25).

To help overcome any lingering resistance to the idea of an African empire, lobbying groups such as the "Comité de l'Afrique" were created. Its members included military officers, financiers, and representatives of big business. Their efforts and those of their allies in the assembly were successful (N'Dongo, 1976, p. 24). A Colonial Department was established in 1883 and became a ministry in 1894. Its budget, starting at 42 million francs, grew by almost 300 percent to 115 million in 1902 (De Gramont, 1976, p. 248).

European powers were colliding with each other in their efforts to bring civilization to the poor benighted Africans. What has been graphically described as the "scramble for Africa" was given a certain organization at the Berlin Conference in 1884-85. Although convened originally to deal with the question of the Congo, the conference laid down guidelines for the partitioning of Africa among Europeans. Whereas the United States was invited, no African representatives were. "A simple rule was laid down that any power might acquire African lands by effectively occupying them and notifying the other powers" (Hayes, 1941, p. 233). The administrative units formed under this rule became the basis for modern African states. The French, British, Germans, Belgians, Italians, et al. wasted no time in grabbing what they could from the rich continent. Looking specifically at France:

> France invaded the . . . kingdom of Dahomey in 1899, subjugated it after a four-year struggle and gradually linked it with the hinterlands of Senegal, the Ivory Coast, Guinea and even Algeria to constitute French West Africa, a huge empire of 1,400,000 square miles and twelve million subjects. Timbuktu was occupied in 1893, and from the French Congo, Lake Chad was reached in 1900. [ibid., p. 234]

France's main rival in the area, Britain, acceded to French hegemony there in exchange for French recognition of English claims on Egypt. "The more Britain worsted France in Egypt, the more France raised her claims on West Africa to strengthen her bargaining position and to provide her politicians with successes" (Robinson et al., 1968, p. 403). In 1898, the Niger Convention was signed, partitioning West Africa between France and Britain. Of course, no one asked the Africans how they felt about any of this. In fact, as we have indicated, conquest was not easy. The Africans rebelled against the blessings of European civilization. Intergroup rivalries among the Africans and the superior weaponry of the Europeans, however, led to colonial dominance. French control was more or less established by 1900, but skirmishes continued for many years. Chad was still being "pacified" up to World War I.

COLONIAL DESTRUCTION

The conquest was destructive for the Africans. In Mauritania, for example, the defeat of native rulers led to the "requisitioning of camels, oxen and sheep." In the process, the camel herds, according to a French historian, "were literally wasted away" (Suret-Canale, 1971, pp. 93-94). In one town, Taoudeni, it was noted that between 1905 and 1912, disruption of the caravan trade and wars caused the death of the entire population (ibid., p. 94). Despite such events, the French described "the bloody conquest of West Africa in all sincerity as the establishment of *La Paix Française*" (Crowder, 1968, p. 5).

The male losers of this war found themselves conscripted by the French for their other battles. A General Magnin argued persuasively that France's relatively low male population required supplementing in times of war (Suret-Canale, 1971, pp. 134-35; De Gramont, 1976, p. 268). According to him, blacks were well suited to this role, since their nervous systems were less well developed that those of whites and they would therefore remain calmer under stress (De Gramont, 1976, p. 269). He does not seem to have drawn the equally logical corollary that, being calmer, they might well be better commanders. Africans were forced to fight in Morocco, Algeria, Syria, and Indochina, as well as in Europe. De Gramont (1976, p. 269) described the fate of the African recruit:

> When the First World War was declared, thousands of native sons of the upper Niger and the Senegal, hardly speaking a word of French . . . were shipped overnight to the freezing trenches of Verdun and the Somme. The cold did more damage than the Germans, and they had to be evacuated during the winter. By the time the armistice was signed there were 134,000 black troops fighting in France, and a total of thirty thousand had died.

Conscription was for three years and reenlistment was permitted. After 15 years of military service, certain privileges were extended, such as pensions, tax exemptions and the right to certain administrative positions. But despite these rewards, young men would hide from the recuiters or from any European they thought might be one. After conscription, some would run away, be chased on horseback, lassoed like so many cattle, and brought back. "When a Negro is conscripted he is mourned by his village as a dead man; justifiably, for the chances that they will ever see him again are slight" (Gorer, 1962, p. 98). If not killed in battles, many of the recruits died from pulmonary and bronchial diseases, and a high incidence of tuberculosis was seen among those returning to their villages. During World War II, Africans were once again placed in uniform and sent to the front. Some—no one has researched how many—were captured by the Nazis and sent to concentration camps along with other "inferior races." Others survived and returned home. Of these, at least 50 were killed and 50 more wounded when a French officer in Senegal gave the order to shoot 1,200 unarmed soldiers who were demanding that they be paid for their services. About another 50 received harsh prison sentences (N'Dongo, 1976, p. 33). Thus, with their blood, sweat, and tears but not their consent, did the West Africans contribute to the building of a French empire.

Even when they were not directly conscripted, enslaved, and beaten, Africans suffered indirectly from European colonial expansion. One of the earliest effects was on the nomadic societies closest to the edge of the desert, the northern Sahelian peoples. With the arrival of European ships off the coast of Guinea in the late 15th century, a new set of trading relations could be established between the forest- and coastal-dwelling Africans and Northern Africans and Europeans. No longer did they ship as many goods across the Sahara in caravans (Caldwell, 1975, p. 39). The loss of the caravans was a severe blow to the nomads, who traded with, taxed, and sometimes raided these caravans. And as European technology developed in the 19th century, railroad lines further supplemented the caravans, making it possible to bring goods from the coastal ports far into the interior. For example, up to the early 1900s, the Sahara salt trade conducted from upper Senegal and Niger accounted for one-sixth of the imports. In 1850, German geographer Heinrich Barth witnessed the drama that marked the annual departure of the salt caravans from Agades, in what is now northern Niger, to the south. He saw "a whole nation in motion, going on its great errand of supplying the wants of other tribes and bartering for what they stood in need of themselves. All the drums were beating, and one string of camels after the other marched up in martial order, led on by the most experienced or steadfast among the followers of each chief" (quoted in De Gramont, 1976, p. 220). But by the end of World War I, the salt trade had become insignificant, the desert traffic replaced by imported salt brought in through ocean ports (Suret-Canale, 1971, p. 190). Most recently, roads have extended the effect of the railways, so hardly a caravan existed by the 1960s (Caldwell, 1975, p. 40).[1]

The decline of the caravans brought general impoverishment of the nomads, in particular reducing their capacity to survive periods of bad weather. This decline is evidenced dramatically by the loss in trading values to the nomads. At the beginning of the 20th century, for example, a camel laden with salt from Amadror could be converted into 15 to 20 loads of millet; by 1945-50, the same salt brought only six to 10 loads of millet, and by 1974, the salt was worth only two loads of millet in a good year but often will bring only an equal weight. Overall, this is a 95 percent drop in terms of trade for the nomadic peoples of the area. Similarly, over the past 30 years, the value of a milk cow in the Ader region (Niger) has declined from 10 sacks of millet to four to five (Bernus, 1974c, p. 140, citing Bonte and Regnier; cf. Keenan, 1977, pp. 165 ff.). Thus the nomads lost their main source of acquiring some valuable, storable goods, such as gold and jewels. With the decline of the caravan trade and the decreasing capacity of the nomadic societies to gain valuables, they began to resort to increasing herd sizes as the only means of "saving" for the future against bad times (Swift, in Dalby, 1973, pp. 73-74).

Other changes had similar negative consequences for nomads such as the Tuaregs. Their military superiority, which had enabled them to raid and tax the savanna farmers, was drastically reduced by the colonial governments. The French even requisitioned their camels, frequently without compensation, and this continued even during a severe drought in the Aïr region of Niger from 1911-14. The Tuaregs lost their estates, pastures, and trading contacts in the south as well as their important animals. In 1916, they revolted and a bitter struggle ensued. Both sides filled in wells, pillaged camels and grain, and laid waste to the countryside. The uprising was harshly quelled, and a large proportion of the population fled the Aïr (Baier, 1976, pp. 55-56; Lovejoy and Baier, 1976, p. 164). The slave trade was also banned, partly as a way of reducing the Tuareg's power. Thus another important source of income was lost to them, and none was replaced. Only the herds were there to be enlarged.[2]

Even the drawing of boundary lines by the European powers led to harmful effects on the nomads, who found their pastures suddenly off-limits. Or they would be required to pay double taxes if they wandered into a region that had been defined as another administrative unit by officials in some far-off capital. And the taxation system itself bred an effect later to be blamed on the nomads as "irrationality" in their herding system: They produced more animals than ever before in order to pay their taxes and underestimated the actual sizes of their herds in order to gain from the tax officials. Later it would be claimed by outsiders that the nomads produced overly large herds for reasons of "social status" and "prestige" only (Swift, in Dalby, 1973, p. 76; cf. Boule, in Copans, 1975, pp. 61-65).

But if the indirect impact of colonial expansion was felt on the farthest edges of nomadic societies, in the regions just to the south of the desert fringe an even more direct and disastrous set of developments was taking place: the profit-oriented system of colonial cash-cropping.

COLONIAL CASH-CROPPING

While African bodies were useful in French wars, the provisioning of their armies was not the main impetus to colonialism. Colonies existed for one main purpose: to provide wealth for interests in the mother country. This view was articulated by Paul Leroy-Beaulieu, professor of Moral and Political Sciences at the College de France. His prize-winning essay *De la colonization chez les peuples modernes*, published in book form in 1874, was discussed throughout the continent. He argued, quite straightforwardly, that "The most useful function which colonies perform is to supply the mother country's trade with a ready-made market, to get its industry going and maintain it and to supply the inhabitants of the mother country . . . with increased profits, wages or commodities" (quoted in Brunschwig, 1966, p. 27).

In French West Africa, the peanut (groundnut) was the primary source of profits. The peanut first made its appearance as a byproduct of the African slave trade. In the 18th century, the captains of the slave ships brought peanut seeds from Brazil to be grown in Africa as provision for the slaves. If food could be provided from Africa, the captains could save valuable cargo space rather than bringing food from America to feed the slaves once they were on board the vessels (Fouquet, 1951, p. 18). The Africans themselves found the peanut a useful complement to their subsistence dishes of millet and sorghum.

In the 1840s France was industrializing, and vegetable oils were becoming an important industry. West Africa was to supply the raw materials from which the oils would be produced. Instead of going to the New World as slaves to produce cotton and sugar, as had formerly been the case, the West Africans would now grow the palm oil and peanuts that European traders required. By 1884, the first regular shipments to Marseilles had begun. In 1892, peanuts were exempted from all duties, to the benefit of the trading houses in Bordeaux and Marseilles (Brunschwig, 1966, p. 87).

ECOLOGY OF PEANUTS IN THE SAHEL

The peanut is, under the right farming conditions, well adapted to the Sahel. While the sandy soil and relatively arid weather that characterize this region are unsuitable for cotton or other tropical crops, the peanut prefers this type of soil and does best with 25 to 30 inches of rain, that is, right on the border of the Sahel and Sudan ecological zones (see pp. 24-25), and it will even grow with only 20 inches. A long dry period is required for the fruit to ripen (Pedlar, 1955, p. 57).

In traditional agricultural systems, before cash-cropping became the dominant form of economic activity, an ecologically sound system of crop rotations was practiced: peanuts alternated with millet. But peanuts became the major crop, with disastrous consequences for the Sahel.

At an early date, the French concluded that it would be more profitable to allow the small grower to bear the whole cost of production rather than try to develop plantations. In 1846, a report of the judge-royal of St. Louis to the governor of the colony advised:

> The groundnut cultivated on a large scale will bring only ruin because the small price of the crop will never cover the cost of exploitation with the aid of dayworkers or captives. These inconveniences disappear for the little household enterprises of the blacks who work at home aided by their families without costs and without expenses. [quoted in Fouquet, 1951, p. 34]

When times have been particularly bad, as during the depression in the 1930s, the peasants have indeed turned to subsistence farming. The colonial administration was thus spared the burden of having to feed landless laborers in order to ensure a labor supply for better times.

What was beneficial to French colonial interests was contradictory to the preservation of the environment. The small peasant with a very low per-capita income could not afford to keep animals whose manure could be used or buy chemical fertilizers when these became available. Nor could the peasant allow the land to lie fallow, and without fertilizers and a fallow period the peanut has a very deleterious effect on the soil. A harvest of 1,000 kilos takes from the ground (Fouquet, 1951, p. 156) 70 kilos of nitrogen, 10 kilos of phosphates, 28 kilos of potash, 12 kilos of magnesium, and 18 kilos of lime.

It is estimated that after three years of growing peanuts, a minimum fallow period of six years is needed. An appropriately long fallow period is of great importance in the regeneration of soils. Particularly, the fallow period allows for phosphorous, potassium, magnesium, and other important elements to accumulate in the topsoil. It also provides for the building up of humus and the addition of nitrogen. Weed growth is also more easily suppressed (Vine, 1968, in Moss, ed., p. 89). The only recourse for the peasant whose land was exhausted was to acquire new land and repeat the process. Thus colonial profit-making in peanuts and African poverty at the producer level combined to set in motion a spreading wave of environmental degradation.

Some additional figures will further indicate what the peanut does to the soil if no fertilizers are used. For the Casamance area of Senegal, it has been estimated that after only two successive years of peanut growing, there is a loss of 30 percent of the soil's organic matter and 60 percent of the colloidal humus (De Wilde, vol. I, 1967, p. 16).[3] In two successive years of peanut planting, the second year's yield will be from 20 to 40 percent lower than the first (Ossewaarde, 1956, p. 88).

As the organic matter diminishes, the soil's capacity to retain water is lessened and there is more susceptibility to drought. Without reserves of moisture, the soil dries out and the harmattan can easily blow it away. This is much less of a problem when millet is planted. After harvesting, the stems and roots of millet are left in the ground, acting as a protection against erosion. But the ground on which the peanuts are harvested is left completely bare, and the shells that are underground are harvested by uprooting. The soil is loosened and the wind can carry away the finest and most important elements (Comité, 1975, p. 58).

COERCIVE AGRICULTURE

The average West African peasant had no incentive to grow peanuts, however useful this crop might be to the French industrialists and bankers. The Africans had to be coerced into cash-cropping. Tax schemes were the keystone in the arch of domination; taxes forced the peasants to produce for a market. Lack of marketable commodities meant no money to pay the taxes, which in turn meant jail and/or forced labor. A member of an ethnographic expedition wrote:

> The idea of colonization becomes increasingly more repugnant to me. To collect taxes, that is the chief preoccupation. Pacification, medical aid, have only one aim: to tame the people so that they will be docile and pay their taxes. What is the object of tours (i.e. military duty) sometimes accompanied by bloodshed? To bring in the taxes. What is the object of ethnographical studies? To learn how to govern more subtly so that the taxes shall come in better. [quoted in Gorer, 1962, p. 92]

To the taxes imposed by the French were added the demands of the local accomplices of the colonial administration:

> The feudal principle of "aid" (an exceptional contribution towards exceptional expenses) was more and more frequently applied. For example, in 1953 the chiefs of Fouta imposed on their subjects a per capita tax for the purchase of a house and an American car, and for financing a pilgrimage to Mecca; they demanded 50 francs per family for each feast day, 25 per head for July 14 and November 11, and 15 francs per head on the occasions of the census.
>
> Taxes were levied on the death of all persons above the age of seven. For an adult over twenty-five years of age, it was 10,000 francs or two oxen, which were demanded for the "right of sucession", failing which the lands of the deceased were confiscated. If the deceased had no children, his (or her) herd was confiscated, and sometimes the empty granaries, without anything being left for the surviving spouse. [Suret-Canale, 1971, p. 327]

Tax evasion was brutally discouraged, and the divide-and-rule technique applied:

> When a village fails to pay its taxes, the administration steps in brutally and ruthlessly. When punitive measures are taken, as they frequently are, the administrator himself is never present, and therefore has a complete alibi; he sends his negro soldiers—naturally always of a different race—to the people they are sent out against . . . with instructions to collect the money. The employment of negroes for the dirty work serves a double aim; it keeps lively the interracial hatred which is so essential for colonies where the subject races are more numerous than the colonizers, and it enables the administration to deny forthright the more inhuman practices in which they tacitly acquiesce, or should the facts be irrefutable, to lay the blame on the excessive zeal of their subordinates. [Gorer, 1962, p. 94]

Techniques used to punish tax evasion, beside the ones already mentioned, included holding women and children hostage until the dues were paid, burning huts, whipping, and tying up people and leaving them without food for several days.[4]

Forced labor was another punishment for trying to avoid taxes. But even when it was not a question of tax collecting, the people were sometimes directly made to donate their labor power to the colonial administrators. The corvée (forced service on roads, etc.), a factor in the French Revolution, was not abolished in the colonies until 1946. As the French Minister of Commerce stated in 1901:

The black does not like work and is totally unaccustomed to the idea of saving; he does not realize that idleness keeps him in a state of absolute economic inferiority. It is therefore necessary to use . . . slavery to improve his circumstances and afterwards lead him into an apprenticeship of freedom. Scorning work, the black is not aware that, for us, work ennobles a man's character; it is necessary therefore to pass through an intermediate stage before giving him freedom as we understand it. [Crowder, 1968, pp. 185-86]

Three decades later, anthropologist Geoffrey Gorer, touring West Africa, described the system:

"Forced labor" and "prison labor" are very adequate descriptions of how nine-tenths of the public work in the French West African colonies are performed. Fifty centimes—one penny at the normal rate of exchange—is considered the proper rate of remuneration for a ten-hour working day; and the "prestation" or work tax, fines and arrears are worked off at that rate. Consequently every adult male negro—in some districts also women and children—does at least forty days' work for the state, chiefly road making, and if it happens that he has to make roads when he should be cultivating his fields, that is just too bad. The more conscientious administrators try to avoid this contingency, but the fields have to be worked during the rainy season, which is also the time when the roads need the most attention. [Gorer, 1962, p. 95]

Very little was spent on a worker's upkeep:

When men are working away from their village, they are meant to be fed and housed. What is more, they sometimes are, though in more than one case that I have seen, the Society for the Prevention of Cruelty to Animals would have prosecuted me if I had given a dog the same quantity and quality of food and shelter. [ibid., p. 97]

THE NEED FOR MONEY

The Africans, for the most part, were reduced to laboring on their own land for another's benefit. The French did develop a small group of more privileged persons who became their administrators at the local and sometimes district ("cercle") level. This African elite often replaced the traditional authority structures of the various social groups and owed their positions entirely to the colonialists.

Africans who had been artisans or traders were ruined, because French cheap manufactured goods were brought in and people encouraged to develop a taste for the European products. Traditional artisans lost their role, although during the depression in the 1930s there was some revival of native crafts. This was an exception to the typical pattern, however, and it had no real effect on the trend toward destruction of traditional artisanry.

The dismantling of native trading patterns was an important part of the process of bringing the West African economy under European domination. Interregional trade became insignificant, replaced by economic relations with France. This was largely a result of conscious French policy. By a decree promulgated in 1905, all goods not coming from France or a region under French control were subject to special taxes (Suret-Canale, 1971, p. 10). Five years after this law was passed, France accounted for nearly half of West Africa's imports. France also received African exports. In 1909, Senegal was sending 73 percent of her exports to France, mostly in the form of peanuts.

Business and trade on any significant scale were not possible for the Africans. Lebanese and Syrians were permitted to play a role at the intermediary trading and retail levels, while the Africans were reduced to becoming sidewalk vendors or itinerant peddlers (Suret-Canale, 1971, pp. 196-97). For the first time in the history of their societies, people had a pressing need for money—money to pay their taxes, money to buy the European products that they could no longer purchase from native craftspeople, and money to pay their debts.

Most West Africans had only one resource to draw upon: their labor power. In some areas, such as Senegal, that labor was used to grow cash crops. In other, more arid parts of French West Africa, men migrated in search of work. Regardless of soil conditions, weather, and the need to grow food in their villages, the tax collector was relentless. In Upper Volta and Mali, the only alternative was to go to the wealthier agricultural areas. Upper Volta in particular was looked on as a reservoir of labor, with men going to the plantations of Sudan (present-day Mali), the Ivory Coast, and Senegal. For example, between 1921 and 1930, 92,000 men from Upper Volta went to build railroads in Senegal and do lumber cutting and plantation work on the Ivory Coast (Crowder, 1968, p. 338).

The seasonal workers from Upper Volta were referred to as *navetanes*, from the Wolof word "navete," meaning rainy season. They migrated to Senegal seasonally to work on the peanut farms (Crowder, 1968, p. 186). At harvest time, workers from Haute-Casamance, called *baraquinies* (from the Mandingo for "I look for work"), came to peanut areas of Senegal and were employed in the harvesting, drying, and cleaning of nuts (Fouquet, 1951, p. 84). The migrants also cleared forests and built railroads and highways. The conditions of work were frequently unhealthy. Epidemics of cerebro-meningitis occurred because of overcrowding under poor conditions (Suret-Canale, 1971, p. 399). The French got their taxes, but the villages lost their young productive men. The usual ages of the migrants were from about 15 to 20 years.

As the population of Senegal has grown, the need for outside workers has become less. Between 1935 and 1940, about 60,000 came each year; between 1949 and 1958, there were approximately 40,000 seasonal laborers per year; but between 1959 and 1962 there were only 11,000 annually (Amin, 1974, p. 74).

COLONIALISM AND HUNGER

French policies resulted in chronic hunger. Production of cash crops meant a reduced production of food. When less was grown, there was less to store as a reserve in case of a natural or economic disaster. Geoffrey Gorer noted:

Far from improving the standard of living the French may be said to have lowered it, for the grain which the negroes cultivate and which practically constitutes their diet, formerly sufficient for their needs, has now to be sold to pay taxes. . . . Moreover their diet, while sufficient for the relatively easy life of a cultivator, is grossly inadequate to support life under the strenuous efforts exacted from the working negro. [Gorer, 1962, p. 102]

In 1949, a Colonel Pales wrote a report on nutrition among the West Africans, noting that with a few exceptions "the people in the whole territory lack balanced nutrition; and this is a *permanent state*" (Suret-Canale, 1971, p. 298, emphasis in original). While harvest time was one of relatively adequate food, "It is followed by a period of deficiency as regards quality and later by a period of shortage." Caloric consumption went from about 3,000 per person per day right after the harvest to below 750 by July.

The daily ration of an adult might even go down to 208 calories per day, not during famines, but simply at times of shortage. So great was the surprise of the personnel in charge of these calculations in France that they suspended their work believing it an error on our part. There was no error. [quoted in Suret-Canale, 1971, p. 298]

On balance, government statistics indicate that per-capita food availability in Senegal went from 240 kgs. in 1920 to only 145 kgs. by 1959, on the eve of independence (Maiga, 1976, fn. 1).[5]

A situation such as this can only be described as terrible. Yet periodically things became even worse as famines ravaged the area. This occurred many times before the most recent situation. Droughts and locusts were the two most immediate causes, singly or in combination, but the root cause was the depradations of the French. This is revealed clearly in a study of the Niger famine of 1931 (Fugelstad, 1974, pp. 18-33).[6] Previous to this, there had been famines in 1900-1901, 1903, 1913-14, 1919, 1920-21, and 1927. They were an almost routine event.

Starting about 1922, Niger suffered more fiscal exactions than the other colonies. In order to pay, the young were obliged to leave and seek work. Military service also lessened the number of able-bodied men available for agricultural work, as did forced labor used in the building of administrative posts and in the construction of railroads. The colonial administrators seemed oblivious to the planting and harvesting schedule when making demands upon people's labor.

Many fled from these demands. Migrations from the French colonies into British ones became a form of political protest. Just after World War I, the governor-general for French West Africa, Vollenhoven, admitted that the problems caused by the colonial administration were motivating people to emigrate to the Gold Coast (now Ghana). Heavy taxes, forced labor, compulsory cultivation of cash crops, and the demands of the French imposed upon local chiefs were the reasons the migrants themselves gave for their leaving (Asiwaju, 1976, p. 580).

Those who stayed asked that they be released temporarily from their taxes, but this was refused. The tax rolls were not even revised to take account of those who had left or died, and the remaining villagers were responsible for the whole burden. When locusts and unusually dry weather occurred, there was no reserve food and no money to buy any. It is not clear how many died. But estimates are that, depending on the particular region, from 25 to 50 percent of the adult population perished, as did large numbers of the children born in 1929, 1930, and 1931.

Directly or indirectly, malnutrition played a major role in the decimation of the population of Africa under French colonial rule. In French Equatorial Africa, the population for 1900 is estimated at about 15 million. The census of 1921 gave only 2,860,868. Famine and disease, whose effects were exacerbated by undernourishment, physical exhaustion of the men, and long separations between the sexes in areas of migratory labor are among the causes for this drastic reduction. As a result, too, of nutritional deficiencies, population growth was slow despite an above-average fecundity (Suret-Canale, 1971, pp. 36; 396-97).[7]

The food situation was bad enough for the French to try to mitigate matters. They created "Indigenous Provident Societies" throughout the West African territory in 1910. These were supposed to store reserves of grain and seeds for the peanut planting. Everyone in each administrative district, or cercle, was obliged to contribute 100 to 150 kilos of grain to the society as provision against famine. This led to the depletion of people's own reserves, while the poor storage conditions destroyed much of what was collected (Crowder, 1968, pp. 316-17). The societies were also supposed to help solve the peasants' debt problems. The interest rates for seed loans and other resources were less than the 200 to 300 percent of the private traders, but they were still quite high, at least 25 percent. Membership, moreover, was compulsory, and essentially the societies were a supplementary form of taxation (Suret-Canale, 1971, p. 237).

In brief, the tax policies of the French plus their demands on African labor meant a below-subsistence standard standard of living, actual starvation on more than one occasion, and a drastic disruption of patterns of social and family life because males were forced to seek work far from their native villages.

EXPANDING PEANUT PRODUCTION

Despite the misery cash-cropping was producing in West Africa, the French continued to seek ways to expand production. As early as 1910, the Chamber of Commerce of Senegal noted that peanuts in that country were showing signs of degeneration. Yields were declining. A scientific mission, looking into this problem, advised in 1912 that an experimental station be established, and in 1913 one was set up at Bambey. The task was to find peanut varieties that would be disease resistant, give high yields, and have a high oil content. It was also hoped that varieties suitable for the varied regions of the area could be developed (Fouquet, 1951, pp. 89-90). For the less humid areas, a creeping variety that would cover the soil with a protective blanket of vegetation was sought, while a more erect plant, allowing for mechanical hoeing, and adapted to the more compact soils of the moister sections, was also to be bred (Pélissier, 1952, p. 54). One type of nut produced was the Cayor variety, with a growing cycle of only 110 days as compared to 125 days for the ordinary plant (Suret-Canale, 1948, p. 354).

The technique used was to have Bambey develop a variety and then have secondary research stations verify the adaptations. If they were suited to the local conditions, seeds would be distributed to the heads of villages for experimental use. If these in turn proved successful, the Indigenous Provident Societies would buy a large part of the harvest and distribute the seeds of the selected varieties to cultivators in the following years (Pélissier, 1952, p. 56).

The French provided the infrastructure that made it possible for the peasants to get their peanuts to market. Particularly important in this regard was the building of the railroads. Between 1908 and 1915, the lines were greatly extended. Wells were dug along the routes of the railroad lines, and this meant water would be available to areas that had little (Pélissier, 1966, p. 305).

The general tendency was for production to go up. There were dips, especially during World War II, but overall the trend is clear. Senegal's production in 1884-85 was 45,000 tons; the 1936-37 yield was 600,000 tons; and the harvest for 1965-66 was more than a million tons (Amin, 1973, pp. 3-4).

Between 1920 and 1927, as a consequence of the rise in peanut prices and the development of credit, making investment easier, there was a spurt in the rate of investment into Senegal. In 1920, there were 300 million francs invested, and by 1927 this had increased to 1,172 million francs (Fouquet, 1951, pp. 25-26).

After World War II, the French oil industry began to expand, and consequently the demand for peanuts was augmented. Peanuts were given protection on the French market, prices to the local producers were increased, and instruction and tools were given to the peasants. As the price of the nuts went up, the area devoted to millet and other subsistence crops declined. Even before the war, the peasantry had been encouraged to eat imported rice, principally from Indochina. Not only did this allow for more intensification of cash crops, but also the commercial trading houses made a lot of money from the rice sales. Imported rice sold for twice the price in West Africa as it did in France (Fouquet, 1951, p. 62). Rice cultivation has been encouraged in West Africa itself, in order to cut down on food imports. Rice is not competitive with the peanut, whereas millet is. Various private and mixed state and private agencies were established after the war to encourage peanut cultivation. For example, in Dakar immediately after the war, a Comité de Propagande de l'Arachide (Committee for the Propagation of Groundnuts) was created, its purpose clearly spelled out by its name. It was organized by commercial interests with the support of the Government (ibid., p. 110).

On a more important scale, in 1946 a plan was created in France for the development of the territories. The growing needs of the metropolis were to be met and the crises in colonial Asia compensated for (Suret-Canale, 1972, p. 99). State planning and state expenditures would be involved in a major way, with a scope much greater than had previously been the case.

The Fonds d'Investissement Pour le Développement Economique et Social (FIDES) was established. A bank that had been originally set up during the war, the Caisse Centrale de la France d'Outre-Mer (CCFOM) was empowered to handle the accounts of the FIDES and give long-term low-interest loans. The private monopolies were well represented in these agencies. The investment pattern is shown in the table below (Suret-Canale, 1972, p. 118):

Investments in West Africa (in billions of C.F.A. francs)

1947	*1948*	*1949*	*1950*	*1951*	*1952*	*1953*	*1954*	*1955*	*1956*
0.4	3.9	7.55	12.25	14.6	17.2	12.35	10.9	12.5	14.2

In addition to FIDES whose loans were made principally to territory governments, the Fonds d'Equipement Rural de Développement Economique et Social (FERDES) was created in 1949. Its funds were used principally for local development projects, irrigation dams, granaries, and so forth. Between 1949 and 1957, FERDES allocated 4.45 billions in C.F.A. francs (Suret-Canale, 1972, p. 105).

The biggest investments were made in the infrastructure, particularly in the development of transportation facilities. Profits could be increased with a more rapid circulation of goods and less storage time for merchandise. Coastal ports were favored, however, and not much was done to improve the hinterland of most of the Sahel. Senegal received about half of the credits allotted during the first four years of the plan. Thompson and Adloff summarize one of the consequences of the investment program: "the great majority of loans granted . . . were made to big companies, chiefly those mixed-economy societies, or to wholly state enterprises. As a result of this policy, the Federation's towns boomed while the vast impoverished hinterland and its inhabitants continued to stagnate in their traditional economy (Thompson and Adloff, 1969, pp. 343-4).

There were other consequences as well. The increased investment was associated with an increase in peanut production and the opening up of new centers for that crop. This led to the further destruction of forest areas, which were sacrificed so that more peanuts could be produced. The importance of trees in the Sahel and Sudan was discussed in Chapter 1.

In theory at least, the French government had recognized how valuable woodlands were, enacting regulations to protect them. In 1935, forest land was divided into two categories, "protected" and "classified." "In the latter, both the commercial and customary rights to fell trees, collect firewood and plants, and station herds were more strictly curtailed and infractions more severely punished than in the 'protected' type of forest"

(Thompson and Adloff, 1969, pp. 343-44). By 1950, there were about three million acres in these two categories in the Sahel countries.

But in practice, the trees continued to be sacrificed. This was clearly evident in the expansionary period of the 1950s, when new wooded areas were opened up by the Compagnie Générale des Oléaginoux Tropicales (CGOT). This organization was established in 1948, in Paris, with 90 percent of its capital supplied by FIDES and the remaining 10 percent by 120 private shareholders (Thompson and Adloff, 1969, p. 374). The CGOT undertook to create the basis of what was supposed to become the most mechanized agricultural enterprise for a dry area in the tropical French African colonies (Pélissier, 1952, p. 70).

The CGOT was granted half a million acres in the relatively undeveloped Casamance area of Senegal. As Maurice Moyal noted:

> By reason of its difficulty of access, Casamance has for long been the Cinderella of French West Africa. But every cloud has a silver lining: the area still has large tracts of virgin land, great stretches of dense tropical forest. Her remoteness and backwardness, have, until now, protected her from extensive cultivation of groundnuts, which has all but exhausted the soil in the rest of the territory. [Moyal, 1952, p. 18]

The CGOT, funded by American aid and by FIDES, moved in heavy equipment for clearing the forests. In 1954, Moyal again described the area:

> Here, the dense forest is being cleared by means of huge steel cables drawn by heavy tractors—two at each end of a cable. Bulldozers push the felled trees right and left of the clearing where the wood is burnt to enrich the soil with its ash. [Moyal, 1954, p. 33]

Despite these efforts, the experiment proved to be a failure. Some of the soil was more clayey than is suitable for the peanut. The plants that grew up after the trees were cut were a bushy type of shrub with roots that were very difficult to get rid of. The rainfall was higher than in areas normally planted with peanuts, and it was very irregular from one year to the next. This made planning ahead difficult, a major problem for a large-scale agricultural enterprise (Pélissier, 1952, p. 74).

MOURIDISM: A RELIGIOUS IMPULSE TOWARD OVERPRODUCTION

In addition to investment patterns, certain social changes that were occurring as the French established their hegemony abetted the spread of the groundnut and its disastrous consequences. The French administration's efforts to turn Senegal into a country of peanut farms was aided by the rise of an Islamic sect called the Mourides.[8] As of 1970, more than half a million people, one-sixth of Senegal's population, were Mourides. Most Mourides are from the Wolof ethnic group.

It has frequently been the case than when traditional ways of life are disrupted by powerful forces that cannot be controlled, a religious movement providing new forms of organization, some solace, and actual social support develops and grows (Worsley, 1968). This religion may be of a rebellious type, offering resistance to the conquerors. Early Christianity has been analyzed in this way. (Thompson, 1954) However, the movement may evolve into a more accommodating form that actually supports the colonizers. Mouridism was the latter type.

The Wolof resisted the French at first. They sabotaged the railway lines, seeing correctly that the "land-ships" thrusting their way into Wolof lands were going to further undermine their already weakened social order (O'Brien, 1971, p. 11). They were finally conquered at the battle of Dekrile in 1886. A year later, a charismatic prophet, Amadu Bamba, appeared. The sect grew rapidly. In the beginning of the 20th century, there were only 500 Mourides. By 1912, there were 70,000, and by 1952, 300,000 (Markovitz, 1970, p. 86).

At first the French were wary of this development. It might, after all, be dangerous to have people loyal to and even fervent about a new religious leader. He might prove to be a rallying point of resistance to the French authority (Markovitz, 1970, p. 88). They exiled Bamba twice, but he counseled only obedience to the French, and the administration discovered they could make valuable use of the Mourides. Mouride social organization was hierarchical, the leadership able to exert a great deal of influence and control over its followers.

The Wolof had been a stratified society with a warrior stratum who now had no army and knew they could win no battles. The Mouride leadership advised young men to join the French armies during World War I. Later, they served as strikebreakers at the docks of Dakar in 1946 (O'Brien, 1971, p. 71).

But it was the attitude toward work and agriculture that proved to be of greatest benefit to the French. The Mouride ideology included a strong work ethic, very suitable at a time in which cash crop agriculture was expanding. Mouridism was able to provide the new way of life with a religious sanction, perhaps softening the harsh reality of what was happening. The colonial administration felt it could rely on the Mouride leadership to increase the area devoted to peanuts, and in the words of one of the French, "to keep the members of the brotherhood entirely disciplined to our authority" (O'Brien, 1971, p. 63).

The Mourides acted as pioneers, opening up new areas for peanut cultivation. Mouridism contained an institution called the *dara,* "a farming group of young men acting in the service of a *shaikh*" (religious leader with disciplines) (O'Brien, 1971, p. 163). In Mouridism, the dara, a word originally referring to a place of religious instruction and as such characteristic of most of Islam, took the form exclusively of a work group. The dara was a source of great wealth for the *shuyukh* (plural of shaikh). For the young men making up the labor force, the *tak-der,* the dara provided an alternative to the traditional occupations that colonialists had made impossible.

The dara worked land provided by its leader, who also supplied the men with seeds and fertilizer. Working in a competitive atmosphere, the tak-der vie to see who will produce the most for the shaikh, who collects the harvest and praises those who have worked the hardest. This is in the best tradition of Mouridism, for Amadu Bamba is supposed to have told his followers, "Be like the little donkey loaded with millet who doesn't eat the load he carries" (Fouquet, 1951, p. 74).

The dara produces the major part of the annual groundnut crop on the estates of the shuyukh. The latter also receive offerings from the small peasants—who make up the main body of Mouridism—amounting to about one-tenth of their own harvest. This is a substantial tithe, considering that these are people with low annual incomes. The *talibes* (followers) work for the religious leader on his "Wednesday fields." The Wednesday field, which is not necessarily worked on that day, is basically a plot of land which is cultivated by the talibes of a given village, and the produce goes entirely to the shaikh. The actual labor time spent this way varies, the minimum being three to four days a year (O'Brien, 1971, pp. 210-11). The talibes not only provide free labor but also do the seeding and provide their own food.

In turn, beside religious leadership, the shaikh will provide food in times of scarcity. He is indeed the only one likely to have any surplus for this purpose, and he will also help care for the old and disabled who cannot support themselves. The shuyukh are also money lenders, their rates being lower than those of the traders, although still quite high. In addition, they have political connections, which may be useful to their followers in the event of an arrest or some other problem. There are clear resemblances between the Mouride structure and that of the old-time urban political machine in industrialized countries.

As the tak-der leave the dara, some will be given land, which is taken from the estates they have been working. As this is depleted, the entire dara is moved to a new location. The tendency then is to expand into new areas. Throughout its history, Mouridism has been an expansionary force, and the French have encouraged this tendency and have given it material assistance.

As the Mourides moved from Baol to the southeastern regions of Saloum and the cercle of Tambacounda, the French allocated large areas of land to the shuyukh. The expansion of the railroads, particularly in the early 1930s, was also an encouragement to the Mouride religious leaders to take their followers to more remote areas, since there would be a way of transporting their crops to market. In 1932, the governor of Senegal praised the brotherhood for its role in "the creation of new villages and the clearing of large areas of virgin land for cultivation" (O'Brien, 1971, p. 65).

Earlier in their history, the Mourides had expanded "along the desert fringe of the Eastern Wolof Zone" (O'Brien, 1971, p. 60). The scrub forest there was chopped down for estates. As a consequence of this movement, the Fulani, the pastoral people who originally dominated the area, were displaced. Since the colonial administration supported the Mourides, they were usually the winners in any dispute between farmers and herdspeople.

The Fulani and their stock were pushed further toward the desert. As one of the major researchers on Mouridism explains:

> The colonial administration encouraged the Mourides to extend the area of cultivation as far as possible even when to do so involved the wholesale destruction of valuable forest; this was especially the case in the last years of the Second World War, when there was a drive to increase groundnut production at any cost. [O' Brien, 1971, p. 196]

The Fulani used the woodlands as pasture without destroying it. In sharp contrast, Jean Suret-Canale (1971, p. 434), a historian of French West Africa, describes the Mourides as the "enemies of the tree." A vivid account from 1937, describes the activity produced in an encounter with the Mourides:

> An audacious *marabout* (religious leader) . . . places himself at the head of 200, 300, 400 *talibes* provided with arms, tools and agricultural implements. . . . At sunrise, the *talibes* place themselves in line and begin to cut down the trees and clear the ground with frenetic zeal. Usually the Fulani immediately leave their villages and move off. The Mourides advance, already they have cut down all the trees, even the useful ones: dye trees, calabash trees, baobabs, etc. The fields of cassava are uprooted, the miserable huts thrown to the ground and burnt. At the same time the brand-new characteristic "hats" of the Mouride huts are placed on solid pillars of wood. The sun has not set before a new Mouride hamlet has arisen amid the freshly cleared fields. [O' Brien, 1971, p. 197]

Other examples illustrate the same process. In 1951, a water hole was bored in a classified forest at Deali. The project's ostensible purpose was to provide a reliable year-round water source for the Fulani herds. Some Mouride marabouts requested that an area near the bore hole be declassified. The government agreed, although it required that tree belts serve as protection against wind erosion. Within three days, 3,000 to 4,500 acres were cleared, and almost no trees were left standing (Pélissier, 1966, p. 361).

ECOLOGICAL DESTRUCTION UNDER THE MOURIDES

At least one authority on Mouride social structure describes them as a people with little history of agriculture, and it should be noted that little has been done to change this pattern. A study done in the 1950s found that Mouride productivity was far less per acre than that of the Serer, who have a long history of peasantry and whose agricultural system includes crop rotation, the preservation of trees, and the use of animal manure (O'Brien, 1971, p. 220).

O'Brien notes that "Mouride agriculture is oriented to the quick cash return and thus has meant a steady overcultivation of groundnuts [peanuts] over the years" (1971, p. 220). Where it is best for the soil to have equal proportions of food and peanut crops, the Mourides will usually allot twice as much land to the peanut. In the Mouride areas, millet has tended to be neglected, although some is grown. The richer landholders grow sanyo, which takes six months to mature but is high yielding. Most peasants cannot wait that long for a food crop and instead grow suna, a quick-maturing variety that takes only half the time to ripen and helps the peasants get through the "hungry" time before their groundnuts are sold (ibid., p. 191).

Some attempts have been made to persuade the shuyukh to cultivate a fixed area by using intensive farming methods. The hope was that soil productivity could be increased and therefore expansion with its deleterious consequences avoided. The first such experiment occurred in 1947, the Bloc Experimentale d'Arachide, in Kafferine at Boulet. Workers were sent by the marabout Bassirou Mback. They were unpaid and could derive little benefit for themselves and their families. The shaikh, however, displeased with the profits, withdrew from the experiment. At least one French commentator criticized the system as one of "semi-mechanization with slave labor" (quoted in O'Brien, 1971, p. 225). This is perhaps an exaggeration, but other experiments have also proved failures. The use of an unpaid labor force, even when combined with fertilizers, rotation, and semimechanization, is not conducive to real improvements. Since the marabouts have the power to control the labor—and their decisions are based on cash returns—they have no clear motivation to change their methods.

The Mourides, who produce about one-third of the peanuts in Senegal, are clearly a major factor in understanding what has happened to the ecology of the area. But it must be underlined that they were not a spontaneous force, a "natural" outgrowth of Senegalese history, or a development that might have been predicted from a study of Islamic religious thought. They were a reaction to French domination. Throughout the period of direct colonization, Mouride leaders had a very favored position: They were used directly by the French to increase the production of peanuts. These were a source of profits for the marabouts and for the French companies, but not for the Senegalese peasants. The profits for these relative few meant the squandering of the soil and forest resources of whole areas of Senegal, making these regions more vulnerable to changes in rainfall.

NOTES

1. The vagaries of European fashion led to a brief revival of the Sahara trade in the 1860s, when ostrich feathers were in vogue. A majority of the plumes came from the area around Timbuktu. This particular traffic seems to have lasted only until the 1880s (Newbury, 1966, pp. 240-41).

2. Thurston Clarke (1978, pp. 22-23) gives a particularly compelling account of a French massacre of nearly 207 Tuaregs in 1917. "As late as 1965, nomads who visited the Tanut wells were still digging up the jewelry of the victims."

3. The effect of peanut production on the soil in Nigeria has been described by I. A. Svandize, 1968.

4. A dramatic literary portrayal of similar French policies in Vietnam as recounted by a Vietnamese novelist during the 1930s is given in Ngo Vinh Long, 1973, esp. pp. 161-75.

5. A fuller appreciation of just how irrational and destructive the colonial economy was can

be gained by considering the relations between French West Africa and another major French colonial possession of the time—Indochina. The needs for food in West Africa were created by the loss of farmer control over the production process. To compensate for these losses, France had imported from Indochina several thousands of tons of Vietnamese rice annually from 1906 to 1915. These imports were insufficient to fully offset the declining food availability in West Africa, however. In addition, they extracted from Vietnamese farmers an output that was also being threatened by rubber production in Indochina. Thus the French appear to have moved rice around the empire to keep people alive so they could continue to produce for French interests, but both the West Africans *and* the Indochinese saw their food availability undergo sharp declines. In 1900, French statistics reveal 262 kg. of paddy available per person per year; by 1913, this had dropped to 226 kg./person/year and fell to 182 kg. in 1937. For details, see Suret-Canale, 1971, esp. p. 49; and Ngo Vinh Long, 1973, esp. p. 124.

6. The 1931 famine in Niger has become the subject of intensive historical research in France. One student has ascertained that there were no unusual climatic trends during the years imeediately preceding 1931 (Derriennic, 1976, pp. 129-33); while a research team at the French National Agronomic Institute has documented through the historical archives the relations among French taxation, labor recruitment, and other forms of impact on the local food production system (Egg et al., 1975). See also the striking account by Salifou, 1975, pp. 22-48.

7. Similar practices in Vietnam are described by Ngo Vinh Long, 1973.

8. Amin (1972, p. 522) refers to the Mouride brotherhood as "the most important vector for the expansion of the groundnut economy and for the submission of the peasants to the goals of this economy: to produce a large amount and to accept very low and stagnating wages despite progress in productivity."

4

On the Eve of the Famine: Independence and Dependency

It appears to be a particularly cruel irony that the great drought and famine of 1968-74 hit the West African Sahel just after the colonial system had finally relaxed its hold over the region. Beginning in 1960, France turned over formal political control of its former French West African empire to the various African political entities now known as Senegal, Mali, Niger, Mauritania, Upper Volta, and Chad. A closer look at the nature of this independence will reveal, however, that far from becoming free of outside domination, the Sahel peoples were merely to see that domination change its form.

The most widely discussed approach to postindependence economic problems of Third World countries in general is known as "dependency" theory. Without entering into a lengthy review of the many issues and debates and points of view within this rather overarching and often contradictory set of concepts, we would propose rather to indicate the ways in which dependency has continued to affect Sahelian economies and societies in general, and then to illustrate with some specific cases the various effects of dependency on actual local social and ecological relationships.

DEPENDENCY

The concept of dependency can easily mislead.[1] In the modern world, all nations are in fact dependent on at least some, if not all, others. Even the

United States, in which politicians often run for office on promises to reduce our dependency on this or that foreign nation or region, is highly dependent on overseas sources of materials, and increasingly so. One study in the 1950s, for example, indicated that of 62 "strategic industrial materials," 52 required at least 40 percent imports, while only seven could be supplied with more than 80 percent within the boundaries of the United States (Bidwell, in Magdoff, 1966, p. 50). More recent estimates give a 96 percent foreign dependence on aluminum, 100 percent for chromium, 88 percent for nickel, 100 percent for tin, and so on for the year 1985, with even higher overseas dependence by the year 2000 (Brown, 1976, p. 94, citing U.S. Department of Interior sources).

Dependency theory, then, is not merely a statement of the internationally *interdependent* character of the modern world economy. Rather, what distinguishes countries with dependent economies is a set of political and economic relationships that render the dependent country relatively powerless to control or affect its course of development. For example, in 1977 and again in 1978, guerrilla attacks in the Shaba Province in Zaire were claimed to have endangered the lives of more than 5,000 Europeans working in the region. In both cases, France, Belgium, Morocco, the United States, and other countries sent in troops, logistics experts, and equipment to occupy towns, carry out search and destroy missions, evacuate Europeans, and so forth. One of the most important official justifications for these operations was that the European forces were invited by a friendly Zairian government to aid in the protection of foreign residents.

But consider the opposite and nearly equivalent situation. In France, there are an estimated 55,000 Senegalese resident workers. Even a cursory reading of the French press over the past few years reveals numerous killings, beatings, mysterious fires in the buildings where these African workers live, and many other forms of intimidation and harassment that the French police and military seem incapable of bringing to an end. Could Senegal drop its paratroopers into Marseilles to protect its civilians?

It is not merely the formal political and military aspects of dependency that are of interest to an analysis of the ecological processes of the postindependence period of the Sahelian countries, however. In our view, four major aspects of economic dependency are of crucial significance to understanding the background to the famine and its aftermath.

The Lack of Diversity

What was the nature of the economies of the Sahelian countries at the time of independence? A survey published by FAO in 1965 conveys a picture of overwhelming dependence on a limited number of exports with which to obtain the many things not produced internally, and a very limited number of market outlets for this limited number of exports. First, it was noted that Sahelian countries as a whole had more than 80 percent of their populations engaged in a single economic activity—agriculture (FAO, 1965, p. 3). As for exports, the U.N. Statistical Yearbook for 1964 showed that the newly independent countries of the Sahel were extremely dependent on a single product: Senegal's exports were 79 percent taken up by peanuts or peanut products, Mali similarly was 59 percent dependent on peanuts and Niger 63 percent, while Mauritania received 58 percent of its export earnings from fish (cited in Hodder, 1969, p. 452).[2] One effect of the extreme single-crop emphasis was noted by FAO (1965, p. 22). "Although many of the countries [of the Sahel] have large commercial production of oil seeds and oil nuts, the consumption of these is low in all zones."

So the high-protein vegetable oils were being exported while little was consumed at home. The FAO study goes on to note the extreme dependence on agricultural products in general for export earnings, reaching altogether as high as 95 percent in several of the countries (FAO, 1965, p. 2). Thus the Sahel countries were unindustrialized, dependent on agricultural products for access to industrial goods, and within agriculture, largely dependent on a single product. FAO concluded that "export prospects from the Savanna [i.e., Sahel] to the rest of the world are not very bright" (p. 62).

But this characteristic is tied to another. Again, the FAO (p. 2) summarizes:

> A second characteristic of the Region [here meaning all of West Africa] is its extreme dependence on international trade. About 30% of the domestic supply of goods is imported from outside the region; even for agricultural goods, in raw or processed form, this proportion is as high as . . . 18% for the region minus Nigeria.

The Sahel countries had to depend essentially on a single crop in order to purchase a varied set of imports from the industrial countries. This problem, however, was further compounded by the fact that through their historical ties to the French colonial empire, the Sahelian countries at the time of independence were dependent for more than 83 percent of all their exports of peanuts, cotton, and fish on just three markets: the United States, Great Britain, and the European Economic Community (FAO, 1965, p. 2).

The combination of having little variety in things to sell and little choice in where to sell it sets up a contradictory situation. On the one hand, the Sahelians would be extremely vulnerable to a decline in the world price for their products, having little if anything to fall back on. This is a classic problem of single-product economies and one of the telling features of dependency. On the other hand, if the outside market countries try to solve this problem by offering a stable, high, subsidized price, there is a constant danger of stimulating overproduction and ecological damage as the artificial price attracts too many productive resources to the crop. It will be seen below in the example from Niger just how devastating this process can be. And "guaranteed" prices have a way of being phased out, as will also be seen in the example from Niger.

Even with rich-country price supports, however, the effects of this dependency on a limited market produce another contradiction: the dependent country is pushed towards higher outputs of its one or two exportable crops both by the price supports *and* by the fact that even these supports are not sufficient to overcome the more rapidly increasing costs of goods imported from the wealthier countries. This phenomenon is usually referred to as the "declining terms of trade". The declining terms of trade for the Sahelian countries in their first decade of independence is dramatically illustrated in the following table:

Table 4.1.
Declining Terms of Trade

		Kgs Produced to Get 100 Units of Market Goods	
Country	*Export Product*	*1961*	*1970*
Senegal	Peanuts	100 kg.	148
Niger	Peanuts/Cotton	100(1964)	130/135
Chad	Cotton	100(1964)	115
Mali	Peanuts/Cotton	100	174/161 (1965)
Upper Volta	Peanuts/Cotton	100	126/118

Source: Comité Information Sahel, 1975, pp. 164-65.

The table shows that in 1961, if each of the countries listed needed to produce 100 kg. of peanuts or cotton for 100 units of imported goods, by 1970 all of the countries were compelled to produce significantly larger amounts of their export crops *just to keep even with imports*. Thus the dynamics of the Sahelian countries' international trade relations were such as to drive them to higher outputs while providing them with an overall negative result.[3]

Dependence on Foreign Funds

The great poverty of Sahelian countries at the time of independence has led to their continuing dependency on foreign funds for investment. The statistics for the decade 1960-70 (Amin, 1973, p. 270) speak so clearly as to preclude comment[4]:

Country	*Foreign Contribution to Investments, 1960-70 (in percent)*
Senegal	81
Mali	78
Mauritania	78
Upper Volta	72
Niger	72

Dependence on the Business Cycle

A major area in which dependency manifests itself is in the cyclical production process in those capitalist economies with which the Sahelian countries emerged from colonialism with their most significant economic ties.

The recurrent boom-and-bust phenomenon of capitalism is familiar to most people in the industrialized capitalist world. High rates of investment produce increases in jobs, wages in many industries are pushed up, production increases, and eventually "recession" sets in as workers are laid off, wages fail to keep up with price increases, and investment money is tight. Then the cycle begins again.

This similar process at home, however, has its implications overseas in forms that are not so easily understood. The effect of the business cycle on dependent countries has not been investigated in as great detail as is deserved, but a few general points can be suggested.

First, the expansionary side of the business cycle is a period in which investments are encouraged, and thus a period in which production is stimulated. This means that materials, such as peanut oil, may be in increased demand according to their uses in the industrial economies. Whatever means are necessary for their production may be offered, either in the form of private investment, foreign aid, loans, or some combination of these. This boom period is also one in which the tendency to offer a guaranteed price in a single-crop economy would be highest, in order to maintain supplies of a necessary material.

By contrast, the recession phase of the cycle in the industrial capitalist world may be characterized by retrenchment of foreign aid, wavering of the commitment to price supports for overseas products, and a contracting market for many of these products. The effects of this retrenchment, severe enough on the poorest groups in the industrialized countries, is even more striking in dependent countries because their greater basic poverty and their lack of diversity of production render them particularly vulnerable to even a single price change.

The recent effects of the business cycle on Sahelian countries have been particularly strong owing to the nature of post-World War II international economic developments. Two processes have dovetailed to create especially strong demands on the Sahelian economies for increased production of agricultural products.

First, the post-World War II upswing in the business cycle was particularly long. From 1949 to about 1968, there was a nearly uninterrupted boom period. In the Sahel, this lengthy expansionary period coincided with the last few years of colonial control and the first few years of independence. This boom helped to determine the economic policies of the French in stimulating ever greater production of peanuts and attempting to establish a meat export industry.

Furthermore, the post-World War II period saw the combination of the

Chinese Revolution, i.e., the expansion of socialism, as well as anticolonial movements throughout the world. In the capitalist countries, the response was in part to increase military expenditures and military alliances and to initiate "foreign aid," "development aid," and other forms of economic assistance to certain sectors of the underdeveloped dependent countries of the world. In the case of the Sahel, most of this aid, both military and economic, was offered by France, although, as we shall see in a later chapter, that pattern is now changing. Its effects, particularly in the form of price supports for peanuts and assistance to veterinary programs, will be documented below. But it is important to keep in mind generally that the eve of the famine in the Sahel was a period of investment and a constant push to increase production.

Dependence on the Effects of Intercapitalist Rivalries

The phenomenon of dependency has yet another aspect. Among the wealthy nations, various rivalries and often open conflicts emerge, and the pressures among and between the different interest groups in these nations can have profound effects on the underdeveloped countries that supply certain materials.

Of particular importance in the case of the Sahel countries during the transition to independence was the situation of the world market in vegetable oils—of which peanuts were a major element—and the relations between France and the United States regarding these oils. In 1957, geographer A. B. Mountjoy wrote a brief article on the world vegetable oil situation, noting several features that related to West Africa and especially to the Sahel. Mountjoy (1957, p. 37) noted first of all that the peanut is a particularly desirable oil-producing plant. "An acre of groundnuts produces 260 lbs. of vegetable fat, one of soya beans 150 lbs. of vegetable fat, whereas the average cow yields only 46 pounds of butterfat per acre."[5]

In addition to the desirability of the productivity of the peanut, there was a particular market problem, in that "The world's greatest consuming area of vegetable oils, Western Europe, produces them only in very limited quantity" (ibid., p. 44). To this was added an additional problem: Several of the major producers, such as China, India, and the United States, had internal markets large enough to absorb their own output of peanut oil. Thus Mountjoy concluded: "The tropical and equatorial possessions in Africa of the great industrial powers, Britain, France, and Belgium offer the greatest opportunities for the expansion of export oil crops. It is clear that already Africa is replacing Asia as the main surplus vegetable oil area" (p. 49).[6]

Mountjoy wrote as well of the potential for increased acreage in peanut cultivation in the Sahelian region of West Africa. The attractiveness of the Sahel's peanut regions was further heightened by the post-World War II economic relations between the United States and France in the matter of vegetable oils. Soybean exports to Europe are among the greatest success stories of American agriculture in the last 30 years. In 1949, U.S. soybean exports were 47,000 tons; by 1973 they had reached nearly 5 million tons of processed beans and another 13 million tons that are crushed in U.S.-owned mills established in Europe (Susan George, 1977, p. 122). The story of this enormous expansion of soybean exports to Europe is one of aggressive marketing, pressure at international economic meetings, and the use of Food for Peace shipments to introduce soya products cheaply to consumers who were accustomed to olive oil.[7]

The massive takeover of the European vegetable oil market by U.S. concerns did not come entirely without resistance, however. The speculations of Mountjoy indicate that the European countries were trying to find more controllable sources for at least part of this production. Of all these countries, France was in a position to put up the greatest resistance because of the alternative sources offered by the Sahelian area. As one French researcher summed up the situation in 1974: ". . . soybeans produced in the United States and peanuts produced in the underdeveloped countries are in competition with each other on the world market." (Marloie, 1974, p. 2)

A double contradiction emerged from this four-way competition of peanuts, soybeans, France, and the United States. On the one hand, the Sahelian countries most dependent on peanut exports—Senegal, Mali, and Niger—found their markets severely limited by the massive and aggressive U.S. campaign to dominate the vegetable oil market with soybeans. Yet, at the same time France put to work much scientific research and foreign "aid" work in Senegal and Niger, the countries where it had the greatest postindependence influence to expand the production of peanuts. (From 1960 to 1968, Mali attempted a radical break with its former colonial master). It was ultimately a losing battle: By 1971, France imported 1,307, 947 tons of soybeans, of which 773,544 tons came from the United States, as opposed to only 318,332 tons of peanuts (Marloie, 1974, p. 13). Nonetheless, in their drive to compete, French governmental and commercial interests extended peanut production rapidly into areas where it had previously been considered insufficiently economical because of transportation costs. This happened especially in Niger on the eve of the famine. The effects will be discussed shortly.

Dependence on Colonial Structures

Earlier chapters have described and analyzed the social structures typical of the Sahelian region during precolonial times as well as some of the major effects of colonial rule on these structures. The independence of the Sahelian countries did not automatically bring with it major transformations of the national or local social structures, and in the absence of revolutionary movements in the region at the time, independence meant the transfer of the highest-ranking political posts from French administrators to those educated members of the French-trained bureaucracy most able to fill these posts. Despite the complexity of the societies in question, and despite the many specific variations from country to country, a number of general characteristics of the postindependence societies can be outlined.

These characteristics will help to explain the pattern of ecological and economic development that was occurring on the eve of the famine. For, like the single-crop, limited-market nature of the economies, the integration into the capitalist business cycle, and the intercapitalist rivalries, the dependence of Sahelian societies on the political and social structures inherited from colonialism sets the context in which these developments were to take place.

In simplified terms, four major social groupings in postindependence Sahel can be identified. First, the French-trained bureaucracy, which inherited the greatest amount of political power, was recruited for the most part from the leading families in the colonies, in particular those who showed the greatest loyalty to the French during colonial rule. While perhaps not a fully consolidated social class, it nonetheless not only had major political control of the society but also was the group that could benefit most directly and completely by carrying out the expansionary policies in peanut-growing; they could hope as well to benefit from the eventual development of a livestock export industry.[8] This same bureaucracy, however, because of the relative poverty of the countries in which it was bequeathed political power—and because of its elaborate social networks of kin throughout the countries—was also particularly prone to exercise its power and control over government funds for the benefit and advancement of these relations. Such use of funds constitutes the phenomenon of corruption, which has also played a role in determining the course of events in numerous development programs.[9]

A second social grouping consists of the merchants or local African traders. While many of these are closely related to the bureaucracy, as a whole they are often competitive with it. In the case of Mali there was a great deal of open political conflict between the two groups as they competed for political and economic privileges. This conflict resulted in riots, arrests, and eventually in 1968 a coup that brought the merchants and their military supporters into power against those elements of the bureaucracy who had tried to mobilize peasant support by adopting a radical socialist program.[10]

In Senegal and Niger, the conflict between bureaucrats and merchants appears more attenuated, but political coups have occurred there in 1962 and 1974, respectively, and in both cases merchants and bureaucrats were elements of the political conflict.[11]

Despite the frequent political tensions between bureaucrats and merchants, these two groups often have interests that coincide. In particular, in the area of economic development, both are in a position to benefit most from a rapid increase in production, since together they can dominate and control prices of agricultural inputs to farmers and market agricultural and livestock products.[12]

For purposes of this study, the most important characteristic of these groups is their position as implementors of foreign-instigated projects and as groups that have an interest in the greatest and most rapid possible return—whatever the longer-term ecological costs.

The third group is constituted by the farmers, who grow subsistence as well as commercial crops. There is a great range across the Sahel in the degree of stratification of land ownership, with some areas having almost-developed rural landlord classes, and others with nearly egalitarian, even collectively run, fields. The implications of these differences will be more closely examined in Chapter 9, for it is in the present period that their effects are becoming more pronounced. For an understanding of the developments on the eve of the famine, it will be sufficient to consider the farming groups as a single social unit, dominated and controlled by the bureaucrats, or the bureaucrats and the merchants together.

Finally, there are the herding populations, which are the most marginal, being farthest from centers of government control, and thus rather free from the bureaucracy, and also somewhat independent of the merchants.

These four social groupings, then, in outline form, constitute the main elements of Sahelian societies on the eve of the famine. The farmers and herders had little political or economic power because they were dominated by merchants, who had traditionally been powerful in the towns and rural areas, and by bureaucrats, whose power had been developed and then partially transferred to them by the colonial power. To see just how these relationships helped bring about the famine, we will examine the case of Niger in some detail and then look briefly at some similar material from Mali and Senegal.

NIGER: PEANUTS, PROFITS AND PASTORALISTS

Niger is a large country, twice the size of France, with a small population of 4.5 million in 1977. Most of the northern part of the country lies within the desert zone (IMF, 1970, p. 402), with the central part devoted to pasture-desert transition that grades into the northern Sahel. Rainfall increases toward the south, creating along the southern border with Africa's most populous nation, Nigeria, a narrow strip in which peanuts can be grown. For centuries, the farming communities of southern Niger have interacted with the pastoralists to the north, producing millet and sorghum in return for animal products, including fertilization of the fields by the herds that move south in the dry season. In some cases, farmers have even developed herds themselves and "lent" them out to the herders during the rainy season when the herds move north to escape the tsetse fly and the farmers are busy tending their crops. It is in this southern, agricultural region that we must first focus our attention.

Peanut Production

Unlike Senegal, Niger does not have a century-long association with the peanut. Owing to the great distances from Niger to the main transportation routes to Europe, the French began developing commercial production of peanuts only after World War I (Péhaut, 1970, pp. 42-43). In the 1930s, there was a small expansion of the area under cultivation, and then, following World War II, the boom began. Peanuts, which had occupied 73,000 ha. in 1934, spread to more than 142,000 by 1954, and had reached 349,000 ha. by 1961 (ibid., p. 48; Raynaut, 1975, p. 36). In 1968 on the eve of the famine, the area planted in peanuts hit the highest mark ever, at 432,000 ha. (Derriennic, 1977, p. 179). The tremendous speed with which the peanut culture spread did not result from a sudden discovery of ways to make its cultivation ecologically beneficial, however.

The potentially harmful effects of overuse of peanut production on Sahelian soils has been previously discussed regarding Senegal. But there are further difficulties that are especially exemplified in the region of southern Niger. Despite its adaptability to relatively dry climates, the peanut is not a very hardy plant unless the growing conditions fall within a certain limited range. Peanuts do not grow well with less than 500 mm. (20 inches) of rainfall during the growing season, although theoretically they can survive on 350 mm. (14 inches) (Péhaut, 1970, p. 14).

Equally important, however, is the timing of the rain, which must correspond closely to the growing cycle of the plant if production of nuts is to be good. For example, there must be a solid rain of 20 mm. in one day, or 25 to 35 mm. in two to three days during the first few days after planting (Péhaut, 1970, p. 22). Similarly, at other points of the growth of the plant, rainfall coming even a few days late can adversely affect the eventual harvest. Close to harvest time, too much rainfall can also be damaging by causing absorption of too much of the acidic elements from the soil into the plant, which has almost stopped growing and is putting most of its intake into the fruits (Péhaut, 1970, p. 25).

The region of southern Niger is close to the 500 mm. isohet, so many areas of peanut production are particularly susceptible to large variations in production from year to year as rainfall varies. In addition, as was noted in Chapter 1, as the rainfall becomes more scarce, it also becomes more erratic in its timing, making further undependability in crop outputs. The result of these climatic circumstances is that peanut harvests in Niger show an extremely varied pattern, with many good years and many bad years.

How have the cultivators adapted to this problem? If peanut production were their sole means of support, each bad year would mean total disaster to the majority of farmers who live only slightly above the subsistence level. A traditional solution has been found, however. Around the farming villages, a certain number of fields have been traditionally given over to millet and sorghum, the main staple crops. Other areas have been left as uncultivated brushland, providing essentially fallow areas that act as ecological "green zones" between villages. During the 1950s and 1960s, peanut cultivation was undertaken in these fallow zones (Péhaut, 1970, p. 34), motivated by the desire of the farmers to maintain their staple crops while expanding the production of the cash crop. Of great significance for the coming of the drought is that these fallow zones had been previously kept unused just for "periods of insecurity" (ibid., p. 34). The peasant cultivation, while not competing directly with staple crops (which were maintained in their previous plots), did lead to a major lessening of "reserve" lands that could be activated in difficult times. Finally, peanut plant residue, while higher in protein content than local subsistence crops such as sorghum, offers only about one-third the amount of total dry-matter yield, or total food provision (van Raay and de Leeuw, 1974, p. 21). Thus the expansion of peanut production over large areas would render even more precarious the dry-season pasture availability of food for nomadic herders and their cattle. The combination of the peanut's delicacy, an unpredictable environment, and cash and subsistence food needs has resulted in a rapid and dramatic decline in the total environmental reserves of the region of southern Niger.

Technology, Expansion, Incentives

How and why did peanut cultivation spread so rapidly in a region where it may not have been most suited—at least when viewed in a long-term ecological framework? The reasons are several, and a look at them reveals much about the developments taking place in the Sahel on the eve of the famine.

First, the peanut was the easiest cash crop to introduce. In neighboring Senegal and in Nigeria to the south, many years of production and research had given techniques for planting, storing, and marketing. As transportation routes into West Africa's interior began to improve, it was logical to push the peanut in as well. In actuality, there were two great surges of peanut production in Niger. One occurred between 1954 and 1957 and was mainly a result of a rapid expansion of the amount of land under peanuts: in 1954, 142,000 ha.; in 1957, 304,000! This remarkable increase in land under peanuts was achieved by two mechanisms. First, there was a government campaign to encourage production, often accompanied by promises of increased income, sometimes made tangible in the form of "gifts," offered by the enterprises that were promoting the government campaign (Péhaut, 1970, pp. 48-49). The gifts, which included commodities such as kola and cloth, bound the producers to companies through local commercial networks. Seeds, tools, and other production costs would be "advanced" along with the gifts and had to be repaid by the farmers at harvest time (ibid., p. 51). In addition, price supports for peanuts were established by the (still colonial) government in France, precisely in order to encourage peanut cultivation.

Second, the research in Senegal achieved new varieties of peanut seeds, which held out hope for even greater expansion, making the peanut appear to be an investment with a future—and local chiefs, traders, and the village elite saw the possibilities along with the French. The research—most of which went on at the Bambey Station in Senegal—led to the development of many new varieties, some with improved yields, some with greater drought resistance, some with greater rainfall tolerance, some with shorter growing cycles. The introduction of these seeds, starting about 1961, just after Niger's official independence from France, brought on a second wave of increase in peanut production. Very few hectares were added between 1961 and 1967, but production increased from 130,000 to 290,000 tons (Péhaut,

1970, pp. 80-82). This "green revolution" in the Niger peanut economy was one of the most statistically dramatic of production increases anywhere in the world—until the drought hit.

Not everyone was pleased with the development of peanut production in Niger. It appears that many local authorities were concerned with the possible effects on subsistence production. Thus the governor of Niger wrote in 1954 to the regional commander in Maradi, one of the main peanut regions:

> Cultivation of peanuts has now reached a level that should not be surpassed: despite the profitable price paid to the producer, its extension, to the detriment of subsistence crops, is dangerous. I order that not a single hectare of millet or other subsistence crop be improperly cultivated because of the attraction of peanut production and request that you invite all the district chiefs to spare no efforts in the coming months to battle this tendency. [Raynaut, 1975, p. 37, cited from Archives de la Présidence de la République, Niamey]

Despite this injunction, just 12 years later the amount of peanuts produced in Maradi had tripled, and 12 new market centers for peanut trade had been opened there (Raynaut, 1975, p. 37).

An American commentator noted in 1966 that "the rapidity with which the peanuts have assumed so important a place in Niger's economy has alarmed the authorities." She went on to state that "the government is reorganizing the local peanut market, discouraging expansion of that crop, and favoring substitute or supplementary agricultural sources of cash income" (Thompson, in Carter, 1966, p. 193).[13] But this "reorganization" of markets mainly shifted control from French companies to Nigerien middlemen and government officials, who benefited from the production of an export commodity. As for the discouraging of the expansion of peanuts, although it is true that the overall area planted in peanuts did not increase much after the surge of 1954-57 (it did go up by some 50,000 ha. more by 1968), some individual localities did witness expansion in land area. In Magaria district, for example, the number of hectares planted in peanuts increased from 82,000 in 1958 to 110,000 in 1961, to 146,000 in 1966 (Collins, 1976, p. 269). In three regions, moving from west to east, the percent of land devoted to peanuts was 13.8 in Dosso, 43.8 in Maradi, and 64.1 in Tessoua (Péhaut, 1970, p. 36). Of equal significance, peanuts came to be an indispensable part of many farmers' incomes. Data from Maradi in 1957-61 indicated that a quarter of the farmers received more than 35 percent of their incomes from peanuts. Another quarter received more than 20 percent, while the remaining half depended on peanut harvest for 50 to 80 percent of their incomes (Péhaut, 1970, p. 64). Along with this increased dependency came a long-term deterioration in living standards. Despite the short-term appeal of peanut growing created by high prices, farmers found their workload increasing as well. One French student has calculated that one hectare of peanut cultivation requires 480 hours of work, as against 375 hours for a hectare of millet (Derriennic, 1977, p. 182). Furthermore, the dependency on outside markets for staple foods resulted in a loss through terms of trade. In Senegal, this has been estimated as follows: In 1913, 110 kilograms of peanuts would buy 118 kg. of rice, while by 1968 the same amount of peanuts would purchase only 34 kg. of rice (Derriennic, 1977, p. 183).

Thus a combination of factors compelled the continuing increase in area and harvest of peanuts—a kind of treadmill in which producers became ever more dependent, worked harder, and needed to produce even more peanuts. More importantly, with the development of seeds for shorter growing cycles, *peanut cultivation in the 1960s began to spread north of its previous boundaries, into regions that brought peanut farmers into direct competition with pastoralists.*

The Fertilizer Problem

As has been noted above, the expansion of production in the 1960s was largely because increased yields were brought about by the spread of improved varieties of seeds. In actuality, these seeds were intended—at least according to the research experiments—to be accompanied by larger doses of fertilizer than were traditionally used by farmers in this region. The need for specific types of fertilizers to protect the soil has been known, if not practiced, for a long time. As one soil expert has commented with regard to Africa generally:

> . . . it was clear forty or fifty years ago that both increased pressure of population and the inclusion of cotton, groundnuts or other crops for export in small-scale cultivators' rotations would sooner or later cause fallow periods to become too short or cropping periods too long for maintenance of fertility by means of natural fallows alone, and that there was definite need of experimentation with alternative methods. [Vine, in Moss, ed., 1968, p. 115]

Earlier we have explained how the fallow period works to restore necessary nutrients to the soils. As the fallow period is shortened—in the case of Niger, as the fallow areas between the villages are put into use next to the millet and sorghum fields—the need for fertilizer increases. In addition, the improved seed varieties for the most part are highly fertilizer-sensitive and get their best results under very specific dosages as determined by the tests on the experiment stations.

During the great production upsurge of the 1960s in Niger, however, it is reported that fertilizer was used on only 1.4 percent of the planted areas. In fact, then, the effects of the improved seeds were felt mostly because of a series of years with very good rainfall patterns rather than because of the most rational use of the new technology (Péhaut, 1970, pp. 82-83). And the more long-term effects of failure to introduce fertilizer along with the more highly productive seeds is likely to have been yet another degree of degradation of the soils.

But why didn't the farmers use the fertilizer? There are several interconnected reasons. First, the production benefits were not clearly and dramatically evident to farmers. Second, the fertilizer distribution was poorly organized and fraught with "abuses," the result being that farmers were not able to keep up with the costs (Péhaut, 1970, p. 83).[14] Finally, fertilizer had to compete with a whole new set of technical inputs, including plows and animal traction equipment, all of which were being pushed on the farmers, who found themselves going ever further into debt to finance an agricultural technology that one critic has stated was primarily suited to European farms and not very beneficial to farmers in Niger (Péhaut, 1970, p. 85). As an indicator of the farmers' difficulties, it may be noted that in 1967, 30 percent of loans to farmers had been defaulted, while in Zinder region, as of March 31, 1968—just on the eve of famine—more than 50 percent of all debts for new technology remained unpaid (ibid., p. 86). Thus the combination of poverty, government corruption, eager European agricultural-implements salespeople, and new seeds drove farmers into debt and prevented the development of fertilizer usage that would help maintain the soils. A USAID-sponsored study in the Zinder region concluded that by 1970 only 26 percent of farmers had "ever" used fertilizer, and in 1973-74, *no* fertilizer was being used on staple-crop production. The report cited "pricing constraints" as the problem (Charlick, n.d.).

By 1972, in the Maradi region, the prefect, a local government official, was charging publicly that: "The fallow periods are shrinking, and so the soil is no longer able to regain its potential fertility. In certain zones, such as Serkin Yama, the soils can be considered totally depleted" (quoted from the newspaper *Le Niger*, in Derriennic, 1977, p. 184).

Price Policy and Production Increases

During the 1950s, the French government maintained an artificially high guaranteed price for peanuts, which was a major stimulant to the rapid expansion of lands under cash-crop cultivation in the 1950s as well as the introduction of high-yielding seeds in the 1960s. The guaranteed French price shielded Niger's government, enterprises, and small producers against shifts in the world market price. It lasted until 1965, when Niger, along with 17 other African nations, joined the European Common Market, with "associate" status. The terms of this agreement included a gradual lifting of the French guaranteed price, which was to be made easier through a year-by-year device of setting a "target cost price." France would pay the difference between this price and the actual world price, but the target cost price was to be reduced each year until it came into agreement with the world market price (IMF, 1970, p. 408). Nonetheless, the actual price paid to peanut producers—the farmers—dropped by 22 percent between 1967 and 1969 (Amin, 1973, pp. 134-35). *This drop in prices to the actual producers occurred just as the drought was beginning.* The associate status with the European Common Market thus brought with it a severe financial burden to an already heavily indebted peasantry, whose farming methods had been stimulated by artificial and unmaintainable international pricing devices and who faced the prospects of a decline in prices, declining soil fertility, and drought—all at the same time.[15]

The Real Meaning of Overgrazing

Despite all the ravages visited upon the agricultural zone of Niger by the expanding peanut culture, it was the pastoral peoples to the north on the edge of the desert—the "true Sahelians"—who suffered most from the drought. But even here, the effects of the peanut were at work.

As was shown in Chapter 2, cooperation and trade developed at the points where farmers and herdspeople came in contact. In much of West Africa, farmers lend out their animals either to transhumant or to fully nomadic herdspeople for part of the year and have them returned during the rainy season. In other arrangements, herds will be brought near a farming area for part of the year in order to fertilize the soil with their dung, while the herdspeople receive payment in the form of cash, trade goods, or agricultural products for the use of their animals. Milk and other animal products may also enter into the exchanges.[16]

Although the trade and contact zones have been unstable throughout recent history, during the last several decades, Fulani pastoralists have been moving slowly from northern Nigeria into southern Niger and spreading along the southern edges of the Sahel zone. These movements have been gradual and orderly, season by season, with the herdspeople making one dry season pasturage into a wet-season stayover and then moving slightly to the north—toward the desert fringe—during the succeeding dry season (Diarra, in Monod, 1975, p. 286).[17] As long as the agricultural zone spread only as rapidly as the nomads, and as long as the nomads were effectively in control of this speed, the delicate system of exchanges and ecologically balanced contacts could be preserved.

But as has been noted above, both in the 1950s and 1960s there was a tremendous surge in lands opened up to peanut production. First, the village reserves where the nomads had traditionally kept their cattle while awaiting their introduction onto the fields were made into cash-cropping zones. Then in the 1960s, with the development of newer peanut seeds, zones to the north were opened by farmers hungry for cash to pay their taxes. These farmers were effectively supported by government administrators apparently unwilling to carry out the legal restrictions on the northern limits to cultivation.[18] The result was a sharp decline in the amount of pasturage available to the Fulani herders, who were not able to readjust their pasture movements as fast as the peanut "pioneers" came in (Diarra, in Monod, 1975, p. 288; cf. Dankoussou, et al., 1975, in Caldwell, ed., p. 683).

This sudden upsetting of the ecological and economic interchanges had many effects. First, the herdspeople and farmers became involved in numerous conflicts, for pastures and peanuts were now in direct competition. As a result, the pastoralists did not receive the pastures they needed, and the farmers no longer received the fertilizing services of the animals (Diarra, in Monod, 1975, pp. 288-90).

Simultaneously, the continued expansion of peanut production in areas farther to the south became more ecologically harmful because the herds no longer could move into these zones, which were being blocked by the politically more powerful cultivators on the northern edges of the peanut zone. Thus chemical fertilizer use was not increasing because people did not have sufficient resources to purchase it, and the number of animals coming to the areas declined, meaning that previous natural sources of fertilizer were no longer available. One French observer noted in 1971 that the cultivated zone of a certain agricultural village had increased far in excess of the numbers of animals available to fertilize the soil. The local farmers well understood that this was related to the drop in yields on their farms (Raynaut, in Copans, 1975, p. 9).[19]

Related to these physical and ecological movements were a series of vast social changes, particularly among the northernmost herding groups (Tuaregs). Former vassals and slave groups moved into the agricultural zones, in some cases claiming their freedom from traditional overlords but at the same time contributing to the eventual ecological overburdening of the land (Bernus, 1974c, p. 142).

Finally, the pressure on the nomads to move north too rapidly meant that more and more herds were converging on the same watering places and pastures. While a number of nomads found it possible to become settled agriculturalists, many were forced to the northern edge of the Sahel, where they and their herds became the victims of the "overgrazing" noted by so many commentators. It would be more accurate to say that the peanut and the profit system were the real "overgrazers"—not the nomads.

A French technical adviser has described this social and environmental process up to and through the famine of 1968-74 and how it affected a small group of pastoralists in western Niger. The Alkasseybaten are a small tribe of 130 persons, inhabiting a zone along and to the north of the peanut belt of Niger, bordering with Upper Volta. While some changes in the ecological relationships of this group, the neighboring agriculturalists, and the pastoralists can be traced to social and political developments in the 1930s, the most significant developments began about 1956. That year, the Alkasseybaten found it necessary to maintain their herds all year in a region that had previously been used only for rainy-season pasturage, even while farming in the same area was being extended. The result was a process of overgrazing, which showed up in a measurable form in the decline in amount of milk produced by the herd. Increasing economic pressures on the Alkasseybaten forced them to sell more and more animals, with the size of the herd dropping as follows: in 1956, 1,500; in 1962, 1,100; in 1968, 700; and in 1972, 63.

This drop in herd size is significant in that, while the drought beginning in 1968 had a major destructive effect, large-scale losses had begun *even before the drought*, attesting to the effects of the overgrazing forced by factors outside the nomads' control. Furthermore, when the drought hit, these herding regions on the fringes of the agricultural zone suffered even more than areas farther to the north.[20]

Overproducing Animals

The spread of nomads into regions where they had not adapted, like the peanut cultivation itself, was not an isolated process. Other outside interventions, particularly in the post-World War II period, made the situation even worse. In particular was the development of vastly increased herd sizes as a result of vaccination and animal health programs. The following figures, while only rough estimates of the actual numbers of animals in Niger, give an idea of the scope of the increase in herds just during the period when land available for pasture was being taken over by peanuts.

Table 4.2. Numbers of Livestock, Niger.

	1938	*1961*	*1966*	*1970*
Cattle	760,000	3,500,000	4,100,000	4,500,000
Sheep/Goats	2,700,000	6,800,000	7,950,000	9,000,000
Camels	50,000	350,000	360,000	n.a.
Donkeys	160,000	300,000	315,000	n.a.

Sources: 1938: British Intelligence, pp. 388-89; 1961: FAO (1961 figures for camels and donkeys, actually 1960, Thompson in Carter, 1966, p. 195). 1966: IMF, p. 423; 1970: Samir Amin, p. 134. For a discussion of some of the problems encountered in estimating livestock numbers in West Africa, along with the various techniques developed, see van Raay, 1974, p. 12.

These figures indicate the period in which the major expansion of peanut cultivation took place, and this was also a period of major expansion of herds. More production was occurring on less and less of an available resource base.

But why the large increase in herd sizes? One important part of the answer lies in the export market to Nigeria, to the Ivory Coast, and to other large population centers in the south of West Africa—those regions that cannot produce their own livestock because of the presence of the tsetse fly.

The increase in herd sizes was thus stimulated by the goal of increasing market sales in the south. In 1937, for example, a total of 317,000 cattle, sheep, and goats was delivered from the entire Sahel region to the Guinea Gulf territories (Thompson and Adloff, 1958, p. 489). By 1970, Niger itself was exporting 170,000 cattle alone (IMF, 1970, p. 422). All these exports were "on the hoof," which had the advantage of low expense, but the cattle had trekked several hundred miles and therefore tended to be low in weight and tough to eat. During the 1950s, the French sponsored attempts to develop fresh-meat shipping facilities, and in 1955, 500 tons of fresh meat were brought to the south by plane from Niger, Upper Volta, and Mali (Thompson and Adloff, 1958, p. 489). Similarly, in Chad a refrigerated slaughter house was opened at Farcha in 1958, and 10,000 cattle had been slaughtered there by 1968. The frozen meat was largely exported to Brazzaville (Rayna and Bouquet, in Caldwell, 1975, p. 570).

In Niger itself, the evolution of export-oriented livestock industries included the establishment before 1966 of a tannery at Zinder, controlled by French private capital, one at Maradi in the late 1960s, and a refrigerated meat abattoir at Niamey specifically to facilitate increased meat exports to the Ivory Coast (Keita, 1974, p. 18; cf. Dupire, 1962a, p. 353). These were followed by the establishment of several experimental ranches, including, in particular, one at Ekrafane, 300 km. north of Niamey, financed by the West European FAC (Fonds d'Aide et de Coopération), which was begun in 1964 and began operations in 1968. This ranch closed off an area of 110,000 ha. to traditional herders, disrupting traditional lines of transhumance. The traditional herders were kept out by a combination of fences and guards (Keita, 1974, pp. 26-32; see also Cohn, 1975, p. 435).

The attitude of the Niger government toward this process is indicated in statements by Hamani Diori, president from 1960 to 1974:

> When France, in order to achieve her policy of price stabilization, wishes to import meat, Niger, with 5 million head of cattle, will be ready to furnish the French market with low-priced beef. [quoted in Keita, 1974, p. 20]

The drive to develop an expanded commercialized meat industry did not stop with the establishment of new marketing and production facilities alone. An entire system of science and technology was brought from Europe (primarily France) in the service of this enterprise. Between 1947 and 1957, more than 5 billion francs (CFA) were invested in livestock (Thompson and Adloff, 1958, p. 337), and the veterinary service, first established at Bamako, Mali in 1922, had by 1957 nearly 1,000 personnel in laboratories and in the field throughout the Sahel region (ibid., p. 339). Programs included immunization, crossbreeding with bulls and rams imported from France, and, perhaps most importantly for the purposes of this study, the construction of wells and watering points along the nomadic trek routes, which provided animals and herdspeople with more water *but not usually with more pasture.*[21]

The pace of these well-digging programs was quite rapid. From 1949 to 1954, for example, FERDES (Fonds d'Equipment Rural et de Développement Economique et Social) dug more than 600 wells in Mauritania, Mali, Upper Volta, and Niger (Thompson and Adloff, 1958, p. 354). By 1955, 50 wells had been dug in the Ferlo desert region of Senegal, helping to open the region both to pastoralists in larger numbers and also to cultivators, "who unfortunately are already beginning to dispute the reclaimed land with the nomads" (ibid., p. 354). Another organization, the

Travaux d'Hydraulique Pâturage, put in more than 500 additional wells in the Sahelian region as a whole (Rayna and Bouquet, in Caldwell, 1975, p. 570).

An additional 170 wells were bored in northeastern Nigeria during the period 1958-62, in a region somewhat resembling that of southern Niger. During the drought years of 1972-73, most of the herdspeople in the region sent their cattle off to the shoreline of Lake Chad. The wells were not providing sufficient water, but the receding lakeshore had left a temporary and unplanned pasture, which helped many of these herders through the drought (James, 1973, pp. 108-11).

Early on, however, it was recognized by some observers that the wells were not merely increasing the size of the herds and stimulating conflicts between nomads and settled farmers. The nomads, who were being driven by the expanding peanut cultivation, were gathering in greater numbers along the trek routes, where the wells were providing water. But this very increase in herd density "led to a destruction of vegetation along the trek routes and has thus contributed to soil erosion," as was noted by two writers as early as 1958 (Thompson and Adloff, 1958, p. 339).[22] Similarly, an FAO report (1962, p. 99) noted in 1962 that,

> concurrently with the increase in animal number, there has been an expansion in the cultivated areas. This is seen on one of the regular grazing routes toward the central delta of the Niger River, along the Senegal River, Lake Maggi, the area around the Office du Niger, the Mopti region in Mali and the borders of Lake Chad. Land has been cleared for cultivation and this has intensified the age-old friction between herders and cultivators.[23]

At about the same time, anthropologist and Fulani specialist Marguerite Dupire reported from Niger that "the localization of creameries on one single route in the sector of Meiganga so rapidly caused the exhaustion of pastures that it became necessary to consider turning the nomads toward less frequented pastures by creating a new route equally well provided with creameries" (Dupire, 1962a, p. 361).

A few years later, a French geographer noted that many of the well sites in the region north of Tahoua in Niger were taking on two, three, and even four times the numbers of animals for which they had been designed, and attributed the overuse in part to government financial and administrative failures. He also noted, however, that the social and political process by which slaves were leaving their Tuareg overlords played a role in the problem. As slaves left to join in the agricultural expansion farther south, the herds, which they had traditionally cared for, were neglected. Thus a virtual labor shortage was created in just the section of the labor force most crucial to proper "herd management"—the herding workers themselves. The wells seemed at first to be a labor-saving device, since they allowed herds to get water more quickly and with less time and work needed to follow them to several dispersed sites (Bernus, 1974b, pp. 121 and 124).[24] Undaunted by criticisms, the well diggers went on with their work, supported and encouraged by the highest organs of Western business and governments. In 1965, the Common Market initiated a program to increase livestock supplies in Niger. The program included vaccination against rinderpest, veterinary services, a cattle ranch, and well drilling. From 1968 to 1970, this program was financed by the Niger government, and as late as 1970, the IMF could proclaim that in Niger "Growth of the livestock population has been hindered by *insufficient watering points* and pumping equipment in the dry season, improper use of pastures, and epidemics" (IMF, 1970, p. 422; emphasis added).

That "improper use of pastures" might be related to an *over*supply of watering points, and the overly expanding livestock and peanut production system does not enter into the IMF's thinking. But this seems to be just the point. The wells, the veterinary services, the slaughterhouses, the increased herd sizes are all related to the beginnings of a development plan for commercialized livestock production in the Sahel. At the same time, however, the pastoral regions were being subjected to rapid encroachments by herdspeople, who were being pushed by the peanut culture into ever more marginal regions. These processes were working together to bring about what might be called the maximization of ecological damage, all for the sake of profits to the colonial economy, international businesses, and the commercial African elite. The "overgrazing" of the nomads, such a common phrase in reports on the Sahel famine, can be seen from the example of Niger to be part of a national and international production system that gave them no other alternative and then provided them with the necessary technology for environmental destruction.

MALI: ECOLOGICAL DEGRADATION

The example of the agriculture-pastoral transition areas is not an isolated one. Although the specifics are different, a similar and ultimately equally devastating process was also underway in Mali in the giant Niger delta.

It has been shown previously how the traditional societies of the Niger delta area had developed internal mechanisms for ecological balance and peaceful relations between herders and farmers. The French colonial development program, with its forced labor, dislocation of villages, and destruction of indigenous political and social systems, played a major role in the environmental degradation of the delta area, an area that was particularly vulnerable because it lies very near the Sahel-desert edge, with low rainfall of uneven distribution.

In the post-World War II period, the same development of livestock populations as has been described above for Niger was added to the Office du Niger project. In Mali, the number of cattle increased from 1.5 million in 1928 to 3.3 million in 1959; and from 1947 to the time of independence in 1960, meat exports from Mali to markets primarily on the southern coast of West Africa increased by 10 to 15 percent annually (Amin, 1970, p. 5).[25] As the new areas were opened up to irrigated rice and cotton agriculture, herders' traditional lines of passage from dry- to rainy-season pastures were disrupted; in some cases, pastures were simply made into polders. In addition, the stimulus for meat exports to the southern coastal areas brought traders who not only had capital to invest in herding but also sometimes set up their own herds. Hervé Derriennic recounts an example of such herds literally invading a traditional grazing area near Gao, Mali, along the eastern edge of the delta. The traders brought along hired, salaried guards for the herds, and they refused to abide by the traditional, more cautious use of the pastures—a use that was evidently not consistent with the traders' needs to get production quickly and in the largest possible quantities (Derriennic, 1977, pp. 251-52).[26]

Cattle thus increased in numbers and became more concentrated along the northern fringes of the delta project (cf. Gallais, 1972a, p. 359). This process continued until the time of the drought, and today some of the most degraded pasture lands of Mali can be found along this delta fringe. Cattle-watering sites are so soaked with urine and droppings that the soil has reached an acidity that defies replanting of nearly any kind of grass. In other, more extensive areas top soils have hardened into a crust. Thus rainwater cannot be absorbed, and the top gradually washes away, while grass seeds embedded only a few mm. underneath do not receive the moisture that would cause them to sprout. The only plants growing are vinelike legumes, which survive because animals do not graze them, and some acacia trees, from which herders chop the upper branches for animal feed (interviews at Niono Ranch, Mali, March 12-13, 1978). As in Niger, the rush to increase production, which would enhance the profits of the colonial enterprise, set in motion processes of degradation that continued through the independence and are still present today.

SENEGAL: THE COMPETITION FOR LAND

In Senegal, competition between herders and agriculturalists, the latter stimulated by Western scientific research, eager local elites, and overseas commercial interests, led to a worsening of the environment.

The role of the Mourides in colonial Senegal has been discussed previously. After Senegalese independence, the Mourides continued to be agents of deforestation. Between 1952 and 1966, 42,000 hectares of forest, one-fifth of that left in the forest area at Deali, was given over to them (Pélissier, 1966, p. 361). What had once been enormous tracts of forest eventually became areas where only sand dunes could flourish (O'Brien, 1971, p. 222). High government officials were anxious to keep Mouride leaders as their political allies, and their requests were usually granted regardless of their ecological ramifications.

In the absence of large plantations, the Islamic religious leaders and especially the Mouride marabouts became the large-scale landowners. In 1966, the Senegalese government drew up a list of large-scale producers of peanuts, using annual tonnage of the crop as their criteria. Of the 29 listed, 27 were marabouts, and 20 of these were Mourides (O'Brien, 1971, p. 202). The connections between government power and local patronage meant that soil protection rules were unenforced or ignored. The disputes with the Fulani continued, with the latter being pushed to the northeast (ibid., p. 198).

The Fulani herders, however, were not being affected only by the aggrandizing agricultural policies of the Mourides. During the 1950s and the 1960s, the government of Senegal, like the government of Niger, conducted a well-digging program ostensibly to aid the pastoralists in their use of pasture lands. One anthropologist saw some positive elements in this program, noting that the Fulani saved time in watering, which then allowed them to exploit local gum sources for an added source of cash income (Dupire, 1962a, p. 361). In addition, she reported a growing sense of "nationalism" among the Fulani, who were beginning to demand more services from the government, although they also had a fear of the wells, which brought on the dangers of "exhausted pastures, contamination [and] conflicts with the sedentary peoples" (Dupire, 1962a, p. 361).

The Fulani political movement was to lead finally to an attempt to establish a "Fulani Union," which could pressure against the agriculturalists led by the powerful Mourides; but this union was not able to prevail.

Even the wells became a disaster for the herders. French observer Claude Reboul witnessed the outcome of well digging and nomad settlement projects in the village of Labgar in the Ferlo region of Senegal. The present community of 1,900 people is based on a well sunk in 1952 to a depth of 285 meters and powered with a diesel pump that runs 12 hours a day. In 1966, the Senegalese government decided to make Labgar a model project village; it installed schools, administrative buildings, a dispensary, and so forth to make the village more attractive to herders who were to settle there. In the haste to settle the nomads, everything was set up, it appears, except a mechanism for rationally controlling the sudden intense concentration of agriculture and herding.

The stark ecological outcome is described by Reboul (1977, p. 19) who visited Labgar as recently as 1977:

> In the immediate surroundings of the borehole, trampling and overgrazing have completely destroyed the grass cover, on a soil base of potential fecundity because of the cattle manure. Less spectacularly, the degradation of the surrounding brush is nonetheless more serious because of the large areas involved.

The only positive thing to be said about this situation is that at least the herders have not been thrown out to the desert.

Another observer in the Ferlo adds that in general, "Around the wells of Diolof and the South and Central Ferlo, all attempts to organize a coexistence between peanut cultivators and herders have ended up in the expulsion of the herders" (Gallais, 1972, p. 308).

The pressure of peanuts, Mourides, Fulani, animals, and wells led to the same kinds of ecological destruction we have observed in Niger. The evidence showed up most dramatically around the herders' wells, where too many cattle had been pushed onto too little pasture. One study conducted in the Ferlo of Senegal showed that wells in the region were 52 km. apart.

But the pasture between the wells constituted a meager diet indeed for the cattle:

Table 4.3. Constitution of Pasture at Various Distances from Drinking Sites in the Senegalese Ferlo (in percentages).

	Distance from drinking site (km)			
Pasture cover	*0*	*½*	*1½*	*26*[a]
Bare ground	100	99	98	95
Grass cover	0	1	2	5

[a]26 km. is half the distance to the next drinking site.
Source: van Melle, 1975, p. 51.

Table 4.3 shows that pastures in at least one section of the Ferlo had become so degraded, so grassless, that they were operating at nearly zero effectiveness. Like the pastures in Niger and those in Mali, they were victims of cattle and nomads, but only because *these* in turn had been victims of peanut cultivators, politically powerful Africans, and overseas commercial interests. It was in the context of these processes that the drought hit the Sahel, and it was these herders and their animals who suffered the most. It was these processes, from colonial times right up to the eve of the drought, that turned that drought into a famine.

NOTES

1. For some of our general criticisms of a current use of dependency theory, see Franke, 1977.
2. More recent figures are cited in Ball, 1978, p. 281, as follows:

	Percentages of Total Exports		
	1968	*1970*	*1972*
Senegal groundnuts (peanuts)	72	48	52
Mali groundnuts (peanuts)	11	14	19
Mali cotton	35	30	33
Mali livestock	29	30	24
Mauritania iron ore	86	80	75
Niger groundnuts (peanuts)	69	65	46
Niger uranium	—	—	18
Upper Volta livestock	48	31	49

All are figures as percentages of total exports. It is evident that the U.N. statistics quoted by Hodder do not include mineral output, but otherwise the statistics appear to be comparable.

3. The generally unfavorable terms of the economic relationship between France and

former French colonies in Africa have been documented in a 1971 study known as the *Gorse Report.* The report was so critical that the French government refused to make the findings available even to the national assembly (see R. Joseph, 1976, p. 6). For a summary of the Gorse report in English, see Robarts, 1974.

4. The figure for Mali is somewhat different than for the other countries, in that the years 1962-68 in particular contain a great deal of investment funds provided by the socialist countries. Samir Amin explains in detail the reasons why the outcome was the same, in view of Mali's ultimate failure to sustain the attempted break with France and the Western capitalist countries. See Amin, 1973, pp. 227-36. A pro-Western analysis of this same period of Malian history is offered by William Jones, 1976. It seems that Amin has the better argument, if only on the grounds that the pro-Western states achieved no more than did Mali, economically speaking, and that Mali, since the reintegration with French governmental and commercial interests since 1968, has continued to suffer from the very economic difficulties the French and other Western support was supposed to overcome.

5. These figures do not necessarily hold for today, but they were undoubtedly relevant in decision-making at the time.

6. It is interesting, in this article written just three years before the independence of many countries in the area, that Mountjoy continued to refer to them as "possessions," particularly since the article is oriented toward the future uses for their lands.

7. For an account of some of this history, see Susan George, 1977, pp. 122-25; for more details, see Berlan et al., 1976.

8. The best summary of the bureaucracy as a semiclass phenomenon is contained in Meillassoux, 1970; cf. Nicolas, in Dalby and Church, eds., 1977.

9. A discussion of the sociological basis of corruption in Third World social structures is contained in Wertheim, 1964, pp. 103-32.

10. The structural elements of this confrontation are outlined in Meillassoux, 1970; a historical analysis of the events appears in Martin, 1976.

11. The Senegalese coup is described by DuBois, 1963, while the Niger coup is analyzed in Higgot and Fuglestead, 1975; and DuBois, 1974.

12. As Samir Amin points out (1973, p. 236), the post-1968 Malian regime continues to be based in large measure on what he calls the "class of urban bureaucrats."

13. This same observer was perhaps too taken with the likely efficacy of the government measures, declaring that "the famines which decimated Niger's population twice during the first half of the 20th century are now a phenomenon of the past" (Thompson, in Carter, 1966, p. 191).

14. The corruption of the Niger government elite was so well known and so widespread that students in the country referred to the president's wife, Madame Diori, as "l'Autrichienne," after Marie Antoinette of "let-them-eat-cake" fame (Higgott and Fuglestead, 1975, p. 390). The corruption in Niger under the Diori government has bred two Nigerien novels and one play, authorized for publication under the current government. (See Ousmane, 1977; Oumarou, 1977; and Keita, 1974.)

15. See also Samir Amin's telling comments on the irrational Common Market-financed transportation system for the peanuts via the *more* expensive route to Coutenou, rather than making use of Nigeria's close-by railway system. As Amin noted, this system "has succeeded in making Niger's groundnuts, even at a rock-bottom price to the producers, unprofitable." This system is a holdover of the colonial period, when France did not want to "lose" continuing revenues to a British rival (Amin, 1973, p. 136; cf. Péhaut, 1970, pp. 57-61).

16. An account of the many complex and often long-distance trading elements in these movements is given in Baier, 1976, p. 3.

17. A map showing several of these trek routes as of 1951 is given in Dupire, 1962, pp. 74, 80-81. Nicolas argues that an earlier wave of pastoral movements was from north to south. Beginning in the 14th century, Tuaregs pushed from Aïr southward, displacing sedentary agriculturalists who previously occupied the oases. The north-south movements were reversed in the 19th century (Nicolas, in Dalby and Church, eds., 1977, esp. pp. 159-60).

18 Edmond Bernus gives a detailed account of the government program to limit agriculture to approximately latitude 15° 10′ north and the system of fines for herdspeople whose animals destroyed cropfields to the south of this border. He affirms that a series of years with good rainfall aided in the spread north of the peanut culture, which the government regulations were not able to stop (Bernus, 1974c, pp. 140-41; Bernus, 1974b).

19. A sketchy and slightly eclectic presentation of similar phenomena from Niger is given in Berry et al., 1977. While noting the importance of French colonial policy, the authors uncritically add population growth to their list of factors and sometimes appear to view the area more in terms of ethnic groups than as different categories of producers. Of note in their presentation is a prophetic quote from French geographer Jean Dresch, who predicted in general terms in a 1959 publication much of what was to happen to the region. The authors also strangely identify the study by the Comité Information Sahel as being primarily an analysis of the relief operation, when in fact it is primarily concerned with the historical development of vulnerability to drought via French colonial policies.

20. This process is described by H. Barral in a mimeographed report quoted at length by Derriennic, 1977, pp. 120-26. A somewhat more abstract theoretical formulation of the processes we describe in terms of social oppositions is given in Derriennic, 1977, p. 255.

21. The expansion of livestock services and the increase in herd sizes does not imply, however, that epidemic diseases had been brought under control. As Gallais notes after a summary of the situation in 1972, "In short, veterinary activities, in spite of substantial results, are far from achieving mastery over the epidemic and endemic diseases which make African herding a game of chance" (1972a, p. 357).

22. It should be noted, however, that this section is not intended to imply that herders trek great distances in the absence of wells, only that they were generally more dispersed. In fact, each group in the past would follow a well-planned path to a region where it would move slight distances as required during the dry season, and then return, again along traditionally determined trek routes (Bernus, 1974b, p. 121).

23. Marty (1972, p. 8) estimates the pasture needs for a nearby section of Niger at 5 km. from a central point during seven to eight months of pasturing, corresponding to 2.5 units of cattle and 5 units of goats or sheep, giving an average of about 3 ha. per animal.

24. This account was written for a U.N. conference in Cairo in 1971, but some of the data on well site overcrowding appear to come from a report of the Livestock Service in Tahoua for 1961. Bernus does not give as much emphasis to the labor losses as an explanatory factor, although his evidence seems to warrant the conclusions we have drawn. More recently, press accounts indicate that the streaming of refugees from northern areas of the Sahel set in motion a final process of breaking the slave-master bonds between Tuareg and Bella herders (*New York Times*, August 12, 1977).

25. Gallais (1972a, p. 359) gives the following statistics for cattle populations in Mali: 1919, 980,000; 1939, 1,830,000; 1946, 2,365,000; 1957, 3,260,000; 1962, 3,923,000; and 1969, 4,872,000.

26. Derriennic (1977, pp. 253-55) notes that the colonial economy had not made substantial progress toward integrating livestock production, as it had peanuts and cotton, for example. But he fails to note that plans were laid and some attempts made, and this was undoubtedly a further stimulus to local capital-holders.

part two

RESPONDING TO THE FAMINE

5

Expert Explanations: Perspectives on the Famine

The Sahel famine has led to numerous commentaries, analyses, research studies, and interdisciplinary projects, all of them offering at least the implicit suggestion of some guidelines by which the Sahel could become a more life-sustaining environment in the future. As might be expected, the various commentators and experts do not agree on what to do, and these disagreements are based in turn on their analyses of the major reason for the famine. In this chapter, we will survey the different approaches taken to the famine in the many publications that have appeared since it became a significant news item in Europe and the United States.

For most experts who have written on it, the famine has been a backdrop for the practice of their own particular specialties. Thus climatologists have tried to assess weather patterns, soil experts have commented on the characteristics of African soils, forestry specialists have looked at forests, anthropologists have analyzed the interethnic relations or have questioned the cultural fit of certain aid programs, and so forth. Journalists and science columnists in turn have picked up one or another of these studies and have disseminated them in the press or in popular magazines, often with melodramatic overtones. A reading of the popular literature turns up such titles as "Climatologists Say Africa's Drought May Intensify and Affect the Whole World," "A Case of Creeping Disaster," "Deserts on the March," or "Ancient Enemy—Too Many People, Cattle Intensify Drought's Effects."[1] Behind and beyond these superficial renderings lie the more detailed accounts of the famine. But here, too, it is often difficult to obtain a thorough understanding of what happened and why.

One of the great difficulties in explaining the famine derives from what appears to be a formidable shortcoming in the approach of scientists studying ecological questions in general. On the one hand, there is a strong tendency to look at a single factor as the sole explanation for the chain of events comprising an ecological development. On the other, a long list of factors may be presented, each with an indeterminate weight. Underlying both extremes are usually some untested assumptions about factors that appear so obvious to the authors that there can be no disagreement about their role in bringing on the events in question. Most of the experts' views on the origins of the West African famine exhibit these features as well, although a few attempts have been made to take a different direction. By looking at the scientific approaches to the famine, we can raise a number of issues about what happened and why. We can also set a basis for some questions about the methods of analysis used in general by the scientific establishment, particularly in the United States and Western Europe, and, by extension, in those countries under their influence or domination.

In brief, six major approaches have been taken: (1) the poverty of the Sahel (this was dealt with in Chapter 1); (2) theories on "overpopulation"; (3) the "tragedy of the commons" theory; (4) climatic explanations; (5) theories about the "encroaching desert"; and (6) discussions of the historical background of the region in recent times.

DID OVERPOPULATION CAUSE THE FAMINE?

A pervasive explanation appearing in both popular and scientific accounts of the famine links the events to the phenomenon of population growth, or, more harshly, to overpopulation. The use of population growth as an explanation for the famine is not particularly surprising, especially in the United States, where, since the early 1950s, population theory has received widespread encouragement and propagation as an explanation for poverty, unemployment, warfare, and most other ills of human society. Summed up in the words of Paul Ehrlich, the veritable dean of population theory who made it popular in the late 1960s and early 1970s, "Whatever your cause, it's a lost cause without population control" (Ehrlich et al., 1973, p. 278).[2]

The population explanation has become so established that analysts rarely, if ever, seem to find it necessary to *prove* that population growth is at the bottom of a set of events. So with the African famine, the *Wall Street Journal* could claim, citing academic experts such as A. T. Grove of Cambridge University and Marcel Roche, of the French Overseas Scientific Research Institute, that the Sahel was overgrazed by too many cattle and that *there were too many cattle because there were too many people.* This theory is implied by placing between paragraphs on ecological destruction and cattle numbers the remark that the Sahel "has one of the highest birth rates in the world."[3] Overpopulation is mentioned in several other parts of the article without questioning its role in the famine.

A *New York Times Magazine* account takes up the population theme from a slightly different angle. Here, it is the paradox of modern medical care that stands at the base of the problem. "The human *population explosion, fueled by the beginnings of health care,* needed the extra cattle, and the frail ecology of the Sahel began to crumble" [emphasis added] (Walker, 1974, p. 42). Thus people in the wealthy nations seem to make others victims of our own willingness to help with aid and development programs.

Even the more optimistic writers seem to be unable to avoid the strongest language when noting the population aspect. John W. Sewell, vice-president of the Overseas Development Council, writing in the *New York Times,* says, "The Sahel is Not a Wasteland"; nonetheless he announced that "population growth, which intensified the impact of the last drought, will continue to exert *inexorable pressures*" [emphasis added].[4] "Population explosion, inexorable pressures" are the typical battle cries of population theorists, whose crisis mentality about birth rates and overall numbers of human beings is apparently enough to explain poverty, malnutrition, misuse of the environment, and famine. If the popular media are only too willing to print without demonstration the idea that numbers of people are sufficient to cause a catastrophe such as the famine, they can at least say they are getting information from established scientific sources.

A case in point is a recent article by Canadian climatologist Derek Winstanley. Referring to the "exponential rate of growth of human and animal populations in the 1960s" (in Glantz, 1976, p. 209), the author's study of climatic factors rather abruptly turns into an essay on the dangers of overpopulation both preceding the famine and in the future. "Clearly, population control will need to be introduced long before a decrease in growth rate can be effectively brought about. . . . Population projections to the year 2030 are far more frightening than to year 2,000" (in Glantz, 1976, p. 211). And, after warning of a likely doubling of Sahelian area populations during the next 26 years,[5] Winstanley (in Glantz, 1976, p. 210) urges readers to consider the dangers of population growth even in Canada:

> And those in North America who think that the carrying capacity of these geographically large Sahelian countries can be increased merely by economic investment and development should ask themselves whether Canada, a rich country with a present population of 22 million, could support 50 million by the end of the century.

To U.S. citizens, living in less space than Canada encompasses, and with 10 times as many people, it may seem strange to read of such concern, but that is just the point about population theory: Wherever you are, apparently, too many people are the problem, or soon will be.

An even more striking example of the pervasive use of population growth as explanation—without ever submitting this variable (or better, set of variables) to any rigorous test—comes from *Science* magazine writer

Nicholas Wade. To judge from the title of the article (Wade, 1974), "Sahelian Drought: No Victory for Western Aid," this would be an essay on the relation between aid programs and the famine. Indeed, much is said on this topic by the author. But, in a four-page analysis, Wade manages to refer at least *six* times to overpopulation, brought about by the introduction of modern science, as noted in the newspaper accounts above. As in all the accounts noted previously, Wade's does not demonstrate the relation between population growth and ecological disaster: apparently, it is just obvious.

In one sense, of course, the population argument is incontestable. To the extent that there were more people to suffer the effects of the famine, there was more suffering when the famine occurred.

But the argument that population growth by itself either caused or exacerbated the effects of the climatic changes that took place after 1967 is far less obvious than might appear once we begin to question the underlying assumptions of population theory. It is assumed by population theorists, for example—even though rarely stated—that people are primarily mouths and stomachs to be fed. That they are also hands to work and minds to think and create is rarely mentioned. The people of the Sahel were not simply producing more people to be cared for during the years preceding the famine: they were also producing more from the land *and* for outside markets as well as for themselves. It could be argued that once the drought came, larger and more dense populations would have had more human resources to put to work in both relief efforts and efforts to salvage the environment and begin the process of reconstruction. That people were *not* put to work at these tasks can hardly be a byproduct of their numbers per se. The explanation must be sought in the organization of these efforts. The same point could be extended to the period preceding the famine if the question is asked: Given the knowledge that droughts in the Sahel are a recurring phenomenon, what steps were taken to organize production in the region so that ecological conditions would be maintained or improved? What use was made of the growing number of workers who could carry out such a program?

The argument here is not that population should be considered totally unimportant in the development of the famine. Rather, by turning the argument around, we can highlight the logical difficulties of assuming that population growth was a major cause. It is just as logical to assume that population growth should have been a major cause of *overcoming* droughts.

POPULATION, POVERTY, AND DEMAND-FOR-LABOR

Recent developments in population theory offer further insights into the relation between population growth and the famine along the general lines suggested above. In particular, the analysis of the concept of "demand-for-labor," as an economic and social variable determining in large part the population growth of a nation or region, has opened new possibilities into understanding the relation between poverty and high population growth rates. Because of the importance of the population argument in present-day Western societies, it is worth looking briefly into the alternative presented by this approach.

One of the most convincing cases given for the demand-for-labor comes from a recent study done in India by economist Mahmood Mamdani (1972). During the years 1953-59, the Harvard School of Public Health conducted a study of its own pilot program to control population growth in a village in the Punjab. In 1969, it initiated a follow-up study on its attempts to introduce birth control devices among a group of Indian farmers. Everyone agreed that the program was a failure. But why would the poor farmers of India, among the world's most impoverished people, refuse birth control when it was offered through the medium of a well-organized, well-financed, intensive program? Population theorists were baffled.

Mamdani, using the idea that children are a form of cheap labor for a farming family, was able to provide an analysis consistent with the findings. He discovered that poor villagers consciously conceive of their children as labor assets. Increasing land fragmentation combines with the new opportunities in postcolonial India to provide special incentives to the poor family for the production of many children. If most of the children could work at agriculture and other jobs, the combined efforts of the family might be enough to put *one* child through school and into a bureaucratic post. Then the family would have some hope of economic security or even advancement. Even if this dream did not come true, the presence of numerous children among the poorest families was viewed as a cost-saving device. One villager explained: "Why pay 2,500 rupees for an extra hand? Why not have a son?" (Mamdani, 1972, p. 77). Although this population growth may or may not benefit Indian society as a whole, each family in the village, competing with other families, must try to keep its labor costs as low as possible, and one's own children are the cheapest form of labor.

But how does a society get into a situation where poor farming families, in order to survive, must produce large numbers of children? A study by anthropologist Benjamin White provides further insight. Making direct use of the concept of demand-for-labor, White attempts to account for the rapid population growth of Java, a region similar in many ways to India. Noting the pressures of the Dutch sugar industry in the 19th century on land and labor available for Javanese family farms, White concludes that traditional controls on population growth had to be lifted in order to produce child laborers who could work the family farms while adults went off to work for the sugar factories. As population thus increased, land holdings became ever smaller, creating further pressures for more laborers to work the small rice fields of Java more intensively (White, 1973).

Putting these two studies together, we can see a line of analysis in which the pressures on individual families to produce large numbers of children were created by the particular needs of the colonial system of profit-making, which in turn is perpetuated by the class structure and land problems that the system has produced or enhanced.

Viewed from the perspective of demand-for-labor analysis, population growth, rather than being an original causal factor in the creation of poverty and underdevelopment, thus becomes a self-perpetuating *result* (or dependent variable) of colonial policies and their effects on production relations. The increase in numbers of people does not come about in a way that allows for the new labor supply to be put to work in an organized fashion to further the needs of the whole society, but under conditions in which they are used to maximize the immediate labor needs of individual family units.

Demand-for-Labor in West Africa

Can the analyses of Mamdani and White help us to understand population phenomena in West Africa, particularly as these might relate to the famine? Several pieces of information suggest a positive answer to this question.

First of all, West Africa's population growth rate is one of the highest in the world. For the period 1960-66, just before the onset of the drought and famine, the crude birth rate was about 46/1,000 for all of Africa, as compared with a world average of 34/1,000. Of all the regions of Africa, West Africa had the highest birth rate at 50/1000 (Ominde, 1972, p. xix). United Nations statistics for 1965-70 indicate a continuing high birth rate, with the all-African average for the period being 46 and the West African rate being 49/1,000, essentially no change over a ten-year period (Hill, in Moss and Rathbone, 1975, p. 108).

Alongside these data on high birth rates can be placed information on the economic situation in the region. Of all the parts of Africa, West Africa had nearly the lowest per-capita income at $74 per year in 1960, as compared with $72 in East Africa, $103 in Central Africa, and $132 in North Africa (Thomas, in Widstrand, 1975, p. 327). The low per-capita incomes in West Africa correlate with its position as the most dependent on agriculture of all the regions of Africa and simultaneously the least industrialized as shown in Table 5.1.

Furthermore, per-capita dollar value of industrial output in Africa ranged from: west, $9; east, $11; central, $21; north, $35; and south, $158

Table 5.1. Industrial Origin of GNP in Africa, circa 1963 (in percentages).

Region of Africa	*Agriculture*	*Mining*	*Manufacturing*	*Other*
West	56	2	6	36
East	47	3	12	38
Central	41	7	14	38
North	35	6	14	45
South	10	13	26	51

Source: Thomas, in Widstrand, 1975, p. 327.

(ibid.). These statistics point toward a fairly clear picture of West Africa as the most underdeveloped, impoverished, least industrialized part of the African continent.

But what can these economic data tell us about the high birth rates? Perhaps surprisingly, in view of what has been said so far, many experts do not consider West Africa to be overpopulated. Indeed, a number have referred to the area as having *insufficient* population. The demographer B. Lacombe, for example, writes of Senegal as "an underpopulated country" (in Ominde, 1972, p. 124). Agricultural specialist John de Wilde (1967, p. 303) notes of Mali that "In general there is not much population pressure," and that "no area of Mali can be considered overpopulated." De Wilde (p. 288) characterizes much of the failure of the Niger River development program initiated by the French in the 1930s as follows:

> It is above all the shortage of manpower that has prevented the scheme from becoming the expected success. Because of the lack of significant population pressures in the former French Soudan, now Mali, it has never been possible to recruit enough colonists. A large proportion had to be recruited in the distant but more densely populated parts of Upper Volta.

Concern with the possibility of underpopulation has been voiced by the noted demographer Etienne van de Walle as well: "Not very long ago wage labor was scarce in Africa. In 1956 Richard Molard was commenting that the supply of manpower in almost all of French West Africa was insufficient" (in Caldwell, ed., 1975, p. 149). And more recently, an agricultural expert commenting on the difficulties of carrying out the development of the Senegal River basin lists seven major blocks to the program, including: need for more labor during the rainy-season harvest and dry-season planting periods; need for more labor power for weeding; competition between different crops for people's labor time, meaning that seedbeds, weeding, planting, etc., must often be sacrificed one for the other; and attacks by birds on nearly harvestable grains, which require more labor to protect the crops. In short, the majority of the problems listed could be solved with a greater availability of labor, that is, a larger population (Trinh Ton That, 1976, p. 5).

Even before the most recent times, there is evidence that West Africa was experiencing a labor shortage. An ethnographic account of the Zarma people, who live mostly in southwest Niger, reports that there was much warfare in precolonial times. The fighting was always over the capture of people for labor, never over land (Lateef, 1975, p. 400). The author of the account attributes the greater emphasis on labor power as a reflection of the climatic uncertainties of the region, making human energy inputs the crucial variable in agricultural production (ibid.).[6]

Thus far, then, it can be established that West Africa has: (1) a high birth rate, (2) low rate and state of economic development, and (3) an undersupply of labor in many areas. According to demand-for-labor theory, these three elements are associated. The underdeveloped state of the economy means that most employment is in agriculture, where child labor would be of greatest relative value, especially as a survival means for impoverished parents. The "undersupply of labor" referred to by some experts is relative to the demand for labor being placed on the society. The high birth rate is one of the responses made by parents to these labor demands.

Demand-for-Labor and Migration

What kinds of labor demands are being referred to? In the case of the Zarma fighting for captive laborers, climatic and production factors at the local level might suffice to explain the high demand for labor. In more recent times, however, the French and British colonial control of West Africa resulted in a vast increase in labor demands throughout the region, but particularly in areas where large-scale plantations or other intensive export-oriented production facilities were established. West Africa thus became a region in which massive human migrations took place and continue to take place as workers leave their home villages and travel hundreds or even thousands of kilometers to work for six months, two years, three years, and sometimes longer. Figure 5.1 shows the major patterns of these migrations.

One example of the adverse effects of migrations on the local economy comes from Upper Volta. Here, villages suffer at certain times of the year from a labor shortage as young men migrate to raise cash for their taxes and other monetary needs. Because of their absence, less bush land can be cleared for new farms, cloth weaving declines, huts cannot be fully repaired, and wells cannot be kept up properly (Skinner, in Kuper, 1965, pp. 70, 72). Although statistics are few, officials in Upper Volta believe that food production has been negatively affected by the migration. This migration also makes it difficult to implement development plans requiring a large labor force (Amin, 1974, p. 99). Clearly, in Upper Volta at least, overpopulation cannot account for the people's hunger. It is interesting to note that the International Monetary Fund's *Survey of African Economics* (IMF 1970, p. 711) approaches matters rather differently. According to this source of major foreign lending and investing agencies:

> This large flow of migrants has been advantageous to Upper Volta. Not only has it reduced considerably the unemployment problem, but it has also contributed to the favorable balance of payments in recent years because of remittances by the migrants to relatives in Upper Volta.

The IMF looks only at national factors, not at the effects on villages, or the needs of farmers and herders and their families.

The migration of labor has taken different forms. Under the French, it was often forced militarily (see Chapter 3). Today, more commonly, laborers leave their homes out of economic need. In either case, the effects on the home village are the same—loss of needed labor power and a consequent pressure to produce child labor by having more offspring. Additional evidence further supports the logically coherent picture provided by the use of demand-for-labor analysis. Two studies in Senegal, for

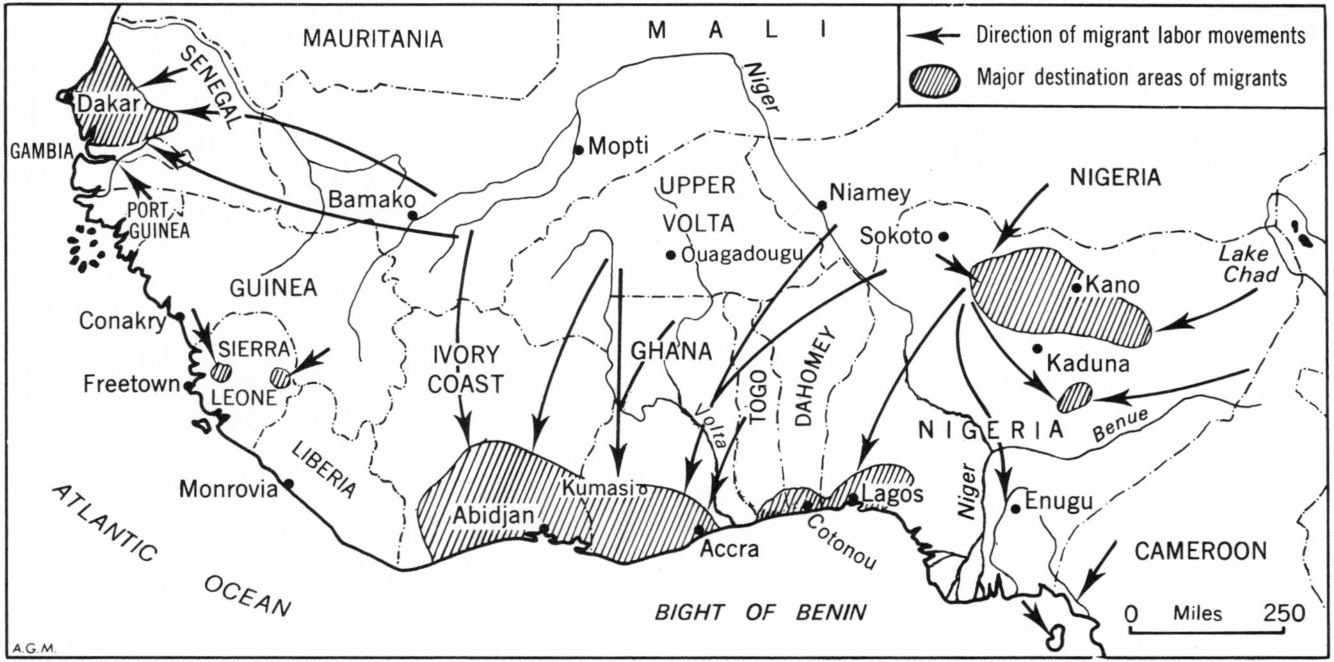

Source: Akin L. Mabogunje, in Caldwell, ed., 1975, p. 156.

Figure 5.1. Labor Migration in West Africa.

example, show that the birth rate for nomadic herdspeople is lower than for other sections of the society (Lacombe, in Ominde, 1972, pp. 123-24). This would tend to confirm the demand-for-labor approach, since the nomads are more autonomous and self-sufficient and would not be placed under the labor pressures as quickly as would the agricultural peoples.[7] Another recent historical analysis shows how the peanut economy of the early 20th century in the Serer region of Senegal may have stimulated the growth of family size far above previous levels (Herzog, 1975). At the other end of the Sahel region, an opinion study of families in Chad reveals that 65 percent of women wanted five or more children, while only 7 percent wanted four or fewer.[8] Most interestingly, when asked *why* they wanted five or more children, the women in that category responded in the following ways:

Table 5.2. Reasons for Wanting Large Family, Chadian Women, 1970 (in percentages).

	Urban	*Rural*
Family support	37	52
Religion	32	34
Will get benefits of modern civilization	8	2
Good of country	4	1
Don't know/No response	19	11

Source: S.P. Reyna in Caldwell, ed., 1975, p. 586.

The author of the study concludes from this table that "Large numbers of children appear to be wanted by most women to continue to provide labor for the family" (Reyna, in Caldwell, ed., 1975, p. 586).[9]

This evidence certainly is not sufficient to *prove* the demand-for-labor analysis, but it does show that fundamental processes can be related to each other, and a potentially comprehensive overview of West African population phenomena might be developed with this type of analysis.

In terms of the famine, demand-for-labor offers an important alternative view that is an immediate challenge to the idea that overpopulation is a basic cause of the tragedy of 1968-74. Demand-for-labor emphasizes that the decision to have large numbers of children is rational, consciously thought-out in many cases, and a necessary response to conditions not created by the parents themselves. It shows us that we must look elsewhere than population theory for an explanation of the famine.

LAND MISMANAGEMENT: A TRAGEDY OF THE COMMONS?

As early as 1972, a USAID "in-house" report cited "Improper land-use practices" as the major cause of the Sahel drought's becoming a famine

(USAID, 1972, p. 1). The report does not elaborate, but other sources soon appeared, giving various renditions of the supposed mismanagement syndrome in the Sahel.

At its most superficial level in journalistic accounts, mismanagement is seen as the unintended result of otherwise well-meaning policies. Thus Claire Sterling could write in *The Atlantic Monthly* (May 1974, p. 102), when the famine was still receiving major headlines in the newspapers, that well-digging programs were the cause of the disaster, coupled with the apparent inability of the Sahel's nomadic herders to remember where they were: "Carried away by the promise of unlimited water, nomads forgot about the Sahel's all too limited forage. Timeless rules, apportioning just so many cattle to graze for just so many days within a cow's walking distance of just so much water in traditional wells, were brushed aside."

Similarly, *Science* magazine writer Nicolas Wade (1974), while listing numerous wrongs committed during the course of the colonial and postcolonial periods, implies that the wells were dug only for the benefit of the herders and their cattle and were somehow themselves the cause of the increase in numbers; although in other parts of his account, Wade refers to the expansion of farming and the forcing of nomads off their pastures and toward the desert fringe.

A most pervasive approach to the mismanagement of Sahelian lands derives from an application of the so-called tragedy of the commons, proposed by biologist Garrett Hardin in a 1968 article in *Science* magazine. According to Hardin, rising population renders the common use of common resources no longer possible without serious environmental damage. The problem lies in the fact that each individual can increase his or her use of a natural resource and gain the full effect of that increase, while the entire community must suffer the consequences of the decline in overall resources that occurs through the single individual's taking an extra share. According to Hardin, the contradiction is not evident until a certain population density is reached. Thus the tragedy of the commons is also a population theory (Hardin, 1968).

A few years after the tragedy of the commons was proposed, van Rensselaer Potter (1974) wrote to *Science* magazine to comment on the applicability of the theory to the Sahel drought. He was provoked by Nicolas Wade's news report on the drought and famine, but he added a slight twist to the argument:

> . . . we see the tragedy of the commons not as a defect in the concept of a "commons" but a result of the disastrous transition period between the loss of an effective bioethic and its replacement by a new bioethic that could once again bring human values into a viable balance.

The lost bioethic was the control over grazing by the "chiefs," from a statement made by Sterling and reproduced by Wade, neither of whom had apparently looked into the historical data on the Sahel. Both the Tuaregs, who have chiefs, and the Fulani, who are essentially egalitarian, have developed effective mechanisms for the use of pasture lands. The absence of chiefs does not contribute to the loss of the "bioethic" but the *presence* of a production system geared to short-range profits does.[10]

A more thorough presentation of the tragedy-of-the-commons approach has been offered by Picardi and Seifert (1977, p. 299), whose research developed out of the MIT project. Using a computer simulation technique, they concluded that the "short-term benefit to the individual [herder and family] outweighs the long-term shared cost—the eventual desertification of common pastures." The apparent factor in all this competition between individual and society-wide needs is an inherent tendency of herders (and anyone else?) to take advantage of their environment whenever they can—even at the expense of their neighbors or their eventual offspring.[11]

The real meaning of the tragedy of the commons is hidden in the ideological choice of a procapitalist writer such as Hardin. By emphasizing the connection between tragedy and commons, he supports the idea that people are just unable to cooperate and that common property will be abused whenever a certain population density is reached. Thus Picardi and Seifert can present a tragedy-of-the-commons model of the destruction of the Sahel environment, ironically using as a data base a part of Niger. Picardi and Seifert, however, have no need to analyze the interractions between farmers and herders, millet and peanuts, French agribusiness and local elites. The cattle and people simply grow in numbers, act selfishly, and denude their pastures. The only conclusions drawn are for the need to increase the marketing of cattle so that the herders' tendency to overproduce can be brought under control (p. 302).

The tragedy of the commons could be more accurately titled the "tragedy of unbridled personal accumulation." If so, its propounders would be able to distinguish those production systems in which such accumulation is a strong tendency and those in which it is not. This would help authors such as Sterling, Wade, Hardin, Potter, and Picardi and Seifert to see that it is the onset of capitalist economic and social relations that has coincided with the development of a tragedy of the commons in the Sahel. It was not simply herders and their lust for greater numbers of animals, but the pressures of the profit system that led to the overgrazing and well construction that so ravished the pastures of the Sahel.

DID A WEATHER CHANGE CAUSE THE FAMINE?

Climatologists have offered three variants of the view that the main causal factor in the famine was a drought brought on by changes in world climate patterns. A common argument links the changes in climate to changes in heat coming from the sun, or, changes in sunspot activities (Lamb, 1974, p. 13). These appear to fluctuate in 200-to-400-year cycles. Another view holds that the earth's arctic regions are expanding—for apparently unknown reasons—and that the cooling of the atmosphere in the temperate zones is bringing about a "push" of the tropical monsoons down toward the equator. Thus in West Africa, the rains are moving south toward the forests, which already have ample moisture, and causing the desert fringe regions to dry up and become deserts. A 1974 workshop on weather patterns held in Bonn, West Germany, concluded over the signatures of experts from several nations that "a new climatic trend pattern is now emerging ... that . . . will persist for several decades, and that the current food-production systems of Man [*sic*] cannot easily adjust" (cited in Bryson, 1976, p. 211).

For some, such as Dr. Reid Bryson of the University of Wisconsin, the African famine is but a symptom and a prelude to an ever-worsening doomsday that the whole world is approaching. Bryson concludes after reviewing data on climate during the 20th century that two factors are contributing to increased cooling of the air in certain places, and greater air turbulence is causing weather patterns to shift in favor of drought. First, until recently, about 83 percent of air turbidity was caused by the effects of volcanic ash in the atmosphere. From 1920 to 1955, volcanoes were at an unusually low level of activity, and so weather patterns were generally more favorable than might normally be expected for the production of food. Bryson points out the difficulty of controlling this factor: "Will the volcanoes please settle down? Probably not" (1973, p. 400).

In more recent times, however, another factor has been added to exacerbate the effects of volcanic activity. This is the increasing amount of carbon dioxide in the atmosphere, produced primarily by the burning of fossil fuels (e.g., oil) in modern industry and in the production of chemical fertilizers and other agricultural aids such as tractors, diesel pumps, and so forth. Various studies have indicated that carbon dioxide combines in the atmosphere with water vapor and ozone to produce what is called the "greenhouse effect." These chemicals together in a certain level of the atmosphere absorb irregular amounts of heat from the sun's radiation, thus setting up bands of temperature variations that bring on air turbulences. These add to the effects of volcanic ash. Bryson calculates that this greenhouse effect now contributes as much as 30 percent of the air turbulence and, when added to the return after 1955 of higher levels of volcanic activity, causes vast air movements that will lead to long-term distortions of the tropical monsoon movements. More rainfall will occur in areas that already have enough, while less rain will fall in areas that now get only enough for agriculture. The effects in the marginal areas, such as the Sahel, will be drought conditions with little chance of a remedy (1973, p. 399). When asked for a comment on the human effects of these weather changes, Bryson was rather blunt about prospects for the near future—"like a billion people dying."[12]

Other experts are not so sure. Using the West African drought as a basis for study, some have calculated the fluctuations in rainfall for long periods of time, combining both geological evidence of past droughts with the more statistically refined information on rainfall year by year, which exists for little more than a century. Comparing different periods of drought and rainfall, it can be calculated that a drought of the severity of the recent one—six consecutive years of rainfall below the mean or average—would occur about every 70 years. A number of French meteorologists have concluded, however, after attempts to produce a mathematical model of cyclical rainfall patterns, that there is insufficient evidence to demonstrate any statistical pattern that would predict the frequency of droughts in the Sahel (Albouy and Boulenger, in Copans, ed., 1975, vol. I, p. 58; cf. Berry, n.d., p. 12). Using the 70-year figure nonetheless, we have not quite so dire a prediction. Other researchers conclude that "there will be no major shifts in precipitation in the region in the near future (50 to 100 years), rather there will be a continuation of major multi-annual variations from the mean resulting in drought periods." What happened in West Africa from 1968 to 1974 was but part of a general trend of climatic fluctuations that will be the curse of certain generations. Only through weather modification will there be a change for the future (Seifert and Kamrany, 1974, p. A15).

Yet another group of experts sees weather modification in quite different terms. For these climatologists, it is the human made modifications in the weather that have brought on the Sahel drought and, perhaps, other droughts and dust bowls in recent times. This third type of climate explanation, while still ultimately a single-factor climate theory, has broader implications for the other kinds of theories and for the explanation offered earlier in this study. It is deserving of some attention.

In its simplest form, this type of theory charges that dust is the immediate cause of drought. Data from the ERTS-1 (Earth Resources Technology Satellite) show that in 1973-74 there was an extremely high level of dust in the atmosphere over West Africa (MacLeod, in Glantz, ed., 1976, p. 219). As dust increases in the air, the amount of sunlight decreases, and thus less of the sun's thermal or heat energy reaches the land and lower atmosphere. This in turn brings on a lowering of the temperature, creating a "cold spot," or air that cannot hold as much moisture as the warmer air; in other words, drought (Winstanley, in Glantz, ed., 1976, p. 206).

But where does the dust come from? Here the satellite must be supplemented by on-the-ground observations, and these observations were made in Niger by Norman H. MacLeod. In touring the Niger countryside, MacLeod noticed that the colors of the soils in many regions had changed from those noted in earlier land studies. Reddish and yellow dirt had changed to white (MacLeod, in Glantz, ed., 1976, p. 219).

Reddish and yellow soils indicate the presence of iron and other chemicals present with a plant cover. When these are replaced with white-colored particles, the meaning is that quartz sands have taken over. Thus the plant cover is no longer there; in other words, desert has replaced crop lands or grass pastures. The dust in the atmosphere may well be the previous iron oxide soil, which has blown up into the air with the loss of the plant cover. MacLeod attributes the drought to this particular dust, the former soil covering, which has left the land surface and become a block against efficient heat energy from the sun.

But why does the soil blow up into the air? Something must happen first to the intricate relation between heat energy on the ground and air currents. If the plant covering is destroyed, MacLeod reasons, the soil is left open to the sun's heat. At first, it might seem that this would actually increase the heat getting in. Another process becomes dominant, however. Since the plant covering regulates the heat intake and loss from the ground level, destruction of the plant covering would lead to the establishment of temperature bands of abnormally high differences from one to the other. These bands in turn would bring on air turbulences or localized wind currents. Once the plant cover has been lost, nothing holds the soil in place, and these wind currents catch up the loosened soils and carry them upward into the atmosphere, where they become the dust cover that inhibits the sunlight and brings on the drought (MacLeod, in Glantz, ed., 1976, pp. 220-22).[13]

It is not so much the drought that destroys the land, but the destroyed land that brings on the drought. We are dealing, then, not so much with a simple act of nature, something beyond our control, but a set of interrelated processes set in motion by the actions of people themselves—a perfect, if horrible, example of what the ecology movement has been warning against. MacLeod's theory, while still unproven, is supported both by observations from satellite photographs and observations on the ground.

The theory, however, poses a further question of perhaps the greatest importance of all. How did the ground lose its plant cover? Here MacLeod stops short of a full analysis, referring only generally to problems of "range and crop management" (MacLeod, in Glantz, ed., 1976, p. 226). Why have land-management techniques deteriorated in the last few decades so that the soil has been denuded of necessary plants? Here we must make connection to another set of theories, the "desertification" studies, in order to see what the experts think has been happening.

IS THE SAHARA DESERT SPREADING?

At first glance, all evidence on this point seems to indicate a resounding "yes." And desertification, the process of expansion of deserts, is linked by many experts with the intensity and timing of the famine.

The spread of deserts on a world scale has led to some doomsday statistics, just as with the doomsday climatologists. Dr. Erik Eckholm, for example, of the Worldwatch Institute in Washington, spoke to a meeting of the American Association for the Advancement of Science in Boston in 1976. Among other things, Dr. Eckholm referred to a U.N. study in which it is claimed that "man-made" deserts now account for 6.7 percent of the earth's surface, "an area larger than Brazil."[14] Specifically, in Africa as much as 250,000 square miles of desert may have been added to the south side of the Sahara alone.[15] In an explicit attack on climatic theories, especially of the type advocated by Bryson and Winstanley, Eckholm charged that North African weather records "reveal no evidence of a decline in rainfall over the last 100 years."[16]

Eckholm was backed up by the highly prestigious Dr. Henri Le Houerou, a French livestock and ecology expert with many years experience in North and West Africa. Eckholm also managed to combine his doomsday approach: the possibility of 60 million people dying of starvation on the fringes of current deserts in Africa, India, Chile, and Argentina, and many hundreds of millions more suffering inflationary food prices—with overtones of violent revolutionary upheavals. "If current patterns prevail, perhaps a fourth of mankind . . . will slowly sink into the slough of hopeless poverty. Whether the deterioration of their prospects will be a quiet one is quite another question."[17]

Finally, one of the most dramatic statements of all, and perhaps a major source of many of the dire press accounts of desertification, was presented by the longtime U.S. food expert Lester Brown to the World Population Conference at Bucharest, Romania, in 1973. Brown claimed that because of

> denudation and deforestation, the Sahara desert has begun to move southward at an accelerated rate all along the 3,500 miles southern fringe, stretching from Senegal to northern Ethiopia. An "in-house" study undertaken by the United States Agency for International Development in August, 1972, indicated that the desert is moving southward at up to 30 miles per year, depending on where it is measured. (Ware, 1975, p. 2)

Significantly, however, the original USAID report was based only on travelers' impressions, a fact not transmitted in most later references to it (ibid.).

Actually, the dire predictions of Eckholm, Le Houerou and others are the most recent statements in a lengthy debate about the question of spreading deserts. This debate goes back to the 1930s and, significantly, has its origins in the Sahel and commentaries about it by various European scientists.

The most important figure in the desertification theory seems to have been Dr. E. P. Stebbing, a British forestry expert with long experience in India before making an intensive study of the forests of West Africa during the 1930s. He noticed in comparing his descriptions of regions of West Africa with those of French explorers of the 19th century that many areas that were desert or grasslands during his visits appeared to have been forests (Stebbing, 1937, pp. 3-4). Extending his historical researches further, he concluded that large parts of the Sahara Desert of his time had once been lush area—the surroundings of the great African city of Timbuktu, for example—but had deteriorated into regions controlled by sand dunes and winds and no longer able to support human life, except for a few nomadic herdspeople. Stebbing saw in the historical record evidence of the drying up of Lake Chad and other water reservoirs, along with a general lowering of the underground water source and the disappearance of rivers that once had carried water to regions covered with sand dunes (ibid., pp. 7-11).

But why was the desert spreading? Stebbing found the answer first in a general climatic change, but later he emphasized the agricultural practices of the people, particularly their use of fire in the technique of slash-and-burn agriculture. Stebbing saw fire as part of a broader attack on the environment by ignorant Africans who wished to clear the tall grasses and trees to facilitate hunting and to get rid of older tough grasses to make way for younger shoots that would be more edible for their cattle and goats

(Stebbing, p. 22). Fire was also used in retreat during warfare (p. 18). Thus, through ignorance of the effects of their "primitive" agricultural system on the land, and through warfare, the people of West Africa are destroying their environment and spreading the Sahara Desert ever southward toward the tropical rain forests, with grasslands destroying the forests and desert taking over the grasslands (1937a, pp. 20-21).

Was Stebbing right in his analysis? We have already seen how more recent views of the use of fire in slash-and-burn agriculture emphasize its positive rather than negative input into forest ecology. Even on the grassland, there is no detailed study showing harmful effects of fire. One French authority, writing in the 1950s, claimed that fire on the savannas results in species selection in favor of "rhizameteuses," whose seeds are better able to withstand the heat than are the more tender annual grasses that would be better for grazing (Pitot, 1952, p. 228). If this view is correct, the herdspeople have been destroying their pasturage for centuries. The study also repeats the charge that fire destroys the forested regions, exposing tree trunks to invasion by fungi and insects and later by termites, which finish off the destruction. The forest canopy is "degraded" to savanna; the savanna undergoes species selection in favor of "rhizameteuses," and, finally, topsoil is transformed into a red ferruginous soil (with heavy concentration of iron), which is like an armor shield in hardness and unusable for agriculture or pasturage (Pitot; cf. van Raay, 1974, pp. 15-16).

The question of the effects of fire has continued to plague the experts, but accumulating data suggest that a far too negative picture has been presented. In the most detailed study to date, a team of French researchers followed the biological-ecological effects of savanna burning for more than 10 years in the area of Lamto, Ivory Coast. The study concluded that burning on a regular basis maintains the savanna in a relatively stable state, the fire essentially substituting for other processes, such as bush eating by large animals and the actions of "termites, earthworms, fungi, and bacteria" (Lamotte, 1975, p. 217). In other words, fire simply speeds up an inevitable process, stabilizing the savanna and making it usable for human productive activities at a faster rate than if left to the termites and fungi.

It is also interesting to note the observations of a range expert hired as a consultant for a USAID project in the grasslands region of Niger in the Agades-Tahoua-Zinder region. The expert notes that observations made during two ground trips in 1975, one in 1977, and one overflight in 1975 indicate that the area of burned grasses is rather small and "does not appear to be as serious as some people state" (USAID, 1975, p. 124; the expert is not named in the report). If this observation is representative, it suggests that the farmers and herders have adjusted their use of fire to ecological conditions, roughly corresponding to those needed to maintain the environment. Other experts have noted that burning of perennial (as opposed to annual) grasses seems to stimulate growth and aid in the process of shoot development (interview notes at Niono ranch site).

Beyond the issue of fire, however, is the more general question of desertification, and here again, the Stebbing report and its consequences are of interest.[18]

Stebbing had called for the appointment of a joint British-French investigation team to check his assertions about the spreading of the Sahara. An Anglo-French forestry commission was set up, but its report, published in 1937 in Nigeria, did not confirm Stebbing's findings (Stamp, 1940, p. 297). Indeed, the four-member commission was unanimous in its findings that "no instance of sand movement on a large scale" was taking place, and that there "appears to be no imminent and general danger of dessication" (ibid., p. 299).[19]

Despite the commission's findings regarding desertification in general, the individual members wrote papers also agreeing with Stebbing's view that fire was a major threat to the environment, and that the problem of soil erosion was more sigificant than desertification (Stamp, 1940, p. 300). Another view put forth was that slash-and-burn agriculture was bringing on soil erosion, but again no specific evidence was brought out (e.g., Jones, 1938, p. 422). At the same time, it was stated that "Bush burning is not causing serious damage in the more arid regions since the grass is too thin and the bush too open to support really destructive fires" (Jones, p. 422). The remedy proposed was fixed farming in place of slash-and-burn, although it was simultaneously noted that "In some districts the soil is so sandy that fixed farming would be impossible without very heavy dressings of manure" (ibid., p. 423). As late as 1966, the issue had still not been clarified, and British geographer Walter Fitzgerald (1966, p. 50) wrote:

> There is no doubt that peoples of the Northern Sudan are tending to migrate in consequence of the dessication of their pasture lands. It is doubtful . . . if decreasing rainfall rather than destruction of vegetation by the Natives, or the drift of sand by the Harmattan is the principal agent of dessication.

And in 1973, at a major Sahel drought conference held at the School of Oriental and African Studies in London, it was reported that "an 'advancing Sahara' could not be confirmed by the evidence presented" (Dalby, 1973, p. 14). More recently, detailed studies of plant cover have revealed at least a temporary movement south of more desertlike species and a disappearance of their less desertlike counterparts. On the Niono ranch in Mali, a region with an average 570 mm. rainfall, the 1968-74 drought resulted in a southern advance of *Blepharis linariifolia*, a Sahelian grass that was also disappearing from regions such as that northeast of Gao, Mali, where the rainfall is only 100 to 200 mm. In the Gao region a desert species was also observed to be advancing, but it may be too early to confirm this as a permanent trend, since a return of the rains could revive these "lost" species, of which many seeds may be lying dormant in the dry ground.[20]

What can be made of all the apparently confusing and contradictory conclusions? Can it be established one way or the other if the Sahara Desert is spreading? Perhaps part of the answer to this quandry lies in the rather common problem of scientific terminology. "Desertification" seems to have developed several interrelated but nonetheless varied meanings. For purposes of understanding the famine, it is not necessary to argue about whether the desert itself is actually spreading dunes where dunes have never been before. But it is important to consider the question as to whether certain ecological zones of West Africa are being rendered progressively less able to support human productive activities such as agriculture and livestock herding. Here it is most important to note the disagreements about the role of fire and the more recent tendency to view slash-and-burn agriculture as a positive adaptation rather than a harmful practice. Despite numerous attempts, no convincing case has been to indict the farming and herding systems for degrading the food-producing ecological zones of West Africa. The experts on ecological decline—as well as on weather and climate—have produced a lot of controversy, but no clear picture of what has been happening to the West African environment has emerged.

RADICAL ALTERNATIVES: SOCIAL AND POLITICAL ORIGINS OF THE FAMINE

The single-variable climatological theories, the often obscure and confused land-mismanagement approaches, the desertification debate, and the obsession with population growth characterize most of the scientific and scholarly writings on the Sahel drought and famine. In the midst of these approaches, however, while largely ignored, a set of alternative approaches has risen that attempts to bring together the interacting variables in a more comprehensive fashion. The radical approach uses history, climatic data, social processes, and, more specifically the effects of the imposition of the colonial economy and its postcolonial dependency relationships between the Sahel nations and the international capitalist system. While to our knowledge the only overall comprehensive statement of the radical approach is contained in the previous chapters of this study, there are several other sources where various elements of the approach have been suggested either in outline form or with specialized points to make.

In a series of articles and notes, for example, Nicole Ball has taken up the question of radical analysis as an approach to the Sahel famine and has tried to familiarize U.S. scholars with some of the available materials from France. She has outlined some of the relationships between dependency and the Sahel drought and famine (Ball, 1975, 1976, 1978). Other writers have made brief statements connecting certain aspects of the Sahel famine to the systems of production in the area (for example, Lofchie, 1975; Warhaftig, 1975; Baier, 1976; and Lovejoy and Baier, in Glantz, 1976, pp. 145-75).

It is from several radical intellectuals in France, however, that the most comprehensive approach to the famine has come. During the height of the 1968-74 drought, the Sahel Information Committee was formed in Paris to bring to the attention of the French public the serious plight of the Sahelian herders and farmers and to criticize the French government for its extremely limited aid program. From this committee came a hastily prepared analysis entitled *Qui Se Nourrit de la Famine en Afrique* (Who is benefiting from the Famine in Africa?) and later a two-volume collection of essays by French experts from many scientific backgrounds. These focused on a selected set of topics such as relief aid, the drought and its victims, the experiences in a number of specific areas, and so forth (Comité Information Sahel, 1974; and Copans, 1975). All of these writings have in common an assumption that the drought and famine are part of a lengthy process of ecological deterioration and some add that that process is directly related to the processes of capitalism in its overseas manifestations of colonialism or the dependency phenomenon.

The research presented in earlier sections of this book seems to bear out overwhelmingly the lines of analysis as set forth in the other radical studies. A full understanding of the forces that led to the dramatic crisis of 1968–74 takes one far beyond climate, desertification, overgrazing, mismangement, population growth, and the like and compels one to study the colonial and postcolonial international economic and political system.

The verification of a general scientific explanation, however, is not the only purpose in studying the Sahel famine. For the Sahel region is today the subject of one of the most ambitious development programs of modern times. The question of how to develop the Sahel's fragile ecology is directly linked to the question of how to interpret the drought and famine. From each of the expert views presented in this chapter, one can derive an approach to the future. If climate is the problem, weather modification is the answer. If population growth is the problem, then family planning is the answer. If overgrazing is the problem, then smaller cattle herds or higher "offtake" rates become the development prescription.

The radical approach differs from these single-variable answers, however. If the economic and political relations have within them the causes of the problem, then it is those relations that must be altered. The altering of these relationships is primarily a task for the Sahelian peoples themselves, while the role of outside "experts" becomes one of encouraging support for the Sahelians' efforts among the people of our own society.

Radical theorists have begun discussion on this difficult and important topic by posing questions about the capacity of Western capitalist societies to develop the Sahel in an ecologically sound way. Nicole Ball (1978, p. 296) has warned, for example, that "The record of previous foreign interventions in the region suggests that environmental protection will take, at best, second place to the pursuit of profits and of economic stability for the industrialized Western governments." And French Marxist anthropologist Claude Meillassoux (1974, p. 28) puts it more bluntly, stating that we should expect "exploitation and not development" as the key aspect of the relationships to be created between the Sahel and its development donors. The problem of the Sahel drought and famine is thus currently the problem of Sahel development, and it is to the Sahel Development Program that we now turn our attention.

NOTES

1. *Boston Globe*, May 19, 1974; *New York Times*, May 27, 1973; *Christian Science Monitor*, November 20, 1973; *Wall Street Journal*, May 24, 1974. More recently, John Updike (1978) has offered a fascinating but highly misleading picture of the problems faced by the Sahelians in his novel *The Coup*. Updike traveled to Africa in 1973 as a Fulbright scholar.

2. For a historical overview of the development of population and overpopulation theories in the United States, see Bonnie Mass, "An Historical Sketch of the American Population Control Movement," *International Journal of Health Services*, vol. 4, no. 4 (1974): 651–76; and *Population Target: The Political Economy of Population Control in Latin America*, 1976.

3. *Wall Street Journal*, May 24, 1974.

4. *New York Times*, June 22, 1976.

5. The time it takes to double a population is a favorite measure of population theorists, although its only justification seems to be that it fits the Malthusian idea of a geometrical or exponential rate of growth, despite the fact that this geometrical rate is logically inherent only in the methods chosen for analysis and not in the phenomenon as such.

6. An elaboration of this suggestion can be found in Hopkins, 1973, pp. 23–27. The author argues that the dispersed population and extensive rather than intensive agricultural production system made the option of hired labor an excessively expensive one. "Slaves were preferred, because the costs of acquiring and maintaining them were less than the costs of hiring labor" (p. 25).

7. But urban rates are also higher than general rural rates, which does not immediately conform to this theory.

8. The "do not know" or "no response" was 28 percent, which the authors believe means that the respondents were mostly astonished at even being asked about reducing family size.

9. The similarities in these attitudes to those of the Indian farmers interviewed by Mahmood Mamdani are striking despite the vast geographical and cultural distance between the two studies and the fact that Mamdani talked mostly with men, while Reyna's data come from women. The author of the Chadian study attempts to show that the women are wrong in their evaluation of their family's labor needs. For the argument being made here, it is not necessary that they be right or wrong, only that they perceive a need to have many children as being related to labor needs of the family. We would like to note, however, that in our view, Reyna's data prove the women in fact are quite *right* about the needs of their families.

10. Indeed, French geographer Jean Gallais claims that in some parts of Mali the creation of a commons was the *result* of abuses of the nobility in those areas who were using their control over the pastures to tax the commoners. As Gallais puts it, however, "this free individualism clashes with the traditional and necessarily disciplined usage of the pastures" (Gallais, 1972, p. 365). The simple model of the tragedy of the commons where herder versus other herders is thus inadequate to deal with the effects of hierarchy and stratification of local elites and/or national governments. The tragedy goes far beyond the commons.

11. Even in their own presentation, however, Picardi and Seifert acknowledge some forms of cooperation and exchange, developed in the Sahel previous to modern times, that have been mutually beneficial to both farmers and herders (e.g., Picardi and Seifert, 1977, p. 300).

12. Quoted by Nigel Hawkes in the *Boston Globe*, May 19, 1974.

13. Other experts have followed similar lines of reasoning, but they have postulated slightly different mechanisms, including loss of "ice nuclei," also having the effect of reducing moisture, or increase in the "reflectivity," causing less light and heat to be absorbed, thus cooling the land and drying up the air (Winstanley, in Glantz, ed., 1976, p. 206).

14. *New York Times*, February 25, 1976.

15. Ibid., March 7, 1976.

16. Ibid., February 26, 1976.

17. Ibid.

18. The most recent statement of concern about fire comes from scientists observing satellite photographs that indicate large amounts of buring in the early part of the dry season. See MacLeod et al., 1977, pp. 269–72.

19. Some of the controversy centered on the concept of a degraded environment. What Stebbing had considered degraded forest was viewed by the commission as climax savanna. In other words, it appeared possible that regions that Stebbing thought were transitional from a climax to a degraded state might just as well be the climax, or most highly evolved, of a different zone of ecology—and they might even be in transition *toward* a more advanced state (Stamp, 1940, pp. 298-99). A recent addition to this debate is offered by MacLeod, 1976a.

20. Breman and Cissé (1977) combined observations from 1952 aerial photographs, a 1970 study by French expert Boudet, and their own research in 1975 at the Niono ranch site, an 11,000 ha. research area 14,20 N and 5,50 W. The observations on plant changes in Gao are cited from Marty (1975) and Diarra (1976). An advance in the understanding of "spreading deserts" may come about as a result of observations from recent satellite passes over the Sahel. Norman MacLeod and Warren Hovis have discovered that the downward movement of cold, dry air from stratosphere into troposphere is the "characteristic atmospheric feature of deserts" (MacLeod, 1975, p. 2). This downward movement requires the presence of a low-pressure air body, which is maintained by absorption of heat from hot sands. Plant cover reflects a different radiation, which is more easily absorbed and dispersed in the atmosphere, while sand, especially quartz sand, emits an infrared light that can be absorbed only when there is a cloud cover. The results of these findings regarding the effects of infrared light qualities, heat absorption, and other highly technical processes are that a mechanism is now describable that would explain how the loss of plant cover could lead to the creation of conditions favoring a desert climate. This climate in turn would greatly inhibit the regrowth of the plant cover once lost. MacLeod and Hovis do not have sufficient data to estimate the number of years of plant-cover loss before desert climate would set in.

6

International Organizations and Regional Plans: Mobilizing Resources for the Sahel

Today, the Sahel has become the focus of one of the most extensive and high-cost development programs in the world, and one that many of its proponents believe has the potential for making numerous innovations in the entire field of development theory and practice. In order to analyze and evaluate the program and the claims made for it, we will continue the approach of previous chapters, presenting Sahel development organizations, projects, and programs in the context of economic, social, and political developments in Africa and between Africa and the rest of the world, in particular the major capitalist nations that are funding and encouraging the programs. The aim of this and the following chapters will be first to present, in analytical fashion, Sahel development efforts in all their various aspects, and then to look critically at some of the social and political forces that will effect the course of these efforts.

The thesis of this section is that, just as past ecological developments were conditioned by the political and economic interest groups in and outside the Sahel, the present development effort will succeed or falter based on its relation to similar forces at work today. On the basis of such an analytical framework, we believe it will be finally possible to deal with the question implicit throughout this study: Can the Sahel be made safe from famine?

CILSS: A REGIONAL DEVELOPMENT ORGANIZATION

By March 1973, the Sahel drought had been underway for five years. Food shortages had become severe in many areas, and United Nations observers predicted mass starvation as a real possibility in Mauritania, Mali, Niger, and Chad especially. Food relief, however, as has been shown previously, was not well underway, and all signs were alarming. In this atmosphere of calamity, representatives of seven Sahelian nations met in Ougadougou, the capital of Upper Volta, to establish the Interstate Committee to Combat Drought in the Sahel, known best by its French acronym CILSS (Comité Interétats de Lutte Contre la Sécheresse). Through the formation of CILSS, the nations of Senegal, Mauritania, Mali, Niger, Chad, Upper Volta, and later Gambia and Cape Verde declared their intention to find and implement a regional plan to overcome the Sahel's vulnerability to drought.

The Interstate Committee to Combat Drought in the Sahel may not seem at first to be original. Since World War II, any number of regional groupings have been set up with the avowed purpose of stimulating economic and political cooperation and development. The European Economic Community (Common Market), the Association of Southeast Asian Nations (ASEAN), the Organization of Petroleum Producers (OPEC), and others have, for better or for worse, promoted regional ties. The West African states themselves, including many of the Sahelian countries, have been or are also members of OCAM, the Afro-Malagasy-Mauritian Common Organization or (in the case of Gambia) the British Commonwealth. Indeed, even as the CILSS was being formed, OCAM was holding meetings to discuss its apparently shaky future.[1] In addition to these various groupings, the U.N. maintains regional offices, such as in Dakar, Senegal, where planning and development are intended to have a regional character.

Why, then, should anyone have a particular interest in the formation of CILSS? USAID official David Shear provides a partial answer: "the governments participating in the development of the Sahel achieved . . . an agreed analysis of the nature of the problems faced by the Sahel and adoption of a dramatic program of development of the entire region" (Shear and Clark, 1976, p. 15).[2] The CILSS and the Sahel Development Program are thought of in many development circles as going "far beyond traditional planning" (Shear and Clark, 1976, p. 15). W. Haven North, acting assistant administrator of the African Bureau of USAID testified at a House Subcommittee Hearing:

> The CILSS has set nothing less than regional self-sufficiency in food production and, in the longer term, sustained economic growth as the goal for the development of the Sahel. Adopting such regional "performance" as the goal of development aid is a fundamental departure from previous planning. Its consequences with regard to program implementation and coordination of the aid resources and diplomatic interests of many states are enormous. If substantially successful, it presents itself as a new model for development in least developed countries, because the program

will have removed the Sahelian states from the status of international dependency and created the basis for sustained improvement" (U.S. House, 1977, p. 69).

Rather than a vague and general set of goals, CILSS formulated a specific set of programs aimed at attacking the problem of drought vulnerability across the entire ecological region that we defined as the Sahel and Sahel-Sudan earlier. Is the CILSS then a new departure in development and development planning? A brief history of CILSS and its supporting organization may shed further light on this question.

THE WESTERN AID RESPONSE

The original CILSS meeting in March 1973 was followed by a rapid succession of events. Just two months later, the United Nations Special Sahelian Office was created. In September 1973, Ouagadougou hosted a second CILSS meeting, with representatives from the United States, West Germany, France, the World Bank, and others (CILSS, 1973b; USAID, April 1976). This meeting was highly organized: From August 31 to September 6, discussions were held among various technical personnel, while September 7-10 was taken up by a conference of cabinet-level ministers. On September 11-12, the heads of state themselves took over (except for Chad), and the entire affair resulted in a series of resolutions and the establishment of the CILSS as a permanent structure with headquarters in Ouagadougou (CILSS, 1973a, b, c).[3]

The first signs of a developing relationship between CILSS and wealthy Western nations appeared in the form of a disagreement over funding levels for Sahel development projects. The technical experts, it appears, had presented a list of drought reconstruction and economic development project totaling more than $3 billion, but, as was reported in the *New York Times*, "the requests were scaled down, according to reliable sources, after some would-be donors had suggested levels that 'could be more seriously considered.'"[4] A figure of $827 million came out of the September CILSS meetings, but as will be seen later, it was to be short-lived as Sahel development plans began to gather momentum.

The forces set in motion by the formation of CILSS were not slowed by the initially low financial response of the Western nations. CILSS itself went ahead with another meeting in Ouagadougou in December 1973 (CILSS, 1973d). This was followed by yet another conference in February 1974, at which U.N. Secretary-General Kurt Waldheim announced that 136 regional projects had been organized and that U.N. experts would visit ten European countries to solicit support for greater aid contributions.[5] Waldheim added a note of high concern to the U.N. efforts: "If sufficient action isn't taken in the next few months, countries could disappear from the face of the map. It is our moral duty to avoid this tragedy."[6] Whatever the role was for those who felt it their moral duty to participate, political events in the Sahel and beyond were also pushing toward a Western reevaluation of the $827-million limit set in September 1973.

In April 1974, Hamani Diori, fifteen-year president of Niger, was overthrown by French-trained army Lt. Colonel Seyni Kountché.[7] While the coup did not alter the overall political orientations of Niger, it did underscore the potential political instability of Sahelian countries with recurrent droughts and famines.[8] Western support activities continued to intensify. In October 1974, the Rockefeller Foundation, USAID, and the National Academy of Sciences convened a private meeting of high-level Sahelian and Western experts at the Rockfeller Foundation's Villa Serbelloni in Bellagio, Italy. This conference endorsed the general orientation of CILSS, concluding in part that "the region's needs are urgent . . . and further help cannot wait" (Rockefeller Foundation, 1975, p. 6).

Within two years, the sense of urgency had increased substantially. In April 1974, left-wing officers in Lisbon had overthrown the fascist Caetano regime, which ushered in the end of Portuguese colonial rule in Africa. In September 1974, Guinea-Bissau, a country bordering the south of pro-Western Senegal, achieved independence under a radical leadership, which, in its thirteen-year guerrilla war, had established a popular peasant and workers army. In June 1975, Mozambique achieved independence under similar circumstances. Almost immediately, the military struggle against the white-dominated minority regime in Zimbabwe-Rhodesia was stepped up. These events were followed in turn by the dramatic left-wing victory in Angola.

Following these developments came one of the most spectacular shifts in world politics in recent years, when the centuries-old feudal monarchy of Ethiopia was overthrown in 1974. Within months, a rapid succession of massive strikes, demonstrations, and military shoot-outs resulted in a political momemtum that pushed, and has continued to push, Ethiopian society rapidly toward socialism. With a potentially rich agricultural and mineral wealth, a strategic location at the crossroads between Africa and the Middle East, and a population of 28 million, second only to Nigeria in black Africa, a revolutionary Ethiopia has come to be viewed as a distinct threat to Western capitalist interests in all of Africa.[9]

The political color of Africa was suddenly changing with astonishing speed. It was noted in the Introduction how then Secretary of State Henry Kissinger expressed his shock at the rapid revolutionary changes that were taking place in Africa at the time. One of Kissinger's responses was to embark on a several-nations tour of Africa, and one of the stops was in Senegal, where, at a "lamb and champagne luncheon given by the Senegalese foreign minister," Kissinger "proposed a $7.5 billion rescue operation to 'roll back the desert' . . . and appealed to the world's industrialized countries to join it."[10]

Kissinger's proposal was not actually new; it had been made at least one month earlier by FAO director Edouard Saouma,[11] but the Kissinger statement was a clear sign that the U.S. government had swung behind a program costing almost *ten times* what the wealthy donor nations had been willing to offer to CILSS in September 1973. By 1977, a joint African-

Western conference in Ottawa, Canada, had called for a $10 billion, 25-year development program.[12]

THE GROWING ROLE OF THE UNITED STATES

Kissinger's public call for a gigantic program to "roll back the desert" was not merely an appeal to others to increase their aid commitments. As the African political pendulum seemed to be swinging toward the establishment of revolutionary governments, high-level debates were going on within the U.S. government, aid agencies, and congressional committees on the need for increased U.S. assistance in Africa. One observer noted in 1974 that "the U.S. has never had any major commitment to seriously develop Africa. The current Sahel operation [including food relief as well as development aid], although modest compared to the major U.S. programs in Asia, is the most important ever untaken by the United States in independent Africa" (Oudes, 1974, p. 52).[13] The relief operation, however, was only a beginning.

Many countries began to increase their aid to the Sahel, but it was the U.S. contribution that underwent the greatest transformation, rising almost 33 times in 1979 over the amounts given in 1974, the time of the early CILSS appeals. The comparative amounts for several Western nations and international agencies are shown in Table 6.1. Of particular note is the rapidly evolving balance between the finances made available by the United States and France, which during this same period increased its aid commitment by less than one-third.

By 1977, the Carter Administration had again increased the U.S. pledge, announcing through spokesperson W. Haven North that the United States was prepared to commit $200 million for the coming ten years, an amount that was estimated by USAID officials would raise the U.S. contribution to as much as 10 or 15 percent of the total Western aid.[14]

Professor Elliot Berg of the Center for Research in Economic Development at the University fo Michigan has estimated that the wealthy donor aid program to Sahelian development will average about $25 per person per year in countries where the overall yearly income per capita is only about $100, as compared to a world average for underdeveloped countries of about $300 (U.S. House, 1977, p. 102). A sense of the relative size of this commitment can be gained by comparison with the U.S. aid to Bangladesh, which amounted to $2.29 per capita in 1978, and to several other countries: for example, India, $ .27; Bolivia, $6.56; Nigeria $ .01; and Indonesia $1.00.[15]

THE CLUB OF THE SAHEL

While the United States was deciding to back intensified development efforts in the Sahel, a United States-Western European organizational structure was being established. Under the aegis of the Organization for

Table 6.1. Commitments of Development Assistance to Sahelian Countries (in $millions).

Country	*1974*	*1975*	*1976*	*1977*	*1978*	*1979*	*Percent Increase*
			(estimated)		*(projected)*		
Belgium	6.5	6.1	6.0	6.5	7.0	8.0	38
Canada	29.0	65.3	50.0	60.0	75.0	75.0	158
France	185.0	222.5	236.8	238.0	240.0	240.0	30
West Germany	76.0	76.7	72.0	90.0	110.0	118.0	55
Holland	2.5	8.4	35.0	36.0	38.0	40.0	1500
Switzerland	2.4	3.2	3.1	6.0	8.0	10.0	317
United Kingdom	7.3	5.1	12.7	13.0	14.0	15.0	105
E.E.C.	157.4	148.4	176.9	140.0	145.0	150.0	–5
I.B.R.D.	42.3	107.9	110.3	150.0	180.0	200.0	373
U.N.	40.0	52.8	22.6	40.0	50.0	50.0	25
African Development Program	16.5	46.7	44.6	45.0	50.0	55.5	233
OPEC	83.7	91.2	75.9	90.0	100.0	120.0	43
Other DAC[a]	12.3	10.3	3.3	18.0	16.0	20.0	62
United States	2.9	5.7	11.5	36.0	67.4	97.1	3,248
Totals	663.8	850.3	860.5	968.5	1100.4	1198.1	80
United States as percentage total	0.4	0.6	1.3	3.7	6.1	8.1	

[a]Including Australia, Austria, Denmark, Finland, Italy, Japan, Norway, and Sweden.
Source: USAID, 1978. Sahel Development Program: Annual Report to the Congress. February 1978, p. 6.
Notes:
Statistics do *not* include drought or emergency aid, at least for the United States. 1974-76 statistics gathered by DAC (Development Assistance Committee) of the OECD.
1979 projections by Secretariat of the Club du Sahel.

Economic Cooperation and Development (OECD), which had come into existence out of an organization coordinating Marshall Plan reconstruction of post-World War II capitalist Europe, an office was set up in Paris and a subgroup formed for donor countries. Maurice J. Williams, then deputy director of USAID and President Nixon's special director for Sahelian relief operations, was appointed chairman of the Development Assistance Committee of the OECD.[16] The Club of the Sahel was officially formed at a meeting in Dakar called by Senegalese President Leopold Senghor in March 1976. Williams and CILSS Chairman Moktar Ould Daddah, then president of Mauritania, drafted a proposal on development policies, and it was accepted by leaders of the CILSS states in December 1975. (Williams, 1976, p. 194).[17]

The aims of the Club of the Sahel were to organize and administer the donor-country aid programs more efficiently and effectively than via straight bilateral country arrangements. To do this, the Club and CILSS established an elaborate structure that provides parallel engagement of both donor and recipient representatives at the regional level, rather than through traditional ministry-by-ministry, country-by-country contacts. The basic orientation of the Club was outlined in the statement issued from the Dakar meeting:

THE "CLUB DU SAHEL"

(Dakar, 29–31 March, 1976)

IN RECOGNITION OF:

–the remarkable courage of the people of the Sahel who managed their survival through bleak years of drought and who wish to continue to devote their energies to reconstruction and development,

–the important efforts of the international community in helping with immediate needs which saved millions of lives and gave renewed hope to the people of the Sahel,

AND CONSIDERING THAT:

–the Sahel countries and the international community have undertaken to work together to avoid a return to the precarious pre-drought standards of life in the Sahel and reduce the disastrous effects of possible recurrent drought;

–planning long-term development will involve new conceptual approaches adapted to the realities of the Sahel and detailed sectoral programmes, as well as careful choice of priorities for action;

–implementing long-term development programmes and projects in the Sahel will require a substantial increase in resources and the most favourable terms;

–the Heads of State of the CILSS Member countries at their meeting in Nouakchott in December 1975 noted all the new initiatives to support the medium and long-term rehabilitation efforts of the Sahel, and welcomed, in particular, the announcement of the creation of the Club du Sahel;

To give tangible expression to their cooperation for the medium and long-term development, CILSS Member countries and their partners from donor countries and organisations

DECIDE TO CREATE THE "CLUB DU SAHEL."

Jointly sponsored by CILSS Member countries and certain donor countries and organisations, the Club is open to all Friends of the Sahel.

THE CLUB WILL:

–Support the work of the CILSS;

–Inform and sensitise the international community on Sahel development prospects and needs;

-Foster increased cooperation among donors for the implementation of actions requested by Sahel governments and regional institutions and facilitate the mobilisation of resources for development;

-Provide a forum for Sahelian states to articulate their long-term development policies and priorities for medium and long-term development and to discuss them with potential donors;

-Function as an informal and flexible discussion group following the principles of mutual confidence, equality, flexibility and consensus among its participants;

-Meet at least once a year; set up working groups to explore specific issues.

The meetings of the Club will be placed under the joint chairmanship of a representative from Sahel country governments and a representative of Donor Friends of the Sahel.

Source: OECD, 1977, pp. 124–25.

Perhaps even more than CILSS, the combination of CILSS and the Club of the Sahel caught the imagination of U.S. aid-and-development personnel. USAID spokesperson W. Haven North, in congressional hearings on CILSS, characterized the Club's donors and their African regional counterparts as "an extraordinary alliance between the developed Western world, several of the OPEC states, and the countries of Sahelian Africa" (U.S. House, 1977, p. 69). The Club was organized into four production sectors: livestock, rain-fed agriculture, irrigated agriculture, and fisheries. These four sectors are intersected by five program areas—in ecology and forestry, adaptation of technologies, human resources and health, infrastructure, transportation, and price policy and marketing. Each of the nine sectors and program areas has a team to direct it, and each of the teams has a formal organization "headed by a senior African representative who is supported by a donor agency specialist" (U.S. House, 1977, p. 69). The work of the nine teams is coordinated by a "synthesis team," and special working groups are set up within and among teams when necessary for the drafting of proposals.

The structure of CILSS and the Club thus brings together Western and Sahelian representatives at frequent planning and discussion meetings; this is intended to maximize regional contacts among Africans as well as those between African and Western experts and administrators.

The Club to date has held numerous symposia and workshops and has drafted strategy statements and development programs for the Sahel. The precise role of the Club in implementing and evaluating programs is less clear. According to USAID spokesperson North (U.S. House, 1977, p. 77):

> The Club is not a management or financial body; it is a co-ordination and program planning body. From the activities that the group decides on, the various donors will identify those that they feel they most appropriately can participate in.

Despite this claim, North had previously listed five basic assumptions underlying the U.S. commitment to the Club. Among them: "The management and evaluation methods now evolving in the Club des Amis du Sahel will provide tight control over and evaluation of the progress of the program" (U.S. House, 1977, p. 70).

MOBILIZING RESOURCES

The massive commitment of Western nations to Sahel development and the influx of U.S. dollars and resources into the Club of the Sahel and CILSS has led to an amazing mobilization of scientific research into problems and possibilities for the region. Many additional resources have been mobilized, not only to explain the recent famine but also to survey the environmental and human potential of the Sahel with the aim of organizing, managing, and putting into motion various forces of economic change. It is from these research studies that much of the Club of the Sahel–CILSS "Sahel Development Program" was assembled.

The first round of studies brought together the resources of French, United States, and U.N. personnel. USAID contracted $968,000 with engineers at the Massachusetts Institute of Technology to produce an eleven-volume technical study, "A Framework for Evaluating Long-Term Strategies for the Development of the Sahel-Sudan Region" (Seifert and Kamrany, 1974; *MIT Tech Talk*, October 18, 1973). Although this study has been widely criticized in private by USAID officials and U.S. academics involved in Sahel research as "not worth the money," OECD's Maurice Williams (1976, pp. 177-94) suggests that the report was somewhat influential in guiding the earliest policy discussions in the Club.[18]

Within a year, USAID had also contracted with the Center for Research on Economic Development (CRED) at the University of Michigan, whose director, Elliot Berg (his congressional testimony is partly summarized above), produced a lengthy analysis of the economic effects of the drought (Berg, 1975). USAID also developed a series of in-house reports, beginning as early as 1972, with a long study, "Development and Management of the Steppe and Brush-Grass Savannah Zone Immediately South of the Sahara" (USAID, 1972), and led up to the time of the first Club meetings with "Development Assistance Programme of the Sahel-Sudan Region" (USAID, 1975).

The World Bank issued a report in 1974 entitled "World Bank Approach to Economic Development of the Sahel" (World Bank, 1974; cf. Williams, 1976, pp. 177-94), while the French development consultancies SEDES and SCET combined with the government Overseas Scientific Research Institute ORSTOM to produce a 1975 study, "Etude sur les potentialites economiques des pays du Sahel" (SEDES/SCET/ORSTOM, 1975; cf. Williams, 1976).

U.N. agencies also followed up their reports on relief problems with a series of documents on the future needs of the Sahel, including the U.N. Special Sahelian Office's "An Approach to Recovery and Rehabilitation of the Sudano-Sahelian Region" (U.N. Special Sahelian Office, 1974) and the UNDP's (United Nations' Development Program) "Progress Report on the Drought-Stricken Regions of Africa and Adjacent Areas" (UNDP, 1974), while the U.N.'s Program on Man and the Biosphere issued a special report, "The Sahel: Ecological Approaches to Land Use" (UN MAB, n.d., published by UNESCO). The most ambitious U.N. work, however, came from the FAO in 1975 in its three-volume *Perspective Study on Agricultural Development in the Sahelian Countries, 1975–1990* (FAO, 1975), which, as the title suggests, attempts to project in quantitative terms the population growth and food needs of the area and to estimate which section of the food-producing economies can best provide this production. The FAO study appears to have had a particularly strong influence on the formation of the major outlines of the Club-CILSS Sahel Development Program.

The OECD itself has commissioned a number of projects, including a map analysis of the drought, "La Sécheresse en Afrique Sahélienne," by geographer Yveline Poncet (1973),[19] and a summary of the studies by other agencies, prepared by Jacques Giri, entitled "An Analysis of Long Term Development Strategies for the Sahel" (1976). In addition to these background and policy studies, the OECD has commissioned the collection of the largest and most comprehensive bibliography, "Elements for a Bibliography of the Sahel Drought," which contained as of August 1978 more than 2,320 source citations and is a continuing project with updating supplements in preparation (Beudot and Joyce, 1976–77). The OECD Development Centre Library maintains a large and well-organized Sahel collection housed in a special office.

At one of the CILSS meetings, in September 1973, U.S. representative Maurice Williams promised to the Sahel development effort "technical help of 'top universities' and the National Academy of Sciences."[20] The mobilization of the resources of the U.S. scientific community has been intense. After the elaborate MIT study, which was judged a fiasco, USAID branched out to other universities with specialized skills.

At the University of Michigan, Elliot Berg and CRED received contracts for the economic study, as well as for research into problems of livestock raising; eventually they were commissioned to conduct a Club-CILSS study of marketing and price policy regarding cereal grains. At Michigan State, a whole series of projects were undertaken, including the training of African students, a research project on aspects of opening new lands in the Sahel where the river-blindness fly prevents human habitation, and the establishment of the Sahel Documentation Center, which has almost certainly gathered the largest collection of Sahel documents and reports in the United States and perhaps in the world. The Center, in addition to cataloging collections and computerizing titles, also publishes a free quarterly bulletin that contains English and French bilingual articles on current research, projects, conferences, and a list of recent acquisitions.[21] A similar and related project has been developed at the University of California at Riverside, where technical scientific literature on the Sahel is being collected and organized within the scope of the larger project on Moisture Utilization in Semi-Arid Tropics (MUSAT).[22]

Another project of note is located at the National Center for Atmospheric Research in Colorado. Professor Michael Glantz has developed a series of research papers, edited books, symposia, and the like on general development problems of the Sahel but with special emphasis on the possible role of weather modification as a partial solution (Glantz, ed., 1976, 1977).

In some cases, the large amounts of funding offered by USAID have helped to catapult entire new consulting operations into existence. The Institute for Development Anthropology, Inc., was organized in 1976 by several university professors to provide anthropological advice and counsel to USAID. The Institute's formal charter lists general goals such as "research and training," "workshops, seminars . . . publications," and the like. Its five reports as of July 1977 include two on the Sahel, commissioned by USAID.[23]

In a more general but related vein, USAID has commissioned studies on the problems and prospects of climate monitoring for regions "prone to desertification." This research, mostly of a background type, has been conducted at Clark University's Program for International Development and includes recommendations on the establishment of desertification monitoring as well as a discussion of certain technical problems (Berry and Ford, 1977).[24]

In addition to the projects and programs mentioned so far, there is also a livestock research program at Purdue University, with a portion devoted to Sahelian livestock problems and a general public health project drafted in part by a faculty member of the Harvard School of Public Health, again funded by USAID (Joseph and Scheyer, 1977).[25]

Government agencies and USAID were not alone with the Rockefeller Foundation in providing research and organizing other informational activities in support of Sahel development. The American Council on Education, funded in part by USAID and in part by the Ford and Carnegie foundations, has also taken a role. In 1975, the Council's Overseas Liaison Committee, through its Rural Development Network, conducted a field trip and workshop via the Senegalese and Malian governments for representatives from ten drought countries to "examine medium-term recovery projects in the field and to advance concrete recommendations to donors on how to impose the design of recovery projects" (Eicher, 1975). The Council went on to publish a study, by long-time African demography expert John C. Caldwell (1975), entitled *The Sahelian Drought and Its Demographic Implications* as part of a series entitled "Development From Below."[26]

THE USE OF ADVANCED TECHNOLOGY

One of the most dramatic forms of U.S. support for Sahel development has come in the form of satellite photography of land-use and weather conditions. In 1973, "as a result of concern about determining both the causes and the effects of drought on the Sahelian resource system, the Drought Analysis Laboratory was established at the Goddard Space Flight Center collaboratively with . . . the American University and the Catholic University of America" (MacLeod et al., 1977, p. 268). The results of various satellite photography experiments have led in several directions. Anthropologists have begun to consider the possible use of satellite imagery for conducting demographic, ecological, and land-use research (Reining et al., 1975). Geographers, geologists, and climatologists now have new sources of information.[27]

Beyond these general developments lies the special concern with the Sahel that partly led to the establishment of the Drought Analysis Laboratory. From the scientists' point of view, the Sahel is an interesting region for applying satellite imagery to the solution of ecological-economic problems. The region is often cloudless, thus facilitating the sharpness and reliability of the photography, although in 1974 experiments dust became a problem (MacLeod, et al., 1977). The Sahel is also an area with specific and dramatic environmental problems that undoubtedly provide a further challenge to many researchers who would like this new technology to be more than a sterile technical exercise. Finally, the Sahel is a region with relatively poor statistical, climatic, ecological and other data, so the satellite program might offer a fast, relatively inexpensive means of making up for data deficiencies.[28] The Drought Analysis Laboratory and the Earth Resources Development Research Institute have already published a series of papers on various aspects of satellite applications to problems such as weather prediction, land use and land management, identification of potential agricultural zones, water resources and mineral detection, plant and animal distribution, effects of human economic activity, and others.[29]

U.S. support, however, is supplemented by aid from many other Western nations. Among many examples are a Belgian-financed vegetable research study in Senegal, Dutch projects to establish the feasibility of "game cropping" and for making computer-ecological models of a Sahelian pasture environment in Mali, French scientific advice to help plan the integration of livestock and permanent irrigated agriculture in the lower Senegal River valley, a Swiss forestry expert for the CILSS planning office, a Canadian veterinarian for CILSS, and so forth. In this list, which could be multiplied many times, most of the elements are postdrought, except, of course, the French, who have been in the region in force for several hundred years.

One additional university source of some importance is the International African Institute in London, which, in collaboration with the United Nations Environmental Program and the African Institute for Development Planning in Dakar (IDEP), has established a series of publications on the African environment. This series appears to have grown out of the University of London symposium on the Sahel drought (Dalby and Church, 1973). Subsequent publications have brought together a wide range of specialized presentations by scholars representing quite diverse points of view, although unfortunately most of the individual papers are extremely brief, and rarely is a topic developed fully.[30]

To all these studies, reports, financial commitments, and discussions has been added an incredible number of symposia, regional meetings, specialized seminars, overseas scholarships, high-paid consultancies, laboratory experiments, and so on. In a few short years since the massive drought and famine of 1968-74, the Sahel has gone from an unknown desert fringe to a region in which hundreds of millions of dollars, major scientific resources, and enormous administrative efforts have been concentrated to develop what is said to be a major new model for development planning. This has culminated in a series of projects and proposals known as "The Sahel Development Program."

NOTES

1. *New York Times,* August 13, 1973.
2. Shear is currently director of the Office of Sahel and Francophone West African Affairs, USAID, Washington.
3. *New York Times,* Septamber 11-12, 1973.
4. Ibid., September 11, 1973.
5. Ibid., February 22, 1974.
6. Ibid.
7. See *New York Times,* April 16-18 and April 23, 1974. Kountché fought with the French army in Vietnam and Algeria and attended officer training school in Frejus, southern France, in 1959 (Kountche, 1978, pp. 8-10).
8. Deposed President Diori was a particularly reliable friend of Western interests. His comments on the availability of his country as a storehouse for cheap meat for France have been noted in Chapter 4. His more general veiws on multinational corporations are quoted from the national paper *Le Niger,* August 7, 1972, in Derriennic, 1977, p. 250: "In the modern world, interdependence has continued to increase, and we all know that in the present situation, multinational corporations are part of an irreversible development."
9. The recent U.S. support for the ill-fated Somali invasion of the Ogaden is clear evidence for this hostility toward the Ethiopian revolution, and this was further demonstrated to us during a research tour of the Sahel when a very high-ranking official of USAID cited Ethiopia as an example of what might happen if the Sahel Development Program does not succeed. Aside from scattered references in the U.S. press (e.g., *New York Times,* February 24, 1974; February 18, 1974; January 2, 1975; January 11, 1976; etc.), few accounts of this highly significant political process have appeared in the United States. One interesting analysis of the land reform program as it relates to development issues is contained in Cohen et al (1976). A sympathetic account of the entire revolutionary process in Ethiopia is given in two pamphlets by Griswold (1978 and World View, 1978). A scathing attack on the prerevolutioary government of Haile Selassie and of the Western aid establishment is contained in Shepherd (1975), whose work demonstrates the importance of the famine in Wollo province and the government's handling of relief needs in setting the stage, perhaps even being the final straw that broke the back of the Selassie regime and ushered in the revolutionary situation (see also Hussein, 1976). A general description and analysis of the Ethiopian revolution has recently been provided by Cuban journalist Rául Valdés Vivó (1978).
10. *New York Times,* May 2, 1976.
11. Ibid., April 4, 1976.
12. Ibid., May 31, 1977; article by Robert Trumbull.
13. For comments on this relief program by USAID assistance administrator for the Sahel Relief and current chairman of the OECD Development Committee, concerned with long-

term Sahel planning, see Maurice Williams, "On U.S. Assistance to Parched West Africa," *New York Times*, February 16, 1974.

14. *Marchés Tropicaux*, No. 1638, April 1, 1977; U.S. House of Representatives, Committee on International Relations, Sub-Committee on Africa, Hearings of March 23, 1977, p. 72. The estimate was offered by W. Haven North, acting assistant administrator of the African Bureau of USAID.

15. The main exception to the U.S. figures is Israel, which received a whopping $215.14 per capita in 1978. A parallel but different persepctive on the U.S. motivations for participating so heavily in Sahel development is given in Robinson (1978).

16. See, for example, the OECD's official history and description (OECD, 1971). The OECD's Development Assistance Centre, formed in 1962, states that "The purpose of the Centre is to bring together the knowledge and experience available in Member countries of both economic development and the formulation and execution of general policies of economic aid; to adapt such knowledge and experience to the actual needs of countries or regions in the process of development and to put the results at the disposal of the countries by appropriate means. The Centre has a special and autonomous position within the OECD which enables it to enjoy scientific independence in the execution of its task. Nevertheless, the Centre can draw upon the experience and knowledge available in the OECD in the development field" (OECD, 1973). The Development Assistance Committee, structurally separate from the Development Centre, functions as a subagency of the Council and Executive Committee of the OECD.

17. Daddah was overthrown in a coup on July 19, 1978; he has since been arrested and charged with corruption.

18. The most recent statement of the Club on the Sahel Development Program cites the FAO, SCET International and SEDES as "quality work," but it makes no mention of the M.I.T. Study, which now appears on its way to development-theory oblivion (Club of the Sahel, 1977, p. 4).

19. Poncet (1974) also contributed a microstudy of the Dallois region of Niger.

20. *New York Times*, September 12, 1973.

21. Information collected in interviews conducted at the Sahel Documentation Center, East Lansing, Michigan, May 22, 1977. Many of the information-gathering problems have been analyzed for the MSU Sahel Documentation Center by Walsh (1976).

22. MUSAT is housed in the science libraries of the University of California at Riverside, 92502.

23. Horowitz, 1976; Tutweiler et al., 1976; Horowitz, 1977; Brokensha, 1977; McPherson, (in preparation). The Sahel reports from the Institute for Development Anthropology cover the same materials and with many of the same experts, whose reports are shortened or expanded versions of those given at other Sahel-related colloquia, probably often also paid for from USAID funds.

In June 1975, for example, the IDA held a colloquium entitled "Colloquium on the Effects of Drought on the Productive Strategies of Sudano-Sahelian Herdsmen and Farmers: Implications for Development." It took place in Niamey, Niger, and consisted of a series of working groups that issued short, superficial reports and a series of "communications." These included presentations by several Sahelian social scientists and several French and American experts. The presentations by Edmond Bernus, Ralph Faulkingham, and R. C. Sawadoga, at least, were re-readings of materials they had presented in one or more other colloquia of a similar type and very likely had some of the same audience (see Horowitz, 1976). Nonetheless, the IDA's reports contain some of the few critical viewpoints on the Sahel Development Program to be found in the USAID-supported literature.

The Institute's *The Anthropology of Rural Development in the Sahel—Proposals for Research*, for example, takes a critical view of the "tragedy of the commons" approach and from time to time raises the issue of popular participation and the example of the People's Republic of China. In general, there is an emphasis in the report on the need for "development from below," but it is not clear how far the Institute would be willing to push this point in view of their funding from USAID. Probably they have reconciled themselves with the position of consultants who will provide data, analysis, and trained researchers on a contract basis so that it is up to the contracting agency to make the actual policy decisions. The actual use of the Institute's work is thus "not their department." See Brokensha, et al., 1977. A general discussion of some of the issues is contained in Almy (1977).

As far as we can tell, there has been no official response to the IDA's controversial appraisals which may have been filed, taken into consideration, or just overlooked. In any case, a major portion of IDA's first reports has been devoted to making a case for the need for social science consulting and research and proposals for various research undertakings that might be useful to development planners and which IDA would presumably be able to carry out.

24. The Program for International Development, Clark University, Worcester, Massachusetts 01610.

25. This source exists in an English edition as well as the French cited here.

26. The origin of the series title is anyone's guess, but presumably it is intended to be in keeping with current trends in development ideology, which call for popular participation, avoidance of "top-down" programs, etc. The question as to whether there is any genuine "development from below" in the Sahel Development Program will be taken up in the following chapter. It is interesting to note that of the OLC's 18 members, two are directly involved with Sahel projects: Michael Horowitz, also of the Institute for Development Anthropology, and Carl Eicher, OLC chairperson, who is also professor of agricultural economics at Michigan State University, where much USAID-sponsored Sahel work takes place. It seems unlikely, however, that these two individuals alone involved the OLC. More likely, it was part of the general mobilization of scientific and academic resources described in this section.

27. A whole new set of special professions is developing in the area of equipment design, processing, and interpretation and vertification of photo materials. Anthropologists involved in the initial experiments with possible social interpretation of the photos have already proposed the establishment of a committee within the American Anthropological Association to take up and make recommendations on the potential moral and ethical issues that may arise from these new endeavors (Reining, et al., 1975). The members of the Research Workshop did not, however, list any of the potential issues, although presumably they would include possible military and counterinsurgency uses.

28. USAID, in fact, has commissioned a report on just this subject, with special reference to the Sahel and with special emphasis on possible uses in development planning. See Earth Satellite Croporation, 1974.

29. Fanale, 1974; MacLeod, 1974a, 1975, and 1976; MacLeod et al., 1975; Reining, 1975; and Earth Satellite Corporation, 1974.

30. See, for example, Richards, ed., 1975, and Dalby et al., 1977. The latter publication is of particular interest because of the introductory essay "Lessons of a Crisis" by French anthropologist Claude Raynaut, printed in French and English in its entirety. The remainder of the papers, however, with one or two exceptions, would seem to indicate that Raynaut's ideas on the intellectual approaches to the famine and to postfamine developments are not widely shared or even thought about by the great majority of his English-speaking colleagues.

7

The Sahel Development Program

In May 1977, OECD published its *Strategy and Programme for Drought Control and Development in the Sahel.* This draft document contains the results of many of the last several years of studies, conferences, symposia, and meetings. It also represents the essential orientation and commitment agreed upon by the various donor countries and their Sahelian counterparts at the CILSS-Club of the Sahel meeting of May 30-June 1, 1977, and previously approved by the CILSS Council of Ministers in Ouagadougou, Upper Volta, on April 25-28, 1977 (OECD, 1977, preface).

The Sahel Development Program is beyond doubt a tour de force. Encompassing a gigantic region, several ecological zones, eight national governments, numerous ethnic and linguistic groups, and several national and international donor organizations, the program has also brought together technical and social science experts, development planners, and government officials to produce an overall plan to rid the Sahel of food shortages and ecological deterioration, to overcome dependency, to raise the incomes and quality of life for 26 million people over widely dispersed zones, and to set a potential model for development planning in other regions.

The program envisions a three-stage process for accomplishing these goals. The period 1977-82 has been dubbed "first generation" projects. These are designed to alleviate the worst effect of the drought and to start the process of food production and ecological recovery. It is also hoped during this period that food production in the area can be doubled on the basis of new seeds and other technological advances (interview with

OECD Sahel adviser in Paris, October 18, 1977). This is to be followed by a "second generation" of medium-range projects running from 1982-90, not yet specified as to content. A "third generation" will encompass 1990-2000, the latter year being the one in which food self-sufficiency is hoped for. The third generation of projects includes water-control schemes such as large dams and irrigation works that cannot be easily begun until appropriate engineering research and planning has been undertaken.

This three-generation approach, with a target year of 2000, is heavily influenced by the FAO's 25-year plan for the Sahel, which outlines the various population projects and food consumption needs of the region and then breaks these down into their possible components in terms of the production resources that might be mobilized to satisfy them. The CILSS-Club of the Sahel program statement adopts many of the FAO statistics as a baseline on which to build various project proposals and pursue directions for research and planning.

But what is the actual content of the Sahel Development Program, and what have the Sahelians and their donors proposed to do? The program is organized around three general issues: major strategic options, sectoral programs, and the question of priorities and interconnections. We will first present the basic framework of the program and then discuss each part in more detail, noting, on the basis of the analysis presented earlier in this study, some of the questions that should be asked about the possibility of the program ridding the Sahel of drought and famine.

STRATEGIC OPTIONS AND GOALS

The strategic options have been chosen in terms of the main goal of food self-sufficiency. This is not to be misconstrued as absolute autonomy; rather it is part of a general pattern of agricultural development that includes the maintainence of export crops and the development of a "new ecological equilibrium." In addition, the document notes that food self-sufficiency will almost certainly have to come first at the regional level; that is, some individual states will not achieve it as soon as others. Therefore, intraregional food exports will be necessary. Based on the FAO study of population-growth projections and environmental resources, the CILSS-Club proposal calls for a doubling of millet and sorghum production by the year 2000, a 70-fold increase in wheat production, a 5-fold increase in rice, an increase of 17 times in sugar production, a doubling in the number of cattle, 2.5 times the number of sheep and goats, and a doubling of fish catch, compared with 1970 statistics (OECD, 1977, p. 9). These increases are emphatically stated to be the minimum necessary for the region.

Agriculture

An important aspect of the strategic-options section is the choice of areas to emphasize in raising general food production. Agriculture is the key, and grain is the major element of crop production. The program document opts for a major emphasis on rain-fed agriculture, or "dryland farming," which, it is noted, will account for 75 to 80 percent of all Sahelian food even in the year 2000 (OECD, 1977, p. 16). Nevertheless, there will be a general shift from emphasis in overseas donor funding on rain-fed agriculture toward irrigated agriculture—especially rice—as the project approaches the year 2000. This is because of the expected larger gains in productivity in irrigated production and its greater capacity to resist drought conditions once dams and other water control devices have been constructed. Overall, the agricultural part of the program revolves around four major goals: to double the dryland production by the end of the century, to make dryland crops less vulnerable to drought, to maintain employment in the rural sector, and to improve the living conditions of rural people (OECD, 1977, pp. 17-18). These four goals are to be achieved by three primary mechanisms: the opening of new lands for production, the increase in productivity of lands currently in production, and the development of new seed varieties that will mature earlier and be more resistant to drought (OECD, 1977, pp. 18-20). Each mechanism is detailed in terms of traditional Western approaches to agricultural development, including fertilizers, crop protection, extension services of the governments to the farmers, and so forth.

Irrigation

A related section of the program deals with the special problems of irrigated agriculture. The report notes that "irrigated farming is as yet feebly developed in the Sahel," and it observes that of the rice consumed in the Sahel in 1976, 40 percent was from irrigated farming, 20 percent from rain-fed agriculture, and 40 percent was imported. The CILSS-Club program calls for an increase of 500,000 ha. under irrigation by 2000, and notes as well that *all* wheat and sugar production will require irrigation (OECD, 1977, pp. 27-29). The potential for irrigation in the Sahel is great, with the

Table 7.1. Irrigated Farm Land in Thousands of Hectares

	1976	*1982*	*1990*	*2000*
Gambia	1.5	9.5	14.0	19.7
Upper Volta	7.7	21.3	58.8	104.0
Mali	107.0	232.0	392.0	524.0
Mauritania	1.4	15.0	30.0	70.0
Niger	4.8	17.5	33.0	52.5
Senegal	96.0	129.3	212.8	372.8
Chad	5.8	23.8	49.3	71.8
Totals	224.2	448.4	789.9	1,214.8

main river basins offering a possible 150 billion cubic meters of water per year to cover a potential 4 million ha. of land, as compared with only 80,000 ha. in 1976 (pp. 27 and 31). The development of irrigation must await long-term planning, however, and even by 2000 it will account for only 15 to 20 percent of all grain output in the region. Table 7.1 gives a picture of the CILSS-Club projections for area coverage of irrigated farming in the three generations of the Sahel Development Program.

Wells

The program calls for a massive increase in well construction to improve village water supplies. The goal is to have 37,000 modern wells, 33,000 village boreholes, and 1,000 pastoral boreholes between 1978 and 1990.

Harvest Protection

The program notes in particular that "due to a reduction of fallow time and the introduction of a smaller number of selected cereal varieties it will be easier for crop pests to attack and reproduce" (OECD, 1977, p. 41), and it calls for a six-point program as outlined in the FAO study: (1) strengthening of national crop-protection services; (2) development of an integrated campaign against the main food-crop pests; (3) strengthening action against migratory pests; (4) protecting infested harvests; (5) rodent control; and (6) creation of a documentation and training center. This program alone has an estimated cost of $69 million for the first generation alone (1977-82), with additional costs to be estimated after evaluation in 1982.

Livestock Production

Increased social and economic knowledge of herding systems and the development of "pastoral management projects" are called for. The major aspects are animal health projects, use of animals for agricultural work (animal traction), and development of marketing institutions and the sale of animals traditionally held by herders.

Fishing

The potential of fishing has long been neglected in the Sahel. The study notes that the 9,500,000 ha. of continental coastal shelf and 8,300,000 ha. of lakes and flood plains make the Sahel a potentially rich producer of fish and fish products. Strikingly, the report notes that fish were consumed in the Sahel at the rate of 15 kg. per person in 1976, as compared to 15.3 kg. of meat, while 60 percent of the of the fish catch is exported. The program calls for research and expert consultation to develop fishing as a source of protein (pp. 59-62).

Human Resources

The health needs of Sahalian populations are to be emphasized, with special emphasis given to the problems of employment and to the need for village-level health systems.

Ecology

This section tries to place the problem of production increases within the broader context of the need for "a new balanced ecosystem" and calls for the development of technologies compatible with ecological equilibrium, measures to protect and restore soil fertility, and, especially, the need for reforestation and the protection of existing forests. The goal is to develop 10,800 ha. of forests near urban areas, 84,000 ha. of rural tree replanting, and 17,000 ha. of "industrial plantations." The program notes that forests are indispensable in protecting soils from water run-off erosion, feeding cattle (which eat the low-growing leaves), and providing firewood to urban dwellers. Forest areas also harbor wildlife species that might make a contribution to the food supply through the development of "game cropping" projects. The main emphasis of the forestry projects is on the training of forestry experts for the various countries. The report notes that "we should not delude ourselves; it will not be possible to reach the objective of a new, stable ecosystem by the year 1990" (OECD, 1977, p. 82).

Technology

The adaptation of technology includes in particular water extraction, remote sensing (i.e., use of satellites to gather data), new sources of energy (solar energy, fermentation of gases), the use of plant-residues storage, and food processing, "since the development of agro-industries could contribute to improving living conditions in the Sahel." Also called for is an examination of the current state of the long-neglected traditional industries and artisan professions in the Sahel, including blacksmithing, rural crafts, and traditional techniques of conservation, such as drying and smoking (OECD, 1977, pp. 85-86.).

Marketing, Prices, Storage

Grains such as millet, sorghum, and rice constitute the main staple foods in the region. The study notes that baseline data are very difficult to obtain and that there is a wide divergence between government marketing agencies, their statistics, and the private grain trade, which accounts for an unknown but probably large part of the marketing process for cereals in many of the countries. The CILSS and Club representatives finally agreed only that there should be collection and analysis of more data in advance of further planning on these issues. On the question of storage, however, a more thorough consensus was reached: to build several storage facilities in certain countries, such as Mali and Mauritania, where grain-relief supplies had been difficult to transport during the 1968-74 drought and famine (OECD, 1977, p. 95).

Transportation

Regarding transportation and other basic infrastructure in the Sahel, the document notes that previous roads and other transport and communications facilities built during the colonial period linked the various Sahel countries with their nearby port neighbors rather than with each other. Thus there is a great need for a "major East-West artery" in the form of a permanent, all-weather highway that would allow trade, imports, development projects, and a means for access of relief supplies during the period before the development program has achieved its goals—and should another drought occur. It also calls for certain special road connections for specific development projects.

"Coherences"

A final section of the program deals with several general problems, such as the interrelatedness of the various sectors and projects, the setting of priorities among and between projects, and the difficult problem of establishing adequate criteria for evaluating projects. Much of this section constitutes a sort of "in-debate" for development specialists and may not be immediately familiar to the outside reader. One of the most pressing problems noted is that of ensuring that a project in one sector (e.g., agriculture) will not harmfully effect the development of another sector (e.g., livestock). Other important problems are the monitoring of the food-increase projects for possible ecological damage and the "coherence" of the projects of short, medium, and long term, or first, second, and third generations, so that each truly prepares the way for the success of the next.

In dealing with the problem of setting priorities, the Synthesis Working Group notes the major need for increased numbers and improved quality in data gathering and basic research for a region that is not well known to scientists. Therefore, the group proposed several criteria (OECD, 1977, p. 113):

1. The role of the project in securing food self-sufficiency for the Sahel.
2. Its contribution to food security in case of drought.
3. Its ecological impact.
4. The possibility it offers for large-scale rural participation.
5. Its acceptability among the people.[1]
6. Secondary effects of the project.
7. Effects on the balance of payments (presumably at the national and/or regional level).
8. Reduction of social imbalances.[2]

9. Reduction of regional imbalances.
10. Cost and duration of the project.

The group also notes the complex problems associated with the preferences given by some Sahelian governments for certain types of projects, and the preferences—sometimes quite different—of certain funding agencies and donor countries based on the historical development of aid programs.

Finally, the report notes that, given the pressing needs of the Sahelian peoples and the long-term nature of the recovery project, the criterion of "profitability" or short-term payback of an aid grant or loan, at least in terms of the national or regional economy of the Sahel, should be set aside. This is presented as though it were a somewhat new step for the Western donor community. In the words of the Synthesis Working Group:

> Experience has shown how unawareness of long-term objectives coupled with the application of classical criteria of profitability, without consideration for non-quantifiable, non-marketable elements, has led to imbalances, desertification, soil deterioration and, finally, an extremely alarming situation for the future of the Sahel, a situation which will require a long time to reverse. It is high time to work on identifying better adapted project selection criteria. In any case, it is useless to attempt to quantify the profitability of actions that are vital to the Sahel. [OECD, 1977, p. 112][3]

In sum, then, the Sahel Development Program appears as a special, intensive, perhaps even "crash" program in which the Western donor countries are prepared to set aside their traditional concepts of profitability to help a desperately impoverished people and region recover their environment, their food supply, and a basis for eventual independent development. It is a program worked out within the framework of a new type of organization, the regional development committee, or CILSS, and with an entire region and several individual nations working together both at the donor and recipient levels. But despite the innovative structures and the innovative terms and proposals, it is still necessary to ask whether the Sahel Development Program is conceived with a real commitment to move in new directions. A closer look at some features of the program in its written form reveals some cause for serious misgivings.

A CRITICAL ANALYSIS

(A) At the very heart of the Sahel Development Program is the planned increase in staple-food production with the goal of food self-sufficiency by the year 2000. The CILSS-Club proposals on this topic reflect, however, some problems and disagreements as to precisely what the concept of food self-sufficiency really means. On the one hand, the Synthesis Group criticizes the idea of the Sahel producing mostly cash crops for sale on the world market and translating these sales into purchases of necessary food goods. In the words of the group, this kind of reasoning "demonstrates a serious misunderstanding of Sahelian realities and the deep aspirations of the people of this region" (OECD, 1977, p. 5). The group also notes the dependency of the region on world market prices for its cash-crop exports and concludes that "after the painful famine experience, it is inconceivable that the Sahelians be asked to rely on potentially insecure foreign sources for the daily food staples" (OECD, 1977, p. 5).

Having stated this, however, the group goes on to propose that cash crops are a necessary item in the maintainance of the balance of trade and for the acquisition of capital goods, including modern agricultural equipment and fertilizers, which it is said cannot be produced in the region. The report summarizes the position of the CILSS-Club countries as one of "stressing food crops while giving proper attention to cash crops" (OECD, 1977, p. 5).

There are at least two major problems with this position. First, it is really an extremely vague orientation when one considers the real-life situation in the Sahel. As we have shown in previous chapters, *peanuts, cotton, cattle, and food crops have often been forced to compete with one another for resources.* It is not at all clear how the program will deal with this problem. If land is taken from peanut production, for example, and turned over primarily to grains, will the donor nations make up for the loss of foreign exchange on the grounds that staple-food production is being increased? Or will they charge the Sahelians with not giving "adequate attention" to cash crops?

Closely related to this is the implication that the CILSS-Club intend the cash crops to be part of the actual financing of the program. Hidden in the vague language of "adequate attention" lies the possibility that if economic problems intensify in the wealthy capitalist donor nations, they may demand more and more Sahelian cash crops to generate the "foreign exchange" needed to purchase necessary industrial products. As we have shown, the dependency situation of the past 30 years has rendered the Sahelian peanut and cotton exports increasingly *ineffective* in producing revenues as fast as the price increases of goods from the industrialized countries. This occurred despite artificially high prices guaranteed by France—and these high prices have been abolished since 1968. The donor nations have apparently made a clear choice of strategy in the vague terms of the program. Instead of making a firm and clear commitment of the estimated resources necessary to achieve food (i.e., staple grain) self-sufficiency by the year 2000, they have left in a kind of contract sleeper clause by which the development program ties the Sahelian countries to the same mechanisms of dependency that played such an important role in producing drought vulnerability in the first place.

Finally, the Synthesis Group never deals with what may be the most important question of all concerning the production of staple foods. As production increases and more of the grains are brought into market exchanges, the so-called subsistence, staple crops will be transformed into cash crops at the local, regional, national, and even international level. The document fails to consider what will happen to grain surpluses produced in one region as a result of a successful development project. Will they be used as staple foods for the country and/or region? Will they be exported by the governments in need of foreign exchange as they become increasingly tied to Club donor nations' industrial equipment for their continued production of food? Will they be slipped out of the region by money-hungry traders who can get higher prices in oil-rich, heavily populated regions such as Nigeria? To give but one example of this range of problems, figures from Mali indicate that in 1975-76 as much as 10,000 tons of paddy rice were sold to markets in the Ivory Coast (Berg, 1977). To the east, all along the Niger-Nigeria border runs an all-weather highway that can be broken off of at almost any point for easy border crossing. Despite the government's installation of police patrol posts every few kilometers, it is suspected that much millet passes through to the Nigerian market.

The CILSS-Club proposals on staple and cash crops remain tied to the superficial notion that a crop is a "cash" or a "staple" depending on whether it forms a major part of the diet or will be devoted to industrial or other uses. To label a crop a "staple" does not ensure that it will be eaten by those who need it most.

Another major element of the program is the long-term plan for an increase in irrigated as opposed to rain-fed or dryland farming. Even though the program planners recognize that by the year 2000, 75 to 80 percent of Sahelian agricultural production will be in dryland farming, they postulate a growing role for the river basins in providing the food supply for the region. It is assumed that irrigated farming will be less susceptible to drought and will provide a dependable baseline production. Evidence from several areas of the world seems to indicate as well that irrigated farming has a very high potential for production increases as compared to dryland farming.

But the Sahel development planners are concerned with the problem of what they call "human resources" as related to the development of irrigated farming. Noting that "passing from dryland farming to irrigated cultivation assumes significant changes in agricultural techniques and human behavior," the report continues with the following assessment of the human resources problem (OECD, 1977, pp. 31-32):

> In the traditional system, man submits himself individually to the climatic conditions and adapts his techniques to the climate. His attitude is semi-passive. Irrigation cultivation requires him to constantly make decisions concerning his production and adopt an adaptive attitude year round. He must work hand in hand with other producers who have equal rights to water. The effectiveness of irrigation depends entirely on the solidarity of the members of the group and the cohesion of the groups themselves.

One cannot help but be struck by the array of uninformed prejudices in this characterization. Readers can check for themselves in Chapter 2 whether the "traditional system" of the Sahel involved individual submission to climatic conditions and the implied lack of organization and initiative on the part of farmers and herders. Terms such as "semi-passive" hearken back more easily to colonial-period racial stereotypes than to appraisals of an economic situation.

Even more revealing, however, is the concluding part of this section, in which it is stated "that is why the 'irrigation farmer' needs special training" (OECD, 1977, p. 32). It is undoubtedly a historical irony that the Western donor nations, having participated actively or observed passively while colonial forces did their best to wreck and destroy the solidarity and cohesion of groups of people in West Africa for so many centuries, are now preparing to undertake the task of training irrigation farmers in group solidarity and cohesion.[4]

Finally, and perhaps most serious of all, we wonder if the Synthesis Group had seen any of the anthropological/sociological research on Sahelian communities today in those areas where irrigation is to be introduced. On what *evidence* do they base their idea that the social prerequisites, as they state them, are not already present, and how do they know that the main problem is not to be found in the relation between these farming groups and government officials, large landowners, and merchants rather than within and among the farmers? We shall reexamine these questions with specific field research data in Chapters 8 and 9.

A third aspect of the program that raises some questions is contained in the section on village hydraulics and the water supply. Here (pp. 37-38) the Synthesis Group calls for 71,000 new wells and boreholes, 1,000 of them in herding areas. Not a word of concern creeps into the program document regarding possible dangers of well digging or even of the need for thorough research into the prerequisites for a successful well-digging program. Given the fairly frequent criticisms of well-digging programs, the omission of even a note in the report suggests that the wells—or at least promises of wells—may be a kind of gift offer to Sahelian governments eager to show villagers and pastoralists their commitment to progress rather than a thoroughly planned and carefully prepared strategy for water control.

The crop and harvest protection program (pp. 41-45) also is seriously lacking in some of the most important of modern cropping techniques, such as intercrop spacing, which provides natural barriers to pest infestation. The importance of pest control is greatly increased by the planned food expansion as summarized in the report:

> . . . the crop intensification programmes advocated for the coming years will almost inevitably cause new outbreaks and crop diseases. Due to a reduction of fallow time and the introduction of a smaller number of selected cereal varieties it will be easier for crop pests to attack and reproduce. [OECD, 1977, p. 41]

After noting this unfortunate relationship between the development plans and crop pests—a relationship which has been established in many other developing countries as a result of experiences with the Green Revolution—the report goes on to outline a strategy mostly aimed at improving the general administrative and scientific resources in Sahelian countries to monitor pests and the establishment of "an integrated campaign against the main food crop pests." Despite the several negative experiences in developed and developing countries with chemical pesticides, no statement is made as to the use of these versus spacing and other biological techniques. The program simply does not mention the new frontiers of pest control research. Many new techniques should be tried in the Sahel *as the program develops*, rather than waiting for painful lessons to be learned. It is difficult not to suspect that the Sahel nations may find themselves recipients of dumped Western chemical pesticides during the course of the next 25 years of development programs.

One of the most interesting sections of the plan deals with livestock production. The livestock team is particularly emphatic in its call for more fundamental research into the "potential of natural resources and range management," including ecological and social research in livestock regions (OECD, 1977, p. 49). The team also provides several pages of commentary on the need for development of research into the relations between herding and agriculture so that an improved ecological balance can be found between animal production and crops in areas where these two systems intermix. The livestock team notes several social elements of these systems and their interrelationships, including the important problem of land rights.

Nonetheless, the livestock group was not able to break through the barrier of oversimplification and euphemism in characterizing the current situation:

> The numbers of cattle in the Sahel increased substantially during the 1960s. Animal health measures and development of watering sites encouraged herd growth. However, this increase was not accompanied by any notable change in methods of raising livestock which remained essentially traditional. As a result, overgrazed areas started developing in several countries and it is probable that by the time the drought set in the herd size had reached a size incompatible with the ecological equilibrium of the region. [OECD, 1977, p. 46]

The "essentially traditional" methods alluded to here are in no way a part of the problem. Overgrazing resulted from a series of historical and social developments, including food-production-increase projects for both crops and animals—the essence of the livestock team's own program.

Further, on the same page, the team notes that "the economic equilibrium of the Sahel was improved through meat exports to coastal countries." We have tried to show that the economic equilibrium of the Sahel countries did not improve at all but rather deteriorated during the recent past. Certainly at the local Sahelian level, the development of meat exports was a major factor leading to the *disequilibrium* of Sahelian ecological systems and did not aid the economy except insofar as these exports may have enriched a small number of Sahelian traders and government officials. Nowhere in the team's report are such issues alluded to. One can only wonder what sort of real program will emerge from a document that ignores much of the recent background to the problems.

The section of the study on the fishing industry also gives rise for some concern. The report notes that fish provided 15 kg. per person annually, as compared with 15.3 kg. provided by livestock. Thus fishing was actually equal to livestock in its contribution to the diet. The fishing team notes, however, that these figures hold *despite the fact that 60 percent of the Sahelian fish catch is exported*.[5]

Given the present situation in the Sahel, and the very difficult immediate future for livestock with the drought-induced massive depletion of herds, one might expect at least a consideration of the possibility that more of the region's fish exports ought to be kept within the Sahel. These could provide protein and other nutritional needs, which are not going to be met by the program for many years to come. But apparently exports are not to be criticized by this group, for the fisheries team waxes enthusiastic about the potential of the region "to envisage the possibility of substantial development of exports which, by the year 2000 could amount to about a million tons or more and thus serve as an appreciable source of foreign currency for the Sahel" (OECD, 1977, p. 60). One wonders if the $700 million proposed for fisheries is to be eventually repaid by the foreign currency earnings of the fish exports while the Sahelian diet continues to be inadequate.

The human resources section of the program contains an explicit call for "mass participation in development" and a rather sharp critique of the education and training institutes of the Sahel for developing specialists with little or no knowledge of how to work in local rural Sahelian conditions. Unfortunately, the working group is not able to go beyond a vague reference to the need to break away from "Western models," and little in the program indicates how mass participation is to come about. Indeed, the report would seem to indicate that the authors of this section consider village health programs to be the highest form of "mass participation." Granted, an effective village health program *presupposes* popular involvement and nonelitist medical technicians, but the team does not even consider how such a popular involvement is to come about. In fact, the question as to whether there might be political reforms necessary to make possible such an involvement is not even hinted at. The only reference is a general comment that "The institutions require substantial modifications" (OECD, 1977, p. 69), but this turns out to be a call for a vague sort of "localization policy" and the possibility of "village assistants chosen by and responsible to the communities" who would receive improved health training (OECD, 1977, p. 69).

In the section on Ecology and Environment (pp. 72-82), the working group notes as important causative factors in environmental deterioration "population growth and the introduction of cash crops which in turn shortened the duration of fallow period, and acceleration of the rate of deforestation, and contributed to further deterioration and erosion of the soil," and "the increase in herd size which resulted in overgrazing." The team concludes that "The drought both intensified and manifested a disequilibrium which was already taking form in many places in the Sahel" (OECD, 1977, p. 72). But the ecology team, having made these observations, then switches rapidly into an elaborate discussion and program on the need for replanting and the less-intensive utilization of Sahelian forests. The team portrays a rather pessimistic short- and medium-term future, concluding that "we should not delude ourselves; it will not be possible to reach the objective of a new, stable ecosystem by the year 1990" (OECD, 1977, p. 82). The team also notes that while several forestry projects have been proposed, donor nations have financed only a few. This seems to indicate that "reforestation in the Sahel is not yet well appreciated" (OECD, 1977, p. 77). The role of various social groups in producing what the team calls the "very alarming situation" of the Sahelian forests is nowhere referred to, nor are the overseas business interests, peanut magnates, merchants and bureaucrats mentioned.

Thus, despite the team's partial awareness of the real processes of change, it has not been able to use that awareness to develop proposals for any specific programs. In the end, the "rural population" in general is called upon for education and a change in its way of life.

"Marketing, prices, and storage" appears to have produced the most controversial part of the program and the most heated debates, at least within the working groups and synthesis team. The problem of storage was rather easily resolved by the proposal to build several facilities, particularly in Mali and Mauritania, where grains could be kept against a possible future drought. But with marketing and prices, CILSS and the Club were forced to debate social and political elements in the Sahel.

The basic disagreement seems to have arisen over the materials presented by the University of Michigan CRED team, which analyzed the Sahel grain trade and marketing structure. Although evidence on all aspects of Sahelian grain trading is rather skimpy, the CRED team concluded that the present marketing boards run by governments ostensibly for the protection of farmer-producers in the economy are not working. The CRED team also surmised that traders were apparently not gouging the farmers and that a return to greater free-market orientation would likely result in a more efficient and effective distribution of grains. The Synthesis Group attempted to portray this position as an "alternate way of viewing the behavior of the farmers . . . called 'cautious farmers and competitive markets'" (OECD, 1977, p. 89), and they contrasted this with the model of "uninformed farmers, rendered powerless when in the grasp of aggressive private traders." Why the farmers are considered "uninformed" rather than merely desperately in need of cash to pay taxes or buy other necessities or to repay loans is not explained.

But at the level of the recommendations implied in these alternatives, the Synthesis Group was compelled to be more specific and less gingerly. After noting the consultants' advice that "legal measures and encouragement for private trade" be made a central issue, the team continued that "nearly all the members of the team, and virtually all the Sahelian representatives strongly opposed this proposal" (OECD, 1977, p. 91).

The most important questions, however, are not investigated. Why cannot the governments of any of the Sahelian countries, many of them under military leadership, better control the grain trade over which they have an official monopoly or near-monopoly? Are the grain traders too clever, too politically powerful? Is the military too corrupt, receiving payoffs to turn over much of its trade to the private sector? Or can the traders offer farmers higher prices at any given time because they are operating in conjunction with outside markets such as Nigeria or the Ivory Coast? The long-term effects of these sales outside the Sahel are to drive up consumer costs and impoverish the country's capital investment budget or put them back on the international dole looking for food replacements for those that have been lost. The CILSS-Club Synthesis Report, by looking at marketing and pricing in narrow technical terms and with two briefly discussed models that include only farmers and traders, cannot begin to come to grips with the full range of problems related to marketing in the Sahel. It can only be wondered if all the necessary types of programs can even be laid on the table for discussion. What *would* CILSS and the Club do about the leakage of grain to bigger, more lucrative markets in the southern coastal countries? What will they do about the possible political ramifications of increasing producer prices, which in turn might bring about protests from urban consumers who do not themselves live off their own farm production and are often highly sensitive to food price changes? The report notes only that "This is a problem related to the problem of income distribution, a policy to be determined by each government" (OECD, 1977, p. 92), and it concludes with a call for additional research. The regional and international organization of CILSS and the Club seem to be unable to transcend the national elites and their interests concerning the control of something as major as the buying and selling of staple foods.

A GENERAL EVALUATION

Finally, what can be said of the Sahel Development Program as a whole? It is definitely an ambitious and massive undertaking, and much of it does break some ground bureaucratically and in terms of the organization of planning and implementation. But the central question of the program, as viewed from the perspective of this study, must surely be: Will it overcome and reverse environmental destruction and set the region on a course that will lead it to some optimum food production system and a base for further economic development? Here there are some overall problems with the program.

One serious difficulty with the entire structure of the program is its strong emphasis on extremely rapid increases in food production. This emphasis is *so* strong that one could almost describe it as a *headlong rush to intensify the exploitation of a dangerously degraded environment.* Despite the language of the program document, which seems to indicate from time to time an awareness of potential ecological problems that will be associated with the drive for rapid food production increases, the drafters of the program have demonstrated no awareness of just how serious those problems have been in other regions of the world where environmental relations are not nearly as delicate.

The Sahel has in some ways only been "discovered" by the international Western community since the drought—or since the drought and the coinciding upsurge of revolutionary activity in Africa. But many other regions, such as Southeast Asia, Latin America, and India, have long been subjected to development programs that, if not similar in their regional sweep and bureaucratic innovativeness, have nonetheless provided ample evidence of serious drawbacks to such rapid increases in food production as that envisioned by the Sahel Development Program in a region far more delicate in its ecology. The numerous studies of the Green Revolution in Asia, for example, have indicated that the headlong rush there to "food self-sufficiency" has often resulted in such tragedies as loss of genetic variability in plants and resistance to local pests, leading to widespread harvest loss, use of chemical pesticides that have killed fish and other necessary protein supplies, and other side effects that have led to *greater* rather than less ecological and food supply vulnerability.[6] The drafters of the program do not even allude to this important body of information. To what extent, then, is the program really a culmination of current scientific knowledge as opposed to a hasty political project?

Related to the headlong rush to food production increases is the relative absence of major programs for ecological regeneration of even maintainance. Although the program document calls for maintaining the environment adequately, the forestry team notes that reforestation—one of the few major specific programs for environmental rehabilitation—is not receiving much attention from funding sources.

Even more seriously, the program contains little if any reference to the idea that there might be more than one general model of development. A few comments on the advisability of mass participation are countered by a general view implied or stated throughout the text: Development means increasing production, which means improved technology, which requires more educated managers and technicians, all of which must be funded from outside. There is no real consideration of the role that different groups in the societies of the Sahel may be playing vis-à-vis each other, of the concept of classes or interest groups, and their potentially inconsistent interests, or even of the more generalized theoretical problem of how the interests of individuals and the society can be made more harmonious. Aside from a few criticisms of French policies, there is little said of the historical conditions that preceded the drought or of the current social and political institutions of the Sahelian countries. Although never explicitly stated, the program is based on a theory of development that ignores the importance of class structures. The importance of this neglect requires a look at some actual projects underway in the Sahel.

THE PROGRAM AT GROUND LEVEL

How well are Sahel development projects doing? We attempted to gain insight into this question in early 1978 during a four-and-a-half month research trip through three Sahel countries—Senegal, Mali, and Niger. We visited project sites, conducted interviews with project directors and/or technical staff, and met with villagers or local staff of several projects. In addition, we were able to attend an eight-day conference of the livestock team of CILSS, which was held in Bamako, Mali, in late February 1978, during which the views of scientific and managerial personnel as well as government officials could be compared. Although only a small portion of the gigantic program, our sample includes projects of every major type and a wide range of social and environmental situations as well as representative projects from the FAO, at least four different countries—France, Holland, Belgium, and the United States—and four nongovernmental agencies. We read project documents, annexes, statistical tables, newspaper reports, evaluations, published articles, and conference presentations. We spoke with embassy personnel, USAID project directors, technical experts, Peace Corps volunteers, U.N. officials, anthropologists, church-aid staff, missionaries, Sahelian social scientists, chauffeurs, other researchers, peasant association leaders, and, in a few cases, Sahelian farmers and herders. We traveled nearly everywhere by ground transport, despite the cost and difficulty, in order to gain as much exposure as possible to actual physical conditions in the Sahel. In nearly every case, we were able to combine several written sources with interviews and on-the-spot observations, so our research, while containing neither an elaborate examination of any single case nor a full cross-section of the entire program, does provide several in-depth perspectives on the current state of the program.

In all the research conducted in the Sahel, we attempted to gain insight into the same kinds of questions that are posed in the analysis of the Sahel Development Program document in this chapter. How will the project contribute toward restoration and preservation or improvement of the Sahelian ecology; how will the project lead to eventual self-sustaining development; how will the project help overcome drought and famine vulnerability; and how will the project benefit the majority of Sahelians—the poorest farmers and animal herders?

After completing the research trip and analyzing the evidence made available to us, we have drawn a general conclusion: *The Sahel Development Program is not working*. Given the finances available, it is not contributing as it should to the restoration and improvement of the environment; it is not leading toward self-sustaining development; it is not leading toward the conquest of famine vulnerability; and it is not benefiting the poorest Sahelians, who are such an overwhelming majority of the producers of wealth that they must be the focus of any truly effective program for environmental and economic reconstruction. When looked at from the level of the projects on the ground, a picture emerges that is similar to the one presented in the last section of this chapter: The Sahel Development Program is fraught with difficulties.

But when examined from the level of the projects, an even stronger picture of failure emerges. While some of the projects are weak in design and application, others are almost totally ineffective or are offset by other social and economic phenomena. *Many of the projects actually appear to be producing the opposite of their intended effects:* they may be producing eventual environmental damage, may be contributing to increased rather than decreased dependency on the technologically advanced Western nations, may be leading to increased drought and famine vulnerability, and may be exacerbating differences between wealthy and poor Sahelians. Indeed, we will argue on the basis of the research undertaken in the Sahel that these several processes are already underway even in the first few years of the development effort and that *they are all interrelated in one way or another.* Furthermore, we will show, as the evidence has presented itself to us, that the apparent shortcomings are not accidental but are more or less inherent in the development strategies generally emanating from the major donor participants in the Sahel Development Program, especially France and the United States.

NOTES

1. This is not necessarily the same as the previous criterion, since "large-scale rural participation" is probably intended to carry the implication of *active* involvement of people in positions other than the government bureaucracy and village leadership, while this fifth criterion could imply that people can be coerced into something even half-heartedly if the planners have decided it is important or necessary.
2. No further explanation is given in the report.
3. The report does not take up the rather interesting implication here, viz. that the Sahel is considered the *only* region to which these statements are applicable. If taken really seriously in all its potential ramifications, this paragraph could be a call for a reevaluation of the fundamental strategy of aid projects in all developing countries and a critique of the entire philosophy on which projects are traditionally developed and evaluated. Apparently the drafters of the statement were content to consider the Sahel such a desperate basket case that the otherwise "normal" procedures of profitability calculation can be set aside in favor of certain "vital actions."
4. See, for example, the discussion in this study of the techniques and effects of French colonialism in Chapter 3.
5. The consumption figures are reproduced without source and page documentation from FAO studies.
6. Some sources on this problem include Franke, 1974, 1975; Lappé and Collins, 1977, chaps. 7 and 22, which include extensive bibliographic citations: George 1977, pp. 87–106; Perelman, 1978, pp. 142–68; and Griffin, 1974.

part three

PROJECTS FOR DEVELOPMENT OR NEW SEEDS OF FAMINE: CONTRADICTIONS IN SAHEL DEVELOPMENT

8

France, The United States, and the Multinationals: International Contradictions in Sahel Development

Despite the enormous range of support from the wealthy donor countries, the Sahel Development Program suffers a series of contradictory effects from its relationship with the Western capitalist nations. In many cases, this relationship seems actually to be undercutting the intended goals of the program. Foremost among the internationally created contradictions are those stemming from the political and economic competition between France and the United States, the contradiction in prices and terms of trade, the effects of multinational corporate investments in the Sahel, and development "showmanship," or the use of projects to court political allies.

FRANCE VERSUS THE UNITED STATES

As shown in earlier chapters, French domination has been a major characteristic of Sahelian social and economic life for the past several hundred years and has continued right up to and through the recent drought and famine. In the most recent years, however, and especially *since*

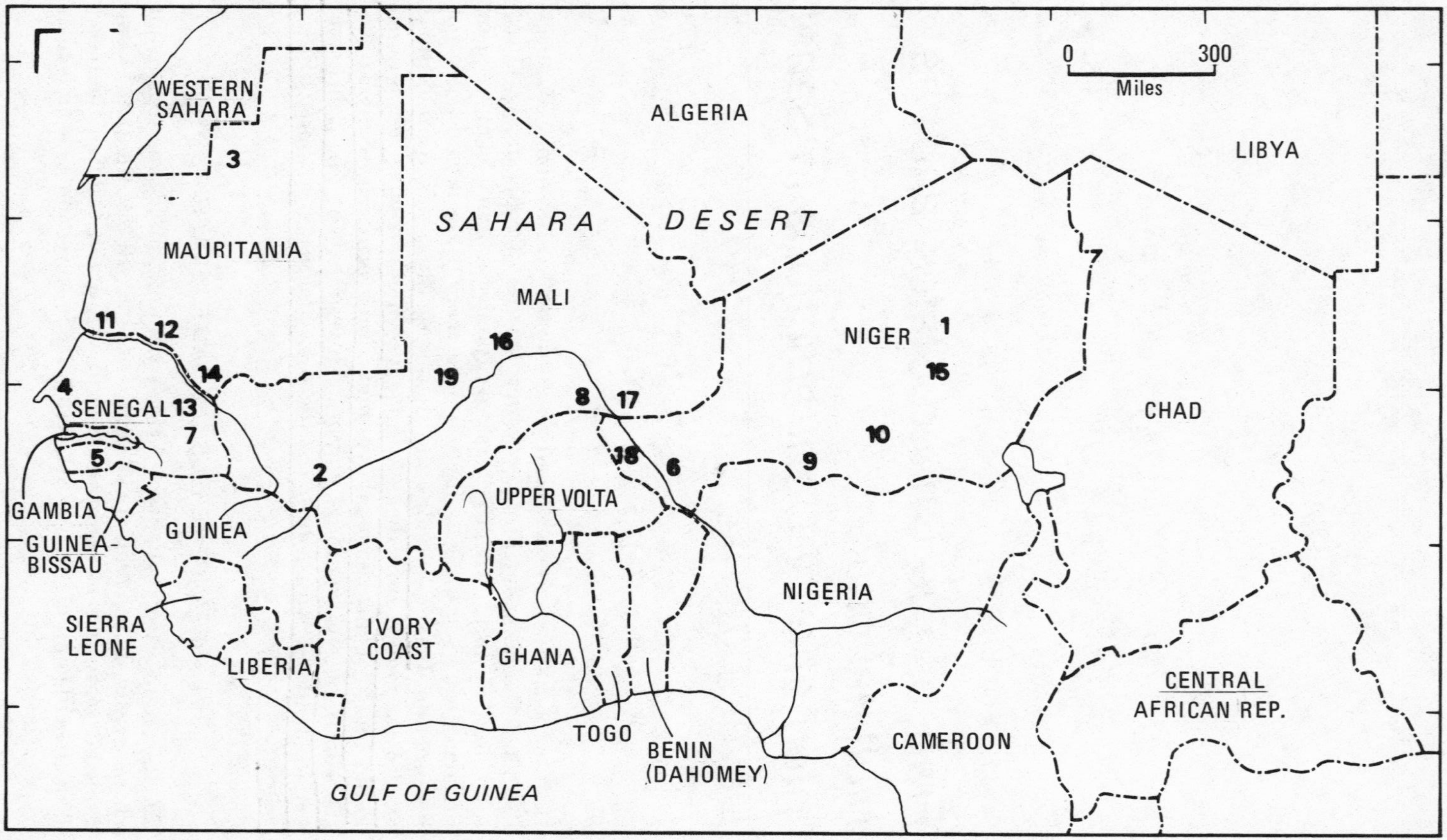
0
300
Miles
WESTERN
SAHARA
ALGERIA
LIBYA
SAHARA DESERT
MAURITANIA
MALI
NIGER
CHAD
SENEGAL
GAMBIA
GUINEA-
BISSAU
GUINEA
SIERRA
LEONE
LIBERIA
IVORY
COAST
UPPER VOLTA
GHANA
TOGO
BENIN
(DAHOMEY)
NIGERIA
CAMEROON
CENTRAL
AFRICAN REP.
GULF OF GUINEA
1
2
3
4
5
6
7
8
9
10
11
12
13
14
15
16
17
18
19

Figure 8.1. The Sahel Region: Places and Projects Discussed in Part Three

The numbers below are keyed to those on the facing map.

CHAPTER 8

1. Arlit uranium mine
2. Malian rototillers and terms of trade
3. Mauritanian iron ore mines
4. Bud-Senegal, SENEGOLD, and the *niayes.*
5. SODAGRI, Citibank, and the Casamance rice scheme
6. Niger River depressions and the World Bank
7. USAID Bakel Livestock Project

CHAPTER 9

8. USAID Gao Rice and Sorghum Project
9. USAID Niger Cereals Project
10. USAID Niger Range Management Project
11. Lower Senegal River Basin of Rice Irrigation Projects
12. Flood recession area of Senegal River Middle Valley
13. SAED and the Soninke Federation

CHAPTER 10

14. Guidimaka
15. Tabelot
16. Timbuktu: Isle of Peace Project
17. Gao: Relaunching herders' cooperatives
18. Oxfam rebuilds Fulani herds
19. American Friends Service Committee "Tin Aicha" Project

the famine, a rising number of U.S. technicians, advisers, Peace Corps personnel, and others have begun to appear in the Sahel. In addition, more and more Sahelians are coming to the United States to study, rather than to France. With its vastly greater resources in money, university facilities, and technical staff, the United States is beginning to compete with France for domination over the political, economic, and cultural life of the Sahel.

This competition between a former colonial power and a formerly "outside" capitalist nation does not remain limited to the development arena, however. The competition between France and the United States extends to political areas, where segments of the Sahelian elites are courted by one country against the other, and especially the area of corporate investment, where non-French interests, especially from the United States, are starting to break into the former French "preserve." This governmental and corporate competition has major negative effects on the attempts to develop rationally the Sahel's productive resources and rehabilitate the environment. A major vehicle for the U.S. inroads into the Sahel has been the development organization itself—the Club of the Sahel. United States officials have become increasingly enthusiastic about the Club of the Sahel in recent years. USAID stated in its report to Congress in April 1976: "AID, acting under explicit Congressional directives, has been a prime mover in the formation of the Club des Amis du Sahel."[1]

Maurice Williams moved from Sahel relief head to OECD development assistance chairman and was a major participant in the formation of the Club. But it is the U.S. financial contribution within the entire aid structure that most likely has had the greatest effect in holding the Club together. Elliot Berg testified to this on the basis of intense experience in the formation and development of the Club: "I think if the U.S. decided not to participate or participated at a very substantial lower level than is projected, I think the Club structure would probably collapse" (US House, 1977, p. 117).

Why should the Club be so dependent on U.S. participation? Why should a 10 to 15 percent contribution be so crucial to the existence of an entire development organization? The answer to this question is not entirely clear, but one element appears to be the reluctance on the part of some donor countries to act with the Club in the first place. This is particularly true of France.

Again, from Berg's testimony (US House, 1977, p. 116), there is a hint of French opposition, or at least concern, with the rather sudden influx of U.S. advisers, technicians, bureaucrats, and money:

> Given the strong French presence in most of these countries, they may have been a little surprised by the recent American initiatives and the club effort. I think there was some initial French reluctance though again these are just casual impressions and they no longer exist as far as I can see.

The French may have been more than "surprised" by the U.S. initiative in setting up the Club; they may have been resistant to have the world's major financial power suddenly moving into "French" West Africa on such a large scale. USAID program officers and staff in the field perceived the French resentment at least one year after Berg felt it had dissipated. One local staffer put it bluntly: "This is their turf and they don't like having us here" (interview in Niger, April 1978).[2]

Whatever differences continue to exist between the United States and France at the diplomatic level regarding the Sahel, it was France's turn to urge increased U.S. contributions in 1978. Following the Shaba rebellion in Zaire, French President Valery Giscard d'Estaing visited Washington and urged U.S. participation in what was described as "a $1 billion one-shot development campaign in Africa by the Western nations."[3]

The report of a Paris-based correspondent analyzes some of the political issues involved:

> Mr. Giscard d'Estaing, buoyed by French military success in Zaire, hopes that the Carter administration has been sensitized to African instability by the Zaire crisis and will be receptive to the aid plan, which hinges on strong U.S. support, informed sources here [Paris] said.[4]

Further indications of differences between France and the United States and even other Sahel contributors are also reported:

> No European government has committed itself to the plan, and West Germany, even more than the United States, is suspicious of possible French intentions of using Western aid to boost French prestige in Africa—an attitude reflecting West German disenchantment over what it perceives as France's channeling of funds in the Sahel relief consortium to French protégés among the recipient governments.
>
> France certainly has its own interests that would be served by the plan. If a fund is organized for a crash program, much of the management inevitably would have come from France's pool of African specialists.[5]

It is worth noting here that the Sahel Development Program and the CILSS-Club of the Sahel combination is viewed in U.S. circles as a "crash program." The difference lies in the U.S. emphasis on longer-term planning and an assertion that it will simply take many years for Sahel development to succeed. The French president, apparently, has a crash program of his own. Also of interest in this revealing press account is a brief note on the historical evolution of French-U.S. aid in Africa:

> The aid effort was broached with the United States in 1976 shortly after the Angola problem. It was received enthusiastically on May 7, 1976, at a meeting to discuss Africa between Mr. Giscard d'Estaing and then-U.S. Secretary of State Henry Kissinger.
>
> Mr. Kissinger promised that U.S. backing for the aid plan would be coming, *but only after trade-offs, which are still secret,* according to sources familiar with the negotiations. [emphasis added][6]

This post-Angolan "problem" meeting took place just at the time of Kissinger's call for massive increases in Sahel development aid. It is also the approximate time of the formation of the Club of the Sahel. But with Giscard d'Estaing's own crash program and "secret trade-offs" between the

United States and France, in the background may lie some sources of disagreement and tension alluded to so cryptically by Elliot Berg at the House hearings. The entire background to this murky area is beyond the scope and methods of this study, but its effects on the character of the Sahel Development Program can be seen in several areas of Sahel development.

Scientific Competition

The contradiction between France and the United States is apparent in at least three arenas of development work. First, U.S. development project personnel take a generally arrogant attitude toward previous French scientific and technical work in the Sahel, and this results in their being unable to draw fully upon the conclusions and implications for future research of French colleagues who, although they may have been working for a colonial administration, provided potentially useful information and analysis. The flippant attitude toward previous work may well stand in the way of the development of research and scientific knowledge.

An example illustrates this problem. During the Bamako, Mali, conference of the livestock team of CILSS, Professor R. E. McDowell of Cornell University's Department of Animal Science presented results of research (McDowell, 1978) he had conducted with the assistance of U.S. Peace Corps volunteers on the use of certain kinds of animal feeds. The information elicited some criticism because the Peace Corps volunteers had not been trained for gathering scientific data. But the most serious and acrimonious debate occurred when several French technicians and scientists charged the author with having completely neglected several highly detailed studies done by French researchers on the same topic. The French participants in the seminar expressed their outrage at American scientific practices that gave credence to informal data collected by inexperienced volunteers over the systematic research of scientists. McDowell replied that he had looked at the French-sponsored studies and had not found them useful. In neither his verbal presentation nor written paper was there specific reference to the French work or any explanation why it was not relevant. During the refreshment break, many French participants grumbled about the sloppy and arrogant methods of U.S. academicians. Perhaps the French were being oversensitive, but a possible cooperative and appreciative concern with each other's contribution was supplanted by an aura of hostility. Later in the conference, one French agronomist inundated the participants with a series of research reports on a variety of topics in several Sahelian countries. Then it was the Americans' turn to grumble at the arrogance of a French researcher acting as if he was the star of the conference.[7] Surely an important element of science—the use of other people's work—is being lost here, and this can only work *against* the needs of the Sahel Development Program. One can only speculate about the response of the several Sahelian witnesses to this affair. Did they quietly choose sides according to some political or financial loyalty, or did they write off the whole debate as a series of Western pretensions?

Political Competition

In addition to the various distortions of scientific research that result from U.S.-French competition in the Sahel, an equally serious problem is the behind-the-scenes political maneuvering. This is not always apparent though, partly because on many issues in Africa outside the Sahel the United States and France act in concert, and the maneuvering itself is mostly secretive and difficult to ascertain. During the first two Zaire crises, for example, in 1977 and 1978, France played a leading role with logistical support from the United States. Especially in the "second Shaba province invasion," France provided paratroopers, while the United States provided equipment.[8]

But if France and the United States were agreed on the desirability of putting a military hold on the most serious uprising against the pro-Western regime of Mobutu Sese Seko in Zaire, they may have been at some odds over the political structure in Niger. As has been mentioned earlier, Niger's pro-Western government of President Hamani Diori was overthrown in May 1974 by pro-Western colonel Seyni Kountché. The coup was in part a response to the drought, the ensuing famine, and widespread public concern with corruption and the abuse of famine relief and other public funds.[9] Yet there is another significant aspect to this coup: Kountché, the coup leader and current head of state in Niger, was a French-trained military officer. By itself this would be hardly surprising, but other important elements surround the coup in Niger. To understand these events it is necessary to consider the importance of Niger as a producer of one of the world's most precious commodities—uranium. As of 1976, Niger was the fifth-largest producer of uranium in the Western world, accounting for 6.5 percent of total production.[10] Uranium was apparently first discovered by French geologists in Niger in 1959, and the French Atomic Energy Commission secured rights to it because it was considered essential to General DeGaulle's plans to create a French independent strike force of nuclear weapons, as well as eventual nuclear-power use for France's energy needs.

The initial uranium rights were secured through a 2.7-billion-franc (CFA, or West African francs) capital arrangement, with 33 percent of the shares held by the French Atomic Energy Commission (Commissariat Française à l'Energie Atomique), 33 percent in the hands of two French companies, 8 percent each by a West German and an Italian firm, and 16.7 percent by the government of Niger (Derriennic, 1977, p. 205).[11] In 1972, arrangements were made for the government of Niger to boost its share of holdings to 35 percent. A company called SOMAIR brought together these diverse investments. Production grew rapidly; from 410 tons (metric) of uranium in 1971, it increased to 948 tons in 1973 and 1,116 tons in 1974 (Derriennic, 1977, p. 206). By 1976, total Niger uranium output stood at 2,000 tons.[12] Western sources have indicated that in the near future Niger is expected to become the third- or fourth-largest producer of uranium in the nonsocialist world.

Despite the production increases up to 1974, the financial returns to Niger were considered disappointing by many. Vice-President and military officer Sani stated to Niger students in February 1975 that the fabulous sums promised to the country through uranium exploitation had been nothing more than a "mirage."[13]

On the very eve of the April 15 coup against Hamani Diori, his government, along with the government of the West African nation of Gabon, had begun negotiations with the French for a reappraisal of uranium. Noting the importance of the OPEC oil price rises of 1973 and 1974, Niger and Gabon had begun to feel that there was a favorable world economic situation for these price increases, and they suggested to France that uranium should sell at a rate comparable to its energy output in terms of oil. According to Vice-President Sani's later account, the French government was "intransigent" in its response to this suggestion. The Niger government invited Esso Minerals of the United States, (a subsidiary of Exxon Petroleum), Conoco, and a West German and Japanese firm to explore for uranium resources.

The coup, however, not only overthrew President Hamani Diori but also ended Exxon's welcome in Niger for at least a few years. Not until 1978 did Esso return; in the meantime, France's Atomic Energy Commission had staked out large concessions, and Vice-President Sani, who had criticized the French even *after* the coup, found himself arrested in August 1975. (He was later killed under mysterious circumstances in prison in 1977.) Esso Minerals finally managed to return and was joined by firms from Germany, Japan, Italy, and Spain, who now compete with the French domination of Niger's uranium supply. Diori may not have been as loyal as France would have liked; and perhaps Kountché bought precious time for French uranium interests when they were threatened by foreign—particularly American corporate—competition.[14]

What has all this to do with Sahel Development? Niger is presumably attempting to organize relief and development programs and maintain a certain bureaucratic stability in order to maximize the experience and eduction of its small fund of trained personnel. Indeed, this governmental stability is frequently cited by politicians in the West and development experts and advisers as a desirable prerequisite to a successfully functioning development program. But how can such stability be maintained if the various donor nations are plotting and intriguing among and between themselves to put in office various people who will be loyal to their immediate interests—such as uranium contracts?

Thus the intrigues of Western governments, in particular France and the United States, may be weakening the very same development programs that the two countries are sponsoring for the region.[15]

PRICES AND TERMS OF TRADE

In the past few years, a great deal has been written concerning the overall economic relationships between underdeveloped countries and those of the industrialized West. Many Americans are now familiar with the idea of a "new economic order" as proposed by several of the poor countries and their Western supporters. Far more have been exposed to the sudden political and economic power of some poor countries that have banded together to raise the price of a strategic material, the most immediate example being that of OPEC and oil.

The background to these recent developments is less well understood in the United States, however. Earlier, we showed how the dependent relationship of the Sahelian countries with France had produced a situation in which peanut or cotton producers had to increase their output just to keep even in terms of imports. What these data show is that, in general, the prices of goods from the industrialized countries have been rising *more rapidly* than have prices for most of the goods sold by the poor countries. The effects of the greater price rises in the industrialized capitalist countries are often described with the expression "declining terms of trade," which works to *increase* the cost of industrial goods purchased by the poor countries vis à vis the wealthy countries, to whom they must sell their raw materials or agricultural products, which are simultaneously *declining* in relative price.

To a development project, this relationship is harmful, especially if the project is based upon the addition of improved technology, which must often be purchased from the wealthy, industrialized countries. In Mali, a French-sponsored aid project is attempting to improve the crop cycles of peanuts, millet, cattle-grazing, and so forth over a huge portion of the rainiest part of the country. One of the important additions to the project is animal power for plowing with a rototiller, a combination of animal-drawn plow, furrower, and weeder. The problem is that the plow increased in price by 500 percent between 1970 and 1977, while peanuts—the crop sold in order to purchase the rototiller—has increased during the same period by 208 percent. As a result, in 1977, it is more than twice as difficult to get improved technology with the output from the agricultural sector, and the agricultural sector is Mali's only export-earning area. (OACV, 1978, p. 9).

Another way to view this contradiction is to consider that, because of it, a large portion of development assistance actually goes only to compensate for the unequal price differences. Thus the French government may be able to offer "aid" to subsidize part of the purchase price of the rototillers, but much of it will simply return from Mali to France as a result of the unequal terms of trade involved in peanuts versus rototillers. As soon as the aid is stopped, farmers in the region will be faced with an impossible situation. They will not be able to continue purchases of new rototillers, nor will they be able to afford spare parts with the revenues from their peanut production.

The "failure" of many development projects once the direct financial aid is stopped is a result, in part or in whole, of these unequal trade relations. The case of rototillers in southern Mali is particularly significant because the equipment is part of a general strategy to link agriculture with herding in order to make possible the more effective use of animals in farming work. It is thus in principle part of an attempt to overcome the destruction of farmer-herder relationships in the past. With the use of the rototiller, which is currently engaged on 10 percent of the farms in the project area, researchers have calculated that farmers can almost double their production (OACV, 1978, pp. 13-14). However, this doubling will not quite keep pace with the loss of revenues through the declining terms of trade if they continue at the same rates as between 1970 and 1977. The final results then, could be that the farmers adopt new technology, work harder, produce more, and find themselves relatively worse off than before. Even when they try to buy spare parts for the technology to which they have become accustomed, they are priced beyond them. It is not difficult to guess what will be their eventual attitude toward the next technical improvements project that might enter the region.

MULTINATIONAL CORPORATIONS VERSUS SAHEL DEVELOPMENT

In addition to intercapitalist political rivalries and the unequal trading system between rich and poor countries, there is a third major stumbling block emanating from the donor countries themselves. Despite its relative underdevelopment, the Sahel is fast becoming integrated into a system of corporate economic relations known to most people through its major institution, the multinational corporation.

Multinational corporations recently have become the subject of much debate in Western capitalist countries. Plant closings and unemployment in the United States, wasted defense expenditures to protect exploitative investments, political instability, and loss of lives of both Third World and Westerners are often blamed by their critics on the profit-seeking of multinational corporations. Supporters, on the other hand, have portrayed the multinationals as "engines of progress" and bearers of necessary capital, management skills, education, and improved working conditions and employment to the poor countries. Many development experts and staff personnel regard multinationals in a somewhat in-between way as "necessary evils" in the process of development.

The Sahel Development Program is not formally tied to multinational enterprises. However, since the donor nations supporting the program are also the same countries from which nearly all the world's major multinationals come, there are many connections. The interests of multinational corporations affect the Sahel Development Program in two slightly different ways. Some multinational investments are not directly part of food and/or ecological reclamation, but nonetheless they have ramifications for those projects that do attempt to increase food output and improve or protect the environment. Uranium mining in Niger is one example of secondary effects. The competition between U.S. and French commercial interests led to political intrigue and subsequent political instability in Niger and may have set back some of the development work in that country. Other potential problems with the uranium mine include the attraction of an excessive work force as the company seeks to keep down wages. To our knowledge, little if any research has been carried out along these lines, but it is worth noting that even some USAID officials expressed private dismay at the enlistment of herdspeople to work in the mines and the difficulties this might create for organizing environmental rehabilitation programs in the pasturelands just south of the mines.

Mauritania's Iron Ore

At the other end of the Sahel, there is a clearer and more dramatic example of the indirect effects of multinational corporate interests on development programs and projects. This is the case of MIFIRMA, an acronym for Société des Mines de Fer de Mauretanie, Mauritania's iron-ore mining corporation.

MIFIRMA is in many respects a classical example of a multinational corporate enterprise operating in an impoverished Third World country. It has a high rate of profit, dominates much of the political and economic thinking and action of the local Mauritanian government, and has brought in its wake modern transport facilities, European technicians, and a salaried work force of several thousand ex-farmers and herders. Founded in 1952, it is composed of several French mining interests as well as British, Italian, and German interests, and a 5-percent share that is held by the Mauritanian government (Gerteiny, 1967, p. 180). In 1960, the company signed a $66 million loan agreement with the World Bank that allowed for greatly expanded investment in what are some of the world's richest iron-ore veins on a large triangular plateau in northern Mauritania. As a correlate of the World Bank loan, MIFIRMA and the Mauritanian government signed a fifteen-year agreement that guaranteed the company certain levels of taxation and rights to repatriate profits. This agreement has been criticized by many observers as essentially a plundering of Mauritania's resources.[16] In economic terms, MIFIRMA became a giant factor, accounting for about 50 percent of the Mauritanian government budget over several years (Bennoune, 1977, p. 9). With the development of several newer enterprises to mine what appear to be attractive copper and perhaps oil resources, mining had by 1976 come to account for 90 percent of the country's exports, as compared with a mere 4 percent in 1959 (Bennoune, 1977, p. 9, citing Westebbe). In 1967, MIFIRMA was using 28.5 of the total 36.5 million kwh of electricity in Mauritania, and the 419-mile railroad—constructed by the French National Railways—has been described as one of the most intensely used in the world (Gerteiny, 1967, p. 177).[17]

The importance of MIFIRMA to France has led some critics to note the closing of several mines in Lorraine and the subsequent unemployment of several thousand French miners so the French companies may use the vastly cheaper labor of Mauritanian herders and farmers. It is interesting that French iron-ore output underwent a substantial decline in 1963, the same year in which Mauritanian ore started coming to France, sold by MIFIRMA (Langer, 1974; Bonte, 1975, esp. p. 93).[18]

In addition to cheap labor in Mauritania, MIFIRMA was able to benefit from vertical integration, since it is substantially owned by European steel producers. This means that MIFIRMA essentially sells raw ore to itself, and the companies benefit by charging themselves what appear to be costs for materials that they have in fact already paid for.[19]

As for MIFIRMA itself, *declared* rates of profit of 18.6 percent in 1968 and 24.1 percent in 1969 illustrate the highly lucrative investment obtained by the European companies. The advantages to the company by its use of impoverished Mauritanian herders and farmers as compared to, say, unionized French miners is illustrated by the fact that between 1964 and 1972, productivity increased from 1,500 tons per workers to 2,100 tons per worker, while salaries did not change at all (Bonte, 1975, p. 99). A brutal government attack broke up the first strike of MIFIRMA's miners, which was organized in 1968. Several workers were killed and many wounded by the Mauritanian army, which was called out to defend the European company against Mauritanian miners (Bennoune, 1977, p. 11). Despite the breaking up of this strike, labor troubles have continued to recur, and there was another series of strikes in 1971. Finally, after some political changes in Mauritania, MIFIRMA was nationalized in 1974, but by 1976 the Mauritanian government had agreed to compensation of $90 million to company shareholders (Bennoune, 1977, p. 12).[20]

Whether MIFIRMA has been and is an "engine of development," creating infrastructure such as roads and railways, electricity, modern management skills, and so forth, or whether the company has been primarily a device to rob Mauritania of its resources and aid European steel companies in disciplining the often militant unionized workers of France, is an important question. For purposes of this study, however, there are other aspects of MIFIRMA that have worked to propel Mauritanian society into its current economic and social shambles. These factors include:

1. The presence of the company, which has led to additional mineral finds.

2. The tremendous potential in valuable raw materials in the Kédia d'Idjil, a triangular-shaped mountain range in northern Mauritania. One scholar lists the estimated reserves as more than 50 outcrops of iron ore within an 85-square-mile area with 125 million tons of high-grade ore (64.5% iron content) and 1 billion tons of quartz rock with lower-grade ore (25–50% iron content), but still commercially exploitable (Gerteiny, 1967, p. 179). Closer to the capital of Nouakchott, there are 9 million tons of high-quality copper and some gold. Gypsum, titanium, lithium, uranium, and thorium may also be commercially exploitable, although further exploration will be required (ibid., pp. 181–84). The tremendous potential of these resources has surely created a desire on the part of Western capitalist nations to maintain a friendly, pro-Western government in Mauritania.

3. The great distance between the mining site and the ocean has necessitated the construction of a 419-mile rail line to bring out the ore for transport overseas.

4. The relative isolation of the mining site at Zouérate necessitated the construction of an artificial town for employees.

5. The use of several thousand European technical advisers and even some unemployed miners from the French Lorraine mines as middle-level technical help created a European enclave.

6. Finally, the general effect of the size of the company's operation was to make Mauritania—which is highly dependent on its single mining operation—and the mining operation highly dependent on a single long rail line, which in turn ran along what was to become a highly sensitive border.

The development of MIFIRMA and the newer mining enterprises, with their subsequent centralizing effects on the Mauritanian economy, would only make that economy actually *vulnerable* in a few situations.

As has been shown in previous chapters, for peanuts, the high economic dependence of a country on a single product is always somewhat dangerous, for if the price of that commodity drops on the world market, it may result in large losses of revenue for the country. In 1976, the worldwide recession caused a major drop in prices for iron ore. The Mauritanian-owned offspring of MIFIRMA witnessed a drop in the selling price for its ore from $17 a ton in 1976 to $14 in the first quarter of 1978 (Hodges, 1978, p. 16). Thus, despite its great mineral wealth, Mauritania's economy has been hard hit as the high dependency on the price of iron ore begins to take its toll, *just at the time when the Sahel Development Program is supposedly going to be increasing the investment funds coming into the economy.*[21] Much of the program, then, may serve merely to compensate for revenues lost through the drop in world iron-ore prices, a drop caused at least indirectly by the economic situation in the very countries that are granting the "aid."

The problems in the Mauritanian mining sector go far deeper, however, than the drop in the world price. For output is also on the decline; from a record 11.7 million tons exported in 1974 to only 8.4 million tons in 1977, and an estimated further drop to just 7 million tons for 1978. As a result of these price and output declines, the government lost perhaps $41 million in 1977 (Hodges, 1978, p. 16). Furthermore, the decline in output of iron ore from the Zouérate area mines is linked to another set of events and processes, which, taken together, are wrecking havoc on the Mauritanian economy. This is the Western Saharan war.

The Struggle for the Western Sahara

An adequate if not complete understanding of the impact on Mauritanian development of the various entanglements centered around MIFIRMA and the multinational interests in exploiting other mineral resources involves

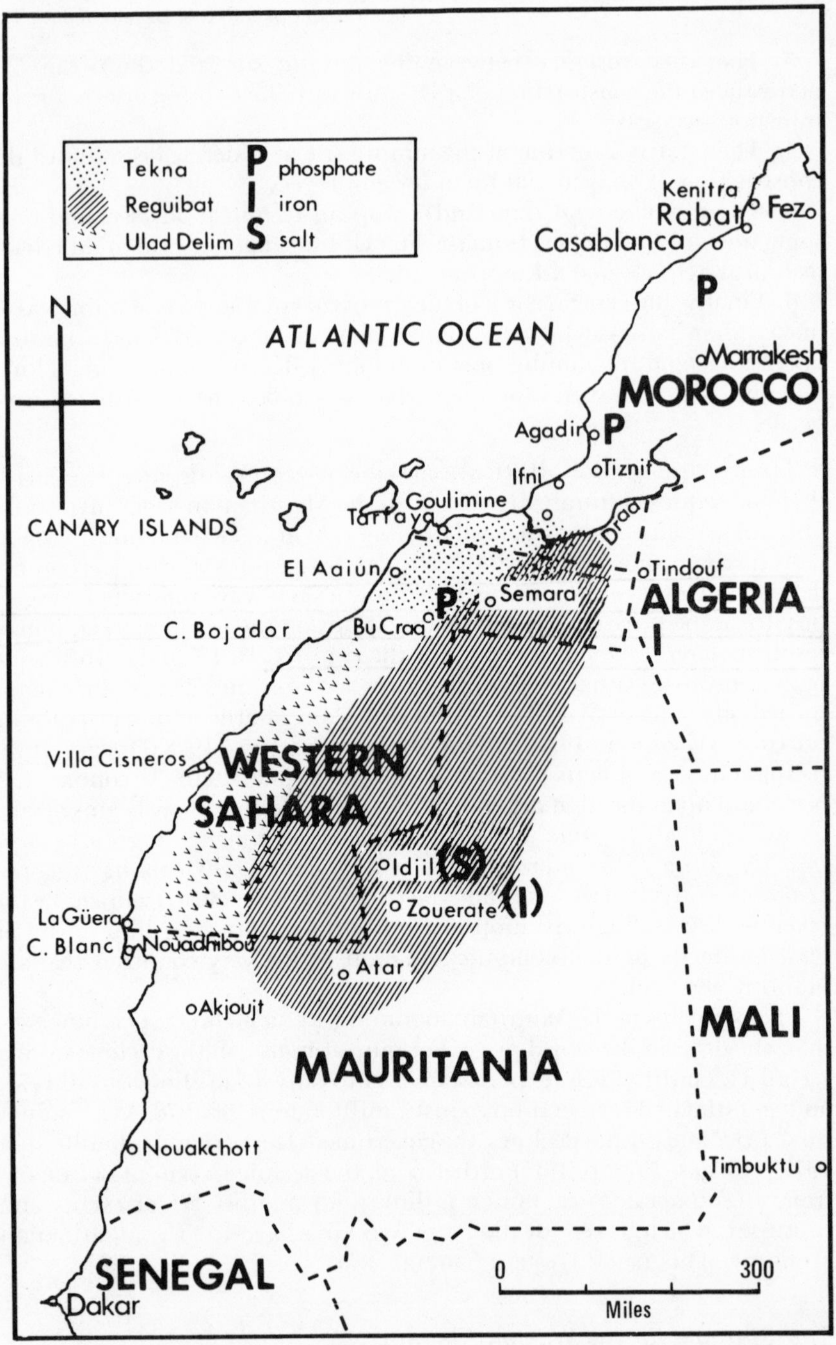

Source: Gretton, 1976, p. 10

Figure 8.2. The Western Sahara and Its Neighbors

the weaving together of several related but nonetheless different elements in what has become a very complicated set of international developments in West Africa. France, the United States, Morocco, Algeria, Spain, the U.N., and, above all, the people of a former Spanish colony are embroiled in a struggle over control of mineral wealth and a strategic military region. The 100,000 or so Saharan tribespeople seem to be obstacles to the vast mineral wealth, and Mauritania has become a pawn in the struggle to control that wealth for the eventual profits of MIFIRMA and its allies.

The current Western Sahara has been known to historians since at least the 11th century, when a confederation of Almoravids developed an empire that included large parts of the Western Saharan region, Morocco, and even part of Spain. As has been described earlier, some of these Almoravids later became part of the Moroccan military invasion that conquered Timbuktu in modern-day Mali in 1591; their hold over that city lapsed in 1727. In 1884, during the height of the European military expansion into Africa, Spain acquired "rights" to a section of the Western Sahara that rests today between Morocco and Mauritania. Because of the lack of interest in the Western Sahara for other than military purposes and the possible defense of the Canary Islands, Spain did literally nothing to develop the mainland region. To give but one indication, as late as 1975, there was not even a single newspaper in the territory in any language (Gretton, 1976, p. 18).

The end of Spanish rule over the Western Sahara came in the mid-1970s as Spain was beginning a transition from decades of fascist rule. In 1947, a Spanish geologist had discovered 57 million tons of phosphates at a site near Bu Craa in the Spanish Sahara. As Spain was making the transition from Franco to post-Franco politics, the Spanish government was negotiating with several American and European multinationals for mining rights over this major phosphate source. Apparently, however, the Moroccan government, itself a grantor of contracts to other rich phosphate and other mineral resources, was able to prevent the United States and European governments from supporting large-scale investment in the territory while it was in Spanish hands (Gretton, 1976, pp. 20–24).[22] In late 1965, rich oil deposits were discovered in Rio de Oro, the southern section of the Spanish Sahara (Gerteiny, 1967, p. 183), and in that same year, Spain announced that the Bu Craa phosphate site would yield up to 1.7 *billion* tons of high-quality material.

Decolonization and Guerrilla War

The end of Spanish colonial rule over the Western Sahara came rather suddenly in 1975. Although Saharans themselves had developed a long political opposition to Spain, and although both a decision by the International Court of Justice in the Hague and a resolution in the 4th Committee (Decolonization) of the U.N. had upheld the basic right of self-determination for the Saharan people (Gretton, 1976, pp. 34–41), King

Hassan of Morocco set off his famous "green march" of peasants, who were to "peacefully" reinstall Morocco's historical control over part of the Western Sahara. The Spanish army temporarily resisted this onslaught, and the Moroccans retreated, but Spain then struck a deal by which the Moroccan Army regular forces were allowed into the country.

The Moroccan takeover of the Western Sahara did not end the political struggle there. The Saharan people themselves had organized a popular movement, the Popular Front for the Liberation of Seguiet el-Hamra and Rio de Oro, or POLISARIO. POLISARIO has offered extremely strong resistance to the takeover and, operating both from within the Western Sahara and from refugee bases in Algeria, has maintained guerrilla control over much of the Saharan people's homeland. As journalist John Gretton has remarked in summarizing his account of the various international intrigues by which the Western Saharan people were denied their self-determination, "In the last analysis, Moroccan control of the Saharan phosphates suited too many people too well" (Gretton, 1976, p. 48). The Saharan people, however, armed and led by POLISARIO, may well upset the intrigues in the long run.[23]

The Mauritanian Connection

Where in this long story about a region on the edges of the Sahel does Mauritania fit in? It is necessary first to recognize Morocco's hostility toward Mauritania itself. For the first nine years of Mauritanian independence, Morocco continued to claim the country as part of a "greater Morocco." Despite this hostility, then Mauritanian President Ould Daddah agreed at the time of the takeover of the Western Sahara that Mauritania would accept a partition of the territory and would thus provide military support for Moroccan control. Mauritania gained nothing (all the important phosphates are in the Moroccan sector), and it had never before made any claims to the Western Sahara. The Mauritanian government was, for all practical purposes, being dragged into Morocco's annexation of rich phosphate deposits, which the Moroccan government would exploit with the aid of several European and American-based multinational corporations.

There are two important aspects of MIFIRMA and the mining reserves in relation to international intrigues to partition the Western Sahara. First, the Mauritanian government, with half its national budget coming from a giant consortium of European multinationals, was not in a strong position to resist quiet pressures from the French advisers and the French government, who undoubtedly saw in the Bu Craa phosphate reserves another potential MIFIRMA. Thus, whether strong-armed or not, the Mauritanians were undoubtedly under effective pressure to support the Moroccan maneuvers, which were clearly approved of by France and at least implicitly by the United States, which made no noises in favor of independence or self-determination for the Western Saharan people. In all this, it is likely that Western corporate interests were most concerned that Saharan phosphates not pass into the hands of a nationalist movement that might eventually set up an Algerian type of socialism.

Second, if the MIFIRMA presence in Mauritania stood as a weight pushing the Mauritanian leadership into joining King Hassan's promultinational adventure, the MIFIRMA mine, with its hundreds of French technicians, its long railway line, its physical isolation, and its absolutely crucial strategic and economic importance to Mauritania, would become a potential target for POLISARIO and an Achilles heel for the Mauritanian army and government.

The POLISARIO guerrillas, in order to weaken the Mauritanian capacity to continue its occupation of part of their territory, have several times attacked the Zouérate mine site and especially the rail line. The rail line is so exposed to attack that in 1977, for example, 150 ore trains had to be canceled because of guerrilla raids (Hodges, 1978, p. 16). In 1977, the guerrillas also attacked and briefly occupied the mining town of Zouérate and took several French hostages, which later became the official basis of increased French participation in the war.

Since 1977, the Mauritanians have been increasingly unable to maintain military control either over the occupied portions of the Western Sahara or over northern Mauritania and the mine site, which the POLISARIO guerrillas have attacked in reprisal against the Mauritanian occupation. French military advisers have been increased, and French Jaguar planes search over Mauritanian territory for POLISARIO guerrillas on the grounds that the guerrillas endanger the lives of French technicians at Zouérate. And now there are perhaps as many as 9,000–10,000 Moroccan troops on Mauritanian soil. One wonders if this was part of Hassan's plan back in 1976.

The war has ravaged the Mauritanian economy. With its dependence on the Zouérate mines and with the mines decreasing their output, Mauritania has been less and less able to finance projects and keep the country running. Pressures from both military and civilian sources led finally, on July 10, 1978, to a military coup against the Daddah regime. The new Military Committee of National Recovery, under the leadership of Lt-Col. Moustapha Ould Mohammed Salek, pledged to arrive at a peaceful settlement of the Western Saharan issue; and there is evidence of a Mauritanian wish to allow a referendum in the parts of Western Sahara that it has occupied (Hodges, 1978). At this time, however, Mauritania is in an extremely difficult position, with thousands of Moroccans and hundreds of French military in the country and still with the dependence on MIFIRMA's technicians to run the mine. It is not clear how many options the Mauritanians have. Meanwhile, development projects are hampered by the financial drain of the war, the deaths and instability within the military, the loss of revenues from the guerrilla attacks on the railroad, and the general political instability and demoralized atmosphere created in the country by the whole situation.

MULTINATIONAL AGRIBUSINESS IN THE SAHEL

Iron ore, uranium, wars, and intrigues contribute to one set of contradictions that prohibit successful Sahel development. Another major area in which multinational corporate interests present themselves in the Sahel is their direct involvement in food-producing schemes.

We have discussed in Chapter 4 some of the ways in which attempts to set up a beef export industry in Chad and Niger in the 1950s and 1960s compounded the forces pushing toward environmental degradation. While there are several large-scale and some small-scale livestock projects subsumed under the Sahel Development Program, it is not evident at this point whether substantial multinational corporate investments are in effect or even planned. There is a possibility that the Sahel's large pasture areas are being eyed by the large meat-producing firms, but the great transportation distances and such factors that led to the relative failure of the earlier projects may still be a brake on investment in livestock at this time.[24] Indeed, the livestock products being sold from the Sahel in nearby African countries such as Ivory Coast and Nigeria appear to be noncompetitive both in price and quality with frozen meats imported from Argentina, Australia, and New Zealand. If the Sahelian meat industry cannot compete in regional markets, it is unlikely to garner much large-scale investment for longer-range international markets unless conditions change.[25] In agriculture, however, conditions have already developed to make corporate investment a possibility.

Winter Vegetables for Europe

Can the Sahel become a supply source for vegetables in Western Europe during the winter months? A positive answer is thought to be possible by several organizations, including the World Bank, the Belgian government, a French importing firm, a Dutch "development financing corporation," and the affiliate of United States iceberg-lettuce corporation, Bud-Antle. The basis for this is a combination of four major factors: (1) The rising demand for winter vegetables in Europe; (2) the relative closeness to Europe by air and sea; (3) climatic conditions; and (4) the low cost of labor. All these factors are spelled out rather specifically in a 1974 World Bank (Annex IV, p. 1) country report for Niger:

> European demand for vegetables is constantly increasing. In addition, consumers want to have throughout the year vegetables that were formerly not available in winter. Except for hothouse-grown vegetables—which rank as luxuries—and early vegetables grown under glass or plastic one or two months ahead of the main season, European production is unable to meet this demand from December 15 to April 15. The Sudan-Sahel region with its long dry season (November-March), in which the temperature is low enough not to damage growing plants, is well placed to produce such vegetables under irrigation. It has the additional advantage of

having inexpensive manpower available for these labor-intensive crops (some 3,000 hours/ha.)

Even as this report was being issued, the World Bank was involved with the government of Senegal and some European companies and financial institutions in providing initial investment funds for "Bud-Senegal." This company, which grew out of the U.S. firm Bud-Antle, was the outcome of some observations by one of its technicians, Fritz Marschall, who had noted that Senegal was superior to some of the Mediterranean countries in its potential for winter vegetable production because there are no frosts in Senegal. Indeed, the country's climate reminded Marschall of California, where Bud has its major operations.

Bud's production of winter vegetables in Senegal began in 1972 with the establishment of a 450-hectare site 38 kilometers east of Dakar, the capital and major port city of Senegal.[26]

The technology of the Bud enterprise involves methods developed in California and Israel for the maximization of water use in areas where water is difficult or expensive to obtain. The technique has been labeled "drip irrigation." This means that water is dripped onto each plant individually from a small hose in a long pipe or plastic hose that runs along the furrows and is connected, along with hundreds of other hoses, to a main water supply source. In addition to irrigation, the method allows for mechanized fertilizer distribution, because the fertilizer can be put in the water (Pels, 1975, p. 15).[27]

Drip irrigation may require substantial investment initially, and in the case of Senegal, water had to be either pumped up from deep underground or run long distances from water sources, all at great cost. As of 1974, the total capital invested in Bud was on the order of C.F.A. 600 million (West African) Francs or $2.4 million (Anon., 1974, p. 319), and recent additional loans and investments of $7.5 million were proposed in 1976.[28]

What exactly does Bud produce, and what happens to it? Reports indicate that melons, green peppers, tomatoes, and green beans are the main items on the company's planting list. Owing to the closeness to Senegal's capital city, the produce can be harvested one morning, taken by truck to Dakar's Yoff International Airport, loaded on DC-8 cargo planes, and landed in Amsterdam, Brussels, Paris, or one of the Scandinavian countries by the next morning (Bunnik, 1975, p. 15). From Europe, the company's distribution agency supplies markets where the produce will get a good price.[29]

The Case for Bud

According to sympathetic accounts, Bud-Senegal can aid in Senegalese development. It brings modern technology into the country along with skilled technicians and management personnel from the advanced Western countries. In addition, since Bud is not only a producer but a major world marketer of vegetables, the company brings its overseas marketing operations to the service of the project. The Senegalese benefit in turn by receiving employment opportunities, added foreign exchange, and better use of otherwise nearly unusuable land.

Viewed in this light, Bud and similar operations could be important elements in the Sahel Development Program, and that is just what their supporters claim.

SENEGOLD: Bud's Smallholder Program

In addition to its own acreage, which is run mostly by European technicians and managers, Bud has undertaken a series of "development" projects. These projects involve one small parcel of 11 hectares and two other areas of 200 hectares each, all along the Senegalese coast. The ecological zone involved was the *niayes*, or depressions, in which water is held throughout much of the dry season or is close beneath the surface. While 4,000 ha. were under cultivation in the niayes in 1971, with a total production of 75,000 tons of vegetables, it is estimated that up to 10,000 ha. might eventually be put into production (Dia, 1972, pp. 110 and 130).[30] To carry out the project, with Bud operating as marketer and buyer for Senegalese farmers, the company hired a former World Council of Churches volunteer. In addition, an American Peace Corps volunteer and his wife somehow became involved in the work (Bunnik, February 13, 1975).

SENEGOLD could be considered a classic small-scale development project in which some technical improvements and some Western advisers worked to introduce new crops and new crop techniques in an impoverished area. According to representatives of the project, it was highly innovative in that Bud's marketing apparatus ensures the farmer an outlet for the improved and increased harvest. This particular aspect, however, is not new at all, and this is something that might cause one to wonder just how experienced the advisers are.[31] In any event, Bud was providing, in addition to advice and marketing outlets, free seeds, fertilizer, and water for one season. After that, farmers were to develop into independent, successful entrepreneurs.

A Critique of Bud

Not all is a rosy picture with Bud-Senegal. Despite the many potential advantages that the company's participation in Senegalese agriculture might seem to offer, there are several serious harmful effects as well. For one thing, Bud's mechanized, highly capital-intensive production system required the uprooting of giant baobab trees, often with two or even three Caterpillars required for a single tree (Lappé and Collins, 1977, p. 259). The general environmental effect apparently has not been studied. Another type of environmental threat was mentioned by several experts privately when they charged that Bud's operation, if expanded, would exhaust the underground water supply in the western part of Cape Verde (cf. Diagne, 1974, p. 149). Furthermore, Lappé and Collins point out that the company's operations tie the Senegalese agricultural economy to the highly irrational system currently in effect in Europe. In 1974, for example, "European taxpayers spent $53 million to destroy [withdraw from the market] European-produced vegetables in order to keep prices up." Nonetheless, at one point, green been prices in Europe went lower than the price of Senegalese beans on the European market. A Bud official commented: "Since the Senegalese are not familiar with green beans and don't eat them, we had to destroy them" (Lappé and Collins, 1977, p. 250; Pels, 1975, p. 16). What kind of development is likely to come from a relationship that requires destruction of the crop at both ends because of organizational features outside the hands of the farmers who are producing the crops?

A 1974 World Bank country report on Senegal notes that the original plans for Bud to control 1,200 ha. and eventually to expand to 3,600 had been "sharply reduced." The report cites the high cost of water for irrigation, which "could jeopardize profitability of the project," and the low quality of the goods produced in terms of the European market as the major problems associated with the enterprise (World Bank, 1974b, p. 149). More recently, Bud-Senegal has apparently suffered additional difficulties, perhaps some of an internal nature. According to a 1976 report of the International Finance Corporation, one of Bud's original backers, the company has suffered from high costs of transportation, inadequate water supply, and "management weaknesses," along with "high personnel costs" (IFC, 1976a, p. 1). As a result, it suffered accumulated losses of $27 million. Nonetheless, the IFC concludes that "the company's losses do not detract from the soundness of developing horticultural production in Senegal for the European winter market" (IFC, 1976a, p. 1). The solutions offered include additional new technology, such as cold storage at the harbor so that the company can switch from air to sea transport (IFC, 1976a, p. 1). In 1978, Bud-Senegal was nationalized, amid suspicions of the Senegalese government that the company had written off many of its profits as losses by selling to its own overseas parent company as marketing agent at exceptionally high prices (on the books at least) and pocketing the difference.

The potential difficulties represented by Bud-Senegal may run deeper than mismanagement, cutting of baobab trees, destruction of crops, and use of Senegalese land for overseas consumers. Claude Reboul, of the National Agronomic Research Institute in Paris, has raised two other serious questions regarding the kind of operation represented by Bud-Senegal, and to which company and World Bank officials seem oblivious. First, the large size of field taken into production by a large corporate investor such as Bud, and the need for uniformity of harvest, leads to the likelihood of large-scale chemical spraying. This spraying would ensure quick profits, but it would speed up the process of pest mutations, so within a few years strains might arise that would be immune to the sprays.

For Bud, this would be a loss but it could always move on to another region. Where would the Senegalese farmers or farm workers move? With the previous cutting of the baobabs, the environment would become especially susceptible to degradation (Reboul, 1976a, p. 38). Thus the more successful Bud is in the short run, the greater the medium- and long-term threat to the fragile Senegalese environment. Biological control systems—a major potential alternative to massive chemical sprays—apparently are not profitable at current levels of scientific knowledge. But But would hardly be expected to wait for its profits, and the World Bank seems ready to continue to come through with the loans.

Second, and more serious for the Senegalese, is another kind of problem analyzed by Reboul. By looking at the implications of Bud through a historical perspective rather than with an eye to immediate or short-term advantages, Reboul concludes that earlier agribusiness enterprises in Senegal have failed because previously it was impossible to produce food products for less than local farmers using outside, capital-intensive methods (Reboul, 1974, p. 37).[32] But with the development of drip irrigation, the relatively low-interest loans from the World Bank and the export factor, meaning that initially at least the company is competing with higher-paid European farmers, it may be possible for the first time to undercut the traditional producers in Senegal. The implications of this possibility are enormous. If Bud or a similar operation were to acquire the means to produce at a lower cost than Senegal's already low-income small farmers, the company could move into the local market as well.[33] Apparently Bud has already experimented with this idea at least once (Pels, 1975, p. 16). Successful competition with local producers would mean driving them out of business and eventually transforming a major portion of the most fertile and best-located lands of western Senegal into agribusiness fields. Farmers would become farm laborers, producing what the management decided in terms of international market conditions. The best-off consumers—those able to pay the higher prices—would set the market conditions, leaving many of the farmer laborers at a disadvantage in getting the very products they were producing. This type of development process has already been observed in northwest Mexico, where winter vegetable production for the U.S. market has led to impoverishment and frustration for the majority of the population (e.g. McCaughan and Baird, 1977).

But could such far-reaching changes occur in a country like Senegal? Isn't the Bud experiment small, isolated, and too much under the control of the Senegalese government to make believable such a dire prediction? Some additional factors give cause for concern.

First, the Senegal experiment is but part of a larger general attempt to develop winter vegetables in the Sahel. In 1970, in Niger, a firm similar to Bud, called SONIPRIM, was established, with 80 percent control by the Niger government and 20 percent by an unnamed French importing firm. In addition to an 87-hectare plot by 1973, the operation was also receiving technical assistance through a West European aid program (FAC) and a French government development agency. A report by the World Bank in

1974 recommended that sprinkler irrigation be replaced by the drip system in use at Bud. The reason: to reduce costs (World Bank, 1974a).[34]

Second, the reader is asked to recall the SENEGOLD development projects. The World Bank and other Bud advocates cite the fact that the company is using land for vegetable production that is otherwise used for little but some extensive cattle grazing—and that not very productive. But in the SENEGOLD project, Bud was involving its technicians and gaining knowledge and experience in producing vegetables for the European winter market in the niayes, a region of Senegal that is relatively densely populated and where the Bud operation, with advanced forms of irrigation, would come into direct competition with local traditional producers. SENEGOLD's own technical expert told the Dutch news magazine *Elsevier* in 1974: "My plan is to plant the entire region of Western Senegal from Dakar to St. Louis in vegetables" (quoted in Stol, 1975, p. 88).

Third, Bud is not alone in the niayes. Despite the impression created both in published accounts of Bud's Senegal operation and from statements by development personnel in Dakar, Bud is not an original experiment in the region. Indeed, since at least 1962, fully nine years before Bud's arrival, several attempts had been made to further develop the niayes region for vegetable production. Combinations of Senegalese government agencies, development organizations, local chambers of commerce, Senegalese businesses, and so forth carried out extensive initial investments in soil and water mapping, pumping tests, insect and pest-control experiments, seed selection, and other preliminary infrastructural work, all of which has been a kind of free preinvestment for Bud (see, e.g., Dia, 1972, esp. pp. 151 ff.). And today the work goes on.

A few miles outside Dakar lies the Center for Horticultural Development at a site called Camberene. Established in 1971 with funds from the United Nations, by 1975 the center was jointly funded by the Senegalese and Belgian governments through a grant to a U.N. trust fund. Despite the continued U.N. affiliation, scientific overseeing of the center was conducted via a visiting committee from Belgium, in consultation with the Western scientific staff (interviews at Camberene Research Station, January 19, 1978).

The Camberene center rests squarely in one of the niayes. Results from the center are thus applicable to the entire niayes region, which stretches up the coast of Senegal to St. Louis, but much of the technical work will also be of value in other nearby regions, including the Bud plot a few kilometers to the east, and the Bud-SENEGOLD projects located directly in the niayes region. Among the various projects underway at the center is a study of drip-irrigation techniques in a niaye—a study requested by Bud-Senegal.

Other work being done includes attempts to improve quality and output of peppers, cauliflower, potatoes, tomatoes, and green beans. Booklets produced by the center are designed to be used by the Senegalese agricultural extension service to make technical knowledge available to local area producers. Much of the technical knowledge has to do with packaging and transport and would be of eventual use to a further expansion of Bud's initial 450-hectare operation into the niayes. One pamphlet even shows different ways to pack the green bean harvest, depending on whether it is to be sold locally or sent off for export. This expansion could take place either by the company being given land rights under Senegal's 1964 land nationalization act or by having Bud expand the SENEGOLD concept of attaching itself as marketing agent for local smallholders.[35] In either case, the warning signaled by Reboul seems worthy of serious consideration.[36]

Finally, whether or not it is known to the company executives, the Bud experiment rests on a highly stratified land pattern that carries with it much of the structure that would lend itself to the outcome predicted by observers such as Reboul and Tiadane Dia. In a study that appears to be totally ignored by the development establishment in Senegal and the Club of the Sahel, Dia has noted that the size of landholding per person in the niayes varies from 0.09 to 20.7 *ares* (i.e., 100 square meters, or 119.6 square yards) (Dia, 1972, p. 110).

In a more detailed examination of the region from Dakar to M'boro, including about one-third of the distance covered by niayes, Dia found that fewer than 3 percent of the farmers controlled more than 50 percent of the cultivated land. Dia (pp. 132–33) also discovered that these "farmers" are mostly military officers, government bureaucrats, religious and customary chiefs, political figures, and well-to-do urban professionals. The size of holding of this 3-percent sector ranged from 5 ha. to 200 ha.; even at the lower end, it is a sizable amount when one considers that 78 percent of the niayes population is farming on 25 percent of the available land in parcels of only 10 to 100 ares (Dia, 1972, p. 133). The development of drip irrigation, the need for uniform quality for export, and the use of other higher-technology inputs and concepts will not likely go first to this group, unless a special effort is made to that end. Even then, it is unlikely that the new inputs would be able to pay for themselves unless the smallholders can be organized into uncorrupt and effective cooperatives. One might wonder how the farmers will avoid the persons from the 5-200-ha. group becoming leaders of these cooperatives, unless special political structures are created to ensure a leading role for the small producers. This does not appear to be currently likely in Senegal.[37]

The high degree of land stratification and the strategic position of middle-class and even upper-class Senegalese urban, military, and political figures in the landholding system of the niayes should constitute a serious warning to development project personnel working in the region. Will a successful transformation of Senegalese vegetable lands from primitive to modern technology simply become another in the long list of development projects that have turned smallholders into impoverished landless laborers or migrants in the unemployment lines in the capital city, while making a few fortunes for already well-off members of the society?[38]

Rather than a future of development, self-sufficiency, and ecological revitalization, the future of the niayes could well become one of wealth versus poverty, of consumer riches purchased from the profits of wealthy land-controllers exploiting cheap landless underfed laborers, and of an environment subjected to the interests of overseas consumers and local entrepreneurs in search of the quickest profits rather than long-term ecological protection. At this stage, of course, such a future is by no means the only possibility. What is dangerous is that all the prerequisites for social and ecological catastrophe are in place, and none of the possible alternative structures seems to be in the plans. It is not even apparent that they are being discussed. And the scientific research at Camberene may only be hastening the destructive process.

Rice for Senegal's Urban Dwellers—By Citibank

Agribusiness appears not only in the form of a corporation involved in producing, exporting, and marketing food products. In Senegal's Casamance, or southern region, a series of banks, engineering firms, government agencies, and development organizations have combined to arrange a high-technology, heavily financed project for the provisioning of rice to Senegal's urban population. It was partly during the colonial period that rice became a major foodstuff in West Africa, being imported from then French Indochina to feed city dwellers and sometimes peanut farmers.

The Casamance region has the greatest rainfall of any region in Senegal. It also has major rivers and tributaries, which implies a potential year-round water supply, and relatively good soils for agricultural production (see Pélissier, 1966, p. 599). The Casamance is also a region of some ethnic diversity, comprising the relatively stratified and Islamic Mandingos, the communal and egalitarian Balantas, and the Diola, who specialize in rice growing in the lower Casamance near the Atlantic Ocean coast.

The Balantas in particular have been the subject of praise by foreign observers for their careful soil management techniques and their use of animals and crops in an ecologically sound interaction (Pélissier, 1966, pp. 557-602).[39] Senegal's recent rice shortage and the need to import 124,000 tons in 1975 have apparently convinced government planners and development experts, however, that there is no time to bother with the knowledge of the Balantas or of other ethnic groups of the region whose techniques may also be appropriate to the environment. Fueled by a $30-million loan arranged by Citibank, and doubled by funds from Saudi Arabia, an ambitious plan has been arranged to cultivate 30,000 ha. of the eastern Casamance in a high-technology plantationlike enterprise.[40] While the Senegalese government, rather than a multinational corporation, is to be the formal organization for production at the local level, most of the technology and much of the planning and organization will be carried out by International Control and Systems of Houston, Texas, a farm implement and agro-industrial firm.[41]

The Senegalese government agency, a development corporation called SODAGRI, will be 50 percent owned by private American capital and will be the official development agency for the project. Hopes are to double current crop yields in the area to six tons per ha., which would mean a total output of 180,000 tons. But as the Center for Research in Economic

Development at the University of Michigan has stated in a report on marketing in Senegal:

A potential problem is that the highly mechanized and centralized operation planned (which would be the most efficient on such a large surface) is not in complete harmony with the Senegalese goal of communal rural development. While some individual rice plots could be maintained and low-level technical assistance given to farmers, a highly mechanized commercial operation relying on hired labor is most feasible. [Berg, 1977, vol. II, p. 40]

The Casamance rice scheme is to be a profit-making venture in which Senegalese farmers will be decertified from their land under Senegal's "socialist" land reform act of 1964; the land will then be rented or otherwise made available to the SODAGRI corporation, which in turn will hire the former smallholders or village communal farmers as wage laborers for its operation.[42]

Much of the Casamance region has been ecologically degraded in past decades by overly ambitious projects to increase peanut output for the entrepreneurs in Marseilles and the colonial administration.[43] Some development personnel in Dakar have also voiced private concerns over possible ecological consequences of the planned dams, which they feel have not been fully studied in terms of harmful effects on water flow, aquatic life, and salt content.[44] Equally important, however, is the social process that is implied by this project. It is as if the warning given by Reboul for the naiyes had been taken as a call to action in the Casamance; for what may result from this giant rice cultivation plan is just that set of outcomes—smallholder impoverishment, bureaucrat enrichment, profit replacing subsistence, and the environment subjected to absentee control by persons whose other financial dealings may compel them to overproduce and damage the already vulnerable Casamance.

THE RUSH TO FOOD SELF-SUFFICIENCY

International financing, and the sometimes subtle but pervasive coaxing that accompanies it, has helped to produce an atmosphere of "let's-get-busy-and-produce-enough-food." This attitude has been prevalent in international capitalist aid circles for three decades now, and it has helped to spur several ecologically and economically harmful developments in many parts of the world.[45]

The idea of rapidly overcoming a severe food shortage is of course potentially attractive to national and local Sahelian officials and development planners. An apparent example of such planning is the series of "river depressions" agricultural projects currently underway along the Niger River in Niger. World Bank financing has helped to encourage the installation of pumping and other irrigation works that may make possible a double-season harvest of up to 8.5 tons rice, which could net farmers an income equal to double the minimum wage in Niger (World Bank, 1974a, Annex X, p. 12).

The World Bank study for the project discusses the integration of the small depressions into the plans for total development of the Niger River, the various costs of production, the kinds of equipment needed, and the possibility that eventually 90,000 hectares could be brought into intensive rice cultivation (World Bank, 1974a, Annex X).[46]

François de Ravignan has looked closely at the situation in a particular village where this development project is underway. Along with students at the Kolo Development Institute in Niger, he collected information on the overall ecological picture, including the relations between herders, fishing people, and farmers, and attempted to calculate the gains and losses from the project not only in terms of short-term increases in rice but also in terms of secondary effects on other related production sectors.

He notes that the depressions, small lowland areas to the side of the Niger River banks, are used for cattle grazing during the dry season. Since the fallow areas for the agriculturalists were mostly destroyed in the last two decades, grazing land is much reduced outside the depressions. As a result of the drought, too many animals have been brought to the river's edge for pasturing. Herders and agriculturalists exchange milk for millet on a one-to-one ratio. Thus the system, while overloaded with animals, is maintaining a certain temporary human equilibrium.

The removal of the depressions as dry-season herding sites, however, would upset this balance. Herders would have to further concentrate their animals on the overused former fallow areas, bringing them into direct conflict with the agriculturalists. The system of milk-millet exchanges would be brought into jeopardy, harming both farmers and herders, and the increased output of rice—the main offsetting factor—would benefit only the farmers, who in turn might be pursuaded to push the herders out altogether. In any case, more rice and less milk and meat would not necessarily mean an improvement in the farmers' diet.

Finally, the herders, forced out of the depressions, would be compelled to overgraze their animals. The nearest alternatives, the already degraded former fallow areas, would be in danger of a possibly final blow to their recuperative capacities. One can only wonder what would then happen to the herders without pastureland, and the farmers without adequate fields or animal dung for their millet. The rice by itself would not be sufficient (de Ravignan, 1977).[47]

The positive cost-benefit calculations of the World Bank experts thus have been achieved by overlooking the delicate and crucial pattern of relationships in the area. Seeing water and soil, the development experts want to add pumps, dikes, seeds, and pesticides. The potential looks good on paper, but not when the entire situation of the villages is taken into account. Are the World Bank experts careless researchers? Are they limited to strict input-output calculations? Are they continuing to carry out the profitability criterion even though this has been set aside in the official program document of the Sahel Development Program? Are they attempting to ensure sales of high-technology waterworks equipment so the project will return much of its investment to Western businesses? Some or even all of these factors may be at work, but the rationale for the project is its purported ability to deliver an output by a certain time. This is the ideology of the quick return at work.

THE USAID BAKEL LIVESTOCK PROJECT

Many hundreds of kilometers to the west of the Niger River depressions, USAID is involved in another type of project that illustrates a different kind of difficulty with Sahel development. Here a project is being continued despite several signs of dangerous potential for human nutrition, animal health, and the environment.

In eastern Senegal near the upper reaches of the Senegal River, some 80,000 to 130,000 hectares of rangelands are being brought into a $2.35-million project to increase output of calves for beef marketing. The Bakel Livestock Project is a small component of a much larger scheme for livestock development in Senegal, first proposed in 1968 but apparently delayed by the drought (Teitelbaum, 1977, p. 125). The idea is to use the nomadic and seminomadic herders to produce calves. These will then be transferred to growth sites under strict management closer to Dakar, the capital city. A third stage, where a fattening ranch or even a feedlot would prepare the animals for slaughtering, has also been under consideration (World Bank, 1976).[48]

As stated in a project report:

> Already, the Ministry of Rural Development officials in Dakar have designated the northern geographical zone, which includes the Bakel and project area, as a breeding zone for a cow-calf operation. This area is to provide yearling animals which will be sent to the peanut growing regions of central and western Senegal. The latter regions are now being planned for irrigation of peanuts, sorghum, and other forage crops. The forage produced in this region will be used for the growing and fattening of the yearling animals. [Consortium, 1977, p. 6]

The 2,500 Fulani and Tukulor herders in the project area will thus become the first stage of a large national cattle production and marketing program. To bring about their participation, the local herding populations will be drawn into cash relations with the outside. Again, as a project document notes: "If the project is to be implemented and rather large cash investments made, then greater cash income must be generated from the area. The economy must become cash-oriented in contrast to traditional self-sufficiency." (Consortium, 1977, p. 324).[49]

A more immediate justification for the project, however, was provided by several different observers and project personnel, who saw it as a means of reestablishing the legitimacy of Senegalese President Leopold Senghor in a region where his political popularity has diminished in recent years. Senghor has been a major supporter of French and U.S. policy in Africa, allowing French military bases in Senegal, from which air operations have been conducted against POLISARIO guerrillas in the Western Sahara and Mauritania and the FROLINAT rebels in Chad. More recently, Senegal offered troops for the French and U.S.-sponsored "peacekeeping" force in Zaire's Shaba province.[50]

At the local level, in Bakel region, the livestock project has several major goals. These include, in addition to the production of calves for the ranches to the south and west, improvements in the standard of living of the herders and the improvement, management, and revitalization of seriously degraded pastures.

To achieve these local goals, the Bakel Livestock Project has designated an initial region around the village of Toulékédi, 25 kilometers southeast of the town of Bakel. In this region, 316 kilometers of fire-break roads are to be constructed, which will divide the area into 18 pasture zones. In the center of each of these zones, a depression site will be dug out with road graders and bulldozers and diked to create a reservoir. When completed, these reservoirs will hold rainy-season water runoff for three to five months, thereby extending the use of the pastures during the dry season and freeing the herders from their need to concentrate animals around the very limited watering sites currently available. In addition to creating the conditions for even more use of pastures and thus less ecological degradation, the project will improve village life by removing the late dry-season competition between herders' cattle and the herders themselves. At present, the wells in the villages must often be used by both animals and people at the end of the dry season, thus creating a potentially dangerous health situation.

The project also envisions the creation of village and herders' associations, which are to provide staffing for fire-fighting associations. A Unimog fire truck is to be ordered and a Peace Corps volunteer has been assigned the task or organizing these associations. Educational meetings to explain and arrange for village-level administration of the project have already begun; they have had 70 percent attendance, according to the Senegalese government officer in charge.[51]

Underneath the official documents and assurances, however, are some severe potential difficulties.[52] First, anthropologist Joel Teitelbaum (1977, p. 130) has noted that the herders in the region often move during the dry season to water and feed their cattle along the banks of the Senegal River. This brings them into contact with Soninke farming peoples, with whom they exchange milk for millet. Interestingly, the Soninke farming villages are themselves the object of another USAID project (which will be discussed in detail in the following chapter). Yet despite the Sahel Development Program's call for association of livestock and agriculture and the idea of integrating development programs with existing beneficial practices of herders and farmers, the Bakel Livestock Project and the Bakel Irrigated Rice Perimeters are completely unintegrated with each other. A serious possible repercussion would be that the creation of the reservoirs for the herders might cause them to modify their dry-season trek patterns. With watering sites available near their villages, the herders may be encouraged to terminate their movements to the Soninke farming areas, depriving the latter of milk to exchange for millet and dung to fertilize their fields. Thus the agricultural project will tend to be harmed by the very success of the livestock project.

A further potential difficulty has been analyzed in some detail by Teitelbaum. As an anthropologist contracted by USAID to write a social analysis of the livestock project, Teitelbaum discovered that the late dry season is a period of extreme nutritional stress for the herders. Much of the cow milk available then is desperately needed to offset the nutritional shortage. This is particularly important for infants, who under current conditions have a less than 50 percent chance of surviving their first year (Teitelbaum, 1977, pp. 127, 131-32). However, as Teitelbaum (p. 134) notes: "Cow's milk will be devoted to hastening calf growth in the early stages [of the project, RF/BC] and calves will be kept with their mothers permanently."

The project document indicates an awareness of this problem when it states that "Under no circumstances should outside change agents oblige husbandmen to do without milk for household consumption as this will turn all the members, including the women who milk the cows, against the project" (Consortium, 1977, p. 355). It advocates the creation of a separate milk herd as a solution to this potential conflict, but as recently as May 1978, there were no indications for the planning or creation of such a herd in the project as it unfolded on the ground in the Bakel region. Teitelbaum (p. 135) notes that "The questions concerning milk use have already become a source of friction between the project planners and the . . . herders."

Finally, in a reference to local inequalities as they may influence the project (a topic to be detailed in the following chapter), Teitelbaum (p. 136) reports that the main supporters of the project in the area are "government officials, foreign experts, and the Soninke cattle-buyers." But no doubt the political and commercial elites who see the marketing of the calves as a source of increased income for themselves will be the main beneficiaries of the project. How will the USAID technicians and Peace Corps staff, however well intended, ensure that a project, administered in the final analysis through local institutions, will place an absolute priority on milk for the herders' children?

Beyond the nutritional aspects of the Bakel Livestock Project is a further set of difficulties that could render it harmful not only to children in the short run but also to the environment in the long run.[53]

The construction of 18 watering sites may seem like a relatively small element in the project, especially when one considers the use of advanced technology such as bulldozers and road graders. It might be presumed that all 18 reservoirs could be finished in a single year. But even with modern technology, the project's local director has estimated 45 machine-days' minimum for each reservoir. In the first season, only two reservoirs were expected for completion, and only one was actually nearly finished in May 1978, just at the onset of the rainy season, when work would have to halt.

The inability to provide the completed project's water and pasture zone means that *each* of the reservoirs, as they are constructed, could become sites for the concentration of animals, just as were the predrought deep boreholes, which have been studied and criticized in such detail. The reservoirs, however, have an additional disadvantage. While encouraging the concentration of animals around a single site and thus aiding in the destruction of pastures, the open-air reservoirs may also become foci for the transmission of cattle and human diseases. The Bakel Livestock Project, intended to befriend the Senegalese president and his need to offer "development" to the Bakel region, could result in an intensified degradation of the region's already depleted pasture resources.[54] The concentration of animals, reservoir by reservoir, could result in an almost total degradation of the project area's pastures. When questioned on this possibility, a project technician replied, "Yes, there is little we can do about this."

CONCLUSIONS: DEVELOPMENT OR RENEWED FAMINE VULNERABILITY?

Whatever the intentions of the planners and administrators, and the project directors and technical experts of the donor countries, the Sahel Development Program is a captive to the overall negative relationships between the Western capitalist nations and the people of the Sahel. Whether it be the trivial bickering of French and U.S. scientific and technical personnel, the profit-seeking of multinational corporations, the ill-considered rush to "get things done," or the subtle pressures exerted on a project by international political alliances, the results of a program created and carried through under current relations between the Sahel and its Western donors may end up being the very opposite of what the program officially intended. If the cases cited in this chapter are representative of what is happening generally in the Sahel, this highly touted "new" approach to development could end up by reproducing the vulnerability to drought that was so greatly increased in earlier decades by the colonial system.

NOTES

1. The name has since been shortened to Club du Sahel, or Club of the Sahel.
2. Additional evidence of French attitudes toward Africa emerged during the Zaire rebellion of 1978. The response of French President Valery Giscard d'Estaing in sending in paratroopers to the rebel-held town of Kolwezi was so rapid and so independent that Belgian Prime Minister Tindemanns complained publicly that France was trying to muscle in on Belgian interests in Zaire. While France never admitted the charge, and the Belgians withdrew it more or less, it is difficult to believe it could ever have reached the stage of being issued by a national leader of a European country if there were not strong feelings in Belgium that it was true. The more recent French initiatives in setting up an African defense force with French and some African participation further strengthens the argument of Richard Joseph (1976) that France has maintained an almost traditional colonial supervision over former African colonies and continues to see Africa much as did French colonial strategists in the 19th century. An interesting view of intercapitalist rivalries in Africa is presented by Soviet scholar Tarabrin (1974).
3. *International Herald Tribune*, May 26, 1978; article by Joseph Fitchett.
4. Ibid.
5. Ibid.
6. Ibid.

7. This series of events contrasts rather sharply with the official ideological view of American science, which considers itself politically neutral.

8. The giant French air base at Dakar was a major refueling depot, and during the Shaba rebellion (a more accurate word for the event than the term "invasion"), U.S. military personnel greatly increased their presence in Senegal.

9. As noted earlier, the Niger coup was discussed in Higgot and Fuglestead, 1975, in several Niger literary contributions, which reflected substantial opposition to Diori's rule by the time of his overthrow, and among intellectuals in Niger society.

10. *New York Times*, June 18, 1977.

11. Derriennic cites François Lancrenon, *La République du Niger, Notes et Etudes Documentaires*, No. 3994–95, Paris, June 1973, p. 20; cf. Donaint and Lancrenon, 1976, pp. 95–96.

12. *New York Times*, June 18, 1977; and *Le Monde*, April 25, 1978, which gives the figure of 1,800 tons as the production expected for 1978, noting as well the discovery by Texaco of oil reserves of unknown size. Also possibly present are lime phosphates, cassiterite, iron, and molybdenum.

13. *Sahel Hebdo* (weekly Niger paper), February 24, 1975, as cited in Derriennic, 1977, pp. 209-10. Sani was arrested that same August, along with Djibo Bakari, who had been a main leader of the opposition to Hamani Diori. These arrests, which took place *after* the fall of Diori, indicate that the new government was *not* principally based upon or at least willing to be based upon the traditional opposition leaders. This in itself raises significant questions as to just how much of a coup it really was, but these questions must be left to historians and political scientists.

14. The various facts cited in the last several sentences come both from Derriennic, 1977, pp. 204–14, who bases his own account completely on moderate journalists' reports and independent verification, unsolicited, from Mr. Alan R. Jager, representative of Esso Minerals, Esso Eastern Inc. in Niamey, Niger, April 12, 1978. It is of note that Jager was the Exxon representative thrown out by Kountché in 1974, so he had his own experiences as well as insights gained later after his return. Significantly, Jager identified Sani as one of the pro-Exxon members of the Niger government in 1974, although Jager claimed Exxon had won the support of many former opponents through its willingness to conduct water resource studies in the area of its uranium and oil prospecting. Jager also had harsh words for the French Atomic Energy Commission's policy of open borehole drilling, which he claimed was causing leaks of subterranean water reserves in the area near the initial uranium finds. We were not able to confirm these accusations from independent sources, but they are at least of note as evidence of U.S. business attitudes toward French counterparts.

15. Recent discoveries of oil and gas in Chad offer the possibility of some French-U.S. competition there as well. Conoco announced finds of as yet unknown size, as reported in the *Wall Street Journal*, November 24, 1975, while an *International Herald Tribune* report, November 22, 1977, indicated both a possible strengthening of U.S.-Chad ties, a Chad request for U.S. military help—which is currently mostly supplied by France—and the presence of several U.S. oil companies, including Exxon, Conoco, and Chevron. A refinery is to be built that will provide some oil for export, it appears. But the presence of strong antigovernment guerrilla forces in the northern part of Chad may be moderating potential French-U.S. disputes over the oil, so Western unity is maintained at least as long as the rebellion continues.

16. The critics include Amin, 1973, pp. 76–82; Bonte, 1975; Bennoune, 1977; and Langer, 1974. Gerteiny, 1967, offers a moderate but skeptical overall assessment, while Westebbe (a World Bank officer), 1971, paints the most positive picture but nonetheless has some reservations. See especially, Westebbe, 1971, p. 11 and pp. 50–57. The most favorable general view in contained in IMF, 1970, pp. 320–26.

17. The IMF study (1970, p. 328) gives a figure of 42.8 million kilowatt hours, "of which the Mining Company [MIFIRMA] consumed about 80%." The figures are thus slightly at variance with those in other sources, but the basic significance remains the same. A table produced by IMF (1970, p. 328) also indicates that the company was using about 50 percent of all petroleum consumed in the entire country over the period 1965–69.

18. See Langer, 1974, and Bonte, 1975, esp. p. 93, in which he contends that French iron-ore production dropped from 62.4 million tons in 1962 to 57.4 in 1963. This drop is all the more significant because the French fourth economic plan had envisioned a *rise* in output of ore from 66.8 to 71.9 million tons in those same two years.

19. This is a phenomenon of the U.S. economy. By double charging for raw materials, a company that is vertically integrated can greatly increase its profits while hiding them in cost categories.

20. Further evidence of the backtracking of the Mauritanian government on the nationalization comes from a decision in October 1976 to promulgate a liberal investment code, and finally at an extraordinary congress of the government political party in 1978, to open—in essence, to *reopen*—state firms to "private and foreign investors" (Hodges, 1978, p. 17).

21. In April 1978, the Mauritanian National Assembly voted to allow up to 49-percent nongovernment ownership in the nationalized company including apparently the possibility of foreign investment as well as local Mauritanian private investment, which is presumably quite small at this time. See Hodges, 1978, p. 17.

22. A critical view of Morocco's economic development is given in Amin, 1970, esp. pp. 164–87.

23. POLISARIO's analysis of the situation in the western Sahara has been presented in several international forums, including: (1) a speech by representatives of the Foreign Relations Committee of POLISARIO to the Liberation Committee of the Organization for African Unity, January 19, 1976; (2) a statement by Bir Lahlou, member of the Foreign Relations Committee of POLISARIO, to the Fourth Committee of the U.N. (Decolonization Committee), September 30, 1976, which includes a list of Moroccan soldiers captured or killed by POLISARIO forces and certain major documents; and (3) a statement by the Foreign Relations Committee to the 32nd Assembly Session, U.N. General Assembly, October 5, 1977. On July 7, 1979, the *New York Times* carried a critique of U.S. military support for the Moroccan invasion in an article by Daniel Volman of the Institute for Policy Studies in Washington, D.C. The article was entitled: "Warning: Stay Out of the Sahara's Quicksand". On August 6, 1979, the *Times* reported that Mauritania had signed a peace agreement with POLISARIO in Algiers, agreeing to withdraw from "the unjust war in the Western Sahara" and referring to POLISARIO as "the representatives of the Saharan people". The article also noted threats from Moroccan King Hassan to occupy the former Mauritanian "share" of the now abortive partition of the Democratic Arab Saharan Republic.

24. Professor Ernest Feder (1978) offers a chilling analysis of the effects of corporate and elite interests in beef production in Latin America, where agricultural lands appear to have been sacrificed for a more profitable but less food-worthy production system. Feder cites recent conferences, including in particular the Rockefeller Foundation (1975), as evidence for a strong myopia on the part of scientists involved in this development. The Sahel, with its large rangelands, may be immune to the kind of difficulty experienced in Latin America; indeed, as will be shown later, the Sahel herders may be the ones more endangered by agricultural policies than vice versa.

25. This problem was the subject of lengthy discussions at the Bamako, Mali, conference on Sahelian Production Systems, February 22–March 1, 1978, but we are not aware of any published documents on it. There was agreement among several livestock and marketing experts that Sahelian meats were not selling as cheaply as overseas imports in the large population centers of the West African coastal areas. Perhaps if the development programs succeed in some way in lowering production and transportation costs, the multinationals will see an investment opening.

26. Bud will be known to some U.S. readers for its role in having United Farm Workers leader Caesar Chavez jailed. Others partake of the company's lettuce production in small amounts as the garnish on McDonald's hamburgers. In 1978, Bud-Antle was acquired by agribusiness giant Castle and Cook which also controls Dole Pineapple, Chiquita Bananas, A & W root beer, Bumble Bee canned tuna, and many other food and food processing subsidiaries. An overview of Bud's history is given by Anne Fredricks in the May/June, 1979 issue of *Food Monitor*. A useful analysis with a brief history of Bud-Senegal is given in Lappé and Collins, 1977, pp. 259-60. Other sources that we have used for this account, graciously provided us in their original form by Lappé and Collins, include Pels, 1975; Bunnik, 1975; and *Landbouw Wereldnieuws*, October 15, 1974.

Claude Reboul (1974, pp. 33-34) identifies a 500-hectare corn plot planted under Bud auspices in the Casamance region of southern Senegal. It is not clear what was the marketing arrangement for this site but it must be in some way geared to local sales; it would not be convenient for quick transport overseas.

27. A description of the drip-irrigation system is contained in Shoji, 1977.

28. International Finance Corporation (the commercial section of the World Bank) 1976a, p. 4. The recommendation is signed by Robert S. McNamara, president of the World Bank.

29. Senegalese newspaper reports indicated that in April 1978 Bud operations had been extended to West Germany, but even before that as many as three DC-8s a week were exporting Senegalese vegetables during the winter season in Europe (*Le Soleil,* April 26, 1978; Lappé and Collins, 1977, p. 259).

30. About one-fourth of the total possible area, 2,500 ha., is located on Cape Verde within 40 km. or so of Dakar and Senegal's Yoff International Airport (Navez, 1974, p. 7).

31. Other evidence of serious weaknesses in the SENEGOLD field technician and perhaps in the peace corps assistant is contained in the account which is extremely favorable to the entire operation. At one point, the Dutch field worker exclaims to his interviewers, "If this project doesn't work, we might as well give up on development aid altogether," adding that he feels the project is essentially perfect in its conception and organization. At another point, he complains of the difficulties in dealing with the farmers' "traditional way of life," with its "siestas, tea drinking, and bowing down three times a day to Mecca"—and all this when the fields need to be irrigated. Nonetheless, the Senegalese farmers are pictured as entirely pleased, even grateful, for SENEGOLD and its resident experts. One wonders what feelings they might have left unstated to their enthusiastic listeners. See Bunnik, 1975.

32. Reboul developed this argument more fully in a report based on a World Bank research trip to Senegal. The report, however, is published not by the Bank but by the French National Agronomic Research Institute (Reboul, 1974, pp. 32-34). Similar fears are expressed by Dia (1972, pp. 127-29).

33. Similar concerns are expressed by Dia (1972), whose research into social and economic conditions in the niayes appears to have been overlooked by all other commentators on Bud.

34. The report gives detailed cost-benefit figures, but it does not appear to offer a recommendation for World Bank financing.

35. A critical discussion of the Senegalese land reform law is contained in Reboul, 1974, and in greater detail in Reboul, 1976b, esp. pp. 77-80. See also Dia, 1972, pp. 61-81. In addition to interviews at Camberene, January 19, 1978, material that illustrates the scientific output of the center includes République du Sénégal (1975 and 1977).

36. In a discussion with several of the senior scientific staff at the Camberence center, we raised the question of Belgian sponsorship of the research and that Belgium is one of the countries that imports winter vegetables via Bud. All agreed that in their view these two facts were unrelated because, as they put it, "most of the produce goes to France, anyway." At the same time, however, they informed us that one of the five major sections of the center's organizational breakdown is marketing, and that the marketing section often influences the technical research. The idea is to get a quality crop for export. Despite the stated idealism of the scientific staff and its willingness to work at a center where pure research cannot be undertaken (only applied studies are considered part of the center's mission), there appears to be a bit of naiveté regarding possible outcomes of its work. Another instance of this was the insistence by one of the technical staff that improvement of nutrition for Senegalese was the main goal of the work, but he could provide no well-thought-out justification for the crops chosen or the experiments undertaken in terms of nutrition. Indeed, as this topic was being discussed, we were passing a cauliflower test plot, which he admitted, somewhat to his own apparent surprise, was not of much relevance to Senegal's nutritional needs. (Interview notes at Camberene, January 19, 1978).

37. A brief critique of Senegal's cooperatives is given in Gagnon, 1976, pp. 365-69.

38. An FAO-sponsored "Technical-Social Study of the Vegetable Regions of Cape-Verde" (i.e., the region of the niayes closest to Dakar) does not even consider the problem of inequality in land ownership and makes no reference to the Dia study. See Navez (1974, esp. pp. 14-16), where the author touches on the edges of landholding. Interestingly, however, some of the statistics provided do give an indirect confirmation of some of Dia's data. For example, the FAO study found that in villages closer to Dakar, up to 40 percent of the land was controlled by people who did not live on it permanently—the only criterion invoked in the study—while villages farther from the city had up to 100 percent of their land held by people who live on it full time. This pattern, along with Dia's study, suggests a process of gradually expanding control by urban elite families over land in the niayes, and it possibly indicates expulsion of former farmers in the villages nearest Dakar. This would seem to be a topic for urgent research before there is any continuation or expansion of the overseas vegetable production system on a high-technology scale, such as that required by Bud or similar enterprises.

39. One development adviser in Guinea-Bissau told us that Chinese technicians in that country had departed after a three-month visit, declaring that the Balantas were sufficiently sophisticated in their rice-growing techniques that there was nothing the Chinese could teach them.

40. Citibank's overseas investments are often placed in the name of the Citicorp International Group. It appears from an announcement placed in the *International Herald Tribune*, April 20 1978, that several other large banks have also subscribed in this project, including Chase Manhattan Limited, First National Boston Limited, Bank of Montreal, The European Bank of Tokyo, and several French and other Western European banks. The World Bank will also play some role in the financing, according to the Citibank loan prospectus.

41. Information gathered from an interview with the commercial officer for the U.S. Embassy in Dakar, May 30, 1978, and from Citibank loan prospectus circulated on London financial markets.

42. From Berg (1977, p. 40) and interviews with the U.S. Embassy in Dakar, May 30, 1978. Other elements in the project include construction of dam and irrigation works, as well as storage facilities, some rice-processing equipment, and an animal-feed production unit.

43. Pélissier (1966, pp. 780–92) recounts these events and processes in some detail. They are similar in many ways to those described in Chapters 3 and 4 on the effects of peanut culture in somewhat more arid parts of Senegal.

44. From interviews in Dakar, January and May 1978.

45. For some examples and discussion, see Franke, 1974a, 1974b; and Lappé and Collins, 1977; as well as Susan George, 1977; and Perelman, 1977.

46. De Ravignan (1977) gives an estimate of 15,000 ha., but this is probably an earlier figure.

47. We have added a few implications that are not explicitly stated by de Ravignan, but they seem to be likely problems on the basis of his analysis.

48. Additional information was obtained from interviews with USAID personnel in Dakar, January 1978. See also our summary of Claude Reboul's account of an earlier, similar attempt in Chapter 4.

49. The possible eventual involvement of multinational corporations in the output end of this program seems likely, particularly in view of the involvement of the World Bank in the financing of the stages *after* the cattle calves will have left the Bakel project area. We received no evidence of this as of 1978, however.

50. Despite his military involvements with France and the United States, Senghor has refused to recognize the People's Republic of Angola on the grounds that the country is occupied by Cuban troops.

51. Information in this section was obtained through several interviews and a field visit of four days to the Bakel Livestock Project area in May 1978.

52. Indirect evidence of the essentially political motivations behind the choice of project site is contained in the intitial project document. Here it is stated: "A number of areas could be selected that, because of their location, would not involve the serious personnel and access problems anticipated in this project. These alternative locations would have a much higher probability of success and would provide an affirmative demonstration of improved range and livestock management practices" (Consortium, 1977, p. 43).

53. The problem of local opposition to the project is raised again and again in Teitelbaum's paper, but it is also dealt with briefly in the project document. In the latter, it is suggested that several "tension management techniques" be considered. The document continues:

"Islamic prayer sessions, magical protective devices, are employed at the outset of any new and important cattle movement. This is part and parcel of current livestock 'management practices.' . . . It is recommended that religious functionaries such as Imams, Marabouts, and fetish priests and other Koranic notables be contacted by the implementers and given incentives to support the project aims. They may be given the honor (and gifts) for blessing the inauguration of new grazing units. Public prayers will be of great use in inducing social change as it shows respect for the established order and traditional wisdom of the elders in association with innovation" [Consortium, 1977, p. 357]

While being reminded of the earlier French practice of trying to co-opt religious leaders to make more palatable otherwise unpopular programs, we would also note that the social location of these religious functionaries is not specified in the study. If they are tied in with the government officials and Soninke cattle-buyers mentioned by Teitelbaum as part of the interest group that would benefit the most from the project, then the document is simply calling for something that will happen anyway. Teitelbaum (1977, p. 136), however, whose study is never mentioned in the project document, distinguishes between "indigenous leaders" and the supravillage officials. The actual positions and relationships between these two groups and their own relations with the villagers is a subject calling for more detailed research.

54. A general statement consonant with our own view comes from the report of a project team working just a few kilometers from the Bakel area, but on the Mauritanian side of the Senegal River: "The advisability of constructing new water supplies in order to shift grazing pressure away from the present zones of degradation is questionable. Similar attempts to disperse grazing through selected establishment of new water supplies elsewhere in West Africa have resulted in the lateral spread of overgrazing" (Bradley, et al., 1977, p. 85).

9

Landowners, Merchants, and Bureaucrats: Privileged Classes Versus the Sahel Environment

Beneath the many contradictions and difficulties stemming from the international relations in which the Sahelian countries are enmeshed, there lies yet a further set of blockages to successful development and environmental rehabilitation. The lack of detailed, analytical studies of Sahelian social structures, among the most pressing research priorities at the present time, should not prevent the formulation of at least one significant, if tentative, hypothesis in this chapter: *Control of resources by elite groups in the Sahel is interfering with the execution of development projects, and indeed it threatens to turn many of them into environmental hazards.* Our investigation of development projects indicates that in nearly every case where relevant data has been gathered, this hypothesis tends to be borne out.

The social-structure impediments to ecologically sound development seem to take two forms: the cleavage between large landowners and merchants versus small landowners and/or herders, and the cleavage between rural producers and government elite bureaucrats. While in some cases both these cleavages may be involved, usually one is more significant. The problem of the relationship between agriculturalists and animal herders is often closely tied to these major hierarchical divisions. We will examine how each of these social cleavages appears to be influencing the course of the Sahel Development Program by examining three projects for each type of division.

LANDOWNERS, MERCHANTS, AND SMALLHOLDERS

Both traditionally and under the influence of French colonial policies, wealth differences have developed in the Sahel. Unlike many parts of Asia and Latin America, Sahelian societies did not involve the overwhelming gulf of estate (or *latifundia*) owners and extremely wealthy trading groups versus an almost totally impoverished and dispossessed rural sharecropping group and proletariat or landless population. But the relatively small differences between rich and poor in the Sahel are nonetheless significant enough to alter the officially intended course of projects in the Sahel Development Program. Evidence for this problem can be seen in one project from Mali and two from Niger.

GAO RICE AND SORGHUM PROJECT

Of all the Sahelian countries, Mali has perhaps the greatest potential for irrigated crop production. Running through the south-central part of the nation is the enormous Niger River inland delta. Both in precolonial and colonial times, the delta area has been the site of major crop development actions, and today the area is a major focus of Sahel development work. USAID, the World Bank, and many other aid institutions are busy along the delta with rice, wheat, livestock, and millet and sorghum projects.

One apparently typical example of a large food-production scheme is USAID's Gao Rice and Sorghum Project, which grew out of a World Bank emergency program in 1973. According to the project document, it is designed to benefit 20,000 poor rural families with a total of 140,000 people (USAID, 1976a, p. 2).[1]

The region of Gao, once an apparently wealthy surplus-producing area, must now import staple foods. The creation of a self-sufficient regional food economy, at least for basic grains, is the major goal of the USAID project. While Gao is not in the inland delta region proper, its flat, floodable plain area is similar. Thus it is likely that many of the accomplishments in Gao will have implications for other projects in the delta area to the west.

USAID's plan of action is straightforward and typical of irrigated agricultural projects. Dikes, improved seed varieties, fertilizers, and pesticides will be added to the farmable strips along the river bank. One area of 5,000 hectares will be given only seeds, fertilizers, and pesticides, while another 5,000-ha. area will receive these plus irrigation construction. The 10,000 hectares will be planted in rice, with expectations for a yield of 500/550 kg. per ha., to be raised to 900 kg. per ha. and eventually even more. An additional 3,300 hectares, to be planted in sorghum, will be designed to increase yields from the current 400 kg. per ha. to 600 kg. per ha. In both crops on the average, it is calculated that the incomes of farmers will be increased by 70 percent, even after they have paid a percentage of the harvest to cover costs of seeds and other inputs (USAID, 1976a, pp. 2-15).

In addition to these standard inputs, the project will experiment with ox-drawn water-lifting wheels and local *bourgoul*, or water reeds, as fences to keep out grass-eating carp, apparently considered to be harmful to the rice plants. The project has even taken account of the possibility that the reed fences will reduce the water flow, which could lead to the development of schistosomiasis. This snail-borne fluke bores into the skin within a few seconds and travels to the liver and other organs, where it lays its eggs and causes internal bleeding. Its prevention is to be accomplished by adding copper sulphate to the water.

The actual implementation of the project will include the hiring of 60 rural project workers (USAID, 1976a, p. 21). A seed station will be constructed to carry out local selection trials to establish the most effective fertilizer dosages, best seed types, and so forth. In addition, a U.N. development program, FAO seed research at Segou, along the delta proper, and trucks and other equipment from Western Europe will supplement the U.S. contribution of $3.5 million. The project, then, is a classical development project in irrigated agriculture, typical of those that Western governments have been engaged in around the world under the general rubric of the Green Revolution.

In nearly all studies of the Green Revolution, planners and implementers have found that landholding patterns are crucial to the outcome of the project. Where landholding patterns are highly stratified, the wealthier, larger landowners are the first to benefit from the improved varieties of seeds and other inputs. Because of their greater political control of the village or regional bureaucracies, they could shut out the smaller, poorer farmers and thus become even wealthier. By buying up the land of the smaller landholders, they establish themselves as a commercial, merchant elite as well as a landowning class, thus forcing the smaller farmers into becoming either landless laborers or refugees to the towns, where they swell the slums. The extra foods produced by the project may never reach the intended beneficiaries—the poor—whose diets may actually decline in nutritional content and overall caloric intake. The emergent landowning and merchant class will sell the surplus grains to other market areas, or wherever the price is justified in terms of their interests.[2] Therefore, the promise of the Green Revolution to solve the food shortage turns into a boon for the already well-off and a disaster for the poorest families.

GAO, MALI

Land Stratification

But does a potential problem of land stratification exist in the Gao region? USAID's project paper notes a technical study done by SATEC (Société d'Aide Technique et de Coopération) and concludes that "the project appears to be feasible in every respect" (USAID, 1976a, p. 33). The SATEC study, however, includes some important data on landholding patterns and historical trends that seem to have escaped the notice of USAID planners. It notes, for example, that there has been increasing pressure on the irrigable zone in the last few years as well as a decline in the village communal land plots. Furthermore, the institution of salaried workers has arisen. This is explained as resulting from a labor shortage, which is itself a result of a "rural exodus" (SATEC, 1975, p. 12).

The increasing pressure on the land and the loss of labor via migration from the area do not seem consistent with each other. There is an explanatory factor, however: the unequal distribution of land. The SATEC study found that 12 percent of the agricultural population was cultivating plots of 3 ha. or more, and that this 12 percent accounted for 32 percent of the total surface under cultivation. Another 50 percent of the population, cultivating plots of from 1 to 3 ha., accounted for 50 percent of the total cultivated area, while 38 percent accounted for only 18 percent of the cultivated area on plots averaging less than an hectare each (SATEC, 1975, p. 13). A further breakdown of the cultivators of more than 3 ha. would be of great use in assessing the current possibility of the emergence of a commercial and landowning elite, but the data are already enough to warrant serious concern on this question.

A more recent study commissioned by USAID itself produced further important information regarding the stratification of land control in Gao. Two Malian scientists compiled and analyzed data from Gao on a series of issues related to the question of whether the USAID project would continue once the U.S. financing is phased out. In the course of their study, Asseya Woldeyes and Boubacar Bah collected information on landholding patterns in three subareas of the Gao region, all within the project zone. While their data are not directly comparable to those compiled in the SATEC report, they found a direct correlation between size of landholding and amount of equipment used.

In the Moudekane subarea, for example, the smallest average farm size reported in their statistics is 2.25 ha. and accounts for 50 percent of all farms. The smaller farmers planted more sorghum than rice, while the farmers with at least 5 ha. to an average of 16 ha. planted mostly rice. All farmers in this subarea sell some of their harvest, and all have access to some animals for working their fields; but only the farmers in the 16-ha. category are listed as having a "perceptible desire for innovation."

In the nearby Gargouna inundated area, more than 50 percent of all farms are less than one ha., have only sorghum planted on them, and the cultivators do not own animals. Plots of 1.5 ha. and 5 ha. are farmed by owners of animals who also have a "perceptible desire for innovation."

The Tacharane flood plain similarly presents a picture of stratified landholding patterns correlating with animal ownership. The farmers with 0.75-ha. to 1 ha. do not have animals, while the 2-ha. and 4-ha. farms do have animals. None of these farmers, however, is listed as having the innovation desire.

Finally, of all the farms studied, only those in Moudekane with 16 ha. had salaried employees, *but these salaried employees numbered 70 to 80 per farm.* This compares with an average of fewer than 10 workers per farm on all other plots. In the Tacharane plain area, the 4-ha. farms make use of an average of 7 workers. These workers are partly from the holder's family and partly former slaves who are working their former masters' land in return for a small plot of their own, approximately equivalent to sharecropping. In the smallest landowning group of Tacharane, the 0.75-ha. to 1.0-ha. farms, a substantial portion of the work force is away in Togo and Ghana (far to the south) for much of the year (Bureau Africain, 1978).

The land situation in Gao, then, is extremely complex, but several danger signs are evident from even these two initial studies. Land stratification and the existence of commercial networks for grains indicate the likelihood of the development of a landed, commercial elite.

With higher prices for agricultural products obtaining in Nigeria and the Ivory Coast to the south, commercial farmers may be induced to sell their surplus production in those markets rather than locally. The official government price for millet was 35.5 Malian francs per kilogram in February 1978. The black market price was 65 francs and up (interview with U.N. observer in Bamako, February, 1978). A Malian government source estimates that in 1975-76 as much as 10,000 tons of rice and 8 to 10,000 tons of seed cotton were smuggled out of the Niger inland delta region to the west of Gao and into the Ivory Coast (Berg, 1977, vol. II, p. 19). Thus a commercial farming elite, when offered technological innovations to increase production, could enrich itself without ever providing more food to the people for whom the project is ostensibly intended.

At Gao, the large number of salaried employees on the Moudekane farms of 16 ha. or more suggests that the process of commercialization of labor relationships has already begun. The introduction of new technology for increased outputs could further stimulate this process.

What is USAID's response to these findings? A project officer in Mali stated: "We don't get involved in the land problem; that is purely the business of the governor and his staff. This project is strictly technical" (interview in Bamako, March 21, 1978). But if the increased production of cereals leads primarily to the formation of a wealthy landed and merchant class, the project will have been much more than technical: It will have created a major social and economic catastrophe for the poorest farming families in the rural areas around Gao.

Herders Versus Farmers

Yet another aspect of the rice and sorghum project requires consideration here. As was noted with the Bakel Livestock Project in Senegal, livestock and agricultural projects are not integrated, despite the call for integration in the Sahel Development Program document. In Gao, we see another variety of this failure. Even though the Malian government is sponsoring a project to relaunch the herders' cooperatives and to reconstitute the herds in the Gao region, the USAID agricultural project is totally unconnected; not even the staff seems interested in the livestock project. As with the World Bank project in Niger, the USAID irrigated-rice project at Gao may cause a decline in pasturelands available to herders. The SATEC study commented upon the "very great reduction in pasture areas" as a result of the concentration and expansion of farming along the river near Gao. This could lead to the same pattern of overgrazing that de Ravignan warned against in his study for Niger.

Nowhere in the project document or in statements by project staff is there a sign of awareness or concern with the effects of agricultural expansion on the herding population and the further effects of the herders on the environment. The commercial interests of the Gao elite, already endowed with a "perceptible desire for innovation," could set in motion again the cycle of ecological destruction through overgrazing.[3]

NIGER

Cereals and the Large Landholders

On a larger scale than the Gao project, USAID has recently begun implementation of the Niger Cereals Project. The goals of the $9.6 million project include a 200,000-ton increase in cereal production by the end of the project, as compared with the 1965-74 average, and increased incomes for 1.5 million families in a zone along the southern strip of Niger, which includes 90 percent of the country's cereal farmers (USAID, 1975, pp. 8 and 30). The Niger Cereals Project is similar to the Gao rice and sorghum project in many ways, but in Niger, a greater emphasis is being placed on specific innovations in millet production. The use of animal traction to allow for cultivation of the soil before the first rains, better timing of planting, improved weeding, the use of fertilizer, composting techniques to make better and more effective fertilizer from cattle dung, and the like are to be integrated with the key Green Revolution element: improved seeds (USAID, 1975, p. 75).

Heavy emphasis will be placed on the distribution of inputs and new techniques. A national seed center will radiate to a series of regional seed farms, which in turn will train "demonstration farmers," who will be given financial incentives to try the new techniques. The Niger cooperatives structure will be mobilized to manage some levels of the production and marketing. All in all, millet harvests are scheduled to rise above their current low levels of 400 to 500 kg./ha., and soil protection is to be implemented by the use of fertilizers. Several senior foreign seed experts are already at work, and use will also be made of available expertise at Bambey, Senegal, and Zaria, Nigeria, and the "ICRISAT" network in India, which specializes in the development of seeds and agricultural techniques adapted to arid environments (USAID, 1975, pp. 46-59). Through this combination of science, technology, and the national and local cooperative structure, an economic and political goal is to be strived for: to end the "country's dependence on food aid" and establish "the economic and institutional base for a predominantly rural society which is needed for sound development" (USAID, 1975, p. 11).

The cereals project in Niger is ambitious and in many ways well designed. It clearly attacks one of the most serious national economic problems. It offers a way out of the bind that the farmers were trapped in in the 1950s and 1960s, when peanut expansion threatened the ecological relationships. Unlike many of the projects, it even has some consideration for the relations between animals and crops, particularly in the use of animal manure as fertilizer. Finally, the project appears to be tied into a cooperative structure that might be able to avoid the problems of land inequality, such as those in Gao with the rice-sorghum project. Unfortunately, beneath the surface, the Niger Cereals Project suffers from the same essential contradictions as were found in Mali.

The most serious contradiction in the project is the existence of a strongly developed hierarchy in one of the major agricultural zones of eastern Niger, which contains a rural elite with geographical and even cultural-linguistic ties to the enormous Nigerian market to the south. Anthropologist Robert Charlick, in an in-house report for USAID itself, outlines the serious nature of land inequality in the Hausa villages of eastern Niger. This is one of the zones in which commercial peanut production was widely extended during the 1950s and 1960s, and the peanut expansion may well have helped to establish the elite in the area.

Whatever the historical causes, the situation at present seemed clear to Charlick. Regarding the development of animal traction, for example, he writes:

> The only farmers who express a real interest in hiring animal traction for use on sandy soils are those relatively well-off individuals whose non-farm occupations take them away from their fields a great deal during the rainy season and their primary interest is in the first weeding of millet or of peanuts.

The demonstration-farmer system is intended to help develop millet rather than peanuts. But what about the social sources for the demonstration farmers?

> Each request for "village participation" in a government program is initially viewed with suspicion. . . . Ordinary villagers do not volunteer to participate in new programs or new offices, and do not present their candidatures for elections. . . . Instead the village notables assign one of their number or one of their close clients to take the job. [Charlick, n.d., p. 14]

And the situation is getting worse, not better. The wealthy "notables" are actually gaining at the expense of the poorer members of the community.

> I would argue from my recent fieldwork that the economic inequalities are increasing as a result of the drought in that *some farmers have been buying land and loaning millet while others have become deeply indebted and nearly landless* [emphasis added]. [Charlick, n.d., p. 16]

Finally, Charlick (p. 18) offers his expert opinion as to what the project might accomplish: "It is . . . clear that training these sons of notables will only serve to increase economic differentiation in the short-run." Charlick expresses the hope that perhaps in several years the project will encourage some members of the poorer groups to go to training centers, but he offers no structural reason why this should occur. Indeed, the experiences from other parts of the world nearly all suggest that the technological inputs to the elite will simply continue the process of rural impoverishment and rural exodus, and, short of a major social structural change, the production increases will be used by this elite in the most profitable ways. The project will even provide a further income benefit to the already wealthy farmers, for many of them will be able to go into business as commercial seed producers with contracts through the project (interview in Niamey, April 4, 1978).

Here the long Niger-Nigerian border becomes significant. The Niger Government has established numerous checkpoints along the border to control the flow of grain to the more prosperous regions to the south, where grain prices are higher, but these controls are of doubtful efficacy.[4] As in Gao, then, the existence of a land-stratification structure entails the likelihood of the subsistence grain crop becoming a new form of cash crop. While millet is less harmful to the ecology than the peanut, the incentive to increase production, when combined with the technological and scientific means to accomplish it, threatens serious dangers to the environment. If the large landowners find the millet output attractive enough, what will prevent them from overplanting and overexpanding their millet acreage in response to market conditions in the south? Will the disastrous peanut expansion of the 1950s and 1960s be replayed with millet in the coming years as a result of the Niger Cereals Project? Charlick's report was loaned to us from the project file in Niger, but neither project staff members nor the scientific personnel on the project were interested in or concerned with its contents.[5] They considered their work to be primarily technical. However, with no substantiation and without reference to Charlick's warnings, the project document expresses a belief that

> The technical innovations . . . should have a positive environmental impact by improving soil structure and checking soil erosion if implemented in a controlled manner. The extension and cooperative components of the project have been designed to provide the necessary supervision required for the introduction of these technical changes. [USAID, 1975, p. 20]

The report does not indicate how the farming elite will be "supervised." Indeed, even if USAID were prepared to attempt such supervision, it is not certain how far they would get before running into World Bank opposition. In a nearby region, the Bank lists the "training of a farming elite" as one of the desirable "first-phase" elements of an agricultural development program (World Bank, 1974, p. VIII-3).

Cattle and Range Management

The cereals project will be at work all along the narrow agricultural strip of southern Niger. Niger's herders are mostly found at or north of the 15-degree line that stretches across the nation. Several ambitious projects have been developed by European, American, and World Bank teams to increase the marketing of cattle, improve animal health, raise the herders' standard of living, and stop the degradation of pasturelands.

In assessing the role of these projects, the analysis in Chapter 4 should be kept in mind because the same combination of factors that so exacerbated the process of ecological degradation during the 1950s and 1960s now exists: animal health programs, expanding agriculture, and range management plans (well digging and trek routes). The question must be raised whether the new projects have overcome the failures and contradictions of the past.

The seriousness of the situation in the herding zone of Niger was summarized in a USAID report by Marieanne Rupp in 1976. Noting that nutritional levels apparently have been low since the drought, Rupp (p. 5) cites information from local Tuareg women whose breasts dried up prematurely when feeding their infants. Children in turn have displayed a lowered resistance to disease, and adults complain of constipation, abdominal pains, and an inability to muster the physical strength to finish arduous physical tasks. Rupp (p. 8) notes as well that supplementary foods in the diet, such as wild grains and plants, are disappearing, along with game animals and birds, all the result of overhunting and indirectly linked to the drought and famine. Tuareg herders complain that their animals are unhealthy as a consequence of the poor quality of the pasturelands and that many of the animals have suffered from disease and have died. Around the many boreholes dug in the 1950s and 1960s, grasses are almost absent for up to 20 to 30 km. (Rupp, pp. 10-11).

As we discussed previously, a major cause of pastureland degradation was the expansion of agriculture under the stimulus of the peanut program. The effects of this process are still being felt. Rupp (p. 25) notes that herders want the crop-restriction laws enforced, but they also want to develop some cultivation themselves. These wishes are apparently opposed by the Hausa cultivators, who want the areas clearly divided into crop and animal zones. A conflict has even arisen about the wells as a result of the spread of farming into pockets around the herders' animal sites. To this combination of factors must be added the severe crop losses during the drought, 50 percent less in millet and sorghum in 1973-74 than the 1969-70 average, and a 39-percent loss of cattle and 10-percent loss of goats and sheep by the herders (FAO, 1976, p. 42).

In this situation of human deprivation and ecological degradation, USAID has designed the Niger Range and Livestock Project to aid herders in raising their standard of living and to help rejuvenate degraded pastures.

The USAID project stands in the center of the several other range and livestock projects in Niger and most clearly straddles the border between herders and cultivators, where much of the conflict and much of the environmental loss is taking place.

The project is initially a three-year experiment to find ways of preserving the pastures in a 4.5 million ha. region that includes 20 percent of Niger's population but produces only eight percent of its GNP.[6]

Animal health, herders' associations, environmental planning, experiments with new types of grasses, fire monitoring, and the like are all included in the $5 million first phase, which is to be renegotiated for a further several years if the project seems successful.

The project, however, like the Bakel Livestock Project discussed in Chapter 8, has as its economic motivation the production of animals for fattening in regions to the south and their eventual sale either within Niger or in Nigeria and the Ivory Coast. This pits the project against the traditional herding practices and philosophy of the project population, especially those of the Fulani:

> A surplus [of animals] is desirable so that one can give animals to a poorer kinsman or to one whose herd has been decimated by disease. This incentive functions as a levelling mechanism whereby those with larger herds give to those with smaller herds. Not only does the donor obtain prestige, but his gift solidifies kinship ties beyond the camping unit. Thus, as a response to both economic and social values the herders have traditionally attempted to maximize herd size. This is especially true for the Fulani who seem to have a closer attachment to their animals [USAID, 1977, p. 43]

The project paper continues with a rationale for increased commercialization of Fulani cattle:

> While these values may have been functional in the past to cope with the harsh ecological realities of the Sahel, they are not so now in an area with shrinking pasturage and a growing population. Clearly the desire to maximize herd size for social and economic reasons must give way to a more utilitarian view of selling excess animals so as to maintain a balance between herd size and available forage. [ibid.]

The USAID project apparently does not consider that the "shrinking pasturage" is a product of the unsound spread of agriculture into the herding zone. Rather than tackle this problem, the project will simply arrange an increased offtake of animals to help ease the overgrazing problem. Neither the project paper nor the project staff indicate any awareness of the inducements to spreading agriculture that may be involved in the cereals project just to the south. If the grain market should become more inflated, the possibilities of increased production will become more apparent to the elite Hausa farmers as a distinct landowning and merchant class.

Indeed, despite statements from the project staff that they do not intend to tamper with local traditions, the project paper states quite clearly that market incentives are in conflict with the current situation among the Fulani. The recommendation is that "the project staff must study how the herders perceive the market systems and how market incentives can be made more relevant to them. In addition, *extension agents must explain carefully to the herders the need to sell animals and to persuade them to do so*" [emphasis added] (USAID, 1977, p. 49). The extension agents may be in for a difficult time. In addition to the barrier of tradition, USAID itself estimates that the project will have ended a full seven years *before* the herds will be back even to predrought levels.

If this were not enough, the selling of animals comes right up against the problem of elite manipulations in the agricultural zone. As USAID notes:

> Demand for animals is usually lowest during the "soudure" [pre-harvest time of shortage] when herders are converting animals to cash for the purchase of cereals. The demand for animals is depressed at this time by the generally poor condition of the animals and the pasture lands. Conversely, the demand for animals is normally strongest immediately following the rainy seasons when animals are in good condition and pasture is available. However, this peak demand corresponds with a period when herders are normally reluctant to sell, and, as a result the supply of animals on the market is low. [USAID, 1977, p. 103]

The situation thus exists for a speculators' market to be set up. The selling of animals, like the selling of grains, is controlled by the swings in the agricultural production cycle. Marieanne Rupp (1976, p. 20) states that one of the herders' main concerns is the speculators' market in grains, and it may well be that this market is connected—or could become connected—to a similar market in animals, much to the disadvantage of the herders.

The likely ecological offshoots of such a situation are not difficult to predict. To the extent that the cereals project succeeds in creating an ever more powerful landed elite in the agricultural zone, the agriculturalist again may begin to encroach on the herders' pastures. The herders in turn will be encouraged to sell their animals, but a speculators' market will hinder this process and perhaps even reinforce the desire to maintain as large a herd as possible. And to the extent that animals are sold, the economic benefits may well go mostly to the agriculturalists/merchants, whose supplies will allow them to manipulate prices by manipulating supplies. Increased conflicts between herders and agriculturalists, further movements by the herders to the north, and further environmental degradation would then be the outcome of the two large USAID projects: a repeat, with slight variations, of the processes of the past that led to the high drought vulnerability of the region in 1968.

One final problem may also turn the project against its stated goals. Although little research is available, some informal data suggest that certain herding groups are themselves so highly stratified in terms of wealth that the development projects could create an animal-based elite, which might itself be tempted toward overproduction in order to compete with the farming elite to the south. The USAID studies note the hierarchical structure of the Tuareg societies in Niger, although World Bank advisers consider the Tuaregs to be less adapted to cattle raising than the more egalitarian Fulani.[7] Nonetheless, some observers claim that, even among the Fulani, there are now some "chiefs" tied in with the local government livestock officers who control up to 10,000 head of cattle. It is this very group of leaders who are in charge of distributing the animals in the herd reconstruction program of the Niger government.[8]

According to one French observer with many years of experience in Niger, the base for a speculators' market in livestock was established under the Diori regime (1960-74) when the president's wife and local bureaucrats joined to set up a "Fulani political party." This party became a means for bureaucrats to invest in livestock (Nicolas, in Dalby and Church, eds., 1977, p. 161). The extent of these investments is apparently not known in Niger, but the same observer considers it to be a major problem which has resulted in many herders becoming deeply indebted to bureaucrats (ibid., pp. 163-64). In this light, it is somewhat alarming to note that a USAID project staff member described the process for implementing the livestock project as one of "getting in with the chiefs and starting some propaganda." As with the cereals project, it appears the development staff will not be able to control the effects of its propaganda once it enters the local society.

SENEGAL

Bureaucrats Versus Producers

Control of land and control of commercial networks are two common bases for the development and crystallization of a wealthy elite. In many of the former colonized societies, however, these bases were often not developed as rapidly as was the colonial administration itself—the bureaucracy. Especially after the end of formal colonial rule, the government administrators often emerged as an elite. The role of this elite in dispensing development funds and administering projects is crucial in determining the course of the Sahel Development Program. To the extent that the government elite plans and carries out projects of long-term economic and environmental rehabilitation, they will surely have to sacrifice many opportunities for immediate personal and group enrichment. But without popular organization and the participation of the producers, foreign development agencies are often left to watch a program become something quite different from what was ostensibly planned. Despite the attractive phrases in the Sahel Development Program document, the Club of the Sahel can itself do little to organize producers or to "police" the actions of self-aggrandizing bureaucrats.

Two projects from Senegal illustrate this contradiction between the projects and their intended beneficiaries on the one hand and the bureaucratic elite on the other.

The Senegal River is a major potential resource. For many centuries a site of relatively affluent African societies and the scene of some major empires, the Senegal River basin greatly impressed French observers. The explorer Mollien, who traveled upriver in 1818 reported: "The fecundity of the soil provides the inhabitants with considerable plenty" (quoted in Adams, 1977, p. 148).

Indeed, the French were so impressed with the environmental potential that then governor Baron attempted to set up a vast colonization program to transform the basin into an export agricultural region. Begun in 1822, the program had ended in failure by 1831 (Adams, 1977, pp. 149-50). In later years, the French colonial administration took the view that the river basin, with its clayey soils unsuited for peanut cultivation, might be a region for surplus production of food provisions to compensate for the nutritional ravages that the peanut crop had wreaked on Senegalese farmers in the peanut basin to the south. Despite this recognition, plans were never developed (Adams, 1977, p. 153). The colonial administration turned instead to rice imports from then French Indochina. During this period, the colonial administration was more taken with the Niger River inland delta, which seemed to offer more immediate potential for development.[9] In 1938, however, the French colonial government established a commission to study the possibilities of developing the basin. Covering 333,800 km., the river valley contains 12 percent of the total surface area of Guinea, Mali, Mauritania, and Senegal and has a current population of 2.4 million (Franco, 1975, p. 207). Cotton growing failed during World War II, so rice was developed (Maiga, 1976, p. 9). From 1944 to 1957, several projects were undertaken, and by 1957, rice was being grown on 6,000 ha. An expansion to 50,000 ha. was planned, but it failed.

Following independence in 1960, Senegal, Mali, Guinea, and Mauritania established an interstate commission for the development of the Senegal River, but this organization foundered on political in-fighting among the various states concerned. By 1972, Senegal, Mali, and Mauritania had replaced the commission with the Organization for the Development and Exploitation of the Senegal River, or OMVS, the French acronym for l'Organisation de la Mise en Valeur du Fleuve Sénégal.[10]

With the OMVS as an umbrella organization, international funding agencies have been drawn to the Senegal River with ambitious plans to succeed where the French had failed. In addition to extensive rice cultivation, current plans for the development of the Senegal River call for the construction of two major dams (one at Manantali, and one in the delta region); control of the water flow at Bakel at approximately 300 cubic meters a second; the extension of sea navigation up the river all the way to Kayes in Mali; and the creation of several smaller-scale rice perimeters in upstream areas to be aided by small diesel pumps (Franco, 1975, p. 209). Several seed and fertilizer research stations are being established or expanded along the river, where teams of experts try to aid the governments concerned with expanding their crop production in the soon-to-be-irrigated paddy fields. According to one of the major studies outlining the river development project, food self-sufficiency in cereals could be obtained by the year 2005, while the export of sugar and vegetables could begin as early as the year 2000 (Franco, 1975, p. 257).

Nearly all the major donors have responded. France, the United States, West Germany, the World Bank, the People's Republic of China, and others are involved in the project, which may well cost more than $500 million, making it one of the largest single components of the entire Sahel Development Program.

Surely the damming of a major river and the increase in acreage for agriculture should be a positive development. But as one of the project's critics has pointed out, there is no awareness of the social variables as they will effect the outcome of the project (Franco, 1976, esp. p. 288). It may be added that, despite the noble words of the Sahel Development Program concerning the need to overcome the profitability criterion, all the major studies for the Senegal River development are based on narrow profitability considerations (ibid., esp. pp. 250-51).

The most serious problem with the project, however, comes from its Senegalese implementation unit, the Corporation for the Development and Exploitation of the Delta Lands, or SAED, as it is known from its French acronym (Société d'Aménagement et d'Exploitation des terres du Delta du fleuve Sénégal). SAED has been described by one observer as an industrial commercial company administered by a board made up of the representatives from various ministries and operating under the auspices of the Ministry for Rural Development" (Maiga, 1976, p. 11). From this simplified description of SAED, one can gather that it represents in its leadership many members of the upper echelons of the government bureaucracy. In effect, they have set up a section of the government as a corporation, with themselves as its officers.

The powers granted to SAED are enormous: to create dikes and roads; settle and resettle families; train farmers in modern production techniques; supervise the creation and functioning of production and marketing cooperatives; supply inputs such as seeds, fertilizers, and pesticides; purchase paddy, and transport and process it as well (Maiga, 1976, p. 11).[11] Founded in 1965, SAED has grown greatly in financial and political power as a result of the influx of development funds in the Senegal River region.

To understand the effects of SAED, it is useful to divide the Senegal River project into three parts. In the lowland regions—about one-third of the total basin—large-scale, semimechanized production of rice, sugar cane, and vegetables is planned. In the middle and upper basins, from about Matam in Senegal to the river's headwaters, smaller-scale diesel pump perimeters are being established. In each of these regions, similar processes of bureaucratic domination are occurring in slightly different ways (see Figure 9.1).

In the lowlands area of the lower basin, SAED's interventions so far have brought on some of the same problems noted in our discussion of other crop-intensification schemes. In particular, herders have suffered from a loss of pasture lands (Diagne, 1974, p. 51). Equally problematical is the contradictory relationship between irrigated agriculture and "flood reces-

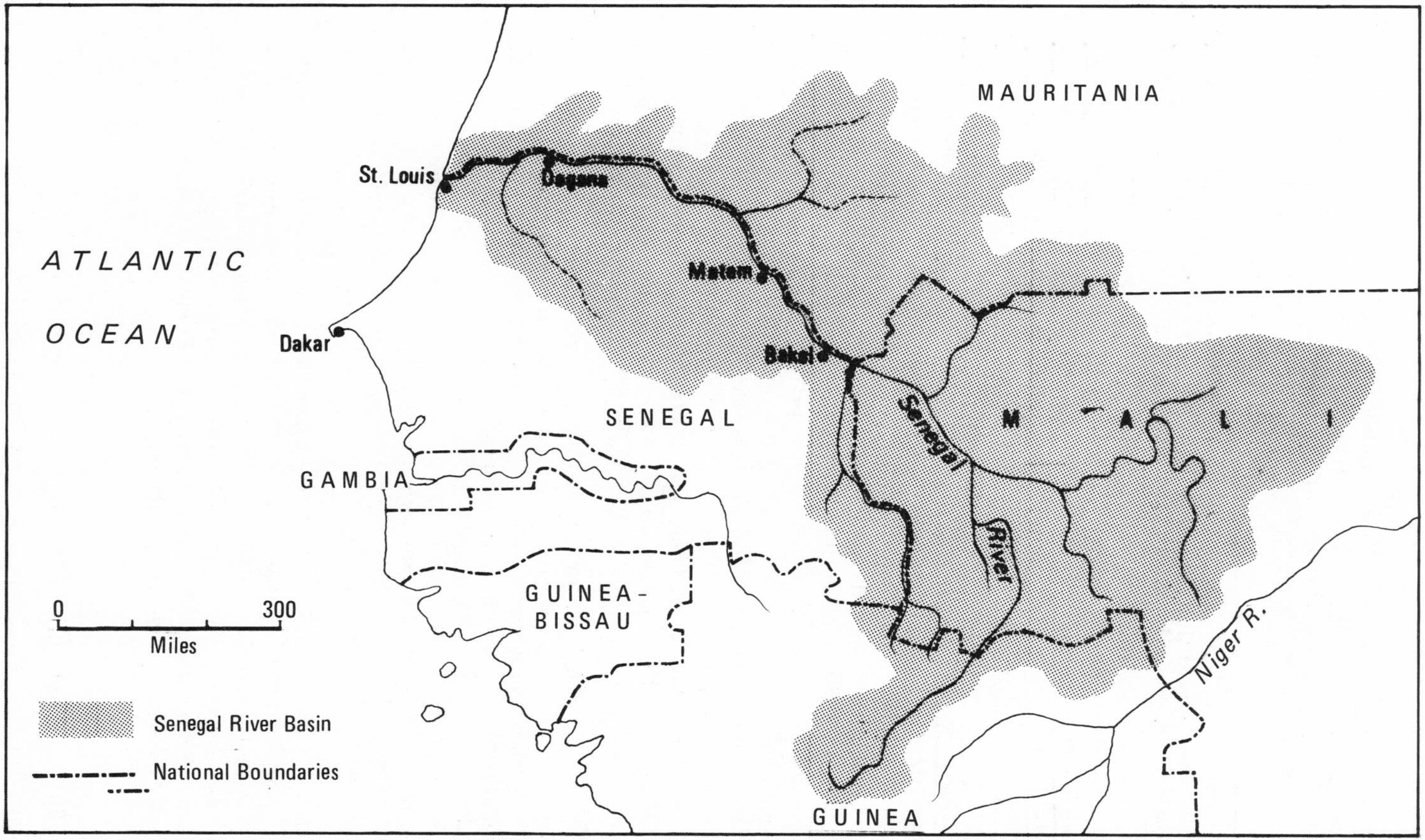

Source: Adapted from Parnell and Utton, 1977, p. 321.

Figure 9.1. Senegal River Basin. The lower valley of primarily irrigated farming runs from St. Louis on the coast to Dagana. The middle region of flood-recession agriculture is from Dagana to a little north of Matam; and the upper basin of primarily rainfed agriculture is upstream from Matam.

sion" agriculture. The former demands a regular flow of water, while the latter requires a rising and falling river. Current plans apparently do not consider this problem (Franco, 1975, p. 215), but the Senegalese bureaucracy is beginning to deal with it upstream in a very special way.

The most serious problem with the rice intensification and dam project of the lower Senegal River seems to be caused, however, by the intensive control exerted by the national, regional, and local bureaucracy over farmers and herders through SAED. Near the town of Podor, for example, a small-scale study was conducted on the depression agriculture (*cuvette*) area of Pété by Moctar Ba in 1977. Ba discovered that the application of Senegal's land nationalization in two villages amounted to a *confiscation* of the land by the government, the creation of a cooperative dominated by the "privileged members" of the community, and the charging of 1,000 francs per family to join the co-op—that is, to get rights to what had previously been their own land. The partial outcome of this development is summarized by Ba: "The peasants find themselves caught in a vicious circle where they have been transformed into farm workers whose salaries are not even fixed before they start work" (Ba, 1977, p. 8). Ba comments that SAED has been increasing its control over the villages through the means of undemocratic, nonparticipatory cooperatives: As an example, he cites the village head who has received four parcels of land (ibid., p. 3).

The problems with SAED have even reverberated slightly in the United States. In congressional testimony, USAID official David Shear responded to a question from Cong. Charles Diggs (D-Mich) at House hearings held on March 23, 1977. Diggs noted "some criticism" of the Senegalese government agency (presumably SAED). Shear replied:

> We have entered into a series of discussions over the last two years with the Senegalese agency charged with assisting in the resettlement of the river basin. We have presented, in the course of the last two years, several plans for increasing the popular participation in those resettlement activities.
>
> I think we can say that we have achieved a fair amount of success in redirecting the efforts of this organization toward getting much greater participation of the local people. I should also emphasize, however, that we are not wholly satisfied with the existing state of affairs and will continue to work with that organization. [US House, 1977, p. 98]

Shear's assessment of the situation apparently is not shared by many of the staff people and Peace Corps personnel either working on the USAID project or frequently traveling in the region. Their general pessimism, cynicism, and criticism of the Senegalese government often turned to the role of bureaucrats and their insensitivity to the general population. Shear did not provide his sources to the committee.

Irrigation Versus Flood Recession in the Middle Valley

Despite the possibly greater potential for large-scale production in the Senegal River delta, it is in the middle and upper basins that much of the immediate development planning is coming to fruition. The middle region, especially the area near Matam (see Figure 9.1), had attracted French interest initially because of the larger population, but it was left more or less untouched because French observers noted strong social ties to the land, which would require major political and military actions to bring under control (see Adams, 1977, pp. 154-65).

The middle basin of the Senegal River is largely inhabited by people of the Tukulor culture group. The area is one of the most important of the "flood recession" agricultural zones of the Sahel. Herders and farmers have developed a traditional association. On the *dieri*, or highland areas, soils are more sandy and water is less available. Millet and groundnuts are typically grown in this area.

Another major zone is the *walo*, or river depressions. Here, farmers sow their millet and sorghum as the river floods recede, leaving watery, clayey soil that is good for grains but not for peanuts (Bradley, et al., 1977, pp. 65-70).

The importance of the flood recession for the agricultural cycle has been noted by river-development critic Mark Franco, who points out that the choice of a dam to manage the water flow throughout the year pits rice against millet and sorghum. This comes about because rice needs a steady flow of water throughout most of its growing season, while the flood-recession millet needs a declining river bank (Franco, 1975, p. 213). Thus, in choosing to construct certain water and irrigation works, the Senegalese government and its Sahel Development Program advisers and donors are asserting their claim to control the kinds of food produced and the techniques of production in the middle Senegal River basin.

The establishment of irrigated ricelands is not awaiting the sudden completion of a large dam. As early as 1973, SAED with French technical assistance began to establish small irrigated rice "perimeters" at Dagana and Nianga in the middle region (Adams, 1977, p. 163). By 1974, SAED had become the official development agency for the entire Senegal River basin, from St. Louis at the Atlantic Ocean to the interior border with Mali. Some of the upper basin fell within this area. Gradually, diesel pumps, rice seeds, fertilizers, and pesticides have been spreading upriver, creating small production regions where irrigation and rice are supplanting flood-recession millet or sorghum as well as the rainfed agriculture which is dominant in the upper basin.

The Upstream Rice Perimeters at Bakel

The expansion of SAED's river development work in the upper basin has run into an obstacle which neither the development experts nor the Senegalese bureaucrats seem to have foreseen. This is the organized social and political determination of a locally built association, the Federation of Soninke Peasants, and its constituent village work groups. Despite its enthusiastic endorsement of the popular participation in the Soninke villages, USAID has effectively joined SAED in a political campaign to thwart local initiatives and impose a development model incompatible with local social and ecological conditions. To understand this problem some historical background is needed.

The Soninke peasants federation grew out of the experiences of a villager from the region. Having spent some 20 years in the military and the merchant marine, he traveled home and then went to France, where he acquired a rototiller and a small pump, which he brought back to the village in 1973. Along with the equipment came the promise of technical aid from a French consortium. The French technician arrived in 1974. A discussion in the village is recalled by the local initiator of the project: "They asked me, 'Will we be working for ourselves, or for the white man?' I replied: 'For us, that's what development is all about'" (quoted in Adams, 1977, p. 135). Despite skepticism among the villagers, the initiators began to hold meetings and discuss how to proceed. A work group was formed using traditional Soninke concepts, and a successful season of millet, corn, tomatoes, lettuce, and onions followed. This attracted others to the collective. By 1975, 200 men and 70 women had joined, creating an agricultural work group, with the original initiator elected president.

The idea of collective work groups and small, motorized pumps spread to three other villages in the region (Adams, 1977, pp. 135-37). Officially organized in 1976, by 1978 the Federation had spread to 19 villages in the region and had elected officers, established local chapters, and developed a written set of principles.

In 1975, the spontaneous local initiatives of the Soninke came face to face with SAED. Having failed to develop the lower and middle basins of the river, SAED moved into the Soninke area with a meeting at the initiator's village in April 1975. In December 1974, USAID had already taken over the financing of the Bakel region rice perimeters, and the French technical expert had been called for private meetings with the SAED staff at headquarters in St. Louis. A rising crescendo of both public and private meetings ensued, with the Federation peasants asserting their willingness to work with SAED but insisting on the right to choose which technical offerings to use and how to organize their plots. It was apparent throughout this time that there were at least three major motivations behind the Federation's opposition to SAED. First, it believed that its main success so far had come about because of the cooperative, locally initiated system of production, over which it was prepared to resist outside control. Second, it knew of the plight of downriver peasants, whose participation in SAED programs had essentially locked them into a system of indebtedness. Third, the high-handed manner of SAED officials led to a strong skepticism on the part of the villagers as to the ultimate motives of the bureaucrats.

The tensions that have developed in the Soninke region have been maintained as a kind of standoff in which condescending Senegalese bureaucrats lecture farmers and their elected cooperative leaders and are responded to with sincere, firm replies as to the peoples' wishes. The government has resorted however, to bribes and pressure maneuvers, including the offer of trips to France for better-off members of one town local of the Federation; it has also attempted to pressure cooperative groups into planting rice and using inputs in the amounts—and with the debt implications—required by SAED's plans.[12]

The expansion of rice cultivation creates a serious economic hardship on farming communities in the Bakel region. The village cooperatives are instructed to use certain inputs and to cultivate rice, which they must then sell to pay for the debts incurred from using the inputs. The rice is intended for the urban market, after providing a profit to the SAED bureaucrats, while the farmers are to be left with an insufficient cash fund. In 1978, rice sold for 60 francs a kilogram, while millet sold for 80. Is it any wonder that the cooperatives hesitate to grow rice? And is it any wonder that the elected president of the Federation has stated: "The SAED works for its own interests, not for the peasants. All the peasants along the Senegal River know this" (quoted in Adams, 1977, p. 175).

Regional bureaucratic representatives are first and foremost trying to implement a plan for their own aggrandizement and to supply the urban rice market. In such a context, it is difficult to see how local environmental needs can be met. What are the views of the donor agency in these matters?

USAID Versus the Bakel Producers

According to the project staff and the project paper, the Bakel irrigated perimeters are an unqualified success story of the first order. With 350 ha. planted in 1978 and an eventual 1,700 ha. planned, the $3.1 million seems like a good investment. Indeed, USAID's Washington office telegramed the Dakar staff in January 1977 to inform them of "the prototype nature of the project in relation to overall Sahel development strategy and its relatively high profile currently in the agency" (USAID, 1977a, telegram of January 28, 1977, in project paper, vol. II).[13]

There are several reasons for the project's current "high profile" in the agency. As USAID has it, the Bakel irrigated perimeters are a development agency's dream, involving donor countries, a local agricultural extension service, and, most importantly, the participation of the local community. As the project paper puts it: "The project already has a tremendous village level, grass-roots impetus and all technical, environmental, and economic analyses are positive" (USAID, 1977a, p. 3). At a more gutsy level, the project's current director explained that "the project has merit because the local people themselves will be running the darn thing" (interview in Dakar, April 25, 1978).

USAID even had a sociological study commissioned to further check on the prospects for success. The Bakel crop-project sociological report "found great support for the project among the villagers and predicted wide acceptance of the project by the target group." The sociologist "further found that the methodology used by SAED and technical assistance in the project area was the approach most likely to succeed . . . . The basic 'hands off' policy of SAED in the area is very appealing . . . to the local population" (USAID, 1977a, p. 7).

To complete its picture of the essential elements of the project, USAID apparently believes that the involvement of SAED came at the request of the farmers in the area. The project's 1978 director explained that "the people hit SAED with the proposition that it provide them with heavier equipment" than the small motorized pumps and rototillers then in use (interview, Dakar, April 25, 1978). USAID is apparently so convinced that the project is on the right track that it is supplementing the seed research, pumps, financial support to SAED, and so forth with a special project for a $1.5 million solar-pump experiment. This pump is intended to irrigate 200 ha., and it is hoped that after seven years the pump will begin to pay for itself in cheaper running costs compared to the diesel pumps currently in use.[14]

When one goes a rung below the official telegrams, project papers, and project directors, the enthusiastic picture fades. For example, one middle-level staffer informed us, completely independently of the information we received in the villages themselves, of the harmful economic effects of the SAED insistence on rice. Corn is a better investment, he affirmed, although he could not say whether the American advisers were in a position to effect a change in SAED's policies. More seriously, this same staffer insisted that the collective work approach was not working and that most of the villages were "going individual" in order to get things done. He added that SAED was explaining to people "in black and white terms" the need for individual plots as opposed to the collective ones (interview, Dakar, April 25, 1978). USAID's enthusiasm for local initiative and peoples' participation apparently does not extend to the inspiration to work as a group and oppose local and regional orders.

Another source for concern comes from a study by the American Public Health Association. Assessing the possible health effects of the irrigated perimeters, John Nebiker cites malaria as a major cause of death and debilitation. Despite the need for shade near the fields, he recommends that the irrigated fields be kept cleared and that dwellings be kept as far away as possible from cultivated zones. Further, he states: "As it now appears, malaria elimination in Africa is impossible, and certainly the Bakel area is not an exception, and therefore prophylaxis will be needed indefinitely" (APHA, 1977, p. 47). Nebiker continues by noting that of an informal sample of mosquitos captured, two-fifths were of the anopheles type, a typical malaria carrier. Additional data to indicate the disease potential of the perimeters are contained in information from two villages on the rate of malaria in the one to nine-year age group. In one, 75 percent of this group was infected with malaria in 1968. By 1977, after several years of drought, the rate had dropped to 53 percent. In another village, by contrast, the rate of infection dropped from 60 percent to 22 percent. Significantly, the second village did not have an irrigated perimeter during this period, while the first had one after 1973. The authors of the study warn against too quickly attributing the higher maintainance of malaria in the first village to the irrigated perimeter, but they do state that the differences in the drop are significant statistically (APHA, 1977, p. D-8).

Finally, Nebiker cites various studies that show high rates of infection of the schistosomiasis parasite in the region. These run as high as 40 percent upstream in Mali and 16 percent in Senegal, with higher rates for certain age groups that are in more frequent contact with water. In a nearby town, a 35-percent infection rate was found.

These data are by themselves indications of the many serious problems that the people of the Bakel region must face in their attempt to create a viable and successful development program. But they also illustrate SAED's general attitude toward the population it is "developing." In response to the schistosomiasis data, for example, SAED claims to have research that shows there are only 28 cases in an area population of 30,000 (APHA, 1977, p. E-4). As for malaria, SAED took a survey and claimed they could not find a single anopheles mosquito! In addition, they denied that there was any likelihood that the irrigation works would create ponds, because even in the dry season the ponds are flushed out every five to seven days, which does not allow the mosquito larvae time to breed. The larvae need seven to eight days, so SAED is cutting it rather close, but they are apparently confident of their ability to control the problem, *and they have thus rejected the suggestion for free distribution of malaria suppressant pills to the population* (APHA, 1977, p. 47).

SAED's arrogant refusal to accept medical supplies, which could do only good for the population, is a sign of the excessive bureaucratic mentality at work. Despite the obvious evidence, however, the doctors of the American Public Health Association glance over the implications in their own report and proclaim that "a distinctive feature of the crop production project in the Bakel region of Senegal is its grass-roots, small size, self-help character. It builds on the initiative, cooperation and continued effort of the effected populations" (APHA, 1977, p. G-10). Except, one might add, where malaria and schistosomiasis are concerned.

SAED Versus the Federation of Soninke Peasants

By May 1978, the situation in the 19 villages united under the Soninke Federation had become increasingly tense. A semilegal battle was developing in which the Federation was attempting, with the aid of lawyers, to get official status from the Senegalese government. The Federation was receiving a lengthy runaround, at great cost in time and resources. At the same time, SAED was pressuring villages to plant crops and use inputs according to their directives, even to the point of telling villagers in one area that all the others had agreed to go along; and sometimes they simply appeared unannounced with a truckload of inputs and loan papers.

Several village work-groups, on the other hand, have continued to resist SAED's attempts to gain control over them. The most remarkable feature of the Federation's approach in many ways is the calm, organized, but flexible and creative manner in which leadership and members go about their planting, harvesting, dike building, meetings, bookkeeping, and mini-confrontations with SAED, all in the same busy weeks. Federation officers are elected but are not paid any additional salary above their share of the collective output.[15]

The land system is changing through a series of continuing experiments. At present, the Federation unit in one village has four specific types of land patterns for agriculture, each with its own special purpose.

First, there are the collective fields. In 1977, these amounted to 7 ha. and are to be expanded to 16 ha. during the 1978 planting season (June to September). The collective fields are designed to make maximum use of the small diesel pump. Land and irrigation-canal patterns are laid out according to the best water-use system, rather than irrationally along private property lines. Work groups rotate on a daily basis to maintain and improve the irrigation infrastructure, so some work is being done nearly every day when necessary, and everyone can expect a certain size of work group to be out for repairs and improvements. Members who must avoid a day's work—and collective members working overseas in France—pay a cash equivalent of a day's salary at high wages. Local members are discouraged from using their money to replace their labor, and collective elected leaders make a point of being present and active on the fields. The collective fields' produce is stored, marketed, sold, and divided up among the work groups according to decisions reached at local meetings. Money brought in from cash sales may be devoted to new inputs, such as fertilizer, repairs on the pump, or purchase of additional grains in a bad year.

A second form of landholding is the household plot. Households contain anywhere from 15 to 100 members. Since all households in the village have representatives in the collective group, all can decide together how much land will be set aside for household plots. These plots usually are in the rainfed or flood recession areas along the river bank. Individual households decide for themselves what to plant there: Most choose crops that are not in the collective plots.

Individual plots make up the third form of landholding. Some areas are left for individuals to plant as they see fit. Younger men often plant vegetables for their immediate families' diet, and women may cultivate specific crops such as beans, from which they make a nutritious sauce for the millet couscous. These plots were begun on an experimental basis by several work-groups in 1978. Far into the interior, as many as several kilometers away from the river bank, women have established small peanut gardens. The women are essentially in control of these plots and their output.

The Federation of Soninke Peasants is bringing together a combination of traditional communal landholding and financial practices with certain organizational forms developed from outside. The overall structure of the Federation is influenced somewhat by the experiences of some local farmers who were members of French unions, in particular the Seaman's Union, in previous years. The collectives function primarily at the behest of local initiative, and there is much room for creative experimentation with land

and labor and labor organization, the absorption of new technical inputs, and local control over the production resources of the villages.

How have SAED and USAID responded to this situation? SAED's response has been noted above. The various forms of attempted intimidation and coercion appear intended to achieve one outcome: the breaking up of the Federation and its local associations, and the establishment of SAED bureaucratic control over the production system so that rice can be grown for the Dakar urban market and SAED officials can reap profits off the system of loans as they have done in the lower river basin.

In an interview with the local SAED official stationed at the district town of Bakel, we received a litany of complaints about the Federation. The collective fields do not make the pump a payable proposition, we were told. And the work groups do not function well; people do not keep up their fields. The peasants are hardheaded about their millet and corn and do not see the increases in output that are possible. SAED is here only to serve the farmers (interview conducted at Bakel, May 16, 1978).

And what is the response of USAID? To judge from the project paper and the statements of the project staff, the American aid community is trying to have the best of all possible worlds. While praising the project for its "local, grass-roots" character and praising SAED for its "go-slow approach," USAID is helping to strengthen SAED's campaign for the destruction of the Federation. The money for the irrigated perimeters goes from USAID to SAED, SAED administers the use of the funds in each village, and SAED now has $3.1 million more than it did. The opportunities for bribery, offering of technology on a selective basis to those willing to break with the Federation, and other tactics will be all the more available. SAED is not an all-powerful body, however, and the Soninke Federation has shown a disciplined, determined ability to survive in the past. But if genuine, participatory development occurs in the upper Senegal River basin, it will apparently be in spite of U.S. donor funds for Sahel development and not because of them.

Bakel and the Environment

Finally, what are the effects of this situation on the problems of the environment? We have mentioned earlier that the Bakel irrigated perimeters are in the same region as the US-funded Bakel Livestock Project. The lack of integration of these two projects means that the uses of the herders' animals will not be available to the farmers. Both animal traction and fertilizing of the soil are thus lost to the farmers (even though some farmers do have their own cattle). Equally important, however, are the effects of SAED's campaign against the Federation.

Despite the willingness of the collectives to take up new technology when they view it to be in their interest, and despite their eagerness for new technical knowledge, the Senegalese Agricultural Extension Service—as represented by SAED in this region—does not make available information that could help increase outputs and maintain or improve soil fertility. During our visit to the area in May 1978, we saw tomato crops, for example, that were far below potential probably because nematodes or root worms had attacked them. A crop rotational method of avoiding this problem has been known to the Senegalese Agricultural Extension Service for many years, but it was never made available to Federation farmers. Similarly, SAED sold bad onion seeds to the Federation in 1977, and there has apparently been a new pump provided in one village to a Moslem school teacher who is cultivating plots in opposition to the Federation. The pump was ultimately purchased by USAID, but the establishment of two competing perimeters is not the best way to manage water and soil resources.

THE SAHELIAN ELITES: GUARDIANS OF THE ENVIRONMENT?

The case of the Soninke Peasants' Federation brings into sharp relief the problem of Sahelian elites. While the officers of the Federation work with their colleagues on the dikes and fields and receive only their fair share of the harvest, the bureaucrats of SAED and of other agencies expect the development projects to make them wealthier and more powerful. The needs of the environment, like the needs of the poorest villagers, may be little more than a handy slogan for personal and group aggrandizement. Anthropologist Adrian Adams reminds her readers of André Gide's comments on development in French colonial Africa: "In the colonies, it is always the most beautiful ideals that are covering the most shameful practices" (Adams, 1977, p. 200).

The political alliance between U.S. and French multinational corporate interests and African elites can be made more palatable to the sincere, humanitarian ideals of many people in the donor countries by reference to the innovations, the large amounts of money, and the desperate needs of Sahelians. In the final analysis, however, even chief spokespeople announce the basically conservative underpinnings of the "new approach" in Sahel development. U.S. representative Maurice Williams told the *New York Times*, on the occasion of the Ottawa meeting of the Club of the Sahel, that "donors have agreed not to look for perfect solutions, but rather to work with and build up existing institutions."[16]

Williams does not seem to have considered that the building up of existing institutions might have negative effects for the program. If the Sahel Development Program, with all its innovative international committees and working teams and all its progressive calls for a rebuilding of the environment, cannot outflank, bypass, or undercut Sahelian elite interest groups most often represented in the government bureaucracies, how will the Sahel Development Program be able to avoid furthering the processes of ecological destruction?

NOTES

1. A later study asserts that 291,000 people will be affected by the project (Bureau Africain, 1978, p. 29).

2. For some critical reviews of the Green Revolution in several parts of the world, see George, 1977; Perelman, 1978; Lappé and Collins, 1977; Franke, 1974, 1974a, 1975; and Griffin, 1974.

3. Dr. James Thomsen provides a parallel but slightly different case of conflicting interests of bureaucrats and villagers in a Niger forest-recovery project. See Glantz, ed., 1977, pp. 57–79.

4. John Davison Collins (1976) describes the illicit trade in peanuts across the Niger-Nigerian border in the 1960s.

5. We interviewed the current and previous directors of the project and three senior scientists working in 1978.

6. Additional information in this section not otherwise given a reference comes from interviews with the project staff in Niamey, March 31 and April 12, 1978. The wealth and population statistics come from the project director.

7. The $16 million World Bank livestock project in the Zinder-Maradi region is summarized as an annex to the USAID project paper. It will create livestock-fattening centers of 25,000 to 30,000 head of cattle and encourage the development of "model herders" somewhat similar to the demonstration farmers of USAID's cereals project.

8. This information was obtained in an interview with a FED project consultant in Niamey, April 3, 1978.

9. Adrian Adams quotes an interesting study from 1934, in which A. Minot illustrates the French attitude toward the Senegal River as a potential source for French profits:

Is there a crop which would be sold in Europe with a beneficial return to Senegalese farmers? Is there for the clayey but irrigable soils, despite the difficulties of the river basin, an equivalent of what the peanut has been for the more sandy soils of Cayor, Baol and Sine? [Adams, 1977, p. 157]

10. A detailed history of these developments is given in Adams, 1977, pp. 159–65. An uncritical overview of Senegal River development appears in Parnell and Utton, 1977.

11. The intensity of SAED's control over the production process is indicated in part by the density of its personnel: an agricultural engineer for each 1,500 ha.; an agricultural technician for each 400 ha.; and a rural project officer for each 100 ha., who is also responsible for the daily organization of labor (Adams, 1977, p. 161).

12. Adams, 1977, pp. 169–70. Some of this information was also obtained in one-the-spot observations and interviews in the Bakel region in May of 1978.

13. Information on the view of American aid personnel comes from USAID, 1977a; American Public Health Association, 1977; and from interviews with the project staff in Dakar in January and May, 1978.

14. The contract for the pump has been awarded to the Thermal Electron Company of Waltham, Massachusetts, and an unnamed French firm (interview, April 25, 1978).

15. One staff person, the keeper of the warehouse, receives a small extra allotment of grain each season as payment for his many hours of work in maintaining the condition of the stores of grains. But this payment must be agreed upon by the local producers' group in each village.

16. *New York Times*, May 31, 1977.

10

Alternatives For the Future: a Development Challenge

Are all Sahel projects doomed to failure? Does the combination of Western government-multinational interests and the interests of Sahelian elites render impossible the successful tackling of the enormous ecological and production problems in the region? Are there meaningful alternatives to present projects?

In our view, there is no simple blueprint for changing current projects, but there are features of several projects that imply general lines of approach. These more promising projects generally lie outside the major donors and agencies. A brief survey of some will set the stage for a few tentative conclusions regarding the possible directions for the future.

GUIDIMAKA: SOCIAL ANALYSIS AND DEVELOPMENT

Directly across the Senegal River from the embattled Soninke federation is a project for agricultural and livestock development in the Guidimaka district of Mauritania, funded with approximately $500,000 from the British-based charity War on Want. The Guidimaka project, however, is anything but a charity program.

Based upon several detailed investigations, the Guidimaka project paper includes a thorough socieconomic history of the area, soil and vegetation data, an outline of the major agricultural practices, and information on the crucial variable of availability of labor to implement the project. Unlike the many USAID projects we have surveyed, which either ignore social variables, filing them in specialized reports or summarizing them with a superficiality that often obscures their content, the authors of the Guidimaka study begin their outline with "The Social Framework for Technical Activities," following historical and other background material (Bradley et al., 1977, pp. 133-38).

This section of the document, based on the traditional organization of the society, begins: "The formation of collective organisations, which would form the framework within which the envisaged technical activities could be implemented, is a fundamental component of the project" (Bradley, et al., 1977, p. 133). This organization is not to be imposed from outside but it will be part of the process by which the Guidimaka district villagers organize their own agricultural and herding activities. The village associations will become units of discussion, planning, and participation in the implementation of the project—not mere actors in carrying out the orders of a bureaucracy. A plan of action is to be developed for each village by the village associations. No specific crops are called for in terms of outside market needs, as is being done by Senegal's SAED across the river. Indeed, instructions are reversed: "The project staff must make sure that they leave the maximum of responsibility for the practical execution of the programme with the groups involved" (Bradley et al., 1977, p. 136).

Livestock management and the interactions between farmers and herders are also to be developed according to principles of collective organization. Unlike SAED, which mistrusts the people and appears eager to break up the collective basis of local culture, the War on Want project takes this organization as a strength through which the people can work together to raise their average technical level and food output. The project design specifically opposes the training of "model farmers" or other individual demonstration innovators, which are such a part of the big donor projects. The outcome of a successful project of this type would be the prevention of the rise of a local elite, and to that extent it would bypass the dangers that such an elite would pose to the environment and to the poorest groups in the society. In addition, the project is designed to emphasize the creativity and knowledge of the entire population, thus holding out hope for a more fruitful interaction between the small number of Western-trained technicians and the people their training is intended to benefit. As stated in the project document:

> The formation of the [collective farming] group will ensure the circulation of information among individuals who confront the same problems, through the continuous discussion of their successes, their failures, and the difficulties which they encounter.

Eventually, it is hoped that the different village associations will also meet to interact across village lines, thus further intensifying the exchange of knowledge and ideas (Bradley et al., 1977, p. 137). As the people themselves experiment, technical support will be provided for various activities, including the cultivation of millet, sorghum, rice, wheat, animal forage, tomatoes, fruits, and other crops, and perhaps crafts and other nonagricultural developments.

The 11,150 Mauritanians in the project area thus face the possibility of a development process in which they will be active participants. The project has only begun, but even from its design, it can be seen as a conscious attempt by a small donor agency to avoid the kinds of problems we have analyzed in the previous two chapters. Needless to say, much is dependent on the Mauritanian national bureaucracy, which must support the project consistently if it is to be successful.[1]

TABELOT: TUAREG GARDENS

Tabelot is situated 850 meters above sea level in the dramatic Aïr Mountains region of Niger. The black cones of ancient, extinct volcanoes contrast with the waving green date palms and other vegetation in the oases that dot the landscape. The area is populated with sedentarized Tuaregs who have been living here for about 50 years. They are thought to be descendents of the former slave castes, and they have a heritage of gardening. Of the approximately 500 families living there, about half are gardeners and the rest herders. Both groups suffered from the drought when wells ran dry and animals died.

Since the end of 1974, two members of the Church of the Brethren, working under the direction of the Church World Service, have been living in the area and assisting the Tuareg in several directions. The aims have been relatively modest, but useful things have been accomplished.[2] The main emphasis has been to make gardening a more viable activity. The area is geologically unusual in that good water is only about five meters below the surface, so wells and simple irrigation systems can be constructed without great difficulty. The church project has helped build some 40 cement wells. These replace the traditional dirt wells, which have a tendency to collapse. The concrete wells do not have to be bolstered by trees and they also help preserve the vegetation. The project supplies the cement, but the work itself is done by the farmers. Attempts have been made to prevent disruptive effects on community life. The wells are built on land that is worked by the owners in order to avoid disputes that might arise if someone put work into a well on land he did not actually own.

The Church of the Brethren has helped people purchase animals by making loans to buy oxen and heifers, which are used to draw the water from the wells into irrigation canals. Wheat, garlic, onions, tomatoes, date palms, and potatoes are the main crops. New varieties of potatoes from France have been introduced with success. More than 200 tons have been grown and 30 tons of seeds have been sent to other parts of the country. The growing of date palms has also been subsidized. These are normally a very slow-growing tree, but it has been discovered that a sprout taken from a tree's side and planted will begin bearing in a year. People from Tabelot were given financial assistance, allowing them to make a trip across the mountains to Timia, an oasis, where sprouts were selected and brought back.

Wherever possible, local resources are used. Crops are fertilized with animal manure and with soil taken from around the Tabiskan tree, a foul-smelling tree whose roots are continually rotting. In order to get the crops to market in Agades, the main commercial center in the Aïr region, 75 miles away, the project organized the building of a road. About 80 men worked for four months, hacking away at the rock-covered ground with crowbars, picks, shovels, and rakes. Food and water had to be brought from the towns of Agades or Tabelot. Herders have also benefited from the road; they now have an easier route for bringing their animals to Agades. The North American project directors speak the local language, Tamachek, and have developed close relationships with people in Tabelot, spending much of their time actually living in the village. Their personal qualities have undoubtedly contributed to the project's success. Warm, outgoing, energetic people who have spent much time in West African village settings, they have a deep commitment to their work.

Not all, however, are benefiting equally from their efforts. Merchants speculate on the crops. For example, farmers will be lent 35 francs a kilo for the promise of their wheat at harvest time. But at harvest, the price may actually be twice that of the loan. Increased wealth mainly manifests itself in the form of luxury-item consumption, such as sugar and radios. More people are now able to afford the very expensive pilgrimage to Mecca.

The project has helped organize a cooperative that runs a small shop and does some buying and marketing. The decisions of the cooperative, however, are influenced by the existing social situation. An individual who is politically powerful in the village may actually be a bad credit risk, but no one dares offend him by refusing him a loan. The organizers agree that the projects themselves may be only temporary, dependent as they are on the vagaries of outside funding and personnel, whereas the villagers are permanent residents. They cannot take the chance of offending someone who may harm them in the future. The existing leadership in the village must be persuaded to support the projects, and this may mean giving them first chance to acquire new things such as the cement wells, thus furthering the inequalities.

The project at Tabelot could be continued when the foreigners leave if the Niger government is willing to continue giving support. If government agents in the area are unenthusiastic about the work, then most likely it will not be funded, people will become discouraged, and some of the gains made will eventually be lost. The hostility between the central government dominated by Hausas and the Tuareg interferes with efforts to improve life in Tabelot. There is also a problem of the local river flooding the garden plots in the rainy season. USAID contributed a small grant to build retaining walls on the edges of gardens bordering the river, but the Niger government was not so helpful. They refused assistance, since some of the officials would rather see the Tuaregs of the Aïr resettled farther south and are not interested in transforming the Aïr into a more viable region. In Tabelot, progress is thus coming to compete with vested interests locally and elsewhere in the national society.

TIMBUKTU: THE ISLE OF PEACE PROJECT

Eight kilometers from the city of Timbuktu lies a fertile flood plain of the Niger River inland delta. In 1954–55, the French colonial government built a 14-km.-long dike enclosing approximately 1,300 ha. where floating rice could be cultivated. The hydraulic works, however, were not properly constructed, with the result that sections of the rice field would flood at the wrong times or would not flood when needed. Timbuktu, with its 15,000 inhabitants and 50,000 farmers and herders in the region, is perennially food-deficient and was particularly hard hit by the 1968–74 drought and famine. Improvements in the water-control system for the Korioume plain and surrounding areas are thus of great significance for people in the area. The lack of roads and the failure of the river to remain high enough for water transport during six to nine months of the year render the area especially susceptible to food shortages.

In 1977, work began on a project to improve and revitalize the hydraulic works and to introduce intermediate technology for the production of floating rice on the Korioume plain. The organization involved, the Dominique Pire Foundation of Belgium, is a small, private foundation funded by the Nobel Prize money of Dominique Pire and supplemented by an annual collection from the Belgian public.

In many ways, the Isle of Peace project is like many of those we have criticized in earlier chapters. Improved water management, introduction of new seed varieties, animal traction, medical and school facilities on a limited scale, a farmers' cooperative, tree-planting for village shade, and the like are being developed by the project team.

There are two important differences, however, between the Isle of Peace approach and many other development projects in the Sahel. First, the project staff is committed to remaining for a minimum of five years. Unlike many USAID staff, who are rotated in and out of a project area on a two- or three-year basis, or World Bank advisers, who pop in and out, often spending little more than a few weeks or even days in a country, the Isle of Peace team will use their accumulated experiences directly in the project area. A second difference is even more important. The project team discovered a major landholding problem at Korioume. Because the plain was uninhabited in the recent past, the French-built rice perimeter was largely taken over by the most powerful bureaucrats and town merchants in Timbuktu. On the basis of input from the project staff, a meeting was organized in June 1978, with the regional governor and the local military commander present. A decision was reached to parcel out the land of Korioume plain on the basis of 50 ares (.5 ha.) per active inhabitant, based on divisions among families and traditional landworking groups, which include six district organizations within Timbuktu and seven rural groups, each with its own elected council (Fondation, 1979, p. 18). While this partitioning does not in itself ensure that the Timbuktu merchants will lose control over the plain, the project's director assured us in an interview (March 17, 1978) that the effect of the redistribution would be to make the land available only to actual farmers and on an equal share basis. According to the official contract drawn up by the Malian local commander and issued through the Ministry of Rural Development, the local groups must partition the land on an equal-share basis and according to the principle of "land to those who work it only."[3]

The Isle of Peace project team has thus achieved, through the channels of the Malian bureaucracy, a potentially significant social and economic reform. If maintained, this reform could ensure that the farming families benefit from the land according to their needs. The problem of control over the marketing of grains and the possibility that the merchants of Timbuktu may find a way to exploit the farmers at the selling end of the production process has not yet been dealt with, but the project has helped to establish a major precedent. At least the stratification among the farming households themselves will be controlled by the equal-shares land division.

The Isle of Peace project faces many difficulties. Even with a five-year stay, the team cannot necessarily control the future of the landholding system. The merchants may be able to exert pressure on the commander, or the commander could be replaced as a result of intrigues in the capital. Furthermore, the project seems to be repeating the errors of previous well diggers in its pastoralist program. The 40 wells planned by the project team could bring about concentration of animals and pasture degradation, but nothing in the project reports or in the interview with the project director suggests an awareness of this problem (Fondation, 1978 and 1979; van Camfort, 1977; interviews at Timbuktu, March 17 and 18, 1978). But the project does show that social reforms can be started on a limited basis within the context of a development project.

GAO: RELAUNCHING THE HERDERS' COOPERATIVES

A day's trip downriver from Timbuktu is the ancient city of Gao, the site of another small but innovative project. Financed by the French-based Catholic Committee against Hunger and for Development, along with several other religious groups, a section of the Malian livestock service is working to reorganize and reestablish herders' cooperatives. The Gao region was particularly hard hit by the drought, with an estimated 62 percent of the livestock destroyed. The Relaunch the Cooperatives program is based upon a historical study of the attempts to create co-ops in Mali during the period 1960-68 and the demise of the co-ops after their funds were frozen by the government that came to power in the coup of 1968. The herders are organized into co-ops with elected councils. The project team conducts lengthy discussions with the councils and the members of the co-ops to ensure that animals are made available to the most needy members on a no-interest loan program. Successive groups of 50 herders each are given means to purchase animals, and they must repay the principle within three years, while a minimum number of animals must be placed in the hands of the cooperative. Advice and discussion of range-management issues and minimal construction of necessary infrastructure are added to the main goals of reconstituting the herds and establishing a viable means of organization by which the herders can themselves control their production resources. Working with limited means, the project may eventually face competition from the effects of the USAID rice and sorghum project nearby. This project threatens to take away herding lands by expanding the agricultural perimeters in a development not integrated with the herding populations.[4]

The project demonstrates the possibility of making social reforms a significant element in a development project. As with the Timbuktu land reform, at least middle-level elements in the Malian government bureaucracy are involved in a positive way.

OTHER ALTERNATIVE PROJECTS

Many other small, privately financed projects are underway in the Sahel. The British-based relief organization Oxfam has aided in the construction of small water-retaining dikes to make possible the replanting of trees and some crops in zones where it is believed the desert may be encroaching. The dikes hold the water, the water nourishes the trees and bushes, and the plant life holds in the soil and holds back the sands. Thus a small degree of environmental protection is achieved. Oxfam has also developed a livestock project in Niger in which traditional social ties are used for the rebuilding of Fulani herds. The project resembles the Gao cooperatives project.[5]

Another small-scale project was undertaken by the American Friends Service Committee in Mali. Resettlement of a few hundred nomadic victims of the 1968-74 drought and famine along the shores of Lake Faguibine offered the opportunity to transform a refugee camp into a viable community. AFSC provided limited funds to aid in the establishment of farming along the receding shores of the lake. This flood-recession type of farming was supported by the organization of cooperatives, the purchasing of a truck to transport some products to Goundam, a local market town, health facilities, and a school. AFSC representatives do not consider the project an unqualified success, but the "experimental community" that has been created has maintained itself for more than four years. A local project council of seven people mediates between the regional bureaucracy and the project population. In July 1978, the AFSC staffer in Tin Aicha could report that the project community's children "are visibly better nourished than those of neighboring villages."[6] The problem still to arise will be that of a potential increase in land values along the lake shore.

The local merchants and bureaucrats at Goundam have so far given the project community more support than interference.

THE SMALL-PROJECTS CONTRADICTION

In all these alternative projects, three key elements stand out. First, the projects are entirely or mostly financed outside the major donor agencies. They are thus independent of the economic and political strings and levers that distort the big donor projects. Second, the alternative projects are of limited size and scope. This feature undoubtedly leads to a more effective use of outside personnel who can spend more time, develop more enthusiasm, and learn more accurately the real problems at the local level. Third, the alternative projects operate on the fringes, or in the interstices, of the major commercial and bureaucratic interest groups, *or* with the assistance of a specific progressive administrator, such as the military commander at Timbuktu. They are thus able to bypass to some extent the effects of the local Sahelian elites—at least for a time.

These three interrelated factors help to explain the apparently greater success of the small, privately financed projects. At the same time, their very success poses a serious contradiction in Sahel development work. If these projects work because they are small, because they are outside the main aid channels, and because they touch only the edges of the local stratification system, then these projects can never supply more than a very small segment of the overall needs of Sahelian development. By showing what can be accomplished *without* the major international and national institutions, the small, private projects only serve to highlight all the more dramatically how serious are the blockages and contradictions in the overall situation.

WHAT ABOUT THE FUTURE?

The alternative projects described above pose the central questions facing the Sahelian peoples in the future. Can the example of Timbuktu's military commander be extended to other regions? Can the herders' cooperatives at Gao withstand the eventual pressures of USAID's agricultural project? Will the Soninke Peasants Federation successfully outflank the bureaucrats of SAED? Will Mauritania's rapidly evolving national political process result in imaginative and progressive bureaucrats coming to positions of power where they can support the Guidimaka initiatives rather than trying to turn them into sources of a lavish elitist lifestyle? These are questions the Sahelian peoples themselves will answer through their own struggles to free themselves of dependency, of multinational corporate exploitation, of intercapitalist political and economic rivalries, and of local, elite self-aggrandizement. From the perspective of this study three general alternative futures for the Sahel seem to emerge.

The Program As Is

For the coming several years, the most likely course is a continuation of the Sahel Development Program as we have described it in this study. Minor technical alterations might be made, but on the whole neither the donor countries nor the Sahelian elites will push for major restructuring on their own initiative. Thus the program may forge ahead replete with the many contradictions we have analyzed in earlier chapters.

The continuation of the Sahel Development Program threatens the majority of Sahelians. To the extent that current large-scale projects are accomplished, the financial and political power of the elites, whose commercial interests outweigh their commitment to protecting and restoring the fragile ecology, will be enhanced. Furthermore, the successful creation of more modern transportation and communications facilities along with the expansion of marketing pressures via the projects could eventually lead to increased multinational investment. As the Mauritanian MIFIRMA and Senegalese Bud cases show, environmental considerations are secondary to profits in the actual behavior of the multinationals, whatever their rhetoric. The multinationals have vastly greater financial resources than the Sahelian elites. Should the Sahel become attractive to them on a larger scale than at present, the overproduction problem—given the delicate ecological relationships in the Sahel—could become serious once again. These processes could bring about an even greater vulnerability to drought than exists at present. Worse famines might well ensue in the future.

Withdrawal

At the other extreme would be a cessation of all development projects. This strategy would have the advantage of stopping the destructive processes inherent in most of the projects. But the Sahel is in a state of ecological degradation so advanced that to leave it to its own devices would be to condemn it to the most limited of recoveries. Selected areas, such as Bakel, Senegal, would probably improve under the auspices of the Federation of Soninke Peasants, and local initiatives would probably arise in other places. But on the whole, the herders and farmers would be left with too few resources to effect the major environmental rehabilitation which the region so desperately requires.

Spreading the Small Projects

A positive line of development emerges from the analysis offered in this study. If the approach of the small projects could be applied to the overall Sahel Development Program, social balance, ecological protection and rehabilitation, and rational use of the region's productive resources would have a much greater likelihood of being achieved. With participation of and decision-making by producers instead of elite bureaucratic domination, with local needs overruling overseas corporate or political interests, the creative powers, the knowledge, the experience and the hard-working habits of the Sahel's farmers and herders could be integrated with advances in modern science and technology in a genuine development of the region.

For such a process to take place, there are several prerequisites. At the level of funding agencies in the donor countries, a wide-ranging debate must occur to determine how, indeed whether in some circumstances, projects can be designed and implemented without the major contradictions we have demonstrated. In the United States, USAID's policies need to be reexamined far more thoroughly. An internal agency review would not be sufficient: Informed and on-going public criticism from outside is necessary to ensure that changes are made in more than rhetoric.

At the level of the Sahelian societies, counterbalancing forces must develop to offset the power of local elites. Outside agency personnel, no matter how well-intentioned, cannot outmanouver local elites except in rare instances. This is what the small projects contradiction illustrates. The major resolution of this contradiction will come from the development and growth of democratic farmers' and herders' political and economic associations. These locally-based organizations in turn should grow into coordinated regional and national movements aimed at alleviating the needs of the Sahel's poorest citizens—its herders and farmers who are the real guardians of the environment. A possible beginning was made in 1978 in Senegal with the formation of a national association of farmers, herders, and vegetable growers that might eventually develop an alliance with progressive intellectuals and others committed to environmental rehabilitation and a rational production system rather than quick profits for bureaucrats or overseas corporations. In Mauritania, the 1978 coup which ousted the conservative pro-French administration could conceivably open a process of political mobilization. In Mali a coup d'état on March 1, 1978, received enthusiastic public support when several ministers, including the one in charge of famine relief, were arrested on corruption charges. A more generalized opposition to elite privilege could also develop. In Senegal, Mauritania, Niger, and Mali, numerous individual members of the bureaucracy already sympathize with the general goals outlined in this chapter and in many instances are attempting to provide support for local and national organizations of producers. For such processes to have the necessary impact, these nascent organizations and progressive groupings must eventually control the political and economic systems of entire Sahelian countries.

Stimulation for the growth of powerful and democratic organizations of producers should be the major priority of all development projects. Planners and technical personnel often balk at such an idea with the claim that they cannot interfere with local institutions. But as we have shown in several examples in Chapters 8 and 9, working with the status quo is also a direct interference. Sahelian societies, like others, are in a constant process of change and development. The strengthening of an elite comes at the cost of those whom that elite exploits. Development projects cannot be neutral from the moment they offer resources to any group in the society.

For development agencies to give genuine and sustained support to local democratic organization and initiative, yet another contradiction must be resolved. Not only must the criterion of profitability be removed from immediate projects as called for in the brave words of the Sahel Development Program document agreed upon in Canada in 1977 (see Chapter 6). The rehabilitation and protection of the Sahel environment will require the forfeiting of Western capitalist profit-making and political domination in general. This will come about only as the result of pressures applied both by the Sahelians themselves and by public pressure from concerned individuals and organizations in the capitalist countries.

From the tropical rain forest, through the Sahel, to the edge of the desert, West Africa is a region with great potential for providing sustenance for its people. Enough could be produced and exchanged from one zone to the other so that a drought would not have to result in a famine.

Looking back over the long history of the Sahel and its peoples, we can see one central element in the complex web of factors that has progressively brought the region to its current state of drought vulnerability and its tendency toward famine. The earliest farmers and herders created production systems that allowed for the support of human life without serious harm to the production resources themselves.

The rise of precolonial elites brought a contradiction into the primitive farming and herding systems. While securing the benefits of interregional trade, the needs of the elites and their mutual competition led to ecological degradation of some areas. The colonial system, however, brought the most severe attacks on the Sahel environment. The destruction of interregional trade and the expansion of slavery and later peanut cultivation for the profits of colonial industries degraded the soil and broke up the ecologically beneficial exchange relationships that had been forged between herders and farmers over many centuries of precolonial history. At present, the continuing domination of the region by international capitalism threatens to renew these forces of destruction by the implementation of profit-oriented multinational corporate investments and short-sighted development projects. The introduction of modern technology has thus not attained the fruits of the Sahel's potential—at least not to the peoples of West Africa.

To achieve the goals of the Sahel Development Program, Sahelians will have to seize control of their resources and reverse the processes that have led to the present situation. In breaking the bonds of dependency, they will find not only their own path to self-reliance in the international sphere but will also overcome the blockages created by the past development of elites, the strengthening of those elites by the colonial regime, and their present continuation as impediments to freeing the creative powers of the producers.

The central resource of the Sahel is its farmers and herders. Their organized political and social power is the key to overcoming the ravages of the past and opening the area to a new form of progress in which the satisfaction of human needs will be accomplished, while, at the same time, the region's fragile ecology is protected and enhanced.

NOTES

1. It is perhaps worth noting that USAID has a livestock project in an area that appears to overlap with the Guidimaka. The Selibaby project is intended to develop herds and range management on somewhat the same lines as the Niger project discussed in Chapter 9. The USAID project paper contains only the most superficial social analysis, being mostly a compendium of specific facts about the region and the project. While the sociological-anthropological section of the paper notes the interdependence of agriculture and livestock, the project ignores agriculture and is aimed at increasing animal production leading to commercialization (USAID, 1974).
2. For a description of several projects in the Aïr, including the one at Tabelot, see Morel, 1976.
3. A copy of the commander's writ on this was made available to us by a researcher in Dakar. It was issued before the June 1978 meeting in Timbuktu and thus does not yet contain the 50-ares figure (Commandant, 1978).
4. Information obtained from interviews and the project document at Gao, March 22, 1978. The speculations on the negative effects of the USAID project are entirely our own and were not made by the staff of the herders' project. The Gao Rice and Sorghum Project was analyzed in Chapter 9.
5. *Oxfam American News*, vol. 1, no. 2, summer 1979.
6. AFSC, "News from Tin Aicha," July 26, 1978.

BIBLIOGRAPHY

I. Works of interest to the general reader.

Adams, Adrian. *Le Long Voyage des Gens du Fleuve.* Paris: François Maspero, 1977.

Amin, Samir. *Neocolonialism in West Africa.* (Translated by Francis McDonagh). New York: Monthly Review Press, 1973.

Ball, Nicole. "The Myth of Natural Disaster." *The Ecologist*, vol. 5, no. 10 (December 1975): 368–374.

Brown, Lester with Erik P. Eckholm. *By Bread Alone.* New York: F. W. Praeger for the Overseas Development Council, 1974.

de Castro, Josué. *Death in the Northeast: Poverty and Revolution in the Northeast of Brazil.* New York: Random House, 1966.

———. *The Geopolitics of Hunger.* 1952. New York: Monthly Review Press, 1977. Introduction by Jean-Pierre Berlan.

Clarke, Thurston. *The Last Caravan.* New York: G. P. Putnam's Sons, 1978.

Comité Information Sahel. *Qui se Nourrit de la Famine en Afrique? Le Dossier Politique de la Famine au Sahel.* Paris: François Maspero, 1974.

Commoner, Barry. *The Closing Circle: Nature, Man and Technology.* New York: Bantam Books, 1972.

———. *The Poverty of Power: Energy and the Economic Crisis.* New York: Bantam Books, 1976.

Copans, Jean, ed. *Sécheresses et Famines du Sahel.* 2 vols. Paris: François Maspero, 1975.

Curtin, Philip. *Economic Change in Precolonial Africa: Senegambia in the Era of the Slave Trade.* Madison: University of Wisconsin Press, 1975.

Davidson, Basil. *A History of West Africa to the 19th Century.* Garden City: Doubleday Anchor, 1966.

Eckholm, Erik P. *Losing Ground: Environmental Stress and World Food Prospects.* New York: W. W. Norton and Company, 1976. Worldwatch Institute with the support and cooperation of the United Nations Environment Program.

Fitzgerald, Walter. *Africa: A Social, Economic and Political Geography of Its Major Regions.* London: Methuen, 1966.

Franke, Richard W. "Miracle Seeds and Shattered Dreams on Java." *Natural History Magazine*, January 1974.

George, Susan. *How the Other Half Dies: The Real Reasons for World Hunger.* Montclair, New Jersey: Allanheld, Osmun & Co., 1977.

Glantz, Michael, ed. *The Politics of Natural Disaster.* New York: F. W. Praeger, 1976.

Gorer, Geoffrey. *Africa Dances: A Book About West African Negroes.* 1935. New York: W. W. Norton & Co., 1962.

Gramont, Sanche de. *The Strong Brown God: the Story of the Niger River.* Boston: Houghton Mifflin Co., 1976.

Griffin, Keith. *The Political Economy of Agrarian Change: An Essay on the Green Revolution.* Cambridge, Mass: Harvard University Press, 1974.

Hopkins, A. G. *An Economic History of West Africa.* London: Longman, 1973.

July, Robert W. *Precolonial Africa: An Economic and Social History.* New York: Charles Scribners' Sons, 1975.

Lappé, Francis Moore, and Collins, Joseph with Gary Fowler. *Food First: Beyond the Myth of Scarcity.* Boston: Houghton Mifflin Co., 1977.

Lerza, Catherine, and Jacobson, Michael, eds. *Food for People Not for Profit: A Source Book on the Food Crisis.* Foreword by Ralph Nader. New York: Ballantine Books, 1975.

Mabogunje, Akin. "The Land and Peoples of West Africa." In *History of West Africa*, Ajayi and Crowder, eds. New York: Columbia University Press, 1972.

Magdoff, Harry. *The Age of Imperialism: The Economics of US Foreign Policy.* New York: Monthly Review Press, 1966.

Mamdani, Mahmood. *The Myth of Population Control: Family, Caste, and Class in an Indian Village.* New York: Monthly Review Press, 1972.

Perelman, Michael. *Farming for Profit in a Hungry World: Capital and the Crisis in Agriculture.* Montclair, New Jersey: Allanheld, Osmun & Co., 1977.

Richards, Paul W. "The Tropical Rain Forest." *Scientific American* 229, no. 6 (December 1973) 58–67.

Russell, W. M. S. "The Slash-and-Burn Technique." In Richard Gould, ed. *Man's Many Ways.* New York: Harper and Row, 1973, pp. 86–101.

Stride, G. T., and Ifeka, Caroline. *Peoples and Empires of West Africa: West Africa in History, 1000–1800.* New York: Africana Publishing Co., 1971.

Suret-Canale, Jean. *French Colonialism in Tropical Africa, 1900–1945.* Translated by Till Gottheiner. New York: Pica Press, 1971.

II. Other references cited in the text.

Ackels, Alden A., et al. A Study and Plan for Regional Grain Stabilization in West Africa. Report No. 21. Manhattan, Kansas: Kansas State University, Food and Feed Grain Institute, 1970.

Albouy, Yves, and Boulenger, Bruno. "Les Facteurs Climatiques" in Copans, J., ed., 1975, Vol. I, pp. 41–59.

Almy, Susan. "Anthropologists and Development Agencies." *American Anthropologist* 79, no. 2 (1977): 280–92.

American Public Health Association Final Report. Environmental Assessment and Health Component Design. Bakel Irrigated Perimeter Project. Senegal Contract No. APHA/AID-AFR-C-1253, 1977.

Amin, Samir. Le Soudan Français, Le Mirage de l'Office du Niger. IDEP: Dakar (Décembre 1970).

———. *The Maghreb in the Modern World.* London: Penguin African Library, 1970.

———. "Underdevelopment and Dependence." *Journal of Moden African Studies* 10, no. 4, (1972): 503–24.

———. *Unequal Development.* New York: Monthly Review Press, 1976.

———. "Introduction" in Amin, Samir, ed., *Modern Migrations in Western Africa.* London: Oxford University Press, pp. 65–124.

Anon. "De Situatie in Senegal." *Landbouw Wereldnieuws,* October 15, 1974, pp. 319–22. (Taken from the 1973 annual report of the Dutch embassy in Dakar.)

Asiwaju, A. I. "Migrations as Revolt: The Example of the Ivory Coast and the Upper Volta Before 1945." *Journal of African History* 17, no. 14 (1976), 577–94.

Awe, Bolanie. Empires of the Western Sudan: Ghana, Mali, Songhay, In *A Thousand Years of West African History,* J. F. Ade Ajayi and Ian Espie, eds. Ibadan: Ibadan University Press (1965), pp. 55–71.

Ba, Moctar. Petit Périmètre Irrigué sur le Fleuve Sénégal: le Cas de l'aménagement de la Cuvette de Pete. Dakar: ENDA/ Doc. No. EV/11543/ECAM, 1977.

Baier, Stephen. Economic History and Development: Drought and the Sahelian Economies of Niger. *African Economic History.* no. 1 (1976), pp. 1–16.

Ball, Nicole. "Understanding the Causes of African Famine." *Journal of Modern African Studies* 14, no. 3 (1976): 517–22.

——. "Drought and Dependence in the Sahel." *International Journal of Health Services* 8, no. 2 (1978): 271–98.

Barry, Boubacar. *Le royaume du Waalo: Le Sénégal avant la conquête.* Paris: François Maspero, 1972. Preface by Samir Amin.

Bennoune, Mahfoud. "Mauretania: Formation of a Neocolonial Society." *Merip Reports* no. 54 (1977), pp. 3–13.

Berg, Alan. *The Nutrition Factor.* Washington D.C.: The Brookings Institution, 1973.

Berg, Elliot. *The Recent Economic Evolution of the Sahel.* Ann Arbor: University of Michigan Center for Research on Economic Development, 1975. (Prepared for the U.S. Agency for International Development.)

——. *Marketing, Price Policy and Storage of Food Grains in the Sahel: A Survey.* 2 Vols. Ann Arbor: University of Michigan Center for Research on Economic Development, 1977.

Berlan, Jean-Pierre, Bertrand, Jean-Pierre, and Lebas, Laurence. "Eléments sur le Développement du 'Complexe Soja' Américain dans le Monde." *Revue Tiers-Monde,* vol. 17, no. 66 (1976), pp. 307–29.

Bernus, Edmond. "Drought in Niger Republic." *Savanna: a Journal of the Environmental & Social Sciences* (Zaria) vol. 2 no. 2 (1973): 129–32.

——. *Les Illabakan (Niger): Une tribu touarègue sahélienne et son aire de nomadisation.* Atlas des Structures Agraires au Sud du Sahara. Paris: ORSTOM, et Maison des Sciences de L'homme, 1974a.

——. "Possibilités et Limites de la Politique d'Hydraulique Pastorale dans le Sahel Nigerien." *Cahiers Orstom,* vol. 11, no. 2 (1974b), pp. 119–26.

——. *"L'Évolution Récente des Relations entre Eleveurs et Agriculteurs en Afrique Tropicale: L'exemple du Sahel Nigérien." Cahiers ORSTOM,* série Sciences Humaines, vol. 11, no. 2 (1974c), pp. 137–43.

Bernus, Edmond, and Bernus, Suzanne. "L'Évolution de la condition servile chez les Touaregs sahéliens." In Claud Meillassoux, ed. *L'esclavage en Afrique précoloniale.* Paris: François Maspero (1975), pp. 27–47.

Berry, Leonard. "The Sahel: Climate and Soils." In *The Sahel: Ecological Approaches to Land Use.* United Nations International Coordinating Council of the Programme on Man and the Biosphere (MAB), Technical Notes no. 1 (n.d.), pp. 9–18.

Berry, Leonard, and Ford, Richard B. *Recommendations for a System to Monitor Critical Indicators in Areas Prone to Desertification.* Worcester, Mass: Clark University Program for International Development, 1977. USAID contract No. AID/ta-C-1407 "on behalf of the United States Task Force on Desertification."

Berry, Leonard, Campbell, David J., and Emker, Ingemar. "Trends in Man-Land Interaction in the West African Sahel." In Dalby, Church, and Bezzaz, eds. *Report of the 1973 Symposium on Drought in Africa,* vol. 2. London: School of Oriental and African Studies (1977), pp. 83–91.

Boahen, Adu. *Topics in West African History* (Schools edition). London: Longmans, 1966.

Bonte, Pierre. "L'élevage et le commerce du bétail dans l'Ader Doutchi-Majya." *Études Nigériennes* no. 23. Niamey, Paris, 1968.

——. "Multinational Companies and National Development: MIFERMA and Maureta- ia." *Review of African Political Economy,* no. 2 (January-April 1975): 89–109.

Boucher, Keith, and Harris, Nicola. *Environmental Research Register.* London: International African Institute, 1977.

Bovill, E. W. *The Golden Trade of the Moors.* London: Oxford University Press, 1968.

Bradley, P. C., Raynaut C., and Torrealba, J. *The Guidimaka Region of Mauritania: A Critical Analysis Leading to a Development Project.* London: War on Want, 1977.

Braudel, Ferdinand. "Monnaies et Civlisations: De l'Or du Sudan à l'Argent, d'Amérique." *Annales: Économies, Société, Civilisations*, no. 2 (1946), pp. 9–22.

Breman, Henk. Beelzebul als Duivelsuitbanner (Plattelandsontwikkeling in de Sahel). *Wending*, vol. 31, no. 3 (1976), pp. 126–36.

Breman, Henk, and Cissé, A, M. "Dynamics of Sahelian Pastures in Relation to Drought and Grazing." *Oecologia* 28: (1977) 301–15.

British Naval Intelligence. *French West Africa: The Colonies*, vol. 2. Geographical Handbook, 1944.

Brokensha, David W., Horowitz, Michael M. and Scudder, Thayer. *The Anthropology of Rural Development in the Sahel*. Binghamton: Institute for Development Anthropology, Inc., USAID Contract No. REDSO/WA-77-91 AID. 1977.

Brown, Lester. *World Without Borders*. New York: Random House, 1972.

Brunschwig, Henri. *French Colonialism, 1871–1914: Myths and Realities*. London: Pall Mall Press, 1966.

Bryson, Reid A. "Drought in Sahelia: Who or What is to Blame? *The Ecologist 3 (1973): 366–71.*

———. "The Lessons of Climatic History." *The Ecologist* 6, no. 6 (July 1976): 205–11.

Buchanan, Keith. *The Southeast Asian World*. Garden City, New York: Anchor Books, 1968.

Bunnik, Jan. Bud maakt Senegal groen. *Vakblad voor groothandel in aardappelen, groenten, en fruit.* (February 6 and 13, 1975), pp. 12–15 and 14–16.

Bureau Africain de Recherches Appliquees. *Riz-Sorgho Gao*. Bamako. (Prepared by Asseya Woldeyes, agronomist and Boubacar Bah, economist.) Bureau Africain de Recherches Appliquees, 1978.

Caldwell, John C. The Sahelian Drought and its Demographic Implications. Paper no. 8. Washington, D.C.: Overseas Liaison Committee, American Council on Education, 1975.

Camfort, E. van. Synthèse des activités de l'Ile de Paix—Cercle de Tombouctou. Huy, Belgium: Fondation Dominique Pire, 1977.

Center for Horticultural Development. Center for Horticultural Development, Dakar, February 1975.

Centre Technique Forestier Tropical. "The role of the Forester in Land Use Planning in the Sahel." In *Man and the Biosphere* Technical Notes no. 1. UNESCO, (n.d.) pp. 41–53.

Chamberlain, M.E. *The Scramble for Africa*. London: Longman Group, Ltd., 1974.

Charlick, Robert. "Sociological Factors in the National Cereals Production Program." Unpublished Report. Niamey: USAID.

Church, R. J. Harrison. *West Africa: a Study of the Environment and of Man's Use of It*. 1957. London: Longman's, Green and Co., 1968.

Cissoko, Sekene Mody. *Tombouctou et L'Empire Songhay*. Dakar: Les Nouvelles Éditions Africaines, 1975.

Club of the Sahel. *Proposals For A Strategy For Drought Control And Development In The Sahel*. OECD (Submitted to Working Group of the Sahel Club N'Djamena, December 6–11, 1976.) 1977.

Cohen, John M., Goldsmith, Arthur A., and Mellor, John W. "Rural Development Issues Following Ethiopian Land Reform." *Africa Today* 23, no. 2 (1976): 7–28.

Cohen, Mark Nathan. *The Food Crisis in Prehistory: Overpopulation and the Origins of Agriculture*. New Haven: Yale University Press, 1977.

Cohn, Theodore. "The Sahelian Drought: Problems of Land Use." *International Journal: Canadian Institute of International Affairs* 30, no. 3 (1975): 428–44.

Collins, John Davison. "The Clandestine Movement of Groundnuts across the Niger- Nigeria Boundary." *Canadian Journal of African Studies* 10, no. 2 (1976), 259–78.

Comité Permanent Interétats de Lutte Contre La Sécheresse (CILSS) *Reunion des Experts. Travaux des Commissions.* 2-4. Ouagadougou, August 31–September 6, 1973. 1973a.

———. *Réunion des Ministres.* Ouagadougou, September 7-10, 1973. 1973b.

———. Conférence des Chefs d'État des Six Pays Touchés par la Sécheresse. Ougadougou, September 11–12, 1973. 1973c.

———. *Premier Conseil des Ministres.* Ouagadougou, December 19–20, 1973. Resolutions. 1973d.

———. *Plant Protection in CILSS Member Countries: Action Proposals.* Dakar, March 23, 1977.

Commandant de Cercle, Tombouctou. *Contrat d'Exploitation d'une Parcelle Agricole sur le Périmètre de Korioume. Timbuktu, 1978.*

Consortium for International Development and the Agency for International Development. Final Design Report Eastern Senegal Bakel Range Livestock Project. Project No. 685-11-120-202, 1977.

Crowder, Michael. *West Africa Under Colonial Rule.* London: Hutchinson and Co., Ltd., 1968.

Dalby, David, and Church, R. J. Harrison. *Report of the 1973 Symposium on Drought in Africa.* London: School of Oriental and African Studies, 1973.

———. 1977 with Fatima Bezzaz, *Report of the 1973 Symposium on Drought in Africa,* vol. 2. 1977.

Dankoussou, Issaka, Diarra, Souleymane, Laya, Dioulde, and Pool, Ian D. "Niger." In John C. Caldwell et al., eds. *Population Growth and Socio-Economic Change in West Africa.* New York: Columbia University Press (1975), pp. 679–93.

DeMarco, Susan and Sechler, Susan. *The Fields Have Turned Brown: Four Essays on World Hunger.* Washington, D.C.: Agribusiness Accountability Project, 1975.

Derriennic, Hervé. *Famines et Dominations en Afrique.* Dissertation, Université de Haute Bretagne, Rennes, 1976.

———. Famines et Dominations en Afrique Noire: Paysans et Eleveurs au Sahel Sous le Joug. Paris: L'Harmattan, 1977.

Deshler, W. "Cattle in Africa: Distribution, Types, and Problems." *Geographical Review* 53, no. 1 (1963): 52–8.

Dia, Tidiane. *La Propriété Foncière dans Les Niayes.* Dakar: IDEP. July 1972.

Diagne, Papa Syr. "La Delta du Fleuve Senegal." Doctorat en Economie Regionale et Amenagement du Territoire, Universite de Paris, Institut de Geographie, 1974.

Diarra, L. "Composition floristique et productivité des pâturages soudano-sahelians sous une pluviosité annuelle moyenne de 1100 à 400 mm." Thesis, Centre Pédagogique Superieur (Ecole Normale Supérieure), Bamako, 1976.

Diarra, M.S. "Les Problemes de Contact entre les Pasteurs Peul et les Agriculteurs dans le Niger Central." In Theodore Monod, ed. *Pastoralism In Tropical Africa.* London: Oxford University Press, International African Institute. (1975) pp. 284–97.

Diop, Cheikh Anta. *L'Afrique Noire Précoloniale.* Paris: Présence Africaine, 1960.

Donaint, Pierre, and Lancrenon, François. *Le Niger.* Série Que sais-je? no. 1461. Paris: Presses Universitaires de France, 1976.

Dorward, D.C., and Payne, A.I. "Deforestation, the Decline of the Horse, and the Spread of the Tsetse Fly and Trypanosomiasis (*Nagana)* in Nineteenth Century Sierra Leone." *Journal of African History* 16, no. 2 (1975): 239–56.

Dresch, Jean. "Les Transformations du Sahel Nigérien." *Acta Geographica* vol. 30 (1959), pp. 3–12.

Dubois, Victor D. The Trial of Mamadou Dia, Part I: Background of the Case. Part II: The Proceedings in Court. Part III: Aftermath of the Trial. American Universities Fieldstaff Reports, vol. 6, nos. 6, 7, 8, 1963.

———. *The Drought in Niger: The Overthrow of President Hamani Diori*. American University Field Staff. West Africa Series. vol. 15, no. 5, 1974.

Dupire, Marguerite. *Peuls nomades: Étude descriptive des Wodaabe du Sahel Nigérien*. Paris: Institut d'Ethnologie, 1962.

———. "Trade and Markets in the Economy of the Nomadic Fulani of Niger (Bororo)." In Paul Bohannan and George Dalton, eds. *Markets in Africa*. Evanston, Ill.: Northwestern University Press (1962a), pp. 335–62.

Earth Satellite Corporation. *Remote Sensing Applications to Resource Management Problems in the Sahel*. 1974. AID, Washington, D.C.: Contract no. AID-afr-c-1058.

Egg, J., Lerin, François, and Venin, M. "Analyse Descriptive de la Famine, des Années 1931, au Niger et Implications Méthodologiques." Institute National de la Recherche Agronomique: Économie et Sociologie Rurales, 1975. Preface by Pierre Spitz.

Ehrlich, Paul R., Ehrlich, Anne H., and Holdren, John P. *Human Ecology: Problems and Solutions*. San Francisco: W. H. Freeman and Company, 1973.

Eicher, Carl. "Preface." In John C. Caldwell, 1975.

Fanale, R. *Analysis of Settlement and Land Use Patterns Using Remote Sensor Data*. Washington, D.C.: Earth Resources Development Research Institute, 1974.

Feder, Ernest. "The Odious Competition Between Man and Animal Over Agricultural Resources in the Underdeveloped Countries." Unpublished. 1979.

Fondation Dominique Pire. *Ile de Paix "Tombouctou": Dossier technique, année 1977*. Huy, Belgium: Fondation Dominique Pire, 1978.

———. *Réalisations de l'an '78. Tombouctou: Troisieme Ile de Paix*. Huy, Belgium; Fondation Dominique Pire, 1979.

FAO. *Africa Survey: Report on the Possibilities of African Rural Development in Relation to Economic and Social Growth*. Rome, 1962.

———. *West African Pilot Study of Agricultural Development, 1960–75. Vol. I FAO West African Meeting on Agricultural Commodity Projections, Dakar, May 24–31, 1965*.

———. *Investigation into the Magnitude of Drought Conditions in the Sahelian Zone*. Accra, Ghana, 1973.

———. *Perspective Study on Agricultural Development in the Sahelian Countries*. 3 Volumes. Rome, 1976.

Forde, Daryll. "The Cultural Map of West Africa: Successive Adaptations to Tropical Forests and Grasslands." In Simon and Phoebe Ottenberg, eds., *Cultures and Societies of Africa*. New York: Random House (1960), pp. 116–38.

———. *Habitat, Economy and Society*. New York: E. P. Dutton and Co., 1963.

Fouquet, Joseph. *La Traite des Arachides dans le pays de Kaolack et ses Conséquences Économiques, Sociales, et Juridiques*. Doctoral thesis. University of Montpelier, 1951.

Franco, Mark. "Le programme de développment du bassin du fleuve Sénégal—Une étude méthodologique." In Samir Amin, Mark Franco, and Samba Sow, *La Planification du Sous-Développement: Critique de l'analyse de Projets*. Paris: Editions Anthropos-IDEP (1975), pp. 207–301.

Franke, Richard W. "Solution to the Asian Food Crisis—Green Revolution or Social Revolution?" *Bulletin of Concerned Asian Scholars* 6, no. 4 (1974): 2–16.

———. "Hunger for Profit—Ten Years of Food Production Failure." In Malcolm Caldwell, ed. *Ten Years' Military Terror in Indonesia*. Nottingham: Bertrand Russell Press (1975), pp. 159–69.

———. "Imperialism and Dependence." *Bulletin of Concerned Asia Scholars* 9, no. 4 (1977): 60–64.

Freyre, Gilberto. *The Masters and the Slaves: A Study in the Development of Brazilian Civilization.* New York: Alfred A. Knopf, 1946.

Fuglestad, Finn. "La Grande Famine de 1931 dans l'Ouest du Niger." *Revue Française Histoire d'Outre-mer* 61, no. 222 (1974): 18–33.

Gagnon, Gabriel. "Cooperatives, Participation and Development: Three Failures." In June Nash, Jorge Dandler, Nicholas S. Hopkins, eds. *Popular Participation in Social Change: Cooperatives, Collectives and Nationalized Industry.* The Hague: Mouton (1976), pp. 365–380.

Galeano, Eduardo. *Open Veins of Latin America: Five Centuries of the Pillage of a Continent.* New York: Monthly Review Press, 1973.

Gallais, Jean. *Le delta intérieur du Niger.* Dakar: IFAN. Mémoires de l'Ifan, no. 79, 2 vols. 1967.

———. "Essai sur la Situation Actuelle des Relations entre pasteurs et paysans dans le Sahel Ouest-Africain." In *Études de Géographie Tropicale offertes à Pierre Gourou.* Paris: Mouton, 1972.

———. "Les Sociétés Pastorales Ouest-Africaines Face au Développement." *Cahiers D'Études Africaines* 12, no. 47 (1972a): 353–68. 1972a.

Gallais, Jean (ed.) *Stratégies Pastorales et Agricoles des Saheliens durant la Sécheresse* 1969–1974. Travaux et Documents de Géographie Tropicale, No. 30. Bordeaux: Centre d'Etudes de Géographie Tropicale. 1977.

Garcia, M. "Pertes sur le Bétail Dues à la Sécheresse en Haute-Volta. Communauté Economique du Bétail et de la Viande." Report of the Mission to Upper Volta, February 2–March 9, 1974.

Gautier, E. F. *L'Or du Soudan Dans l'Histoire. Annales d'Histoire Économique et Sociale* 7 (1935): 113–23.

Geertz, Clifford. *Agricultural Involution: The Processes of Ecological Change in Indonesia.* Berkeley: University of California Press, 1963.

Gerteiny, Alfred G. *Mauritania.* New York: F. W. Praeger, 1967.

Gillet, H. "Plant Cover and Pastures of the Sahel." Man and the Biosphere. Technical Notes No. 1 UNESCO (n.d.) pp. 21–27.

Giri, Jacques. *An Analysis and Synthesis Of Long Term Development Strategies For The Sahel.* Paris; OECD, 1976.

———. "L'avenir à long terme du Sahel." *Revue Juridique et Politique, Indépendance et Cooperation,* no. 4 (1976b), pp. 461–90.

Goldsmith, William W. "The War on Development." *Monthly Review* 28, no. 10, (1977): 50–57.

Gray, Ronald. "A Report on the Conference: 3rd Conference on African History and Archaeology, 3–7 July, 1961, School of Oriental and African Studies, University of London." *Journal of African History* 3, no. 2 (1962): 175–91.

Greene, M. H. "Impact of the Sahelian Drought in Mauretania." *African Environment* 1, no. 2 (April 1975): 11–21. Originally published in *The Lancet,* June 1, 1974.

Gretton, John. *Western Sahara: The Fight for Self-Determination.* Research Report no. 1. London: Anti-Slavery Society and Committee for Indigenous Peoples, 1976.

Griswold, Deirdre. *Eyewitness Ethiopia: The Continuing Revolution.* New York: World View Publishers, 1978.

Grove, A. T. "Desertification in the African Environment." *African Affairs* 73, no. 291 (1974): 137–151.

Hall, Anthony L. *Drought and Irrigation in North-East Brazil.* New York: Cambrdige University Press, 1978.

Hance, William A. *The Geography of Modern Africa.* New York: Columbia University Press, 1964.

Hardin, Garrett. "The Tragedy of the Commons." *Science* 162 (1968): 1243–48.

Hargreaves, George H. *Water and Conservation Programs for Cape Verde.* Washington: USAID, Contract No. AID/afr-c-1203. March 1977.

Hayes, Carlton, J. H. *A Generation of Materialism: 1871–1900.* New York: Harper and Row, 1941.

Heiser, Charles B., Jr. *Seed to Civilization: The Story of Man's Food.* San Francisco: W. H. Freeman, 1973.

Herzog, John. "Population Change and Productive Activity Among the Serer of Senegal: Some Hypotheses." Paper No. R/2680. Dakar: United Nations African Institute for Economic Development and Planning, 1975.

Higgott, Richard, and Fuglestad, Finn. "The 1974 coup d'Etat in Niger: Toward an Explanation." *Journal of Modern African Studies* 13, no. 3 (1975): 383–98.

Hightower, Jim. *Eat Your Heart Out: How Food Profiteers Victimize the Consumer.* New York: Vintage Books, 1975.

Hightower, Jim and DeMarco, Susan. *Hard Tomatoes, Hard Times: The Failure of the Land Grant College Complex.* Cambridge, Mass: Schenkman Publishing Co., 1973.

Hill, K. H. "Population Trends in Africa." In R. P. Moss and R. J. A. R. Rathbone, eds. *The Population Factor in African Studies.* The Proceedings of a Conference organized by the African Studies Association of the United Kingdom, September 1972. London: University of London Press (1975) pp. 107–14.

Hodder, B. W. "West Africa: Growth and Change in Trade." In Ralph M. Prothero, ed. *A Geography of Africa.* London: Rutledge and Kegan Paul, Ltd. (1969) pp. 415–69.

Hodges, Tony. "Mauritania After the Coup." *Africa Report* 23, no. 6 (November-December 1978), pp. 13–18.

Horowitz, Michael, ed. *Colloquium on the Effects of Drought on the Productive Strategies of Sudano-Sahelian Herdsmen and Farmers.* Binghamton: Institute for Development Anthropology, 1976.

Horowitz, Michael. *Social Science Consultant Network (TA/RD).* Binghamton: Institute for Development Anthropology, 1977.

Hussein, Abdul Mejid, ed. *Drought and Famine in Ethiopia.* African Environment Special Report No. 2 London: International African Institute, 1976.

International Finance Corporation (IFC). *Report and Recommendation of the President to the Board of Directors on a Proposed Third Investment in Bud Senegal, S.A. Report* #IFC/P-229 Senegal, March 3, 1976.

International Monetary Fund. *Surveys of African Economies.* Vol. 3; Dahomey, Ivory Coast, Mauritania, Niger, Senegal, Togo, and Upper Volta. Washington, D.C., 1970.

Irons, William and Dyson-Hudson, Neville, eds. *Perspectives on Nomadism.* Leiden: E. J. Brill, 1972.

Jacobs, Alan. "African Pastoralists: Some General Remarks." *Anthropological Quarterly* 38, no. 3 (1965): 144–54.

James, A. R. "Drought Conditions in the Pressure Water Zone of North-Eastern Nigeria: Some Provisional Observations." *Savanna* (Zaria, Nigeria), vol. 2, no. 2 (1973) pp. 108–114.

Johnson, Douglas L. *The Nature of Nomadism: A Comparative Study of Pastoral Migrations to Southwestern Asia and Northern Africa.* Chicago: University of Chicago, Department of Geography, 1969.

Jones, Brynmor. "Dessication and the West African Colonies." *Geographical Journal* 91 (1938): 401–23.

Jones, William. *Planning and Economic Policy: Socialist Mali and Her Neighbors.* Washington: Three Continents Press, 1976.

Joseph, Richard. "The Gaullist Legacy: Patterns of French NeoColonialism." *Review of African Political Economy* no. 6 (1976), pp. 4–14.

Joseph, Stephen and Scheyer, Stanley C. "Une Stratégie de Santé, Composante du Programme de Développment du Sahel." Washington, D.C.: Family Health Care. Prepared under contract No. Aid/afr-c-1138, Work Order No. 8. 1977.

Joyce, Stephen J. and Beudot, Francoise. *Elements for a Bibliography of the Sahel Drought.* 2 vols. Paris: OECD, 1977. Updated November 1977 and August 1978.

Kafando, Talata Wendlassida. "L'Agriculture et l'Élevage dans la Stratégie du Développement Integré du Liptako-Gourma." Dakar: IDEP, January 1973.

Kassas, M. "Desertification versus Potential for Recovery in Circum-Saharan Territories. In Harold E. Dregne, ed. *Arid Lands in Transition.* Washington, D.C.: American Association for the Advancement of Science, 1970. Publication No. 90, pp. 123–142.

Keita, Joseph. *Corruption* (Pièce inédite en 5 tableaux). Niamey. Imprimerie Nationale du Niger, 1973–74. Preface by Amadou Ousmane.

Keita. Michel. "La Stratégie d'Intervention des Sociétés Multinationales dans l'Élevage Sahélian: Le Ranching-Étude du Cas Sahélian." Dakar: IDEP. October 1974.

Kjekshus, Helge. *Ecology Control and Economic Development in East African History.* London: Heinemann, 1977.

Klein, Martin A. "Social and Economic Factors in the Muslim Revolution in Senegambia." *Journal of African History* 13, no. 3 (1972): 419–41.

Kountché, Lt.-Colonel Seyni. *Citations.* Niamey: Conseil Militaire Suprême. Service de Presse, 1978.

Lacombe, B. "Fertility and Development in Senegal." In S. H. Ominde and C. N. Ejiogu, eds. *Population Growth and Economic Development in Africa.* New York: Heinemann (1972), pp. 123–24.

Lacoste, Yves. "Bombing the Dikes: a Geographer's On-the-Site Analysis." *The Nation* (October 9, 1972): 298–301.

Lamb, Hubert H. "Is the Earth's Climate Changing?" *The Ecologist* 4, no. 1 (January 1974): 10–15.

Lamotte, Maxime. "The Structure and Function of a Tropical Savannah Ecosystem." In Frank B. Golley and Ernesto Medina eds. *Tropical Ecological Systems: Trends in Terrestrial and Aquatic Research.* New York: Springer-Verlag (1975) pp. 179–222.

Langer, Elinor. "Chemical and Biological Warfare." *Science* 155. January 13 and 20, 1967.

Langer, Frédéric. "L'Exemple du Minerai de Fer en Mauritanie." *Problèmes de Développement,* no. 146 (April 1974), pp. 31–32.

Last, Murray. "Reform in West Africa: the *Jihad* Movements of the Nineteenth Century." In J. F. A. Ajayi and Michael Crowder, eds. *History of West Africa,* Vol. 2. New York: Columbia University Press (1973), pp. 1–29.

Lateef, Noel V. "A Techno-Environmental Analysis of Zarma Cultural Organization." Bulletin de l'I.F.A.N." vol. 37, series B., no. 2 (1975): 388–411.

Laya, D. "Interviews with Farmers and Livestock Owners in the Sahel." *African Environment* 1, no. 2 (April 1975): 49–93.

Levinson, Alfred, Rosenberg, Charles, and Yansane, Aguibou. "The Political Economy of Energy and Agriculture in the Third World." Paper presented at the Center for the Biology of

Natural Systems Conference on Energy and Agriculture. St. Louis, Missouri, June 16–19, 1976.

Levtzion, Nehemia. *Ancient Ghana and Mali*. London: Methuen & Co. Ltd., 1973.

Lewallen, John. *Ecology of Devastation: Indochina*. Baltimore: Penguin Books, 1971.

Lewicki, Tadeusz. *West African Food in the Middle Ages*. London: Cambridge University Press, 1974.

Livingstone, F. B. "Anthropological Implications of Sickle Cell Gene Distribution in West Africa." *American Anthropologist* 60 (1958): 533–62.

Lofchie, Michael F. "Political and Economic Origins of African Hunger." *The Journal of Modern African Studies* 13, no. 4 (1975): 551–67.

Lovejoy, P. E., and Baier, S. "The Desert-Side Economy of the Central Sudan." In Michael Glantz, ed. *The Politics of Natural Disaster*. New York: F. W. Praeger (1976), pp. 145–75.

Mabogunje, Akin L. "Migration and Urbanization." In John C. Caldwell, ed. *Population Growth and Socioeconomic Change in West Africa*. New York: Columbia University Press (1975), pp. 153–68.

McCaughan, Ed, and Baird, Peter. *Harvest of Anger: Agro-Imperialism in Mexico's Northwest*. North American Committee on Latin America (NACLA), Latin America and Empire Report. vol. 10, no. 6, July-August, 1976.

McDowell, R. E. "Feed Resources on Small Farms." Paper presented at the Seminar on the Improvement of Farming Systems, Bamako, Mali, February 20-March 1, 1978.

MacLeod, Norman H. *Use of ERTS Imagery and Other Space Data for Rehabilitation and Development Programs in West Africa*. Washington, D.C.: Earth Resources Development Research Institute, 1974.

———. *Food Production in Deserts*. Washington, D.C. Earth Resources Development Research Institute, 1975.

———. "Dust in the Sahel: Cause of Drought?" In Glantz, Michael ed. *The Politics of Natural Disaster*. New York: F. W. Praeger (1976), pp. 214–31.

———. *Climax Agriculture (plus an analysis of the Process and Stages of Desertification/Aridification/and Rehabilitation in the Arrondissement of Filingue, Niger)*. Washington, D.C. Earth Resources Development Research Institute, 1976a.

MacLeod, N. H., Schubert, J. S. and Anaejionu, P. *Skylab V.O.T. Sl4 Report on African Drought and Arid Lands (An Epistemological Experiment)*. Washington, D.C.: Earth Resources Development Research Institute, 1977 (Reprinted from *Skylab Explores the Earth*, NASA Scientific and Technical Office, Washington, D.C.)

McPherson, Laura, Horowitz, Michael M., and Scudder, Thayer. *Anthropology and the Agency for International Development*. Binghamton, N.Y.: Institute for Development Anthropology, n.d.

Magasa, Amidu. *Papa-commandant a jeté un grand filet devant nous: les exploites des rives du Niger 1902–1962*. Paris: François Maspero, 1978. Introduction by Claude Meillassoux.

Maiga, Mahamadou. "Situation des Études de Projets D'Aménagement et de Développement du Bassin du Fleuve Sénégal." Dakar: IDEP. February 1974.

———. "The Policy of Rice Import Substitution. The Case of the Senegal River Valley and Delta." *Africa Development* 7, no. 2 (September 1976): 44–57.

Marchés Tropicaux. "Sahel: un programme d'aide américaine de $200 millions." No. 1638, April, 1977.

———. "Sahel: La mise au point du programme d'aide américain." No. 1641 April 22, 1977.

Markovitz, Irving L. "Traditional social structure, the Islamic brotherhoods, and political development in Senegal." *Journal of Modern African Studies* 8, no. 1 (1970): 73–96.

Marloie, Marcel. *Le Marché Mondial des Tourteaux Oléagineaux: Une Nouvelle Division Internationale du Travail.* Paris: Institute National de la Recherche Agronomique: Économie et Sociologie Rurales; 1974.

Martin, Guy. "Socialism, Economic Development and Planning in Mali, 1960-1968." *Canadian Journal of African Studies* 10, no. 1 (1976): 23-46.

Marty, André. *Les Problèmes d'Abreuvement et le Fonctionnement des Stations de Pompage vus par les Éleveurs de l'Arrondissement de Tchin Tabaraden.* République du Niger. Secrétariat d'État à la Présidence, Commissariat Général du Développement, Service de la Promotion Humaine. Niamey: Tchin Tabaraden, 1972.

———. "Contribution à la rélance des coopératives d'éleveurs en 6e region (République du Mali)." CILSS/AD (FAO), 1975.

Mass, Bonnie. "An Historical Sketch of the American Population Control Movement." *International Journal of Health Services* 4, no. 4 (1974): 651-76.

———. *Population Target: The Political Economy of Population Control in Latin America.* Toronto: Latin American Working Group, 1976.

Mauny, Raymond. *Tableau Géographique de l'Ouest Africain au Moyen Age.* No. 61. Dakar: Mémoires de l'Institute Français d'Afrique Noire, 1961.

Meillassoux, Claude. "A Class Analysis of the Bureaucratic Process in Mali." *Journal of Development Studies* 6, no. 2 (1970): 97-110.

———. "Introduction" in Meillassoux, ed. *The Development of Indigenous Trade and Markets in West Africa.* London: Oxford University Press (1971), pp. 3-86.

———. "Development or Exploitation: is the Sahel famine good business?" *Review of African Political Economy* 1, no. 1 (1974): 27-33.

van Melle, G. "Wildlife utilization: Het gebruik van wilde fauna voor melk- en vleesproduktie." *Intermediair* 11, (January 3-17, 1975): 47-51.

Messiant, Christine. "La Situation Sociale et Matérielle des Populations." In Jean Copans, ed. *Sécheresses et Famines du Sahel,* vol. 1. Paris: François Maspero (1975), pp. 61-73.

Meunier, Roger. "L'Aide d'Urgence et les Nouveau Projets de Développement." In Jean Copans, ed. *Secheresses et Famines du Sahel,* vol. 1. Paris: François Maspero (1975), pp. 109-29.

Morel, Alain. "Faire Renaître le Sahel: Expériences de développement agricole dans le Massif de l'Aïr-Niger." *Cultures et Dêveloppement,* vol. 8, no. 2 (1976), pp. 266-86.

Moss, R. P., ed. *The Soil Resources of Tropical Africa.* Cambridge: At the University Press, 1968.

Moss, R. P., and Rathbone, R. J. A. R., eds. *The Population Factor in African Studies.* Proceedings of a conference organized by The African Studies Association of the United Kingdom, September 1972. London: University of London Press, 1975.

Mountjoy, A. B. "Vegetable Oils and Oilseeds." *Geography* vol. 42 (1957): 37-49.

Mountjoy, Allen B., and Embleton, Clifford. *Africa: A New Geographical Survey.* New York: F. W. Praeger, 1966.

Moyal, Maurice. "French West Africa: Trouble Ahead for Senegal." *West African Review* vol. 23 (1952): 18-21.

———. "Economic Development in Senegal." *Colonial Development in Senegal* 1, no. 19 (1954), pp. 33, 35, 37.

Murdock, George Peter. *Africa: Its Peoples and their Culture History.* New York: McGraw-Hill (1959).

Navez, S. Y. *Résultats et considérations sur l'Enquête Technico-Sociale Effectuée dans les Zones Maraîchères de la Région du Cap-Vert.* République du Sénégal. Ministère du Développement Rural. Cambérène-Dakar: Centre pour le Développement de l'Horticulture, 1974.

Newbury, C. W. "North African and Western Sudan Trade in the 19th Century: A Re-evaluation." *Journal of African History* 7, no. 2 (1966): 233–46.

New York Times. Give Us This Day—A Report on the World Food Crisis. New York: Arno Press, 1975.

Ngo Vinh Long. *Before the Revolution: The Vietnamese Peasants Under the French.* Cambridge, Mass.: M.I.T. Press, 1973.

Nicolaisen, Johannes. *Ecology and Culture of the Pastoral Tuareg.* Copenhagen: The National Museum of Copenhagen. Etnografsk Roekke IX, 1963.

Nicolas, Guy. "Rémarques sur divers facteurs socioéconomiques de la famine au sein d'une société subsaharienne. In Dalby, Church and Bezzaz, eds. *Report on the 1973 Symposium on Drought in Africa*, vol. 2. London: School of Oriental and African Studies (1977), pp. 159–69.

O'Brien, Donal B. Cruise. *The Mourides of Senegal: The Political and Economic Organization of an Islamic Brotherhood.* London: Oxford University Press, 1971.

OECD. *OECD: History, Aims, Structure.* Paris: OECD Information Service, 1971.

———. *The OECD Development Centre: Activities, Publications, Documents.* Paris, OECD Development Centre, 1973.

———. "The Sahel: Time for a New Approach." *The OECD Observer*, no. 79, January–February 1976.

———. *Strategy And Programme For Drought Control And Development In The Sahel.* Paris: OECD, May 1977.

Ominde, S. H., and Ejiogu, C. N. *Population Growth and Economic Development in Africa.* London: Heinemann Ed. Books Ltd., 1972. In association with Population Council, New York.

Opération Arachide Cultures Vivrières. "Communication sur la Culture Attelée à l'OACV". Présentée au colloque sur l'amélioration des systèmes de production au niveau des exploitations agricoles dans les pays du Sahel. February 20–March 1, 1978.

Ossewaarde, J. G. "The C.G.O.T. Ground-Nut Scheme in French West Africa." *Tropical Agriculture* 33 (April 1956): 86–94.

Ottenberg, Simon, and Ottenberg, Phoebe, eds. *Culture and Societies of Africa.* New York: Random House, 1960.

Oudes, Bruce. "Crocodile Tears Over American Aid." *Africa Report* (March-April 1974), pp. 52–54.

Oumarou, Idé. *Gros Plan.* Dakar-Abidjan: Les Nouvelles Editions Africaines, 1977.

Ousmane, Amadou. *15 ans, ça suffit.* Niamey: Imprimerie Nationale, 1977. Preface by Idé Oumarou.

Owen, John. "A Contribution to the Ecology of the African Baobab." *Savanna* (Zaria, Nigeria) 2, no. 3 (1973): 1–12.

Paddock, William, and Paddock, Paul. *Famine 1975!* Boston: Little, Brown and Co., 1967.

Parnell, Theodore, Utton, Albert E. "The Senegal Valley Authority." *Ekistics* vol. 43, no. 258 (May 1977): 320–23. Reprinted from *Indiana Law Journal* 51, no. 2 (1976): 253–56.

Pedlar, F. J. *Economic Geography of West Africa.* London: Longmans, Green & Co. Ltd., 1955.

Péhaut, Yves. "L'Arachide au Niger." *Études d'Économic Africaine.* Série Afrique Noir, no. 1 (1970), pp. 11–103.

Pélissier, Paul. "L'Arachide au Sénégal: Rationalisation et modernisation de sa culture." *Problèmes Agricoles au Sénégal* Etudes Sénégalaises No. 2 Centre IFAN Sénégal; Saint Louis du Sénégal, 1952, pp. 48–80.

———. "Les Paysans du Senegal. Saint-Yrieix: (Haute-Vienne) Imprimerie Fabrègue, 1966.

Pels, Kees. *Stijgende invoer van Afrikaanse groenten.* (1975), n.a. pp. 15–17.

Phillips, John. *Agriculture and Ecology in Africa.* London: Faber & Faber, 1959.

Picardi, Anthony C., Seifert, William W. "A Tragedy of the Commons in the Sahel." *Ekistics* 43, no. 258 (May 1977), 297–304.

Pitot, A. "L'Homme et les Sols dans les Steppes et Savannes de l'Afrique Occidentale Française." *Les Cahiers d'Outre-Mer* no. 19, (1952), pp. 215–40.

Poncet, Yveline. *La Séchéresse en Afrique Sahélienne.* Paris: OECD, 1973.

——. *La Sécheresse en Afrique Sahélienne: Une Étude Micro-Régionale en République du Niger: La Région des Dallois.* Paris: OECD, 1974.

Porteres, Roland. "Primary Cradles of Agriculture in the African Continents." In Fage and Oliver, eds. *Papers in African Pre-History* (1970), pp. 43–58.

Potter, Van Rensselaer. "The Tragedy of the Sahel Commons." *Science* 185 (Sept. 6, 1974): 183.

President's Science Advisory Committee. *The World Food Problem.* Washington, D.C.: US Government Printing Office, 1967.

van Raay, Hans G. T. *Fulani Pastoralists and Cattle.* Occasional Paper No. 44. The Hague: Institute of Social Studies, 1974.

van Raay, Hans G. T., and de Leeuw, Peter N. *Fodder Resources and Grazing Management in a Savanna Environment: an Ecosystem Approach.* Occasional Paper No. 45. The Hague: Institute of Social Studies, 1974.

Ravignan, François de. "Un Village du Niger devant les Experts Occidentaux." *Le Monde Diplomatique*, November 1977.

Raynaut, Claude. "Le Cas de la Région de Maradi (Niger)." In Jean Copans, ed. *Sécheresses et Famines du Sahel.* vol. 2. Paris: François Maspero (1975), pp. 5–43.

——. "Lessons of a Crisis." In Dalby, Church, and Bezzaz, eds. *Report of the 1973 Symposium on Drought in Africa.* vol. 2 (1977), pp. 17–29.

Reboul, Claude. *Economie de la Production Agricole Sénégalaise.* Paris: Institut National de la Recherche Agronomique, May 1974.

——. "Sénégal. Le développement contre les paysans?" *Actuel Développement* (1976a), pp. 36–41.

——. "Causes Economiques de la Secheresse au Senegal." *Bulletin d'Information du Departement d'Économie et de Sociologie Rurales.* no. 2. Paris: Institut National de la Recherche Agronomique (INRA) (1976b), pp. 59–93.

——. *Danger D'Oasis? Aléas d'une politique de sédentarisation. Le Forage de Labgar, au Sénégal.* Paris: INRA, March 1977.

Reining, Priscilla. "Satellite Potentials for Anthropological Studies of Subsistence Activities and Population Change." Report of Research Workshop, May 27–30, 1975, Washington, D.C.

Républic of Cape Verde. *Petit Monographie du Cap Vert,* n.d.

——. *Résume des Characteristiques Climatiques, Physiques, et Démographiques.* Praia, October, 1976.

République du Sénégal. *Centre for Horticultural Development.* République du Sénégal. Ministere du Developpement Rural et de l'Hydraulique. Direction Generale de la Production Agricole. Dakar, 1975.

——. *Compte Rendu de Quelques Essais D'Irrigation au Goutte a Goutte.* République du Sénégal. Ministère du Développement Rural et de L'Hydraulique. Direction Générale de la Production Agricole. Camberene-Dakar: Centre Pour le Developpement de l'Horticulture, 1976.

——. *La Récolte, le Conditionnement, le Transport et la Vente du Haricot Vert.* Ministère du Developpement Rural et de l'Hydraulique. Direction Générale de la Production Agricole.

Cambérène-Dakar: Centre pour le Développement de l'Horticulture, 1977. Fiche Technique No. 3.

———. *Classement des donées de l'enquête socioéconomique de base menée dans la zone de Toulékédi.* Secrétariat d'État à la Promotion Humaine—Project Élevage Bakel: PH/USAID Promotion Humaine en Milieu Eleveur, 1977a.

Richards, Paul, ed. *African Environment: Problems and Perspectives.* African Environment Special Report No. 1. London: International African Institute, 1975.

Robarts, Richard C. *French Development Assistance: A Study in Policy and Administration.* Beverly Hills: Sage Publications, 1974.

Robinson, Pearl. "The Political Context of Regional Development in the West African Sahel." *Journal of Modern African Studies,* December, 1978.

Robinson, Ronald, Gallagher, John, and Denny, Alice. *Africa and the Victorians: The Climax of Imperialism.* Garden City: Doubleday Anchor, 1968.

Rockefeller Foundation. International Development Strategies for the Sahel: A Conference held at the Bellagio Study and Conference Center, Italy, October 1974. The Rockfeller Foundation, 1975 Working Papers.

Rosevear, D. R. *The Bats of West Africa.* London: The British Museum (Natural History), 1965.

Rupp, Marieanne. "Report of the Sociological Study conducted in the districts of Tanout, Dakoro, Agades from March 30 to April 30, 1976."

Salifou, A. "When History Repeats Itself: The Famine of 1931 in Niger." *African Environment* 1, no. 2 (April 1975): 22–48.

SATEC [Société d'Aide Technique et de Coopération]. "Étude de Reconnaissance de la Vallee du Niger dans la Région de GAO." Paris, 1975.

Sawadogo, Patrice. *Enquête sur les Nomades Refoulés par la Sécheresse: Zones de Maradi et Dakoro, Niger, 1974.* Dakar: IDEP, February 1975.

SEDES/SCET/ORSTOM. Étude sur les Potentialités Économiques des Pays du Sahel. Paris. 1975.

Seifert, William W., and Kamrany, Nake M. *A Framework for Evaluating Long-Term Development Strategies for the Sahel-Sudan Area.* 11 volumes. Cambridge: Massachusetts Institute of Technology, Center for Policy Alternatives, 1974.

Shear, David, and Clark, Bob. "International Long-Term Planning for the Sahel." *International Development Review* no. 4, (1976), pp. 15–20.

Sheets, Hal, and Morris, Roger. *Disaster in the Desert: Failures of International Relief in the West African Drought.* Special report, Humanitarian Policy Studies. New York: The Carnegie Endowment for International Peace, 1974.

Shepard, Jack. *The Politics of Starvation.* New York: Carnegie Endowment for International Peace, 1975.

Shoji, Kobe. "Drip Irrigation." *Scientific American* 237, no. 5 (November 1977): 62–68.

Sík, Endre. *The History of Black Africa,* 2 volumes. Budapest: Akademiai Kiado, 1970.

Singer, Max, and Bracken, Paul. "Don't Blame the US." *New York Times Magazine.* November 7, 1976. pp. 34–35, 119–120, 124.

Skinner, Elliot P. *The Mossi of the Upper Volta.* Palo Alto: Stanford University Press, 1964.

———. "Labor Migration among the Mossi of the Upper Volta." In Hilda Kuper, ed. *Urbanization and Migration in West Africa.* Berkeley: University of California Press (1965), pp. 60–84.

Smith, Susan E. "The Environmental Adaptation of Nomads in the West African Sahel: A Key to Understanding Prehistoric Pastoralists." In Wolfgang Weissleder, ed. *The Nomadic*

Alternative: Modes and Models of Interaction in the African-Asian Deserts and Steppes. The Hague: Mouton Publishers (1978), pp. 75–96.

Stamp, L. Dudley. "The Southern Margin of the Sahara: Comments on Some Recent Studies on the Question of Desiccation in West Africa." *Geographical Review* vol. 30 (1940): 297–300.

Stanford Biology Group. *A Legacy of our Presence: The Destruction of Indochina.* Palo Alto: Stanford University, 1970.

Stebbing, E. P. "The Encroaching Sahara: Threat to the West African Colonies." *Geographical Journal* 85, no. 6 (June 1935): 506–24.

———. "The Threat of the Sahara." *Journal of the Royal African Society.* Supplement to vol. 36. 1937.

———. *The Forests of West Africa: A Study of Modern Conditions.* London and Edinburgh: W. R. Chambers Ltd., 1937a.

Stenning, Derrick J. *Savannah Nomads: A Study of the Wodaabe Pastoral Fulani of Western Bornu Province Northern Region, Nigeria.* London: Oxford University Press, 1959.

———. "Transhumance, Migratory Drift, Migration: Patterns of Pastoral Fulani Nomadism." In Simon and Phoebe Ottenberg, eds. *Cultures and Societies of Africa.* New York: Random House (1960), pp. 139–59.

Sterling, Claire. "The Making of the Sub-Saharan Wasteland." *Atlantic Monthly* 233, no. 5 (May 1974): 98–105.

Stol, Albert. *Schijn en Werkelijkheid in de Sahel.* Bussum: Uitgeverij Agathon, 1975.

Sundström, Lars. *The Exchange Economy of Pre-Colonial Tropical Africa.* New York: St. Martin's Press, 1965.

Suret-Canale, J. "Quelques aspects de la géographie agraire au Sénégal." *Cahiers d'Outre-mer* no. 4 (1948), pp. 348–67.

———. *Afrique Noire Occidentale et Centrale:* vol. 1 *Géographie-Civilisations-Histoire,* Paris: Editions Sociales, 1958.

———. *Afrique Noire, Occidentale et Centrale:* vol. 3 *De la Colonisation à nos Jours: 1945 à 1969.* Paris: Editions Sociales, 1972.

Svanidze, I. A. "The African Struggle for Agricultural Productivity." *Journal of Modern African Studies* 6, no. 3 (1968): 311–28.

Swift, Jeremy. "Disaster and a Sahelian Nomad Economy." In Dalby and Church, eds. *Report on the 1973 Symposium on Drought in Africa,* vol. 1 (1973), pp. 71–78.

Tarabrin, E. A. *The New Scramble for Africa.* Moscow: Progress Publishers, 1974.

Teitelbaum, Joel M. "Human Versus Animal Nutrition. A 'Development' Project Among Fulani Cattlekeepers of the Sahel of Senegal," in Thomas K. Fitzgerald, ed. *Nutrition and Anthropology in Action.* Assen/Amsterdam: van Gorcum (1977), pp. 125–43.

Thompson, Archibald. *The Origins of Christianity.* New York: International Publishers, 1954.

Thompson, Virginia. "Niger." In Gwendolyn M. Carter, ed. *National Unity and Regionalism in Eight African States.* Ithaca: Cornell University Press (1966), pp. 151–230.

Thompson, Virginia, and Adloff, Richard. *French West Africa.* 1958. New York: Greenwood Press, 1969.

Thomas, Clive Y. "Industrialization and the Transformation of Africa: An Alternative Strategy to M.N.C. Expansion." In Carl Widstrand, ed. *Multinational Firms in Africa.* Dakar: African Institute for Economic Development and Planning; Uppsala, Sweden: Scandinavian Institute of African Studies (1975), pp. 325–60.

Thomson, James T. "Ecological Deterioration: Local-Level Rule-Making and Enforcement Problems in Niger." In Michael Glantz, ed. *Desertification.* Boulder, Colorado: Westview Press (1977), pp. 55–79.

Trimingham, J. Spencer. *A History of Islam in West Africa.* London: Oxford University Press, 1962.

Trinh Ton That. "La Double Culture du Riz dans la Moyenne Vallée du Sénégal: Orientation des Recherches." Centre National d'Experimentation Agronomique et de Developpement Agricole de Kaédi, 1976.

Tutwiler, Richard, Murdock, Muneera S. and Horowitz, Michael M. *Problems and Prospects for Development in the Yemen Arab Republic: the Contribution of the Social Sciences.* Binghamton, N.Y.: Institute for Development Anthropology, 1976.

UN Development Program. *Progress Report on the Drought-Stricken Regions of Africa and Adjacent Areas.* 1974.

UNESCO. *The Sahel: Ecological Approaches To Land Use.* Man and the Biosphere (MAB). Technical Notes, No. 1, n.d.

UN Special Sahel Office. *An Approach to Recovery and Rehabilitation of the Sudano-Sahelian Region.* 1974.

Updike, John. *The Coup.* New York: Alfred A. Knopf, 1978.

USAID. *Development and Management of the Steppe and Brush-Grass Savannah Zone Immediately South of the Sahara.* In-House Report Prepared by the Agency for International Development, October, 1972.

———. *Mauritania Livestock Project.* Noncapital Project Paper (PROP), May 28, 1974.

———. *Niger Cereals Production.* Niamey, 1975. Project No. 683-11-130-201.

———. *Report to the United States Congress: Proposal for a Long-Term Comprehensive Development Program for the Sahel. Major Findings and Programs.* April 1976.

———. *Mali Crop Production Project Action Riz-Sorgho Gao.* No. 688-11-130-202. Bamako: USAID, 1976a.

———. *Niger Range and Livestock.* USAID Project Paper, 1977. Project No. 683-0202.

———. *Bakel Crop Production Project.* 2 vols. USAID Project Paper, 1977a. Project No. 685-0208.

———. *Sahel Development Program: Annual Report to the Congress.* February 1978.

US House of Representatives. *The Drought Crisis in the West African Sahel.* Hearing before the Subcommittee on Africa of the Committee on Foreign Affairs. 93rd Congress. July 16, 1973. Washington, D.C.: US Government Printing Office, 1973.

———. *Foreign Assistance Legislation for FY 1978. Part 3: Economic and Military Assistance Programs in Africa.* Committee on International Relations. Subcommittee on Africa. Hearings of March 23, 1977. Washington, D.C.: US Government Printing Office, 1977.

US Senate. *World Hunger, Health, and Refugee Problems.* Joint Hearings before the Subcommittee to Investigate Problems Connected with Refugees and Escapees of the Committee on the Judiciary and the Subcommittee on Health of the Committee on Labor and Public Welfare. Part I: *Crisis in West Africa,* July 25, 1973; Part IV: *Famine in Africa,* March 21, 1974; Part V: *Human Disasters In Cyprus, Bangladesh, Africa;* Part VI: *Special Study Mission to Africa, Asia, and the Middle East.* Washington, D.C.: US Government Printing Office, 1973–1975.

Veyret, P. "L'Elevage dans la Zone Tropicale." *Les Cahiers d'Outre-Mer* no. 17 (1952), pp. 70–83.

Vivó, Raúl Valdés. *Ethiopia's Revolution.* New York: International Publishers, 1978.

de Vries, F. W. T. Penning. "Results and Perspectives of the Project 'Production Primaire Sahel'—A Sketch Halfway." Bamako: February 1978.

Wade, Nicholas. "Sahalian Drought: No Victory for Western Aid." *Science* 185 (July 19, 1974): 234–237.

Walker, Martin. "Drought." *New York Times Magazine* (June 9, 1974), pp. 11–14, 43–46.

Walsh, Gretchen. *Access to Sources of Information on Agricultural Development in the Sahel.* Working Paper No. 17. East Lansing: Michigan State University African Rural Economy Program, 1976.

Ware, Helen. "The Sahelian Drought: Some Thoughts on the Future." United Nations Document ST/SSO/33. March 26, 1975.

Warhaftig, Alan Matt. "Famine in Africa: No Act of God." *The Nation*, February 22, 1975.

Weber, Fred P. *The role of Forests in Sahelian Rehabilitation Efforts.* CILSS/UNSO/FAO Consultation, 1976.

Wertheim, W. F. "Sociological Aspects of Corruption in Southeast Asia." In *East-West Parallels: Sociological Approaches to Modern Asia.* The Hague: W. van Hoeve Ltd. (1964), pp. 103–31.

Westebbe, Richard M. *The Economy of Mauritania.* New York: F. W. Praeger, 1971.

White, Benjamin. "Demand-for-Labor Analysis and Population Theory: Population Growth in Colonial Java." *Journal of Human Ecology* I (1973): 217–36.

———. The Economic Importance of Children in a Javanese Village. In Moni Nag, ed. *Population and Social Organization.* The Hague: Mouton (1976), pp. 127–146.

Wiesenfeld, Stephen L. "Sickel-Cell Trait in Human Biological and Cultural Evolution." *Science* 157 (1967): 1134–40.

de Wilde, John C. *Experiences with Agricultural Development in Tropical Africa.* Vol. 2, *The Case Studies.* Baltimore: International Bank for Reconstruction and Development and Johns Hopkins Press, 1967.

Williams, Maurice. "Development Strategies for the Sahel: The 'Club des Amis du Sahel.'" Paris: *OECD Review.* (November 1976), pp. 177–96.

Winstanley, Derek. "Recent Rainfall Trends in Africa, the Middle East, and India." *Nature* 243 (1973): 464–65.

———. "Climatic Changes and the Future of the Sahel." In Michael Glantz, ed. *The Politics of Natural Disaster.* New York: F. W. Praeger (1976), pp. 189–213.

World Bank. *Current Economic Position and Development Prospects of Niger*, vol. 3, The Agricultural Sector (Annexes). Western Africa Regional Office, August 20, 1974. Report No. 487a-NIR. "Not For Public Use". 1974a.

———. *Senegal: Tradition, Diversification, and Economic Development.* Washington, D.C.: World Bank, 1974b.

———. *République du Sénégal: Etude du Sector Agricole.* Vol. 1, Rapport Principal. Vol. 2, Annexes. Western Africa Regional Office, November 3, 1975.

———. "Report and Recommendation of the President to the Executive Director on a Proposed Credit to the Republic of Senegal for a Livestock Project." May 24, 1976. P-1771a-SE.

World View Publishers. *The Ethiopian Revolution and the Struggle Against U.S. Imperialism.* New York: World View Publishers, 1978.

Worsley, Peter. *The Trumpet Shall Sound.* New York: Schocken Books, 1968.

Index

About the Authors

Richard W. Franke is assistant professor of anthropology at Montclair State College, where he has taught since 1972. Professor Franke has carried out field research in Surinam, Bougainville and Indonesia, in addition to the research in West Africa. He has published articles on problems of underdevelopment, food production (with emphasis on the Green Revolution) and ecology, and is currently on the editorial board of *The Bulletin of Concerned Asian Scholars*.

Barbara H. Chasin is assistant professor of sociology at Montclair State College, where she has taught since 1970, and has taught at the University of Massachusetts in Boston. She is coauthor of *Power and Ideology: A Marxist Approach to Political Science* (1974). Professor Chasin has published articles on various topics including sociobiology, and the sociology of death, liberalism, and hunger.

Drs. Franke and Chasin began their research on the Sahel drought and famine in 1974. In 1976 they joined the World Agricultural Research Project at the Harvard University School of Public Health. In 1977, as part of the Project, Drs. Franke and Chasin traveled to France and in 1978 spent five months in the Sahel gathering data on current development projects and problems.

THE HUMAN REVOLUTION

DAISAKU IKEDA

The HUMAN REVOLUTION

VOLUME ONE

with a foreword by Arnold J. Toynbee

and illustrations by Teikichi Miyoshi

New York · WEATHERHILL · *Tokyo*

This book contains a condensed English translation of Volume 1 and Volume 2 of the original Japanese version of *Ningen Kakumei* (Human Revolution) as first published serially in the daily newspaper *Seikyo Shimbun,* Tokyo, during the period of January, 1965, to February, 1966, and then published in book form by Seikyo Press, Tokyo, in October, 1965, and April, 1966. An earlier English translation was published by the Seikyo Press in October, 1965, and May, 1966.

First edition, 1972

Published by John Weatherhill, Inc., 149 Madison Avenue, New York, New York 10016, with editorial offices at 7-6-13 Roppongi, Minato-ku, Tokyo 106, Japan. *Printed in Japan.*

LCC Card No. 72-79121 *ISBN 0-8348-0074-8*

CONTENTS

FOREWORD

THE HUMAN Revolution is an English translation of the story of Soka Gakkai, Society for the Creation of Value, as told by this society's third president, Daisaku Ikeda. The present book comprises the first two volumes of the original, and translations of further volumes will follow. There is also a French translation in progress, and, in thus making this book accessible to the English-reading and French-reading public, Mr. Ikeda has done a service to his contemporaries all over the world. These now include an appreciable number of adherents of Soka Gakkai; for, though this society was founded in Japan, and gained momentum in response to Japanese experience, its concern is for all mankind, and *The Human Revolution* is an accurate description of its objective. Soka Gakkai is inspired by a belief that a revolutionary change of mankind's spiritual values is urgently needed in all spheres of life, and its adherents believe that this worldwide spiritual revolution can be achieved by embracing, and acting on, Soka Gakkai's tenets.

The pursuit of this objective is an act of religious faith, and in fact Soka Gakkai is the lay association of the adherents of the Nichiren Shoshu sect of Buddhism, whose head temple is Daiseki-ji at Fujinomiya, near Mount Fuji. Nichiren Shoshu is one of the communities of followers of the thirteenth-century Japanese Buddhist prophet Nichiren.

"Prophet" is an appropriate description of Nichiren; for in many ways Nichiren has more affinity with the prophets of western Asia than with any of the other propagators and interpreters of Buddhism in India and in eastern Asia. Zoroastrian, Muslim, Christian, and Jewish readers of this book will recognize Nichiren's affinity with Zarathustra, Muhammad, and the prophets of Israel and Judah, and this impression will be confirmed if they read the English translation of Nichiren's collected writings that Soka Gakkai has published.

Like the West Asian prophets, Nichiren has inspired other dynamic personalities in later generations. The common ground between Nichiren Buddhism and the West Asian religions is extensive and important. The source of the spiritual power of Nichiren and his followers was, and is, faith, in the meaning that this word carries in the histories and doctrines of the West Asian religions.

Faith, in this sense, is an absolute belief in the truth and saving power of a religious community's object of worship and in the supreme spiritual authority of the founder. Indeed the founder and ultimate spiritual reality have, in some cases, been identified with each other. For instance, the followers of Nichiren Shoshu, unlike those of other Nichiren sects, firmly believe that Nichiren claimed to be and in fact was a manifestation of Buddhahood; this conviction has given them, as it gave Nichiren himself, the confidence and courage to play an active part in public affairs, secular as well as religious.

To take a strong line on controversial public issues exposes a prophet and his followers to persecution. Their faith gives them the moral strength to remain true to their convictions, even at the price of martyrdom. Nichiren himself narrowly escaped being put to death by the *de facto* government of Japan in his day (the Hojo regents of the Kamakura shogunate). Nichiren had made himself unpopular by his outspoken criticisms of the representatives of schools of Buddhism other than his own. He maintained that his school was the only right one. He warned the Japanese government and people that, if they rejected his formulation of the essence of the Mahayana Buddhist Lotus Sutra, they would bring calamities on themselves. The calamities came. A civil war was followed by two Mongol attacks, and Nichiren won the reputation of being a prophet in the popular sense of being endowed with a gift for foreseeing the future, besides being a seer of ultimate spiritual reality.

Japan's situation in the thirteenth century after Christ was much like that of Israel and Judah in the eighth century before Christ. In both instances an aggressive empire (the Assyrian in the earlier case and the Mongol in the later), which had already achieved vast conquests, was poised to strike. In the case of Japan, however, the attackers were repulsed, and though he was persecuted, Nichiren escaped Isaiah's martyrdom. Mr. Ikeda's book deals with a later chapter in the history of Japan and of Nichiren Shoshu, in which the Japanese people suffered the worst tribulations that they had yet experienced, and in which the followers of Nichiren Shoshu were challenged, more harshly than ever before, to have the courage of their convictions.

This time Japan herself, like her thirteenth-century Mongol assailants, was led into aggression and consequent disaster by the wickedness and folly of militarists, who had dominated the government; and the adherents of Nichiren Shoshu were being pressed to betray their faith by paying allegiance to State Shinto—a political perversion of an ancient worship of the forces of nature, in which this non-Buddhist religion had been converted into a cult of the Japanese people's collective power. State Shinto had been fabricated since the Meiji Restoration, and it was enforced—as an instrument for maintaining national solidarity—when, in World War II, in which the militarists had involved Japan, the tide was turning against her. The Christian church underwent a similar ordeal between A.D. 250 and A.D. 311, when the Roman counterpart of State Shinto was forced upon the Christians for the same reason.

The English edition of *The Human Revolution* covers the period of July, 1945, to October, 1947—a testing time for Soka Gakkai and also for the whole of the Japanese people. The leaders of Soka Gakkai had distinguished themselves by their steadfastness in refusing to be intimidated into paying lip service to a religion that they did not believe to be true, and that they saw to be leading Japan into disaster. The first president of Soka Gakkai, Tsunesaburo Makiguchi, died, a martyr in prison, in 1944. The present book opens with a moving account of the conditional release from prison of the second president, Josei Toda, only a few weeks before the war ended. Toda is the hero of this chapter in Soka Gakkai's history. Though sick and penniless, Toda immediately set to work to rebuild Soka Gakkai. Under his presidency and then under that of his successor, Daisaku Ikeda, Soka Gakkai has achieved its astonishing postwar resurrection—a spiritual achievement that matches the Japanese people's material achievement in the economic field.

What have been the causes of Soka Gakkai's triumphant postwar success? The fundamental cause was the faith with which this community and its leaders in our time have been inspired by the founder, Nichiren, whose spirit is still potent in the seventh century after his death. This faith has given them the courage and constancy to endure persecution, and the sincerity that they have demonstrated by their endurance has opened their countrymen's hearts and minds to this teaching and has helped to win Soka Gakkai its huge increase in numbers. When religious persecution was suddenly ended in August, 1945, by the collapse and liquidation of the military régime in Japan, Soka Gakkai had a free field for its missionary zeal.

The situation in Japan in 1945 is described vividly and

harrowingly in Mr. Ikeda's book. It was like the situation in the Roman Empire in 311, when the persecution of Christianity was reluctantly abandoned by the Roman Imperial Government. In both cases, there was a spiritual vacuum and a material crisis. The Roman Empire had been devastated by barbarian invasions and at the same time the old religions had lost their hold on the people's minds and hearts. In Japan, State Shinto—the adulation of corporate national power dedicated to military aggression—had been discredited by the catastrophic denouement of half a century of successive military victories that had culminated in the sensational but ephemeral exploits of 1941.

When the Japanese people became the targets of their previous victims, they suffered a long-drawn-out agony before the militarists were compelled at last by force majeure to release the country from a war that had become a nightmare. By then, the people were bankrupt and starving, and many of them no longer had roofs over their heads. But their material straits were surpassed by their spiritual bewilderment. They had been led to imagine that Japan was destined to conquer the rest of the world; instead, Japan had fallen under foreign military occupation for the first time in her history.

This partly accounts for Soka Gakkai's postwar success. In the midst of despair and disillusionment, this little community was sure of its objective and was confident that it could and would attain it. No wonder that, within the next three decades, Soka Gakkai has grown to its present stature.

The postwar rise of Soka Gakkai is not solely the concern of the country in which it started; already Soka Gakkai is a world affair, as is indicated by the translation of Mr. Ikeda's present book into French and English. Soka Gakkai is a Buddhist society, and Buddhism was the first missionary religion to address its message to all mankind. Nichiren, like his followers in present-day Nichiren Shoshu, loved his country, but his horizon and his concern were not bounded by Japan's coasts.

Nichiren held that Buddhism, as he conceived it, was a means of salvation for his fellow human beings everywhere. In working for the human revolution, Soka Gakkai is carrying out Nichiren's mandate.

Arnold Toynbee

PREFACE TO THE ENGLISH EDITION

THE INSPIRATION for the Japanese original of this novelized biography came to me one day many years ago while Josei Toda, the late second president of Soka Gakkai and my mentor, was still alive. We were just about to begin publishing the newspaper called the *Seikyo Shimbun,* which later became the daily organ of our society. Toda said to me with a smile and a pat of his pocket, which obviously contained something important: "I've just finished a novel. Now that we're ready to put out a newspaper, we'll want a serial story for it." The novel he had started was called *Ningen Kakumei* (Human Revolution). This conversation took place one spring day in 1951.

By 1956, Toda's health, never very good after his imprisonment during the war, had failed completely. Only a few months before his death, *Ningen Kakumei* was published at last in book form. One evening in the rest home in Karuizawa, where he was being treated, Toda asked me what I thought of his work. I answered honestly that I felt the earlier sections dealing with Tsunesaburo Makiguchi had been powerful but that he had been unable to write as convincingly about himself. He agreed with me in such a way that I knew that his wish was for me to take up his task and to write a sequel telling his own story. The Japanese version of this book and now this English translation are the results of my efforts to fulfill his wish.

Since it deals with my own life as well as with that of Toda, I know how difficult writing about oneself is. In titling his autobiography *Dichtung und Warheit* (Poetry and Truth), Goethe underscored something very important about the process of telling a personal story. That is, facts are not always true, because the human mind sometimes distorts them accidentally and sometimes deliberately fictionalizes them for poetic or other effect. Goethe and all great writers have known that in order to create an image of the truth the author must dissect his own heart into its component parts and discover what is true and what is false within himself. In my attempt to produce a lasting and true image of Josei Toda, I have had to perform a similar dissection of my own heart.

This project has been a long one and is still continuing in spite of the fact that I am busy and am also aware of my own limitations in the field of literature. Nevertheless, Josei Toda devoted his entire life to the task of spreading the true Buddhism throughout Japan and to all mankind; and I, as a representative of Soka Gakkai, feel that it is my duty to continue and expand that great work.

But perhaps even more important is the urgent need to lead people to the revitalizing hope and faith possible through the kind of human revolution that Toda taught and that I, as a believer in Nichiren Shoshu, have experienced. Today, excess concern with wealth, power, and material possessions has submerged much that is priceless in humanity. The human revolution of Nichiren Shoshu teaches how the reformation within one man can transform not only his karma, but those of a nation and of all mankind as well. If in telling the story of Josei Toda and the dramatic history of Soka Gakkai, I can help even one person to know this revitalization I shall be very happy. I am an ordinary man, but a man of faith. I believe that by striving to learn the truth about myself and by battling to live a meaningful life I shall be true to the principles of both Buddhism and democracy.

In writing this book I have used no real names aside from those of Toda himself, his great teacher Tsunesaburo Makiguchi, and those of a few well-known historical personages. During his lifetime, Toda came into contact with thousands of people. Obviously they cannot all be included in a book, but I have selected the ones who were closest to him and whose personalities and activities had the greatest influence on him and on the development of Soka Gakkai. I have treated them all in the manner of fiction; that is, I have sometimes combined a number of real people into one character and sometimes used traits of one person in the composition of several fictitious characters. In general, the line of development of the story follows that of the true history of Soka Gakkai, though a few incidents have been fabricated to improve the narrative or to make special points.

As of this writing, the Japanese version of the book has now run to seven volumes. In all of them, in spite of a certain unavoidable amount of difficult Buddhist terminology, I have enjoyed the understanding and encouragement of many readers. To them I am very grateful. But I must also express my gratitude to Nittatsu Hosoi, the sixty-sixth high priest of the Nichiren Shoshu head temple, Daiseki-ji, for the guidance and help he has unfailingly offered, and to senior members of Soka Gakkai who have supplied me both with important information about the society's earlier history and with continued moral support.

In preparing this English-language edition, which is a condensed version of Volume 1 and Volume 2 of the original Japanese edition, an attempt has been made to make the story as straightforward as possible and to simplify the vocabulary so that people unacquainted with Buddhism will be able to understand the meaning of Nichiren Daishonin's teaching, as well as Toda's guidance. A glossary has also been included to aid readers who may be unfamiliar with some of the Buddhist personages and terminology that appear in this book. For their efforts, I must thank an international group of translators; Richard L. Gage, who assisted in the preparation of the manuscript; Rebecca Davis and other editors of John Weatherhill, Inc., for their valuable assistance and advice; and Meredith Weatherby and Takeshi Yamazaki, president and vice-president of Weatherhill, for their interest and encouragement.

BOOK ONE

1. DAWN

WAR IS barbarous and inhuman. Nothing is more cruel, nothing more tragic.

In July, 1945, Japan had been at war for eight years, and her people were near despair. Many had lost their parents and children; most had been left homeless and starving. Day in, day out, they lived in fear of American bombers; yet they endured in silence. When the rumor began to spread that an enemy invasion of the home islands was imminent, however, deep foreboding and dread swept the nation.

About seven o'clock on the evening of July 3, 1945, three people standing outside the forbidding iron gates of Toyotama Prison gazed into its empty compound. They had been waiting for two hours, faces drawn with anxiety and expectation. Dusk had fallen; only intermittent muted sounds from within the prison broke the hush. In the dreary dusk of the deserted street, the high concrete prison wall loomed ominously. Heat and humidity still hung thick in the air, but as dusk wore on, cool breezes blowing from the Musashino Plains brought hope of relief from the rainy season.

A tall, slender man in his forties appeared from a small side gate. It was Josei Toda, a man destined to play a vital role in the history of his nation, but a most unimposing sight at that moment. He carried a large cloth-wrapped bundle in his hand. As the gate closed, he looked about uncertainly in the gathering dusk. Though gaunt and emaciated, his figure was unbowed; and behind thick glasses, his deep eyes were alert and penetrating. As he started to walk away, the three people waiting recognized him and rushed forward calling excitedly. His glasses glinted as he halted.

"Ikue!" he said, "you've come."

He smiled. Overcome with emotion, his young wife nodded.

"I'm so glad," he said. "How is everybody?"

"Fine," replied Ikue, fighting to keep back the tears.

"Our house—is it safe?"

"Yes, dear."

"Thank heaven! It must have been trying for you during this long time, Ikue. But you don't have to worry any more." He put his hands on her shoulders consolingly, reassuringly.

"Welcome back, uncle." A youth who had been standing to one side broke in.

"Kazuo!" Toda stretched out his hand to pat the boy on the head.

"Welcome back," called a feminine voice charged with emotion. Toda's myopic gaze sought out the speaker in the semidarkness.

"Sister, how good of you to come."

For two seemingly interminable years, Toda's wife, elder sister, and nephew had awaited his release from prison. At last he stood before them, free. Although he looked absurdly frail and thin in an incongruous summer kimono, he nonetheless seemed surrounded by an aura of inner strength. But a glimpse of his twiglike legs, momentarily revealed as a gust of wind parted the skirt of his kimono, told his wife that the strength they discerned was not physical. She wanted to take his bundle, but young Kazuo seized it by the knot of its cloth wrapper and raised it to his shoulder.

"It's heavier than it looks," he said cheerfully.

After two years of separation each of the four people had many things to say, but a strange diffidence checked the excitement of reunion, making words useless. They continued their walk beside the prison wall in silence.

The man's attire contrasted sharply with the clothing of his

relatives. His light cotton kimono was better suited to a public bath house than to the streets of a war-torn city. His wife and sister wore the heavy bloomerlike trousers called *mompe* and the cloth hoods common to all women in Japan in those years. The boy, prepared for the almost certain air raids, wore leggings and had a steel helmet strapped to his back.

The little group came to the end of the prison wall and turned right, into a deserted street. Darkened houses lined the road for several blocks, and then suddenly there was nothing. The whole street fell away into an empty plain of desolation. Toda stopped, his eyes riveted on the stark darkness that seemed to fill the horizon. Here and there he made out looming shadows, fragmented ruins, twisted pillars, crushed roofs, fallen trees. A pungent sulfurous smell clogged the air. Though stunned by the sight, Toda resumed his walk.

For countless nights, lying in his prison cell he had seen the red flames of the holocaust outside his small, high window. He could hear the eerie screaming of sirens, the roar of airplanes, and the explosions of bombs. Dread and anguish filled his heart as he suffered from ignorance of the fate of his wife, children, and loved ones, of Tokyo, and of all Japan. Was everything being destroyed?

In prison he had seen only flickering lights and phantoms; tonight, for the first time, he confronted the appalling reality. It shook the very core of his being. In November, 1944, American bombers based on the Mariana Islands began indiscriminate bombing of Japanese cities. By May, 1945, they had demolished large areas of Tokyo, Osaka, and other major cities and were daily raiding smaller provincial cities. On the main islands an estimated three million homes had been razed, and more than six hundred thousand people had been killed or wounded. Ten million had suffered lesser damage of one kind or another. Isolated in his prison cell, Toda knew no details of the casualties and destruction, but he sensed colossal devastation. Now from his wife he learned that the downtown area of Tokyo was in almost total ruin and that more than half his friends and acquaintances had suffered from the bombings. And still the war raged on. In fury and indignation he asked himself: "How much longer will this madness continue?"

Picking his way through the black wreckage, he thought of the long ages in which peace and happiness had been the universal aspiration of mankind and of how these hopes had always been frustrated by war. In his heart he knew that war is always evil, no matter what its causes, since it inevitably brings destruction and misery. In modern history, Japan has frequently gone to war, staking the national destiny on armed conflict and undergoing tremendous hardships. But never before had war brought such disaster. "Is Japan doomed to fight forever?" he wondered. "Is there no way to save the country and the people from this horror?" Alone in his meditation, solitary and assailed by a sense of powerlessness in the face of apparently insurmountable problems, from deep within himself he tried to muster the strength he knew would well up from the mystic vision he had seen in his prison cell. The light from that vision slowly grew into radiant hope.

Josei Toda, though reduced by two years of confinement to a thin, frail man of forty-five, had once been hearty and strong. There was nothing unusual about the way he was freed from prison. He was simply one more of the many wartime prisoners, confined but unconvicted, who were ultimately released on bail. The cropped hair, plain kimono, and unassuming manner gave no indication of the true distinction and greatness of this man who was to become the second leader of Soka Kyoiku Gakkai, the society that was later to be called Soka Gakkai. Tsunesaburo Makiguchi, the founder and first president of Soka Kyoiku Gakkai and Toda's revered teacher, had died in prison the year before.

Toda was now free. The death of his teacher had shaken him profoundly but had not defeated him because of the great faith he shared with Makiguchi. It had supported them both throughout their tribulations. Though death causes many human beings grief, Toda and Makiguchi could face it unperturbed because they believed that both life and death are an inseparable unity, no more than phases in the great operation of an immense universal law. These two men also derived great strength from the knowledge of their important mission of *kosen rufu*, spreading the true Buddhism to all men, while striving for *obutsu myogo*, the fusion of that Buddhism with all phases of society. Though still in prison when he learned of Makiguchi's death, Toda did not give in to despair. He knew that he had great work to do now that his teacher had passed on to him the legacy of a great religious revolution. On the other hand, his own imprisonment and the death of Makiguchi made Toda hungry for revenge, not against the military, but against the invisible force of evil that had cost untold numbers of lives and had brought Japan to the brink of total disaster.

Seven centuries ago Nichiren, the founder of Nichiren Shoshu, the religion in which Toda and Makiguchi believed and to the propagation of which they devoted their lives, had proved that misguided or perverted philosophies and religions are the true cause of all human misery. The Shintoism of the Japanese militarists had shown how perspicacious Nichiren was. Because Toda knew the cause of the misery, he was able to survive it secure in the hope that once free he would be able to do something to remove its causes.

Just after his release from prison, however, his condition did not permit great physical activity. Even the short walk he had taken from the prison gate taxed his strength. And now he stopped suddenly as a sharp pain stabbed his heart. He stood gasping in the darkness, which reeked of scorched and charred debris. When the pain had subsided, he resumed his walk and turned onto Waseda Avenue. All the houses were blacked out against the air raids, and a pallid gray strip of sidewalk seemed to float into the night. Soon the little group turned toward Nakano Station, where heavily shaded platform lights speckled the night. Tired from the walk but relieved that it was not far to the station and the electric train, Toda sat down on a stone wall capped with grass growing in tangled profusion.

"Let's take a rest," he said to the others.

With a groan, young Kazuo swung the bundle off his shoulder.

"Whew!" he said. "This thing's heavy."

"Full of books."

"Books?"

"Yes, I had a lot of time for reading."

"You read in prison, uncle?"

Toda began to scratch his side vigorously. "Reading is what prison's for, my boy."

Seeing that her husband was sweating, Ikue took out a small towel and crouched to wipe his brow.

"Don't come too close, or you'll get some souvenirs you don't want," Toda laughed.

Ikue looked at him inquiringly.

"Lice, my new blood relatives. They're quite cute."

Ikue leaped away in panic as the others laughed.

Still breathing hard, Toda wiped his forehead and cheeks; his wife dried his neck and shoulders. Free at last from the confinement of a cell, he greedily savored the pleasant breeze. With eyes closed he inhaled the sweet, delicious air and luxuriated in freedom. The air was good indeed after two years in a stale solitary cell. Although all around him was dark, a radiant light shone in the depths of his being. Alone with a flame that had been kindled in a prison cell, he basked in its glow. The calm, sure light of faith burned unwaveringly in his heart. Just then he had no means to make that radiance known to others, but he was certain that it would never be extinguished. Rising and brushing away the mosquitoes that swarmed around his face and legs, he said: "Let's go."

In the dim light of the platform, Toda was surprised to see that everyone had on clothes that looked like uniforms. The men wore service caps and leggings; some carried helmets and others air-raid hoods. The few women about were all clothed in the same baggy *mompe* and cloth hoods that Ikue and her sister had on. In all this drabness, Toda's light summer kimono, a garment designed for relaxation, aroused suspicion. The prolonged hysteria of war had distorted the people's way of thinking to the extent that a man in a summer garment looked abnormal, out of place, almost obscene. Unaware of the unbalanced nature of their own attitudes, the passengers stared at this tall, wispy, ridiculously clothed intruder. Their expressions seemed to brand him as disloyal, a traitor.

But Toda remained indifferent to their accusing glances and, by his presence alone, demonstrated that he was a man of great personality and a born leader at ease with everyone. Before long Toda started a conversation with the person sitting next to him, an energetic-looking man in his fifties who carried on his lap a battered frying pan and a wash basin. He held these objects as if they were priceless treasures. At first disarmed, then charmed, by Toda, he told of a massive air raid that had taken place one May night.

"Hellfire couldn't be more horrible. By daybreak the whole place had burned to the ground; nothing was left except an air-raid shelter here and there. My house was destroyed, but our shelter is fairly solid. We live there now, me and three others. We're lucky; at least we have a place to live."

Listening to the man, Toda recalled the great Kanto Earthquake, which struck Tokyo in 1923, when Toda was twenty-four and only three years after he had come to the city from Hokkaido. The whole downtown section had burned for two days, and one blanket or a single radish was worth a fortune. Now, riding the train with his new acquaintance many years after that early disaster, Toda remembered a delicious bowl of soup he had drunk then, his first food in four days after the disaster.

"Was the air raid as bad as the fire after the Kanto Earthquake?" Toda asked.

"Far worse," said the man. "Three times bigger and five times more terrible."

"What about food?"

"We had nothing for days. But where do you come from?"

Faltering briefly, Toda decided not to tell the man about prison but to make up something instead.

"I evacuated to Ome and I have only recently come back to Tokyo."

"I see. My house was burned in the Kanto Earthquake too. This is the second time. To be burned out twice in one lifetime really is too much, don't you think? The earthquake, at any rate, was a natural disaster. We couldn't do anything about it. But this is different; it's the Yankees. Just to think about it makes you mad, the senselessness, the whole war! It's nerve-racking, don't you agree? I really wonder what the military people are going to do about it. As things stand now, it's exactly like a fight between grownups and kids. Really. . . . "

Suddenly the man stopped and pursed his lips. He looked frightened. Toda continued talking to him, but he replied in monosyllables. Evidently he was afraid of being overheard by the civil or military police, who were said to lurk everywhere, spying on people.

At Shinjuku, Toda and his family changed trains, and once again the tall, thin man captivated those around him with his open charm. When asked about their houses and families, many people were at first mystified, perhaps even alarmed, but they soon relaxed under the influence of Toda's amiability and spoke freely to him about their trials. As the train pulled into Harajuku Station, however, something happened that seemed strange to Toda. All of the passengers stopped talking, turned to the right side of the train toward a dark grove of trees, and bowed low. Puzzled for some time, Toda finally remembered that the grove contained the shrine to Emperor Meiji. The people, caught up in the militarists' emperor-worship doctrine, made obeisance even while riding a train. Toda murmured to himself: "It is religious ignorance of this kind that has ruined the country."

Unfortunately, Buddhist protection had not been forthcoming because the Japanese had abandoned Buddhism for the false doctrines of Shinto. As Nichiren said: "Buddhist deities do not listen to false prayers. Without belief in true Buddhism, there can be no protection from Buddhist deities." As he pondered the misery and despair around him, Toda was reminded of the injustice that had both jailed him and killed his great teacher. And he knew that it and the plight of the nation sprang from the same source.

In one corner of the battered train car, beside a broken window, four or five workers were engaged in a boisterous argument that aroused Toda's curiosity. Listening closely, he found that they were discussing the steel in shells from spent American incendiary bombs.

"I don't know what kind of steel it is, but it's good. I made a shovel out of one shell, and it was first-rate."

"I made a good kitchen knife out of a shell. You can get about ten knives out of one shell. That's what you should make; the steel's too good for shovels."

"You can't get ten knives out of one shell. Five or six at the most."

"I know what I'm talking about, and I say ten. Out of one bomb."

"Don't be crazy. Five or six is the limit."

"Ten. With that kind of top-grade steel, it's easy to get ten."

The irony and inventiveness of making shovels and kitchen utensils out of enemy bombs amused and pleased Toda. Rising and approaching the men, he said: "You men have the right idea. Keep on making lots of shovels and kitchen knives."

At first the men were surprised at this intrusion; they looked at each other thinking perhaps one of them might know the man. No, he was a stranger, but they laughed cheerfully anyway. At Meguro, Toda got off, waved to his new friends, and wished them good luck. Though the encounter had been brief, Toda had obviously encouraged the men.

Only two years earlier he had easily climbed the creaking, dingy staircase leading from the train platform, but now the ascent tired his emaciated body. At each step memories of the past flooded his mind. At the ticket gate, Toda paused to catch his breath; he leaned on his nephew for support while Ikue rushed to search for a taxi. In those troubled days such luxuries were scarce. She was unable to find an empty car, but a dark, empty trolley car stood waiting. After making inquiries about its departure, she hurried back to her husband.

"There are no taxis, but there's a trolley."

She knew from experience that the trolley schedule was erratic, but it was the surest way of reaching their destination. As they started across the station plaza, Toda suddenly turned and began walking in the opposite direction.

"Aren't we taking the streetcar, dear?" asked Ikue, puzzled.

"There's something I want to see first," Toda replied, pointing to a lane leading up a hill away from the plaza.

Sensing what her husband wanted to see and knowing the disheartening desolation that awaited him, Ikue felt a sharp stab of pain. On the right side of the lane was the site of the Jishu Gakkan, the private night school Toda had founded in 1923. It had burned two months ago; only blackened debris remained. Their footsteps echoed in the dark of what had once been a familiar part of town but was now a strange, charred rubble heap. When he saw the ruin that had been his school, Toda was overcome with a sense of futility. "Build and destroy, build and destroy. Is this the mad cycle to which man is forever condemned? Are peace and harmony for all peoples impossible?" He slumped against a stone and slowly ran his eyes over the wreckage, the bare lifeless trees, and especially a large, once familiar old plane tree now uprooted and tilting crazily, like a beached ship.

"Have you any cigarettes?" he asked.

Ikue, knowing her husband's fondness for cigarettes, had exerted every effort to provide this rare luxury for him but had completely forgotten about them till then. She gave him one and lit it. Toda inhaled the blue smoke deep into his lungs, then released it in a pale plume that faded in the darkness.

These ruins had once been Toda's castle, the private night school he started in order to put into practice the pedagogic theories of his teacher Makiguchi. In 1922, Toda resigned a teaching post in a primary school and from that time devoted himself to the night school and the application of Makiguchi's

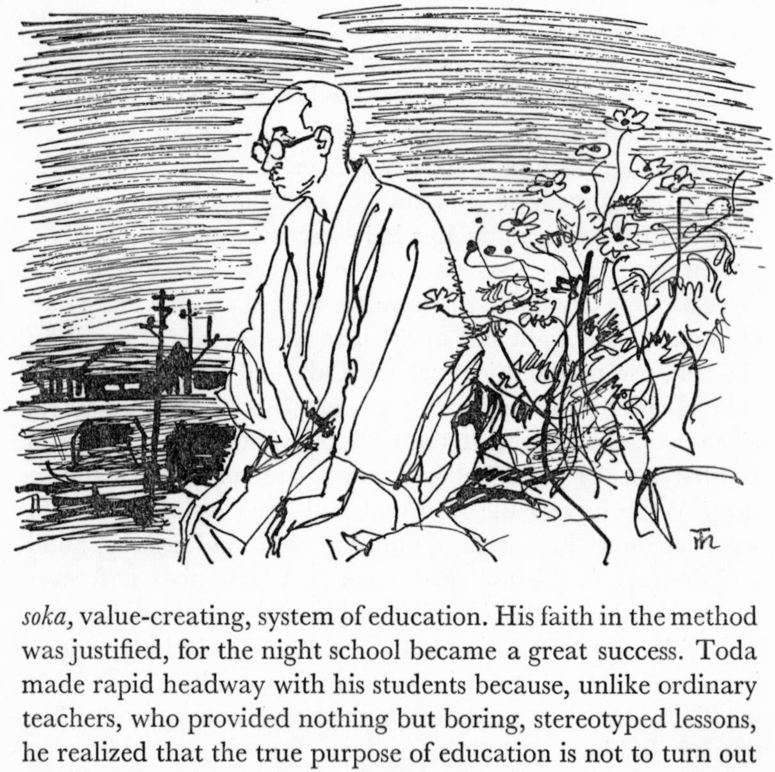

soka, value-creating, system of education. His faith in the method was justified, for the night school became a great success. Toda made rapid headway with his students because, unlike ordinary teachers, who provided nothing but boring, stereotyped lessons, he realized that the true purpose of education is not to turn out automatons that are all of one pattern but to cultivate the individuality of each person. So well trained were graduates of the Jishu Gakkan that many families in the neighborhood came to prefer it to the municipal primary schools. Obviously the principals and teachers of those institutions took a dim view of Toda and his enterprise.

Toda was a superb teacher, skilled in child psychology. He knew how to exploit curiosity and thirst for knowledge and how to give abstract concepts understandable, concrete forms. Most important, however, he held the children's interest. He had a way with his pupils. Though his daily greeting was always warm and friendly, he demanded both respect and undivided attention. And he got them, even from mischievous boys. He brought home the significance of the Chinese writing system by offering to give a dog to anyone who wanted it and then writing the character for dog on the blackboard. "Any boy who wants this dog may have it," he said. The children immediately understood from this that an ideogram is not, and yet in a sense is, the thing it represents. He was good in all phases of teaching, but perhaps his greatest achievement was devising a new way to teach arithmetic. He first compiled his method in a mimeographed textbook, which he distributed to his pupils; but later, at the suggestion of his friends, he published the book under the title *A Deductive Guide to Arithmetic*. It became an immediate best seller because it was a fine original work. At the Jishu Gakkan, Toda put Makiguchi's educational theory into practice, but in his business ventures and daily life, he followed the life philosophy of Nichiren fully and creatively. He was of the opinion that all theories, no matter how well developed and distinguished, are worthless unless they lend themselves to the creation of values in actual life.

His approach paid off. Using the royalties from his book as capital, he established a number of publishing companies, a loan company, and a securities firm. His enterprises prospered and multiplied until by 1943 he owned seventeen companies and was on the verge of acquiring a coal mine in Kyushu and an oil and fat company in Osaka. But on July 6 of that year, his hopes were dashed. On that day Makiguchi was arrested. Two days later, Toda and ultimately twenty leaders of Soka Kyoiku Gakkai were sent to prison. Everything that had started with the night school suddenly collapsed.

Now, after two years in prison, he had returned to his ruined castle. Though all around him was ashes and rubble, memories of smiling faces, hard work, success, and prosperity filled his mind. He was not yet defeated. Something indomitable welled up in his soul and blended with the holy light kindled within him by the mystic experience he had in prison. He was sad, but stronger, as he put out his cigarette, rose, and taking one last look at the darkened town dotted with faint lights, walked down the hill to the waiting, empty streetcar.

After a ride through familiar streets and a short walk, Toda was home at last. Miraculously, his house had been spared. The Western-style living room, with its sofas, clocks, and other familiar objects, was intact. When he had taken a few minutes to enjoy the sensation of being free and among known and beloved surroundings, Toda suddenly said: "Bring me some fresh clothes, and boil these. I've had enough of prison lice."

While she helped her husband into fresh underwear and a summer kimono, Ikue silently mourned for his thin legs and swollen stomach, a sure indication of advanced malnutrition. But even more heart-rending was the way he held his emaciated body erect and proud.

"Go upstairs and rest, my dear," she said.

"I think I will."

But as he said this the living-room door opened, and his father-in-law, Seiji Matsui, entered. Rising and bowing respectfully, Toda said: "It's been a long time, father. I am afraid I have caused you a great deal of trouble."

"How are you?" the old man asked, glancing anxiously at Toda's face.

"I'm all right."

"How glad I am to hear that," said Matsui, laying his hand on his son-in-law's shoulder. "Now we are all safe. You know I've been living in your house since spring. Mine was pulled down as a fire hazard, and I sent the family to the Shonan coast for safety. I stayed here in Tokyo to work."

Toda's house in Shirogane had become a bustling place during his absence. His elder sister, Tatsu Yamamura, and her teen-age son, Kazuo, had joined the rest of the family after her home was bombed.

"The bath is ready," said Matsui. He had scraped together enough firewood to heat the bath and had lit it himself while waiting for Toda's return.

"You take your bath first, father," said Toda.

"No, after you," was his reply.

"That's kind of you, but I want to go upstairs for a few minutes. Please don't wait. I'll be down in a little while."

When Ikue followed him upstairs after a moment, she found him prostrate in front of the family altar.

As he gazed at the Gohonzon a sense of peace came over him. He was like a child returned to his mother after a long separation. The compassionate presence of the Gohonzon enfolded him, comforting his spirit, assuaging pain, and erasing the bitter memories of prison. Feeling whole and real again, he began to chant the Daimoku. Ikue, who had been sitting in silence, took out her rosary, intending to join him, but the sight of his gaunt neck and thin body pained her so that her voice failed. Silently, she prayed ardently to the Gohonzon for his recovery. Toda's chant was strong and resonant. Finally, realizing that after countless hardships her long-cherished dream had come true, she followed her husband in the chant.

Downstairs, Kazuo was asking for his dinner, and Toda's sister was busy with preparations. After Toda had his bath, everyone sat down to a happy meal of delicacies truly rare in those war days—boiled green soybeans, salted cuttlefish, grilled cod, and most wonderful of all, sakè. Ikue poured for her husband and father, but as Toda took a sip, the first in two years, he muttered: "It is so bitter."

"Is the sakè bad?" asked Ikue, knowing her husband's fondness for the drink.

After tasting his, Matsui said he thought it was fairly good, but Toda, turning his cup over as a sign that he would take no more, said: "It's not the sakè. It's my body; it rejects the drink."

At the time, Toda was suffering from malnutrition, chronic tuberculosis, asthma, heart disease, diabetes, hemorrhoids, and rheumatism. Moreover, he was diarrheal, as victims of malnutrition usually are, and his myopic eyes were failing—one eye was almost totally blind. Nevertheless, he was in good spirits and ate heartily of the green soybeans. Though he was gravely ill and a mere shadow of a man, his spiritual vitality bore him up. Life force, mysterious and unfathomable, cannot be explained in material terms. By surviving a terrible ordeal, Toda had proved the life philosophy of Nichiren that mind and body are one.

During the meal he began to tell his family about his experiences in prison. Though it had been a dismal, wretched, sometimes even lurid life, he retold it all dispassionately in a style relieved by humor. The little group followed his tale with intense interest and from time to time broke into laughter, a sound that the house had not known for a long time. Reunited with his family, Toda felt happy and greatly enjoyed the dinner. It was a feeling he had missed for two years. The war had broken up nearly every home in Japan, depriving people of the only happiness left to them—that of home life. This was another thing that angered Toda.

Four days prior to his sudden release, for reasons unknown to him, Toda had been transferred from the Tokyo Detention House to Toyotama Prison. Though this was odd, he was even more surprised at being set free when he believed he would probably remain in confinement another two or three years.

"This is good enough. We are all well, and so is Kyoichi at Ichinoseki. I can't complain. Things could have been much worse."

Nodding, Ikue refilled her husband's teacup. But his mind was suddenly filled with thoughts of his only child, Kyoichi, a fourth-grade primary-school student.

At the time of Toda's arrest, one of his younger sisters agreed to care for the boy at her remote and relatively safe farm in northeastern Japan. From prison, Toda had written him: "My dear son Kyoichi, I have just had word that you have moved to Ichinoseki. You are only ten now, and though traveling and living away from home may seem hard, remember that you are equal to the trial. It will help you grow into a good man. Be strong and noble. The basis for all discipline is strength. In order to become strong, you must first have the will to accomplish what you set out to do. Your mental resources will take care of the rest.

"I cannot see you for a while yet, but let us make the following agreement. Every morning at a fixed time I want you to recite the Daimoku one hundred times before the Gohonzon. I will recite it, too, at the same time. Our spirits will be together in this way. We might even be able to converse. We could include mother, grandfather, and grandmother in our pact if you like. It is up to you. Please let me know your morning prayer time."

Toda had written his son frequently in the same vein. Every morning and evening he chanted the Daimoku two thousand times and an additional one hundred times for each member of his family. Foreseeing inevitable defeat for Japan, he prayed fervently to the Dai-Gohonzon for the safety of his loved ones and, most of all, for the success of his mission. Naturally there were no candles, incense, or Gohonzon in prison, and Toda had to improvise a rosary by stringing together paper caps from bottles of milk sent by his wife.

His prayer was that the Dai-Gohonzon would protect his family. If they must die at the hands of the enemy or suffer humiliation, he prayed that they would enter the Land of the Buddha as the wife and child of Josei Toda, votary of the Mystic Law, Myoho, and be received warmly by Nichiren. He was prepared for his own death and the possible deaths of his wife and son, but inwardly he knew his prayer would be answered. He felt convinced that he would survive his ordeal and eventually launch a great campaign for the propagation of the true faith.

Now, once again free and in the happy circle of his family, he was loquacious: there seemed to be so many things he wanted to say. Kazuo was already asleep. Matsui and Toda's sister were quiet, and Ikue, though afraid that the exertion of too much talk would overtax his weakened body, did not have the heart to tell him to go to bed. But suddenly, at a few minutes past midnight, screaming sirens shattered the quiet of night.

"Air-raid alarm," whispered Ikue.

Her face turned pale as she glanced at her calm husband. She and Tatsu sprang to draw the blackout curtains over the windows. Then Ikue turned on the radio to hear an announcement that a formation of 120 P-51s led by 3 B-29s had been sighted approaching the sea off the Boso Peninsula, southeast of Tokyo. Huddled around the radio, they listened for further news as the cacophony of sirens pierced the sky.

"We must go into the shelter," said Ikue.

"I'll stay here," her husband replied.

"You can't." But as she said it, Ikue knew that Toda was not to be persuaded.

"Don't worry about me. I'll be all right here," he added as his wife reluctantly followed the others out of the house. After sitting still for a few seconds, Toda rose and climbed the stairs.

In the dingy, musty air-raid shelter, Ikue fell prey to a fear greater than she had ever known. She was terrified that something would happen to them. Until now, this courageous woman had never allowed herself to be afraid during air raids or to complain about food shortages and deprivations. For two years her only thoughts had been of her imprisoned husband; her only hopes and wishes had centered on his release. Her life had been empty without him. Today he had returned, and the void in her life had been filled. He had said affectionately: "Don't worry. I'm back now; everything will be all right." Ikue knew then that her long years of struggle had ended. Peace and a sense of the joy of being just an ordinary person changed her whole world. But now she shuddered with fear of the shrieking sirens. If death came now she had too much to lose.

In the black-curtained second-floor room, Toda sat in silence in front of the family altar. In his mouth he held a shikimi leaf.

Standing and removing his glasses, he approached the altar and slowly removed the Gohonzon scroll. Bringing it close to his weakened eyes, he scrutinized each written character.

"Yes, it is as I knew it would be. No mistake. It is just as I witnessed it in prison."

One night in his barren cell, Toda had had a vision. He was taking part in a mysterious rite on Ryoju Peak in the eternal land of Buddha. With him were Viśistácaritra and numerous other Buddhas, Bodhisattvas, and deities. The scene he beheld in his vision was wondrous and strange, but now, here before him in a room in his, own house, he saw that it was represented exactly on the Gohonzon in his family altar. The vision, in which he experienced a mysterious identity of the substance of his life with the essence of the cosmic life force, kindled an unquenchable flame in his heart. It was a brilliant symbol of promised strength far greater than he could have derived from his own body or will. At that moment, in Toda's soul there dawned the eternal brightness of determination to spread the life-giving faith to all men.

Finally, he returned the scroll to the altar, and as he looked around, a tremendous sense of solitude enveloped him. He heard within his soul things no human being could have told him. "Do not hurry. Be patient and thorough; do what you must, no matter what happens." In the dark of that night, where no one heard or knew, there sounded within this man the bell of a new morning—not for him alone, but for all Japan, as well. It was dark, very dark. Darkness engulfed the nation and surrounded Toda, but in his heart the light of a new day shone brightly. He thought: "The darker the night, the nearer the dawn."

In a shrill voice the radio announcer said that after having attacked Chiba and Ibaraki prefectures the P-51s were headed out to sea.

The all-clear sounded.

2. RECONSTRUCTION

ON THE third of July, 1945, the day of Toda's release, the government announced a ten-percent cut in staple-foods rations. Already reduced to a near starvation diet, the people were forced to subsist on ten ounces of rice a day for each adult. Furthermore, in ration calculations, allotments of white potatoes, sweet potatoes, soybeans, bean cake, and sorghum—in Japanese eyes by no means substitutes for their favorite cereal grain—were deducted from an individual's daily rice quota. Fish, allowed only once every four days, consisted of one sardine for each person. The average daily intake of the Japanese before the war had been 2,160 calories; it had now dropped to 1,200. The dire shortage of food, aggravated by the Allied maritime blockade, drained the people's physical energy. They became thin, their eyes were hollow, and their breathing grew short. Many lapsed into lethargy and torpor, and it is not surprising that months of deprivation had alienated the people from the militarists. In spite of the government's blind and persistent cry for the "last crucial battle on the home islands" and its insistence that the people die rather than surrender, the exhausted Japanese were no longer to be deceived. Their morale had disintegrated, and their confidence in the government had vanished. Neither statesmen nor militarists had any effective plans for peace negotiations. The unconditional surrender of Germany in May made ultimate defeat a certainty for Japan, but nothing was done to avert disaster. From May till the final blow in August, the nation was in a vacuum.

American bombers continued to ravage cities and towns, but they no longer met opposition from the now powerless Japanese army and navy. Ninety cities had been all but totally destroyed, and almost one-third of the nation's urban areas had been razed. Still the systematic destruction did not cease. Army preparations for the last crucial battle consisted in rallying the entire nation toward final war efforts. Between February and May, army headquarters mobilized the so-called defense soldiers, who were in fact ill-equipped civilian groups deployed in various parts of the country for the last bloody encounter. The navy, deprived of all its seaworthy ships, could do no more than attempt to defend the coast. By 1944, eighty-nine percent of all healthy males had been conscripted; in the following year, the percentage rose to ninety. Only the deformed and the ill were spared. For most of these slavelike soldiers, military service meant no more than digging air-raid shelters and tunnels. A great many promising youths who would have created a new future for Japan had already perished in battle. Countless homes had been destroyed. Silently the Japanese had endured the unendurable, but at last they began to harbor in their hearts contempt and hatred for the fanatic stupidity of their leaders.

Okinawa, the supposedly impregnable fortress, ultimately fell to the Americans in one of the most bloody and costly battles of the Pacific War. Japanese soldiers stationed there resisted courageously for a hopeless cause. By June, it was all over; Okinawa, a charred heap of ashes and earth, fell. Entire squadrons of kamikaze pilots had plummeted to flaming death against American warships. Some 100,000 Japanese soldiers had died; 150,000 men, women, children, and the tragic Lily Corps—a unit of schoolgirls mobilized to serve as field nurses—had lost their lives.

Okinawa, however, was only a portent of the total defeat to come.

The extended strain of a nightmarish existence began to take the form of physical and mental exhaustion throughout Japan. In the flickering light of burning homes, countless people tugged and dragged what few odds and ends they had managed to salvage. The hysteria of pain and imminent defeat echoed in hollow voices as a kind of deadly gaiety.

"My house burned last night."

"Got yours too, eh? Mine went ten days ago; everything I owned. Ha, ha, ha."

Wiping the soot and sweat from their brows, the stricken people talked of the horror of their lives as if it were all happening to someone else.

As his nation hurtled toward doom, Josei Toda slept at home for the first night in two years. Waking at dawn, blinking, and looking around him at the unfamiliar familiarity of the room, for a moment he could not remember where he was. A second look and a second thought, however, confirmed for him the joy of his freedom. Rising to open the window, he inhaled the cool morning air and with it the smell of the small, carefully tended garden below, where a purple hydrangea bloomed boldly. Ikue was a good gardener. As he returned to his bed and heard the chirping of sparrows outside, time seemed to stand still in an almost magical instant of peace.

Mornings were important to Toda because it was in the early hours, when his mind worked best and ideas came thick and fast, that he was able to think effectively about the problems facing him. On this morning, one thought dominated everything: the reconstruction of Soka Kyoiku Gakkai. Where should he begin? What action must he take? Obviously, the first step was the rebuilding of his business enterprises, for without financial support the great project of reviving the society would be impossible. It must be done, however, and no consideration of personal sentiment or comfort could be allowed to stand in the way. While still in prison he had learned that his business world had crumbled, but he did not yet know the full extent of his loss or the actual condition of the national economy. He needed to ascertain both before taking any other steps. First he had to see if there was anything of his own left to salvage. He quickly made the first decision: he must visit the office of his lawyer in Shibuya. That would be a start.

After morning Gongyo with his wife, then breakfast, he asked Ikue to bring him his summer clothes.

"You're not thinking of going out?" she asked, appalled.

"Yes, I am," he replied.

"But you are not well enough."

Kneeling before him in the Japanese manner, she begged him to remember his weakened condition. It had taken him two hours to make the trip from prison, a distance that a healthy man could have covered in half the time. The heat was oppressive; it would be reckless of him to attempt the trip. Could he not postpone the visit a day or two, until he was better? Why not ask the lawyer to come to him? None of her arguments had any effect; Toda remained determined.

"I must go today. I'll be all right. I couldn't possibly ask him to bring the stacks of papers I must examine. I know what I am doing. Ikue, bring me my summer clothes now."

Lips sealed in silence, face turned away, she refused to budge.

Toda's father-in-law, who had been observing the contest of wills, intervened.

"Why don't you go with him, Ikue?" he asked with a smile. "If he must go, you can make sure he doesn't strain himself. And if he takes his time and rests now and then, he'll make it."

After a moment's reflection, Ikue reluctantly rose and opened the chest of drawers.

Laughing aloud, Toda said: "Well, father, Ikue has developed quite a mind of her own."

"I certainly have," she broke in, "and it's only natural. After all, I've been what they call a woman on the home front for the last two years."

Toda laughed again.

"Yes, but you've been on the home front while I was in jail, not in battle."

His summer clothes hung loosely on him, as if they belonged to a much larger man. Even his Panama hat drooped over his eyes. True, his hair had been cropped short in prison, but even so, the hat was much too big. Could his head have shrunk like the rest of his body? Knowing that the scorching sun would be unbearable without some protection, Ikue took out a hunting cap and carefully wiped away the mold that had grown on the sweatband.

In the vestibule Toda was shocked to see that his shoes were too big. "I can't walk in these," he said as he shuffled his thin feet in their overcapacious containers. Ikue retied his shoestrings more tightly.

"I'm afraid that is the best I can do," she said wistfully.

"It's all right; I'm not going to run anywhere," he joked with a playful stamp of his foot.

His first outing in two years took him up the slope outside his house to a nearby main street. Though he felt like a schoolboy on an excursion, he looked more like an invalid in the company of a nurse incongruously clad in coarse cotton *mompe*. He had no time to lose, not even one day's rest after his long confinement.

To reach Shibuya they had to take a streetcar and then transfer to the elevated train at Meguro. Everywhere Toda looked, Tokyo lay in blackened ruins. The walk from Shibuya Station to the lawyer's office was arduous, through streets crowded with people and cluttered with debris. Several times he had to pause to recover from attacks of dizziness or breathlessness, but his spiritual vitality, his sense of mission, and the firm arm of his wife sustained him to his destination.

In the office the lawyer briefed him on the grim state of affairs. All seventeen of Toda's firms were insolvent.

"I'm terribly sorry, but there is nothing I can do. Most business enterprises in the nation are bankrupt. I only wonder what will happen next."

The lawyer launched into a discussion of the war and the national economy, but this was not what Toda wanted to hear.

"What is the balance?" he cut in.

The lawyer handed a pile of documents to a clerk who immediately went to work with an abacus. After a short time, the clerk wrote a figure on a slip of paper and gave it to his employer, who examined it in silence, then passed it to Toda. Removing his glasses and bringing the paper close to his eyes, Toda read a staggering figure.

"In the red?" he asked.

"In the red," was the reply.

"A deficit of more than two and a half million." Toda groaned.

Ikue shuddered. All his companies were ruined. After a long, awkward silence, Toda left.

He retraced his path through the clutter of the destroyed streets, as destroyed as his whole business world. Everything reduced to ashes. Worse still, he was burdened with colossal debts. For a moment defeat threatened, but he refused to give in to it. He knew that he had to begin again from scratch. The odds were hopelessly against him. He had no money, no connections, no immediate prospect of help; but something would turn up.

"Don't worry, Ikue," he said to his troubled wife. "Don't let this upset you. Things are not over yet."

Deep in his heart, he knew there would be a way out of this apparently hopeless situation. Although his encouraging words brought Ikue to the verge of tears, the strange radiance shining from his face eased her mind.

"How do you feel, dear?" she asked, looking up at him. "I think you should try to rest and not think about business for a while."

Smiling, Toda replied: "Don't worry about my health; it can't get any worse, and besides, I know I'll get better now that I'm out of prison."

When the two returned home, they heard of further bomb raids on airfields in Ibaraki, Tochigi, and Chiba prefectures.

The following day, Toda was very tired and remained at home. Though he stayed in bed and rested, his mind functioned as actively as ever. He received a few guests, mostly former employees, aged, out of work, and seeking advice. They talked desultorily for a while, then took their leave. Toda knew that these people were not the ones he could count on in this desperate moment. As Toda lay awake until late one night, out of the myriad thoughts and ideas that flooded his mind he finally found one that seemed promising: start a correspondence school.

Government preparations for the last crucial battle had suspended schools for a year. All primary school children had been evacuated from Tokyo, and most junior high school students had been mobilized for work in munitions factories. From long teaching experience, Toda knew that even when deprived of formal educational opportunities young boys and girls remained eager to learn. Nothing, not even surrender, could quench their thirst for knowledge or reduce the importance of trained people to the nation. A correspondence school would require only a small staff, but the most pressing problems were funds and the timing of the school's opening. Of the two, the graver difficulty was financial. Penniless and in debt, how could Toda manage? Was the idea hopeless? Then Toda remembered something the lawyer had told him the day before.

"Here are your fire-insurance policies. Eventually some of the indemnities may be paid, as they were after the Kanto Earthquake. Not all, of course, and not right away. But I think the government will take some measures sooner or later. These scraps of paper may be valuable someday."

Yesterday Toda had paid no attention to the policies; today he suddenly realized that many of his buildings had been

burned and that, though the insurance companies would probably resist paying, public opinion and government pressure might force them to make compensation. At least some of the indemnities might be forthcoming, and if so, his policies would help him to raise money now against the hope of their future value. Making up his mind to seek help and advice from Kiyoshi Ozawa, an old friend and a lawyer, Toda fell asleep.

Impatient to lay the groundwork for the rehabilitation of Soka Kyoiku Gakkai, Toda had the insurance policies sent to his house the following day. In the sultry heat of the overcast afternoon, he and Ikue set out for the Ozawa residence. The part of town they traversed was less badly bombed than the Shibuya district, but the heat and the hills demanded more than Toda's worn body could give. Halfway up a hill that he thought might even be the wrong one, he was forced to pause and sit for a moment. His face drained of blood, and Ikue, thinking herself a fool for letting her husband make the trip, sheltered him from the merciless sun as best she could with her own body while chanting the Daimoku. After a few minutes, faint tinges of color returned to Toda's face, and he was able to resume the walk. It later appeared that he had suffered a mild attack of cerebral anemia.

Wiping the sweat from his brow and leaning heavily on Ikue, who was herself tired and overheated, he climbed the hill leading to the imposing Ozawa house. Ikue pushed the doorbell button. Shortly Mrs. Ozawa opened the door, greeted them warmly, and ushered them into the spacious, high-ceilinged living room, which overlooked a well-tended, freshly sprinkled garden. Huge steppingstones led from the then dry pond to the edge of the veranda. Ozawa entered the room, and the two old friends greeted each other. Not attempting to conceal his shock at Toda's appearance, Ozawa said: "You've grown thin. Are you all right?"

"I'm thinner, but no one comes out of prison fat," Toda replied, smiling.

"Are you sure you're well?" Ozawa asked as he examined Toda's gaunt face.

"It's just the steep walk to your house."

"Yes, I know. It's good to see you again. You've gone through a terrible ordeal," said Ozawa.

Having had no news of the outside world for two years, Toda was anxious to hear about the true political situation. A man once associated with a minor faction in the formerly all-powerful military hierarchy and a member of a group that had made an unsuccessful peace overture, Ozawa was in a position to explain what the leaders were thinking and how their minds worked. After listening to his friend's well-informed comments, Toda asked: "When will the war end?"

"It's hard to say," replied Ozawa, frowning and stroking his mustache. "Peace efforts are still being made, but it's largely up to the other side. And then the government must unify public opinion."

"Slow death? It's unbearable."

"You're as impatient as ever, I see," Ozawa laughed.

"I've reason to be. After all, I've got my own problems to worry about."

After a short silence, Ozawa said: "It's difficult to say for sure, but I give the war another six months, maybe a year."

"That long? It can't go on that long."

"The delay's not my fault, you know." Both men chuckled.

"Now to get to my problems." Toda told his friend about his business collapse and his project for a correspondence school. Finally, he asked for the loan of ten thousand yen on his fire-insurance policies.

Ozawa readily agreed and brought his checkbook from his study. He took up a pen, but after glancing at the checkbook, he said that his present situation would permit him to offer only half that amount. Fully aware that ten thousand yen was the absolute minimum he would require, Toda hesitated. Then, observing the anxiety on his friend's face, he said cheerfully: "It'll do. I'll scrape the rest together somehow."

"I am sorry," Ozawa said as he wrote a check for five thousand.

"Don't be sorry. I'm very grateful for this much. Thank you," said Toda as he handed his wife the check. It was natural for Toda to turn to this man for help; they had known each other for twenty-five years.

They first met in 1920, when they were both enrolled in the third-year course of night school. In March of that year, Toda had come to Tokyo from his home in Hokkaido; Ozawa had arrived in April from Yamagata Prefecture. Toda was older by fifteen months. The two young men had entered the school in preparation for high school entrance examinations because they realized the need to fill in the inevitable gaps in their basically self-gained educations. Older than most of their classmates, Toda and Ozawa soon struck up a fast friendship. The intelligent and lively Toda, who could talk on a wide range of interesting subjects, soon gathered a group of followers for whom the steady, quiet Ozawa was a kind of guardian. Toda wanted to become a successful businessman, whereas Ozawa dreamed of first becoming a lawyer and then beginning a political career.

Both were diligent in class. Toda, who had passed the examinations qualifying him for a teacher's license and had already taught in a Hokkaido primary school, excelled in mathematics and the Japanese language. His method of study was ambitious and aggressive. When faced with a problem in English he would accost any college student he happened to meet and ask for help. If something in mathematics proved too difficult, he sneaked into the classroom of a preparatory school and, when the lecture was over, consulted the teacher directly. Toda did this often, but because of his apparent studiousness, he was never suspected as an interloper. Eagerness and enterprising methods helped Toda make rapid progress, which impressed Ozawa greatly. Gradually the two saw each other more frequently and became very close. But Toda was soon to form a more important personal relationship.

In the summer of 1920, he met Tsunesaburo Makiguchi, the man who was to become his life-long teacher and mentor. Makiguchi, then principal of Nishimachi Primary School, assisted Toda in obtaining an instructor's post there. Not only did this kindness solve most of the young man's immediate financial problems, but it brought him into closer contact with Makiguchi, whose spiritual and intellectual powers proved a constant source of advice and counsel. A man who has a teacher to guide and advise him is indeed blessed. No matter how successful and famous one becomes, one is forlorn and isolated without a teacher. Unfortunately, Ozawa never realized the importance of an intellectual guide and therefore could not understand the relationship between Toda and Makiguchi. By the time the relationship with Makiguchi had reached a truly profound level, Toda and Ozawa were already treading two entirely separate paths of life.

Working at the primary school by day and attending night school in the evening, Toda shared a single room with eight, sometimes nine, other young men from Hokkaido. All of them, except the regularly employed Toda, were struggling through school, doing what odd jobs they could find as newspaper delivery boys and rickshaw pullers. Toda paid all the bills most of the time.

Whenever Ozawa visited the messy room in which all of them slept and cooked, he could not understand why Toda lived this way in the first place or why he had to pay for all the others. Toda's reply to his friend's query was simple: "If I leave the rooming house, they will all be thrown out in no time. None of them has a regular income, but I get fifty-five yen a month. Out of it I save five for myself, and the rest goes into rent and food."

"Don't the others chip in?" Ozawa asked one day.

"Certainly, but it's hardly enough. It costs a lot to feed and take care of eight or nine people."

"I still can't understand why you have to support them," Ozawa remarked.

"They'll stand on their own feet soon, but until then I can't leave them in the lurch."

Though amazed and speechless, Ozawa found himself admiring Toda more than before. "I could never do that; he is better than I am," he thought.

In 1922, both graduated from middle school with good

grades. Ozawa entered the law department of Nihon University in 1923 and passed the bar examination the following year. Later he returned to Yamagata, where he started a practice of his own and married the daughter of a wealthy man. Though Makiguchi continued teaching at Nishimachi Primary School for a while, he was later transferred to a slum-district school. Toda chose to follow him. When Makiguchi became the principal of Shirogane Primary School in 1923, Toda left his post to open the Jishu Gakkan, his private tutoring school.

The bond of friendship between Toda and Ozawa did not dissolve, but the passing years attenuated it. Returning to Tokyo to establish a prosperous law practice, Ozawa seemed to conduct his life according to an organized plan. Toda, on the other hand, was the constant victim of insecurity. Shortly after he had gone through the labor of creating the Jishu Gakkan, he lost both his infant daughter and his first wife. Then he contracted tuberculosis. All but crushed by loss and illness, he plumbed the depths of despair; and since in those early days he was ignorant of the strength and encouragement to be gained from the teachings of Nichiren, he could find no way out of the darkness. Nevertheless, Toda was not a man to succumb to hardships. After regaining a measure of health, he made a new start. Because of the vicissitudes of his life, Ozawa and other friends often compared Toda to a lark.

"You are like a skylark," Ozawa was in the habit of saying. "You lie hidden in dark undergrowth, apparently nursing some wound; then you suddenly soar into the sky, higher than the rest of us can go. But the next thing we know, you are down hiding in a bush again."

Toda often replied that the life of a skylark is far from filled with ease and happiness; certainly his had not been.

Out of prison, but weakened and faced with staggering difficulties, Toda was down again. This was perhaps one of the greatest crises of his life, and Ozawa read signs of doom in his friend's face. In all previous times of hardship Toda had recovered. Could he do so now when the nation was on the brink of calamity? Ozawa mused glumly that there was little chance that Toda would rise again like a lark into the sky. But that was not all Ozawa was thinking. Toda had been indicted on charges of lese majesty and of violating the Public Peace Preservation Law. What danger might his presence in Ozawa's house invite? The Ozawa family had been lucky so far; their home was still standing, they were alive. Ozawa preferred not to get involved with Toda under such circumstances.

Friendship, precious in any form, is more ennobling when it is based on a common belief in some great cause. Purely worldly friendship, though often beautiful and valuable, does not always go deep; it may even disintegrate in the face of difficulties and adversities. Friendship between people of common faith, however, endures anything and inspires the friends to risk their very lives in the struggle toward their common goal. Although the relationship between Toda and Ozawa was longstanding, it had always lacked the vital basis of a common faith. Ozawa's feelings in the early days had been pure and unsullied, but as he grew older the material world claimed a large part of his interest. Even as he sat in his living room with one of his oldest and closest friends, in the back of his mind he was calculating the practical value or peril of continued association with this weak and wasted man. Suppose the police found out about his connection with an ex-convict. Would it not endanger Ozawa's position and future? From that day, their relationship became almost entirely one-sided; Toda's sincerity was never again truly reciprocated, for Ozawa dismissed his friend as doomed to an abyss of failure from which he was not likely to rise.

As they spoke, apparently two old friends rejoicing in reunion, Toda sensed a subtle change; but he disregarded it as a delusion and suddenly said: "I have wanted to tell you; the Lotus Sutra was a tremendous inspiration while I was in prison."

Aware of his friend's religious associations and reverence for Nichiren Shoshu, Ozawa listened half-heartedly to what he said.

"I've come to realize," Toda continued, "that my belief in the Lotus Sutra is truly profound."

"Is that so?"

Ozawa's perfunctory answers and absent-minded nods clearly revealed to Toda that there was no point in telling his friend about his own life mission. He would never understand the importance of devotion to the spreading of the one true faith. Disappointed and oppressed by a sense of solitude, Toda changed the topic to his adventures and misadventures in prison. But as if inevitably drawn to more important conversation, after a few minutes of witty, sometimes spicy, storytelling, Toda returned to what was uppermost in his mind.

"Thanks to those years in prison, I have learned to read the Lotus Sutra easily. I understand all the difficult Chinese words."

"You must have studied a lot."

"Study is not enough. I think I grasped the essence of the Sutra through profound suffering. Then it became easy for me to comprehend."

Suddenly, there flashed through Toda's mind the thrilling moment when at last he knew what the final chapter of the Lotus Sutra means: "If one professes faith in this Sutra, if he forgets one word or phrase, I will teach him and recite the Sutra with him, and this shall be to his benefit."

Although Toda had grasped the inner meaning of this passage, he feared that his old friend was deaf both to its wisdom and to all that Toda's life stood for. In Ozawa's eyes the Lotus Sutra was no more than mystic jargon, but Toda could not suppress the desire to share his faith.

"I now know what I must accomplish before I die, and I will do it."

A ringing assurance in Toda's voice caused Ozawa to look up at his friend, whose eyes blazed with enthusiasm. Though

Ozawa dimly sensed that this man was not the same Toda he had known for twenty-five years, it was beyond his wisdom and insight to fathom the nature and depth of the change because his whole soul was concentrated on his own worldly future.

After World War II, Ozawa was elected to the House of Representatives from his electoral district in Yamagata Prefecture, but the happy fulfillment of a cherished ambition was short-lived. In the next election he not only was defeated but was charged with violation of the election law. No longer a member of the House, no longer well known and wealthy, he began a downhill course that lasted for many years. When Toda was finally on the way to recovery, he never refused his old friend's frequent requests for money. If he was unable to scrape up the amount Ozawa needed from his own funds, he would find some way, even if it meant borrowing from his employees. These loans put Ozawa back on his feet again, and he deeply respected the man who had done so much for him; but the gap between them, caused by the lack of a common faith, was never filled.

In the dark days before the surrender, however, it was Ozawa's five thousand yen and other funds that Toda scraped up that enabled him to make a start on the reconstruction project. He had some money, but the times were inauspicious. Japan was in her death throes. Not only did American bombers have complete freedom of attack now that the Marianas and Okinawa had fallen, but also the United States fleet cruised Japanese waters unmolested. Massive bombing raids continued throughout July. The people began to sense that both the army and the navy, which put up only minimal resistance against attacks, had already disintegrated. A difficult period was drawing to a close.

But Toda's new work had just begun. He lost no time laying the groundwork. Air raids and rubble could not keep this man from his task. His weakened body would not always obey his will, but with the aid of a cane he forced himself to run errands in the stifling heat, amid the crumbling remains of the metropolis. Soon, through the miracle of unflagging effort and driving faith, Toda accomplished the apparently impossible. He had an office, printing facilities, and an ample supply of paper. The only problem was the timing of the opening of his correspondence school. Convinced that it must begin the moment the war ended, he had to know when the hostilities would cease. Perhaps the one man to tell him was Kazuo Kojima, a senior politician of long experience and great influence, who, though retired, appeared on the scene whenever major governmental change and upheaval were in the offing. Toda decided to visit him.

Shown into the living room of Kojima's home, Toda found the elderly gentleman engrossed in a game of *go,* his passionate addiction to which was well known. Toda's cordial greeting met a mute nod and a return to the game. It seemed that Kojima had forgotten about his guest. From time to time he would refer to a textbook or place a *go* stone on the board but gave no indication of willingness to speak. Fidgeting and impatient, Toda recalled tales of visitors being kept waiting for hours while the old man silently worked out *go* strategies. Toda also knew that Kojima was vain of his game. Three-quarters of an hour passed and still no sound. Suddenly, Toda had an idea.

"Mr. Kojima, I have heard that you are a very poor *go* player," he said.

"What?" Kojima at last broke silence.

"They say that you do not play as well as you claim."

Provoked, Kojima faced his guest for the first time. Toda continued:

"What is your *go* standing among politicians?"

"My standing is well known, young man."

"And?"

"Among the best, of course," Kojima pronounced, then lowering his head, chuckled.

"Well, perhaps, but rumor has it . . ."

"Never believe rumors," the man cut in, then burst into

laughter as he cleared away the stones on the *go* board. Kojima leaned back in his seat and gazed for a moment at his visitor. Toda had been imprisoned and released. This much Kojima knew, but there was no point in commenting on it now. What difference could one old man's opinion make in a bedlam of fanatic militarists? The aged, lined, but noble face was like a Noh mask that though actually immobile often seems to change expressions. This wrinkled visage, too, reflected its world and the hardships and vicissitudes of the three reigns through which Kojima had served his nation.

"How will this war end?" asked Toda.

"Everyone already knows."

"Defeat for us?"

Kojima lit a cigarette and gazed intently at the curling smoke.

"When?" pressed Toda.

With half-closed eyes and in a voice that almost reflected his personal interest, Kojima asked why Toda wanted to know.

"I'm about to start something new, and timing is important."

"Something new? Is it a business?"

"Yes."

"It's about time someone started something new."

After Toda outlined his project, Kojima remarked: "Yes, I can see that timing is important to you."

"Well then, six months?"

Averting his face, Kojima shook his head.

"Three months?"

Another negative sign.

"One month?"

Kojima scooped a handful of *go* stones from a bowl and, sighing, threw them on the board to indicate both that Toda had guessed the answer and that the interview was ended.

The war was nearly over; there was no time to lose. Excitedly Toda began final preparations. Advertising was essential, but where was he to get the money? In these times no one would invest in a new company, and the stocks and shares he held were worthless. The national economy had gone primitive, with bartering the only reliable form of transaction. Suddenly, Toda remembered an old and very prized sword that he had kept in a closet for many years. Fishing it out, he reluctantly decided to sell it. If it was to fetch anything at all, the sale must be completed before the end of the war. He called a curio dealer, who, to Toda's great delight, gave him a handsome price. So far so good; now he must confine himself to his home and work on textbooks and a general teaching plan.

Throughout the ensuing period of hard work, Toda's health gradually improved. For exercise he took regular morning and evening walks, which led him past a nearby temple called Zuisen-ji, where countless homeless children had sought shelter. One afternoon, Ikue heard him call from the vestibule:

"My dear, come here a moment. I've guests."

His wife was startled to find five ragged children standing next to her husband.

"Who are they?" she asked.

"They are my friends," he said as he invited them to take off their dirty shoes and come up the step from the vestibule into the entry hall.

Although annoyed at first, Ikue soon saw in these deprived children a temporary outlet for the love she felt for her own son, separated from her for so long. She often gave them sweets to eat, and when she had none, Toda would offer them small amounts of money. She saw purity and innocence radiating from his face as he chatted with his little companions, and Ikue knew that her husband's thoughts too were of their son. The small visitors returned with increasing frequency and in greater numbers till the sight of the tall, gaunt man surrounded by droves of children became familiar in the neighborhood. The friendships that Toda formed with these children lasted for many years.

But this bright, restful spot in his life, though comforting, in no way dimmed the ardor of his devotion to the great task of rebuilding the society. Devastation and the horror of war had dispersed the membership and gravely shaken the faith of many. He could not forget for a moment the death of his teacher Makiguchi. And in the back of his mind he was deeply concerned about the condition of Daiseki-ji, the head temple of Nichiren Shoshu. Many obstacles littered his path, and he was impatient to clear them all away. But a wise inner voice warned him that this was no moment to be rash. After all, he was still on parole. He did not know the whereabouts of most of the principal leaders of the society, and he had heard nothing from members sent to the battlefront or from his fellow teacher-members who had evacuated to the country. Those who knew of his release from prison did not dare make contact with him for fear of the police.

3. CEASE-FIRE

AUGUST, 1945, was a nightmarish month unlike any other period in the history of Japan. The rain of American bombs continued unabated while the militarists and politicians squabbled over the terms of the Potsdam Declaration, issued by the Allied Powers in July. What did it mean? Would the emperor's sovereignty remain unimpaired if the nation surrendered to the enemy? And there was still the fear that the Soviet Union might break its neutrality pact with Japan and enter the war on the side of the enemy. Germany had capitulated; Italy was long out of the war. The Japanese army and navy were virtually powerless, and the nation's morale had sunk to its nadir. President Truman's motives will probably always remain clouded in mystery. He claims to have made the decision in order to hasten the end of hostilities; it seems likely, however, that political motives were not without weight in his thinking. Be that as it may, in compliance with his orders, on August 6 a B-29 flying serenely in the cloudless sky over Hiroshima opened its bomb bays. A few seconds later a blinding white cloud transformed the town below into a writhing, screaming inferno of death and flames. An estimated two hundred thousand citizens lost their lives in the holocaust. The Japanese became the first people on earth to suffer an atomic-bomb attack, just as seven hundred years earlier, when the Mongols attempted to invade the country, they were the first people ever to be subjected to gunpowder attacks. But even faced with this destruction, the Japanese government failed either to understand the nature of or to grasp the ominous meaning of the new weapon until August 9. On that day, before daybreak, the Soviet Union entered the war against Japan; and at eleven o'clock, a second atomic bomb leveled Nagasaki.

On the following day, the foreign minister sent a message to both Switzerland and Sweden for transmission to the Allied Powers. It said that Japan would accept the Potsdam Declaration on the following condition: "with the understanding that the said declaration does not include any demand that prejudices the prerogatives of His Majesty as sovereign ruler." The Allied reply, received from Washington on the twelfth of August, did not touch on the question of the emperor's status. Confusion prevailed in the Japanese cabinet, but on the fourteenth the emperor himself convened an extraordinary meeting of the ministers and ordered immediate acceptance of the American demand: unconditional surrender.

As these portentous events rocked the capital, an American task force of ten aircraft carriers plowed through the waters off the Kanto region, and bombers ceaselessly pounded the cities. Throughout all this, however, Josei Toda never sought the refuge of an air-raid shelter, not because he was reckless, but because he was confident he would be spared to complete his great work. To start his correspondence school, Toda had rented a nearby building owned by a Mr. Kurikawa, a good-natured, middle-aged businessman who had lately become a frequent visitor to Toda's home. Early on the morning of August 15, Ikue was interrupted in her breakfast preparations by an excited cry from Kurikawa, who had just entered the vestibule.

"It's all over," he called.

Drying her hands with a towel, Ikue went to greet him.

"My, my, Mr. Kurikawa you are up early. Come in for a cup of tea. Why are you so excited?"

"Haven't you heard the radio?"

"No; why?"

"The emperor, he's going to make an important speech at noon."

"His Majesty? I wonder what about."

"It's over, I tell you."

Coming down the stairs, Toda caught only snatches of the conversation.

"Good morning Kurikawa," he said. "You're an early bird this morning, aren't you?"

"Who could sleep on a day like this? The war is over, and the emperor will make an important talk at noon."

"Unconditional surrender; I know. A newspaperman told me last night," Toda half whispered. "I must say, Kurikawa, you look happy about it."

"Of course; no more war!"

Both men laughed; then after a moment's silence, Kurikawa asked: "What does unconditional surrender mean to all of us?"

"It means we must be ready for an ordeal," Toda replied. "Punishment for the sins the nation has committed. But Nichiren Daishonin's true teachings will save us."

"Do you think we can be saved?" Kurikawa inquired softly.

"It will depend on our strength in the face of hardships but most of all on our faith." There was an odd, suppressed fury in Toda's voice as he said this. Though Kurikawa could not grasp the full import of Toda's words, they moved him nonetheless.

After the morning Gongyo and breakfast, Toda changed clothes and left for the office, where he said he would be all day if visitors asked for him. As he stepped into the bright morning sun he said to himself: "Now my battle begins."

At noon, silence blanketed the entire nation as the Japanese people huddled around radios to hear the grave words of the emperor's message, which was couched in classical Chinese phraseology only vaguely grasped by most of the listeners. Still, they understood his meaning: for the first time in her history, Japan had surrendered to a foreign power. When they learned the emperor was to address the nation, most of the people thought he would announce the long-heralded decisive battle on the home islands. Consequently, the universal first reaction to the contents of his speech was shock. Then as the gravity of the emperor's statement settled heavily in their minds, many sobbed; others shouted in frustrated rage. Strange mixtures of emotions beset almost everyone. The disgrace of defeat stung their pride, but it was good that the killing, burning, and bombing were over. On that cloudless day, some Japanese felt like celebrating; others—mostly soldiers—committed suicide.

Death, waste, futility, and more death. By the end of the war, virtually the entire nation had been mobilized in one way or another for a struggle that it could not possibly win. Including both military personnel and noncombatants, three million precious human lives had been lost. But even the people who survived the war had suffered much. Bombings, fires, and compulsory destruction to reduce fire hazards left fifteen million people homeless. Three million were out of work; three and a half million students had been called to work in munitions factories; and another three million young women had been forced to leave home to work in factories and on farms. Though it turned their world upside down, the war was only vaguely understood by the majority of the people. The emperor had said they must go to battle; they went. Then, without further explanation, His Majesty announced that it was all over. Few people ever really understood the reasons behind either proclamation. On the night of August fifteenth, in defiance of the still-official blackout, lights burned bright throughout Japan; but the hearts of the people were dark. Shame, the threat of foreign occupation, and unpredictable ordeals loomed in the future. For those who had sincerely believed in the Shinto doctrines thrust down the nation's throat by the ultranationalist militarists, who had used emperor worship to serve their own ends, the very foundation of life had crumbled away; there was no longer any reason to live.

That same night, crowds flooded the plaza before the Imperial Palace. Many people sobbed as they prostrated themselves in front of the wooded palace compound wherein dwelled the man they had thought to be a personal god. Military men whose whole beings had centered on that article of faith offered their last prayers to their sovereign and then put bullets through their brains. High-ranking officials and their wives took their lives in expiation for the shame of defeat. Statistics show that on or about the day of the imperial rescript more than five hundred members of the military services killed themselves. Upon hearing of the surrender, ten rebels attempted to assassinate Lord Privy Seal Koichi Kido but he hid in an air-raid shelter in the Imperial Palace grounds. Frustrated in their first try, the rebels made another vain attempt to kill Prime Minister Kantaro Suzuki. Later they entrenched themselves on a hill in the part of Tokyo called Shiba. When police encircled them, they blew themselves up with grenades. Other fanatic Shinto nationalists chose equally drastic courses. Why had intelligent men accepted the militarists' perverted version of Shintoism as a sound religious truth? Because it was a religion, and a man without a religion is condemned to a lonely life as vulnerable and helpless as an uprooted blade of grass blown about in the wind. Wrong religion, however, inevitably drives its believers to doom.

False religion brings misfortune. Nothing is more frightening than belief in the untrue, for a man deluded into such belief is destined for disaster no matter how diligent he is or how good his intentions are. The downfall of Shintoism, which had been abused by the militarists for war purposes, testifies to this truth. Belief in something is indispensable to human life; it is the basic driving force compelling men to action. In addition to religions and ideologies, man may believe in science, technology, medicine, or any number of things. Even so-called agnostics and atheists subconsciously believe in something and act in accordance with their beliefs. In short, all human life consists of a repetition and accumulation of actions based on belief. Faith is not the monopoly of a special group. It is within the reach of all; however, each man must carefully seek the true faith, for misguided belief is the cause of great misery.

Is there a religion in which one may safely put his trust? Yes. Seven hundred years ago, Nichiren propounded the one pure, true faith. But for all these long centuries people have turned deaf ears to his teachings. At the end of the war, when the whole world had come to the sad state Nichiren had prophesied, the age of awakening was close at hand. Nichiren had once written the following passages in a letter to one of his followers.

"The priests in Japan today are vicious and wicked. And since the people respect and make offerings to them, this country will be transformed into an eternal hell plagued by great famines and pestilence, the likes of which have never occurred before in history. Moreover, the country will be invaded by a foreign power. . . . Such is the divine will of the Buddhist deities. Of this divine will only I, Nichiren, am aware, though I hesitated at first to reveal it."

The prophecy had at last come true. Japan, a nation three thousand years old, lay prostrate. Nichiren's vision had proved deadly accurate, and Toda was now convinced that the time had come for Nichiren Shoshu to rise to full stature, for the founder had also foreseen the appearance of multitudes of followers of the true Buddhism who would come to the wasted land to propagate his teachings. At last, all of Japan would know the unparalleled happiness achieved only when the true faith is spread to all people.

But Toda faced a serious problem; he lacked friends who would help him alleviate the heartbreaking misery and unhappiness he saw around him. Clearly realizing the peculiar social phenomena that were going to take place in postwar society, Toda longed to rush out to teach the word of Nichiren. But he knew he must bide his time until he could find trustworthy fellow believers and could build a small, devout circle around them. He also knew that searching for those few people might prove more difficult than converting millions. But without the foundation of a small but totally trustworthy and diligent group of friends, nothing could be accomplished. He had to be patient; he had to go about this most important work slowly and cautiously.

Nichiren himself had written in his *Shoho Jisso Sho:* "In the beginning, I, Nichiren, chanted Nam-myoho-renge-kyo all alone. Then, one by one, those chanting with me increased to two, then to three, then to hundreds. Thus it will be in the future, for the Lotus Sutra has prophesied that an infinite number of Bodhisattvas will spring up from the earth to propagate Buddhism. Therefore, just as an arrow aimed at the earth cannot miss its mark, when the faith has been spread to all, the entire Japanese nation will chant Nam-myoho-renge-kyo."

Toda felt as if this passage had been written especially for him. He understood how Nichiren must have felt when he first proclaimed his doctrine. The nation was vanquished, as Nichiren had foreseen; and the time for the spreading of the faith was ripening, also as Nichiren had prophesied. If these things had come true, was it not time for the guardians of the true Buddhism to spring up in multitudes? The will of the Buddha is truly unfathomable. "Those chanting the prayer increased to two, then to three, then to hundreds." To cry out alone now would be to cast the priceless message to the winds, but to wait and gradually gather together the faithful in small numbers at first and then in the thousands and millions was the way to bring relief and salvation to countless people suffering untold humiliation, anxiety, and fear.

The day the war ended, Toda returned to his home for supper and then retired to his upstairs room, where he wrote the copy for a newspaper advertisement. It was printed in a corner of one of the two pages—all papers were only two pages then—of the *Asahi Shimbun,* a major national daily, on August 23. It was the only advertisement in that issue:

> THE CORRECT WAY TO STUDY AND TO SOLVE PROBLEMS IN MATHEMATICS AND PHYSICS (BY CORRESPONDENCE) FOR STUDENTS IN THE FIRST THREE YEARS OF JUNIOR HIGH SCHOOL. The major topics in the physics and mathematics textbooks will be given expanded commentaries and explanations twice a month. Examinations will be given monthly. Commentaries and notes, when filed, will make an indispensable reference book. The correspondence course to be completed in six months. The fee is 25 yen for each six-month course. Payment in advance. Membership limited because of scarcity of printing materials. No samples available.

From that time, Toda, though not yet fully recovered from his illness and still nursing a neuralgia that gave him a slight limp, was at the office every day. After he hired a few clerks, things began to move according to plan. However, one thing troubled Toda: the absence of the brilliant young man named Sumida, who had worked diligently for him before and during his imprisonment. Although for some weeks after his release he continued to hope that Sumida would turn up, Toda finally resigned himself to the fact that this youth, like many of his former friends, had forsaken him. True, Toda was ill. Moreover, starting a new business in those troubled times was practically impossible. Still, to have been abandoned and betrayed by a trusted friend and associate saddened Toda's heart.

But it by no means dampened spirits in Toda's office, where he employed an elderly Mr. Okumura and a few young girls. With battered desks and no decoration of any kind, the new office contrasted sharply with the large, well-equipped rooms Toda had enjoyed before. But spirits were high, and in view of the brief time they had been in business—since August twentieth, five days after the end of the war and only forty-nine days after Toda's release—things looked very promising.

Though the newspaper advertisement heavily underscored the shortage of supplies by refusing to send samples and by

informing prospective students that they would do well to keep all work papers and notes as references, it nonetheless brought numerous, speedy responses. Toda waited. Time passed, and applications for the course poured in. Thirty to fifty applications each morning made the first half of the day buzzingly active, but after lunch everyone sat idle. On one such afternoon as Toda sat puffing a cigarette, he said: "What do you say to a sukiyaki party—when we get ten thousand yen's worth of applications in a single day?"

No one spoke. To people who had eaten no meat for years, the luxury of sukiyaki seemed beyond the realm of credibility.

But ten thousand yen in one day? One hundred applications only brought in twenty-five hundred yen. The boss must be kidding. Still, Okumura's mouth watered in anticipation of the feast.

"Why not have the party before we get ten thousand yen? It could be a celebration for a successful beginning and an encouragement to do even better in the future," he hastened to say.

Toda chuckled and the clerks laughed. Toda was confident, but he was also a shrewd, patient businessman.

"Perhaps you have a point there, but I think we should wait a little," he said to the crestfallen Okumura, who probably doubted that the happy party would ever materialize.

The nation was in turmoil over the impending arrival of the occupation forces. Furthermore, millions of Japanese servicemen had begun returning to their homes. Shinjuku, Ueno, and Shinagawa stations were packed with bundle-bearing demobilized soldiers and sailors. They crammed into the train coaches and even rode hanging from the locomotives.

The office of Toda's company, the Nihon Shogakkan, was modest, but it was a comfortable haven from the chaos outside; and Toda's warm personality inspired his employees to work hard willingly. His encouragement reaped rewards, for one day, to everyone's surprise, the goal of ten thousand yen was not merely reached but was surpassed. That morning the mailman arrived with two enormous bundles of mail tied with string. Signing the receipts for the registered letters alone was a chore, but when the clerks began opening and reading them they could scarcely believe their eyes. Applications were flooding into the office from distant prefectures.

"I've already counted four hundred and fifty applications, and there are still more," screamed one excited girl.

"Amazing! We've gone past the ten-thousand mark," Okumura exclaimed.

Laughing aloud, Toda said: "Well Okumura, you'll have to

start hunting for some good beef. I don't know where you'll find it, but it's your job."

"Leave it to me. I'll get it if I have to risk my life."

"And don't forget the sakè," Toda added. "Try to get several bottles of good sakè."

"Where will we have the party?" asked Okumura.

"At my house, upstairs," replied Toda. There were no sukiyaki houses left standing in Tokyo in those days.

"We'll ask Kurikawa to join us. Let's finish up work early and celebrate," Toda called as Okumura hurried out on his shopping trip. "Oh yes, and get some cakes and fruit and some soft drinks for the ladies." Though happy and excited, Toda thought of even the small details.

That evening everyone gathered at Toda's house. They had left word for Kurikawa to join them when he got home. Okumura's shopping had been a great success, and he was in the kitchen helping with the preparations. Upstairs the juicy meat was cooking in the black iron skillet; the very sizzling sound made mouths water. As Ikue filled the small porcelain sakè cups, everyone toasted the correspondence school.

After a sip, Toda gazed at the clear warm wine and said: "This is very good sakè, Okumura, where'd you get it?"

"It is good, isn't it? But where I got it is my secret."

"Very well," Toda smiled, "everyone has some talent, and yours is ferreting out the best sakè in town."

They sat in almost total silence as each person relished the rare luxury of meat. After a long pause, Okumura, beaming, said how happy he was that everything was going well. At that moment, Kurikawa appeared, offering his congratulations.

"Thank you, Kurikawa. Sit down. Have a drink," Toda urged.

"I was amazed when my wife told me about it." Kurikawa glanced around at the guests. "At a time like this, with the whole nation in shreds, you were able to take in ten thousand yen's worth of business in one day. It's fantastic."

"Do you envy me?" asked Toda.

"Of course I envy you. The only thing that costs in your business is paper, isn't it? And paper's cheap. Ten thousand in one day; you'll get rich overnight. Anyone would envy you."

"And not just anyone could have done it," said Toda as he refilled the sakè cups.

"You're right there. I admire your ideas and your resourcefulness."

After a brief silence Toda remarked: "You don't understand. Our good fortune is no accident, and it is not entirely thanks to me. It was a reward from the Gohonzon for my two years of suffering in jail. It's not talent alone that has brought this about. It was the wish of the omniscient and marvelous Gohonzon."

As Toda said this, his eyes shone with happiness.

4. OCCUPATION

ATSUGI Air Base was the home station of the navy's 302nd Air Group, which had vowed to resist the enemy in spite of the emperor's announcement that the war had ended. Nevertheless, the Allied Powers chose it as the place of their initial landing in Japan, because it was the only airfield that had escaped bombing. The decision was made over the objections of Japanese military authorities, who feared that the personnel at Atsugi were capable of fighting the Allied forces to their deaths. Two days before the occasion, an advance party of 150 Americans arrived at the base. Then, at 2:05 P.M. on August 30, General Douglas MacArthur, Supreme Commander for the Allied Powers, arrived on an aircraft named *Bataan*.

The general's first appearance in Japan in his new role was quiet and undisturbed because for several days prior to it the crumbling military had rallied themselves to ensure order. Recalcitrant elements at Atsugi and elsewhere, outraged by the imperial rescript of August 15, had cabled the Navy General Staff Headquarters that they would refuse to obey all orders. On the fifteenth and sixteenth of the month, they scattered leaflets reading: "There is no surrender for the imperial forces. Acceptance of the surrender terms in the Potsdam Declaration is tantamount to high treason." The Atsugi contingent appealed to other rebels. Navy General Staff, driven to their wits' ends by the defiant group, attempted to dissuade them from taking rash action, but the inherent weakness of the Japanese military organization was at last laid bare.

Seventeen Japanese government and military representatives, dispatched to Manila on August 19, learned that the United States planned to send an advance party to Atsugi on or about August 23. The naval commanders had no choice but to use force to quell rebellious elements. To this end they formed a special armed battalion, which on August 21, under orders from the fleet commander, emptied all the gasoline tanks and removed the propellers from all airplanes at Atsugi. Learning of this operation, the insurgents seized and somehow repaired twenty-three fighters and flew to the Sayama and Kodama army air bases, where they were immediately arrested and interned. During a violent storm on August 22, deactivation of the naval squadron at Atsugi began. Pilots sympathetic to the rebels were disarmed and sent to their homes before their comrades were demobilized. Once they were gone, civilians from the neighboring areas broke into the base and looted warehouses. Such occurrences were rare, but utter poverty and starvation drove them to it. Nobody could have stopped them. Rebellious groups existed in other parts of the country, but their spirit, together with that of all other military personnel, was broken. Suppressing them presented little real difficulty, and after preparations on the part of the Atsugi reception committee, complete calm reigned when the *Bataan* touched down on the runway.

The engines stopped and MacArthur appeared in the doorway, confident and casual. He wore his usual khaki shirt and trousers and the familiar sunglasses and held a corncob pipe jauntily in his right hand. As he posed for photographers, it was immediately obvious that he carried no weapon. At the foot of the ramp, he took his first step on the summer grass of the country he had conquered. He then exchanged greetings with General Robert Eichelberger, commander of the Eighth Army.

Standing on the runway, the stylish MacArthur must have been proud: he had conquered Japan and now held her destiny in his hands. But he was unarmed. The war was over; he had come to bring peace. The image he wanted to convey was that of a mighty man bearing an olive branch. In his statement to the press, he commented that the road from Melbourne to Tokyo had been long and tedious. He complimented the Japanese authorities on the way they had disarmed and removed dangerous elements, and he expressed the wish that the surrender would be accomplished without incident. His words were free of the arrogance and hauteur that might have been expected of a victor.

As the motorcade bearing the general and his party traveled from Atsugi to Yokohama, they passed what must have seemed an enigmatic sight. Along the highway stood thirty thousand armed Japanese soldiers mobilized to protect MacArthur, but they had all turned their backs on his procession. Doubtless the Americans failed to realize that this was a special posture of deference reserved only for the emperor. MacArthur, riding in a Lincoln of uncertain age, which was placed at his disposal by the Japanese government, observed the spectacle with a cool gaze. Although ninety-five percent of Yokohama lay in ruins, three thousand students had been recruited to clear the debris from the undamaged New Grand Hotel, where the general was quartered. The students also cleaned the area around the Yokohama Customs Office, the temporary site of general headquarters, which were later moved to the Dai Ichi Life Insurance Building in Tokyo, across the street from the Imperial Palace. The first day of Allied occupation of Japan ended peacefully. On the same day a great number of Allied warships sailed into Sagami Bay on their way to Tokyo Bay.

MacArthur had known nothing of the completion, let alone the projected use, of the atomic bomb. He had believed the war would probably continue for at least another year and had prepared to make two-pronged landings at two places on the Japanese islands before establishing military rule. Consequently, he was surprised when it all ended abruptly with the Hiroshima and Nagasaki tragedies. At that time he lacked a firm blueprint for the military government of the defeated nation. Coming as a conqueror, he knew that a great battle remained to be fought and won, for the seeds of ultimate defeat are latent in all victories. Much of his plan for the rule of Japan had been thought out during the flight from Manila to Atsugi. As he walked about the cabin of the plane, he paused now and then to dictate ideas like the following to General Whitney, who accompanied him. First of all, destroy Japan's military capability, then establish a parliamentary political system. Enfranchise women. Emancipate the peasants. Establish free labor movements. Help develop liberal and responsible newspapers. Abolish police oppression. Liberalize education. Decentralize political power.

During the six years of the occupation, the policies of this idealist were largely realized; and throughout this period, the United States, instead of attempting to colonize Japan, tried earnestly to steer her in the direction of modernization and democracy. One can only wonder what the nation's fate would have been had Soviet Russia or China been the occupier. Even more doubtful would have been the fate of an occupied United States had the Japanese generals won the war.

Peoples everywhere were crying out for peace; MacArthur, too, must have had the same feeling, because World War II had left deep scars on the victors, as well as on the defeated. Britain lay weak and wounded. Russia's vast territories had been ravaged. Even America's great resources had begun to show the strain of prolonged warfare. The plight of the conquered nations was obviously more dire. Italy, Germany, and Japan lay like beggars in the ruins of their own lands. Then too, the atomic bomb, a byproduct of the desperation of war, had changed the nature of combat from a grim, though relatively limited, affair in which comparatively small numbers of combatant and noncombatant lives are lost to one involving the possible destruction of mankind. Even should some few wretched human beings survive a nuclear war, they would be left to wander blighted mountains, forests, and plains, like beasts.

In the wilderness of ruin, MacArthur cherished the hope that he could transform bellicose Japan into a truly pacifist nation. After the signing of the formal surrender document aboard the U.S.S. *Missouri,* on September 2, he made this statement:

> A new era is upon us. Even the lesson of victory itself brings with it profound concern, both for our future security and the survival of civilization. The destructiveness of the war potential, through progressive advances in scientific discovery, has in fact now reached a point which revises the traditional concept of war.
>
> Men since the beginning of time have sought peace. Various methods through the ages have attempted to devise an international process to prevent or settle disputes between nations. From the very start, workable methods were found insofar as individual citizens were concerned, but the mechanics of an instrumentality of larger international scope have never been successful. Military alliances, balance of power, leagues of nations all in turn failed, leaving the only path to be by way of the crucible of war. . . . We have had our last chance. If we do not devise some greater and more equitable system, Armageddon will be at our door. The problem basically is theological and involves a spiritual recrudescence and improvement of human character that will synchronize with our

almost matchless advance in science, art, literature, and all material and cultural developments of the past two thousand years. It must be of the spirit, if we are to save the flesh.

Taught by the militarists to dread the Americans as devils, the people of Japan feared the occupation and the humiliation it might bring, but MacArthur's words and subsequent actions belied their anticipation. After learning that the occupation forces came in peace to rebuild the nation on a new pattern, the Japanese first experienced relief that the bloodbath was over and then, gradually, stirrings of hope for the future. Still, in the face of a paralyzed economy and a disrupted social order, securing sufficient food to ward off starvation remained uppermost in all minds.

During the first momentous days of the occupation, Josei Toda closely followed the policies and activities of the new ruler on whom the fate of Japan depended. Reflecting on the national condition and the tactics of General MacArthur, Toda recalled a passage in the *Gosho* of Nichiren in which it is said that when a nation follows false religions and persecutes true Buddhism, it will become filled with heresy. At such a time the Buddha will send the guardian deities Bonten and Taishaku to mete out punishment. It suddenly became quite clear to Toda that MacArthur corresponded to Bonten in his role of judge of those who had ignored the true faith and led Japan to destruction. This was as it must be. MacArthur-Bonten had his work cut out for him.

Toda's own task was to establish the true Buddhism of Nichiren. In order to accomplish this, however, greater financial power was essential. How should he go about expanding his enterprises? As he observed the increasing numbers of American military personnel walking the streets of Tokyo, he had an idea.

While his staff was busily working one day, Toda suddenly asked some of the girls what they thought of the droves of

American servicemen now living in and around the city. Slightly apprehensive of the outcome of the conversation, the girls lowered their heads and remained silent. Toda pursued the point.

"What would you do if an American asked you to show him the way somewhere?" He puffed a cigarette, and the girls, after examining his face, relaxed, seeing that ability to use the English language was his topic.

"I would show him like this," said a plump, pink-faced girl as she raised her hand and pointed.

"That's a language everyone understands. I'd do the same," said Okumura.

"Just like a mute," Toda teased. "All of Tokyo becomes a town of mutes. The Americans will think no one in Japan can talk."

"Yes but they speak no Japanese, and we don't know enough English to get by," said another girl.

"Would you try to learn it if someone taught you?" Toda asked after a pause.

"Of course," chimed the girls in unison.

"I'm all for it, too," spoke up a young man who had been listening.

"That's it. Let's publish a book on English conversation right away," cried the suddenly enlightened Okumura.

"Right."

"A good idea."

"It'd sell like hot cakes and probably run through several reprints."

"But," Toda interrupted the gleeful chatter, "every publisher in town has probably had the same idea, and many of them may have their English conversation books in print at this very minute."

Not long afterward, everyone in the office was surprised to see cheaply printed and bound English conversation texts selling briskly in such bustling parts of town as Ueno, Shinjuku, and Tokyo stations. More appeared in the following weeks, and soon the market was flooded with them. As early as the day after the end of the war, an enterprising man had already opened an English conversation school.

"Well," said one enthusiastic young man, "let's put ours out now and get the jump on the others."

"Before long, you won't be able to get ahead in the world unless you know English." Toda went on: "The Americans are going to rule this country, and unless we learn to communicate with them we are headed for serious trouble. This is going to be the age of English."

Still remaining noncommittal on the subject of the merits of a textbook, Toda asked Okumura for his opinion.

"I'm absolutely for it. The correspondence school is going smoothly. We have the money. Paper's still scarce, but if we pay cash, I think we can get enough. It may be a golden opportunity."

"So everybody's for it—except me." Toda smiled. "It's too late now. Companies that are going to make money by being first with English books are already well on the way to publication. All the books are going to be more or less similar, and latecomers will be losers."

"But I think it's a good idea," one young man said, unwilling to give up.

Toda countered: "Maybe, but we have to go one step further. From now on, people are going to want to know more English than just 'Good morning' and 'Where's the train station?' What they will need is a thorough text on written and spoken English with carefully supervised study plans. Probably some of the bookstores are already thinking of putting out such a book. What we must do is use that book and build a correspondence course around it. And to do that we have to start right now rounding up the best teachers available."

Not everyone on the staff was convinced. In the first place, where would the teachers come from? All the universities were closed and the faculties scattered. What kind of course would be most suitable? Beginner's course? Advanced course? A simple book on English conversation seemed much easier and more lucrative.

"I think it would be difficult to organize a course like that," put in a clerk, timidly. All the others nodded in agreement.

"That's true, but every worthwhile project demands work and effort. In times like these, you'll never accomplish anything with a defeatist attitude." Toda continued: "Set yourself difficult tasks; then overcome them. Weaklings are afraid of difficulties, but I know I don't have any weaklings in my office. Besides, I assume full responsibility. Have I ever blamed anyone when things went wrong?"

"No sir; I think I understand," said a penitent Okumura.

"I don't think you do," pronounced Toda.

As if goaded into action by Toda's apparent disappointment in them, Okumura and the others began busily thumbing through educational magazines in search of universities with good English departments. One of the girls brought Toda a telephone directory in which he rummaged intently, jotting down notes from time to time. Soon some organized information was available. Most university professors had either evacuated to rural areas or had not yet returned from the battlefront. Nevertheless, in a few hours the office staff had contacted several of them and had made arrangements to meet those interested in collaborating on the project. Even the office workers who had been skeptical of Toda's idea were now impressed by the rapid progress.

"When we are all of one mind, we can succeed in anything," Toda said with a smile. "And even when we fail, failure opens up new paths and new vistas for other attempts. When we work together, there will always be a way. This is the strength given to believers in true Buddhism."

The next day negotiations with teachers began. At loose ends and with nothing to occupy their minds because all schools were closed, most of them were eager to apply for work on the course, especially since no one had any idea when campuses would reopen. The office began to buzz with preparations. Convinced at last that the idea was a good one, the staff worked with renewed vigor. Steadily increasing returns from the correspondence school spurred them to greater efforts. The English course was completed in a remarkably short time, and the advertisement announcing its opening appeared in the *Asahi Shimbun* on September 25, only forty days after the end of the war. In addition to his business activities, however, Toda was constantly building the framework for his secretly avowed plan to propagate the true faith. He was concentrating on the future of Japan.

But the present was a time of hardships. Repatriated people, demobilized soldiers, and American military men thronged the streets. MacArthur accomplished the demilitarization at a rapid pace. In less than two months, four million Japanese soldiers stationed on the main islands returned to their homes as civilians. All of this took place without bloody incident. But the road to political reconstruction was less smooth.

On August 17, Prince Higashikuni had formed a cabinet under the ludicrous motto "Repentance by the Entire Japanese Nation." Suggested by the Christian Socialist leader Toyohiko Kagawa, the slogan enraged many people who felt that the government and the militarists, not the people, must repent for the immense wrong committed. Although this first postwar cabinet was effective in pacifying and disarming the military, it overlooked the pressing problem of hunger. Instead it concentrated on the relatively minor questions of preserving the status of the emperor and the old political structure. On September 2, the formal surrender was signed aboard the battleship *Missouri;* and on September 4, the eighty-eighth extraordinary session of the Diet unanimously adopted the resolution "Obedience to Imperial Order." New political parties began to be formed.

Instead of establishing direct military rule of the kind that was to be proclaimed in Germany, MacArthur chose to rule indirectly through the Japanese government with administrative, legislative, and judiciary authorities subordinate to his office. The Japanese very narrowly escaped martial rule, war-

crimes trials held in military tribunals, and issuance of military scrip to replace Japanese currency, for such a plan was scheduled to go into effect on September 3. The idea caused so much confusion and unrest, however, that Foreign Minister Mamoru Shigemitsu and his aide Katsuo Okazaki were finally able to persuade MacArthur to act through the government while enforcing rule in accordance with directives from the office of the Supreme Commander of the Allied Powers (SCAP). This step helped the cabinet save face to an extent. Further attempts to mitigate the disgrace of defeat included using phrases like the "war's end" and "forces stationed in Japan" in lieu of "defeat" and "occupation forces."

On September 10, the General Headquarters of the Allied Powers made its administration policies public. On the next day, Hideki Tojo and other war criminals were arrested. Though making their intentions perfectly clear on the war-crime trials, occupation authorities maintained an enigmatic silence on the fate of the emperor, who was at the head of the lists of the war criminals in Britain and the Soviet Union. Greatly concerned over the possible indictment of His Majesty, the Japanese government arranged a meeting between him and the general. It took place on September 27, in the Dai Ichi Life Insurance Building.

After greeting the emperor in the reception room and dismissing everyone but an interpreter, the general offered his royal guest a cigarette. The emperor accepted, but as he lit it, his hands trembled. MacArthur immediately realized the agony of humiliation this man was undergoing. The general was stunned when the interpreter translated His Majesty's opening remarks:

"I come to you, General MacArthur, to offer myself to the judgment of the powers you represent as the one to bear sole responsibility for every political and military decision made and action taken by my people in the conduct of this war."

The emperor of Japan had not come to plead for his life, but to claim responsibility for a war instigated by the militarists. MacArthur was first surprised, then moved, by the man's courage. Before the emperor left, the general said: "Please come whenever you have problems."

Realizing that because of the deep historical connection between the people and the imperial throne it would probably require one million troops to quiet the nation if the Allies were to attempt to prosecute the emperor, MacArthur strongly cautioned Washington against complying with the adamant British demand that he be tried as a war criminal. Although

Japanese government leaders heaved sighs of relief when they learned that the meeting between the two men had gone well, the picture of the short, mild-looking emperor contrasting sharply with the much taller American hero dismayed them. Fearing the effect this photograph might have on the public, the government banned the sale of newspapers carrying it. They suffered a loss of face, however, when the Allied authorities immediately demanded a retraction of the ban.

MacArthur soon expressed displeasure at a series of blunders committed by the Higashikuni cabinet. Their efforts to retain the Imperial Guard Division of the army, to convert the hated military police into a civil police force, and to channel discharged servicemen into the police force met with severe disapproval from SCAP. But a still more serious reversal awaited this basically conservative government. The sudden death of imprisoned liberal philosopher Kiyoshi Miki, who had been arrested during the war on charges of sheltering a Communist friend, brought to light the apparently forgotten incarceration of numerous so-called political offenders who had been imprisoned under the infamous Public Peace Preservation Law, which had enabled the militarists to silence anyone whose thoughts ran counter to theirs. The public was stunned to learn that more than one month after the end of hostilities this law was still in effect. Hot on the track of just such news items, foreign correspondents interviewed Home Minister Yamazaki, who made the following statement:

"The secret police in charge of thought control are still active and will continue to arrest Communists engaged in anti-imperial propaganda. . . . Anyone advocating the abolition of the emperor system as the basis of the political structure will be regarded as a Communist and arrested under the Public Peace Preservation Law."

Dumbfounded that the minister could make such a scandalous statement as if it were a matter of course, the correspondents immediately clarioned the news, which quickly found its way into the pages of the *Stars and Stripes,* the United States military newspaper in Japan.

Though the Japanese government cooperated with the occupation in demobilization, it was still intent on retaining the old political structure and, above all, the emperor system, at a time when the emperor's responsibility for the war was attracting worldwide attention. But their efforts were soon to be thwarted, for on October 4, SCAP ordered the government to remove all restrictions on political freedom, human rights, and religion. This meant the abolition of the Public Peace Preservation Law, legalization of the Communist party, and release of all political prisoners. Occupation authorities also ordered the dismissal of the home minister and of leading national police officials, as well as the disbanding of the Special Political Police. All of these steps, though part of democratization, had been prompted by the home minister's stupidity in baldly making shocking statements to foreign correspondents, whose reporting of the incident alarmed world public opinion.

Less than fifty days after it came into power, on October 5, the Higashikuni—so-called repentance—cabinet resigned in a body, pleading that if the directives were enforced, it would be impossible to maintain public peace. With its unmourned demise, postwar reforms got under way in earnest. On October 9, Kijuro Shidehara formed a new cabinet, abolished the Public Peace Preservation Law, and released five hundred political prisoners from prisons throughout the nation. Many other prisoners on parole, among them Josei Toda, received full freedom. More than because it liberated him, Toda exulted in the October 4 SCAP memorandum because it guaranteed freedom of religion. On that fine autumn day, as he walked to his office Toda looked at the sky and said: "Mr. MacArthur-Bonten, you're doing a fine job." An alien conqueror had given to Japan religious freedom of a kind she had not known since the days of Nichiren. This was the turning point Toda had awaited, for he knew that without this freedom he could never achieve the true spreading of the word of faith to all men.

As he took a deep, thankful breath of clean air, the autumn sun warmed his face. His step was light and buoyant, health and vigor surged through his body. Silently, he renewed his vow to dedicate himself to his great mission. Not a Japanese, but a foreign conqueror had effected this reform. It was indeed the work of Bonten, as prophesied in the *Gosho*. No longer could the government hinder religious activities; the Japanese people would be saved. Though many political prisoners had cause to rejoice on their first day of freedom in many long years, none had more reason than Josei Toda. But experience had taught him to moderate his enthusiasm, and as he stroked his mustache—now restored to its prewar luxuriance—he thought: "This will do for the time being."

In the midst of his pleasure at his own prospects, however, he was haunted by the misery around him. The impotent government could not cope with the nation's darkest trials. Had it not been for the occupation, who knows what riots would have flared up all over Japan. The masses had no one to turn to in their hardships. Even in starvation, they knew that outcries to the government would produce not so much as a bushel of rice. It was equally futile to attempt to rise against the occupation forces, for that would only begin the hated fighting again. Bereft of hope, frustrated, and discontent, eighty million hungry Japanese had no outlet for the pessimism and despair that had become nearly second nature to them. The grim conditions pained Toda's sensitive heart and outraged his sense of justice. As he walked through the crowded streets he felt a strong urge to call out to the distraught passersby: "This is not your fault. False religion has led us to this cruel state. You may not understand it yet, but you will in time."

At the corner of the street, a pale, anemic young man bumped into Toda and, without apology, scurried on. An old woman jostled him roughly with her large, rag-wrapped bundle. She too said nothing. Shabby, ill-fed, unhappy, the people of Tokyo hurried from place to place in search of something, they knew not what. And in his heart Toda continued to address them:

"This is what happens to a country that vilifies and persecutes the true Buddhism. Nichiren Daishonin foresaw this misery. No one believed him, but now the time has come when all must have faith in his teachings. I will give you his teachings, no matter what the cost to me. When you understand them, your lives will begin anew. Your horizons will be bright. But what about now? I believe that Mr. MacArthur-Bonten will take some steps to see us through. He must, for it is his appointed task."

Although Toda had never met the great soldier, he had accurately assessed his role as the new ruler of Japan. In fact, Toda may have been the only man to do so. It was tragic that Japan had been defeated and was now occupied by foreigners, but it is even more tragic when the minds of a whole people are dominated by hatred, anger, and animality and when nations and societies are ruled by wicked philosophies. No historical phenomena, however, are meaningless when viewed in the light of Buddhist principles. Japan had suffered great misfortune, but the day was dawning when she would become Buddha's world. A nation embracing true Buddhism can turn poison into the elixir of life and misery and poverty into happiness and prosperity.

5. STANDING ALONE

INITIALLY, the Americans, vividly recalling both the fierce fighting of the Japanese troops in the Philippines, Okinawa, and other Pacific islands and the suicidal attacks of kamikaze pilots, were puzzled by the people's meek acceptance of occupation policies. What had happened to the formidable energy and death-defying courage with which the Japanese soldiers had fought? The Americans had failed to understand that both the Japanese reaction to the end of the war and the first steps taken by the American leaders had created a favorable climate for the occupation authorities. When they finally realized this, they were enough encouraged to issue directives to intensify the drive toward democracy. On October 11, SCAP headquarters instructed newly appointed Prime Minister Kijuro Shidehara to carry out its program to enfranchise women, encourage the formation of labor unions, liberalize education, abolish autocracy, and democratize the economic structure. They followed this program with successive reforms that disbanded big-business groups, known as *zaibatsu;* froze the assets of the imperial household; suspended indemnities for properties procured by the government during the war; created taxes on wartime profits and property; instituted land reform;

separated the state and Shintoism; and established new rules concerning the preparation, execution, and revision of the budget. During this early period, apprehension of war criminals accelerated; in the month of September, Prince Nishimoto, former lord keeper of the privy seal Marquis Koichi Kido, and three-time prime minister Prince Fumimaro Konoe were arrested. During the following two years, two hundred thousand people in political, financial, and cultural fields were purged from public office for the part they had played in the war. The accomplishment of such great political reforms in so brief a time is rare in world history, but it is unfortunate that an alien military commander, not the voluntary will of the Japanese people, was the agent through which it was effected.

While the nation was undergoing transformation, Toda pursued his own objectives steadily and calmly. Only a month and a half after the opening of the correspondence school, he heard of a building for sale in West Kanda, near the heart of the Japanese publishing world. It was close to the bustling main street of the district and near the bus and streetcar lines but removed from the noisy elevated trains. He quickly bought the three-story structure; and he and his staff moved from their cramped Meguro office to more spacious, if scarcely new and gleaming, surroundings. Looking back on the heartbreaking loss of his beloved Jishu Gakkan, Toda realized that it is possible to recover from any blow, no matter how crippling. One day, seated by the south window in his new, second-floor office, Toda was talking with his employees.

"I hope none of you thinks it was pure chance that enabled us to move from Meguro into the center of Tokyo," he said.

All nodded mechanically, but they were too filled with excitement over the move to pay much attention to what Toda was saying. Okumura, who was impressed by the new quarters, said: "You've found a wonderful place; ideal location, too."

"It's a sign that our new Nihon Shogakkan will make even

greater strides than before the war," Toda added as he smoked a cigarette.

"It's the divine reward of the Gohonzon," put in Okumura, who remembered Toda's earlier conversation along these lines.

"Yes, remember that. But there isn't much divine reward

in that lunch of yours, I see," joked Toda as he watched Okumura open a bundle wrapped in old newspaper. It contained nothing but several pieces of sweet potato.

"Joking aside, though," Toda continued, "this office really is a reward from the Gohonzon. Less than two months ago we started this business with nothing. Now look at us. It's unbelievable, but it has happened. The building, too. It's a gift from the Gohonzon, and it's going to play an important part in our future. We have to take very good care of it."

Though not fully understanding Toda's meaning, all the

clerks agreed because they were grateful to have a pleasant working environment and to enjoy the good living Toda provided, especially in times of general unemployment and misery.

Toda remained busy with his daily work, but he sometimes had a free moment to sit back and envision the future: not just the business future, but the whole course of growth of the new Soka Kyoiku Gakkai. He had decided that the name must be changed. The title, Soka Kyoiku Gakkai, Value-Creating Education Society, was too limited for the new era. He would propose to call it the Value-Creating Society, Soka Gakkai, and to expand its activities from education alone to political, cultural, economic, and social fields, as well. In this way, the everlasting philosophy and truth of the Three Great Secret Laws of Nichiren could flow into all phases of the life of the nation and thus revitalize the people. This building in West Kanda would be the cradle of the new organization. By day it would serve Toda as his business headquarters; by night it would become the meeting place of adherents of true Buddhism. The time would come when its sooty walls and scarred wooden posts would resound to the first cry of the true faith proclaimed to all people.

Whenever he thought about these things, he was reminded of a school called Shoka Sonjuku, founded in the nineteenth century by Yoshida Shoin, a great Confucian scholar. From that institution had come a score of brilliant youths who later played significant roles in the Meiji Restoration. It too had started on a modest scale, no more physically impressive than Toda's Kanda office, but it had become the birthplace of many important leaders, such as Kusaka Genzui, Takasugi Shinsaku, and Prime Minister Ito Hirobumi. Toda was certain that from the very rooms in which he sat other brilliant young men and women would someday emerge. The age of the Confucians had ended in failure. But now a new age was dawning, a new world of young people trained in a philosophy infinitely greater than the secular thought of Confucius. Disappointed in the egoism, irresponsibility, and lack of integrity of the older generation,

Toda put all of his hope in youth. He constantly exhorted the young workers in his office to work diligently, for the true battle of their lives was only beginning.

"What you've seen up till now," he would say, "has been only child's play. Work, study, and train yourselves for the real battle of the future."

Though unaware of the inner meaning of his words, the clerks were happy to follow him because they could sense his vision of the future. They all worked hard, and the office atmosphere remained cheerful and animated.

This aura of happy industry must have impressed visitors, who came daily in increasing numbers. Most of them were businessmen; but significantly, members of Soka Kyoiku Gakkai, which was in a state of collapse, began coming to see him one by one. Toda did not attempt to conceal his joy upon receiving them, for these were the brave people, the ones who had persevered throughout the hell of war. They had not fled to the countryside, as many of the members had done, but had remained in the burning, crumbling capital. The nightmare of the war was over, but many of them still lived in fear and unrest. In the old days, they had all received guidance from Tsunesaburo Makiguchi, and his death had affected them greatly. Hoping that their society would become active once again, they longed for help but did not know where to turn. Some, however, recalled Josei Toda, the former General Director. Although unacquainted with him personally, they were aware of the great faith Makiguchi had had in him and felt that he would be the proper man to trust in their difficulties.

Old and young, men and women wearing threadbare military uniforms and crushed caps or ungainly *mompe,* and obviously in reduced circumstances, timidly approached Toda's receptionist to ask for interviews.

"Mr. Toda will not know my name, but he may remember my face," some would say.

The puzzled receptionist, suspicious because of their shabbiness, would ask the purpose of the visit. The most frequent answer was a simple wish to say hello and to make themselves known as former members of the society.

Toda always found a few minutes to talk to these unfortunate people. Though the interviews usually opened with reminiscences of past society activities under the leadership of President Makiguchi, they invariably ended with discussions of losses and with requests for advice and guidance. Toda knew that people who negligently allowed their Gohonzon to be burned in air raids suffered much more intensely than those who had preserved theirs intact. Neglect of the Gohonzon brings retribution, and on hearing vivid proof of this fact, Toda realized anew the unavoidable severity of the law of causality. Had times been better, he would have sharply admonished those who had been careless of their Gohonzon, but he was mild because they were too weak and miserable to face reprimand. Furthermore, they all knew their failings and suffered for them. Sensing this, Toda repressed his desire to point out the principle of cause and effect in human actions and gave benign counsel instead. He told them of the great intangible benefits the Gohonzon always conferred on those who follow the true Buddhism. Toda rekindled the flame of hope and faith in the hearts of these afflicted people. He stressed the Gohonzon's immense power to transform poison into elixir. He urged them not to let the present crisis cast them into despair but to have faith in the infallible teachings of Nichiren. As an illustration of his meaning he often quoted the founder of their faith, who once said: "I and my disciples shall attain Buddhahood as a matter of course even in the face of the severest ordeals, as long as we practice faith without doubt." Toda usually concluded his talks with admonitions to adhere to the faith in spite of present hardship, for in that way a follower of Nichiren not only would be strengthened but would also be blessed with indestructible happiness in this life. All who heard him were moved and encouraged. Some wept, some smiled radiantly. As they left, eyes glowing with new hope, they always thanked Toda, who told them never to hesitate to bring their problems to him.

These visitors were a joy to Toda; certain others, however, were a burden. They were the ex-members of Soka Kyoiku Gakkai, businessmen who had once occupied responsible positions in the society and who had been close to Toda for years. About twenty of them once formed an organization called the Economics Reform Club, with Toda as its nucleus. For their activities in the society, they, like Toda, had been persecuted and imprisoned; but unlike him, they had compromised with the authorities and had renounced their faith. Some had returned their Gohonzon to the temple; others had been released from prison on the condition that they sever ties with the society and volunteer for military service. A number of them escaped internment and deviated for fear that once discovered as members they would be thrown into prison. Doubting the teachings of Nichiren, these men betrayed their faith; and as punishment they were in serious financial and emotional straits when the war ended.

Even after Toda was released from prison, they avoided him out of fear that association with him might injure their reputations with the militarists. Being shrewd businessmen, however, they hastened to attempt financial comebacks and frantically dashed about the city in search of quick and easy profits. When they heard of Toda's initial success, they were first surprised and then bitten with envy as his good fortune continued, whereas theirs showed no signs of even beginning. One by one, they called at Toda's offices in the hope of capitalizing on his success. Toda never turned them away. He was fully aware that these were not the true comrades who uphold the faith in spite of all adversity; but their faces, once so proud and assured, were marked with suffering. Their wan smiles did not conceal their fears. Though he received them warmly, he was surprised to see them. In prison a prosecutor had baited him with the number of the so-called faithful who were renouncing the society in order to be released. At that time Toda seethed with rage at their betrayal. But now, faced with his miserable former colleagues, he felt only pity. His office assistants, knowing of the kind of men these were and of Toda's tendency to have angry flare-ups, were puzzled at the calm with which he was able to conduct himself during the visits. Once, when a clerk criticized Toda for tolerating the men who had slandered him during his imprisonment and who had caused trouble in his company when they should have done all in their power to be helpful, Toda explained his attitude in this way:

"You are too hard on them. Never forget that these men were subjected to imprisonment and torture. Many people would break down under the treatment they received. It is scarcely surprising that they deserted the society. Of course, those of you who have not experienced the horror of prison life cannot understand; but the important thing is that all people will be saved, even if they waver in their faith and desert the Gohonzon at one time, because Nichiren Daishonin is infinitely compassionate and forgives all those who ask forgiveness. Human judgment is meaningless, but nothing is more severely just than the judgment of the Gohonzon. Man is sometimes foolish; but once judged by the Gohonzon, he realizes and repents his waywardness. These men who have failed in their faith are miserable now, but they couldn't live without the Gohonzon. They realize that their only hope is in worshiping and preserving the Gohonzon."

Among the businessmen who visited most often and who had been members of the Economics Reform Club, Yoichi Fujisaki, Naosaku Kitagawa, Kizo Iwamori, and Yoichiro Honda seemed especially anxious to revive their friendship with Toda. Mid-autumn saw a great improvement in Toda's health and a return of his fondness for sakè and whiskey. He frequently had drinks with his former associates, many of whom were able to bring him good whiskey because they had contacts with the black market. Toward the end of October, bars, restaurants, and teahouses had been permitted to operate again. One day, as Toda and a few of these men were having a snack and some after-work sakè at a local sushi shop they knew, the conversation gradually turned to the past activities of the society and the importance of reviving it as the first step toward the propagation of the true faith. The men's manner was glib, as if the great task were something that might be easily accomplished. Their frivolity irked Toda, who considered both rebuilding the society and spreading the religious truth to be matters of the gravest importance.

Kitagawa, who owned a printing company, dogmatically announced: "Our first step is easy enough. We simply have to revive the old society."

"Who has to?" Toda asked.

"We, all of us. There's no one else, is there?" Iwamori, the proprietor of an optical-instrument plant ventured timidly. He had escaped imprisonment during the war.

"I suppose we can leave the whole thing up to Iwamori," Toda suggested ironically. "But the road of propagation is long and rugged. You can't see the end of it with Iwamori's best telescope."

They all burst into laughter.

"But we have to do something," persisted Iwamori.

Toda's face suddenly became stern.

"You keep talking like parrots about spreading the true faith, as if it were something easy to accomplish. It's a colossal task; and it demands devoted men—a great leader and dedicated followers."

Toda weighed each word, and as he made his statement smiles faded; silence fell over the group. Finally, Yoichiro Honda, owner of a recently bankrupt food supply house and a childhood friend of Toda's, broke the spell.

"Well, you are the General Director, and you should assume the leadership, Mr. Toda—you should do it," he said.

Slowly sipping his sakè, Toda said nothing. Then Fujisaki, a clever businessman, said: "No one is as well suited to replace President Makiguchi as you are. If you were the leader, I would follow you to the best of my ability. I'm that determined."

After another brief silence, Toda said softly: "The society must never break up again."

"But it won't, the times are different—completely different. How could we make the same mistake again? It's going to be a whole new world," Kitagawa said.

"I grant you *times* have changed," put in Toda, "but how about men? It's men that count. Unless we have strong and dedicated men who are willing to give their lives for the true Buddhism, the whole thing could happen again." Toda's voice was low and calm.

"But the militarists are gone; the enemy has collapsed. It'll be a simple matter to rebuild now."

Toda gazed at Kitagawa and said: "The collapse of the military gives us greater freedom of action, but remember that tens of thousands of misguided religions have lain dormant all this time. They are going to spring to life again and take advantage of the present social confusion. In no time, the nation will be infested with false religions. Conditions have changed, but they have not necessarily improved. Spreading the true faith is going to be hard today because the masses will find it difficult to distinguish between what is valid and the thousands of unfounded religions that are bound to spring up like weeds. That is why I think the old Soka Kyoiku Gakkai organization will not work in the new Japan."

"Do we have to start all over again?" asked Fujisaki.

"That's not what I meant. If we are to spread the saving faith, we must have completely new concepts and policies." But as he said this he could tell from his friends' faces that they did not grasp the meaning of his words. He fell silent in his disenchantment with these men, and when Fujisaki asked how they might arrive at new concepts and ideas, Toda, rising to pay the check, said: "Let's drop it for now."

As Toda paid the cashier, the other men stepped out of the restaurant and expressed their appreciation of the delicious sushi. It was the first they had eaten in a long time. Plans immediately got under way to investigate a new tempura shop that had recently opened in Shinjuku. The men were busily discussing the relative merits of different kinds of good food when Toda approached them. From the bits of their conversation that he overheard it was clear that food, not the remodeling of the society or the spreading of the faith, occupied their minds. At the corner they parted company.

As Toda walked along, disillusioned with his shallow, superficial friends, he came to understand that these were not the loyal comrades he sought. They had not repented of their wartime betrayal of the faith; they had been and remained obtuse and worldly. Looking up at the velvety autumn sky and the sparkling stars, he felt very alone. But at that moment he seemed to have a vision of the smiling, bright face of Tsunesaburo Makiguchi. So vivid was it, in fact, that he nearly cried out to his teacher. The vision uplifted him and strengthened his faith, and as tears welled up in his eyes, he recited to himself a poem he had written in prison:

"My master from this world is gone,
Offering his life in sacrifice.
But how can I, left alone,
Serve the will of the Buddha?

Pure flower of life is all
That is left of my slender body;
And I will pluck it from its stalk
For my country and friends.

A storm rages in the eastern sky,
Where devils go wild and rampant.
I shall save my fellow men,
Haunted by evil shadows.

In my hands the mystic jewel,
Granting me infinite power.
'Salvation for all men,' I cry;
And my master smiles approval."

Reassured, Toda continued on his way, but now he felt a poignant awareness of his own solitary being, no more than a pinpoint in the vast glittering universe. Pure limpid starlight cleansed his heart; a wave of strength surged within him and made him confident and free.

The first anniversary of the death of President Makiguchi was to be observed on the evening of November 18, 1945, at the Kankiryo temple in Nakano. Toda left the office early that day, since it was necessary to walk the distance between Nakano Station and the Kankiryo. As he walked under autumn trees trembling in a chilly breeze, he recalled the agony of another trip he had made to the same temple, in the heat of July, only two days after his release from prison.

On July 5, he stayed in bed most of the day but arose in the late afternoon to visit the priest Taiei Horigome at the Kankiryo. Though Ikue was opposed to her husband's making the trip, she finally relented because she knew how ardently Toda desired news of the condition of the head temple, Daiseki-ji. After an arduous walk, Toda, accompanied by his wife, reached the Kankiryo at about six in the evening. The compound was deserted; only the shrilling of the cicadas punctuated the stillness. Leaning on Ikue's arm, Toda slowly climbed the steps of the temple and, kneeling before the Gohonzon, reverently began reciting the Daimoku. Toda raised his eyes to find the familiar figure of Horigome, who had been about to greet his old friend when the sight of Toda's wasted body silenced him. This priest, who later became the sixty-fifth high priest of Nichiren Shoshu, was the mainstay of the head temple throughout the war. Not only did he fight courageously for his faith, he also risked his life to oppose state authorities when they attempted to suppress his religion. He and Toda had much in common. Both had suffered for their belief, both had undergone persecution; and most important of all, both shared a common bond of faith. Naturally, the war had interrupted their relationship, and some staff members who were jealous of Toda's rapid rise in the society had attempted to stir up trouble between them. But now the war had ended, and the misunderstanding was cleared up. These two men had kept the pure stream of the true Buddhism unsullied in the face of cruel religious persecution. Nichiren Shoshu, destined to be the salvation of mankind, had weathered its most violent storm in seven hundred years because of the strength in the priesthood represented by Horigome and of the lay organization headed first by Makiguchi and later by Toda.

Now that the outlook had brightened, they met again after a long separation. Toda lay prostrate before the priest, who came to him, asked him to rise, and took his hand. The two stood in front of the Gohonzon.

"I've waited a long time for this moment, Mr. Toda. You have no idea how happy I am to see you. But you look ill. It must have been very hard for you."

"I had quite a time," Toda said, referring to his imprisonment. Then he laughed heartily. Ikue, deeply moved by the long-awaited encounter, quietly dabbed her eyes with a handkerchief.

"When did they release you?"

"The night before last, on parole."

The priest smiled warmly and, leading his guests toward his house beside the temple, said: "Both of you, come with me. It's cooler in the house." As they entered his study, he invited them to remain for dinner.

Seated among stacks of books, the two men talked of many things, as if they were anxious to make up all at once for the two years that had passed since they had last met. Toda told of the wretchedness of prison life, but also explained how he had made good use of his time by studying the Lotus Sutra day and night.

He also tried to explain the mixture of rage and sorrow that had filled his heart when he first learned of the death of President Makiguchi. Horigome listened in silence, but his face flushed deeply in sympathy with Toda's reactions. Then he told of the fate of the head temple, which lay in near ruin. The military authorities had requisitioned the beautiful sprawling temple compound, and shortly afterward, vandals had broken in and trampled the gardens. On June 17, 1945, a fire had destroyed the Reception Hall. As he heard these things, Toda wept silently in indignation and grief, because the desolation of the head temple vividly symbolized the decayed state of Soka Kyoiku Gakkai. The war was not yet over at the time of this meeting between Horigome and Toda. The Mappo era, the prophesied Latter Day of the Law, had begun in reality.

At the conclusion of the priest's account, Toda said: "My experience in prison was horrible, but it gave me discipline and strength. I am sure that trial was intended by the Gohonzon. The society may be down now, but I will not admit defeat. With the divine help of the Gohonzon, I will strive with all my strength to rebuild it. I must ask for your help."

The priest replied: "Nichiren Shoshu is faced with a grave crisis. But I interpret it as a sign of an unprecedented rise in our religion."

"I pray that it will be so," said Toda.

"Leave the head temple to me," Horigome continued, "and I will depend on you for lay activities."

In answer to the urgent prayer implied in the priest's tone, Toda said: "I pledge myself to protect the head temple as long as I live. You can count on me. But I've just come out of prison, and my business prospects are still vague. I shall need a little time."

After vowing to rebuild his business in order to contribute to the wider propagation of the true faith, Toda joined Horigome in the Daimoku, then left the temple. This three-hour meeting had reaffirmed the bond of faith between the two men. It had signified the dawn of a new era for Nichiren Shoshu and the renewed unity of clergy and the laity after an interval of two years.

During the one hundred days that had passed since their reunion, Toda had regained his health and had gone far toward rehabilitating his businesses. Now, as he once again walked

along the road to the Kankiryo, he felt a sudden intensification of the urgency of his life mission. November 18, 1945, would mark the first day of his active role as initiator of reform and reconstruction.

After entering the gate of the Kankiryo temple, Toda first chanted the Daimoku before the Gohonzon, then went to the priest's residence, where he met members of Makiguchi's immediate family and other relatives. He had not seen them for a long time. During the ensuing greetings, Horigome complimented Toda on his quick recovery but neither of the men said anything about the vow made three months before. Nevertheless, both understood that it was vibrantly alive and that they were firmly united in their unswerving will to attain the supreme objective.

In attendance at this memorial service for the first anniversary of Makiguchi's death, aside from the family and relatives, there were roughly twenty of Makiguchi's followers. Toda's heart sank when he remembered the society's earlier membership of three thousand. To be sure, not all of the members had returned to Tokyo from the rural areas or from the battlefront, but even so, more should have come to this service. On his way to the temple, Toda had secretly prayed for a large turnout of faithful adherents who would help pave the way for the rebuilding of the society. Though his disappointment was great, he suppressed it to chat for a while with the few who had come to pay their respects. Soon the talk stopped, and Toda moved to the side of the room to await the beginning of the service in memory of his great mentor.

Tsunesaburo Makiguchi had been in prison one year and four months when, at the age of seventy-four, he died in the hospital of the Tokyo Detention House in Sugamo. Until his last day he fought against unjust police oppression and upheld the doctrines of Nichiren Shoshu. Ruthless interrogations, repeated tortures, and humiliating treatment that ignored basic human rights failed to force him to give way to police pressures. Finally, however, age and malnutrition weakened his frail body; he became gravely ill, and the prison authorities advised him to transfer to the prison hospital. He adamantly refused. On November 17, one day before his death, he consented to be moved to the hospital. Before going he changed his underclothes, dressed himself in formal Japanese attire, shaved, and combed his hair, as if for a solemn death rite. When the warder came to escort him, he was waiting patiently but refused to be carried. He preferred to walk to the hospital himself, in spite of his weakened condition. A doctor examined him at once and prescribed medicine, which Makiguchi would not take. In the evening, an attendant, peering into his face in the dim light, saw that he had fallen into a deep sleep. Early on the morning of November 18, he passed away peacefully. The shadow of death had not fallen on him, and his cheeks were rosy. The doctor took his pulse several times because he found it difficult to believe that Makiguchi was dead. A strangely sweet smile lay on his noble face, which was peaceful and serene, a vision of Buddhahood itself. But his heart no longer beat; his hands were cold. A young man carried his body to his home, and his family accompanied him on this last journey.

As Toda participated in the memorial service for his beloved teacher, his heart was torn with grief over the tragic loss. The priest, Horigome, was assisted in the service by the reverends Nittatsu Hosoi and Hoki Chigusa. Hosoi was later to become the sixty-sixth high priest of Nichiren Shoshu and had been a valued assistant to Horigome during his wartime struggle against pressure from the military government. The ceremony began with the chanting of the Daimoku, included recitations from the Lotus Sutra and a unison chant of the Daimoku, and ended with offerings of incense. Throughout the ritual, Toda's mind dwelt on the battle Makiguchi had fought long and well.

When the militarists were in power, the state attempted to force belief in the Sun Goddess, Amaterasu, on the followers of Nichiren Shoshu. As the president of Soka Kyoiku Gakkai, Makiguchi held that it was the society's duty to teach the religiously blind nation what true religion was. He felt to do so was the only way to save the nation from ruin.

Makiguchi and the followers of Nichiren differed with the established government theology on a number of points. First, in their attempt to glorify the emperor, the militarists naturally supported his claim to divinity through the Sun Goddess, traditionally held to be the ancestress of the imperial family. The militarists held that the intercession of the Sun Goddess saved Japan from invasion by the Mongol fleet in the thirteenth century. Since the Sun Goddess had worked this miracle, the Shintoist-militarists argued, she could perform others of equal magnitude. But the Nichiren followers staunchly resisted this fabricated doctrine and refused to bow to the *kamifuda,* or Sun Goddess worship-tablets, that were ordered to be displayed on family altars in all Japanese homes. The government counted all who refused to do reverence to the Sun Goddess as traitors. Because they knew that Amaterasu is only a minor guardian deity of the Gohonzon, Nichiren Shoshu Buddhists were largely unwilling to give in on this point. Their unyielding stand and their attempts to show the true nature of the Sun Goddess earned them the displeasure of the military authorities, who attempted to submerge Nichiren Shoshu by ordering it to recognize the leadership of Minobu Nichiren Shu. Some priests yielded, but so many held firm that the government intensified its persecution.

In June, 1943, acting under pressure from the government, a leading priest of Daiseki-ji summoned Makiguchi and other staff members of the society to an interview during which he instructed them to accept the *kamifuda* as a means of appeasing the authorities. Makiguchi knew that if he refused, his fate and that of the three thousand society members would be uncertain. He hesitated, but only for a moment. There suddenly flashed through his mind a passage from the writings of Nikko Shonin, the second high priest of Nichiren Shoshu and the founder of Daiseki-ji: "You must not accept dogmatic interpretations, even those of a high priest, if they run contrary to true Buddhism."

Makiguchi saw then that acceptance of the *kamifuda* was out of the question. He raised his head and said: "We will never bow to the Sun Goddess." Turning his back on the priest, Makiguchi left Daiseki-ji for the last time.

On the way home, Makiguchi, trembling with rage at the injustice the government was attempting to force upon him, said to Toda: "I don't fear the downfall of one sect as much as

I fear the destruction of our whole nation. I fear the sorrow this would cause Nichiren Daishonin. Isn't it time to admonish the government, Toda? What are the priests afraid of? What do you think about this?" Toda did not know what to reply, apprehensive as he was of the old man's frail health.

"Well, what do you think?" Makiguchi pressed the point, his voice calm now.

Toda looked up at the sky, then replied in a quiet but vigorous tone: "As long as I live, I will follow you faithfully. I'm ready to die for our faith."

Makiguchi smiled and nodded his head contentedly. They walked down the sun-baked road in the blazing afternoon sun, Mount Fuji towering serene and majestic above them. Less than one month later, both were arrested and imprisoned.

The last echo of the final Daimoku of the memorial service roused Toda from his recollections. Horigome was about to address the congregation.

"I am happy to see you gathered here to pay tribute to the memory of the late Tsunesaburo Makiguchi, for the repose of whose soul we have all just prayed. He was a rare, noble man, a martyr to the cause of true Buddhism and to the Lotus Sutra. The very memory of him arouses deep emotion in all of us." Horigome continued his gentle, touching memorial address, as the widow, her daughter-in-law—the Makiguchis' only son had died in battle—and her seven-year-old granddaughter sat in silence. Toda regarded these people as affectionately as he would his own family; and when the courageous and steadfast Mrs. Makiguchi died in 1956 at the age of eighty, he held a splendid funeral for her at Jozai-ji, a Nichiren Shoshu temple in Tokyo.

When the memorial address was over, Yozo Terakawa, formerly a top member in the educators' group of Soka Kyoiku Gakkai and a fine orator who held himself in high esteem, rose and asked permission to speak. Though he had often claimed to be Makiguchi's favored disciple, when arrested and sent to the detention house, he immediately obtained release by turning apostate. At the memorial service this nimble man with the mind of a small-time politician eloquently harangued against the militarists, who had robbed Japan of a great treasure in causing Makiguchi's death. Toda listened carefully, but he and the others who knew of Terakawa's betrayal of his faith heard only hollow falsehoods in his words. Standing naked before the lucid mirror of Myoho, the Mystic Law, Terakawa was trying desperately to conceal his faults, but he could not. A short time after this, he left the society again and lived in misery and misfortune for ten years. A year before Toda's death, Terakawa came to him to beg forgiveness for his wartime betrayal. He later died a lonely man.

At the memorial service, Terakawa spoke at great length but to little purpose. When he was finished, Tatsuji Miyajima rose to add his comments. Like many other former leaders, Miyajima had renounced his faith upon being imprisoned. Nevertheless, he now loudly bewailed the disasters called down by the militarists, the Meiji constitution, and the emperor system. He bemoaned the death of Makiguchi and referred to himself as the late president's most trusted follower. In fact, he too had once been a leader in the educators' group and had served as a society theoretician, but his faith had not been strong enough to withstand severe trials.

Both of these men denounced the misdeeds of the military and the persecution of the followers of Nichiren, but neither of them said a word about the most pressing problem: the reconstruction of the society. Somehow to Toda their main purpose in speaking seemed to be self-exoneration. When they had finished, Toda rose quietly and began speaking in a low voice:

"In my cold, solitary prison cell I prayed that all of the charges brought against President Makiguchi might fall on me. I was young and strong; he was seventy-four years old and unable to bear the hardship of prison life. The news of his death cast me into the depths of a grief greater than I had thought existed. Mr. Makiguchi left that prison in death. I, his unworthy disciple, walked out of it alive. What I must do now is clear."

Some of the congregation wept silently, but some others seemed hostile toward Toda. Sensing this, he almost stopped, but suddenly he felt he could no longer restrain the flood of a message that had to be expressed.

"While he was still with us, President Makiguchi often exhorted his followers to work toward the propagation of the faith with greater devotion. We failed then to understand what he meant, and our obtuseness caused him worry and unhappiness. Only during my long stay in prison did I finally come to understand his meaning. Today I announce to you that I know what he wanted us to do, and I declare that I intend to make amends for my past mistakes.

"Our lives are eternal, without beginning and without end. And we are on this earth for one reason. To give to all men the true faith of the Myoho and the inexhaustible benefits of the seven characters of the holy chant, Nam-myoho-renge-kyo. The Latter Day of the Law has arrived, the degenerate age is upon us, and we—you and I—are the Bodhisattvas prophesied in the Lotus Sutra to come to save the world. In one of his important works, Nichiren says:

'Do not make light of my followers for in their origins they are the great Bodhisattvas who have served the Buddha for eighty trillion ages. In the future their services will prove greater than those of people who served Sakyamuni in the eighty years of his earthly life. They are as worthy and splendid as princes in precious swaddling clothes or as a great dragon rising for the first time into the sky.'

"We are those Bodhisattvas, and because I know this, I solemnly vow to achieve the spreading of the faith no matter what the cost to me.

"My teacher, now resting in the other world, forgive me. As your dedicated disciple, I vow to spread the true faith to all men. From this day, rest peacefully in the knowledge that I will carry on our great work."

When he had finished, a moment of silence passed; then a rustling of conversation and comment began. Some people whispered to their neighbors. Others cast their eyes down with a sneer of contempt for Toda's audacity. Expressions of distaste and distrust crossed many faces. The looks were soon gone, but they all too clearly revealed the deeper feelings of the listeners. Toda's proclamation had been ill-received.

After the final incense offering, the congregation drifted out. Toda remained behind to see the Makiguchi family safely on their way. Then, after a last word with Horigome, who wished him good health, Toda departed. He was oppressed with loneliness by the chilly reception his earnest desire to carry out the great work had received. In the dark night, he joined a group of friends walking toward the station. A brisk autumn wind blew as he said to encourage his companions:

"Faith now will protect us from remorse later. Remember that our work in the next two or three years will determine whether our names will be finally recorded in the history of true Buddhism. As Nichiren Daishonin said, faith is the substance, life its manifestations. Let us strive for the rehabilitation of the society and for success in business as well."

Walking along in the dark night Toda recited one of his own poems:

"From Buddha I received the task,
To give the Mystic Law to all.
Holding high the flag, I stand alone.
Friends are few; foes are many.
I fight this war without support.
Wind howls on the battlefield.
But my heart is brave and strong.

All I can have is my single life,
And that I give without regret.
Now I call the young, the banner bearers.
Where are you? Appear!
Can you not see the pure and
Lofty peak of Fuji?"

As confidence flooded Toda's heart, tears of gratitude coursed down his cheeks, and he remembered something he had once heard: the lion seeks no companions. Suddenly he realized that the sense of solitude he had felt so often in recent days stemmed from a craving for friendship. Now he had undertaken a noble and lofty task, worthy of the king of the beasts. Therefore, like the lion, he must stand alone. Doubt had fled. Toda knew in his heart that he must lead, that he must emulate the noble lion if he was to attract enough followers to give the word of the Law to the world.

As the small group of friends drew near the station, Toda turned to them and said with assurance born of the conviction of right: "Next year we will hold a grand memorial service for President Makiguchi. This will be a year of hard work, but it will also be the year when we hold a general convention of the society." Unaware of the great transformation that had just taken place within this man, his friends could only watch him in puzzlement as they parted to go to their homes.

Thus, November 18, 1945, marked the historic first declaration of Toda's resolution to achieve the spreading of the true Buddhism. And on that cold, star-studded night, he walked home with firm, sure steps.

Schiller said that he who is strong when he stands alone is a true hero.

6. THE THOUSAND-MILE JOURNEY

AS A MAN of action, Toda immediately decided to take steps toward the fulfillment of the great task that lay before him. Because he recognized it as the source of the power to start the desperately needed religious revolution that would lift the Japanese people from the misery and hardships they suffered, he planned to institute a lecture course on the Lotus Sutra. General MacArthur had already cooperated by issuing an order that religion and the state be completely separated. This officially brought Shinto to a level with all other religions and created the atmosphere of freedom that Toda required to make his work a success.

To give lectures, however, Toda needed an audience. Many of his acquaintances and friends were preoccupied with the problems of daily life. At a time when the nation was on the verge of starvation, who would listen to talks on the Sutra? He decided to try the four businessmen who visited him frequently and who loved drinking. They were men of some means and might show interest; at any rate, they had four excellent pairs of ears, to which Toda very soon addressed himself.

One evening when they were enjoying a few cups of sakè Toda remarked: "Why do we waste our time just drinking? Let's start a study course on the Lotus Sutra."

"What? The Lotus—Sutra," Honda mumbled through now sakè-thickened lips.

"Yes, the Lotus Sutra, all twenty-eight chapters," said Toda. "What's the good of parroting phrases like 'true faith' and 'spreading the faith' without even understanding what the scriptures mean? You should know that book. It's a great work."

The men listened, fascinated, as Toda told them how he had seriously studied the Lotus Sutra during his confinement and how it had enlightened him and given him joy.

"Why not ask Toda to lecture on it then?" Iwamori asked Kitagawa.

"Good idea. I've been meaning to read it, but all those difficult Chinese words! Toda seems to know a lot about it, though. I could never read it by myself, but I'd love to hear what he has to say."

"It's a wonder how he learned to read it so easily, and in prison too," put in Honda.

There was a moment's silence; then Toda said: "I know that I will be punished if what I teach you is mistaken."

"Don't worry about that," said Fujisaki. "No one doubts your intelligence or your knowledge. Anyway, it's about time you did something constructive for the society. I'm ready to become your student."

They had all been drinking. Toda was not sure they meant what they said; but for the time being, they were the only people willing to listen to him. "I will start with them," he thought.

Refilling the sakè cups, he said: "A toast to the new lecture course on the Lotus Sutra."

After they had drained their cups, Fujisaki asked: "Now that we're all agreed, when do we begin?"

"Tomorrow," blurted Kitagawa, who was a little drunk.

"I can't," said Honda. "I haven't got a copy of the Sutra."

"Neither have I," said Iwamori, "I'll have to get one."

"The year's drawing to a close. It will soon be New Year. Let's visit Daiseki-ji on New Year's Day and begin our lectures there. By that time you'll have copies," Toda said. They agreed and headed home in a spirit of harmony.

As Toda walked along, he noticed that many people wore no overcoats. Probably they had sold them to buy rice; the nation was nearer to starvation than ever before. More than ten million people were unemployed. Many had become black marketeers, and almost everyone lived from hand to mouth. The New Year holiday, the most important in the Japanese calendar, promised little joy because the minimal rice rations in the city made the traditional and much-loved rice cakes out of the question. Although the occupation authorities were going ahead with reforms, inflation, which was symptomatic of the postwar economy, spiraled.

On December 9, 1945, a drastic land-reform directive freed farmers from the bonds of feudalism and thus was the first step toward democratic reconstruction of rural life. On December 17, women were granted the right to vote, and the election law for the House of Representatives was revised to adopt the majority-electorate system. On the following day the Imperial Rule Assistance Diet was dissolved, but the general election scheduled to be held thirty days later was postponed until April, 1946, to allow more time for a thorough reform of the political structure. Furthermore, a new constitution was being drafted. Finally, on December 21, General MacArthur announced the completion of the first phase of the democratization program in a statement in which he said that the last source of the emperor system had been eliminated when Shinto was reduced from the status of the state religion. But all of these political steps failed to make New Year's Day of 1946 bright for the hungry, confused people. Nevertheless, Toda continued working steadfastly toward his objective. The life philosophy of Nichiren, with which his whole being was deeply imbued, fired his passion to share the faith with all people. He was convinced that this life philosophy was the only possible foundation for a truly democratic Japan.

At three o'clock in the afternoon, on New Year's Day, 1946, Toda, accompanied by Fujisaki, Kitagawa, and Iwamori, alighted at Fuji Station on the Tokaido Line. They had stood all the way from Tokyo in a packed train, and they learned that the local train to Daiseki-ji would not leave for two and a half hours. Tired of traveling, they left the station in search of a taxi. It was a fine day, and although the houses in front of the station sadly lacked the traditional pine gate-ornaments, majestic snow-clad Mount Fuji rose high above the town.

During the war, American bombers had used the famous mountain as a landmark, but now, as the location of Daiseki-ji and its grove of monumental cedars, it was about to become the center from which the message of Buddhism and world peace and culture was to travel far and wide. Sacred to the Japanese and unrivaled in the world for its serene beauty, Mount Fuji is called *Taho Fuji Dai-Nichirenge-zan,* a wonderful title because it prophetically contains the name of Nichiren. Its summit, shaped like eight leaves, symbolizes the eight petals of the lotus and the eight volumes of the Lotus Sutra. As he admired the sacred mountain, Toda thought how like it was to the soaring personality of Nichiren himself.

But they were standing at a spot thirteen miles from Daiseki-ji, and there was neither bus nor taxi to take them there. A suggestion that they walk was immediately rejected because they suddenly remembered a small taxi company nearby. They had used it often in the past, but today it was closed. Still, after spying two battered, apparently long-unused cars in the garage, Kitagawa knocked on the door. The proprietor emerged.

"Would you be kind enough to take us to Daiseki-ji?" inquired Kitagawa.

"Daiseki-ji? No, I'm afraid I can't today."

"Won't your cars run?" Kitagawa persisted.

"It's not exactly that they won't run, but they might not make it that far. Besides it's New Year's Day."

"We have a sick man with us," said Fujisaki, meaning Toda. "We'd be grateful if you would take us to the temple."

"We'll pay extra," Kitagawa added discreetly.

Saying nothing and turning his face slightly away, the proprietor gave no sign of relenting; yet the situation did not seem entirely hopeless. Kitagawa took out his wallet.

"We'd be very grateful," he said as he opened it.

The taxi owner named an exorbitant sum, but Toda's group thought it was better to pay than to walk. The driver added: "If the car breaks down on the way, you'll have to walk." After changing into work clothes, he began the laborious preparations required to start the charcoal-burning engine. These not always effective contraptions had been used by all civilians during the war. Scarce gasoline was reserved for military use. Since the low-powered charcoal burners took a long time to start and often failed, drivers disliked them. After forty minutes of commotion with the fuel and a fan to encourage the weakly glowing coals, white smoke rose from the engine and black soot covered the driver; but they were ready to go.

The road was uphill all the way, and the driver quite naturally lacked confidence. In the sunset, the great mountain loomed pink against the bleak winter landscape as the temperamental vehicle wheezed, gasped, and bounced, often sending the passengers' heads crashing into the roof. They were in good spirits, however, and clutching two large bottles of sakè, Iwamori joked between bumps: "This is hard work." Sometimes the car seemed to falter in its ascent, and then all four held their breaths for fear the ride was over; but at last they sighed in relief as the towering cedars of the temple came into sight. "We've made it," said Toda. At the entrance to the temple they dismissed the taxi.

Surrounded by trees thought to be six or seven hundred years old, the stately gate was built in the Tokugawa period and was donated to Daiseki-ji by Tennei-in, wife of Ienobu, the sixth Tokugawa shogun. Majestic enough to be worthy of its role as the entrance to the main temple of Nichiren Shoshu, it belongs in a class with national treasures. Long ages of wind and snow have scoured away the red paint that once covered it.

After chanting the Daimoku in front of the familiar gate, the group silently proceeded up the stone-paved path that leads to the Mieido Temple. This path is flanked by twelve lodgings for pilgrims. No one was in sight in the temple compound. The innermost lodging on the left side, called the Rikyobo, was set aside for the exclusive use of Soka Kyoiku Gakkai members. Toda and his companions left their luggage in the hall and greeted a friendly priest who, while pouring hot tea for them, recounted the series of events that had led to the present shabby state of the temple. Toda was shocked to hear the details of the fire that had destroyed the Reception Hall; and after tea he and the others went to the site across the stream behind the Rikyobo. Where once the handsome building had stood, there were only charred ruins. A tour around the compound revealed further desolation. The roof of the Mieido Temple, in which is enshrined one of the life-size statues of Nichiren, was in disrepair, and the bell tower leaned sadly. A cold winter wind rippled the weeds clogging the once beautifully kept compound. But even worse than the physical dilapidation of the old temple compound was the complete absence of pilgrims. During New Year's Day in 1942, the place had echoed to the prayers of over a hundred faithful, including President Makiguchi. In contrast, throughout all of 1945, only about one hundred pilgrims had come to the temple. Taiei Horigome had tried to prepare Toda for the bleakness and emptiness of Daiseki-ji, but he had not imagined it would be as bad as it was. The buildings were crumbling, and the temple was in dire financial straits. During the fire that destroyed the Reception Hall, the granary too had caught fire, and a great quantity of stored rice was lost. Furthermore, the postwar occupation land-reform policy prompted the government to confiscate a large tract of land and to purchase at a low price roughly 250 acres of outlying forest and arable land. Even some of the land within the temple compound had been seized by a Communist member

of the local village agrarian committee. The situation was dismal indeed. As Toda began to think about the fate of Nichiren Shoshu in this severe ordeal, he recalled the passages in the *Gosho* prophesying the decline of Buddhism, the loss of its redemptive power, and the constant warrings in the Latter Day of the Law. The Pacific War was testimony to the prophecy. Until true Buddhism is universal, all men must continue to suffer meaningless strife and conflict. But Toda's firm resolution to tread the path toward his goal remained unshaken. Standing before the ruins of the Reception Hall, he renewed his pledge to rebuild the head temple.

When he and his followers returned to the Rikyobo quarters, they found that the priest had delayed evening services for their sake. Toda was very happy, since this was the first worship service he had attended at the head temple in two years. Later, during dinner, as they all sat around a charcoal brazier by the table, Iwamori took out one of the bottles of sakè and began to open it. But Toda stopped him by saying: "Let's wait a little while for that. I think we should study the Lotus Sutra first, don't you?"

"Ah, yes, the Lotus Sutra; well, I can wait a while, I suppose," said Iwamori, blushing and giving the bottle a wistful glance.

"I'm as thirsty as you, but we can have a good time with the sakè after we study," smiled Toda.

"Right," broke in Kitagawa, "study first; sakè later."

The Lotus Sutra and the *Gosho* stood on a small table. The electric light was dim, and Toda's eyes so weak that he had to bring the book very close to his face. "I want to begin with the introductory chapter, but my eyes are too bad for this light. Let's read in turn. Fujisaki, you begin."

Stumbling over the difficult language, Fujisaki began, but soon gave up. "I don't understand a word," he said frowning.

"Don't worry," consoled Toda. "Read the translation in modern Japanese. Then you'll understand better."

Enunciating each word clearly, Fujisaki read: "Thus have I heard. Once when the Buddha was on Ryoju Peak, he found himself in the presence of twelve thousand monks, all of whom were Arhats."

"This," Iwamori said, "I can understand better." Fujisaki chuckled in agreement.

Only occasional gusts of wind from Mount Fuji broke the perfect still of the icy winter night, but in the dim light of the room three faces glowed with dawning understanding. Toda began his talk:

"Sakyamuni, the historical Buddha, who was a prince, renounced his worldly life at the age of nineteen and attained enlightenment at the age of thirty. He preached for fifty years after this, until his death at the age of eighty. His teachings are generally classified into Five Periods and Eight Teachings. Of all of his works, the Lotus Sutra reigns supreme. It is at once the basis and the essence of Buddhism. Without understanding its twenty-eight chapters, true comprehension of Buddhism is impossible. Although Sakyamuni himself said that the Lotus Sutra is the most important of his numerous sutras, in the past other Buddhist sects neglected it, with deplorable consequences."

Toda then went on to explain the Lotus Sutra of Nichiren as embodied in the seven characters of Nam-myoho-renge-kyo and pointed out that it was one of the two great currents of Buddhism, the other being the Lotus Sutra of Sakyamuni.

"The two must not be confused, however, because a distinction exists. The Lotus Sutra in eight volumes totaling twenty-eight chapters is the essence of Buddhism as expounded by Sakyamuni, whereas the Lotus Sutra of Nam-myoho-renge-kyo is the core of Nichiren Daishonin's Buddhism. Sakyamuni gave the world his Lotus Sutra as the way to salvation for the first two millennia after his death, in other words, for the eras of the Former Day and the Middle Day of the Law. Sakyamuni prophesied that the Buddhism he taught would become invalid two thousand years after his death and that a great votary of the Lotus Sutra would arise at that time to teach true Buddhism for the era of the Latter Day of the Law. That great votary was Nichiren Daishonin. He distilled the essence of Sakyamuni's Lotus Sutra into Nam-myoho-renge-kyo and exalted it to the supreme Law for those living in the Latter Day.

"Throughout our study of the Lotus Sutra, it is vitally important that you bear in mind this important fact. Nam-myoho-renge-kyo is the Lotus of the Mystic Law; it is the final and supreme teaching of Nichiren Daishonin and the one and only way to salvation."

After a pause for a sip of water, Toda continued:

"Our next problem is to examine the substance of Nam-myoho-renge-kyo. In *Ongi Kuden,* his most important work, Nichiren Daishonin says something to this effect: the character 'myo' means supreme enlightenment; 'ho,' on the other hand, means ignorance and confusion. 'Myoho,' or the Mystic Law, embodies both. 'Renge' means the two laws of cause and effect, here fused into one substance. 'Kyo' represents the languages and voices of all mankind. This interpretation, however, is not the only possible one. Chang-an holds that 'kyo' means life eternal: past, present, and future. Putting these interpretations of the individual characters together, we see that 'myoho' represents the universe, or all things subject to the laws of cause and effect; that is, all things. Consequently, though you may find it a little difficult to grasp at first, 'myoho-renge-kyo' is the fundamental law governing all universal phenomena, which change incessantly from moment to moment. In contemporary language, I might call it the cosmic life force."

At this point, Kitagawa asked: "What is the position of man in relation to this law?"

"In his essay *Totaigi Sho,* Nichiren Daishonin said: 'What is the substance of myoho-renge-kyo? It is the totality of living beings and phenomena and of the ten states of life. If this is the case, are we common mortals also part of myoho-renge-kyo, the cosmic life force, itself? The answer is yes.'

"The ten states of life are the whole range of modes and ways of life from Hell to Buddhahood. They cover all spheres of life in the universe, which is composed of subjective life and objective phenomena."

In his further attempts to paraphrase the life philosophy of Nichiren in understandable terms, Toda called on other great Buddhist thinkers like T'ien-t'ai and Nan-yueh.

"Both T'ien-t'ai and Nan-yueh," he went on, "have told us that we common mortals can become the substance of myoho-renge-kyo because it is the embodiment of the mystery of all life. It is the fount of our life force. Nichiren Daishonin himself made this perfectly clear in a passage in *Ongi Kuden.*"

Toda found the place in the book and gave it to Fujisaki, who read:

"Nyorai, Tathagata, is Buddha, who exists in an eternity of time and space. He is Nichiren, the trinity of life, wisdom, and the body, which exists in the universe with no beginning or end. Nyorai is also the disciples of Nichiren and the votaries of true Buddhism."

"Yes, that's fine, stop there," said Toda. "Nichiren Daishonin, then, makes it clear that we common mortals can become nyorai and thus the embodiment of myoho-renge-kyo. We fail to believe this because of our stupidity and lack of faith. Since we do not believe what he teaches, we are perpetually tormented by the karmic cycle and never attain true, constant happiness. Nichiren Daishonin taught us that Nam-myoho-renge-kyo is the honorable name given the votaries of the Lotus Sutra in the Latter Day of the Law. This means that Nichiren is the True Buddha of the Latter Day of the Law and is Nam-myoho-renge-kyo itself. In other words, the essence of 'myoho-renge-kyo' is cosmic life force, with which we can identify our own lives. Therefore, the Buddha-nature is inherent in all of us."

The lecture had been lucid and inspiring. All three men had listened intently, but sensing that he had said enough for one evening, Toda closed his books. "Too much study at one time will strain our brains, small as they are. We've finished our first lecture. And since it's New Year's Day, let's celebrate with a little sakè."

Iwamori willingly brought the bottle and cups, and all four helped themselves. The wine was excellent, just right for this important occasion. They exchanged drinks and congratulations on the New Year, and then in the still of the night, they talked over some points in the lecture that they had not quite grasped. Iwamori said: "I wonder; can ordinary men become Buddhas?"

"Some Buddha you'd make, Iwamori," teased Kitagawa.

"And how about you, Kitagawa?" asked Fujisaki. "A prodigal Buddha, that's what you'd be."

Everyone laughed and Toda said: "So here we are—a conclave of Buddha rejects."

All laughed again, except Iwamori, who said in earnest: "But I can't possibly imagine myself a Buddha."

At this all the others guffawed.

"Don't worry," Toda assured him. "We're all called common mortals because we don't have faith in Nichiren Daishonin's teachings. But once we have faith in the Gohonzon and perform our religious practices with conviction, all of us can attain Buddhahood. Don't try to understand everything in one night. It'll become clear to you in time."

Gradually, the conversation returned to the Lotus Sutra, and all four men, lost in conversation, forgot about the passing hours.

Early the following morning, they were granted an audience with Nichiman Akiyama, the sixty-third high priest. After the interview they participated in the ceremony for opening the Treasure Temple, where the Dai-Gohonzon is enshrined. Its very presence overwhelmed them. Throughout the service, Toda thought of nothing but the Dai-Gohonzon and his joy in beholding it for the first time in two and a half years. As he gave thanks for protection in his darkest hours, he chanted the Daimoku and renewed his vow to do all in his power to spread true Buddhism to all men. While praying, Toda was unconscious of the passage of time; he felt as though he had shed both past and future. He was aware only of the Dai-Gohonzon, himself, and a sense of eternal life. Then he realized in a flash of inspiration that eternity was a continuation of moments, that the root and the substance of the moment was Nam-myoho-renge-kyo. When at last the great doors swung closed, ending Toda's moment of blissful communion with the Dai-Gohonzon, he felt overjoyed and renewed, ready to continue the study course, which resumed in the afternoon of that fine, sunlit day.

In the evening, Yoichiro Honda arrived, bringing with him Miss Katsu Kiyohara, who was a primary-school teacher, and Mrs. Tame Izumida, both of whom had been students of President Makiguchi. Mrs. Izumida's husband, a career soldier, had not yet been repatriated; in fact, no one knew whether he was alive or dead. There had been no transportation at the Fujinomiya Station, and since they had walked, all three were sweating and tired, but their arrival enlivened the atmosphere of the Rikyobo Lodging Temple. At the cheerful dinner, Kitagawa, Iwamori, and Fujisaki told the newcomers about the previous night's lecture.

"We're having a marvelous time studying the Lotus Sutra. You know, it can change your whole life," said Kitagawa.

"It can certainly change your appetite. I've been eating like a horse," chimed Iwamori.

"And even sakè tastes better. Can you beat that?" put in Fujisaki.

It rained on the third of January while Toda continued his lectures to the larger group. But the fourth was a beautiful day. By then the students had finished Hobenbon, the second chapter of the Lotus Sutra, and were studying Hiyubon, the third chapter. In the warmth of the afternoon sun, with the paper-covered sliding windows open to let in the fresh mountain air, all of them were deep in study and happy with the progress they were making. The Lotus Sutra was not impossible to understand, after all. As Toda watched their glowing faces, he promised himself that he would complete the lecture series, no matter how many new people came or how many old ones dropped out. The important thing was to carry on with the talks on the sacred text.

On the fifth of January, their last day at the head temple, the little party strolled around the compound. They worshiped at the Sanctuary and visited the Mieido Temple, then they crossed the Oto River and climbed the hill to the site of the sadly ramshackle five-story pagoda. From there they returned to the site of the ruined Reception Hall. Nothing remained except the foundation stones, but in the distance Mount Fuji, the holy mountain, loomed in lotuslike serenity.

Originally built in 1465 and reconstructed in 1869 by the fifty-second high priest, Nitten, the historically important Reception Hall had been a spacious structure housing a large sanctuary and hall, the scene of many important temple rituals including the nightly midnight prayer service. During the war the militarist government immediately cast their eyes on the convenient Daiseki-ji buildings and began using them as living quarters for conscripted workers. In July, 1943, the library of one of the priests' quarters, called the Daibo, was requisitioned as headquarters for the Chubu Regional Training Center for munitions factory workers. Center officials went so far as to enshrine and worship the *kamifuda* of the Sun Goddess in the Daibo. The temple leaders immediately lodged a complaint with the authorities. They argued that the use of a Buddhist building to enshrine other gods was a violation of the sanctity of the temple, but the officials dismissed the complaint as unworthy of consideration. When approached on the subject, officials of the Training Center condemned the priests as unpatriotic and traitorous.

During their occupancy, the worker-trainees and many evacuated primary school pupils who sought shelter in the temple ravaged the buildings and the grounds. The workers left the temple library in 1944, but more than two hundred conscripted Korean soldiers immediately replaced them. The Koreans were unruly and caused more damage to the compound than the workers, but it was the Japanese officers and noncommissioned officers who were true terrors. Behaving like feudal lords, they were contemptuous of both the priests and the farmers in the neighborhood. Although the cause is still unknown, the fire that destroyed the Reception Hall on the night of June 17, 1945—two months before the Japanese surrender—broke out in the reception room of the Daibo, where the Japanese officers were quartered. By the time the priests discovered the fire, flames had already engulfed the roof of the Reception Hall. One group of priests forced their way in to salvage what they could, while another group hurried to the Treasure Temple to guard the Dai-Gohonzon. However, all of them were either child acolytes or aged priests with little strength, for able-bodied priests had been drafted into military service. In the Reception Hall was a Gohonzon inscribed by Nikko, the second high priest of Nichiren Shoshu. In the roaring inferno the priests struggled to remove its great bulk from the wall. At last they succeeded and hauled the treasured object to a nearby cedar grove where they left two of their group on guard. The remainder then rushed back to the Reception Hall to save the life-size statues of Nichiren and Nikko enshrined there. In the meantime, a battered fire engine manned by a feeble old crew arrived. This sorry band and a battery of children who lived in the priests' quarters seized buckets and fought the fire as best they could. Fearing mass escape, the Japanese officers forbade the Korean conscripts to leave their quarters to assist in fighting the fire.

Suddenly, one of the priests left to guard the treasure in the cedar grove remembered that he had not seen the high priest.

"I saw him a moment ago on the porch," said his companion.

"Where could he have gone?"

The helpless priests chanted the Daimoku, their prayer beads gleaming in the light of the flames swirling and roaring as the mountainside echoed to the crackling of burning wood. Soon shouts announced that the Dai-Gohonzon, the statues of both Nichiren and Nikko, and other important treasures had been removed to safety. This brought some relief, but the merciless fire continued to consume the Reception Hall. It was beyond saving.

The hellish night passed, and in the graying light of a dawn that smelled of smoke and destruction, one of the priests ran about wildly, searching and crying out: "Where is the high priest; where has he gone?"

Other priests joined the search, saying:

"Where is he?"

"Has anyone seen him?"

"I saw him by the porch, but that was some time ago."

"Maybe he's in one of the small temples or in the priests' quarters."

"Perhaps the Mieido."

Frantic searches of the entire compound failed to produce a trace of the aged man. The first gray of morning turned to pink. The fire had subsided, leaving behind a smoldering ruin. The second-floor inner chamber of the Reception Hall had not burned, but loomed black at the top of a charred section of the structure. The priests' anxiety over their head priest mounted, until at last they permitted themselves to look through the sulfurous smoke toward the damaged inner room. The staircase remained intact. Suddenly, one priest broke from the group and dashed toward it. Paralyzed with apprehension, all the others watched as he mounted the stairs one by one, beating each step with a stick to make certain it could support his weight. Finally reaching the top, he broke into the inner chamber. The next moment a scream of grief and horror broke from the second-floor room. Two or three more priests hurried to mount the blackened steps.

In his vestments as the high priest of Daiseki-ji, the head temple of Nichiren Shoshu, sat the burned remains of the old man. He was turned to face the Treasure Temple, where the Dai-Gohonzon was enshrined. His was the only death caused by the fire. No one knows with certainty why he chose self-immolation, but something he had said to his friends a few days earlier sheds some light on the mystery.

"This country may perish any day now. I might die any day. But if something should happen to me, there is nothing for you to worry about. The two retired high priests Nichiko Hori and Nissho Mizutani are still in good health."

A few days prior to making this remark, the high priest had visited the Ministry of Education to lodge a vigorous protest, in the style of Nichiren himself, against the proposed merger of Nichiren Shoshu with Minobu Nichiren Shu. He had sternly announced to the minister that "even if you behead me I will oppose a merger with the Minobu or any other misguided sect."

The sight of the ruins of the Reception Hall and the memory of the tragic death of the high priest, coupled with the loss of Tsunesaburo Makiguchi, revealed the ruthless persecution to which true Buddhism was being subjected. In keeping with the relentless law of karma, the Japanese nation had all but perished because of this persecution. As he looked up from the black scar on the earth where the stately hall had once stood to the flawless blue of the sky glowing through the cedar tops, Toda recited a prayer from the *Gosho:*

"The Nirvana Sutra says: 'All suffering endured by mankind becomes the suffering of the Buddha.' I, Nichiren, declare that the sufferings of mankind become my sufferings."

Nichiren had also said that when a great calamity occurs, a great good fortune is near at hand.

Nichiren Shoshu had already undergone a supreme ordeal. Surely an unprecedented rise in fortune and the prophesied universal propagation of the faith must come soon. The way ahead was precipitous and thorny, but the horizon was clear and bright. As he started to walk away Toda whispered: "This is the beginning."

Toda and his friends left the temple in the early afternoon, and after waiting two hours at Fujinomiya Station and four more at Fuji Station, they finally arrived well past midnight at a cold, dark, and deserted Tokyo Station.

7. PRELUDE

ON NEW Year's Day, 1946, as Toda was delivering his first lecture on the Lotus Sutra, an imperial rescript containing the following paragraph was issued:

"We stand by the people, and we wish always to share with them their moments of joy and sorrow. The ties between us and our people have always been based on mutual trust and affection. They do not depend upon mere legends and myths. They are not predicated on the false conception that the emperor is divine and that the Japanese people are superior to other races and fated to rule the world."

Later regarded as a document of great historical importance, the rescript was reportedly drafted by Prime Minister Kijuro Shidehara and issued in accordance with General MacArthur's directive concerning the separation of Shinto and the state.

A pleasant surprise awaited Toda upon his return late on the night of the fifth of January. His son, Kyoichi, who had insisted on spending the New Year's holidays with his parents, was home from northeastern Japan and sleeping soundly in his bed. Kneeling beside him and looking lovingly into the young face, tanned and golden from sun and snow, Toda murmured softly: "How healthy you look." As he stroked the fourth-grader's forehead and cheeks, he stifled an impulse to awaken the child and hold him in his arms. When Kyoichi had arrived, accompanied by his aunt, he had been disappointed at his father's absence, but Toda had not known that homesickness had driven the boy to harass his aunt into allowing him to come to Tokyo. The boy was no longer a child; the sight of his strong body, clear complexion, and close-cropped hair melted his father's heart with joy. Kneeling before the family altar, with its offering of rice cakes brought by Kyoichi, Toda performed the Gongyo in gratitude to the Gohonzon for his son's well-being.

As soon as he awakened on the following morning, Kyoichi burst into his father's room and threw himself into Toda's arms. All day he shadowed his father wherever he went, even to the toilet. He could not accept being separated from Toda for an instant. At the breakfast table, where the entire family gathered, the boy, speaking in the thick accent of the northeastern region, told his father of his experiences. "The war didn't scare me, father, but the avalanche in the snow country was awful." At first Toda and Ikue grinned at how rustic their son's speech had become, but later they could no longer suppress their laughter. In only two years, he had changed so much.

Not understanding the cause of the hilarity, the boy asked: "What's so funny?"

"You seem to have picked up a good case of the northeastern dialect, son," replied his father.

"Whaddaya mean, I didn't say nothing funny," Kyoichi protested.

In order that his son might see the ravages of war and from them learn to appreciate the glory of peace, Toda took Kyoichi to his office that morning. The boy's excitement and curiosity were boundless. Accustomed to the peaceful landscape of the northeast, he was bewildered by the ugly spectacle of the ruins of downtown Tokyo.

"They dropped lots of bombs, father. There's hardly a house left. But we're lucky. Ours didn't burn. Were you scared, father?"

"I wasn't at home when it happened."

"Poor mother. You gone, and me too. She must've had a terrible time alone in the house."

"Yes, Kyoichi," said Toda, laying his hand on his son's shoulder, "your mother was very brave, and the Gohonzon watched over her and our home and all of us."

The boy smiled and said proudly: "I chanted the Daimoku in Ichinoseki, father."

"You got my letter, then."

"Yes, our father-son pact. Aunt put it in the drawer of the family altar."

After half a day at the office and among the crumbling debris of the city, Kyoichi was very tired and went home alone. The devastation had strained his sensitive young nerves.

When Toda came home late that night, peering curiously at the sleeping boy's face, he wondered what would be the best step to take now. An argument ensued between him and Ikue, who wanted the boy to go back to the country, whereas Toda wanted him to remain in Tokyo. Both were adamant and in the end agreed to leave the decision up to Kyoichi. On the following morning, when asked to choose, the boy thought for a moment, then said: "I like Ichinoseki better." Though Toda was disappointed, Ikue persuaded him that it would be safer to let the boy return. Tokyo was not yet a fit place for children. At the end of the New Year's vacation, Kyoichi went back to the snow-blanketed north.

The lectures on the Lotus Sutra, into which Toda poured all his energy and passion, were given two nights a week in his second-floor office. Some minor difficulties plagued the gatherings, but they were generally easily overcome. For instance, electric power in those days was unreliable, and the lights went out from time to time. But a few well-placed candles solved that. More serious was Toda's poor eyesight, which often prevented his reading the passages from the Sutra and the scriptures of Nichiren. When this happened, one of the others would read for him, and Toda would comment and interpret. He seemed to know all of the *Gosho* and the Lotus Sutra by heart and was able to clarify even the most obscure passages. His students found his knowledge and insight amazing.

On one occasion, Iwamori, unable to contain his curiosity, asked Toda: "How and when did you manage to master these works so thoroughly? Merely memorizing the Sutra and the *Gosho* is a tremendous task in itself, but your insight is so profound. It's a mystery to us."

"I don't know what to say," Toda replied. "All the scriptures of Sakyamuni concern our lives. While in prison, as I recited the Daimoku and studied the Sutra I gradually remembered them. Before my imprisonment I was too busy making money to have time to study them."

Somehow his explanation did not satisfy, and there was much head shaking.

"Did you say you remembered them?" Honda, who had been Toda's classmate in primary school, said: "Your lectures have been wonderful. I thought I knew you fairly well, but I never suspected you could do anything like this. It's almost superhuman. I'm certainly with you from now on, Toda."

"No, I'm not superhuman. I can understand the Sutra and the scriptures of Nichiren Daishonin only because of my faith. If you have faith, you will soon come to understand them just as well as I do," Toda replied.

After lighting a cigarette, he continued: "Nichiren Daishonin taught us that those who chant Nam-myoho-renge-kyo in the Latter Day of the Law automatically become Bodhisattvas. He said: 'None but Bodhisattvas will be able to chant it.' Maybe you think it sounds too good to be true, but if we revere the Gohonzon and chant the Daimoku, we will become the Bodhisattvas prophesied to arise from the earth in order to save the world. We have a great mission: to save our fellow men and to propagate true Buddhism. Nichiren Daishonin's teachings are infallible. For us to carry out our duties to ourselves and others, all we need is faith, willingness, and good health."

Toda followed these remarks with an explanation of his conviction that Nam-myoho-renge-kyo is not only the essence of true Buddhism, but also a great driving force for national prosperity and cultural and creative fruitfulness. He cited examples of the cultural heights reached by ancient India, China, and Japan when the Lotus Sutra exerted great influence over these nations. In the Latter Day of the Law, the last of the three eras of gradual decline in Buddhism, the Lotus Sutra of Sakyamuni has lost its power of redemption, if not its great structure. The Nam-myoho-renge-kyo, the Lotus Sutra of Nichiren, must open new horizons and give rise to a new civilization and culture. Viewed in this light, Nam-myoho-renge-kyo is the one way out of the conflict between spiritualism and materialism.

Toda's personal charm helped make his lectures a success, and gradually his group of businessmen, concerned primarily with their business affairs, came to relish their struggle with abstruse Buddhist terminology and philosophy. Their faces virtually glowed as they studied the Lotus Sutra and the *Gosho;* and before long, all of them regarded the hours spent in study and listening to Toda's enlightened commentaries as the happiest in their lives. The scriptures came to be meaningful to all of them, but the most impressive aspect of the series of lectures was the transformation they saw in Toda himself. He was no longer the man they had known before the war. When asked about this change, he always said that it was the result of his faith and of applying the Myoho of Nichiren in practical cases. He also said that this was the way in which he was bringing about his own human revolution. He taught his students that this revolution had transformed his life and karma without compromising dignity or individuality. He added that a great outpouring of life force from individuals was the quickest, most fundamental way to reform culture, politics, science, education, and all society.

Japanese society of the immediate postwar period was far from blossoming. On February 17, 1946, the government issued a series of economic measures designed to decelerate inflation and thus remedy the grave economic crisis facing the nation. The new policy froze all bank accounts, issued new currency, and limited the amount of old currency that could be converted into the new. In addition, it established a ¥500 ceiling on cash salaries. This meant that overnight most of the people of Japan, aside from highly placed bureaucrats and government leaders, had to subsist on a totally insufficient amount of money. In certain respects, Japanese economy took on a slight Communist color. Though severe, the austerity measures failed to halt the inflation, and the people suffered as a consequence. Furthermore, staple-food distributions were often late. When that happened, people were forced to purchase necessities on the black market at exorbitant prices. In the final analysis, only the big capitalists felt any relief as a result of the government's favorable economic measures, while other people often died of hunger and cold.

The economic crisis rocked the nation, and Toda's enterprise felt its effect, too. His correspondence-course students paid their fees in advance regularly, but inflation raised the prices of printing and paper to such an extent that Toda was often unable to keep up. He felt he could not raise the tuition fees or demand any additional charges of the students, yet, unlike large business concerns, he lacked hoarded commodities to fall back on. Fortunately, his business initiative at last enabled him to procure, at least temporarily, a steady supply of paper; and he resolved to use it more effectively than he had in the past. He decided to revive the publication of some of the popular novels his prewar publishing firm had issued. He still held the copyrights, and he went to work immediately on the project. While engaged in this, he had an idea that seemed good to him. The word democracy was on all lips at that time, but few people understood what it truly meant. Why not commission someone to write a special course on democracy? He quickly organized an editorial staff and gathered a group of intellectuals and scholars well versed in political science to write five volumes on the topic. Toda appointed Yuzo Mishima, one of the twenty-one society leaders arrested during the war, as editor and gave him a staff of young editorial workers including Chuhei Yamadaira, a university student who had taught at Toda's night school before being drafted into military service to become a pilot. After the war, Yamadaira returned to Tokyo, sought Toda out, and came to work on the editorial staff on a part-time basis. All of the staff members were eager, and when their task was finished and the book on the market, everyone was delighted to learn that they had an immediate best seller on their hands.

Books were scarce in those days. The minute new ones were on the stands, they sold out immediately. But publishing firms were faced with two serious problems: shortage of paper and constantly rising paper prices. One way or another, Toda managed to overcome these difficulties. He worked hard, and by exploiting all of his business skills, managed to ensure a paper supply most of the time. Furthermore, if he ever had a surplus, he saw to it that smaller, less fortunate companies got a share. This naturally boosted his reputation in publishing circles, where he soon had a great following. The connections he made through his publishing activities provided the framework on which he later built a loan company.

One of the methods Toda used to obtain supplies of paper was prayer. In one particular instance, when a very important project threatened to fail because of a lack of paper, he sat up in bed one night and invoked the Buddhist deities. "We need paper for our work, which will eventually become the foundation of a spreading of the true faith. Why don't you help us?" he finished in a reproachful voice. On the following day, a company with which he had been out of contact for some time delivered the paper he needed for his project.

Two elements in Toda's personality made him an overwhelmingly successful businessman. First, he spared no effort to solve a problem. But once the difficulty had been surmounted, he was able to forget it completely. Second, though not completely healthy, he was tireless. He might work late at night or go out on a drinking spree with his friends, but he never missed a day at the office and was never late.

Gradually his office, which was a veritable business battlefield by day, became the scene of great spiritual progress at night, for it was there that he continued his enlightening lectures on the Lotus Sutra. On study nights—Monday, Wednesday, and Friday—in addition to the original four businessmen, new faces appeared from time to time. Among them were Katsu Kiyohara and Tame Izumida, who had been part of the earlier study session at Daiseki-ji. On March 28, 1946, about three months after its beginning, the series of lectures came to a close.

"That, then, concludes this series on the Sutra. I want to thank you for your patient attention and faithful attendance, and I would like to have a little ceremony to mark this special occasion."

The students were surprised that Toda felt called upon to thank them. They felt that the profit had been all theirs, and Iwamori said as much. The others agreed with him and added that they hoped they would be able to use the knowledge they had gained to spread the true faith.

Opening a box containing an inkstone and taking out a brush and a clean sheet of white paper, Toda said: "You have been excellent students." He then wrote a certificate stating that the undersigned had completed Toda's course on the Lotus Sutra and asked the four faithful men to sign. When they had done so, Toda announced: "Our little ceremony is complete. Perhaps we should sing 'Auld Lang Syne,' but since we all have such poor voices, let's skip that and have a little liquid refreshment." Saying this, he went to a cupboard and took out a bottle of whiskey and gave it to Kitagawa to open.

"This is terrific," Kitagawa cried as he happily filled five glasses.

"Bottoms up, then," said Toda. "You know, I've saved this bottle especially for tonight."

But the others hesitated. They were embarrassed by Toda's thoughtfulness and generosity.

"What can we say?" asked one of them sheepishly. "For three months you've taught us without taking a penny, and now you give us a party. We are the ones who should try to repay you."

"No, you've been patient listeners, and I'm very grateful," said Toda, lowering his head.

The four men were puzzled by Toda's attitude; they had no way of knowing that he was then recalling this passage from the Lotus Sutra:

"After my Nirvana there shall appear a man who will preach the Lotus Sutra of the Latter Day of the Law, even if in secret and to only one person. That man shall be acknowledged as a messenger of the Buddha. As an emissary of the Buddha, he will perform the function of the Buddha and propagate the Lotus Sutra among the people."

The phrase "after my Nirvana" alludes to the Latter Day of the Law, the age in which Toda was living. Because he had found attentive students, Toda had become a messenger of the True Buddha. Deeply conscious of the glory and honor, he felt grateful to his friends.

"Well then, let's drink," said Toda. "Why are you so quiet?"

Fujisaki said: "Yes, here's to you, Toda." They all raised their glasses.

The series of lectures was over, but that was by no means to be the end. One morning Miss Katsu Kiyohara called on Toda. She had heard that the lectures were finished and wondered if

Toda would be good enough to repeat them for another group. Sensing her sincerity, Toda agreed to do so if there were people who earnestly wanted to study.

"Wonderful," cried the young woman. But when asked the names of the prospective students, she had to admit that she did not know as yet.

"But I'll get a group together right away," she said. "The last time I attended one of your lectures, I was so moved, and I thought it really ought to be heard by more people. I'll have the students ready whenever you begin."

"All right, we'll begin in mid-April," said Toda.

Thrilled that he had agreed but dubious about her chances of organizing a seminar from the inhabitants of ruined Tokyo, Miss Kiyohara started on a round of calls on all of her old friends who had been believers. She urged them to attend the lectures, which she said were to be a prelude to a reorganization of Soka Kyoiku Gakkai. In addition, she prayed fervently that the lectures would be a success. She worked very hard to that end, since she believed that after three years of persecution the society was going to get back on its feet again.

Most of the ten people who appeared at the first lecture, on the evening of the twelfth of April, were strangers to Toda. Dispensing with the formality of introductions, he immediately began his lecture:

"Conveniently, we call this series a course on the Lotus Sutra, but what matters most is that you fully understand the meaning of Nam-myoho-renge-kyo, taught to us by Nichiren Daishonin. Therefore, I will begin my remarks with an explanation of this vital point. First of all, do not be misled by the meanings of the Chinese characters used to write the word 'namu.' They are only a transliteration of a Sanskrit word meaning devotion or believing with body and soul. So then, the first word of the Lotus is 'namu'; that means we are devoted to something. That something is the Gohonzon. By worshiping the Gohonzon, we become one with the great cosmic law, the Mystic Law, or 'myoho.' The Buddha that we worship is, then, the personification of Nam-myoho-renge-kyo, or in short, Nichiren Daishonin, the True Buddha. Each of the words 'myoho,' 'renge,' and 'kyo' stands for profound philosophical doctrines."

As he paused to light a cigarette, Toda could see that his audience was tense.

"If this line of thinking sounds strange to you, it is because you have been taught in school to employ the Western philosophical method of inductive reasoning; that is, reasoning from the particular to the general. The method we apply here is the Oriental one of reasoning from the general to the particular, or the deductive method. Throughout our discussion, bear in mind the fact that the inductive method is not applicable in this case.

"Now to turn to 'myoho-renge-kyo.' These words are a translation into Chinese characters of the Sanskrit *Saddharma Pundarika Sutra*. In plain terms, these three elements embody the substance of cosmic life force."

As Toda continued, his audience gradually warmed to the subject and, as often happened, fell under the spell of his personality. His lucid explanations held their attention.

In discussing the true Buddhism, he said that most people had long regarded the no longer valid Buddhism as both difficult and totally divorced from ordinary life. True religion should never be mere discipline of mind. True Buddhism, however, is fundamentally concerned with life in its myriad manifestations. Its aim is to help people attain enlightenment and happiness through the practice of faith. He also talked on the difference between religion and science and clarified their aims and functions. Finally, he delved into the concept of oneness of mind and matter, one of the cardinal doctrines of Nichiren Shoshu. Mind and body are inseparable and their perfect fusion is the ultimate life state to which man can attain. It is also the object of 'namu,' or devotion.

The talk was long—over two hours—and when it was finished, Miss Kiyohara, noticing that no one had fallen asleep, was secretly pleased with her group.

At the next session, however, only two people attended, Miss Kiyohara and Mrs. Izumida. Although Toda said nothing, Miss Kiyohara pulled her small body into as inconspicuous a knot as she could and prayed for the lecture to pass quickly. She was very embarrassed. When Toda finally closed his book, he announced that because of business appointments he would be unable to meet with the group on the following scheduled day, but would see them on the nineteenth.

When the two women were in the street, Miss Kiyohara took Mrs. Izumida's hand and asked what in the world she could do: only two people!

"Don't worry, my dear, we'll find more people by next time," Mrs. Izumida said unconvincingly.

"Oh, but how?" wailed Miss Kiyohara. "I was so ashamed. And just think, it was all my idea."

The two women agreed that something must be done and resolved to send invitations to everyone they knew. But most of the letters came back because the person did not live at the address given, the house had burned, or the person named had not yet returned from either battle or his wartime place of refuge. Miss Kiyohara was disheartened indeed on the afternoon when she accidentally bumped into Takeo Konishi, a former disciple of Tsunesaburo Makiguchi.

"Well, Miss Kiyohara, what a surprise." Konishi's healthy sun-tanned face beamed with a smile.

"Mr. Konishi, after all these years. How have you been?"

After exchanging news and small talk about mutual aquaintances, it suddenly occurred to Miss Kiyohara to invite Konishi to Toda's lectures.

"Are you still practicing your faith?" she asked by way of drawing him out.

"Oh yes," was the reply. "My house didn't burn, so Harayama and Seki—you remember them—are living with me. We have no money and no sakè, but we spend a lot of time together studying the *Gosho*. The other day we held a discussion meeting, but the young people who attended the meeting were smart alecks."

Heartened at this, Miss Kiyohara asked: "Have you seen Mr. Toda?"

"No, I heard he was very ill after they released him from prison."

"Oh, no. He's well and runs a publishing firm in Kanda. He has even started giving lectures on the Lotus Sutra. I go, wouldn't you like to join me?"

"Indeed I would. Just tell me how to get in touch with him."

Konishi, who was a primary school teacher, had evacuated with his pupils to a mountain temple in the northeastern part of the country. His friends Harayama and Seki, also teachers, had taken their pupils to safety also but to different locations.

After the war, when they returned, they found their homes had burned. They moved in with Konishi, whose house in Kamata was still standing. During the war, the authorities had treated all three badly because of their Buddhist associations and activities, but they had escaped imprisonment because they were not leaders in the society. These three close friends often read Nichiren's *Kaimoku Sho* together during air raids.

The lecture on the nineteenth was given to a large and lively audience. In addition to the three teachers from Kamata, three men from Toda's office also attended: Mishima and Yamadaira from the editorial department and Okumura, the accountant. Since most of the people attending were young, vitality and eagerness prevailed. The atmosphere was vastly different from that of the first series. Seated in the front row, proud and attentive, Miss Kiyohara already regarded Toda as the new leader of Soka Kyoiku Gakkai.

During his lecture, Toda became aware of a responsiveness in his audience; it was something new, vital, and strangely challenging. When he was only half way through, he sensed that he was close to winning devoted followers; and in the back of his mind, he could see the society reborn. The audience perceived in him a new passion and fervor, an uncommon determination; and although they could not know which way the society would go in the future, they sensed that Toda was the man to lead them along the new path.

When he finished and closed his book, Toda looked up to see a small group of radiant faces, a splendid prelude to the accomplishment of the supreme mission.

8. GEARS

THE SOCIETY was now called Soka Gakkai instead of Soka Kyoiku Gakkai. The lectures on the Lotus Sutra, now held regularly each Monday, Wednesday, and Friday, enjoyed steadily increasing attendance. Toda, with his earnest desire to give his pupils a firm knowledge of the canon of the Lotus Sutra and a basic understanding of the essence of Buddhism, lectured with compelling zeal. At the same time, he decided to revive the Tuesday, Thursday, Saturday, and Sunday discussion meetings, held by Makiguchi in the past but suspended for three years. Toda either presided at or participated in most of these meetings, which were sometimes held at Miss Kiyohara's home, sometimes at Konishi's house, and at other times in the Morikawa home in Tsurumi.

Though, by and large, both the lectures and the discussion meetings were successful, Toda gradually sensed a point of doctrinal difference between himself and the students of President Makiguchi. These people were disappointed in Toda's apparent lack of interest in the former president's philosophy of value. Toda attempted to explain his feelings to them. He believed that the philosophy of value, important as it is, must be regarded as only a preface to the true burden of their study:

the life philosophy of Nichiren. Consequently, he strongly emphasized Nichiren's doctrines of the oneness of mind and matter and the theory of the three existences of life: past, present and future. Some of the students, while understanding the value philosophy, found the life philosophy of Nichiren difficult to grasp.

"You must believe in the existence of three lives, because it is a cardinal principle of Mahayana Buddhism," Toda said. "When you believe, new horizons will open for you. The philosophy of value, which I admire greatly, is only a stairway to the greater edifice of Buddhism."

The gap between Toda and his students arose from their failure to understand the relationship between Nichiren Shoshu and Makiguchi's philosophy of value. Makiguchi felt that the pursuit and creation of values are the ultimate purpose of life, and he established goodness, beauty, and gain as the three greatest values. He denied truth the place Immanuel Kant gave it among the other values because he felt that truth can only be perceived or recognized, not created. In order that man may lead a life of goodness, beauty, and gain he must depend on religion. In Nichiren Shoshu, Makiguchi found the ideal of his value theory as well as an object of worship, for he believed that the Dai-Gohonzon embodied the highest and greatest value possible in this world.

While recognizing the originality and merit of his teacher's philosophy, Toda refused to admit that the Dai-Gohonzon and the teachings of Nichiren could be assessed on the basis of a philosophy of value, since they exist and will continue to exist apart from all theories. Consequently, in his teaching he omitted discussions of the philosophy of value and concentrated on the Lotus Sutra, which he believed to be the legitimate path to an understanding of Nam-myoho-renge-kyo. Although some of his audience persisted in preferring the value philosophy, in their desire to learn about the Lotus Sutra Toda found encouragement that someday he would be able to correct the misconceptions they held.

As his lectures and meetings progressed, Toda grew more and more certain that the time had come for the reorganization of the society. Often after lectures the audience was so fired with enthusiasm that they stayed on to discuss the new organization or to exchange information on the whereabouts of former members. Some even suggested the formation of chapters in rural areas, where a sizable proportion of the membership still lived. On the first of May the first postwar leaders' meeting was held. Less than a dozen members attended; but the historic meeting marked the beginning of the revitalization of the society, this time organized around Josei Toda. The conference discussed rebuilding and revamping the virtually disintegrated society structure, establishing new departments, and preparing schedules for discussion meetings in the four principal Tokyo chapters. All the participants were overjoyed that things had begun again, but in his closing speech Toda explained that the way was not free of hazards.

"I thank you for attending today. Finally our society has gotten started again. This is a new beginning. But I warn you that great obstacles lie ahead and that the current of our times will overwhelm us unless we perform our task with unwavering faith and conviction.

"This is one of the most turbulent times in the history of Japan. Today half a million workers participated in the May Day demonstration in the Imperial Palace Plaza. They demanded more food, the abolition of the emperor system, and the establishment of a democratic government. Turmoil envelops the political scene now that the Shidehara cabinet has fallen, and prospects for the appointment of a new prime minister remain uncertain.

"The aftereffects of war and defeat burden our nation, but we must remember that we have the Gohonzon and our faith.

As we are taught in the Lotus Sutra, where there is faith, there is peace. With this conviction to strengthen our hearts and bodies, we can march toward the great goal of spreading the true faith to all men."

After this inspiring message, everyone joined in singing "Song of the Comrades." They sang it twice, three times. Moving into the street, faces glowing and eyes sparkling with tears of happiness, they continued to talk cheerfully as they walked toward the train station. As they dispersed, Toda told them jokingly that they had just had their own demonstration of a sort and that they should all tell their families and friends about it.

On May 22, at the second leaders' meeting, Toda, acting as chairman of the board, appointed three new directors—Harayama, Konishi, and Seki—to join Toda's four original pupils, Iwamori, Honda, Fujisaki, and Kitagawa. Less than a month had passed since the first postwar meeting of the society; and though neither was large in terms of numbers, both conferences were of gigantic consequence to the religious movement that was to unfold in years to come.

For the society, things began to brighten, but Japan's political and social conditions failed to improve. On May 12, residents of Setagaya Ward, in western Tokyo, staged a demonstration in the Imperial Palace Plaza demanding more rice and asking to be told what the emperor ate. As a result of the elections of April 10, the Liberal party, led by Ichiro Hatoyama, obtained a majority. The Progressive party, under Shidehara, was second, but Socialists and Communists together captured a total of ten million votes. Although the Liberals and the Socialists agreed to form a coalition government, on May 3, just as Hatoyama was about to form a cabinet, the occupation authorities ordered him purged. Thus the political world was once again plunged into turmoil. Several people, including Kazuo Kojima, whom Toda had visited just before the end of the war, were mentioned as possibilities, but on May 13, Shigeru Yoshida, a former foreign minister, was chosen to lead the government. However, his attempt to form a cabinet was to meet many obstacles.

On May 19, the Communists made good use of the people's hunger and caused a riot in the Imperial Palace Plaza, where 250,000 workers, under the leadership of Kyuichi Tokuda, cried out for more food and an interview with the emperor. In their hysteria, the people lost all sense of pride. They staged mass riots that created a state of virtual moral anarchy. Some demonstrators carried placards bearing abusive slogans, the most notorious of which read: "I eat heartily; you may die of hunger." It was signed: "The Emperor." The author of this slogan later became a hero among the workers. The demonstrators had the support of organizations outside their own immediate associates. For example, the National Railway Workers Union ordered members employed at key stations throughout Tokyo to give all demonstrators free train rides. Rioting demonstrators flooded the streets. One group, led by Tokuda, staged a sit-down strike in front of the Liberal party headquarters, where at that moment Shigeru Yoshida was unsuccessfully trying to form a cabinet. Under pressure from the popular front, Yoshida's hopes dwindled to such an extent that by seven o'clock in the evening he had announced failure. On the following day, however, General MacArthur issued a severe warning in which he said that unless the violence and rioting were quelled he would be forced to take stringent measures. This statement crushed dreams of overthrowing the government and enabled Shigeru Yoshida to form a cabinet two days after the general's warning.

On June 11, a momentous event for the society took place: the revival of the publication of the monthly magazine *Kachi Sozo*, "Value Creation." Originally founded in July, 1941, the periodical had run to nine issues by May, 1942, when it was banned by the militarist government. The paper and printing in the early postwar issues were of poor quality, but Toda and his associates rejoiced to see this further step toward the dawn of their long-awaited religious campaign.

Other important developments soon followed. On June 22, Toda organized the Youth Division of the society; on July 3, the first anniversary of his release from prison, he convened a meeting of the leaders and the board of directors. On July 20, the Women's Division began meeting, the young men's round-table discussion meetings started on July 24, and the young men's discussion meetings began on July 27.

Though not yet the vast machine that he envisioned, the gears of the organization had begun to turn. But Toda realized two very important things. First, each gear, each tiny part of the machine, must be kept in top running order all the time if the whole is to function as it must. For this reason, he paid careful attention to the smallest details. The discussion meetings were friendly but serious. Toda would not allow compromise with other religious dogmas. He insisted that each member be equipped with a firm background of doctrinal knowledge about Nichiren Shoshu.

With this feeling, he departed from the methods employed to gain new members in the prewar society, when the philosophy of value had been the first step for new members. He insisted on the importance of the teachings of Nichiren and of the Lotus Sutra as an auxiliary, to the exclusion of all else. Once he told his audience: "This is an age requiring a powerful guiding principle, a powerful religion. Without these we will be unable to survive as happy human beings. This religion must be one that brings good fortune. Everyone desires such a faith, but nothing is more disastrous than believing in the wrong religion. There can be only one sun in the heaven, and there can be only one religion for this age and world, the religion that Sakyamuni prophesied and Nichiren Daishonin expounded. As the testimonials you hear at these meetings prove, Myoho is a universal doctrine applicable to every man, every family, and every nation. Although at first you may find these things difficult to understand, hold firm to this: Nichiren Shoshu is a great religion, and it will make you happy if you accept and believe it."

Toda's uncompromising method of conversion, based on the concepts of divine benefit and rewards, differed essentially from that of the prewar members, who had adhered to Makiguchi's philosophy of value and the concept of retribution. He was sure that, armed with a firm doctrinal discipline in Nichiren's life philosophy, his members would be better able to win new followers.

His battle was growing more intense every day, since the separation of Shinto and the state and the emperor's renunciation of divinity had left a religious vacuum in the land and thereby created conditions favorable to the sprouting of iniquitous, profit-seeking religions. It was with these fraudulent religions that Toda and his followers had to do battle in order to save the millions of innocent people being led astray. Toda redoubled his efforts toward rebuilding and strengthening the lay organization. As he trained young members, he had only one thing in mind: the spreading of the true Buddhism. He knew that he must awaken the people of Japan to the cosmic philosophy and all-embracing saving powers of Nichiren. He must prove to those yet ignorant that only by accepting Nichiren could they attain enlightenment and salvation.

Part of his campaign toward this end was reopening the summer training course formerly held yearly at Daiseki-ji but suspended since 1943. On August 7, 1946, he and twenty-nine others, among whom were seven new converts, traveled to the foot of Mount Fuji to relax in the beautiful surroundings and to study. The training course consisted of lectures on the *Gosho,* question-and-answer sessions, discussion meetings, and excursions to Shiraito Falls. Toda, aside from conducting the vital morning and evening Gongyo, which lasts two or three hours, talked with his young companions and offered them fatherly advice on personal problems. The four-day course was refreshing and rewarding, and when the group passed through the main gate on their way home they seemed to be transformed with religious assurance and joy.

Robust, pure, happy, and united in thought and purpose, these young people set out on the sun-baked road leading to the station and to their great work. As he walked along with his friends, Toda conceived an image of the group as a cluster of sacred flames in a dark wilderness: a small fire destined to spread its cleansing power.

BOOK TWO

1. TOWARD THE END OF SEPTEMBER

AUTUMN red and gold made the mountains and hills of the northern Kanto district beautiful. In farm gardens, vermilion persimmons glowed against the blue morning sky. Wild chamomile, purple and serene, and lingering evening primroses bloomed beside the road. Swaying silvery stalks of pampas grass whispered the arrival of the calm, clear days of fall. Having left the village of Kurobane early that morning, Josei Toda and a party of seven were wending their way along the old Riku-u pass, by the twisting Shirakawa and Nakagawa rivers, to the small village of Ryogo, where they were to hold a lecture meeting. This trip was the first step in a postwar rural evangelizing campaign. The small group soon left the highway to trudge along a mountain path that was characteristically unpaved, strewn with stones, and difficult to climb, even though it was only moderately steep.

The towering ranges of the brilliantly colored Nasu Highland Mountains dominated the scenery, and a column of white smoke spiraled into the clear sky from the crater of the Chausu volcano. As Toda thrilled to the peaceful landscape, he recalled the poem "The Spring View" by the Chinese poet Tu Fu:

> Even though the nation has fallen,
> The hills and rivers prevail,
> For spring has come to the castle,
> Amid lush trees and grass.

Though in a different age and place, with no sign of a castle, Toda felt in tune with the poetic images of grasses and trees. Looking back on his companions, he knew that they too, long accustomed to the hideous ravages war had wrought on Tokyo, were delighted and joyous at the beauty of the peaceful scenery sparkling with amaranths, dahlias, and China asters. As they entered a valley, from which the nearby hills obscured the view of the mountains, these newly happy people shouted and pointed to the golden persimmons and the burrlike chestnuts as if they were great discoveries. The travelers' dress was out of keeping with the scene. Toda himself was clothed in a summer suit, open-necked shirt, and an ill-fitting hunting cap; but the attire of the others varied wildly from flimsy wartime uniforms to rusty, formal black coats that contrasted bizarrely with khaki officers' trousers. The women's strange combinations included *mompe* and excessively large jackets from which their fingers sometimes peeked. The five-mile mountain road had tired Toda, and he called out to Takeo Konishi, who was leading the way: "It's been a long walk; are we there yet?"

"Almost," Konishi answered over his shoulder.

"You've been saying that all morning, but we still don't get any closer," grumbled Miss Katsu Kiyohara, who was leaning on some of the others for support.

"Konishi's idea of distance seems to be different from ours," smiled Toda. "Are you sure we're on the right road?"

"Of course," replied Konishi. "There is only one, and it is perfectly straight. I tell you we're almost there."

Toda and his party had left Tokyo at noon the previous day to conduct the three-day guidance program that the Soka Gakkai headquarters had decided to hold in the provinces from September twenty-first through the twenty-third, during the important autumnal equinox holiday. The areas chosen were the village of Ryogo, in Tochigi Prefecture, and Kiryu, in Gumma Prefecture. In both places, members of both the society and another Nichiren Shoshu sect had been carrying out membership drives during the year that had passed since the end of the war.

In those days trains were scarce, and passenger control was in effect at all stations. Toda and his friends had been forced to stand in line for nearly twelve hours at Ueno Station in order to obtain tickets. Even after buying them, they stood up most of the way, because the trains were packed with black-market peddlers and people in search of the food that was more readily available in rural areas than in town. A strange collection of people, including many repatriated soldiers, filled the coaches, hung from the boarding-platform handrails, and even clung to the front of the locomotive. To allow the hordes to get on and off at local stations, the trains had to make long stops; and when they did, the strong odors of sweat, breath, and too many people in a small place became overpowering. The dark and desperate faces of the passengers seemed to mirror the gloom of postwar Japan.

Though exhausted from the trip, Toda was able to say a prayer for his group and to offer a word of gratitude for the bright, vital faces of his friends. There stood Miss Kiyohara, flushed but smiling. Yuzo Mishima was animatedly talking with a stranger, and Konishi and Seki were engaged in conversation over the shoulders of other passengers. Affection for these brave people filled Toda's heart, especially since he knew that they had been forced to economize to scrape together the money for the trip. The society was not yet in a position to finance such expeditions. Toda thought: "Though we look like scavengers and ragpickers, we are the vanguard of the Buddha's force."

At sundown, at Nishi-nasuno Station, they changed to a local line, which took them to Kurobane. There they stayed in a riverside inn, where they were able to relax and enjoy the murmur of the clear Nakagawa river and the exhilarating freshness of the mountain air.

After dinner, a maid brought in a special treat, a large plate of steamed corn. Biting into a golden ear of it, Toda smiled as reminiscences of home flooded his mind. Corn, the sweet tender corn of his native Hokkaido, had been part of his childhood. He had often nibbled it as he read the works of Byron, Napoleon, the prominent educator Yukichi Fukuzawa, and the statesman Taisuke Itagaki that had helped form his young mind, just as the salt air and leaden skies of his home on the cold Bay of Otaru had tempered his young body. So clearly did the corn bring back his fishing-village home of Atsuta that he began to describe it to his friends. Although the population was usually only about ten thousand, it rose to thirty thousand during the herring season, between April and July. Then millions of silver fish racing to the beach to spawn turned the waves gleaming white. Everyone who could take time off from regular work participated in the catch. Toda's father, who was a seafood dealer, made a point of taking part each year. And how delicious the fresh herring were! Carried away with the excitement of the memory and especially the nostalgic recollection of fresh, baked fish, Toda continued with abandon till he suddenly caught himself. "We always end up talking about food," he remarked wryly, to his companions' amusement.

When the little group arrived in Ryogo, the villagers mistook them for food scavengers from the city. Later, after noticing that Toda and his friends had neither the sacks nor the desperate, rapacious faces of most people from the cities but were instead cheerful and disciplined, the local people began to wonder who the visitors might be. However, they had already been announced, as Konishi proudly pointed out when he saw a crude poster tacked to an electric pole.

"Look at that," he exclaimed. "Now I know we're here."

MR. JOSEI TODA IS COMING! HE WILL GIVE A LECTURE ON THE LOTUS SUTRA AT 2 P.M., SEPTEMBER 22, AT RYOGO ELEMENTARY SCHOOL

"That's the work of the Masuda family," said Miss Kiyohara. "We must give them all the help and moral support we can. They're our first rural guidance team since the war."

Amused by the boldness of the poster, Toda grinned and said: "I'll bet they've never heard of Josei Toda around here, but I do hope they'll come in big numbers, even if it's only out of curiosity."

The group proceeded toward the Masuda farmhouse, and when they drew near it, Konishi announced: "Here we are. I told you it wasn't far."

"I certainly am glad," said Toda. "I never thought we'd make it."

"Five miles indeed," teased one.

"More like fifty if you ask me," chimed in another.

Hearing the chatter, the Masuda family came out to greet Toda and his party.

Kyuichiro Masuda, who had once been a police officer in Tokyo, joined Soka Kyoiku Gakkai while Makiguchi was president. He retired from police service before the war began and joined a business firm, where he remained until bombings made Tokyo uninhabitable. Then, after purchasing a home in his native village of Ryogo, he evacuated his family to it in May, 1944. His family consisted of his wife, two daughters, and his elder daughter's husband. Both of his daughters taught at the village elementary school; his son-in-law had become a farmer. After the war ended, Masuda himself left Tokyo to help work his small farm. Because both he and his son-in-law lacked experience, the villagers laughed at their clumsy initial efforts. Indeed, many obstacles made their task very difficult; but with the strength and determination granted them by the Gohonzon, to which they prayed morning and night, they persevered.

However, times got worse before they got better. In the summer of 1946 a drought threatened to wipe out even the skilled farmers. What would it do to poor sixty-year-old Masuda and his city-bred family? Nevertheless, these people, the only believers in Nichiren Shoshu in their neighborhood, were determined that with the help of their faith they would reap a good harvest, even under apparently hopeless circumstances. Day and night Kyuichiro prayed. He chanted the Daimoku, even while hoeing, as energetically as if he were determined to produce fire from moist wood and water from parched earth. The mocking villagers labeled him a madman, but one day his prayers were answered in the form of a life-giving rainfall.

Overjoyed and reconfirmed in their faith, the Masudas began to teach all those around them the wonderworking power of the Gohonzon, and before long their neighbors came to respect them for their efforts and unwavering belief. Their history reflects Nichiren's teaching: "The Mystic Law does not spread by itself, but when propagated by believers, both the Law and its adherents radiate greatness and glory."

In late July of 1946, the Masudas learned to their joy that the society had gotten a new start under the leadership of Josei Toda. On a trip to the school where she taught, Konishi, then a director of the society, met Masuda's daughter Naoe. They had met in Tokyo before the war, and she remembered him immediately. Happy to see a fellow believer in her remote village, Naoe said: "You are Mr. Konishi, aren't you?" Konishi did not recall her at once. He soon did, however, and they had a cheerful reunion in the school courtyard. When she returned home in the evening, the delighted Naoe described the meeting to her family and told them everything she had heard about the society's present activities, including the summer training course.

Because both of them were eager to catch up on all the society was doing, Naoe and her sister Masako went to Tokyo immediately after the school closed in the early summer. They visited fellow members and attended Toda's lectures on the Lotus Sutra, which made a profound impression on them. In time, Naoe was introduced to Toda, who gave her special guidance. She then told him of the difficulty of winning new members in her village, where there were no other believers in Nichiren Shoshu. In spite of their efforts, so far they had made no headway in their missionary work. Realizing the depth of her concern over her neighbors, Toda promised to go to her village to help her and her family. Overjoyed with the exciting news, the Masuda sisters hurried home to tell their parents that Ryogo was to be the first village Toda would visit on his new rural membership campaign. It might also become the heart of a sacred flame that would carry the true Buddhism all over the country.

Fired with new zeal, the two sisters visited from door to door in their eagerness to convert their neighbors. Out of deference to them, most of the people on whom they called listened patiently; but few understood the message, and none resolved to follow the path of Nichiren. The villagers found the talk too difficult but sensed that the sisters were sincerely devoted to their faith. Several days later, when the Masuda family learned that Toda and his party would arrive in Ryogo on September twenty-second they were proud to be able to offer their home to the top leaders of the society, though they were disappointed and embarrassed that so far they had failed to convert a single villager. They discussed the situation together. Whereas the younger Masako was overjoyed at the prospect of the lectures, Naoe was worried.

"I thought there would be only a few of the leaders, but a whole party of them is coming. What shall I do?"

The women continued to discuss the matter in perplexity. Kyuichiro, who had been listening in silence, finally spoke up: "This is a great opportunity, and we must be grateful for it instead of worrying."

Unconvinced, Naoe said: "Suppose no one comes to the lecture? These important leaders are coming all the way from Tokyo."

"Yes, we've done our best," Masako said, "but no one responds to our invitations. Father, I am afraid you don't understand the situation."

"I understand this," said the unperturbed Kyuichiro, "if we are sincere and pray to the Gohonzon, the villagers will respond."

Moved and encouraged by their father's words, the girls agreed to renew their efforts, and everyone else in the family promised to help. The sisters prayed constantly and put up posters, not only in Ryogo but in other distant villages, as well.

Their advertising campaign explained the large number of crude but direct signs Toda and his party saw all along the way to the Masuda's house.

The lecture on the Lotus Sutra began promptly at 2:00 P.M., on September 22, in the tatami-floored sewing classroom of the village elementary school. There were eighty people in the audience. By way of an opening address, Kyuichiro Masuda made a few remarks. Standing tall and erect among the people seated on the floor, he said that he deplored the ruination of Japan and that the only way to save the country and her people was through faith in the teachings of Nichiren. His impassioned tone at once surprised and interested his audience, some of whom had been nonchalantly chatting or smoking. But his speech was brief, and after a slight pause he presented the speakers for the day. There was scattered applause. Konishi was first, with the topic "Recognition and Evaluation." He introduced himself by saying that though born the son of a farmer he had, by some strange quirk of fate, become a teacher. He went on:

"We are often asked what the purpose of life is. Scholars and academicians say that its purpose is the pursuit of truth, by which they probably mean such things as the discovery that the earth revolves around the sun. But many others ask: 'What practical value does such knowledge have?' This question implies that human beings are always seeking value and that abstract truths in themselves are valueless.

"The purpose of life is the pursuit of happiness, or the quest for value. Recognition and evaluation are often confused because we tend to equate truth and value. The first person to point out the mistake in this approach and to establish a philosophical system of value was the late Tsunesaburo Makiguchi, the first president of our society. He made it clear that things assume true value only when they come into contact with or make an impact upon our daily lives and sensory perceptions. However, he also cautioned us against attempting to evaluate things without recognizing or understanding them fully.

Correct evaluation, in other words, depends on correct recognition. I have brought up this topic in order to prepare you for the discussion of the teachings of Nichiren Daishonin, which my colleague Josei Toda will present later."

After Konishi left the platform, Hisao Seki rose to speak: "Continuing the train of thought begun by my colleague,

I should like to say first that human happiness depends on both the amount and the nature of the value we create. Kant says that the supreme values are truth, goodness, and beauty; but our teacher Mr. Makiguchi showed that this conception is mistaken. Since it can be recognized but cannot be created, truth has no independent value. Mr. Makiguchi's revolutionary system established goodness, beauty, and gain as the three greatest values of human life. He further taught that values arise only in man's subjective relations with his environment. For example, knowing how to produce rice is a good thing, but it will not ease the pangs of hunger as the rice itself can.

"Mr. Makiguchi also taught us that three negative values exist as well. These are ugliness, evil, and loss. The positive values make life happy; the negative ones make it wretched. Values arise only in relationships between man and his exterior environment. For that reason, a life manifesting the positive values indicates harmony with the outer world. Conversely, a life marked by the negative values is one of discord with its surroundings. The kind of life a person leads, then, becomes the most important issue. This is where religion enters the picture because the fundamental purpose and problem of religion is the exploration of the mystery of human life.

"Now there are both true and false religions, and it goes without saying that selection of religion determines human destiny because only a true religion can bring happiness. Nichiren Daishonin declared that false religions lie at the root of all misfortune and that this principle applies to all men, all families, all nations. Japan's defeat in World War II and her postwar misfortunes stem directly from the false nature of Shinto.

"The staggering task of reconstruction, which we face right now, can only be accomplished successfully if we take into account the fundamental problems of human life. Only faith in a true religion can help us solve these problems. Our colleague Miss Kiyohara will explain what true religion is and how we can practice it when she speaks next on the topic 'Purification of Life.'"

The audience applauded politely when Seki left the platform. When the small and unprepossessing Miss Kiyohara began her talk, the villagers were puzzled to find a woman in the speaker's place. Many of the women in the audience exchanged suspicious and disapproving glances. Nevertheless, Miss Kiyohara began:

"I am nervous, and what is more, I am not a good speaker. But I will begin my remarks by stating my conclusion, so there will be no misunderstanding when I finish."

She smiled, and the audience muffled its laughter.

"We can only attain happiness if we lead pure lives." As she overcame her initial stage fright and began to deal with a subject about which she felt very deeply, Miss Kiyohara gained confidence. Her assurance was reflected in her voice and manner.

"True purification can only be the result of faith, and faith can only grow from practice and experience, because it is much more than a mere idea. Only the practice of true faith can purify human life, but what is true religion?"

At this point she gave a brief history of Buddhism. She pointed out the supremacy of the Lotus Sutra in the hierarchy of the teachings of Sakyamuni, the historical Buddha. She then went on to outline the state of Buddhism in the final, decadent Latter Day of the Law and talked about the teachings of Nichiren and the importance of Nam-myoho-renge-kyo, the prevailing article of faith in that period.

"Many people today labor under the misconception that only the teachings of Sakyamuni embody the true Buddhism. For them, real faith is dead. They rely on faith only at times of funerals and memorial services. They don't even try to understand the Mystic Law of Nichiren Daishonin. Modern man's greatest misfortune is his refusal to understand the meanings of the true Law. As there are no two suns in the heaven, so there is only one true Buddhism, the Three Great Secret Laws of Nichiren Shoshu, the one orthodox sect that has preserved the true essence of Buddhism that it inherited almost seven centuries ago.

"Once I was a bitterly unhappy, disillusioned woman—perhaps more so than any of you—but today I am joyful because of my faith. And I will remain happy as long as I live. Each of us can achieve the purification of life that brings joy if we have faith in the Gohonzon, which is the essence of Buddhism."

Although Miss Kiyohara's obvious devotion to her faith won applause from many, there were still some skeptical faces when she left the platform.

The next person to speak was Mrs. Take Sakata, a chubby, middle-aged housewife, who walked timidly to the platform and bowed deeply to the audience. Sensing her shyness, Toda applauded warmly to encourage her; the others followed suit. But after a faltering start, Mrs. Sakata fell silent in embarrassment and fright. "Easy does it," whispered Toda. Taking heart, she began again:

"I would like to tell you about my experiences. My family ran a small steel plant. During the war we made munitions. When I was converted to Nichiren Shoshu, my whole family opposed it violently. My husband even threatened to divorce me. I was an orphan and had been unhappy all my life, but my new faith gave me peace and happiness. At home I had no one to talk to about it. I suffered all kinds of hardships and mental persecution, but I clung to my faith. Then, in one year, eight of the people who had been against my conversion died, miserable and impoverished. When my maid saw the terrible consequences of making fun of the true Buddhism she became frightened. She too was soon converted to the faith, but not my husband. He continued to oppose my religion, but his life gradually took a turn for the worse until he became very unhappy. I wanted to save him and our marriage, so I prayed sincerely for him. But I had to do so in silence. Finally, in June, 1942, my husband saw the light and accepted Nichiren Shoshu. I was so overcome with joy that I wept before the Gohonzon. That was the most unforgettable day of my life."

Mrs. Sakata paused to dab her eyes with a handkerchief; the villagers were clearly moved by this woman's simple story of suffering and triumphant faith. She continued:

"I'm no speaker, but I will do the best I can. As I had expected, after my husband accepted the faith, our factory began to prosper. Soon, the air raids began. Bombs often fell on our neighborhood and turned everything into a sea of flames. Still, we all knelt and prayed before the Gohonzon, and sometimes when it was too dangerous to stay at home, we sought shelter somewhere else but we always took our Gohonzon with us. I was easily upset and frightened before, but during that whole awful period my faith gave me courage to organize my own family and to become a leader in the neighborhood. All our neighbors came to count on me. We fought the fires together, and there were many of them. In fact, by the end of the war, Kamata, where I live, was reduced to a charred ruin. But our house and six neighboring houses escaped unharmed. In all that burned area, only our few houses stood. And it was all thanks to the Gohonzon.

"Not only that, but after the war our factory continued to do well. We used our house for discussions among believers in Nichiren Shoshu. Now I know in my heart that the Gohonzon protects us wherever we are and whatever happens. I believe that all people who do not have the Gohonzon to rely on are very unfortunate."

With a quick bow, the timid Mrs. Sakata left the platform, but the audience responded with great warmth. Obviously they believed the artless sincerity of her story and the wisdom she had acquired through unpretentious devotion and daily faith. She did not theorize; she spoke in terms of everyday experiences. This is the kind of thing that truly moves people.

Toda saw that human experiences are the most powerful tool for converting people to the faith. Theories, learned arguments, and doctrines interest bookish people, but not the masses. He began to understand that it was a mistake to use too much sophisticated dogma in speeches to audiences of uninitiated people. The beneficial power of the Gohonzon cannot be understood by means of theory alone; it must be grasped through the actual practice of faith and through experience. Similarly, faith in the teachings of Nichiren is, above all, a real experience, not an empty theory. The universal propagation of true Buddhism can be effected only if the masses see the everyday grace of Nichiren's teaching. Toda felt keenly that it was time to modify the society's methods of winning members.

Next, Koichi Harayama spoke on the establishment of faith, and Yuzo Mishima followed with remarks on the way he had sought value. Both of them related their own turbulent pasts and emphasized the help of the Myoho, without which they would have been defeated in their struggles for survival. Finally the moderator announced that Josei Toda would speak on the topic "There Is No Buddhism in Japan Today."

The shouts of children playing outside the building had long ago died. Stillness filled the air and the western sun threw shafts of gold light into the room as the audience concentrated on the tall, lean man, who rose, placed his hands on the lectern, and began explaining the ten states of human life:

"Man exists in one of the ten human states, *jikkai,* at any given moment, which range from hell, through rapacity, animality, anger, tranquillity, rapture, learning, absorption, and the Bodhisattva nature, to Buddhahood. Hell is the state of infernal sufferings both in the mind and the body. Rapacity is the state of being dominated by various desires. Animality is the state of ignoring the fundamental moral principles and abandoning oneself to beastly instincts. Anger is the state of being angry, acrimonious, and contentious. Tranquillity is a peaceful, tranquil, meditative state. Rapture is the state of happiness and joy one experiences when aspirations and wishes have been fulfilled. Learning is the state of intellectual pursuit and enjoyment. Absorption is the state of perceiving truth intuitively in natural phenomena. The Bodhisattva nature is the state of compassion, wisdom, sincerity, and of striving toward happiness and enlightenment for others. Buddhahood is the supreme state of enlightenment."

Toda continued: "Furthermore, the entire universe and all its phenomena are constantly in one of these states. Obviously, everyone prefers a good state—that is happiness—to a bad one. But wishing alone is never enough to make us happy. True religion, on the other hand, has the power to give us vitality and set us on the right road. At the risk of his life, Nichiren Daishonin taught that we cannot attain lasting happiness by means of our own unaided will. We must have an object of worship strong enough to set in motion the Buddha nature inherent in all men. The one object that can do this is the Dai-Gohonzon, which, by means of the power of its Myoho, can change ugliness into beauty, evil into goodness, and loss into gain. It alone can fill our lives with manifestations of the everlasting Buddhahood. This is the true significance of the advent of Nichiren Daishonin, the True Buddha of the Latter Day of the Law, the period we are now living in."

Toda's sincerity and conviction of the truth of his faith moved the audience, especially when he said that the hellish conditions suffered by Japan were the result of the nation's having slandered Nichiren's Buddhism for seven hundred years. He continued:

"I am deeply grieved by the state of our nation at present because, if we are to recover from the crippling blows we have suffered, we must have a truly practical philosophy. Philosophy without practical application is only playing with ideas. Today we Japanese are faced with the necessity of selecting a true faith. Belief in Shinto obviously led to failure.

"Now, as false cults and destructive Communist ideas delude the people, Soka Gakkai is endeavoring to contribute to rehabilitation by practicing the philosophy of Nichiren Daishonin. In order to rise again as a peace-loving nation, Japan requires a true religion and a rational philosophy that can be beneficial to all fields: politics, economy, and culture. Nichiren Daishonin's Buddhism meets the nation's urgent spiritual need, and the Gohonzon is the very basis of that Buddhism.

"Although the Dai-Gohonzon has existed at Daiseki-ji, the head temple of Nichiren Shoshu, for the past seven hundred years, most of the Japanese people have either ignored it or refused to devote attention to it. I am sure that most of you are now hearing about the Dai-Gohonzon for the very first time, but it is my fervent prayer that you will believe in it and bask in its compassion and blessings for the sake of the nation as well as that of yourselves and your families."

His message and the power with which he delivered it created a profound silence among his listeners until the moderator announced a period of questions.

"Sir, will you please explain the relation between the Lotus Sutra and democracy?" asked a young man.

After saying that he thought the question a good one, Toda explained: "It is only natural that democracy should be a topic of frequent discussion now that the end of the war has brought about so many changes. Because the Japanese suffered bitterly under a totalitarian military dictatorship, we now realize that sovereignty must rest with the people. The three democratic principles, freedom, equality, and philanthropy, are fine. I am all for them. But viewed in the light of Nichiren Daishonin's philosophy, democracy is less than perfect because it embodies only part of the truth. Though originally a Greek idea, democracy has been deeply influenced by Christian philosophy, which fails to clarify the vital law of karma and the three existences of past, present, and future. Democracy deals only with the present. Of course social systems and political structures are important to mankind, but they pale in the face of the problems of true spiritual freedom and ultimate destiny. Western democracy limits itself because of its failure to take these things into consideration.

"Only the Buddhism of Nichiren Daishonin has the power to purify present life and solve problems of the past and future, and true democracy is impossible until these problems are settled. Western democracy, because of its strong Christian leanings, is spiritual and idealistic. So-called peoples' democracies, on the other hand, are usually materialistic. It goes without saying that both approaches are only partial. Buddhist democracy, based on Nichiren Daishonin's philosophy, is complete because it is neither idealistic nor materialistic and because it teaches the oneness of mind and matter, of body and spirit; therefore, only through its teachings is it possible to establish democracy in the fullest sense. Perhaps you will see my meaning more clearly if you study this question for a while on your own."

"I think I understand now, sir," said the naive young man.

Toda replied with a smile: "I wonder. If you do, you are quick indeed." The audience laughed.

Questions followed one after another, all of them serious, some of them critical. Toda answered them with conviction and sometimes with wit. The discussion period promised to go on much longer, but the moderator cut it short at five o'clock. He announced that Toda would hold another similar period at the Masuda house beginning at seven in the evening. After thanking the villagers for their interest and attendance, Toda and his party went out into the cool autumn air and the fiery red of the sunset.

At the Masuda house, after a cheerful dinner and evening Gongyo, everyone chatted merrily over tea and an after-dinner snack of the steamed corn that Toda loved. Later, the villagers began to arrive for the discussion meeting. After a lively question-and-answer period and some quiet person-to-person conversations, the first convert was introduced to Toda. He was the young man—a schoolteacher of twenty, as it turned out—who had asked Toda the question about democracy and the Lotus Sutra. Two aged farmers seemed anxious to join Nichiren Shoshu, but for a while they hesitated. The idea of discarding other deeply ingrained traditional forms of worship worried them. Soon, however, they were won over. Finally, a lively seventeen-year-old girl came forth voluntarily to accept the faith. These four converts heartened Toda and his party and overjoyed old Masuda, whose cheeks flushed with happiness as he ordered his wife to bring out all the good food they had in the house. He wanted to have a feast in celebration. And he himself left immediately to go to the barn for a bottle of his own home-brewed sakè.

Soon everyone was chattering happily over a table laden with rustic delicacies—steamed pumpkin and potatoes, roasted eggplant, wild grapes, chestnuts, pickled vegetables, burdock root braised in a rich sauce of soy and sesame, fresh river fish, and the sakè. First Toda suggested that someone sing a song, then the festivities got under way in earnest. There were dances, folk songs, and laughter. They sang the bright and popular "Apple Song," which was written after the war in an attempt to cheer a downhearted and gloomy nation. Toda himself danced a noble and graceful traditional dance. Amid singing and laughter the evening wore on. It was well past midnight when Toda at last reluctantly said good night because he and his party had to be on their way at 4:30 the next morning. After the new converts and their friends departed, only the chirping of the crickets disturbed the silence of the night.

At four o'clock the following chilly morning, Toda and his

party, accompanied by the Masuda sisters, started for Kurobane. In the dark the rugged road was especially trying for Toda because of his poor eyesight; before long he had slipped into a stream. He was wet up to his thighs. In alarm, Miss Kiyohara and Mrs. Sakata rushed to help him, but he calmed their fears by joking: "Lucky it wasn't the night-soil pit." As

the group at last neared their destination, the sky was turning pearl gray with dawn. The younger Masuda sister, Masako, came up to Toda and whispered: "Mr. Toda."

She seemed to want to say something but hesitated.

"What is it?" Toda asked encouragingly.

"Mr. Toda. I want to go back to Tokyo."

"But why? Oh, I think I see. It has something to do with marriage, doesn't it?"

Surprised that Toda read her thoughts so easily, Masako blushed and nodded.

"Don't be impatient, Masako. It isn't always necessary to go long distances to find happiness."

"But, Mr. Toda, I've been in this village for three years now. Oh, I've had several marriage offers, but none of them was suitable. I'm afraid I'll never find a husband in the country. I'll have to go back to Tokyo for that."

Like many girls of her generation, Masako's coming of age had coincided with the dark years of the war. Now she was disturbed because she felt that her chances for marriage were dwindling, especially if she remained in the remote Nasu Mountains.

"So you think that by coming to Tokyo you can find the right man?"

"I think so."

"You're wrong. No good will come of hurrying an important thing like marriage." Toda's voice was firm, and, disappointed, Masako hung her head. Toda went on: "Devote your whole heart to your faith, and someday—I can't say when or how, but someday—the ideal person for you will come along. It makes no difference where you are; faith, not the place where you live, determines what will happen. If this were not true, the Gohonzon would be deceiving us. Isn't that so?"

Toda knew that the best way to console and assist with personal problems was to apply the Myoho, and for this reason, as he took the girl's hand, he said gently: "Be brave. Your hometown is where you are needed now. Devote yourself to the faith, and everything will work out all right." The young Masuda girl said no more, but the depth of Toda's advice brought gentle, warming tears to her eyes.

The sky continued to brighten as the sun mounted the sky. The little party arrived at Kurobane Station just in time for the six o'clock train. In a flurry of thanks and farewells to the Masuda sisters, Toda and the others boarded. As the train pulled out of the station, Miss Kiyohara and Mrs. Sakata waved their handkerchiefs out the window until the Masuda girls were out of sight. Then, worn out—they had not slept the night before—all the party but Toda fell sound asleep. He watched range after range of mountains filling the northern horizon and the plains swaying with silvery pampas and dotted here and there with gilded autumn trees. And as he drank in the beauty he fell into meditation, thinking:

"If I walk steadily and without faltering, there is no physical mountain, no matter how high, that I cannot scale. But what about the mountains of trouble, the great obstacles that stand in the way of the spreading of the true faith? What are those mountains like? How many raging rivers of difficulty and strife must we ford before we reach our goal? What demons dwell in those mountains? In this weekend tour we are taking our first steps, but the road ahead is long and strewn with obstacles. Demons lurk everywhere."

Toda realized the difficulty of his task, but he was not afraid. He recalled his own faith-giving vision of Nichiren and quietly chanted the Daimoku to himself.

After several changes of trains, the little group at last reached the city of Kiryu, where a few friends greeted them and took them to the house of Mr. Miyata, an old and staunch follower of Nichiren. During the war, Miyata's house, which stood near the main street of the city, had been the scene of frequent discussion meetings that had helped the believers keep their faith burning bright in dark times. There was also a small Nichiren Shoshu temple in the city; therefore, Toda had expected a better reception than he found. To his disappointment, when he began Gongyo at Miyata's house, he learned that few of the local leaders were able to read the Sutra. After a subsequent discussion meeting at the house of a new society member named Mizuta, Toda strongly sensed that something was wrong with the faith in Kiryu. He said as much to Yuzo Mishima and suggested that Kiryu would need frequent visits and close guidance for several years. At the conclusion of the discussion meeting, Toda announced his personal intention to achieve the universal propagation of true Buddhism and called on all those present to follow him in this supreme task. Many, realizing the vital importance of the task, began to sense their roles in it; one newcomer decided to accept this faith.

This was the end of the first postwar rural guidance tour. It was a modest undertaking, but the results had been encouraging. This trip was to pave the way for a great spreading of the faith throughout rural Japan. Finally the meetings were over, but Toda's group of fellow members had one more trying ordeal to face before they could lay their heads on the comfortable pillows of home.

The day spent in Kiryu had fallen on the autumnal equinox holiday, and the trains were overflowing with food-seekers from the city who had seized their brief leisure to scour the countryside for whatever they could find to augment their meager diets. The train was so crowded that even angry and frustrated people who might have picked fights over very petty issues could not do so: there was no room to fight. By the time the train heaved into Asakusa Station in Tokyo, Toda's legs were numb with weariness.

2. OVERTURE

LIKE A great flowing river, the times of mankind are perpetually changing. One great alteration occurred in Japan on November 3, 1946, with the promulgation of a new constitution declaring that the emperor is a symbol of the state and of the unity of the nation and that his position devolves from the will of the people. Not only did this important document remove the emperor from a position of divinity, it also took an even more momentous step by renouncing both war and all war potential. Article Nine says that the Japanese people forever renounce war as a sovereign right of the nation and the threat or use of force as a means of settling international disputes. It adds that land, sea, and air forces will not be maintained and that the right of belligerency on the part of the state will not be recognized. It is doubtful that Prime Minister Shidehara or even General Douglas MacArthur realized the true import of the new constitution, but Josei Toda, lying in bed one morning enjoying his early hours of clearest thinking and taking quiet pleasure in the scurrying of the rats overhead—their presence indicated a better store of food in the larder—thought about the document and knew in his heart what it meant to himself, those round him, and the entire country.

Clearly the constitution was idealistic. Shidehara and his group were concerned with the preservation of the imperial family at all costs. They gave little thought to the true democratization of Japan; for them the constitution was a compromise to an end. But Toda saw immediately that the document promised a new era for Japan if a system could be found to put it into effective practice.

To be sure, the true pacifism promised in Article Nine of the constitution never became a reality, but peace was nonetheless the fervent aspiration of a people who had suffered the full horror of war. Fulfilling this great hope was a task of the greatest importance, but to accomplish it the nation required a completely new political concept. Neither communistic nor capitalistic ideas would do, nor, for that matter, would a theoretical synthesis of the two. A concept based on the life philosophy of Nichiren was essential. Toda was convinced that only when Japan followed a policy based on the life philosophy taught by Nichiren would true pacifism be proclaimed to the whole world. Such a political climate would do something even more important: it would pave the way to the global propagation of the true Buddhist faith and the resultant salvation of mankind and the harmonious fusion of Buddhism with all aspects of human society.

Perceiving that the time was ripe for bold action, Toda renewed his vow to strive tirelessly for the spreading of the faith. As the writings of Nichiren teach: "It is as certain that the true faith will someday achieve universal propagation as it is that an arrow aimed at the earth is certain to hit its mark."

Toda knew this, but at that time he was the only person who did. He also realized that though the goal is great and perhaps distant the only way to reach it is to deal immediately with the problem of the moment; and at that moment, Toda had several problems. First he faced the imminent third memorial service for Tsunesaburo Makiguchi and, equally important, the first postwar general meeting of the society. Early rumors had it that hundreds of people from all over Japan would attend this meeting. Thinking these things over carefully as he lay in bed, Toda prepared himself to face the great day.

On November seventeenth, in the old auditorium of the Education Hall in Kanda, retired high priest Nichiko Hori

presided over the third memorial service in honor of the late Tsunesaburo Makiguchi. A photograph of this great man, hanging in the middle of the platform, moved many in the audience to tears, especially as the services brought back memories of their leader and of his martyrdom. At the end of the solemn ritual, as the heady fragrance of incense lingered in the air, Toda introduced the first man to make a memorial speech, the seventy-nine-year-old high priest Nichiko Hori, a small, vigorous man with bushy white eyebrows.

"Old as I am, I made the long trip to Tokyo without hesitation when I heard that the faithful followers of late President

Makiguchi were planning a ceremony to commemorate his tragic death. Your sincerity and devotion to his memory move me deeply.

"Although time forbids my talking at length about my personal relations with President Makiguchi or about my connections with Soka Gakkai, I feel impelled to say this: with great compassion, Nichiren Daishonin courageously remonstrated with the state for neglecting true Buddhism, and he preached the benefits of the Gohonzon. Now, I am convinced that until the very end Mr. Makiguchi obeyed the teachings of Nichiren Daishonin and that he never wavered in his determination to spread the faith in true Buddhism.

"I think the commentary of Chang-an, a disciple of T'ien-t'ai the Great, on the teachings of Sakyamuni's final sermon—embodied in the Nirvana Sutra—is pertinent to a discussion of Mr. Makiguchi because it deals with the disciples' faith after the historical Buddha passed from this earth into the blessed state. 'To be an uncompassionate friend is to be an enemy, but to cleanse a man of his evil is the act of a parent.' This means that those who remain indifferent to the slandering of the true Buddhism are false disciples. No one could have said this of Mr. Makiguchi. Though a layman, he strove harder than many priests for the propagation of the faith and the realization of the will of Nichiren Daishonin. Yet he died the death of a martyr at the hands of hostile authorities. This is not an unusual thing, for in all ages those who love humanity with a pure mind and true compassion are often hated and persecuted by those in power. Nichiren Daishonin's Buddhism has a long history of martyrdoms, much of which I have described in an account of religious persecutions at Atsuhara and in a later book about the trials of the followers of Nichiren Daishonin throughout the history of our group. The Atsuhara incident, in which three peasant brothers were barbarously beheaded in Kamakura in 1280 for attempting to convert people to the faith, is only one of a long list. Thousands of laymen and priests in all parts of

Japan have met similar fates, but the point that must be underscored is that all of us are called upon to give our best to the faith. The martyrs of the distant past and President Makiguchi have made the supreme sacrifice. Our duty is to devote ourselves to the spread of the true faith for the sake of society, this country, and all mankind. In attempting to do this, each of you will leave his name in the sacred sea of the true Buddhism."

As Nichiko Hori returned to his seat, many of the older members of the audience reflected on the life and works of that distinguished scholar and great man of faith. Born in Kyushu in 1867 and converted to Nichiren Shoshu in 1885, when he was only eighteen, Hori later compiled the monumental 134-volume *Complete Works of the Studies of Nichiren Shoshu*, containing discussions of all existing teachings and dogmas and interpretations of the True Buddha's thought. In this work Hori clarified beyond all doubt the right of Nichiren Shoshu to be called the only truly orthodox branch of Buddhism. Not only did this book establish Hori as a masterly scholar, it also irrefutably fixed the position of Nichiren and gave Soka Gakkai a firm theoretical foundation for its great work of universal propagation of the faith. Without Hori and his scholarship, the movement might have been delayed fifty years.

Following the speech of the retired high priest, another priest and an intimate associate of Makiguchi, Taiei Horigome, spoke of his emotions on attending the ceremony. During a few moments of reminiscences of past experiences with Makiguchi and their studies of Buddhist literature, he said that Makiguchi and his probing of the question of value had penetrated to the very heart of vital issues. After Horigome, Nittatsu Hosoi spoke about the anti-Buddhist activities of violent exponents of Shintoism—for example, Norinaga Moto-ori and Atsutane Hirata—and commented on the prejudices that their attitudes had spawned against Nichiren. In conclusion, he remarked pointedly: "Japan was defeated by Shintoism, and the thoughts of Shinto scholars still poison the land. It is now your duty and mine to prepare ourselves for the great propagation of the faith by study of and meditation on the true meaning of Buddhism and by attempting to follow in the footsteps of President Makiguchi."

After the gratifying comments of three of the most distinguished priests in all Nichiren Shoshu, many of the faithful rose to testify to their debt to the late leader and to speak of the dire consequences of backsliding that many of them had experienced during the grueling war years. At last Josei Toda rose to speak, but instead of turning to the audience, he addressed himself to the photograph of Makiguchi in the intimate tones used between close friends:

"The last time I saw you, in September, 1943, when they took you from the Metropolitan Police Office to the Sugamo Detention House, I was too angry at the injustice of what was happening to do more than say: 'Take care of yourself.' You nodded silently, but in your face I saw boundless courage and compassion. Not long after, when I followed you to the detention house, I prayed morning and night that you would be released. I knew you were old and in poor health. You could not stand the rigors of prison life.

"Then, when, on January 8, 1945, they told me you had passed away, shock and sorrow crushed me. You, my guiding light for so many years, were gone."

Toda's stifled sob was echoed by many of those listening to him. He composed himself and went on in a stronger voice:

"You were no longer on this earth, but your love lived on to work wonders in many hearts. Your infinite compassion had allowed me to accompany you even to prison. There, inspired by the concept of the inseparability of master and disciple, as taught in the Lotus Sutra, I read and reread the Sutra until its profound meanings gradually became clear to me.

"Because I am conscious of my unworthiness and lack of talent, I have long hesitated to become your successor. But now I pledge myself anew to the attainment of the supreme goal for which you died: the universal spreading of our faith. This I am determined to accomplish before I join you someday in the Land of Buddha."

Lifted on the wave of Toda's enthusiasm, the audience carried the mood of happy tension with them when, after an hour's intermission, the first general meeting of the newly renamed Soka Gakkai began. Of all the fresh starts made after the end of the war none was more splendid in human meaning than this, for, completely untainted by motives of self-seeking greed, it was devoted entirely to the development of harmonious unity between the clergy and the laity, and the masters and their disciples. After a brief opening message and a longer report by Naosaku Kitagawa on the recent activities of the society, an announcement was made of the new organizational structure. Nine departments, including General Affairs and Study, had been established; their officers were introduced to the gathering. This was followed by the notice of the formation of fifteen local chapters, ten in metropolitan Tokyo and five in rural areas. It was explained that during their membership campaigns Toda and his co-workers had added two hundred new converts to the membership. In short, only one year after the conclusion of the war, the society was steadily moving toward rehabilitation and rejuvenation.

The good news infected the audience with enthusiasm for progress. They greeted each announcement of advance with loud applause. But Toda felt a nagging fear that the heat of fervor might cool when the members were away from the direct influence of the society leaders. After all, the *Gosho* teaches that when in the immediate proximity of the Buddha one burns with faith, but when far removed from him, one tends to neglect his teaching. Unwavering faith should be like water, constantly flowing. In the knowledge of the need for loyal supporters and of his own responsibility for the growth of the society, Toda prayed for guidance and for steadfastness among the members.

The general administrative report came to an end, and one

by one, members of the audience rose to testify to the great power of the true faith. They told tales of their experiences with despair and poverty during the war years and of how the Gohonzon had been the only thing that gave them hope. Great experiences were related; but the audience, deeply convinced that true Buddhism sheds light on the law of cause and effect, had no trouble accepting the most marvelous stories as absolute fact. Touched by the experiences of their fellows and encouraged by the progress the society was making, everyone present was at a peak of excitement and happy expectation when Toda addressed them.

Using only the plainest words, he laid before his audience a flaming truth. "Today various deities and Buddhas compete with each other in doling out rewards and punishment to mankind, but this role is not theirs alone. All aspects of life are governed by laws of punishment and reward. Only scale and content differentiate punishment and reward as seen in, say, the fishing business from those of the highest realms of finance. But this very aspect of the problem is of great importance because the greater the content of the issue at hand the richer the rewards and the more horrendous the punishments that are implied.

"The Mystic Law is the most all-embracing doctrine in the universe; therefore, belief in its teachings is the highest act of mankind. It is obvious that when activity is of this magnitude the rewards accruing to it are inexpressibly great. According to the law of causality, however, the punishments are terrible beyond human knowledge.

"Our beloved leader suffered persecution on this earth in the name of the faith, but now his praises are sung by Buddhas and Bodhisattvas. On the other hand, those who slander or misuse the Mystic Law or this society—which is dedicated to the Law and to its propagation—have the torments of the damned in store for them. Furthermore, the *Gosho* and the Lotus Sutra have warned them of their fate."

On this fiery note of hope and warning, the general meeting ended. Toda was satisfied with everything that had happened, but he was especially elated at the changing of the name of the society from the old Soka Kyoiku Gakkai, Value-Creating Education Society, to the more inclusive Soka Gakkai, Value-Creating Society, because this symbolized the newer, wider foundation on which Toda knew his future endeavors must be built. From now on, salvation for millions of distressed people would flow directly from the Myoho without the intermediary of the philosophy of value.

One year after the end of hostilities, Japan had emerged on a new path of growth with its first true constitution, and Soka Gakkai had begun its path of startling progress. Both events thrilled Toda's heart. Warmed by the assurance of the society's new start, Toda and a group of young people left the hall in the chill dusk of the evening. Through the gray, light golden paulownia leaves fluttered down from a nearby tree. Toda was happy for the companionship of his young followers, and he joined them in song as they strolled toward the train station:

"As clouds of glory pass away,
  Ambition's revels close,
Faith in falsehoods fades from sight,
  But Buddha's power glows.
Time to spread our faith has come,
  Desired by all the world;
Young soldiers, now go to the fray,
  With banners all unfurled!"

3. LIGHT AND SHADOW

BECAUSE the Reception Hall of Daiseki-ji had burned to the ground, it was necessary to use a lodging temple called the Renzobo for midnight prayers. On the night of November 15, 1946, that building was brightly illuminated, as was the Main Hall of the temple, because rites of succession for a new high priest of Nichiren Shoshu were to take place. Deep darkness and silence engulfed the rest of the temple grounds. The Gohonzon, transferred from the Treasure Temple for this important occasion, was in the Main Hall. All the priests of the temple stood as symbolic guards at the four corners of the building. A few days earlier, for reasons of ill health, the sixty-third high priest, Nichiman Akiyama, had resigned after only one year in office, and an extraordinary meeting of councilors suggested Nissho Mizutani to succeed him.

The teachings of Nichiren have been passed down through an unbroken line of chosen disciples, beginning with Nikko, whom Nichiren himself selected. The essence of true Buddhism has been handed down in much the same way as water is transferred from one vessel to another in endless succession. Therefore, the water of the Myoho bequeathed to the sixty-fourth high priest was the same as that bestowed by Nichiren seven hundred years ago; its purity, clarity, and taste were unchanged. Some two thousand years before Nichiren, Sakyamuni, too, had chosen the same method of passing on his teachings and had bequeathed them to his disciples. First he gave the Hinayana teachings to Maha-Kasyapa and then to Ananda. Next he passed the Mahayana teachings to Manjusri. But the essence of the Lotus Sutra he gave to Viśistácaritra, disregarding all others. Naturally, a ceremony as exalted as that of an ordination in this venerable tradition entails a great amount of pomp. The retiring and acceding high priests are closeted for many hours behind vast gilded screens. During the ceremonies, tension throughout the temple steadily builds to reach a peak when the symbolically newborn high priest conducts his first midnight Gongyo in continuation of the seven-hundred-year-old tradition of praying nightly from 2:00 until 4:00 A.M. for the attainment of the universal propagation of true Buddhism and for the peace and happiness of mankind. On this night, as on every night throughout that long period, the prayers rang strong and clear into the night air, but the voice intoning on this occasion was that of the man who was to become a driving force in the post-war rehabilitation of Nichiren Shoshu and especially of the head temple.

The problems facing the high priest Nissho Mizutani when he assumed office at the age of sixty-eight seemed insurmountable. The Reception Hall had to be rebuilt as quickly as possible. Even more important, it was vitally urgent to reconstruct some twenty Nichiren Shoshu temples burned in all parts of Japan during the war. Undaunted even in the face of these difficulties, Nissho began work immediately. His first step was to organize a special temple-reconstruction committee to work out concrete operational plans based on the utilization of timber from the forests of the head-temple compound and on appeals for aid from affluent believers.

At first these plans were apparently frustrated by the two-phase agrarian reforms sponsored by occupation authorities.

According to these regulations, no landowner was allowed to possess more than twelve and a quarter acres of land; he was obliged to sell everything over this amount to the people who had previously farmed the land as tenants. A noncultivating landowner was allowed to possess no more than two and a half acres, and religious institutions were forbidden to own any arable land at all. The problem facing Daiseki-ji as both a noncultivator and a religious organization was grave indeed. In addition, a local agrarian commission, headed by a Communist, forced the temple to sell 245 acres of land at ludicrously low prices. Of this area, 147 acres were farmland; the remainder was forest. This loss clearly crippled Nissho's rehabilitation program, but the priests were by no means at a loss for an alternate plan.

Ignorant of affairs of the world but keenly aware that the agrarian commission might force further land sales, the priests saw what they must do. They must become farmers themselves. So eager were they to preserve Daiseki-ji property that they doffed their priestly garments and voluntarily became tenant cultivators of temple lands. Picking up spades and hoes, to which their hands were little accustomed, they set out to cultivate the five acres of the temple compound and thus to both protect the head temple and provide food for themselves.

Plowing, weeding, and all the other farm chores gradually became the daily routine of these devout men. But about once a month, when pilgrim visits occasioned services in front of the Dai-Gohonzon, they put aside their farm implements, once again donned priestly garments, and for a brief time returned to their old way of life. This way had all but vanished from the ordinary round of duties, however. When demobilized monks gradually began coming back to Daiseki-ji, some of them were so shocked at the changes that they could not bring themselves to remain with these strange farmer-monks. The priests of Daiseki-ji took this title themselves in remembrance of the warrior-monks who had turned to the sword and the lance to protect themselves from tyrannical lords in the late Heian period. In a somewhat similar sense the postwar priests of Daiseki-ji had turned to the plow and the hoe for survival. In spite of dissatisfaction in some quarters, the wise policy of Mizutani kept food on the tables of the temple through a period when the entire nation was tightening and retightening belts because of dire shortages.

Nissho was not alone in striving to rebuild the faith in a struggling war-torn nation, nor were his disgruntled demobilized monks the only people to express great dissatisfaction with the way things were going. Josei Toda continued his lectures on the Lotus Sutra and the *Gosho*. Attendance had taken such a turn for the better after the first general meeting of Soka Gakkai that extra meetings were necessary. At times, especially when discontented young people attended, exchanges became heated. The schedule was arduous, but Toda made every effort to preside at all the meetings because he realized that though many of his most faithful followers were already capable of putting up convincing arguments for Nichiren Shoshu on theoretical and philosophical grounds they sometimes lacked the warmth to substantiate their claims with appeals to true humanity. With his charm and his genuine interest in the welfare of all who came to learn, Toda was exactly the man to add this needed element to the discussions.

Meeting conditions were never luxurious in those days. Streetlights were scarce, and the nearsighted Toda often stumbled as he nightly made his way through remote parts of the city to attic rooms in dilapidated houses where the faithful gathered. Dim light made reading a chore. Tatami floor mats were invariably soiled and ragged. Sometimes wooden structures, seriously shaken during the war, tilted so crazily that merely sitting straight demanded a considerable part of the audience's attention. Floorboards shrieked when anyone took a step. But such minor inconveniences disappeared the moment Toda made his entrance and began his cheerful greetings.

Because he abhorred the spiritually crippling effect of formality, Toda always insisted on casual meetings. Generally only about twenty or thirty people could squeeze into the rooms, but there were rarely fewer than that. Everyone had a multitude of questions, all of which Toda heard willingly and attentively. After answering the questions, he would pose some of his own

about the history of Buddhism, the true purpose of life, the meaning of happiness, and certain Buddhist doctrines, like that of the ten states of life. This was done to stimulate discussion and to bring to light whatever doubts might lurk in the minds of his audience. Toda was never afraid of honestly expressed doubts because he believed deeply that true understanding is always born of serious doubts resolved through faith.

The meetings were open to all ages, classes, and kinds of people. Each had a perfect right—in fact was actively encouraged—to participate in the discussion no matter whether he was an old society member with years of experience or the greenest of newcomers. Seniority and rank had no meaning because a spirit of democracy always prevailed. Toda regarded discussion meetings as one of the most important activities of the society and for this reason avoided prepared lectures, which tend to separate speaker and audience and to create a barrier between the masses and a small group of so-called leaders. The discussion meeting was a place where people sincerely communicated with one another in their search for truth and salvation.

Sometimes people of limited mental abilities asked silly questions, but no inquiry was ever rebuffed. Toda always treated each person with the dignity due an individual human being and gave all questions his closest attention. The most challenging questioners were the dispirited young men. Physically weakened by warfare, many of these youths were only recently demobilized and had returned to a world they did not understand, where they were trying to give life some meaning. With sunken cheeks and hollow eyes, they often challenged Toda to prove what he said. At one meeting, in the midst of a discussion of the great promise inherent in belief in true Buddhism, a young man arose and interrupted Toda.

"Oh, no, you're trying to trick me, but I won't let you. What you are saying is too good to be true. It's a fraud, and I'm fed up with frauds."

Friends who had brought the young man to the meeting leaped up in embarrassment and tried to make him sit down and be quiet, but Toda instructed them to allow him to finish. Toda knew the emptiness and hopelessness in the hearts of these young people; he realized that their only release was emotional outburst. For a moment the young man was taken aback by Toda's permissive attitude, but he soon stoked the fire of his fury and shouted afresh:

"I'm not going to be fooled by your talk of building a peaceful Buddhist land. How can you expect me to believe that? Ever since I can remember, high-flown talk of the Imperial Army, the invincible navy, the sacred war, and universal harmony has been crammed down our throats. Empty words! But I didn't know it then. I believed them, and my belief led me to join a kamikaze squadron because I truly thought that by dying for my country I could contribute to the eternal prosperity of all peoples. All of us, we actually swallowed that stuff, but when the nightmare was over and I could think clearly, I saw that it was all lies. Oh sure, the ones who tricked us were scoundrels, but we were such idiots! I vowed then and there that no such fine talk would ever fool me again, and I'm not going to let you trick me either."

Toda watched the young man as he scowled and twitched his way through his bitter tirade, hands clenched against baggy khaki trousers left over from his kamikaze days. When he had finished he stood for a minute staring into space. Toda thought: "This man might be possessed of a strong will or he might be just stubborn." But true to his policy of equal courtesy and interest for everyone, he began to speak quietly:

"Perhaps you're right. You know your own experience, and experience must be true. You have learned an invaluable lesson: never let yourself be fooled. But you are still very unhappy."

"How do you know?" snapped the young man. "I won't be called unhappy. I'm not anything. Not happy, not unhappy."

"Then what state would you say you are in?"

"No state; that's all there is to it," the young man laughed derisively. But sensing nihilistic despair in the snarling laughter, Toda suddenly felt a rush of affection and pity. Beckoning the young man to sit near him, Toda invited him to discuss his problem more seriously. At first the youth hesitated, but since his fury had burned itself out, he did as he was requested.

"Now then," smiled Toda, "you've been raging for over a year and a half. Don't you think it's time you calmed down?"

Some in the audience giggled, but the still bitter look on the young man's face quickly stifled their untimely mirth. Toda then went on:

"You say you've been tricked, but before you realized the fraud, you truly believed the things you were taught. Didn't you?"

"With all my heart. That's what makes me so angry now."

"Then you are not to blame for having believed." Toda nodded, as if calming a wayward child. "You believed because you didn't know that what you were taught was wrong. As you now realize, nothing is more terrible, more dreadful than blind belief. It can plunge you into the depths of misery. This is a law that no one, no matter how great or how humble, can get away from. Have you ever thought about it this way?"

Not replying, the youth lowered his head.

"It's not just my idea," Toda continued. "About seven hundred years ago Nichiren Daishonin made all of this crystal clear when he warned against the danger of belief in false religions. Think of it this way: since your childhood you have been taught that militarism and all it means are righteous. Your belief led you to act as you did and ultimately brought you to the condition you find yourself in today. Obviously, the people who taught you these ideas are to blame, but they too were unaware of their mistake. Now they are in as great a quandary as you. As you say, they are neither happy nor unhappy. Because you have been deceived once in the past, you now close your mind against anything that smacks of religion or religious devotion. It's understandable."

Surprised at Toda's insight into the deep recesses of his mind, the young man glanced up. Toda lit a cigarette, and after a few leisurely puffs, continued:

"The thing for you to think seriously about now is whether there is anything in this world worth believing in. I have a suggestion, and I think you know what it is.

"In his own time, Nichiren Daishonin, in spite of severe persecution, dared to share the Mystic Law of Nam-myoho-renge-kyo with all men who were willing to accept it. Out of his profound compassion and in the knowledge of the sorrows that would befall man in the Latter Day of the Law—our own time, in fact—he gave the Mystic Law concrete form in the Gohonzon, which we all venerate. The Law is no empty theory, and our reverence for the Gohonzon is by no means idolatry. The Law is a true religion that helps us regenerate our lives and revolutionize our fortunes and destinies. The Gohonzon is

the intermediary through which we can train ourselves toward our ultimate goal of Buddhahood.

"Perhaps this line of thinking seems to have illogical gaps, but that is because you still do not understand the difference between true and false Buddhism. Obviously, in any field of study, without learning the basic elements, grasping higher aspects is unthinkable. If you study this Buddhist philosophy, the immense differences between a religion that is true and one that is not will become apparent to you. For me to try to unravel complicated philosophical problems for you now would be a waste of your time and mine. But the Mystic Law exists, whether human beings are aware of it or not. And I do not want you to be unaware of it, because as long as you are in your present state you are bound to go astray. On the other hand, with a knowledge of the Law and with the help of the Gohonzon, a whole new universe opens itself to you. Certainly you realize that I am not trying to deceive you. You don't think that I am telling you all of this for my own profit, do you?"

"Of course not."

"Right now you may not know it, but I think you have a bright future ahead of you. However, you will need the support and guidance of a true religion. Remember this: if you accept Nichiren Shoshu and embrace the Gohonzon, your life will be filled with blessings and achievement; if you reject them, false freedom and darkness await you. The choice, of course, is yours."

"Maybe you're right, but I'm too confused tonight to be able to judge. Let me think it over later when my mind is clearer."

The confusion in this young man's heart was multiplied millions of times throughout the entire nation, where living conditions continued to deteriorate as inflation spiraled. The usual symptoms of such a social malady—antagonistic labor movements and intensified strikes—spread like wildfire. In October, workers in all industries, including newspapers, broadcasting, motion-pictures, theaters, and manufacturing, among others, struck for higher wages. Overwhelmed by the pressure, management relented and met the demands. Although in fact the increases only contributed to rising inflation and thus brought the working man small recompense for his efforts, at least labor had a taste of victory. Through this episode it learned the importance of collective action.

As a result of this knowledge, in November, 1946, all government and public office workers formed a joint struggle committee to lead a group of nearly two million members. On December 17, at the Imperial Palace Plaza, hundreds of thousands of workers joined together in what was called a "rally of the national congress for securing workers' livelihoods and for overthrowing the Yoshida cabinet." Wave after wave of rallies followed this first Communist-inspired mass meeting. Red flags and placards proclaiming revolution flooded the streets of Tokyo. The labor offensive, shaking the foundations of the nation by now, assumed the coloring of a political struggle. Encouraged by their initial successes and convinced that revolution was imminent, the Communists mounted a huge January labor offensive and scheduled a general strike involving six and a half million workers. The strike was to begin on February 1, 1947. All this turbulence reflected the misery and poverty of the people and boded ill for the future.

Though he followed the developments on the labor front with great interest, Toda remained aloof from political questions and concentrated on his lectures on the Lotus Sutra and the *Gosho* and on his numerous discussion meetings. He never allowed current affairs to distract him, because he knew that the only path to salvation for the nation was the propagation of true Buddhism. The troubled nature of society had convinced him that the time was ripe for the achievement of his goal. The Japanese people needed the teachings of Nichiren in those dark days as they had never needed them before.

Others, too, were aware of the deeper implications of the trouble. One day Toda read in a newspaper a letter written by General MacArthur to a Christian leader in the United States to the effect that the Japanese people were now experiencing a moral emptiness and that Christianity would fill that vacuum.

Whereas Toda agreed that the Japanese people were experiencing a spiritual vacuum, he did not think that Christianity would fill the need or even manage to take root in Japan. Only the true Buddhism had the power to awaken the people from their spiritual torpor and to inspire them with vitality and energy for the rejuvenation of the state. Life-giving like the sun, Nichiren's Buddhism alone could work this miracle.

Not all of Toda's followers, however, saw things this way. At lectures and discussions, it became clear that one element of the group—an element frequently conspicuous by its absence—believed strongly that building a democratic society was more important than the activities of Soka Gakkai. Toda had an answer for them:

"Don't think that I fail to understand your problems. I sympathize with you in your struggle for a better way of life, and if you really need me I don't object to helping you wave your union flags. But bear this in mind: you are attempting to relieve the symptoms without curing the disease. The labor movement has a part to play, but it is insignificant in comparison with the real problem: saving Japan and solving once and for all the difficulties that plague the people. Only the Mystic Law can do this. Keep on fighting. You're right; therefore, you must win. But do not forget to pray to the Gohonzon, for without it you are powerless.

"Compromise is the way to settle political, economic, and labor problems. But when essentials are at stake, no compromise is possible. Think of it this way: by fighting for improvements in labor conditions you are bailing out a tiny boat tossed on a raging sea of profound difficulties. The thing to do, however, is to try to calm the sea so that all boats, not just the labor one, can sail in safety. To calm the storm of our times, we must devote ourselves to the propagation of the true faith. We need a revolution, but it must be a religious one, a more profound revolution that solves all human problems on a high level, completely free of compromise."

Toda persevered. His lectures continued, and when he and his closest followers visited Daiseki-ji on New Year's Day, there were thirty-nine people in the group. A year before, there had been only six.

But the turmoil on the labor front continued. On January 28, a mass rally involving three hundred thousand people was held in Tokyo. A tension that seemed to prophesy revolution strangled the nation. If the general strike scheduled for February took place, the entire country would come to a standstill; and the conservative Yoshida government would face certain downfall. Once again, however, General MacArthur stepped in, called off the strike, and saved the day—at least temporarily.

Obviously, the strike had been a question of vital interest to most people, and one evening, during a discussion meeting, Toda found himself besieged with questions pertaining to it. His answer not only revealed his own indomitable faith in the march toward universal Buddhism but also gave hope and courage to those who heard him:

"Doctors can cure colds, but they cannot touch the inner problems of mankind. By the same token, strikes and activist movements can solve labor problems or political difficulties, but they are ineffectual in the face of the profundities of karma, birth, life, advancing age, disease, death, family and personality problems, and so on. Nations, societies, and all groups are made up of individuals. If one man cannot attain true happiness until he has found a solution to his inner problems, how can a collective group of men hope to solve the problems of a nation without relying on a true religion?

"Strikes may recur; they may effect temporary gains, but since they do not reach the heart of the trouble, man will ultimately be forced to see that only the teachings of Nichiren Daishonin can provide answers to the fundamental questions and, by putting them in proper perspective, make minor difficulties simple to solve.

"What we are doing now in our discussions and lecture meetings may seem small and insignificant compared to the turmoil surrounding the labor and political issues of the moment. But, in fact, these political problems are insignificant compared to the harmonious fusion of Buddhism with society, which is the goal of the propagation of the true faith. This is the task of each of us. Our duty is to continue to march steadily toward that goal."

4. SKIRMISH

IN THE warm spring sun of a late March afternoon, a group of six young men and women waited at a streetcar stop at Nogizaka in the Akasaka district of Tokyo. Their clothes were neat, if nondescript; the men's faces were clean shaven and the women's hair neatly combed. They were obviously waiting for someone; they had hopeful looks on their faces as they watched people alighting from the streetcars. After several cars had gone and their friend still had not arrived, one of the young women began to fret.

"I wonder what's happened to Iwata," she said as she looked at her watch again.

"He'll be here any minute now," replied a tall, thin young man wearing glasses.

"But it's already twelve forty," continued the girl.

"Impatient as usual, Miss Mikawa," replied Kinya Takimoto, the young man she had been talking with. "Don't worry. He's our leader. He has to come."

Iwata was not on the next streetcar or the one after that, and even Takimoto started to be concerned. As the little group began to think of going on without him, Iwata suddenly turned up from nowhere and greeted them cheerfully.

"Here at last, and about time too."

"Do you know what time it is?"

"What!" said the imperturbable Juichi Iwata. "One o'clock already? Sorry, but I don't have a watch. Anyway, I didn't keep you waiting for nothing. I did some scouting on my way, and by my count there must be at least one hundred people at the meeting." Iwata continued his briefing in his clear but strangely thick voice: "Let's carry out the plan just as we decided last night. We'll go in one at a time so they won't suspect anything and try to stop us."

With this, the little group of conspirators set off. As they mingled with the Sunday pedestrians on the streets, no one would have taken them for anarchists or Communist unionists, which, indeed, they were not. They were only members of a young people's group devoted heart and soul to the propagation of true Buddhism. After a few minutes' walk, they arrived at their goal, the headquarters of a religious organization called the Unity Order. After entering one by one, the group dispersed inconspicuously among the members of the congregation.

This Unity Order, one of countless similar groups to sprout up in postwar Japan, took advantage of the prevailing moral vacuum left by war and defeat. It taught a monstrous, eclectic blend of Christianity, Buddhism, and Shinto called the Oneness of All Religions. Its guiding tenet was that anyone can be saved if he believes in the dogma of the order and reads two books, *The True Aspects of Life* and *The Truth*, both—as might be expected—written by Kishiharu Taniyama, the founder of the sect. But salvation was not offered only to the literate; Taniyama explicitly made allowance for the unlettered, who could enter the doors of paradise if they merely carried copies of these two miraculous works about with them. As is often the case with the spiritually starved, many people took the Unity Order teachings at face value and spent good money for these worthless books as well as for other printed material made abundantly available. In reality, the Unity Order was less religion than profitable business, very profitable indeed, since it was able to thrive on the pennies and small change of hundreds of people who swallowed the false teachings of Taniyama.

Nor were the sins of this man limited to his postwar activities. During the heyday of the Japanese militarists, Taniyama had cooperated fully with government schemes by loudly acclaiming both Shinto doctrines and ultranationalism. However, when the militarists fell, the resourceful Taniyama, not willing to join them in defeat as he had walked hand in hand with them in success, called on the assistance of a heady concoction of mingled and muddled religious ideas to convince the weary and unhappy people of the city that he, Taniyama, was the doorway to a richer life.

At the March meeting attended by the group of young people who had been waiting at the streetcar stop, several of Taniyama's deluded followers went to the rostrum one after another to talk about how they had come to accept the teachings of the Unity Order and to recite the benefits they had enjoyed as a result of that step. But, no matter with what assumed fervor they attempted to reveal the bliss they found, the pale and sickly complexion, downtrodden attitude, and worn appearance of the middle-aged woman with tangled hair and unkempt clothes, the beaten ex-convict, and the gloomy ex-soldier belied all their good words. Although the testimonials lasted for almost an hour, their lack of foundation in religious faith and their emptiness repelled the seven young people scattered throughout the drab audience. The high point of the meeting, Taniyama's sermon, was yet to come. This was what the young people were waiting for. After a few more testimonials—in all of which, incidentally, frequent mention was made of the wonderworking powers of Taniyama's literary efforts—the great man himself at last took the rostrum amid loud applause. After glancing lovingly at his group, he began to speak:

"I can say without fear of contradiction that the surest way to illuminate the mind with the clear light of truth is to peruse with care—for only one hour daily—my *True Aspects of Life*. Let me say immediately that I by no means claim that my poor writings will cure your illnesses. Oh no, illnesses are only the result of false ideas, wrong beliefs. But in the end, they are of no consequence, for as I have always taught you, the body is only the shadow of the mind. When one is ill, one must remove the pain from the mind and it will then leave the body."

Taniyama continued his edifying discourse at great length. Decorating his speech with liberal quotations from the Bible and the Buddhist scriptures, he soothingly told his innocent listeners how all religions were ultimately one.

Glancing around him, Iwata could see from the emptiness in the faces of the crowd that none of Taniyama's pap was, in fact, allaying the desperation of the audience. He felt both pity for the fooled and contempt for the foolers. When Taniyama had finished, Iwata raised his hand and requested permission to ask the speaker a question. Surprised by this unusual request, the people on the platform whispered hurriedly among themselves; then the moderator rose to announce that although Mr. Taniyama was extremely busy he would be kind enough to entertain a question period of half an hour.

Four or five people raised their hands to ask questions. The moderator, carefully avoiding Iwata as an obvious troublemaker, pointed to another unknown young man in the back of the room indicating that he might open the discussion period. Unwittingly, however, the moderator had selected Takimoto, who said: "Sir, you have been speaking about the god of the Unity Order. I am not sure that I understand you. What kind of god is he? Could you please explain in more concrete terms?"

"The matter is essentially one of faith. By saying that we are children of God, we mean that the absolute and infinite deity dwells in all of us. The deity, however, assumes various manifestations. This of course brings one to the question of monotheism versus polytheism, but we resolve the apparent difficulty.

We believe that all deities fall into one of three categories symbolized by the God of Christianity, the Buddha, and the Sun Goddess, Amaterasu. No matter what category they belong to, all are manifestations of what I call the mysterious spiritual wave of salvation, which emanates from one fundamental godhead. Now, the deity of our Unity Order, too, is a manifestation of this mysterious wave."

Since there seemed to be no imminent end to Taniyama's rambling, Takimoto interrupted him. "Yes, thank you, I see. Now for my next question. As well as I can understand, you say that the god of the Unity Order resides in your book *True Aspects of Life*. Is that correct?"

"You have understood me correctly, young man. My book conveys the spiritual wave of salvation, thus it delivers us from our sufferings and anguish."

"How about this Sun Goddess, Amaterasu? Is she distinctly Japanese, is she American, or Chinese?"

"She is Japanese, of course, but she sheds her light on the entire universe. However, the Sun Goddess protects the Japanese particularly."

"Is that so? Well, how can you explain her notable failure to protect the Japanese people during the war?"

The ensuing lengthy silence made it clear that Taniyama had no answer prepared for this impertinence. Takimoto continued:

"I would like an answer to my question. If Amaterasu is a goddess and if her duty is, as you say, to protect the Japanese, why did she let us down so miserably? Doesn't her failure to come to our assistance cast some doubt on her very existence?"

"You speak of duty," Taniyama stumbled, "but I don't think deities have duties."

"Very well then, a role. Why did the Sun Goddess fail to display her love?"

"Yes, well you see, I interpret it this way. . . ."

But no clear interpretation was forthcoming because Taniyama's embarrassment conveyed itself to the audience, who immediately set up a restless buzzing. Takimoto now delivered the final blow.

"A god that fails is a god out of a job, right? You have set up a hierarchy of divinities. Now explain just where the Sun Goddess of the Japanese, who lost the war, stands in relation to the Christian God of the Americans, who won it."

As his audience laughed and snickered, Taniyama stood still, pale and stricken. But he was not to be so easily defeated. After a moment's flustering, he recovered sufficiently to outwit Takimoto.

"You asked about the god of our order, and I have done my best to explain. Nevertheless, you do not seem to understand. I am convinced of your intelligence, and if you still sincerely want to know more about our beliefs, I urge you to join a spiritual training group we have established for people like you. Now, the next question, please."

Takimoto tried to get in a few more words, but the moderator had already given the floor to someone else. That someone turned out to be another member of the youth group—Juichi Iwata. Takimoto was able to retire from the floor, pleased and relieved.

Deliberate and confident, Iwata said: "I am afraid I can't quite swallow what you have to say about the body's being only a shadow of the mind. Do you mean that all material phenomena are shadows and that only the world of the spirit truly exists?"

"That is correct," said Taniyama.

"Well, what about science and the things it teaches concerning the physical world?"

"After all, my dear young man, science may seem real, but essentially it belongs to the realm of shadows, of the insubstantial. Unfortunately, too many people fail to understand this, and the world is suffering today as a result of the general mistaken idea that science is omnipotent." As he spoke, a disdainful grin curled Taniyama's lips, and a note of pompous confidence crept into his voice.

"But surely you are not refuting all the scientific truths and laws that govern the physical world," countered Iwata.

"I neither refute nor affirm your so-called truths. I only insist that man must not overestimate the power of science," said Taniyama.

"Do you say that the universally accepted law of gravity is a shadow?"

The smirk was gone from Taniyama's face, and irritation replaced the confidence in his voice as he said: "You are certainly a persistent young man. But surely you can see that the physical world is essentially nonexistent. And what does not exist simply does not exist. No one can grasp truth until he has abandoned the world of matter. Of course, not everyone can achieve this. Even some of the chief disciples of the Buddha were held in bondage to the physical world."

Iwata finally lost patience. "Nonsense. How can a person abandon the world of matter. It's perfectly obvious that even you cannot perform such a feat." Turning abruptly to the audience and taking out a box of matches, Iwata continued: "I ask all of you, does this box of matches exist? Is it a shadow? And do you really believe that my body is only a shadow of my mind?"

The dumbfounded and confused congregation looked first at Taniyama, then at Iwata, behind whom a few of the Unity Order strong men were now looming in a menacing way. Suddenly, a voice broke the tension:

"Mr. Taniyama, please enlighten this man. Help him to salvation through the teachings of the Unity Order. I am sure that what you have to say will be of great use to all of us." The young man speaking, though apparently sympathetic to Taniyama, was in fact Giichi Sakata, still another member of the group that had deliberately come to refute the false teachings of the Unity Order. The predetermined plan had included just this turn, because the group thought that if they could induce Taniyama to drag out his explanation he would inevitably sink deeper and deeper in his own muddle. Taniyama, unsuspecting, took the bait.

"Young man, are you a professed materialist?" he asked Iwata.

"No, I don't deny either the body or the spirit."

"Then you must understand this about the Unity Order: our belief is that only by repudiating the existence of matter—and of the body—can mankind attain freedom. We are completely opposed to materialism." Having delivered this statement, Taniyama looked at his watch, as if to make it clear that his valuable time was running out.

"And how do you propose to repudiate the human body and the physical world we live in? Your ideas don't make sense. You are a phony. You poison the minds of innocent people, and I think it is time you stopped. What do you say to that?"

With this challenge, Iwata brought the views of his group clearly out in the open. The remainder of the congregation, however, unaware that the entire questioning session had been carefully manipulated to bring about this final confrontation, looked to Taniyama to put the young upstart in his place. Taniyama stood stonily silent. He glanced tellingly at his watch again. As he did so, two of his officials rose from the back of the hall and started forward. One of them announced that the question-and-answer session was over. Encouraged by their action, Taniyama attempted to recoup his losses. "Young man, it is not for you to tell me what I may and may not teach. Today's meeting is now over. I must hurry to another hall where many of our faithful followers are waiting for me."

With this feeble rejoinder, Taniyama scurried from the platform in his eagerness to escape the humiliating exposure of the shabbiness of his doctrine. But Iwata was determined not to let him off so lightly.

"Wait! Don't run away, you phony," he called to the retreating figure.

On hearing this, the Unity Order strong men rushed to Iwata and tried to seize him by the arm, but Sakata, Takimoto, and Yusuke Yoshikawa formed a protective ring around their friend. "I wouldn't try any rough stuff if I were you. He has a right

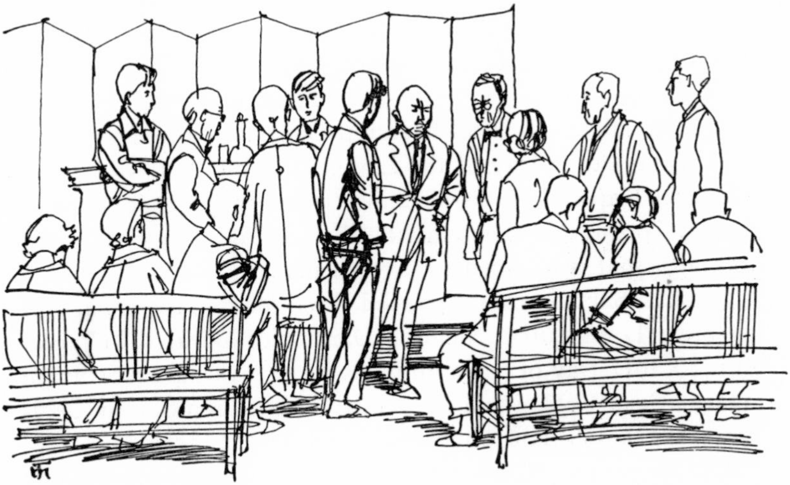

to speak his mind," threw in Yoshikawa. This remark almost touched off a fight, but as the strong men were closing in, shouts arose from the congregation.

"Let him talk; remember the freedom of speech."

"We don't want any fighting."

"If you start a fight with them you'll only disgrace the order."

After a few minutes of confusion, the moderator succeeded in calming the assembly. Because he could see no other way out of the situation he said: "Very well, young man, you may have the floor. But only for ten minutes."

Iwata rose to the platform and began: "First, I should like

to introduce our group. We are members of the Youth Division of Nichiren Shoshu Soka Gakkai."

The name meant nothing to most of the audience, but the officials of the Unity Order now knew with whom they were dealing. Only a week earlier, members of Soka Gakkai had attempted to convert some of them. Now, in front of a full hall, their leader had been discredited and humiliated by another member of that organization. The six other members of the Youth Division joined Iwata on the platform as he began speaking with sincerity and composure:

"Nichiren Shoshu is the only Buddhist group adhering to the legitimate teachings of Nichiren Daishonin, the True Buddha of the Latter Day of the Law. Seven hundred years ago, Nichiren bequeathed his teachings to the second high priest, Nikko. To this day they embody the one and only Buddhism, the faith that is destined to save all mankind.

"Just as Sakyamuni prophesied three thousand years ago in his great Lotus Sutra, Nichiren Daishonin appeared in Japan in the Latter Day of Sakyamuni's Law to save the unfortunate masses. Soka Gakkai is a lay society of Nichiren Shoshu dedicated to religious and philosophical activities. It strives to save the Japanese people from misery and to promote the ultimate salvation of mankind. Time prohibits my going into the historical evidence, but I ask you to believe that Nichiren Shoshu is the only orthodox sect of Nichiren Buddhism. A country has only one king, and Nichiren Daishonin's Buddhism has only one truly orthodox sect.

"What are the teachings of the Unity Order? As you have heard me prove today, they are a preposterous mishmash of bits of Christianity, Buddhism, and Shintoism, palmed off on you as religious truth. This Taniyama apparently intends to set himself up as some kind of deity. According to the words of both Sakyamuni and Nichiren Daishonin, a man who attempts to do such a thing is a devil. Consequently, you are unwittingly being made devil's disciples. Taniyama has been using sweet words to deceive you in your innocence."

As Iwata's remarks became increasingly astringent, the Unity Order leaders, who had been whispering among themselves, interrupted:

"Your ten minutes are up."

"No, they're not; there are still two minutes to go," shouted Takimoto who had been keeping a careful eye on his watch. Takimoto then addressed the audience: "Since my colleague has been rudely interrupted, I ask you to be patient and to grant him a little more than ten minutes."

Scattered applause indicated that at least the young people had the initiative. Iwata resumed his remarks:

"Has Taniyama ever broached the cardinal Buddhist doctrine of the law of cause and effect or the life philosophy on which we must base all our activities? No, of course not. Instead he has been clouding your minds with the stupid notion that matter is a mere shadow of the spirit. Because Nichiren Daishonin taught us that false religions—like this one—are the source of mankind's misfortunes, we feel it our duty to obstruct people like Taniyama and his order in their attempt to lead thousands and tens of thousands of people astray.

"As to the question of mind and matter, Nichiren Daishonin long ago explained that they are inseparable, that enlightenment depends on one's understanding of this basic fact. Today it is a universally accepted truth that neither spiritualism nor materialism can bring salvation to mankind. The only teaching that is in a position to reconcile and harmonize these two ways of thinking is Nichiren Shoshu. Nichiren Shoshu alone can give peace and happiness to the hundreds of millions of suffering people in the world today."

The audience listened closely to what Iwata said. He had suddenly become such a fine orator that his colleagues were surprised and impressed. A poorly educated factory worker,

Iwata was not speaking from books. He was opening his heart and sharing with others the truth that he felt.

"We cannot sit idly by while a bogus religion of this kind saps you of your vitality and plunges you deeper into misery," he continued. "How many of you truly believe that the Unity Order dogmas can save you? Those who believe that raise your hands please."

In response to Iwata's audacious move, a few people in the audience haltingly raised their hands and then lowered them when they saw that they were a clear minority. The officials chose to ignore the question.

"I see," Iwata went on. "Now I will tell you of a religion that can save you. Nichiren Daishonin left us his teachings and he also left us the Dai-Gohonzon enshrined at the head temple, Daiseki-ji, at the foot of Mount Fuji. Believe in the universal Dai-Gohonzon and, as a sign of your belief, chant the Daimoku prayer, and you will be on the road to salvation and happiness.

"Of course, today I cannot give you all the information you need and want to know. All I can do now is point out to you the existence of a true religion and of the Dai-Gohonzon, a wellspring of prosperity and world peace. I urge you to accept Nichiren Daishonin as a savior, for seven centuries ago he said: 'You must be converted to the only legitimate Buddhism.' Renounce your mistaken religion and accept the Nam-myoho-renge-kyo of Nichiren Daishonin. Only in this way can you lead a rich, fulfilled life."

Iwata concluded his remarks, gave the address of the Soka Gakkai headquarters, and bowed courteously. His six colleagues also bowed together, and leaving the platform, the little group marched boldly up the aisle and out into the warm sunlight. In the hall, some shouting and a few angry protests followed the Unity Order leaders. The young Soka Gakkai people spoke little, but the triumphant smiles on their faces showed pride in having accomplished the mission they had set themselves.

The next day, following Toda's lecture on the Lotus Sutra, Iwata reported to the gathering about the skirmish at the Unity Order meeting. He explained in detail how the idea had originated, how they had worked out the strategy, and finally how they had carried out the plan. The audience was at once delighted and envious of the success of the seven youths. Generous applause and approval greeted the conclusion of Iwata's remarks. Encouraged and self-assured, Iwata turned to Toda and said: "In obedience to your instructions, we of the Youth Division swear to fight relentlessly against wicked and false religious sects. Nothing stands in the way of the mission of true Buddhism. The enemy is a straw man that tumbles at the touch of our hands. I think my report makes that clear. We ask you to continue to guide and instruct us."

More hearty applause greeted this speech, and Iwata, returning to his place, felt very much like a hero. Everyone followed him with admiring eyes, everyone, that is, except Toda, whose face was grim. At the beginning of Iwata's talk, Toda had listened with a gentle smile on his lips, but that look gradually gave way to pain and finally to open anger. Now in a sharp, loud voice he commanded: "Stand, all of you who went to the Unity Order yesterday."

Bewildered, Iwata and his colleagues slowly stood. Instead of being praised, it seemed they were going to be severely reprimanded. Why?

"You are as happy as kings just because you managed to put down some small fry like Taniyama. Your arrogance and conceit displease me more than I can say. I've never taught you to behave this way. Are you really my pupils? Iwata, tell me whose disciple you are."

Too puzzled to reply, Iwata hung his head in silence; the others in the room were dumbfounded by Toda's unexpected and violent outburst.

"You can't tell me, can you? Well, I'll tell you. You are no disciples of mine, because if you were, you would realize that no religious doctrine is a match for Nichiren Daishonin and, furthermore, that your little success yesterday was thanks only to the Gohonzon. You speak as though you had accomplished this feat on your own. Nonsense! You act like little heroes, and I am ashamed of you."

Turning to the directors, Toda asked: "Konishi, Kiyohara, Harayama, do you know how I feel?"

Although they had earlier joined in the general applause for the young people's exploit, these men now nodded in embarrassment.

"I repeat," Toda went on, "I'm grieved that you are swollen with pride and conceit at having defeated one petty charlatan. The universal propagation of true Buddhism is a supreme mission of Buddha's disciples; the enemy who awaits us is far more formidable than you imagine. I'm not condemning you for trying your hand at activity of this kind. Neither do I especially encourage you, but if you feel you must do such things, I suppose it is all right. The point I am making is this: such small-timers as Taniyama and the Unity Order are no gauge of the power of the enemy with whom we will all have to struggle in the future. If you let insignificant success, like yours yesterday, turn your heads and if you allow yourselves to become overconfident, you will be unprepared when the true battle begins. And I'm afraid you will not be equal to the task. We can't stop converting people, but don't think that incidents like yours represent the most important kind of converting. In fact, it is often more significant for a housewife to win over her neighbors than for groups like yours to attack even the headquarters of another religious organization. Right now you must concentrate on developing ability and power in preparation for the great fight, which is yet to come. Learn patience and give no thought to personal honors. Concern with one's own glory is the surest path to failure.

"Now I hope you understand why I am scolding you." As he said this Toda's face relaxed into a smile, and his audience, especially Iwata and his group, bowed their heads in penitence. Some even dried a few tears. To these Toda said: "Don't cry; after all, no one is saying you lost your fight with Taniyama."

5. UP FROM THE EARTH

ON APRIL 1, 1947, a controversial six-year-three-year system modeled on the American plan officially went into effect in all Japanese schools. According to the new system, courses in ethics and Japanese history and geography were suspended. All passages smacking of militarism or ultranationalism were deleted from textbooks. Because he felt that the occupation was attempting to impose the American system without taking into account the opinions of the Japanese people, Toda was dissatisfied with the educational reform. He regarded it as the least successful of all occupation policies. It is true that an educational mission from the United States had surveyed the Japanese situation and had made certain recommendations—the division of public schooling into six-year and three-year periods, for example. But the occupation authorities had accepted most of the mission's proposals almost without consulting responsible Japanese specialists. The mission had gone so far as to recommend the abolition of the Ministry of Education, but the occupation saw fit to overrule them in that case. Toda's thought on the new system was summarized in his protest that the Americans understood neither the national character of the Japanese people nor the Oriental mind. He felt taht the occupation educational reform would be interpreted as an attempt to make Japan permanently subservient to the United States. Toda was not alone in his disappointment. Some people found the new reforms so distasteful that they began to criticize the very idea of democratizing the educational system.

Occupation reforms also extended to other areas. A new labor-standards law was passed on April 7, an antimonopoly law on April 14, and a local autonomy law on April 17. In spite of these changes, however, the Japanese people made their feelings known through the elections held on April 20 for the Upper House of the Diet and on April 25 for the Lower House. Winning 143 seats in the Lower House, the Socialist party came out on top. They were followed by the Liberal party with 131 seats and by the Democratic party with 124 seats. The Communist party, as a result of their mismanagement of the abortive general strike scheduled for February of that year, came in a poor fourth with only four seats. The Democratic party was formed when Hitoshi Ashida, a former leader in the actually conservative Liberal party, broke away and established a new group advocating progressive capitalism. Although the Socialists had an edge, the division of seats in the Lower House was close enough to require a coalition cabinet, formed on June 1 and headed by Tetsu Katayama, the first Socialist premier ever to hold office in Japan. Unfortunately, the attempts of the Katayama cabinet to curb mounting inflation and to alleviate the economic crisis were unsuccessful. Consequently, as the national economy weakened, the government became the target of attacks from the opposition, the labor unions, and the leftist elements within the Socialist party itself.

No matter what reforms were getting under way or what turmoil was raging in the high places of politics, the people of Japan continued to endure great hardships. Merely to exist in those days involved staggering difficulties. Food was the primary problem everywhere, especially in the eastern part of the country, where people were on the brink of starvation because deliveries of staple foods often came too late. Even with the assistance provided by the occupation forces—600,000 tons of food in the spring and a total of 1.6 million tons, including 43,500 tons of canned foods, in the period between December, 1946, and October, 1947—frequent two-week delays in delivery caused widespread hunger and sometimes death.

Like everyone else, Toda and his followers suffered. Unlike many, they were neither unhappy nor discontent. Though not a few who attended Toda's nightly lectures in the Kanda headquarters of the society were hungry and shabbily dressed, all were lively and cheerful. The religious revolution inspired by Toda's passionate teaching of the life-giving philosophy of Nichiren transformed misery into hope. The members of his group were proud of their training as religious revolutionaries. Attendance at the meetings was always good because many of Toda's followers thought nothing of braving packed streetcars and trains or of missing meals in order to save money for transportation. Newcomers to the meetings increased, although the number of new converts remained a modest twenty or so each month.

The Tokyo meetings were not the only society activity forging ahead. Guidance tours to rural provinces, which had begun in the autumn of 1946, continued, as did campaigns to convert people from all walks of life. Leaders and teachers were dispatched not only to the nearby prefectures of Gumma, Tochigi, Nagano, and Shizuoka, but also to remote areas of Kyushu. No power is greater than a supreme mission carried out under the inspiration of devotion and faith. Nothing can stand in the way of the triumphant march of those dedicated to peace and freedom for all mankind. Without a sense of mission, man is at his weakest; with one he is invincible. It was this sense of a great job to do that filled Toda's disciples with happiness and that inevitably brought their conversations around to the imminent human revolution.

Following their successful bout with the Unity Order, Giichi

Sakata and Miss Mikawa redoubled their efforts to convert their friends, acquaintances, and especially their former classmates. Both of these young people were about twenty years old and lived in the Kamata section of Tokyo. Their parents had been converted to Nichiren Shoshu shortly before the outbreak of World War II. Although many of their old classmates had fled the city during the hostilities and had not yet returned, Sakata and Miss Mikawa enthusiastically strove to convert those who remained in the vicinity.

Among the friends whom these two ardent members of Toda's group were anxious to win over to Nichiren was a studious, frail, but amiable young man named Shin'ichi Yamamoto. Though physically weak and consumptive, Yamamoto had intellectual powers that set him apart from the average man. Both Sakata and Miss Mikawa knew that he would be an excellent addition to their circle, from which they felt sure he himself would gain immeasurably. Yet for a while they hesitated to invite him to Toda's meetings. From time to time they visited him in his small room lined with shelves on which stood a heterogenous collection of works by great writers of both the Eastern and Western worlds. Novelists like Doppo Kunikida stood side by side with Nietzsche, Montaigne, and the Japanese philosophers Kitaro Nishida and Kiyoshi Miki. The poems of Byron shared a shelf with the Greek classics, Carlyle, works on Confucian ethics, and Chinese poetry of the T'ang and Sung dynasties. A poor young man, Yamamoto treasured his library as his most prized possession.

Miss Mikawa and Sakata always found him either reading or writing at his desk. In front of him there was usually a notebook in which he jotted down summaries of his reading and his comments in a small, neat hand. Neither of the two young people was familiar with the books Yamamoto read. Regarding him as something of a mystery, they felt that the way to get to know him better, and thus to sound out the most effective way to approach him as a prospective member, was to limit their initial discussions to such topics as wartime episodes, old acquaintances, and the good old primary-school days. They intended to broach more important subjects later. After a few visits in which conversation followed these comfortable, if uninspiring, lines, Miss Mikawa and Sakata discerned that Yamamoto's ruling interest was philosophy. As a valuable man still floundering in uncertainties, he was in great need of conversion to the true Buddhist faith. Sensing their own intellectual inferiority, however, they suspected that the task of reaching him was beyond them. They therefore decided to bring him into contact with Toda's great personal magnetism, intellectual powers, and religious faith as soon as possible. One sultry summer night, Miss Mikawa said to Yamamoto: "Listen, we're having a discussion of philosophy at my house on the fourteenth. Why don't you join us?"

"Philosophy?" half questioned Yamamoto.

"Yes, life philosophy," spoke up Sakata in support of Miss Mikawa.

"You mean Bergson?" Yamamoto was aroused, because at that time he was especially interested in Bergson and his idea of the *élan vital* pervading all organisms. However, the French thinker was unknown to Sakata, and he discreetly declined to answer.

"Who is giving the talk? Is he a professor at some school?" inquired the now eager Yamamoto.

"Josei Toda. He's a great man."

"Toda? Is he a philosopher? I've never heard his name before."

"Yes, and his philosophy goes to the very roots of life. It's a great philosophy, and he's a great man. Please come. You'll enjoy listening to him. I'll come by to pick you up on the night of the fourteenth." Miss Mikawa was now determined to have Yamamoto join them.

"Well, I suppose so." Yamamoto suppressed a cough and continued: "I'll come if I can bring some friends."

"Oh, as many as you like. Everyone is welcome," chimed the overjoyed Miss Mikawa.

The friends Yamamoto had in mind were the members of the small but serious intellectual study group called the Kyoyukai. During the chaotic postwar years, many young Japanese, eager to acclimate themselves to the changed and still changing times, formed such study groups. Though the older generations plodded on lethargically, the young people, like buds bursting into bloom after a long, severe winter, hungrily sought knowledge and enlightenment. Not all of the study groups springing from this desire maintained lofty ideals, however. Some degenerated into black-market rings or gangs of hoodlums. But Yamamoto's Kyoyukai never wavered from its initial high aims. At their regular nighttime meetings, the members exchanged books, phonograph records, and opinions. They studied foreign languages and sometimes went to hear lectures by scholars and journalists. Their sphere of study was comprehensive, covering the arts, economics, politics, philosophy, and the humanities. Since military service or labor duties during the war had interrupted the regular education of these young people, they were eager to catch up on what they had missed. The twenty members of the group were young men from many walks of life: students, engineers, technicians, factory workers, and office employees. A well-known economist who was a friend of Yamamoto's introduced them to intellectuals with whom they discussed Dante's *Divine Comedy,* democracy, communism, inflation, the Weimar Republic, the status and function of the Japanese emperor, European and Oriental philosophy, and many other topics. Though he sometimes found them difficult to understand completely, Yamamoto was especially drawn to Bergson and Schopenhauer.

For all their extensive study, Yamamoto and his friends knew that they were engaged in no more than intellectual play. They were not approaching solutions to the great problems of life. As a result of this awareness, Yamamoto was anxious to establish a philosophical foundation for his life, something solid that would give him a sense of purpose and direction. Like other serious and sensitive youths of that chaotic period, Yamamoto and his friends tended to be skeptical and pessimistic. In their search for a purpose, doubts and unanswered questions constantly assailed them.

Among these doubts, patriotism and its nature loomed large. Yamamoto loved his nation as he did his own mind and body. But the concept of patriotism in the accepted sense held no meaning for him. He knew that the ultranationalistic patriotism of the wartime military had been not only mistaken but also iniquitous. On the other hand, he sensed an artificiality and unnaturalness in the devotion to the Soviet Union then prevalent among the Communist workers in Japan. He considered their struggles valiant but their dedication to another country misguided. Secretly and hopefully, Yamamoto dreamed of finding someone who would remove his doubts and elucidate the deep meaning of life. In his innermost heart he longed for a guide who would set him on the right path, give his existence a clear direction, and assist him in finding truth. So far, in all of his meetings with intellectuals and literary leaders he had failed to meet such a person.

When Miss Mikawa and Sakata called for Yamamoto on the evening of August fourteenth, they found him slightly feverish. He was waiting for the friends who were to accompany them. After thirty minutes' wait the friends still had not come, and Sakata suggested that they go without them. Yamamoto refused. "They will turn up soon," he assured the other two. Fever had lessened Yamamoto's enthusiasm to meet Toda that night; he hoped that the appointment might be postponed. But he said nothing because Miss Mikawa's eagerness to bring him and Toda together was all too apparent. With typical feminine sensitivity, Miss Mikawa was aware of both this and Yamamoto's illness, though the young man insisted the fever was slight. Still flushed and coughing, Yamamoto projected his inner turmoil and anguish more clearly than usual. Miss Mikawa was almost certain that Yamamoto and Toda would take to each other immediately. And she knew that for the sake of his salvation Yamamoto must meet Toda without delay. But the friends did not come, and the little party continued waiting. After a while Miss Mikawa asked Yamamoto: "Are you all right?"

"Yes." He smiled. "I'm used to this kind of fever."

An hour after the agreed time, the tardy friends arrived, and after repeated inquiries about Yamamoto's condition, the group set out along the unlighted street that led to Miss Mikawa's house. They arrived at about eight o'clock.

Miss Mikawa's father was a naval engineer; he and her mother had been converted to Nichiren Shoshu before the war. In the ruins of Kamata, an industrial part of Tokyo that had been heavily bombed, their house was one of the very few still standing. Upon entering the vestibule, Yamamoto heard the husky, energetic voice of a middle-aged man. In a large room at the end of a corridor he found the speaker, who was wearing thick glasses and lecturing quietly but intently to a group of about twenty young people, housewives, and elderly and middle-aged men and women.

Although surprised to find fewer young people than he had expected, Yamamoto listened attentively to a speech that for a while passed over his head. Miss Mikawa whispered to Yamamoto that the lecturer was Josei Toda. On this occasion he was speaking on Nichiren's treatise *The Security of the Land Through the Establishment of True Buddhism,* "Rissho Ankokuron." As a young woman read from the ancient text, Toda gave commentaries.

The young woman read: "How grieved I am to learn that millions of people have for decades been deceived and led astray by misguided sects."

Toda then explained the meaning of the text:

"In this passage, Nichiren Daishonin is referring to the Nembutsu sect of Amida Buddha, founded by Honen. By following this false teaching, millions of people who were ignorant of true Buddhism were plunged into misery. No matter how pure and ardent a person's faith, if the object of his worship is false, he is bound to meet misfortune. This is no less true now than it was in the past. Since religions today have sunk lower than ever before, their adherents are certain to be victimized

by wrong doctrines. As Nichiren Daishonin taught us, all misfortune and misery in this world is caused by ignorance of the true Buddhism."

After Toda's remarks, the reader began the next passage:

"People neglect the true Law in favor of ephemeral, wicked teachings; will this not incur the wrath of the Buddhist guardian deities? The deluded masses abandon perfect doctrines and cling to false ones; will not this arouse the demons?"

"This passage," Toda continued, "represents one of Nichiren Daishonin's firmest beliefs. Today, many people who are ignorant of Buddhist philosophy find the belief strange, even superstitious. Once one comprehends the true Buddhist life philosophy, however, the meaning becomes clear. Unfortunately, too many people today know nothing of the philosophy embodied in Sakyamuni's theory of eternal life, the life philosophy of T'ien-t'ai the Great, according to which human life is in three thousand states at any given moment, or of the true Buddhism of Nichiren Daishonin, which perfected this theory into a great life philosophy that teaches that the universe can be embodied in any mind and eternity in any moment. A perusal of the teachings of orthodox Buddhism convinces one that Japan today not only wallows in decadence but also lacks a legitimate guardian deity. The false gods, objects of worship, and other paraphernalia of Shinto exert only an evil influence on the nation and seduce the people into unhappiness."

When he saw that the lecture concerned Buddhism, Yamamoto was disappointed, but as he listened, he got the impression that the speaker was dealing seriously with the practical problems of life. Toda's self-mastery, sincerity, and zeal were clear to the young man, even though the Buddhist terminology was strange to him. The speaker was obviously dedicated and learned. Something elusive set him apart from the other intellectuals Yamamoto had met. At first when Toda fixed his gaze on Yamamoto it was sharp and penetrating, but gradually it became so warm and friendly that the young man felt as if he alone was being spoken to. Timid by nature, he averted his eyes, but while embarrassed at being closely scrutinized, he also felt a kind of warmth he had never known. The Buddhist terminology got no easier to understand, and fever and pain muddled Yamamoto's mind. Still, he listened attentively, vaguely glad that he had attended the lecture, which now continued with another reading from Nichiren's text.

"It is better that you abandon faith in this evil than that you offer tens of thousands of meaningless prayers." Toda's comment followed:

"Only Nichiren Daishonin could have made this daring, courageous statement. In it he defies the false faith in Amida

Buddha that had been established as almost a state religion, worshiped by all strata of society, ranging from the regent Hojo Tokiyori in Kamakura to the common people. Denouncing it as 'this evil,' Nichiren Daishonin went on to condemn the rulers of the nation for sanctioning a mistaken religion. His courage, however, incurred the wrath of the people, persecution, and eventual banishment by the Kamakura shogunate. Nevertheless, because he was the True Buddha of the Latter Day of the Law, he was willing to do anything to save people of all classes.

"I, as a disciple of Nichiren Daishonin and as a Bodhisattva who has sprung from the earth, have no choice but to demand the worship of the one true religion and the abandoning of all false sects. Only in this way can Japan be saved.

"Well, that should be about enough for tonight. The few passages we have learned disclose the profundity of the essence of true Buddhist philosophy. They prove that Nichiren Daishonin alone embodies this philosophy and that his words, spoken seven hundred years ago, are applicable to the present day. Those of you who have already accepted Nichiren Shoshu will inevitably gain enlightenment, but a great multitude remain ignorant of the saving powers of the Dai-Gohonzon of Nichiren Shoshu. To save all mankind and to banish unhappiness and misery from the world, I ask each of you to join our tireless efforts for the propagation of the true faith."

Yamamoto and his companions were impressed with the eagerness and spontaneity of both the leader and his group. He had an instinctive distaste for charlatans and fakes, but Yamamoto found nothing in the moving directness of the speaker or in his audience to arouse suspicion about their sincerity. During the question-and-answer period following Toda's remarks, many people put stimulating problems to their teacher, who answered with clarity and wit. From time to time he glanced at Yamamoto as if to ascertain the effect of the proceedings on the young man. At the conclusion of the question period, Miss Mikawa rose to present her friends to Toda. To Yamamoto, Toda said: "I am very glad to have you with us tonight. How old are you, young man?" Toda's voice was open and friendly.

"I'm nineteen, sir."

"Nineteen? You remind me of myself when I was your age. I had just come to Tokyo for the first time from Hokkaido, and I was lonely, penniless, and jobless." Lighting a cigarette and smoking meditatively, Toda lapsed into a silence. He seemed to be thinking of something far away in time and place.

As Yamamoto watched Toda he was both fascinated and puzzled. Obviously, Toda was sympathetic toward him, and Yamamoto sensed a spiritual affinity. But was Toda the teacher Yamamoto had been seeking? For a number of reasons, Yamamoto was not sure. For one thing, there was Buddhism. Toda's whole outlook was Buddhist, and Yamamoto, infatuated with European philosophy, held the ancient religion in disdain, as did many young postwar Japanese. To their way of thinking, Buddhism was a dead religion, nothing more than antiquated rites and outmoded thought. Still, Toda insisted with fervor and sincerity that Nichiren Shoshu was not only the sole orthodox Buddhist sect but also the single way to salvation in an age of chaos and misery. But what in fact was Nichiren Shoshu? Yamamoto had seen Nichiren monks parading the streets to the beat of drums, but he could not connect those men with what he considered true religion. Perhaps there was some other branch of Nichiren Buddhism of which Yamamoto knew nothing. He felt compelled to discuss the matter, to make contact with Toda, to draw him into conversation. After a while he broke the silence by saying: "Excuse me, Mr. Toda, but I would like you to tell me something."

Waking from his reverie, Toda said quickly: "I'll be happy to explain whatever I can. What is it?"

"What is the true meaning of life? Does such a thing as a true life philosophy exist? The more I think about this problem, the more confused I become."

In asking such a sweeping question, Yamamoto had almost unwittingly given expression to the anguish that had tormented him for a long time. Feeling that he had been too forward and sensing that the attention of the entire room was now centered on him, Yamamoto hung his head in embarrassment. Neverthe-

less, he felt relieved of a great burden because he had asked the question. Toda smiled and said: "Well now, that is a tall order." A look of joy came into his eyes as he stubbed out his cigarette and gazed intently at the young man with the timid face. Toda was happy that Yamamoto had the courage to pose such a weighty problem. He intuitively recognized the inner suffering behind the question, and he loved that suffering as he loved the purity and innocence of the young man. Toda felt himself warming to Yamamoto just as though he had known him for many years.

"I suspect that very few other people in Japan today could answer you with conviction. I am in a position to do so because I have studied and practiced the life philosophy of Nichiren Daishonin and am fortunate enough to understand it. Life holds many problems for everyone: career, love, illness, family troubles, war, food and housing shortages, and so on. Each of these aspects of life creates certain struggles and demands certain efforts, but all of this pales in comparison with the one truly profound issue: life and death. Until one has a correct understanding of this ultimate issue, life in the fullest sense is impossible.

"Buddhism organizes the life of man in the following series: birth, aging, illness, death. Each of us is fated to grow old, no matter how much we would like to remain nineteen forever. Similarly we are all subject to illness and to the infirmity and weakness of age. Finally, no one can avoid the stern reality of death. Rich and poor, exalted and humble, all must face this great truth.

"In the past, for want of a solution to this problem, truly abundant life sometimes seemed so impossible to attain that many people despaired at the incomprehensibility of existence itself and committed suicide. Nichiren Daishonin, however, has pointed the way to enlightenment. Even at your young age, you are concerned with the problem of the true life; and it is good that you are. I urge you to accept and practice Nichiren Daishonin's teachings, for I am convinced that in doing so you will find yourself. You will learn to lead the kind of life you now seek."

The warmth and sincerity in Toda's voice and his undoubted eagerness to help encouraged Yamamoto to ask another question. "What is a patriot? How do you define patriotism?"

"The concept in the most accepted sense alters with the age, but loyalty to nation and people is the primary element of a patriot. As times change, this loyalty may assume different forms. For example, the nineteenth-century thinker Yoshida

Shoin was a patriot, as was General Maresuke Nogi, who fought in the Russo-Japanese War. But there is another kind of patriot, one who transcends the age in which he lives and whose deeds withstand the test of time. The many adherents of the Mystic Law who save their fellow countrymen through religious devotion and good works certainly contribute to the peace and prosperity of their nation. They, too, deserve to be called true patriots. This is not empty talk. It is the will of the Buddha of the Latter Day of the Law that a new society based on the Myoho emerge in the future. A close scrutiny of history, ideologies, and the races points to this.

"Their right to that honor becomes easier to understand when one realizes that by believing in the Mystic Law the followers of the Buddhism of Nichiren Daishonin are destined to propagate their saving faith not only in Japan but also in the rest of the world. Perhaps now, when we are only a small group, this assertion seems farfetched, but the time is coming when our numbers will multiply to the astonishment of all mankind. The Buddhism of Nichiren Daishonin, as embodied in Nam-myoho-renge-kyo, has the power to achieve this. Historians in coming ages will testify to the truth of what I am now saying."

Caught up in the discussion and flattered that Toda devoted so much attention and care to answering his questions, Yamamoto continued: "You mentioned Nam-myoho-renge-kyo. What is that, sir?"

"To define it exactly and fully demands both time and knowledge. Ultimately, virtual mountains of Sakyamuni's scriptures were compiled to explain it, but I think that put in easily grasped terms Nam-myoho-renge-kyo is the fundamental law of all universal phenomena, humanity, and all plant and animal life. It has the power to transform even man's karma, because it is the force governing the universe. In Buddhist terminology, it is the inherent nature of all things. In addition, it is the name of the eternal Buddha of the Latter Day of the Law. As Sakyamuni prophesied, two millennia after his death Nichiren Daishonin became the Buddha. He inscribed the essence of his Buddhahood in the form of the Gohonzon. This manifestation of the Law has become the substance of Nam-myoho-renge-kyo. In the preface to the Lotus Sutra, Sakyamuni said that all phenomena are born of one universal law. This one law is Nam-myoho-renge-kyo. I realize that all of this is a little too much to take in at one time, but remember that until one grasps the meaning of Nam-myoho-renge-kyo, the true life is impossible. Well, I could go on all night, but it is about time to bring the meeting to a close. Let's go into this more thoroughly after you have done a little more studying on Buddhism."

Although he did not completely understand everything Toda had said, Yamamoto was elated by the discussion and by the intelligence and warmth of the man. Not yet ready to say good-bye, he hurried to put in one more question: "What do you think of the emperor?"

"From the Buddhist viewpoint, the emperor system is not a major problem. We see no need either to abolish it or to give it special treatment. After all, in the eyes of the Buddha, the emperor is no more than another mortal. Today, in relation to the happiness of the Japanese people, he has no significant role to play. Times have changed greatly. I am not opposed to the provision in the constitution that gives sovereignty to the people and limits the emperor to a symbolic function. Right now, the important thing is for the nation—including the emperor—to recover from the devastation of war and to rise to a peaceful and highly cultural level as quickly as possible. Of course, this is no easy task, but it must be undertaken with boldness and courage. Halfway measures will neither help Japan nor contribute to the well being of mankind."

As he listened to Toda's straightforward explanations, Yamamoto suddenly thought that perhaps he had at last found a teacher and guide. Perhaps under Toda's leadership he might discover the true meaning of life. But suddenly the idea came to him that he had thoughtlessly monopolized too much of everyone's time. In embarrassment he turned to his comrades to ask if they had any questions. They all shook their heads.

Most of the leaders and society staff members had attended this meeting. All of them were impressed with the eagerness and wholesome curiosity Yamamoto displayed. The seriousness of his questions clearly set him apart from most young people. The keen interest Toda had paid Yamamoto suggested that he too was both impressed and interested in him as a prospective convert. Everyone present earnestly hoped that it would not be long before Yamamoto made the decision to join them. Quite naturally, Miss Mikawa and her friend Sakata were proud that their newcomer was a success. They had been right in their appraisal of him. A certain suspense filled the room as, for some reason, the meeting, though formally over, did not yet adjourn. Toda smoked calmly and watched Yamamoto, who was nervously aware of the expectant gazes focused on him. Presently he rose and, after thanking Toda for his interest, said: "As the Chinese sage says in the *Book of Rites:* 'It is better to think again when you disagree with someone; it is also better to think again when you agree.' I will be doing a great deal of thinking about all you have told me before I make a final decision. But I agree that I ought to apply myself with the energy of youth. And I would very much like to study under your guidance and to practice the faith as you have suggested. This meeting has been a revelation to me. I have been deeply moved. In gratitude, though I'm afraid it is not very good, I should like to recite this poem:

Dear traveler,
Where do you come from?
And where do you go?
The moon has set,
And the sun has not yet risen.

In the darkness before dawn
I fumble
In search of light.
To dispel the dark clouds in my mind
To seek a great tree unbowed by the storm,
I spring from the earth."

Some applause and much surprise greeted the recitation; few there had seen anything of the kind before at a discussion meeting. But as he listened, Toda smiled with contentment, especially at the last line of the poem, which reminded him of the Bodhisattvas springing from the earth as they are prophesied to do in the Lotus Sutra. Apparently the similarity between Yamamoto's poem and the passage in the scriptures was a coincidence, if a wonderful one, for Nichiren had said that his disciples, devoted to the propagation of the true Buddhism, would be "Bodhisattvas springing from the earth."

Yamamoto had in mind the lush, exuberant growth of plants springing from parched ground and the sense of wonder that always accompanies the resurgence of the beauty of nature. Images of this kind had been running through his head for the past few days and found expression in the poems he frequently composed. Flushed with emotion and shyness, he sat down as Toda said: "Your poem was fine, but from the look of you I would say you are not entirely well. How is your health?"

The question startled Yamamoto, who wondered how Toda had come to suspect his poor physical condition. "In fact, I am not as well as I might be. I have a kind of lung ailment."

"Tuberculosis? Well it's not the most pleasant thing in the world, but if you take care of yourself, rest, and eat plenty of nourishing food, you'll be all right. I know what I'm talking about because I've had it too. One of my lungs was badly affected, but it healed before I knew it. Do you have a fever?"

Touching his forehead, Yamamoto said: "I had one earlier,

but I feel much better now." In fact, Yamamoto was surprised to find that the weakness and fever had passed. He seemed to have forgotten about them in the excitement of the discussion. He was still tired, but that was all.

"Still, take care of yourself," said Toda. "You are young. You have plenty of time to regain your health. Only nineteen." As Toda said this he seemed to lapse again into a musing reminiscence. Everyone else in the room was still deeply concerned about Yamamoto and the possibility of his accepting Nichiren and becoming a member of Soka Gakkai, but Toda seemed almost sure of the young man. Presently, rising and bidding farewell to the group, Toda remarked in passing: "I'm sure I'll be seeing you again next month, everyone." It was nearly ten o'clock when he left the room. He bade farewell to the Mikawa family and disappeared into the night, accompanied by some staff members.

After Toda had gone, Yamamoto felt lonely and deserted. He suppressed an urge to follow Toda and continue the talk. Two leaders of the society began explaining the formal technicalities of joining the group, but none of this interested Yamamoto. The important thing for him was Josei Toda. The idea of joining a religious organization disturbed him, but all doubt and fear were allayed at the thought of Toda, his voice and gaze and the unforgettable impact of what he had said. Bergson seemed to recede into a hazy background. His two friends, unable to make up their minds, remained noncommittal; but Yamamoto told them: "It is just possible that in the Buddhism Mr. Toda explained I might find the way to the true life. I haven't found it anywhere else. I must give this a serious try."

On his way home Toda was absorbed in recollections. He had been only twenty when he first met his teacher, Tsunesaburo Makiguchi. That meeting had transformed Toda's life, and he could not help wondering what kind of impression he had made on the eager and serious young man who had plied him with deeply felt questions. Perhaps this meeting was no accident; perhaps Yamamoto was predestined to meet Toda, as Toda had been predestined to meet Makiguchi twenty-seven years ago.

Until March, 1920, Toda had taught at the Mayachi Elementary School in the small, coal-mining mountain town of Yubari, in Hokkaido. He had obtained a substitute elementary-school teacher's license in 1917, while working for a wholesale dealer in his hometown on the coast of Hokkaido, and through a connection of his mother's had managed to get the job at Mayachi Elementary School. The town was remote and lonely. There was no train service in those days, and in order to reach Numanozawa, the nearest town of any size, it was necessary to rely on horse-drawn carriages in the summer and sleighs in the winter. Since Toda had lived his young years near the sea, the monotony of mountain life depressed him to the extent that he developed something very like claustrophobia. For about two years he lived in a small rented house and took his meals at the home of one of his pupils. In spite of the loneliness of the town, Toda found joy in his work. He was one of the most popular teachers in the school. Students flocked to his house to study and to have a good time with the lively and personable young instructor. But the grayness of the environment often led Toda to urge his young charges to get out of the town as quickly as possible. In fact, Toda was eager to take his own advice.

Studious and diligent, he obtained his full-time teacher's license in the summer of 1919 and added another license as teacher of mathematics and physics at the end of the same year. Though severe with indolent youngsters, Toda was warm and understanding with the majority of his students, for whom he felt genuine affection. He even forgave them when they mischievously stole his glasses, without which Toda was nearly blind.

In February of 1920, Toda suddenly abandoned his work and left Mayachi. Although he knew that his departure—only one month before graduation—would sadden and disappoint many people, he had a burning sense of ambition. Certain that something better waited for him in later life, he was convinced that it would never happen in the remote mountains of Hokkaido. Tokyo was his destination, but before starting on the longer journey, he returned to his hometown to say goodbye. From there he traveled to northern Honshu, where he stayed a few days with his elder brother.

He arrived in Tokyo in late March, 1920. While still in Hokkaido, he had dreamed of the glittering metropolis where he would succeed immediately. Instead he found a cold, unfriendly city of busy, indifferent people. Staying with a friend from Hokkaido, Toda met nothing but difficulties for the following few months. He could find no work; he ran out of money and gave up the self-education plan he had initiated upon arrival in the city. His life became an ordeal, but he persevered. Oddly enough, it was because of this trial that he ultimately met Makiguchi. If he had found work in a school at once, the initial encounter with this educator and thinker might never have taken place; and Toda's life might have taken an entirely different course.

In spite of Toda's determination to be true to himself and to work to the utmost of his ability for his future development, his circumstances did not improve immediately. By the middle of July, when the Tokyo humidity and heat were nearly intolerable—especially to one born and bred in the dry cold of Hokkaido—Toda still had not found a regular job. His funds were exhausted, and he felt that he could no longer endure his hardships without assistance from somewhere. Although he had long hesitated to take the humiliating step, it finally became unavoidable for him to visit the home of General Okamoto, a distant relative of his mother's, in the hope of some kind of help.

Because he had no other clothes, he wore a quilted kimono, and by the time he reached the Okamoto house, perspiration poured from his face and ran down his arms. Shabby and miserable in the heat, he entered the comfortable drawing room of his relative's home. Mrs. Okamoto, who received him after a brief delay, was polite as propriety demanded, but she was unable to conceal her contempt for this ragged country boy clearly come to beg for money or food. Immediately sensing the lady's true feelings, Toda cut his visit short. As he started to leave, she wrapped a bit of cake in some paper and handed it to him with a patronizing smile. Angered and disappointed, Toda refused her charity and left, vowing never again to set foot in that house.

Humiliated at having been judged on the basis of his appearance alone, Toda now found himself in worse straits than ever. He managed to struggle on till August, when he read about a distinguished educator who had recently made a bold, if somewhat shocking, pronouncement to the effect that Emperor Meiji's famous Educational Rescript, the basis of Japanese education, was "of the lowest moral order." Puzzled yet attracted by this attitude, Toda decided to visit the man. The author of the statement was Tsunesaburo Makiguchi. Armed with a letter of introduction from a Hokkaido friend, Toda called at Makiguchi's home in mid-August.

Mrs. Makiguchi, who was drawing water from the well when Toda arrived, immediately conducted him into the living room. Makiguchi was then principal of the Nishimachi Elementary School, and his reputation in educational circles was high because of his unusual theories and teaching techniques. Naturally, the newly arrived country boy had never met this well-known man, and as he awaited Makiguchi's arrival, Toda wondered what kind of person Makiguchi was and whether he would give Toda a job in his school. In Toda's financial straits, a job was of the utmost importance, but from the psychological standpoint he was in even greater need of a teacher and mentor.

At last Makiguchi entered the living room. He was a dignified, middle-aged man with penetrating eyes. After the customary courtesies, Toda presented his letter of introduction, which Makiguchi read at once. He then asked Toda a few questions about his background and experience. Though at first somewhat shy before this taciturn man, as he related his past experience and plans for the future, as well as his opinions on education, Toda was soon encouraged to talk more freely. Makiguchi listened with interest and curiosity. When Toda finished, Makiguchi asked, smiling gently: "Have you brought a *curriculum vitae?*" Toda said that he had and offered it. As Makiguchi perused the paper, Toda watched the calm, observant face of the man. Suddenly, he came to a decision: he would immediately ask for employment in Makiguchi's school, for he felt sure that at last he had found the man who would be his intellectual and spiritual guide.

"Please, Mr. Makiguchi, hire me to work with you at the Nishimachi School. I promise that if you do, you will never regret it. I can make honor students out of all your backward people. Please believe me."

Makiguchi immediately perceived that what seemed to be aggressiveness and self-confidence was in fact ardor and enthusiasm to do good work. He nodded with a smile and, when Toda renewed his plea for a job, promised to do what he could. Before Toda left, the two new friends had a chance to engage in a long discussion on serious aspects of educational theory and practice. When they parted, Makiguchi was decidedly impressed, and Toda was filled with hope. Nor was his hope betrayed, for shortly after this initial meeting, Toda was appointed an instructor at the Nishimachi Elementary School.

Thus began the association that continued until Makiguchi's tragic death. During all those years, Toda worked hard and revered and obeyed his teacher and friend. Makiguchi rarely praised Toda, but Toda had both profound respect and deep affection for him. Their friendship and professional relationship bloomed into what in Buddhist terms is called "the oneness of teacher and disciple." In 1928 both were converted to Nichiren Shoshu.

The first meeting between Yamamoto and Toda took place on a night three years after the death of Makiguchi. Toda was forty-seven, and Yamamoto was nineteen. Makiguchi had been forty-nine and Toda twenty when they first met. Suddenly, Toda knew in his heart that this strangely handsome, intelligent, and spiritually disturbed young man, so different from others of his generation, was destined to be the true disciple for whom he had waited. Although Yamamoto was yet unaware of his future, Toda was convinced that he was to be the person to share the great task of propagating the true Buddhism to all mankind. The two of them together would instigate the human revolution that would lead the world to peace and happiness. Toda's heart swelled with hope and gratitude as he thought about young Yamamoto and his destiny.

On August 24, 1947, Yamamoto formally joined Nichiren Shoshu in a rite conducted by the priest Taiei Horigome at the Kankiryo temple. During the lengthy ritual, composed of recitations of the Sutra and chanting of the Daimoku, Yamamoto's face revealed his mixed emotions. He took his religious commitment seriously, as he did all things. He knew that his will was strong, but aware of his physical weakness, he feared that his body would be unequal to the immense task of spiritual reformation.

6. ROOTS

IN 1947 the postwar misery of the Japanese people plunged to its depths. Metropolitan Tokyo, which had been razed by incendiary bombs, remained in ruins; there were no signs of true rehabilitation. Half-starved citizens swarmed the streets in search of food and clothes. The underground passages at major railroad stations were crowded with hordes of vagrants, hooligans, and homeless children with vacant stares. Though the actual fighting was over, another kind of war had taken its place: a war against chaos, spiritual anarchy, nihilism, poverty, and hunger. World War II was finished, but peace had not yet come to Japan. Only black marketeers thrived, while honest citizens suffered in hunger. Because the food supply remained far short of the demand, people, in desperation, behaved like starved beasts. The government's attempts to import rice from Southeast Asia failed, forcing Japan to depend entirely on the flour and corn released by the occupation forces. Rice gradually became unobtainable; even the substitutes—white potatoes, corn, and sweet potatoes—were distributed only in minimal quantities.

The clothing situation was no better. Only flimsy staple fiber was available. Men were most often dressed in jackets of this unsatisfactory cloth and leftover army trousers; around their shoulders, women wrapped such sweaters and shawls as they could find and wore baggy *mompe* in place of skirts and wooden clogs instead of shoes. Those who obtained clothing of even this wretched caliber were lucky: many less fortunate people were clad no better than beggars.

The housing shortage visited still another nightmare on the nation. Air-raid shelters, shacks of corrugated tin sheeting, and jerry-built barracks were homes for countless people. As the demobilized soldiers and the repatriated colonials of the now defunct empire flooded back to the Japanese islands, every house was crammed to overflowing. Often a small room housed ten people, young and old, men and women. When it rained, the poor hovels leaked like sieves; when winter winds blew, they were only slightly warmer than the outdoors. Still, even in the face of almost unbelievable conditions, the government remained powerless to help.

If staying at home in crowded, cold, or leaky rooms was unpleasant, venturing abroad was worse because the transportation system was chaotic. The electric trains, the only remaining means of transport, were few and far between. Dark and drafty because of their boarded windows, they were invariably jammed to capacity, and in order to buy tickets, people waited for hours in line.

It is scarcely to be wondered that deprived of the basic necessities of life and confronted with ever-spiraling inflation many people died. Among the most notable losses from hunger were a professor of philosophy and a judge who starved rather than buy black-market food.

Under these trying conditions, Toda and his followers continued their lectures and discussion meetings, visited the head temple, and journeyed to rural areas to offer guidance to society members. The odds they faced were extremely stiff, but their dedication and faith enabled them to carry on the work and to conduct Gongyo every morning and evening. As Toda sadly mused on the affliction of the nation, he could not help observing that everything had turned out precisely as Nichiren had prophesied in his treatise *The Security of the Land Through the Establishment of True Buddhism.* Seven hundred years after he had written it, at least two of the seven major calamities Nichiren had foreseen were repeating themselves: foreign invasion and internal strife. The Allied forces were occupying Japan, and the entire nation was disintegrating in fierce internal battles over food, housing, wages, economics, politics, and religion. Turmoil reigned. In one instance a man was killed by a member of his own family over a trifling morsel of food. Passengers on the stifling and overcrowded trains and trolleys quarreled among themselves; and on a larger scale, prolonged labor disputes stalled production and thus paralyzed the national economy. Fragmentation of political parties meant that the group managing to gain even nominal control spent all of its time consolidating its position and devoted little energy to solving the pressing problems of the moment or trying to alleviate the suffering of the people. All religions, both the established older ones and the new postwar sects, were torn by schism.

In the light of this confusion and disorder, Toda spent much time pondering the course and the structure Soka Gakkai must take. Sensing the increasingly important role the society would inevitably play in the future of Japan, he conceived plan after plan for its advancement and growth. Because he firmly believed in the Buddhist axiom "the deeper the roots, the more luxuriant the branches," Toda intended to ensure that the society took firm root so that it might grow into a great tree and bear rich fruit.

But the society was still young. Its membership was increasing at a satisfactory rate, though its foundations were still far from solid. Although they worked hard, some of his followers entertained somewhat superficial ideas of the universal propagation of the true faith and were as yet spiritually incapable of manifesting the essential fortitude and integrity. One night, at a meeting of an intimate circle of his closest disciples, Toda delivered the following remarks in order to strengthen the faith of his people and to avert any possible disunity among them:

"Today it is difficult for any organization in Japan to remain unaffected by internal strife. There are many reasons for this, but the chief one is the current widespread abuse of the true Buddhism. It only follows, then, that since we are devoted to the upholding of true Buddhism and since we are rooted in the life philosophy of Nichiren, Soka Gakkai is the only possible group in the country that can escape internal contention and discord. No matter how large our organization becomes, if we remain true to the one faith, we have nothing to fear. I am doing all that I can to deepen and strengthen the roots of our faith because without them we are powerless.

"Pay no attention to the flashy activities of other pseudo-religious groups. They are all inevitably doomed to self-destruction from within. Furthermore, do not listen to foolish talk about splits in our society after we have grown to power in the future. People who say such things speak in jealousy of our vigor and strength. Remember, as long as we remain true to the one Buddhism, we need have no fear of splitting. Only by remaining together and devoting all of our energy and strength to the great task can we achieve our ultimate goal. Never neglect your duty or let the supreme mission of the society slip from your mind, for if you do, the threat of internal dissension will emerge. In such a case, I will disband the group. Our society is growing like a tree. Its main root is buried deep in the faith of Nichiren Daishonin, but each of you is a rootlet. The main root and the entire tree depend on the rootlets for sustenance and strength.

"We differ from other organizations in that our aim is the spreading of a life-giving faith, whereas most other groups seek only profit. Anyone who harbors in his heart a motive of self-gain had best leave us now. We must be unified to carry out our great work. True unity is not achieved through the wills and intentions of men alone. It is born of the bonds of pure, firm faith in the Gohonzon. According to Buddhist thought, the act of disturbing harmony and unity is one of the five capital sins. Consequently, since the introduction of desire for self-gain into the purity of our attitude amounts to disruption of harmony, it

cannot be tolerated. But as long as we march together toward the achievement of our goal, nothing can stop us, for we will be united firmly by the bonds of faith.

"Do not think that ours is the only age in which members of the group have renounced their belief. Even during the lifetime of Nichiren Daishonin, several priests abandoned their faith and slandered their great leader. After his death, in the days of the second high priest, Nikko, five of Nichiren's leading disciples turned away from the faith for the sake of gain. But all of these men ultimately met retribution and died in misery. Let their stories be a lesson to us all. Each of us is like a rough diamond that must be polished before it manifests its inherent beauty. Polish yourselves by strengthening your faith, and you will be richly rewarded.

"Finally, although we are fundamentally unlike the rapidly burgeoning labor unions of today, I foresee our developing into a body of unprecedented size and power. In order to make this growth possible, we require a solid structure and an efficient organization. Let us all devote our talents to the creation of such an organization, for it will not only advance our mission but also infinitely benefit each individual member of the society."

In this way Toda revealed part of his vision of the society's future in order to make his disciples realize the importance and urgency of fortifying the group's foundation. It disappointed him, however, to see from the faces of his audience that many failed to grasp his vision.

On October nineteenth, Soka Gakkai held its second general convention in the Education Hall in Kanda. Taking part in the proceedings were the sixty-fourth high priest of Nichiren Shoshu, Nissho Mizutani; his predecessor, Nichiman Akiyama; the retired high priest Taiei Horigome; and other leading clerics, including Nittatsu Hosoi. At both sessions of the convention—one in the morning and one in the afternoon—attendance exceeded that of the previous annual meeting. Yuzo Mishima, a director of the society, opened the conference with a report on achievements:

"Our society presently consists of six divisions: General Affairs, Doctrinal Study, Information, Youth, Women, and Finance. Each department functions smoothly. We now have twelve chapters in Tokyo and eleven in the provinces. Discussion meetings are held once every month for the practicing of the faith and for membership drives.

"Since the first general meeting, held on November seventeenth of last year, a new series of lectures on the Lotus Sutra has gotten under way. The first series began on New Year's Day last year at the head temple. The fifth series began in September of this year. An average of fifty people attend these meetings, which are held every Monday, Wednesday, and Friday evening from six to eight at the second-floor headquarters in the Nihon Shogakkan Publishing House. Our people are so eager to learn about the Sutra that some come from as far as Chigasaki, Hiratsuka, and Sagamihara in the south and Shiki in the north of Tokyo. Their pressing desire to become cornerstones in the edifice of the universal propagation of true Buddhism inspires these people to make the long trip to town to hear the words of our General Director, Josei Toda, who conducts the lecture meetings. I would now like to say a few words about the activities and development of a few of our leading chapters.

"The Suwa chapter, in Nagano Prefecture, by increasing to twenty members under the guidance of Mr. Toda and other leaders, gives every indication of continuing its dynamic growth. Similarly, after Mr. Toda and his group visited the Izu Peninsula in January of this year, the chapter there has rapidly increased to a few dozen members. Each month, three of our leaders visit the city of Ito, and thanks to their efforts, the Ito chapter now has a membership of over thirty eager people and holds discussion meetings on a regular basis. Even in distant Kyushu the work of a small group of leaders is now bearing fruit. Their guidance trips to Fukuoka and Oita prefectures in January touched off brisk activity among the members of the Kyushu chapter.

"In September of last year, Mr. Toda conducted the first postwar guidance trip to the Nasu chapter. While there, he held a meeting in the home of the Masuda family; and now membership is increasing. Mr. Masuda has been elected to the local village assembly. The Kiryu chapter demonstrated its interest and fervor in growth and expansion by inviting Mr.

Toda and other leaders to hold discussions and lectures in their region on two occasions since the spring of this year.

"Not to be overshadowed by the provincial groups, the chapters of metropolitan Tokyo, thanks to the untiring efforts of many of our colleagues, are making great strides forward. The Kamata chapter has made outstanding progress: it created two new chapters in Urayasu, Chiba Prefecture, and another in Shiki, Saitama Prefecture. It makes me happy to say that the Kamata group has reached its prewar level of activity. In addition, the chapter in Adachi Ward is expanding its efforts, not only into neighboring Saitama Prefecture but also as far as Aomori Prefecture in the north. Especially impressive is the establishment of the new Honjo chapter, in an area reduced to ruins by the war.

"Eighty persons attended the summer course held at Daiseki-ji this year. This is a fine increase over the twenty-nine who attended last year."

Naturally, as he listened to the lengthy catalog of impressive society achievements, Toda rejoiced over the progress being made; but somehow he felt that the general atmosphere of the meeting lacked vitality and dynamism. There seemed to be no new, talented disciples to inject fresh life into the organization. The older staff members could justly take pride in their work, but they were deficient in the essential regenerating spirit. They were prosaic and uninspired in outlook.

Following the opening remarks by Mishima, several people gave testimonials, after which the high priest Mizutani spoke on the age of the propagation of the true faith. He appealed to the lay believers to do their utmost to spread the belief in the Mystic Law. He then said a few words about conditions at the head temple:

"As you know, the head temple is currently in urgent need of reconstruction. The occupation-sponsored agrarian reform has stripped us of almost all the arable land that has belonged to Nichiren Shoshu for centuries. The outlook is by no means bright, but if we reflect on the days of Nichiren Daishonin himself, we see that we have little cause for complaint. He and his infinite teachings prevailed then, as they are bound to do in this evil world. The time has now come for laity and clergy alike to follow his example and to devote maximum effort to the rehabilitation of Nichiren Shoshu and our nation through the unceasing practice of our faith."

The high priest's words pained Toda's heart and inspired him with a deepened sense of anxiety and of his own responsibilities. As the lay leader of the group he must undertake the reconstruction of Daiseki-ji. The high priest then brought his speech to a close:

"I fervently pray that the society will grow in a spirit of cooperation, study, and devotion to the speedy realization of the universal propagation of true Buddhism under the divine guidance and assistance from the one True Buddha."

Rising from his seat and bowing to the high priest, Toda swore silently: "If you give me a little more time, I promise to strive with all my heart for the rehabilitation of the head temple and for the universal propagation of our faith. To this mission I dedicate my entire life and strength."

Following the high priest's remarks, the retired priest Taiei Horigome ascended the rostrum. He opened his speech with a short discourse on the great seventeenth-century poet Matsuo Basho, who had swept decadent schools of verse from the field with his work toward the perfection of the haiku, the pithy, association-rich, seventeen-syllable verse style that has persisted to this day. He moved from the achievements of this great poet to the even greater triumphs of Nichiren, whose teachings had destroyed the very base of degenerate and misguided religious sects.

"Seven centuries have passed since the founding of Nichiren Shoshu, but its orthodox doctrine still remains undimmed. Yet, even today much remains to be done to spread the word of our faith."

He then spoke on the essence of true Buddhism and appealed passionately to the faithful to intensify their attempts to win new followers.

Toda made two speeches that day, one in the morning and another in the afternoon. In his morning speech, he emphasized that rehabilitation of Japan must be carried out through true Buddhism, which teaches a life philosophy based on the concept of karma ranging over the three lives of the past, present and future. "Only by understanding the law of causality, or karma, as expounded in true Buddhism can the Japanese people change their destiny and prosper," he declared.

He then went on to expound the essence of true Buddhism as taught by Nichiren, after making it clear that although the Lotus Sutra of Sakyamuni is supreme among the sutras it is no longer valid in the Latter Day of the Law.

"It becomes imperative for us to acquire a law that will lead us to enlightenment and thus overcome the karma that binds all common mortals. Nichiren Daishonin, however, founded the very law that can help us break free from the bondage of our past lives and change our destiny. That law is Nam-myoho-renge-kyo. Chanting it and worshiping the Gohonzon is the only way to change our karma.

"Of all the evil deeds committed since time immemorial, slandering true Buddhism is the most serious. It condemns us to the Ten Evil Deeds and the Eight Great Difficulties. By fervently believing in the Myoho, we can purge ourselves of karma from past lives. Without the Myoho, however, it would take eons to change our karma. Since karma works on us continually, we must not lose faith when we are confronted with a succession of difficulties and ordeals. Instead we must realize that our trials are a necessary process in our eternal life and enlightenment. In other words, they are the will of the Buddha."

His afternoon speech was entitled "On the Mission of Our Society." In it he alluded to the troubled conditions of the nation and the people and stressed the importance of spreading the teachings of Nichiren for the sake of the salvation of the Japanese people and mankind. He said that he wanted to share with his fellow men the enlightenment he had experienced in prison, the realization that common mortals can attain Buddhahood through faith in the Gohonzon.

"The desire to share the life philosophy of Nichiren Daishonin with others makes us emissaries of the Buddha. Our membership drives represent our wish to give people the source of salvation, clothed in compassion.

"Converting others is the heart of the mission and the creed of our society. Those of us who are fortunate enough to understand the meaning of worshiping the Buddha must share our conviction with our fellow men. There can be no poverty in the Buddha, for he is protected by the Bodhisattvas and guardian deities. His strength and power ensure peace and plenty in this existence. Our society is an assemblage of emissaries of the Buddha. It is our duty to bring all troubled and perturbed people before the Gohonzon of Nichiren Shoshu. But I must emphasize one thing: we must never seek personal convenience or gain. I need hardly say that the retribution for such an act would be dreadful, for self-interest in this instance is far worse than other sins. Nor is this true only on an individual level: the society as a whole must never work for fame, money, or donations."

In rounding out his speech, Toda said a few words about the founder of the society, the late President Makiguchi:

"In spite of all the criticism and abuse heaped upon him in the later part of his life, our founder and teacher worked tirelessly for the spreading of Nichiren Shoshu. Finally, imprisoned by the militarists and police officials, he gave his life for his faith. Like him, we must maintain undying faith in Nichiren Daishonin's teachings and strive always for the universal propagation of the faith. No matter how great the obstacles in our way or how fierce the attacks and criticisms leveled against us by nonbelievers, we must continue our work. Only in this way will we be able to face the Dai-Gohonzon with pride and clear consciences when we die and return to the Land of the Buddha."

At the conclusion of Toda's talk, the entire assembly joined in singing "Song of the Comrades," and as he listened, Toda discreetly wiped away a few tears. They were not entirely tears of joy, for though the general meeting had been an apparent success, something seemed wrong. The meeting lacked vigor and spontaneity, and Toda suspected that this might be because some of the leaders were losing their pioneering sense of mission. Force of habit was blunting their spirit of reconstruction. Toda began to fear that the foundation of the society was less secure than he had hoped; perhaps his efforts to transform the society into a lay organization primarily devoted to the life philosophy of Nichiren, instead of to the philosophy of value, had not succeeded. As these suspicions ran through his mind, Toda became more convinced that steps must be taken to strengthen the organization. Most of the leaders of the postwar group were the same ones who had controlled the society in the prewar days. As the society showed signs of regaining and even surpassing its former strength, the leaders tended to lapse into complacency. Their faith clearly had its limitations. In fact, many of them had renounced their faith during the dark days of the war, because of persecution by the militarists. It was only thanks to Toda's good offices that they regained their positions on the board of directors and in other high places after the society got under way again. True, there were some active young members on the staff. They had the right idea, but unfortunately, they were still immature. The lack of vigorous young leaders deeply concerned Toda, who impatiently awaited the arrival of new men who would be more creative in their approach to Soka Gakkai's great task.

In the old society, the driving force of the organization had been the middle-aged people, but realizing the importance of preparing for the future, Toda laid great stress on training the young. He insisted that the Youth Division concentrate on giving its members a firm foundation in Buddhist doctrine so that their faith would be strong and they would be prepared to do doctrinal battle with other Buddhist sects when the occasion arose. So thorough was their training and so eager their spirit that many of the members of the youth group grew impatient to cross verbal swords with their doctrinal enemies.

Looking for opportunities to engage in religious argument, they often visited temples, where they invariably caused a great stir. Toda never tried to restrain his young followers because he knew that encounters with the clergy of other Buddhist groups and of new religions would help them understand firsthand the evils of false teachings and would strengthen their faith in Nichiren Shoshu. Thrilled by ideological battles with priests and religionists, these young people quickly defeated their opponents with the incisive sword of Nichiren's doctrine, but they were bewildered when their polemic success proved short-lived in practice. The misguided sects did not disintegrate as—in the opinions of the vigorous young people—they should have. On the contrary they seemed to thrive. At a meeting on one December night, a certain young firebrand asked: "Mr. Toda, we've always defeated our opponents in religious debates, but their influence doesn't seem to fade. In fact, some of them seem to grow stronger. Why is that?"

The naiveté of the young man amused Toda, who explained the situation this way: "Don't take this thing too seriously. It is about time you learned that religious polemics are not what they used to be. In the old days, religious debate was a deadly serious matter. The loser was usually converted to the sect of the winner, whose disciple he willingly became. For instance, in the ninth century, Dengyo the Great, the founder of the Tendai sect in Japan, conducted a religious debate with leading priests of the six older Nara sects. The discussion took place in the presence of Emperor Kammu. In his treatise *The Security of the Land Through the Establishment of True Buddhism,* Nichiren Daishonin wrote that Dengyo the Great completely defeated fourteen priests, representing six sects, who realized on the spot that they had been degrading true Buddhism by neglecting the Lotus Sutra. After writing a letter of apology to the emperor, these prominent priests accepted Tendai and became disciples of Dengyo the Great. This is a famous story. Naturally, since the leading priests of the six sects were converted to the Tendai school, all other priests throughout Japan had to do the same. In 827, as a result of this provisional *kosen rufu,* a high sanctuary was built on the summit of Mount Hiei. This period, known as the Heian, was among the most peaceful and prosperous in Japanese history. It may be regarded as an approximation of *obutsu myogo.*

"Since the culture and society of the times were aristocratic, however, only the emperor and the ruling classes worshiped the Lotus Sutra. The Buddhism taught then was a provisional teaching for the Middle Day of Sakyamuni's Law. Though the fusion of Buddhism with society was achieved, it was shallow and superficial in comparison with the truly profound union of the two that we are now beginning to undertake. Because the results achieved in the distant past lacked profundity, certain leading priests of the Tendai school adopted the false doctrines of the Shingon sect and defiled the great Tendai tradition. Nichiren Daishonin deplored this in his *Treatise on the Three Great Secret Laws.* Let me quote him now:

> 'Jikaku and Chisho, third and fourth chief abbots at Enryaku-ji, the head temple of the Tendai Sect, on Mount Hiei, betrayed their masters Dengyo the Great and Gishin by adopting false doctrines and ridiculing the teachings of their own sect. In doing this they defiled the mystic teaching of the Perfect and Immaculate Truth, which had been nurtured at Enryaku-ji. This state of affairs is truly regrettable.'

"Although the establishment of the fusion of Buddhism and society and the spreading of the provisional teaching of the Lotus Sutra actually lasted for no more than thirty years, the glory of the achievement resulted in three centuries of peace. Dengyo the Great's polemic victory over the priests of six false sects was of special significance because it was instrumental in the attainment of a general, if short-lived, propagation of the provisional teaching. Incidentally, in those days, the rules of polemics were strictly observed.

"Time and time again, Nichiren Daishonin demanded that the Kamakura shogunate government allow him to hold a public debate with priests from other Buddhist sects. When he presented *The Security of the Land Through the Establishment of True Buddhism* to the then all-powerful regent Hojo Tokiyori, he announced bluntly that if the government doubted the contents of the tract they should allow him to prove the truth of his position by means of public debate with other priests. But the priests knew they did not stand a chance of winning in a debate with Nichiren Daishonin.

"Toward the end of the Kamakura period—which lasted from 1185 to 1333 and was the opening of the Latter Day of the Law—cunning priests not only avoided public debates, in which they ran the risk of ignominious failure, but also conducted smear campaigns against Nichiren Daishonin and gradually manipulated the government into persecuting him.

"Nichiren Daishonin was aware of what these people were doing, but he did not allow it to discourage him. He continued to press for public religious debates, and in one instance, the long-awaited duel seemed on the verge of materializing; but it was canceled at the last minute. Nichiren Daishonin then wrote his famous eleven letters to the government, in which he denounced it for espousing false religions and prophesied calamities if it did not accept the Myoho. Nichiren Daishonin acted in a noble and courageous way that puts modern revolutionaries to shame.

"As a result of his insistence on religious debates he was banished to Ito on the Izu Peninsula and then to remote Sado Island. He suffered further tribulations as well, but he never ceased demanding the right to speak in public. Still, the corrupt people with whom he had to deal saw to it that he never got his chance. Because they were afraid of the power of his polemic abilities, the priests avoided open confrontation but relentlessly continued their covert intrigues against him.

"Today, in contrast to the times of Nichiren Daishonin, religious circles are so chaotic and evil that not even the rules of polemics are observed. Religious organizations concentrate solely on making money, and faith does not exist. The old tradition, whereby religious leaders bowed to the victor in religious debates and willingly followed the leadership of those who triumphed, is now a forgotten thing of the past. This kind of depravity is typical of the Latter Day of the Law, in which we live.

"Our age is a terrible one, for even when a person has completely defeated his religious opponents in open debate and has proved all their doctrines false, they refuse to admit defeat. Propagating the truth under such circumstances is certainly a difficult thing. Unlike times gone by, when it was enough to convert the leaders of the nation to assure the conversion of the whole citizenry, today sovereignty rests with the people. This means that we must convert each individual. The religious revolution we are about to carry out cannot be achieved without fervent faith, great courage, and wisdom. This is the key to the religious revolution that we must bring about.

"Religious debates no longer offer a possibility of fruitful results. Our age is so wicked that even international treaties and nonaggression pacts are callously violated. No matter how often you defeat false priests in fair debates, you will be doing little to destroy their religion and even less toward the propagation of the true faith. Our activities must be carried out on a person-to-person basis. Although some may call this method old fashioned, it is both democratic and the best way for us to achieve our goal. As you make converts, one by one, you will set up waves that will eventually sweep over the entire world."

All in the audience felt that Toda's words had given them a heightened sense of mission and had set them on the proper path toward their goal. Though it was long past time to break up the meeting, no one made a move to leave. For a while they continued talking about the temples and headquarters of false religious orders they had visited and seen. Finally, one of the young men, looking up at the flaking paint on the walls and the soot-covered ceiling, said to Toda: "But all the false sects have fine buildings to meet in. I wish our hall would hold at least two or three hundred people."

Toda answered sternly: "We are not a business enterprise. Our aims are fundamentally different from those of the false sects that cow their followers with splendid architecture and frighten them into giving generously. We are not looking for customers. If, during the course of our struggle for universal propagation of the faith, we need buildings for legitimate purposes, we will build them with contributions, which are the fruits of true faith, from Soka Gakkai members. The Gohonzon will see to it that we get what we need. Do not envy the temples and headquarters of corrupt religious orders. That is not the spirit of our society. Faith is paramount, and right now, good men are much more important and urgently needed than fine buildings."

As he spoke, Toda himself glanced round the room in which they sat. It was both the office of the Nihon Shogakkan Publishing House and the Soka Gakkai headquarters. There was no doubting its shabbiness—peeling paint, leaking ceiling, and bare walls. But in spite of all that, the mood of the room was bright and hopeful. Toda continued:

"For the time being at least, this room is big enough. Remember, most places in Japan are in much worse condition. It is our duty to become a pillar of the nation and to assume the fate of Japan. It is our mission to change the fate of Japan entirely. Instead of worrying about buildings, first you ought to improve yourselves and devote all your energy and your unwavering faith to the attainment of universal propagation of true Buddhism. In this way you can become the indestructible core of the society. As Nichiren Daishonin said in the *Gosho,* in the Latter Day of the Law those who have faith in the Mystic Law are the noblest and the most worthy. Have faith in yourselves as young revolutionaries. Many things are far more important than this headquarters building. More important in the architectural line is the Reception Hall at the head temple. As you know, it burned down just before the end of the war. Even now, two and a half years later, it is still in ruins. As you may have guessed from his speech at the last general meeting, the high priest is deeply worried about it. As far as building is concerned, the Reception Hall must take top priority. After we have rebuilt the head temple we will have plenty of time to think about building a new headquarters building for the society.

Till then be patient, and let's take care of what we have. Oh yes, some of you need to have your socks mended. After all, when we do get that new building, you must all be dressed properly."

Everyone joined Toda in laughing, though some of the young men in the room furtively pulled their feet under them to hide the holes in their socks.

As 1947 drew to a close, the islands of Japan still lay in stark misery. Icy winds blowing across the land chilled both the minds and the hearts of the people.

Cold, freezing mornings.

Cold, dark nights.

Day after day of misery and anguish.

The economy of the nation paralyzed, the people stricken with dire hardships, the prospect for rehabilitation was by no means bright. Disaster followed on disaster. A devastating typhoon caused unparalleled floods and damage in the Kanto district. Relief measures were slow, and in mountainous areas, roads went unrepaired. The cold war between the free world, led by the United States, and the Communist countries, led by the Soviet Union, still gripped the international scene. In China, civil war raged as the Communist forces mounted an all-out offensive against the Nationalists. Darkness seemed to cover most of the earth.

In November, 1947, Foreign Minister Molotov announced that the Soviet Union possessed an atomic bomb, thus breaking the United States' monopoly of nuclear weapons. But this news brought little joy to the people of the world, who now found themselves facing the horrendous possibility of nuclear warfare. Though the sun's brilliance daily flooded the sky, gloom filled the minds of people throughout the world. Toda seemed to stand alone and upright, holding the banner of the faith high over the raging seas of darkness and disturbance.

GLOSSARY

AMIDA BUDDHA: The Buddha of Infinite Light (Amitabha); the Buddha of Infinite Life (Amitayus).

ANANDA: A cousin of Sakyamuni and one of his ten major disciples. He accompanied the Buddha for more than twenty years as his favored disciple. Under the guidance of Maha-kasyapa, Ananda is said to have attained enlightenment after the demise of Sakyamuni. He was famed for his excellent memory and is said to have recited all of Sakyamuni's teachings at the First Council, at which they were compiled.

ARHAT: A saint in Hinayana Buddhism who has learned all things and freed himself of desire and rebirths in this world. Also a Buddhist leader.

BODHISATTVA: A being aspiring to enlightenment or a future Buddha. The Bodhisattva seeks salvation for others and therefore concentrates on altruistic aims.

BONTEN AND TAISHAKU: The Japanese names of Brahma and Indra, the central Buddhist guardian deities, who promised to safeguard believers in true Buddhism when Sakyamuni preached the Lotus Sutra.

CHAN-AN (561–632): A disciple of T'ien-t'ai the Great, he collected all the teachings of his master.

DAI-GOHONZON: The fundamental and supreme object of worship enshrined in the high sanctuary of the Nichiren Shoshu head temple, Daiseki-ji. It was inscribed by Nichiren Daishonin on October 12, 1279, to save all mankind from distress and unhappiness. The Dai-Gohonzon is the embodiment both of the profound theory of the Three Great Secret Laws and of the life of the Daishonin himself.

DAIMOKU: The invocation Nam-myoho-renge-kyo, chanted in worshiping the Gohonzon.

DENGYO THE GREAT (767–822): The founder of the Tendai sect (Japanese reading of T'ien-t'ai) in Japan. Dengyo the Great completely refuted prevalent misguided Buddhist sects in the presence of Emperor Kammu and achieved wide propagation of faith in the Lotus Sutra during the Middle Day of the Law.

THE EIGHT GREAT DIFFICULTIES: Retributions for sufferings caused by slandering true Buddhism in past and present lives. These difficulties are: being slighted, having an ugly physical form, lacking suitable clothing, lacking food, seeking vainly for wealth, being born into a poor family, being born into a family believing in a misguided religion, and being persecuted by temporal rulers.

GOHONZON: The object of worship in Nichiren Shoshu, first inscribed by Nichiren Daishonin himself in 1279. At present it is inscribed only by the high priest of Nichiren Shoshu and bestowed upon followers. "Go" is an honorific prefix; "honzon" means object of worship.

GONGYO: The prayer service performed before the Gohonzon every morning and evening. During Gongyo, believers recite the *Hoben* and *Juryo* chapters of the Lotus Sutra and chant the Daimoku.

GOSHO: The complete works of Nichiren Daishonin, consisting of religious theses and letters to his disciples. For the followers of Nichiren Shoshu, it serves a function similar to that of the Bible in Christianity.

HINAYANA BUDDHISM: Generally speaking, there are two main historical streams of Buddhism: Northern and Southern. Northern Buddhists call their own branch Mahayana, or the Larger Vehicle, and call the Southern branch Hinayana, or the Lesser Vehicle, because of the limitations and self-concern of its teachings. Southern Buddhists call their own school Theravada, or the Doctrine of the Elders. Hinayana Buddhism is practiced mainly in Ceylon, Burma, and Thailand; Mahayana Buddhism is practiced mainly in Japan, Korea, and China.

KAIMOKU SHO (Opening of the Eyes): One of the ten major writings of Nichiren Daishonin. Written in February, 1272, while Nichiren Daishonin was in exile on Sado Island, it was dedicated to Shijo Kingo and other disciples. In it Nichiren Daishonin revealed that he is the True Buddha of the Latter Day of the Law.

LOTUS SUTRA: The next to last sutra expounded by Sakyamuni, it is his highest teaching, though the term also refers to the highest teaching of any Buddha, and its implications may vary with time. For instance, the Lotus Sutra of the Zoho, or Middle Day of the Law, is the Maka-shikan of T'ien-t'ai; and that of the Mappo, or Latter Day of the Law, is Nichiren Daishonin's Nam-myoho-renge-kyo, or the Gohonzon.

MAHA-KASYAPA: One of the ten major disciples of Sakyamuni. About three years after Sakyamuni attained enlightenment, Maha-kasyapa became his disciple. Following Sakyamuni's death, he presided over the First Council of believers.

MAHAYANA BUDDHISM: *see* Hinayana Buddhism.

MAKIGUCHI, TSUNESABURO (1871–1944): The first president of Soka Kyoiku Gakkai. Converted to Nichiren Shoshu in 1928, he published *Value-Creating Education Theory* in 1929 and established Soka Kyoiku Gakkai in 1930. Because of his antimilitaristic stand, he was arrested and imprisoned in 1943, together with Josei Toda and other leaders of Soka Kyoiku Gakkai. He died in prison in 1944.

MANJUSRI-BODHISATTVA: Also called Manjushiri, Monjushiri. The Bodhisattva of meditation, or of supreme wisdom, he is regarded as the idealization or personification of the wisdom of the Buddha. He is usually shown mounted on a lion, and in groups he is seen on the left of Sakyamuni.

NAM-MYOHO-RENGE-KYO: Literally, Devotion to the Wonderful

Law Lotus Sutra. Initiated by Nichiren Daishonin, the True Buddha in the Latter Day of the Law, this invocation is the basis of universal life—the most fundamental law of all phenomena in the universe.

NAN-YUEH (515–77): Another name for Eshi, the second patriarch in the lineage of the Chinese T'ien-t'ai sect.

NICHIREN DAISHONIN (1222–82): The founder of Nichiren Shoshu, whose teachings are the basis of Soka Gakkai. A fisherman's son, he inherited the doctrine of Sakyamuni and in 1253, at the age of thirty-one, distilled the essence of the Lotus Sutra into Nam-myoho-renge-kyo. In 1279 he exalted it to the position of the supreme guide for people living in the Latter Day of Sakyamuni's Law and embodied it in the form of the Dai-Gohonzon, the ultimate object of worship of Nichiren Shoshu. Daishonin is an honorific suffix that is interpreted to mean "the True Buddha in the Latter Day of the Law."

NICHIREN SHOSHU: The Buddhist sect that has faithfully preserved the orthodox lineage of Nichiren Daishonin's Buddhism for the past seven hundred years. Its head temple is Daiseki-ji, located on the southern slope of Mount Fuji. Soka Gakkai is the lay organization of Nichiren Shoshu.

NIRVANA SUTRA: So named because Sakyamuni expounded this his final sutra just before he entered Nirvana.

ONGI KUDEN: The oral teachings of Nichiren Daishonin written down by Nikko Shonin, the second high priest of Nichiren Shoshu. It clarifies Nichiren Daishonin's profound life philosophy by interpreting the important passages of the Lotus Sutra from the viewpoint of true Buddhism.

RISSHO ANKOKURON: *see The Security of the Land Through the Establishment of True Buddhism.*

RYOJU PEAK: Grdhakuta, or Vulture Peak, near Bodh Gaya, in the North Indian state of Bihar. The sacred mountain where Sakyamuni preached the Lotus Sutra.

THE SECURITY OF THE LAND THROUGH THE ESTABLISHMENT OF TRUE

BUDDHISM (Rissho Ankokuron): The treatise written by Nichiren Daishonin in 1260, at the age of thirty-eight. It reveals the cause of disaster and unhappiness as being the proliferation of misleading religions and philosophies. This treatise is a remonstrance against the Kamakura shogunate, which then ruled Japan.

SHIKIMI: An aromatic Chinese anise symbolizing the eternity of life. It is placed in front of Nichiren Shoshu altars. In Nichiren Shoshu, flowers are not offered because, withering soon, they signify transience and mutability.

SHOHO JISSO SHO: One of Nichiren Daishonin's important writings. In it he revealed his profound philosophy of life and predicted future universal propagation of Nichiren Buddhism.

SOKA KYOIKU GAKKAI: Literally, Value-Creating Education Society. Founded in 1930 by Tsunesaburo Makiguchi, the first president, and Josei Toda, the second president. The military government suppressed the society in 1943, because of its antiwar orientation and anti-Shinto policy. Josei Toda reestablished it in 1946 under the name Soka Gakkai (Value-Creating Society).

TAISHAKU: *see* Bonten.

THE TEN EVIL DEEDS: According to Buddhist thought, the ten evil deeds are: murder, adultery, theft, falsehood, flattery, duplicity, slander, avarice, anger, and stupidity.

THREE GREAT SECRET LAWS: Another name for Nichiren Daishonin's Buddhism, which is composed of three vital elements: Hommon-no-Honzon (supreme object of worship as the embodiment of Nam-myoho-renge-kyo), Hommon-no-Daimoku (invocation of Nam-myoho-renge-kyo), and Hommon-no-Kaidan (high sanctuary for the enshrinement of the Dai-Honzon).

T'IEN-T'AI THE GREAT (538–97): Another name for Chih-i. A great Chinese Buddhist leader and the founder of the T'ien-t'ai sect. He is considered the Buddha of the Middle Day of the Law.

TOTAIGI SHO: One of the most important of Nichiren Daishonin's writings. In it he identifies believers in true Buddhism with the entity of Nam-myoho-renge-kyo. Although the facts are uncertain, it is said that Nichiren Daishonin wrote this treatise while in exile on Sado Island and sent it to Sairenbo, one of his disciples and a former priest of the Tendai sect.

Treatise on the Three Great Secret Laws: One of Nichiren Daishonin's important works, written in April, 1281, one year before his death. It is dedicated to Ota Kingo, one of his lay disciples. In this treatise Nichiren Daishonin clarified the Three Great Secret Laws. This work contains the first written mention of the construction of a high sanctuary.

Viśistácaritra: The leader of the Jiyu-no-Bosatsu, or the Bodhisattvas who rose from the earth when the Lotus Sutra was proclaimed and vowed to propagate the Three Great Secret Laws in the Latter Day of the Law. Nichiren Daishonin appeared as Viśistácaritra to propagate true Buddhism, although he is in fact the True Buddha in the Latter Day of Sakyamuni's Law.

The "weathermark" identifies this book as having been designed and produced at the Tokyo offices of John Weatherhill, Inc. Book design and typography by Meredith Weatherby. Text composed by Samhwa Printing Co., Seoul. Printed by Kenkyusha Printing Co., Tokyo. Bound at the Makoto Binderies, Tokyo. The text is set in Baskerville 11/13, with hand-set Baskerville for display.